Praise for *The Blackwell Companion to the Bible and Culture*

"This volume is a delight, full of interest and surprises. It contains a wealth of fine scholarship made readable and the book is highly recommended . . . Immensely varied, accessible, and fascinating."

Journal of Contemporary Religion

"A sweeping and magnanimous overview . . . admirably achieves its goal with wit, aplomb, and a disciplinary breadth that is all too rare in biblical studies today . . . A welcome addition to the growing corpus of literature on the important relationship between the Bible and culture."

Review of Biblical Literature

"A unique manual which demonstrates that biblical studies are no longer done exclusively in departments of theology."

International Review of Biblical Studies

The Wiley-Blackwell Companions to Religion

The Wiley-Blackwell Companions to Religion series presents a collection of the most recent scholarship and knowledge about world religions. Each volume draws together newly-commissioned essays by distinguished authors in the field, and is presented in a style which is accessible to undergraduate students, as well as scholars and the interested general reader. These volumes approach the subject in a creative and forward-thinking style, providing a forum in which leading scholars in the field can make their views and research available to a wider audience.

Recently Published

The Blackwell Companion to the Bible and Culture

Edited by

John F. A. Sawyer

A John Wiley & Sons, Ltd., Publication

This paperback edition first published 2012
© 2012 Blackwell Publishing Ltd

Edition history: Blackwell Publishing Ltd (hardback, 2006)

Blackwell Publishing was acquired by John Wiley & Sons in February 2007.
Blackwell's publishing program has been merged with Wiley's global Scientific,
Technical, and Medical business to form Wiley-Blackwell.

Registered Office
John Wiley & Sons, Ltd, The Atrium, Southern Gate, Chichester, West Sussex, PO19 8SQ, UK

Editorial Offices
350 Main Street, Malden, MA 02148-5020, USA
9600 Garsington Road, Oxford, OX4 2DQ, UK
The Atrium, Southern Gate, Chichester, West Sussex, PO19 8SQ, UK

For details of our global editorial offices, for customer services, and for information about
how to apply for permission to reuse the copyright material in this book please see our
website at www.wiley.com/wiley-blackwell.

Wiley also publishes … formats. Some content that appears
in print may not be available in electronic books.

Designations used by … panies to distinguish their products are often claimed as
trademarks. All brand names and product names used in this book are trade names, service
marks, trademarks or registered trademarks of their respective owners. The publisher is not
associated with any product or vendor mentioned in this book. This publication is designed
to provide accurate and authoritative information in regard to the subject matter covered.
It is sold on the understanding that the publisher is not engaged in rendering professional
services. If professional advice or other expert assistance is required, the services of
a competent professional should be sought.

Library of Congress Cataloging-in-Publication Data

The Blackwell companion to the Bible and culture / edited by John F. A. Sawyer.
     p.   cm.—(Blackwell companions to religion)
   Includes bibliographical references and index.
   ISBN 978-1-4051-0136-3 (hardback : alk. paper)
   ISBN 978-0-4706-7488-8 (paperback : alk. paper)
1. Bible—Influence.   2. Christianity and culture—Biblical teaching.
3. Bible—Criticism, interpretation, etc.   I. Sawyer, John F. A.   II. Series.
   BS538.7.B62 2006
   220.09—dc22

                                        2005034703

A catalogue record for this book is available from the British Library.

Cover image: Gerrit Dou, Old Woman Reading, 1640 © Rijksmuseum, Amsterdam.
Cover design by Nicki Averill.

Set in 10/12.5pt Photina by SPi Publisher Services, Pondicherry, India
Printed in Malaysia by Ho Printing (M) Sdn Bhd

1   2012

Contents

Notes on Contributors

Ibrahim Abraham is a research assistant and case worker in the Centre for Studies in Religion and Theology at Monash University, Australia. His work explores the intersections of religion, law and culture.

Alice Bach is Archbishop Hallinan Chair of Catholic Studies at Case Western Reserve University, Cleveland, Ohio. 'My main scholarly interests parallel and reflect my amateur pleasures: watching the media, film, and politics hammer out startling versions of religion, while the religious hammer away at the media, filmmakers, and politicians.' She is the author of *Women, Seduction and Betrayal in Biblical Narrative* (1997) and *Religion, Politics, Media in the Broadband Era* (2004).

Andrew Ballantyne practised as an architect, and then moved into academic work. He has held research and teaching posts at the universities of Sheffield, Bath, and Newcastle, where he is now Professor of Architecture. Among his publications are *Architecture, Landscape and Liberty* (1997), *Architecture: A Very Short Introduction* (2002) and *Architecture Theory: A Reader in Philosophy and Culture* (2005).

Roland Boer is Senior Research Fellow in the Centre for Studies in Religion and Theology at Monash University, Australia. Among his many publications are *Knockin' on Heaven's Door. The Bible and Popular Culture* (1999), *Last Stop Before Antarctica: The Bible and Postcolonialism in Australia* (2001) and *Marxist Criticism of the Bible* (2003).

Sharon A. Bong currently lectures in the School of Arts and Sciences at Monash University, Malaysia. Her key research interests are women and religion in a post-colonial context. She is the Executive Coordinator of the Ecclesia of Women in Asia, a forum of Asian Catholic women. She was a journalist with the *New Straits Times Press*, based in Malaysia.

Euan Cameron is Henry Luce III Professor of Reformation Church History at Union Theological Seminary, New York. He is the author of *The Reformation of the Heretics: The*

Waldenses of the Alps 1480–1580 (1984), *The European Reformation* (1991) and *Interpreting Christian History* (2005), and is the editor of *Early Modern Europe: An Oxford History* (1999).

Jo Carruthers is AHRC Academic Fellow in 'Performativity, Place, Space' in the Arts Faculty at the University of Bristol. Her interests are in the intersection between biblical, literary and cultural studies. She is currently working on a cultural history of the Jewish festival Purim as well as writing a reception history of Esther for the Blackwell Bible Commentary series.

Kate Cooper is Senior Lecturer in Early Christianity and Director of the Centre for Late Antiquity at the University of Manchester. She is the author of *The Virgin and the Bride: Idealized Womanhood in Late Antiquity* (1996), and co-editor of *Studies in Church History*. She has written numerous articles on gender and religious change in the late Roman Empire, and her forthcoming publications include the monograph *Passion and Persuasion: Gender, Violence, and Religious Change in Late Antiquity*.

Philip R. Davies is Research Professor of Biblical Studies at the University of Sheffield, and the author of numerous books and articles on Israelite history and archaeology, early Judaism and biblical interpretation, including *In Search of Ancient Israel* (1992), *Scribes and Schools: The Canonization of the Hebrew Scriptures* (1998) and (with George Brooke and Phillip Callaway), *The Complete World of the Dead Sea Scrolls* (2002).

Mary Dove is a Reader in English at the University of Sussex, and was previously at the University of Melbourne. She has published widely on medieval biblical interpretation, particularly interpretation of the Song of Songs, and is the editor of the *Glossa Ordinaria in Canticum Canticorum* (1997). She is currently completing a book on the first English Bible.

Jonathan A. Draper is Professor of New Testament at the University of Natal, Pietermaritzburg, South Africa. He is the editor of *The Didache in Modern Research* (1996), *The Eye of the Storm: Bishop John William Colenso and the Crisis of Biblical Interpretation* (2003), *Orality, Literacy and Colonialism in Southern Africa* (2003) and *Orality, Literacy and Colonialism in Antiquity* (2004).

Erhard S. Gerstenberger studied theology at the universities of Marburg, Tübingen and Bonn. He has taught at Yale, the Lutheran Seminary of the Igreja Evangelica de Confissão Luterana no Brasil (IECLB) and the universities of Giessen and Marburg. Among his publications are *Yahweh – the Patriarch* (1996), *Theologies in the Old Testament* (2002) and commentaries on Leviticus (1996) and Psalms (1988, 2001).

Tim Gorringe is St Luke's Professor of Theological Studies at the University of Exeter. He has taught in St Andrews, Oxford and India. His publications include *Fair Shares: Ethics and the Global Economy* (1999), *A Theology of the Built Environment: Justice, Empowerment, Redemption* (2002) and *Furthering Humanity: A Theology of Culture* (2004).

Heidi J. Hornik studied at Cornell University and Penn State University and is now Professor of Italian Renaissance and Baroque Art History at Baylor University, Texas.

Her archival research is on the sixteenth-century Mannerist painter, Michele Tosini. With her husband Mikeal Parsons, she co-edited *Interpreting Christian Art* (2004) and co-authored *Illuminating Luke: The Public Ministry of Christ in Italian Renaissance and Baroque Painting* (2005).

Edward Kessler is Founding Director of the Cambridge Centre for the Study of Jewish-Christian Relations. He specializes in contemporary Judaism and Jewish-Christian relations. His publications include *Bound by the Bible: Jews, Christians and the Sacrifice of Isaac* (2004), and he is co-editor of *A Dictionary of Jewish-Christian Relations* (2005).

Stephen N. Lambden received his PhD in 2002 from the University of Newcastle upon Tyne. His research spanned the fields of Biblical and Islamic Studies, focusing upon the Isra'iliyyat phenomenon, the Islamo-biblical tradition, and the emergence of the Babi-Baha'i interpretation of the Bible. He is currently a Research Scholar at Ohio University in Athens, Ohio, working on Shiism, early Shaykhism, and doctrinal dimensions of the Babi-Baha'i religions.

Scott M. Langston teaches Religion and Biblical Studies at Texas Christian University in Fort Worth. He has also taught American history and is a member of the Southern Jewish Historical Society. Among his publications are articles on Jewish history and the New Testament, and the *Exodus* volume in the Blackwell Bible Commentary series (2005).

Burke O. Long is the William R. Kenan Jr. Professor of Religion Emeritus, and Research Professor of Religion at Bowdoin College in Brunswick, Maine. His recent publications include *Planting and Reaping Albright: Politics, Ideology, and Interpreting the Bible* (1997) and *Imagining the Holy Land: Maps, Models and Fantasy Travels* (2003).

Gerard Loughlin is Professor of Theology and Religion at the University of Durham. He previously taught at Newcastle, where he developed his interests in the theology of culture, with reference to film and sexuality. He is the author of *Alien Sex: Desire and the Body in Cinema and Theology* (2004) and editor of *Queer Theology: Rethinking the Western Body* (2005). He is also a founding co-editor of the journal, *Theology and Sexuality*.

Peter Matheson is a Fellow of the Department of Theology and Religious Studies at the University of Otago, New Zealand. His recent books include *The Imaginative World of the Reformation* (2002), and *The Rhetoric of the Reformation* (1997). He is currently writing the biography of Luther's contemporary, the woman theologian, Argula von Grumbach.

Mikeal C. Parsons is Macon Professor of Religion at Baylor University, Texas, where he has taught since 1986. He has published numerous articles and authored or co-authored eight books, including *The Departure of Jesus in Luke – Acts* (1987), *Rethinking the Unity of Luke and Acts* (1992) and (with Heidi Hornik) *Illuminating Luke: The Infancy Narrative in Italian Renaissance Painting* (2003).

Anne Primavesi is a systematic theologian focusing on ecological issues. She is a Fellow of the Centre for the Interdisciplinary Study of Religion, Birkbeck College,

University of London, and the author of several books including *Sacred Gaia* (2000), *Gaia's Gift* (2003), and *Making God Laugh* (2004). She has lectured widely in the British Isles, Europe, North America and South America.

Ilona N. Rashkow teaches at Stony Brook University, New York. Her primary interests include psychoanalytic literary theory as applied to the Hebrew Bible. Her books include *Upon the Dark Places: Sexism and Anti-Semitism in English Renaissance Biblical Translation* (1990), *The Phallacy of Genesis* (1993) and *Taboo or Not Taboo* (2000). She is currently writing a book-length study on 'forgetting' in the Hebrew Bible from a Freudian and Lacanian perspective.

John W. Rogerson is Emeritus Professor of Biblical Studies at the University of Sheffield. His many publications on the history, sociology and geography of ancient Israel, the history of biblical interpretation and the use of the Bible in social and moral questions include *W.M.L. de Wette: Founder of Modern Biblical Criticism* (1992), *The Bible and Criticism in Victorian Britain* (1995), *The Oxford Illustrated History of the Bible* (2001) and *Theory and Practice in Old Testament Ethics* (2004).

Deborah F. Sawyer is a Reader at Lancaster University. Her publications include *Women and Religion in the First Christian Centuries* (1996), *Is There a Future for Feminist Theology?* (co-edited with Diane Collier, 1999), and *God, Gender and the Bible* (2002). Her other publications in the area of gender and religion include her contribution to the *Encyclopedia of Religion* (2nd edn, 2005) and articles in *Feminist Theology* and *Religion and Sexuality*.

John F. A. Sawyer is Emeritus Professor of Religious Studies at Newcastle University and of Biblical Studies and Judaism at Lancaster University. His books include *The Fifth Gospel: Isaiah in the History of Christianity* (1996) and *Sacred Languages and Sacred Texts* (1999). He is co-editor of the *Concise Encyclopedia of Language and Religion* (2001) and the new reception-history-based *Blackwell Bible Commentary Series* (2003–).

Choan-Seng Song is the Distinguished Professor of Theology and Asian Cultures at the Pacific School of Religion in Berkeley, CA, and Director of the GTU project, 'Partnership for Transforming Theological Education in Asia, the Pacific and North America'. He has taught in Taiwan, Princeton, Kyoto and Harvard, and his many books include *Third-Eye Theology* (3rd edn, 1991) and *The Believing Heart* (1999).

Andrew Tate is a Lecturer in English at Lancaster University. He has published articles and book chapters on a wide range of topics, including nineteenth-century religion, Victorian visual culture and post-modern fiction and spirituality. He is currently working on a full-length study of Douglas Coupland, and a book about contemporary fiction, Christianity and re-enchantment.

Meg Twycross is Professor Emeritus of English Medieval Studies at Lancaster University. She is Editor of the journal *Medieval English Theatre*, and a Co-Director of the York Doomsday Project. Her publication, *Masks and Masking in Medieval and Early Tudor England* (2001), written with Sarah Carpenter, won the David Bevington Prize. She is currently engaged in a detailed study of the York *Ordo paginarum* using virtual restoration techniques on high-resolution electronic scans.

xii   NOTES ON CONTRIBUTORS

Gerald West teaches at the University of KwaZulu-Natal, Pietermaritzburg, and is the Director of the Ujamaa Centre for Community Development and Research. His publications include *The Academy of the Poor: Towards a Dialogical Reading of the Bible* (1999) and (with Musa Dube) *The Bible in Africa: Transactions, Trajectories and Trends* (2000).

Figures

Preface to the Paperback Edition

Since the publication of the hardback edition of *The Blackwell Companion to the Bible and Culture* in 2006, there has been a veritable explosion of academic interest in the reception history of the Bible. In addition to two new journals, *Biblical Reception* and the online open access *Relegere: Studies in Religion*, there are at least three reference works: my own *Concise Dictionary of the Bible and its Reception* (2009), the *Oxford Handbook of the Reception History of the Bible* (2011) and the projected 30-volume *Encyclopaedia of the Bible and its Reception* (2009–). Out of numerous other recent publications by biblical scholars I might mention Bernhard Lang, *Joseph in Egypt. A Cultural Icon from Grotius to Goethe* (2009), Martin O'Kane, ed., *Biblical Art from Wales* (2010), Chris Rowland, *Blake and the Bible* (2011) and *After Ezekiel. Essays on the Reception of a Difficult Prophet*, edited by Paul Joyce and Andrew Mein (2011). Six more volumes in the Blackwell Bible Commentary Series have also appeared, three on Old Testament books, Esther (Carruthers), Ecclesiastes (Christianson) and Psalms I (Gillingham), and three on New Testament books, Galatians (Riches), Thessalonians (Thiselton) and the Pastoral Epistles (Twomey). Despite all this, thanks to the pioneering work of a large and very remarkable team of contributors, I think the *Blackwell Companion* is still in many respects ahead of the game, and will continue to provide a useful reference source as well as a starting point for future research in most of these rapidly expanding areas of postmodern Biblical Studies.

The other thing I want to refer to that happened in the years following the publication of the hardback edition, is the untimely death of Paul Fletcher in September 2008 at the age of 43. The original conception and overall structure of the volume owes almost everything to his scholarship and the breadth of his vision, and I would like to dedicate this paperback edition to his memory, with affection, nostalgia and great respect.

John F. A. Sawyer
Perugia

Introduction

John F. A. Sawyer

If we exclude those parts of the world where the Bible was entirely unknown before the advent of Christian missionaries, there are few aspects of culture, ancient, mediaeval and modern, European and non-European, religious and secular, that have not interacted in some way with the Bible. Outside the United Nations building in New York the representatives of at least 191 countries are daily confronted by a bronze statue, 3 metres high, entitled 'Let us beat our swords into ploughshares' (cf. Isa. 2:4; Mic. 4:3). According to the latest statistics provided by the United Bible Societies, there are 2,377 languages in which the Bible or parts of it can be read, while another, probably rather less reliable, calculation sets at more than six billion the number of copies of 'the world's best-seller' sold since the invention of printing. The title of this *Companion* reflects the scale of the subject and sets no boundaries on the areas to be explored, chronological, geographical or thematic. The only limits are arbitrary and practical, namely the size of the volume and its date of publication. As the authors faced with the challenge of contributing to it have frequently pointed out over the past few years, they could not possibly give adequate coverage to every aspect of their topic and have had to be selective. The same is true of the editor. There are many topics that would have been relevant and interesting and which some readers will be disappointed to find missing. What no-one can say, however, is that this project was too narrowly defined, or that the vast range of material covered is not broadly representative of the extraordinary phenomenon implied by the title.

The word 'Bible' in the title is itself comprehensive and includes both Jewish and Muslim definitions, although it must be said that, apart from the two chapters specifically devoted to Judaism and Islam, the authors are working by and large with the Christian Bible in the sense that the texts discussed are in the vernacular (mostly English) rather than the original Hebrew, Aramaic or Greek, and include the New Testament. The interaction between the Christian Bible and culture, however, goes well beyond Church history, and well beyond a survey of Christian interpretations of the Bible. The title of the volume deliberately presents a relationship between two terms that can be described as both tension-filled and mutually generative. The focus through-out is the interaction between the text, the specific context of the Bible's readers, and the weight of the historical past and tradition(s) that impact upon the readers' present. The aim is to provide a series of assessments of the ways in which the various 'prac-tices' of culture – aesthetic, political, religious – inform and are informed by scripture. It offers a coherent challenge to assumptions that the Bible is a static and univocal phe-nomenon. Just as the text and its readers have challenged dominant cultural assump-tions in every age or period, so too changing cultural forms constantly question the validity of the biblical text and its interpretations.

Only a minority of the authors – and the editor – would describe themselves as having had a conventional training in biblical studies. Most come from other disci-plines, and the variety of fields of study and topics selected is matched by the variety of scholarly approaches adopted. A few are concerned to show how the meaning of certain biblical texts can be or has been illuminated by the application of insights from aspects of contemporary culture such as, for example, architecture and psychology. Others, less interested in the niceties of biblical interpretation, explore the impact of the Bible – or particular biblical texts – on the Reformation, politics in general, ecology, and the like, or on specific peoples and communities, especially in Asia, South Africa and Latin America. Another group, the largest group, focuses on types of interaction between the 'Bible' and 'Culture' which illuminate both, as for example in the chapters on Literature, Film, Music, Art, the Theatre, the Body, Gender, Nationalism and Postmodernism.

A recurrent theme in these essays, designed to make students of the Bible and other disciplines more aware of what kind of a text they are working with, is the multi-faceted nature of the Bible and its after-lives. Christopher Hill, whose book *The English Bible and the Seventeenth-Century Revolution* is also a recurring motif in *BCBC*, argues that 'the polysemy of Scripture undermined its political power' (1993: 428). If the text can mean more or less whatever anyone wants it to mean, then how can it be used as an author-ity on which social policies, ecclesiastical dogmas, ethical codes or the like are based? The evidence of this volume is that, far from undermining the political power of the Bible, its many meanings seem to have provided its readers with all the inspiration and authority they need, whether to justify a theological doctrine or to create a work of art or to rebel against an oppressive regime.

It is no postmodern discovery that a text can and often does have many meanings. As the rabbis of the second century CE put it, 'Just as a hammer striking a rock makes several sparks, so too every scriptural verse yields several meanings' (Talmud Sanhedrin 34a). The same is true of most patristic exegesis, where, for example, allegorizing was one of the main methods used to interpret scripture, and for mediaeval Christian writers and artists, for whom the literal sense of the Bible was of little consequence in comparison to what they considered to be deeper, more relevant spiritual meanings, including the countless traditional christological interpretations of the Old Testament which they inherited. The subject of the original meaning of the text, or its literal meaning, hardly ever arises in this volume. Indeed, one can imagine the reception an ageing professor of biblical Hebrew would have received if he had interrupted a bibli-cal discussion group in Brazil or South Africa or Korea with the words, 'But that is not what the original Hebrew means.' Maybe not, they would say, but that does not mean we are wrong. Who is to say that our reading of the text is not more inspiring or more relevant to us than the original meaning?

The rabbis tell the story of how Moses, once given the opportunity to attend a lecture being given by Rabbi Akiba (*c*.50–135 CE), was happy with a rabbinic interpretation of something he had said in the Torah, even though he could not understand it himself (Talmud Menahot 29b). We can speculate, *mutatis mutandis*, on what Jesus would have said if he had had the chance to discuss the interpretation of his parables with Joachim Jeremias; and what is he saying to St Catherine as they discuss the Psalms together in the painting by Domenico Manetti (1609–63) in the Palazzo Pubblico in Siena? On the evidence of the gospels (e.g. Matt. 27:46; Mark 15:34), we can be reasonably sure he would not have rejected out of hand many of the Church's traditional eschatological or christological interpretations.

If we accept the value and validity of the new quest for non-literal meanings of the Bible, whether rabbinic, patristic, mediaeval, modern or postmodern – without which the present volume together with a good many other recent monographs would not exist – is there any control over how the Bible can be interpreted? Is it a helpless victim in the hands of its readers? To protect it, Jewish tradition laid down in minute detail precisely what instruments and materials are to be used in the production of Torah manuscripts, where they are to be kept and how they are to be used. Likewise Islamic authorities have sought to prevent the translation of the Qur'an into the vernacular, and to ensure that it is used only for correct religious purposes and not, for example, as a text for non-Muslim students of Arabic to practise on. For many centuries the Church too strictly controlled the process of reading the Bible, who could read it and how it should be interpreted or translated: they even put to death some of those who challenged their control of scripture. In modern times, the historical critics have attempted to impose their view that biblical texts have only one meaning, the original or literal meaning, and that all other readings are wrong. If these and other such controls are removed, and there is plenty of evidence that for many, if not most, readers of the Bible today, they have been, is there anything to prevent the wholesale rape and dismemberment of the biblical text?

The first answer to this charge would be to point out that when it comes to dismemberment, it is in fact the historical critics who are most guilty of this, in their wholesale fragmentation of the biblical text – one thinks of JEDP, the three Isaiahs and the synoptic problem – while the new readers by and large show far greater respect for the sacred text of the Bible as it has come down to us. Clearly, there can be no theoretical objection to the continuing application and refinement of historical critical methods, with their limited goals and expectations. But by the same token the value and success of other methods of interpreting the Bible, informed by structuralism, feminism/womanism, psychoanalysis, postcolonialism and the like, can no longer be denied. Second, the material collected in the present volume is immensely rich in examples of people searching the scriptures, desperately at times, for help and inspiration. Their seriousness, their respect for the text, their expectation that it will speak to their need, are beyond doubt. There are some like the supporters of Nazi anti-Semitism and the apartheid regime in South Africa, or the Jewish extremist settlers on the West Bank, who use the Bible to give authority and respectability to what most would consider to be an unjust cause. However, their crimes are not against the original meaning of the text – indeed, their interpretation may on occasion come very near it – but against humanity. Third, let us agree that the Bible has been roughly treated down the centuries by millions and millions of readers, including bishops, theologians, political activists, artists and preachers, as well as by the historical critics and uneducated ordinary folk. Those who would have liked to control the process and protect the Bible from ill-treatment – with whatever authority, ecclesiastical, academic or political – have been singularly unsuccessful. The text has suffered at the hands of its readers. For Christian readers, at any rate, it would be nothing new to find revelation in a broken body. 'Wounded for our transgressions, bruised for our iniquities . . .', the Bible is nevertheless still alive and millions still hear the Word of God or the voice of their Saviour when they read it.

A challenge of a different kind to the enterprise undertaken in this volume, is implied by Walter Brueggemann's out-and-out rejection of traditional Christian interpretations of the Hebrew Bible in his commentary on Isaiah (1998, vol. 2: 6). Not only do they fail to do justice to the Hebrew text, he says, but they are also anti-Jewish. I have argued elsewhere that the Hebrew Bible and the Old Testament are not the same thing: their contents are different, the arrangement of the books is different and, above all, the language in which they are written is different (Sawyer 1991). I therefore have some sympathy with Brueggemann's view that there is something wrong in attempts to find direct access from the ancient Hebrew text into Christian tradition. While continuity between the Old Testament and the New is spelt out, in many editions of the Christian Bible, by cross-references on almost every page, direct continuity between the self-contained scriptures of the Hebrew Bible and the Greek New Testament is much more problematical. The Christian interpretations and appropriations of the Old Testament that are the subject of this volume, take place almost entirely in Greek, Latin, German, English and the other languages of global Christianity.

Childs' 'struggle to understand Isaiah as Christian scripture' (Childs 2004) does not really begin until the seventeenth century because he is primarily concerned with the Hebrew text, and, before the seventeenth century, a knowledge of Hebrew is not only relatively rare among Christian interpreters, but also remained subordinate to Christian tradition (ibid.: 230–64). Christian uses of the Hebrew and Jewish sources down the centuries had for the most part been directed at exposing the errors of the Jews, and many Christian interpretations of Isaiah were violently anti-Jewish (Sawyer 2004). On the other hand, the Hebrew Bible has always been at the heart of Jewish life: in the words of Rabbi Jose ben Kisma (second century CE) 'when you walk, it will lead you (i.e. in this life); when you lie down, it will watch over you (i.e. in the grave), and when you awake, it will talk with you (in the world to come)' (Prov. 6:22, in Mishnah Aboth 6:9). Christians have much to learn from Jewish literature, art and music, not least about the meaning of the Hebrew text. Furthermore, the 'back to the original Hebrew' movement of the past three centuries, informed initially by historical criticism, Semitic philology and archaeology, and more recently by Jewish studies, has added an important new dimension to the reception history of the Book of Isaiah, and of the Hebrew Bible generally. However, it would be wishful thinking to imagine that it could ever have as much to say to Christians as the wealth of 2000 years' dialogue between the Christian Old Testament (not yet, so far as I am aware, available in a Hebrew edition) and its Christian readers.

There remains in this discussion of the Bible in its global context, the question of whether it is the case that the Bible can mean anything you want it to mean. Is there any interpretation of scripture that is illegitimate or invalid or untrue? Let us take an extreme example. Members of the gay community in Israel noticed that the words normally translated 'Every valley shall be exalted' (Hebrew *kol ge yinnase'*) can be read in Modern Hebrew as 'Any gay person can get married' (Isa. 40:4). What are we to do with this modern reading of the text? Of course, the words are taken out of context and the interpretation is millennia away from the original author's intention, but so are many, if not most, of the Jewish and Christian non-literal readings of the text that make up the subject matter of the present volume. It is clever and maybe mischievous, but it expresses the hope of a particular community that, in the topsy-turviness of a new age, when 'the glory of the Lord shall be revealed and all flesh shall see it together' (v. 5), they will be redeemed like everyone else.

If it is the case, as many believe, that the text without a reader has no meaning, and the Bible is 'like a sheep that before its shearers is dumb', then it is its 'shearers', the readers and interpreters that must be scrutinized, their presuppositions, their aims, and their methods, not only their readings and interpretations. In the chapters that follow, readings of the Bible by fascists, sexists, imperialists and the like are condemned in terms probably acceptable to most readers. Other interpretations are cited with approval on what are probably less universally agreed aesthetic, ethical, political or other criteria. One suspects, for example, that many critics would seek to silence the gay reading of Isaiah 40:4 just cited, not because it is anachronistic or linguistically unsound in itself, but because of their attitude towards gay and lesbian marriages. Thanks to the achievements of modern biblical scholarship, we can sometimes hear, albeit faintly, the individual voices of the men and women through whose wisdom and creative genius, some would say guided by the hand of God, the Bible came into existence. Our aim in this *Companion to the Bible and Culture*, however, is to listen to some of the much louder and clearer voices of the millions of readers and interpreters of the Bible, who down the centuries have looked to it for guidance, authority and inspiration, and ensured that it is not isolated from the world in which they live, but remains, in the words of another second-century CE rabbi, 'a tree of life to those who lay hold of it' (Prov. 3:18; cf. Mishnah Aboth 6:7).

The thirty chapters are organized into four parts based on various key themes. Part I, *Revealing the Past*, considers the Bible's journey through time from the Ancient World, from which it emerged and in which it barely existed (Davies, Chapter 1), to the modern world where it was challenged, dismembered and rewritten by scientists, historical critics, theologians and others (Rogerson, Chapter 7). During the intervening millennium and a half, the Bible was for the most part in the hands of its powerful custodians, the bishops and scholars of the Christian Church (Dove, Chapter 3), though the voices of lay people, including women, can be heard even in the Patristic Period (Cooper, Chapter 2). The translation of the Bible into the vernacular marked a major turning point in the history of European culture (Rashkow, Chapter 4). In the hands of the

Reformers 'it burst on the sixteenth century with the force of a revelation' (Matheson, Chapter 5), and, in response, Catholic orthodoxy was obliged to develop new strategies to safeguard the authority of the Councils, the Fathers and papal primacy (Cameron, Chapter 6).

Part II, *The Nomadic Text*, traces the global appropriations of the Bible. Judaism, insep-arable from the Hebrew Bible, is considered mainly in the context of Europe and the Middle East (Kessler, Chapter 8). Iran and the Arab world are the setting for a discussion of the complex relationship between Islam and the Bible (Lambden, Chapter 9). The remaining four continents have a chapter each devoted to them, with the exception of America which is divided into North America (Langston, Chapter 12) and Latin America (Gerstenberger, Chapter 13). A comprehensive study of the evolution of truly Asian forms of Christianity assesses trends common to the whole of South Asia, East Asia and South-East Asia (Song, Chapter 10). By contrast, the Bible in Africa is exam-ined in the microcosm of Zulu culture (Draper, Chapter 11), and the Bible in Australa-sia in the sub-cultures of Vanuatu, outback Australia, and suburban Melbourne (Boer and Abraham, Chapter 14).

Part III, *The Bible and the Senses*, looks at some aesthetic and performative renderings of the Bible. A chapter on literature examines the history of the Bible's reception in lit-erature as 'one of re-writing, supplementation and defamiliarization', with examples from many periods of English literature (Carruthers, Chapter 15). In an essay on the Bible in film, the focus is not on Gibson's *Passion* or the Hollywood epics, but on more unexpected examples like Pasolini's short and controversial *La Ricotta* (1962) and the western *Shane* (1953) (Bach, Chapter 16). The chapter on music considers the rela-tionship between libretto and biblical text in a selection of choral and operatic works from Handel to Vaughan Williams (Rogerson, Chapter 17). Painting as 'an expansion of the (biblical) text' is surveyed by reference to images from early Christian art, the Byzantine period, the Renaissance and Baroque, and the nineteenth and twentieth cen-turies (Hornik and Parsons, Chapter 18). A professional architect reads the descriptions of Rahab's house in Jericho, the Tower of Babel, the Temple of Solomon, the New Jerusalem and other biblical monuments and buildings (Ballantyne, Chapter 19). Biblical drama is the subject of two chapters, one a critical study of the origins and development of mediaeval dramatizations of the Bible (Twycross), the other a socio-economic and political study of a dramatization of the 'Fall of Nineveh', first per-formed by a travelling circus in Philadelphia in 1892 (Long, Chapter 20). 'The Body' considers the application of biblical texts about the body of Adam, created in the image of Christ, to Christian teaching on homosexuality (Loughlin, Chapter 21).

Part IV, *Reading in Practice*, looks at disparate applications and practices of scripture in the modern world. A theologian argues, against Karl Marx, Christopher Hill and others, that throughout the twentieth century, from Russia to Africa, from Europe to Asia, the Bible remained a 'profoundly disturbing political text' (Gorringe, Chapter 24). An ecologist traces the origins of her subject to the Reverend Gilbert White, Carl Lin-naeus, Ernst Haeckel (who invented the term 'ecology') and others down to the present day, mostly with reference to texts from Genesis, Leviticus, Psalms and Job (Primavesi, Chapter 25). The chapter on 'contextuality' finds increasing socio-economic awareness in African theology and biblical studies, using as a case study the work of the Ujamaa

Centre for Biblical and Theological Community Development and Research at the University of KwaZulu-Natal (West, Chapter 23). A critique of psycho-analytical approaches to biblical interpretation leads to a new reading of a biblical incest narrative (Rashkow, Chapter 26), and a brief history of feminist and womanist re-readings of Scripture demonstrates how feminist theology brought a breath of fresh air into western academia (Sawyer, Chapter 27). The chapter on nationalism from the sixteenth century to the present day argues that various nationalist impulses have their origin in the pages of the Old Testament (Carruthers, Chapter 28). Postcolonialism is examined in the context of Asia where euro-centric meanings of the Bible have been broken down and Christianity has become a spiritual tradition of the East (Bong, Chapter 29). The final chapter explores the multiple manifestations and interpretations of the Bible in our own complex historical moment, an epoch frequently identified by the name 'post-modern' (Tate, Chapter 30).

Acknowledgements

On a personal note, I would like to say what a pleasure it has been to work with scholars from so many different fields and to thank them all very warmly for their cooperation. Among the many who have helped and encouraged me along the way, I want to acknowledge in particular the huge contribution made by Paul Fletcher to the project in its initial stages, and that of Francis Landy who, by a happy coincidence, was a near neighbour in Cortona during the final stages. My thanks are also due to the editorial staff at Blackwell Publishing, especially Rebecca Harkin, Sarah Edwards and Louise Cooper, and the production team of Karen Wilson, Linda Auld and Susan Dunsmore. Finally, I would like to mention my two daughters, Hannah and Sarah, whose labours coincided with mine, and to whose firstborn Alice and Sophie I proudly dedicate this volume.

References

Brueggemann, W. (1998). *Isaiah* (Westminster Bible Companion). 2 vols. Louisville, KY: Westminster/John Knox.

Childs, B. S. (2004). *The Struggle to Understand Isaiah as Christian Scripture*. Grand Rapids, MI: William B. Eerdmans.

Hill, C. (1993). *The English Bible and the Seventeenth-Century Revolution*. Harmondsworth: Allen Lane.

Sawyer, J. F. A. (1991). 'Combating Prejudices about the Bible and Judaism', *Theology* 94: 269–78.

Sawyer, J. F. A. (2004). 'Isaiah and the Jews: Some Reflections on the Church's Use of the Bible', in C. Exum and H. Williamson (eds), *Reading from Right to Left: Essays on the Hebrew Bible in Honour of David J. A. Clines*. Sheffield: Sheffield Academic Press, pp. 390–401.

'Swords into Plowshares', http://www.un.org/Pubs/CyberSchoolBus/untour/subswo.htm

United Bible Societies Translation Statistics, http://www.biblesociety.org/index2.htm

PART I

Revealing the Past

CHAPTER 1
The Ancient World

Philip R. Davies

From the twenty-first century, we look at the ancient world through two pairs of eyes. One pair looks back over the sweep of human history to the civilizations of Egypt and Mesopotamia, Assyria, Persia, Greece and Rome, which played their successive roles in shaping our modern world. The other set of eyes looks through the Bible, seeing the ancient world through the lenses of Scripture, not only directly from its pages but also through two millennia of Christian culture that long ago lodged itself in the imperial capitals of Rome and Constantinople yet saw its prehistory in the Old Testament and its birth in the New. The museums, galleries and libraries of Western Christendom bulge with representations of scenes from a biblical world dressed in ancient, medieval or modern garb.

Although the rediscovery of ancient Egypt, for which we should thank Napoleon, preceded by a century and a half the unearthing of the ancient cities of Mesopotamia – Babylon, Nineveh, Ur, Caleh – these cities captured the modern imagination because they were *known to us from the Bible*. These discoveries heralded the phenomenon of 'biblical archaeology', and the kind of cultural imperialism that brought ancient Mesopotamia (Iraq) and Egypt into the 'biblical world'. Although the 'Holy Land' was a small region of little consequence to these great powers, the biblical vision of Jerusalem as the centre stage of divine history has been firmly embedded in our cultural consciousness. The 'biblical world' can therefore mean both the real world from which the Bible comes and also the world that it evokes. In this chapter we shall look primarily at the former, with a final glimpse of the ancient world *in* the Bible.

How does one introduce 'the ancient world' in a short space? Obviously with the aid of great deal of generalization and selectivity. What follows is obviously painted with a very broad brush, focusing on major motifs such as kingship, city and empire – institutions that are not only political, but also economic and social configurations. The growth and succession of monarchy, cities and empires both dominated the world of the Bible but also occupy much of its attention. The climax of this ancient world's history is the interpenetration of two spheres: the 'ancient Near East' and the 'Greek', effected by Alexander's conquest of Persia. The 'kingship', by then lost to the Greeks, was revived in an ancient Near Eastern form, Greek-style cities sprang up, and a civilization called 'Hellenism' developed. This great cultural empire fell under the political governance of Rome, under which it continued to flourish, while Rome itself, after years of republic, adopted a form of age-old ancient Near Eastern kingship.

A Historical Sketch

The worlds of the eastern Mediterranean and the ancient Near East were contiguous both geographically and chronologically. The eastern seaboard of the Mediterranean lay at the intersection of a maritime world and a large stretch of habitable land from Egypt to Mesopotamia, the so-called 'Fertile Crescent', curving around the Arabian desert to the south-east and fringed on the north by various mountain ranges (see Figure 1.1). Egypt and the cities of Phoenicia were engaged in sea trading with each other and with various peoples that we can loosely call 'Greek' (Minoans, Myceneans, Dorians, Ionians and Aeolians) from very early times. The Greeks colonized parts of Asia Minor and islands in the eastern Mediterranean, and the Phoenicians founded colonies in North Africa and eventually Spain also. What was exchanged in this trade included not only wine, olive oil, papyrus, pottery and cedar wood, but 'invisibles' such

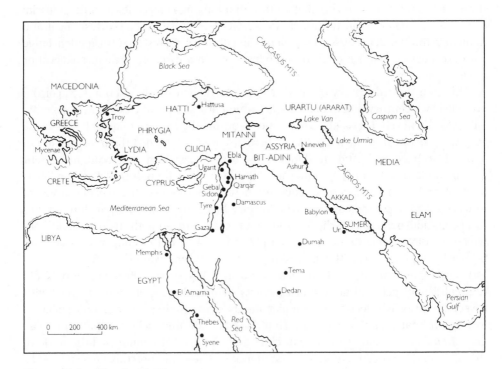

Figure 1.1   The Fertile Crescent

as the alphabet, stories, myths and legends. Traders (including tribes who specialized in trading caravans, such as the Ishmaelites and Edomites) and their wares penetrated eastward via Damascus and the Euphrates and across southern Palestine to the Red Sea. During the second millennium BCE, Egypt was in control of Syria and Palestine; but during the Iron Age and up to the advent of Alexander, its grip loosened and political power lay well away from the Mediterranean, in Mesopotamia.

The ancient Near East

The word 'civilization' derives from the Latin *civitas*, 'city', and civilization is insepara-ble from urbanization. Cities mark the emergence of human diversity, a proliferation of social functions. They also mark a differentiation of power, for cities and their activities (in the ancient Near East at any rate) represent a form of social cooperation that is always governed by a ruler: major building projects, organized warfare, taxation, bureaucracy. In Mesopotamia, as throughout the ancient Near East (except Egypt) during the Bronze Age (c.3000–1200 BCE), cities were individual states, each compris-ing not only the fortified nucleus but also a rural hinterland of farms and villages, forming an interdependent economic, social and political system. Within the 'city' proper lay political and ideological power: administration, military resources, temples, the apparatus of 'kingship'. Economically, the ancient city was a consumer rather than a creator of wealth, its income drawn mostly from the labours of the farmers, who were freeholders, tenants or slaves. Farmers comprised well over nine-tenths of the popula-tion; but they have left us little trace of their mud-brick houses, their myths and legends, their places of worship, their daily lives. Their houses have mostly disintegrated, their stories, customs and rituals left only in their burials, and whatever has survived of their material culture. We see them only occasionally as captives in war on an Assyrian relief or as labourers in Egyptian scenes of building enterprises. (We glimpse them in the Bible, but not fully; we know mostly about kings, priests, prophets and patri-archs.) They subsisted as the climate permitted; their surpluses went to their ruler, the king and to the gods (the temple and priests), who were usually under royal control. In return, the ruler defended them (as far as he could) from attack and invasion, which could also destroy their harvest and their livelihood.

We know more of the rulers than the ruled: we can visit the remains of cities and walk through the ruins of palaces and temples; we can read texts from ancient libraries, which reveal rituals and myths, lists of omens, prayers and tax receipts, accounts of battles and the boastful inscriptions of royal achievements such as buildings, laws or military campaigns. Inevitably, our history of the ancient world is a skewed one: we know who commissioned a pyramid (and was entombed in it), but not a single name of one of the thousands who constructed it.

Whatever had preceded the advent of kingship is lost to history. One of the earliest preserved texts, the Sumerian King List (the surviving tablet is dated 2125 BCE), opens with the words, 'After the kingship descended from heaven . . .'. The gods handed laws to the kings, who, in their own words, always ruled justly, served the gods and destroyed their enemies. Kings of course, were frequently usurped, even assassinated, but kingship always persisted. No other system ever seems to have been envisaged (even among the gods). Warfare was endemic, since it constituted a justification for kingship and the existence of standing armies; it also provided a source of wealth in booty and slaves. In Mesopotamia, as in most of the ancient Near East, cities fought each other for supremacy. The Sumerian King List describes this process as follows: 'Erech was defeated; its kingship was carried off to Ur . . .'. The successive supremacy of Mesopotamian cities is sometimes reflected in the mythology: our text of the Babylonian Creation Epic (from the twelfth century BCE) features Marduk and his city of Babylonia; but it adapts older Sumerian epics, and in turn an Assyrian copy replaces Marduk with the Assyrian god Asshur.

Egypt was in some ways dissimilar to Mesopotamia. It was a politically unified country (theoretically, a union of two countries, Upper and Lower Egypt), not a group of city-states. Unlike the lands 'between the rivers', it was seldom threatened from outside, though in due course it did succumb to Assyria, Persia, Alexander and Rome. It enjoyed a stable agricultural economy, since the annual flooding of the Nile was more reliable than the flooding of the Tigris–Euphrates basin (which often inundated cities). The pharaoh reigned supreme as the son of the god Amon, the king of a large society of gods. Hence the chief religious preoccupations were the sun and the underworld; in the Egyptian cosmos, the sun sailed (how else did one travel in Egypt?) daily into the underworld and back, just as the pharaoh and at least the upper classes would pass, after their death and judgement, into that world where Osiris ruled.

Egypt and Mesopotamia formed the two ends of the 'Fertile Crescent' and each exerted a strong influence on the lands between. Palestine was under Egyptian control until the end of the Bronze Age (thirteenth century BCE), when some kind of crisis, possibly economic, saw a collapse of the political system. Mesopotamia, where a Semitic population had overlain the non-Semitic Sumerians in the late third millennium, gave a cultural lead to the largely Semitic peoples of Syria and Palestine. The language of Mesopotamia, Akkadian, became the literary *lingua franca* of the entire Fertile Crescent in the second millennium, as we know from the letters written by kings of Palestinian city-states to the Pharaoh Akhenaton in the fourteenth century BCE and found in his capital at Tell el-Amarna.

In the thirteenth century, an influx of what were called 'Sea Peoples', which included Philistines, settled in Palestine, having been repelled from Egypt by the Pharaoh Merneptah. These peoples, whose origins lay somewhere among the coasts or islands of the Eastern Mediterranean, quickly absorbed the indigenous culture, but the Philistine cities of Gaza, Ashkelon, Gath, Ashdod and Ekron remained powerful and politically independent for several centuries (giving, of course, their name to the land of 'Palestine'). At this time, new territorial states also arose in Syria and Palestine, including Israel and Judah. But a new age of empire soon arrived.

Empires are a natural extension of the social processes that governed kingship: patronage, in which protection was offered by the 'patron' to the 'client' in return for services (in our own day, the best-known example of the patron is the 'Godfather'). Chiefs and kings ruled in precisely this way, and it was by making other kings into clients that empires were constructed, by extracting loyalty in the form of tribute and political allegiance. However, as the trappings of kingship tend to expand, they require more income, and also empires consume huge amounts of wealth. City-states had tried to establish military superiority over each other for the purpose of extracting economic surplus, and this is how empires begin, with the extraction of wealth by annual subscription, often requiring a military threat or even military action. This typically gives way to more direct administration of territories as provinces (the history of the British Empire is an excellent illustration). Trading had always been an instrument of royal administration and a source of income (including imposing duties on the passage of goods). This too was more effective if directly stimulated and controlled by the 'king of kings'.

The first great empire builders of the ancient world were the Assyrians, and they drew the map of the ancient Near East early in the first millennium. All empires face external and internal threats, more or less continually and in the end they succumb, as did Assyria late in the seventh century. To the extent that empires create any kind of political or economic system, they persist under new ownership. The Assyrians' immediate successors, the Neo-Babylonians, took over the Assyrian Empire, though they learnt very little in doing so. (The Persians, by contrast, learnt much.)

Assyria was under-populated, landlocked and culturally dominated by Babylonia. It expanded aggressively in two waves between the tenth and seventh centuries, subduing its neighbours and driving westwards towards the Mediterranean coast where lay material wealth, manpower and trade opportunities. Its system of patronage, making vassals of the rulers of territories it wished to control, was inscribed in treaties in which the commitments of each side were made public and sealed with an oath. Such a format is clearly visible in the 'covenant' (treaty) of the book of Deuteronomy, where Yahweh is the patron and Israel the client. However, the Assyrians did not invent the vassal treaty: before them, the Hittites and others had used it. Patronage is an age-old mechanism.

Assyria found itself converting vassals into provinces, as it did in Israel after it put down yet another rebellion, killed the king, effected some population transfers and carved out three provinces. Judah was left, however, with a vassal king. In the ruins of the city of Ekron (Tell Miqneh) lie the remains of a very large olive oil production installation, from the mid-to-late seventh century, producing over a million litres a year. It is likely that Judah's own production was also integrated into a larger economic system. The Ekron facility shows us how the Assyrians managed an empire, and also how Judah's political independence was nominal.

Kingdoms, cities and empire, however, are not simply political machines; they also create and sponsor cultural activities. The ruler of Assyria in the mid-seventh century was Ashurbanipal, who could probably read and write (very unusual for a king) and who spent much of his life accumulating a library of classical Mesopotamian literature, without which we would know much less about the literature of ancient Mesopotamia than we do. His collection was assigned to different rooms according to subject matter: government, religion, science, each room having a tablet near the door that indicated the general contents of each room. Libraries were already a well-established institution of the great cities of the Near East and have been excavated at Ebla, Mari, Nuzi and Ugarit.

His cultural activities did not prevent Ashurbanipal from extending his empire, but it fell a few decades later. The Neo-Babylonian kings (of whom Nebuchadrezzar is the best known) inherited an empire that the Medes and Persians in turn overcame less than a century later, when Cyrus marched into Babylon as the ruler appointed by Marduk. The Persians were faced with a highly diverse empire, and a highly expensive one. Rule of the empire was confined to the Persian aristocratic families, while the territories were divided into satrapies and subdivided into provinces, where their inhabitants were encouraged to enjoy cultural autonomy. The satraps were mostly Persian, but governors of provinces would often be local. The Persians were not Semitic, like most of the peoples from Mesopotamia, Syria and Palestine, and the religion of the rulers (from the beginning or almost) was different from what had previously been known in the Fertile Crescent: Zoroastrianism. Here was a monotheistic system (though with a dualistic aspect) which has no deification of the female but believes in a judgement of souls after death, and afterlife in heaven and hell.

We actually know more about the Persian Empire from Greek sources than Persian ones. The Persians engaged with the Greeks, first, as a major trading presence but then in a struggle with the Greek colonies of Ionia, leading to a Persian attack on Greece itself (480 BCE), and ultimately to the campaigns of Alexander of Macedon. The Greek account of that war is contained in the *Histories* of Herodotus (440) who also tells us about the history and customs of the people of the empire. In addition, Xenophon wrote the *Anabasis*, a story of the march home by Greek mercenaries who had been enlisted by a rival to Artaxerxes (another Cyrus) to try and take the throne (401–399 BCE). He also wrote a life of Cyrus the Great, the *Cyropaedia*.

The classical world

The political system of Greece evolved later than Mesopotamia or Egypt and urbaniza-tion did not begin until about 800 BCE. Greece was never a politically united system: its cities fought for dominance, formed leagues and alliances, traded extensively and founded colonies elsewhere. The cities were at first ruled by kings or by aristocrats, who also controlled religious activities: there was no separate priestly caste. Increasingly, political and religious power was shared by more of the inhabitants of the individual cities. The absence of a powerful kingship or priesthood constitutes a highly important distinction between Greece and the ancient Near East, which remained in most aspects dominated by totalitarian categories of thought and culture. Yet, having never achieved political unity or stability, the Greek cities gave way to Philip of Macedon who united them under his kingdom and whose son Alexander went on to conquer the Persian Empire. The change that this brought within these territories was more than merely political. The entire Fertile Crescent, together with Persia itself, as far as the borders of India, plus Egypt and Sicily, were to be hugely influenced by Greek culture. Greek colonies were implanted, and colonial cities, modelled after the self-ruling Greek city (the *polis*), but now multi-ethnic, flourished almost everywhere. Antioch and Alexandria were among the most important of these new foundations, but cities that were already long established also sought this status (including Jerusalem itself, a policy that precipitated the Maccabean wars).

The older civilizations of the Near East were all torn between resistance, reasserting their own history and customs, and embracing the new. Histories of Egypt and Babylon from the earliest times were written by Manetho and Berossus – but in Greek! Yet cultural influence was not in one direction only: Alexander and his successors adopted much of the style of traditional ancient Near Eastern monarchies, while religions such as the cult of Demeter, of Mithras and Isis and philosophical systems penetrated the Eastern Mediterranean where they had a mass appeal in a world where religious affiliation was more elective than in the ancient Near East. In the realm of religion, syncretism was rife: not only gods and goddesses but legendary heroes were blurred together: Tammuz and Adonis, Thoth and Hermes, Samson and Heracles, David and Orpheus, Isis and Demeter. With Alexander the Great two worlds that already knew each other not only collided but also began to mix – though socially 'Greeks' made little effort to mix with the 'locals' who lived alongside them in the cities. Politically, his empire quickly shrank and split into smaller kingdoms, governed by his generals – largely following the contours of earlier civilizations: Egypt (the Ptolemies) and Syria–Mesopotamia (the Seleucids), with Palestine, as before, sandwiched between the two and passing in 199 BCE from the control of the Ptolemies to the Seleucids.

There was never a 'Greek Empire': the 'Hellenistic' world in some ways perpetuated the older Near Eastern monarchies but in a quite different cultural guise. The Hellenistic monarchies had ambitions, but were no match for the organized ambition of Rome (even when Rome was torn by civil war, as it was in the first century BCE). Rome had also fallen under the Greek spell, and perhaps rather like Assyria with Babylon, it found cultural self-confidence only once it had achieved political hegemony over its more illustrious neighbour. Like the Greek cities, Rome had once been ruled by a monarch but had developed into a republic. Victory over Carthage (202 BCE) won it control of most of the Mediterranean, and having consolidated Italy under its rule (by the third century BCE), it annexed Macedonia and Egypt in the second century, and quickly extended its influence over the remainder of Alexander's former empire, except for Babylonia, which had been gained by the Parthians in 250.

Like Assyria, centuries earlier, Rome's problem was manpower. Although it followed the policy of granting citizenship liberally (including to freed slaves), it never had the resources to assimilate conquered territories, and generally proceeded by creating clients from local rulers and using local elites to govern. Here again is something of a repetition of the original Assyrian practice; certainly, it again exemplifies the patron–client mechanism. Thus, for example, in Palestine, the dynasty of Herod the Great ruled as client kings (with the euphemism *socius*, 'ally') until finally direct Roman rule was imposed as a result of that dynasty's failures and of popular unrest. Even so, while Roman armies and a Roman governor were present, administration here was left largely in the hands of the local aristocracy.

Under Rome, the Jews of Palestine lost their temple in 70 CE and their land in 135. But Jews were, like some other nationalities in an increasingly mobile population, already a largely dispersed *ethnos* (a recognized national identity) and now without temple or priesthood, the religion was severely threatened. Having enjoyed a favoured status under the Romans since the time of Julius Caesar, they lost it under Hadrian (135 CE). The rabbis struggled to impose their authority in the face of assimilation and the growing influence of Christianity. However, the triumph of Christianity under Constantine (who died in 337) also may have secured protection, yet with a rather ambivalent status, for Jews and the great era of rabbinic Judaism ensued, culminating in the completion of the Talmuds. Yet it was Babylonia, under the Parthians' successors, the Sassanids, that became the intellectual and religious centre of Judaism, while Christianity divided, as had the empire, into eastern and western domains, ruled respectively from Constantinople and Rome.

The impression of a succession of world empires from Assyria to Rome is, of course, a simplification: there were always revolts, gaps, and power vacuums. Empires decay and shrink as new ones grow. There is a certain continuity from one empire to another, but also (as in the case of Macedonia) clear discontinuities also. As for gaps: at two junctures in the long history just reviewed, Palestine enjoyed brief moments of independence from the imperial powers, and both were crucial. As mentioned earlier, in the tenth century between the decline of Egypt and the rise of Assyria, Israel, Judah and several other small kingdoms arose and briefly flourished here, until they all succumbed to Assyria. Again, in the second century BCE, between the decline of the Seleucid kingdom and the arrival of Roman control, Judah gained independence under the Hasmoneans, and expanded its territory to include Idumea, Galilee and parts of Transjordan, consolidating Judaism as a dominant religion of Palestine, at least outside the Hellenistic cities. The spread of Judaism and of Christianity – and thus their ultimate survival – were due entirely to the existence of the great empires, while kingship and city remain highly potent symbols in both religions ('king' is still a popular epithet for the Jewish and Christian god), reminding us of the ancient world from which they draw political and social conventions.

Social and Cultural Configurations

The ancient Near East

If the political life and history of the ancient world are usually described in terms of the deeds and territories of rulers and their servants, social and cultural life requires a broader vision. There is only a limited extent to which rulers control daily life. First of all, they do not necessarily control even all the territory they claim. The patron–client relationship operated at a series of levels, and even kings ruled through their own clients, such as local landowners or tribal leaders, or even warlords. Indeed, ancient monarchies often relied upon the loyalty of such powerful local 'barons'. Apart from slaves, at the bottom of the hierarchy were the farmers, whose world was largely circumscribed by their own (extended) family and village, with its own dialects, stories and customs. Kinship, not nationality, held these societies together, and genealogy was the normal way of expressing social liaisons and loyalties, even when such kinships are not really biological – as any reader of the Bible can quickly see. A village would be bound to the urban centre, where its ruler lived, where some religious festivals would be attended, markets held, and where security might be sought in time of war. Beyond that, identity was largely meaningless: the inhabitants of the city of Dan, for example, would hardly see themselves as essentially 'Israelite' or 'Aramaean': they might from time to time be controlled (paid taxes) to a ruler in Samaria or Damascus or Hazor; they belonged permanently only to their village and beyond that, its mother city. It was through marriage, collaboration in times of harvest or assembly for major religious events that social bonding was maintained.

The life of the farmer depended on the climate and the weather. Without rain at the right time, or too much rain, or locusts, or indeed a ravaging army devouring and despoiling the crops, death was likely. If the local patron fulfilled his obligations, surplus might be distributed, but if food had to be acquired by incurring debt, slavery and forfeiture of land could result. In systems where the land was in theory the property of the king, and farmers were his 'servants' (as in Egypt), individual freedom was sacrificed to greater security. But in less secure and prosperous lands than Egypt (which did not have to rely on local rainfall, since the Nile annually flooded), the success of the harvest was the dominating concern, and ownership of one's own land was not always a benefit; it could be a liability. Popular religion was therefore understandably about fertility; gods of war or dynastic gods were of little relevance: reproduction was the giver of life. The Bible may decry the goddesses and 'abominations' of the 'Canaanites' at their local shrines, but the female figurine is the commonest of artefactual remains from Iron Age Palestine, including the kingdoms of Israel and Judah. The religious preferences of the urban elites were different: they worshipped at their temples the god of the city and of the king, and the gods of their professions, such as the god of writing (Nabu, Thoth).

The culture and values of village farmers were transmitted from parent to child, justice was administered by parents and village elders, and through communal festivities (religious celebrations, story-telling, births, weddings and funerals). However much rulers claimed to control the administration of law or temples, or the proper conduct of the cult, such influence was probably weak. Such control would have gained the ruler little benefit. Occasionally a ruler imposed a new cult (Akhenaton, Nabonidus), but these reforms had as much to do with politics as religion; neither was long-lasting and neither had any great effect on the rural populace.

As noted earlier, urbanization stimulated the emergence of dedicated professions, mostly associated with the ruler: soldiers, temple personnel, administrators, but also certain artisans. The feeding of the ruler's own retainers was paid for from the produce taken from the land, whether owned by the ruler or the temple or owned privately, in which case produce was taxed. It is unlikely that the farmers retained much surplus, but owners of extensive land could accumulate wealth. Armies could pay their way by securing booty and slaves – if victorious; but on campaign they lived off the land (some farmers' crops), and they still required regular sustenance at other times. Temple personnel may have been as important in securing divine favour for good weather, freedom from illness or security in war, but to our modern eyes they were unproductive. In short, a small elite lived at the expense of a large underclass. However, we must not conclude that there was an antagonism between rural and urban populations; the evidence we have is of a real symbiosis of the two.

The country did come to the city, and the social heart of the city was the gate, or rather the space immediately inside the gate. Here was the ancient equivalent of the

Greek *agora* and the Roman *forum*. It was where legal hearings were conducted before elders, where (probably) prophets would have delivered their speeches, where markets were held, where representatives of the king would be present to speak or hear. It was also a place where people met and where rural and urban culture mixed, where travellers sought accommodation and refreshment. Here more than anywhere else in the city, the unity of the city and its surrounding countryside was evident.

It is needless also to say that ancient societies were patriarchal (as many still are today) and polygamous – but only where economics and availability permitted. In practice, monogamy was determined by these and not moral factors, and the poorer men must have been largely monogamous. Women's functions were confined largely to the household, but included agricultural labour. Like the rest of the household, a woman was subject to the authority of the (male) family head (father or elder brother) until married, when that authority was transferred (in return for payment of a dowry) to her husband. On being widowed, she often depended on the generosity of her children. Women did not normally inherit in ancient Near Eastern societies, though there is evidence that they could in Sumeria and also in Egypt.

In most ancient Near Eastern and Mediterranean societies, women played important roles in religious cults: in Greece and Rome as priestesses, in the Near East more usually as intermediaries (prophetesses); in the religious life of the village, women also played various roles as religious specialists. Everywhere we have to bear in mind the contrast between the public and official place of women as reflected in the literature, and the reality, in which individual women might in fact exercise effective control of their own husbands as well as their children. Our knowledge, unfortunately, must always be patchy since our only sources are archaeological and literary. But from literary sources such as the *Epic of Gilgamesh* (see below) and the biblical books of Ruth, Proverbs and Song of Songs, attitudes to females and the limits of female behaviour were complex and cannot easily be generalized.

The classical world

The world of the Greeks was not monolithic. They all spoke the same language, and worshipped the same gods, but the cities had their own laws and customs. From the fifth century BCE onwards, wealth and political power were not confined to a small elite as in the ancient Near East. There was no scribal class, no priestly class, literacy was more widely spread and, apart from the usual economic tasks (in which slaves – up to a quarter of the population – and women carried much of the burden), Greeks engaged in the political life of their city, in athletics, games, horse-riding, music, theatre and dining. Boys were educated at schools. But women, too, were sometimes educated, and many Greek (male) writers praise the delights of educated female companions. Nevertheless, classical Greece was also patriarchal, stressing the role of women as bearers of children and ornaments to their husbands, and in fact Athens was less liberal in this respect than Sparta, where, for example, women came to own a good deal of property. Women were not citizens and did not participate in political life. Their role was in the home, where they were excluded from the banquets enjoyed by their husbands. And the Athenian tragedies, perhaps surprisingly, focus very often on the fate of women (Clytemnestra, the Trojan women, Antigone, Elektra and many others). In the Graeco-Roman world reflected in the New Testament, there are no women priests or leaders, but women are depicted among the followers of Jesus, and among influential leaders in Christian communities. Priscilla is always named with Aquila, four times in Acts and the Pauline letters. 1 Corinthians 1:11 refers disparagingly to the 'house of Chloe'; and Revelation fulminates against a 'Jezebel'. If Christianity was indeed especially popular among women (including the upper classes), it would not be surprising to find women leaders. But other religious cults also appealed especially to women, including the mystery cults. Again, then, it is impossible to generalize about the role that women could play in classical society.

The advent of (partial) democracy in Athens, for example, had been achieved by wresting power from oligarchy and vesting it in the citizenry. From Homeric times to the sixth century BCE, Athens, a typical example, experienced monarchy, then aristocracy, then tyrants, then democracy. The laws of Solon in 594 were a crucial stage in this last transition, as a result of which the citizen was politicized (the root of 'politics' aptly being *polis*), so that in the famous speech of Pericles (as Thucydides tells it, at any rate), the term *idiotes*, meaning non-political person, became pejorative. Every citizen participated, or was expected to participate, in the running of the city, and this involved the exercise of reason and judgement. It involved weighing priorities, and it involved the assessment of human motivation. Decisions were now taken in a way that focused the attention of every member of the assembly on his own personal responsibility.

The Greek city, then, had citizens: it was 'owned' and run by those who lived in or near it (excluding women and slaves!). Citizens were expected to participate in administration, in judgement, in determining political and economic policy. This, whatever the other similarities between Greek and ancient Near Eastern cities, made a vital difference to their character. If the words 'totalitarian' and 'democratic' are too blunt (and unqualified) to express the contrast, they point to that difference. The overwhelming role of kingship and state, not only with its entrenched bureaucracy but also its heavy ideological apparatus, is absent in Greece, and the stratification of producers and consumers of wealth, ruler and ruled, in the ancient Near East does not apply as absolutely in Greece or in Rome. The intellectual achievements of Greece (see below) cannot be explained without reference to the elevation of human judgement, both corporate and individual, in the organization of life, rather than the gods and their royal representative on earth.

The Ancient World of Ideas

The ancient Near East

One important cultural configuration of the ancient Near East was the scribal class. The bureaucratic apparatus required a class of persons who were official guardians and producers of knowledge, writing everything from royal propaganda to economic records, including myths, annals, prayers – anything that required recording permanently on clay, wood or papyrus. Their competence included diplomacy (hence knowledge of more than one language) and record-keeping (archives, libraries). They might well be thought of as the ancient civil service, indispensable to the running of any state. Yet they also formed an intellectual class, who regarded writing and reading as a divine gift that enabled knowledge, whether political, ethical or metaphysical, to be explored and classified. Apart from maintaining the necessary instruments of state government, these people took upon themselves the role of the intelligentsia, exploring knowledge, including natural science (e.g. cosmology), social sciences (e.g. history and social policy) and ethics ('wisdom'). They systematized myths, created lists of astronomical observations and omens (which they also tried to correlate), and thought incessantly about the meaning of human life and the battle for control of human existence with the gods who determined everything. Their specialized range of skills required them to provide an education for their apprentices, and examples of their textbooks and their exercises have been found in Mesopotamia and Egypt. It will have been these people in Israel and Judah who were responsible for the contents of the Hebrew Bible.

The culture of the ancient Near East was religious and we have no literature at all that reflects an awareness of the world as an autonomous system, or one subject to ultimate human control. The existence and power of the gods were everywhere taken for granted. Only with the scientific philosophy of the Greeks of Asia Minor does speculation begin about immanent laws of nature and how they can be understood. Astronomical observation was highly developed already in Babylonia and geometry was certainly well advanced among the builders of the pyramids, both 2,500 years before Thales of Miletus (624–547 BCE). But the Mesopotamian astronomers regarded the heavenly bodies as signs of events on earth. The difference is in the abandonment of mythology, just as in the political sphere divine kingship was rejected in favour of a more 'democratic' form of government. The same is true of history: while Herodotus seeks to know the 'causes' of the war between Persia and Greece, Near Eastern cultures produced myths of origin, ancient 'king lists' of a mythological character, texts celebrating royal military campaigns, buildings or victories, and – the closest approximation to what we would call 'history' – the Babylonian Chronicles. In the Hellenistic period, however, national histories proliferate, drawing on whatever ancient sources (including mythology) were available. The biblical history from Genesis to Kings has features in common with these Hellenistic histories but the dating of the biblical literature is still disputed; it is not ruled out that the work as a whole belongs to the early Persian period, i.e. the time of Nehemiah, who was a contemporary of Herodotus; indeed, some have claimed to detect the influence of Herodotus, though the general opinion regards the biblical work as at least based on older historiographical documents.

The intellectual and artistic range of ancient Near Eastern scribal literature is impressive, and can be exemplified in the very old, originally Sumerian, *Epic of Gilgamesh*. The oldest long poem in the world, it tells the story of Gilgamesh, king of Uruk (Erech) *c*.2700 BCE, two-thirds divine and one-third mortal. It opens:

> He saw the great Mystery, he knew the Hidden:
> He recovered the knowledge of all the times before the Flood.

He journeyed beyond the distant, he journeyed beyond exhaustion,
And then carved his story on stone.

Gilgamesh starts as an oppressor of his subjects, who cry to the gods and in response a wild companion is provided for him, Enkidu. Enkidu becomes civilized through a temple woman and loses his strength; but she introduces him to Gilgamesh. The two fight but then become friends and decide on a great adventure, to kill the demon guardian of a forest and destroy the trees. Enkidu forces Gilgamesh to slay the demon, who curses him: may he die before Gilgamesh. Later in Uruk, Gilgamesh refuses the advances of the goddess Ishtar, who in revenge obliges the chief god Anu to send a raging bull against his city. Gilgamesh and Enkidu kill the bull and the gods decree death for Enkidu. Enkidu first curses all those he has known, then, realizing how he has enjoyed life, blesses them and is dragged off to the underworld before he dies. Gilgamesh's grief is increased by awareness of his own mortality and on the advice of another mysterious woman, Siduri, he seeks the gift of eternal life from the one human granted it, Utnapishtim, survivor of the great Flood, whom he reaches after a fabulous journey and hears his story. Gilgamesh is told that if he can stay awake six days and seven nights he will achieve immortality; he fails, falling asleep instantly for seven days. Utnapishtim offers Gilgamesh a plant to restore youth, which Gilgamesh retrieves from the ocean floor but does not eat immediately. On the way home he stops to sleep and a snake devours the plant. Gilgamesh returns to Uruk and dies.

The story is a reflection upon many facets of human life. Urbanization (civilization) is still a recent achievement, and the dialectic of wild and tamed is nicely conveyed through the main characters. The taming of Enkidu may be a metaphor for the cultivation of the land, the domestication of herds and crops, but is also about the civilizing influence of women (likewise, Siduri teaches Gilgamesh). Women may seduce, but they also have their own wisdom. Mortality is another theme, threatening not only oneself, but one's friendships. Mortals cannot live forever; but they can compensate by being remembered and by building cities; the city and kingship are yet another theme. Yet the city must also be left in the quest for what is valuable: security does not bring wisdom: it must be sought out, at risk, if necessary. This too is probably a metaphor for human life, in which there is ultimately no security. The epic teaches that life is a journey towards wisdom as much as towards death, and while immortal fame may be acquired, the value of life and of the quest is friendship. As Siduri says to Gilgamesh, 'Fill your belly with good things; day and night, night and day, dance and be merry, feast and rejoice. Let your clothes be fresh, bathe yourself in water, cherish the little child that holds your hand, and make your wife happy in your embrace; for this too is the lot of humans.' The poem also criticizes tyranny and ambition and celebrates the virtues of the pleasures of human companionship, love, food, and drink. Gilgamesh begins as a tyrant, but it is his friendship for Enkidu that tames and teaches him.

Classic texts like these were copied and preserved in the major cities of the Fertile Crescent, such as Ugarit, Ebla and Mari. They point us to the existence of a widely known Akkadian 'canon' that also included laws (such as the codes of Hammurabi) and divinatory texts as well as other myths such as the *Creation Epic* that, like *Gilgamesh*, also began as a Sumerian story and migrated via Babylon to Ashurbanipal's library, where the best-preserved copies were found. The 'Akkadian canon' continued to be copied well into the Graeco-Roman period, and its contents would no doubt have been familiar in the scribal schools of Palestine. These texts were not only copied but studied, stimulating the ongoing debate about the meaning and values of life and the universe (see the poem of Job). We find motifs from *Gilgamesh* in the Eden story of Genesis 2–3 (immortality, the snake), in Ezekiel 28 and 31 (the semi-divine figure), and in Ecclesiastes' recommendation to enjoy life while it lasts, illustrating an intellectual stream that flows through the Bible too – as witness also the obvious affinities between the laws in Exodus and those of Hammurabi and the collections of prophetic oracles from Mari and Nineveh. The book of Job, too, has its antecedents in Mesopotamia, while the book of Proverbs contains sayings identical to those in the Egyptian Wisdom of Amenemope, written in the fourteenth century BCE. It is not necessary, or possible, to date such parallels to a specific time or place: they were accessible everywhere.

Gilgamesh also claims to be a written account by the ancient king himself of his exploits and discoveries, which points us to another widespread cultural phenomenon of the ancient world: revealed wisdom from the past. It inspired the blossoming of apocalyptic literature, especially during the Graeco-Roman period. Apocalypses are revelations or heavenly secrets typically given to an ancient figure who then writes them down; the writing is then 'discovered' at a later time. They typically reveal the origins and ends of the world and of history and the answers to the problems of evil. Among the techniques of apocalypses are heavenly journeys and descriptions of the heavenly mechanisms that govern earthly phenomena. Some of these ingredients can already be seen in *Gilgamesh* (see the quotation above), but an even more important influence was manticism, the culture of divination.

One of the obsessions of Mesopotamian culture was divination, predicting the future. This activity generated hundreds of writings in which observations about omens and their consequences were recorded, in the belief that there was a system by which the future could be intimated to humans through signs, known to a professional guild. Dreams, heavenly phenomena, sacrificial entrails and many other devices were used. An excellent instance of this tradition is Matthew's *magoi* who come 'from the east' following a star that would predict a Jewish Messiah. Although the Old Testament deplores divination, we have Enoch (a figure based on an antediluvian ruler from the third millennium BCE Sumerian King List), who 'foresees' the future and writes it down for future generations. Daniel, too, is trained in the mantic lore of Babylon and by direct divine revelation unlocks secrets of the future. Apocalypses also typically deal with the final resolution of the problem of evil, however that is seen. Usually evil is personified in a wicked king or emperor (Daniel, Revelation) or angel (Enoch). In Jewish and Christian belief the figure of Satan emerges as an amalgam: the ancient snake, the fallen archangel, the head of a legion of evil spirits, the 'tempter' of individuals (as in the book of Job). 'Evil' was often equated with 'death', the great obsession of much of Graeco-Roman religion, and the age-old theme of *Gilgamesh*, immortality, was thus integrated into a new religion in which the triumph of good over evil, the abolition of sin and the defeat of death were all brought together in a synthesis, much of which seems to be the work of Paul, who as a Greek-speaking Jewish Roman citizen personifies almost the whole cultural background of the ancient world. Seen in this light, the triumph of

Christianity is not surprising: it covered almost every religious question and problem, with the added sparkle of a 'divine man', not the hero of an ancient myth but of recent history.

The classical world

In fifth-century Athens the intellectual tradition was not vested in a class, but in citizens themselves. The individual existed as a separate, clearly defined entity, aware of individual selfhood and moral responsibility for their actions. Rather than Greek philosophy, which has already been briefly compared with ancient Near Eastern thinking, Athenian tragedy offers a striking illustration of the Greek 'world of ideas'. Its roots lie in religious ceremony, its stories are drawn from myth and the gods are involved in the action, and this may be precisely why its subject matter is about the human. Athenian tragedy is about people, and what they do to each other. It deals with human relationships and decisions in relation to family and to politics: loyalty to the gods, the race, the family and the city often conflict. Athenian politics was not essentially about principles but about the management of conflicting claims, about individual cases, about expediency.

Because citizens had to do public service, they were interested in moral dilemmas, moved by the impulses of pity and fear, and concerned about the bases of choices in matters of moral conduct. What made a person guilty or not? Or a course of action wise or not? Here the gods themselves are little more than glorified humans, morally speaking. Whether Zeus himself comes to be seen as a transcendental guarantor of order, or a personality of desperate conflict (a precursor of the Wagnerian Wotan?), his own instinct is at war with what he is supposed to represent. In Athens what is right is decided by the democratic court, by public opinion, and not by regal or divine decree, not by verdict of the elders, and perhaps only to an extent by traditional laws and within the household. And that is why it is in Greece and not the ancient Near East (nor the Bible) that ethics was born.

The ancient world in the Bible

How is the ancient world seen in the Bible? What is the place of the universe in its various schemes? We might start with the stories of Genesis 10 and 11, which both account for the spread of humanity across the world after the Flood. In Genesis 10, the so-called 'Table of Nations' assigns nations and territories to the descendants of Noah (a scheme still reflected in our modern use of 'Semitic' and 'Hamitic'). Here everything is orderly and divinely willed. In Genesis 11, humanity is scattered from Babel (Babylon) to curb its ambition, and the proliferation of language symbolizes the disunity of the human race ever since. But the following genealogy focuses on Shem and narrows down to Terah, the father of Abraham, who is then called by God. One nation is chosen, and the ensuing story is about the descendants of Abraham (indeed, only some of them). Thereafter other nations play only incidental roles. This chauvinism would have been characteristic of any ancient society, but because of the influence of the Bible, the idea of a 'chosen race' has embedded itself in our culture.

In the so-called 'historical' and prophetic books of the Old Testament/Hebrew Bible, the world is divided into the land, near neighbours and other nations. With Ammon, Moab, Edom and Aram, there is a recognition of kinship, though perhaps precisely because of this they are quite distinctly distanced from membership of 'Israel'. One looks hard to find a friendly face painted on any of these nations. The prophetic books are full of 'oracles against foreign nations' (a curiosity that is quite hard to explain), and while oracles against Israel and Judah are also plentiful, there are usually compensating calls for repentance or promises of future restoration or prosperity. The nations as a whole are often depicted as being used by Yahweh to punish his own people, but also to then incur punishment for the punishment they inflict. In the Priestly writings (e.g. Leviticus) where the key is holiness, the region beyond the camp of 'Israel' is beyond the reach of the divine presence, a place to which the unclean are sent, a place corresponding perhaps to the chaos that lies outside the divinely created cosmos. In writings from the second century (1 Maccabees, Jubilees) the sense of an Israel besieged on all sides by all other nations, whether militarily or culturally, is strong. It is not unfair to say that in the discourse of the Old Testament/Hebrew Bible, the outside world is hostile. It threatens Israel politically and religiously, because it worships 'gods of wood and stone'. It may be that the book of Jonah is, among other things, a protest against this attitude, portraying both foreign sailors and the king and people of Nineveh as responsive to the word and deeds of Yahweh.

There is one curious exception: Persia. Nowhere are we told anything about the religion of Persia, though in Isaiah 45 proclaims Cyrus as the 'anointed' of Yahweh, and it is Cyrus who in 2 Chronicles 36:22 has his 'spirit stirred' by Yahweh to decree the rebuilding of the temple in Jerusalem. Perhaps behind this is the recognition that the religion of Zoroaster was seen as compatible or complementary with that of Judah or that, writing under the Persians, the biblical authors felt free to criticize only preceding empires, this is significant, and supported by the fact that while Persian kings can be portrayed as pawns of their courtiers (Esther, Dan. 6), they are never wicked.

A fundamental antinomy exists in both the Hebrew Bible and the New Testament about empire and its embodiment of all worldly power. In Daniel, we find, on the one hand, the notion that the kings of the world rule in orderly succession under the overall direction of the 'Most High' (Chapters 1–6). Yet in the later chapters, the successive kings, depicted in the guise of monsters, rebel and have to be destroyed. In the New Testament, written for those generally loyal to Rome, the Roman victim Jesus is portrayed rather as persecuted by the Jews; Paul uses the empire, and his citizenship, to spread his gospel, and seems to accept the empire as ordained by God. Yet in the book of Revelation, Rome is the great 'whore of Babylon'. In these cases, it is the experience of persecution that makes the difference. But if we probe, we find that throughout the Bible the world-rejecting and the world-affirming lie side by side, as does the representation of the world as orderly and as chaotic. In one view, a benign divine providence sustains everything; in the other, a final intervention will be needed at the end to establish justice.

Further Reading

Austin, M. M. (ed.) (1981). *The Hellenistic World*. Cambridge: Cambridge University Press.

Boyce, Mary (1979). *Zoroastrians*. London: Routledge & Kegan Paul.

Braudel, Fernand (2001). *The Mediterranean in the Ancient World*. London: Allen Lane.

Burckhardt, J. (1998). *The Greeks and Greek Civilization*. New York: St Martin's Press.

Liverani, Mario (2005). *Israel's History and the History of Israel*. London: Equinox.

Marks, John H. (1985). *Visions of One World: Legacy of Alexander*. Guildford, CT: Four Quarters.

von Soden, Wolfram (1994). *The Ancient Orient: An Introduction to the Study of the Ancient Near East*. Grand Rapids, MI: Eerdmans/London: Gracewing.

Walbank, F. W. (1993). *The Hellenistic World*, rev. edn. Cambridge, MA: Harvard University Press.

CHAPTER 2
The Patristic Period

Kate Cooper

What impact did the Bible have on the early Christian laity? While we know at least something about the reading habits and theological interests of community leaders and men of literature in the early Church, the evidence for how ideas circulated among Christians of the 'silent majority' is much more difficult indeed. As far as we can tell, the Christian writings, from the mid-first-century letters of Paul to the Gospels a generation later, were not perceived as 'Scripture' at the time they were written. It has long been understood that until the second century, when Christians talked about Scripture, they meant the Septuagint, the Jewish third-century BCE translation of Hebrew and Aramaic Biblical texts into Greek. We know that the Septuagint was central to the early Christian imagination not least because so many of the first- and second-century writings see the life and death of Jesus as a fulfilment of biblical prophecy.

The process by which 27 disparate first- and second-century texts came to be chosen as part of a canon, an authoritative group of texts by which the soundness of new or unfamiliar Christian writings could be measured, seems to have begun around the beginning of the second century. The Book of Revelation refers to a collection of letters to the Seven Churches of Asia; though the collection is clearly imaginary, there is significance in the author's visionary awareness of the idea that disparate letters (for example, by a figure such as Paul) could be revered as a sacred collection. In the mid-second century, the heretic Marcion's attempt to define a canon of Christian writings was symptomatic of a wider need to rationalize the terms of the new faith's rapid expansion. Marcion, however, wanted to use this canon as a substitute for – rather than a supplement to – the authority of the Septuagint, and this did not gain acceptance. From the second century onwards, we have manuscript evidence of Christian sacred texts circulating widely, often in translations, such as Armenian, Gothic, Latin, or Ethiopic, to reach Christian communities within and beyond the boundary of the Roman world. But in the first centuries, Christian texts circulated individually or as part of small clusters – such as the letters of Paul – rather than as part of a single definitive book. This meant that the canon of Christian Scripture remained fluid until the fourth century at least.

Writing during the reign of the Emperor Constantine in the fourth century, the first historian of Christianity, Eusebius of Caesarea, suggested that the very earliest Christian communities had enjoyed a doctrinal and intellectual unity that later communities could only envy. According to Eusebius, heresy had emerged at a second stage of the Church's development, when envy of the leadership caused some of the congregation to draw away from the early union of hearts. In the early twentieth century, however, Walter Bauer argued that the myth of early unity was Eusebius' invention. The hallmark of the earliest churches was in fact tremendous doctrinal diversity, born of the process by which the Christian message had circulated across the Roman Empire. Wandering charismatic teachers had carried and developed the message, drawing in equal parts on tradition and inspiration. These teachers, of course, had little opportunity to consult with one another to confirm whether or not their respective prophetic improvisations on tradition had resulted in compatible theologies.

In 1979, Elaine Pagels argued that the emergence of a canon of normative Christian Scriptures reflected the struggle of second-century bishops to develop a network of established institutional authority. As part of this process, it became important to harmonize the independent theological traditions of the ancient communities. In so doing, Pagels suggested, the bishops placed as much stress as they could on precedents for institutional authority, and on their own status as recipients of an institutional role handed down directly from the apostles. Toward the end of the century Irenaeus of Lyons, for example, told the story of the succession from Peter to Eleutherus, his contemporary as Bishop of Rome, and elsewhere how as a youth he himself had sat at the feet of Bishop Polycarp of Smyrna, who in turn had sat at the feet of John of Ephesus, apostle and evangelist. At the same time, Irenaeus suggested to his readers that despite the existence of a diversity of Gospels handed down in the name of the apostles by the second-century Church, there could only be four – those of Matthew, Mark, Luke, and John – which held authority. He saw them as breathing incorruption into the Church, their number reflecting that of the four principal winds.

At the same time, Christian men of literature across the empire asked themselves how biblical tradition could be brought into a meaningful relationship with the literary, historical, and philosophical currents of the wider Graeco-Roman cultural milieu. It is a commonplace that 'high' biblical interpretation in the patristic period clustered around two schools. That of Antioch, exemplified by Theodore of Mopsuestia (d. 428), made every attempt to respect the historical sense of both Old and New Testaments. It was understood that *theoria*, the search for a more elusive spiritual sense, could also bear fruit, but only if the result bore an evident relationship to the historical sense. The Alexandrian tradition, by contrast, sought a freer relationship between text and meaning through allegorical interpretation. Here, the key was the identification of a parallel relationship between events in the biblical text and an encoded spiritual message. Its opponents felt that the allegorical method left too much open to the inspiration of the interpreter, that the allegorical sense of Scripture was no more than the spiritual sense come unmoored from any accountability to tradition. But the allegorical tradition in fact bore a very distinguished pedigree. Reaching back through its most famous Christian exponent, Origen of Alexandria (d. *c.*254), to the Jewish Platonist Philo of Alexandria (d. *c.*50) and beyond, allegorical exegesis had been central to diaspora Judaism as a means of mediating the relationship between Jewish and Hellenic intellectual traditions, allowing educated Greek-speaking Jews to resolve the tension between otherwise conflicting identities. Meanwhile, in late antiquity, pagan philosophers were working with the same methods in order to find new philosophical and spiritual meanings in Homer and other touchstones of Hellenic tradition.

Christian ethics seems to have been biblically based from the outset, even where the reading is allegorical or tangential. If we take as a starting-point the first-century letters of Paul of Tarsus or those of Ignatius of Antioch at the turn of the second century, we see men who are deeply immersed in the imaginative landscape of the Septuagint. In her imaginative study, *The Making of Fornication,* Kathy Gaca has demonstrated that even comparatively non-intellectual matters such as sexual ethics were debated through an exegesis so learned that even the interlocutors could not be sure of following one another's learned use of both the Septuagint and Hellenic philosophical sources.

When Paul, for example, developed his central metaphor of the community as Body of Christ, he layered in what Gaca calls a 'sexual poetics' based on the metaphor of God's marriage to Israel. Individual Christians were to be understood as 'limbs' 'or 'members' of the Body of Christ, in contrast to others, the 'limbs of a harlot', who failed to show allegiance to the community. As with the Septuagint, the metaphor gains force from evocative layering: 'Do you not know that he who joins himself to a prostitute becomes one body with her? . . . Do you not know that your body is a temple of the Holy Spirit within you, which you have from God?' (1 Cor. 6:16, 19). The relationship of metaphorically linked images, though not precisely aligned in a rational order, derives power from layering, overlap, and repetition. The metaphors do not really 'line up' – but this is part of their power. If the reader or hearer was confounded in the face of the metaphor, this may have been all to the good.

While *porneia* in pagan texts referred in a comparatively neutral descriptive sense to prostitution, in the Septuagint it refers to sexual transgressions against the authority of God. According to Gaca, 'Sexual defilement and dishonor are incorporated into a new order of wrongdoing – disobeying a deity who requires unconditional obedience and devotion.' As imagined by both Jews and Christians, God is a jealous lover, whose people must humble themselves on the model of an adulterous wife hovering in fear of punishment. Here a specific demographic threat to the growth of Israelite religion – that of inter-marriage with women who will raise the couple's children in a gentile faith – takes on a metaphorical life of its own. Thus, for example, Israel is collectively likened to an adulterous bride while the male Israelites are individually enjoined not to 'betray' their God sexually by engaging in relations with women who worship other gods. Again, the metaphors do not really 'line up' – but they do not need to.

Turning again to Paul, we see in his sexual ethics an attempt to balance biblical tradition with eschatological urgency. Paul did not see much value in procreation, given his firm expectation that the end of the world was approaching. More importantly, his plan of action in the battle against fornication was to fight fire with fire. Paul saw what Gaca calls 'the pure blue flame of marital sex' as his most powerful weapon. It is significant that in the face of the eschaton, Paul made every attempt to achieve vivid-ness and force in his language, and to be understood. But across the centuries the impor-tance of being widely understood seems to have become less urgent. At the same time, readers and hearers could still not be trusted to recognize complex biblical inter-textu-alities when they were brought into play. There is evidence, as we will see below, that the learned exegetes of the later patristic period often felt they were speaking in a void.

Two landmark studies of the last decade have changed the landscape against which the question of widespread participation in debate over Scripture and tradition must be viewed. Harry Gamble's *Books and Readers in the Early Church* (1995) reminds us that the well-documented conversions of the second century, such as that of Justin Martyr, were not typical, in that they involved literate men whose spiritual identification with the new faith was the culmination of a sustained process of philosophical inquiry. To be sure, this is a point which has been made in previous generations. In 1963, H. J. Car-penter went so far as to suggest that the late second- and third-century figures such as Origen and Tertullian of Carthage (d. 225), who had attempted to develop a specula-tive and systematic theology, were in fact at odds with the ethical and pastoral interests of the wider Christian population:

> In a sense, the future belonged to these men, at least on theological issues, but they were all acutely aware of swimming against a tide, and their work passed into the future with its content and direction profoundly modified as the result of this force which opposed them. They stood in varying degrees for a new kind of interest in the faith which was not welcome to the great mass of Christians. (Carpenter 1963: 295)

For Carpenter, it was Irenaeus, with his ferocious repudiation of the speculations and esoteric traditions of the Gnostics, and his relentless interest in matters of authority and in the plainest meaning of the biblical text, who stood closest to the ground of popular Christianity.

But it is possible that even Irenaeus was fighting a losing battle if he expected the faithful to understand the biblical basis of the Church's ideas. Literacy, Gamble reminds us, was rare indeed in the Roman Empire; perhaps 10–15 per cent of the early Christ-ian community could read, and even these would have done so with difficulty. Obvi-ously this does not mean that the majority of Christians had no exposure to the biblical text, but their exposure was through hearing it read aloud or paraphrased in preach-ing. This meant that where the Bible ended and the wider and often disputed contours of Christian lore began would have been unclear to most, even after the canon had emerged as a fixed point of reference.

We can deduce from the late second-century *Acts of the Scillitan Martyrs* that com-munities pooled together their resources to buy books (or have them made), for in this text, written in North Africa in 180, the community leader, Speratus, brings 'books and letters (*libri et epistulae*) of a just man named Paul' with him when he and his com-panions are brought before the proconsul. Questions of literacy aside, book ownership would have been well beyond the economic means of ordinary community members. Where books were owned by individuals, intense piety and high economic standing must have stood in alignment. We will see below, however, that even where the individual possession of books was a realistic possibility, the biblical text was some-times linked to modes of piety which were a far cry from our post-Reformation idea of Bible study.

As the Christian message spread out into a largely illiterate gentile society, biblical literacy was probably restricted largely to exposure through preaching and the liturgy. Second-century writers such as the author of 1 Timothy and Justin Martyr himself record that the 'public reading of Scripture' (1 Tim. 4:13; Justin, *Apology* 1:67) was a standard element of early Christian corporate worship. The medium of exposure would have been the same for the emerging corpus of Christian writings as for the Septuagint. As the arbiter of what elaborations of biblical material would be made available though preaching, the bishop would play an all-important role as the guardian and expositor of the Christian message.

The second landmark study is that of Rodney Stark, *The Rise of Christianity: A Sociologist Reconsiders History* (1996). Stark offered compelling evidence from modern field-work-based study of religious evangelism that interest in the ostensible 'message' of a religious group is not an important factor in predicting whether or not an individual will pursue a relationship with a religious group after first contact. In fieldwork during the 1960s with his colleague John Lofland among the early followers of the Reverend Sun Myung Moon in the USA, Stark discovered that an individual's memory of 'first contact' with the group would change dramatically if he or she eventually became a member. A consistent feature of retrospective answers to the 'Why did you join?' question put to converts was that the magnetic influence had been exerted by the group's theology. But this did not line up with the data on initial reactions collected directly after the encounter – even where the same informant was interviewed. When Stark and Lofland interviewed individuals after 'first contact' and then traced the eventual decision of those individuals whether or not to join the group, what they discovered was that the individual's recollection of 'first contact' would be distorted by ideas and values which had later come to seem significant. Equally, the people who eventually converted did not begin by being especially attracted to the group's ideas. Rather, they began by liking members of the group as individuals. (Indeed, future converts sometimes specified in interviews that they liked members of the missionary team despite a perception that their ideas were strange.) From Stark and Lofland's work, it became clear that personal relationships, not religious doctrine, were at the core of the movement's unusual appeal. Related work by Stark and William Sims Bainbridge on interpersonal bonds between Mormons and non-Mormons in the 1970s led to complementary results. In one Mormon mission, the statistical return on door-to-door missionary activity was a disheartening 1 in a 1,000 visits. But where 'first contact' took place in the home of a new contact's own friends or family, the success rate was 1 out of 2. In other words, to attain a high conversion rate, missionaries needed to target their activity toward the existing non-Mormon contacts – friends and family – of members of the group itself.

Stark argued that a similar strategy must have been in play among the early Christian communities. His main aim in *The Rise of Christianity* was to present a model that would account for the stunningly high growth rate of the early Church – *c.* 40 per cent per decade, a rate roughly comparable to that of the Mormons. With growth of this kind, similar to the compounding of interest, seemingly small gains could be multiplied if they were compounded by repetition, and if new converts themselves were invited to take up a key role as mediators between the faith community and the 'outside' world. Friendship, personal magnetism, and a sense of belonging were probably the driving factors in this process.

So what was the place of books in the early Christian communities, and what was the place of the Book? How deeply aware were the Christian laity of the Christian scriptural tradition, and how closely did awareness of the teachings of this tradition govern lay ethics in the early Church?

The epitome of the third-century *Acts of Andrew* made by Gregory of Tours in the late sixth century preserves the story of Trophime, the repentant former mistress of the Proconsul of Achaea in Patras, who begins frequenting the proconsul's palace with a new motive, in order to hear the preaching of the apostle Andrew, who is acting as a kind of palace chaplain. When the proconsul's wife discovers her presence in the palace, she summons the *procurator* and has Trophime condemned to a brothel. But like many a heroine of hagiographical romance, Trophime avoids contact with the brothel's clients to the degree that she can:

> Trophime entered the brothel and prayed incessantly. Whenever men came to touch her, she would place the Gospel which she had with her (*evangelium quod secum habebat*) on her breast, and all the men would fail to approach her. A particularly shameless rogue came to violate her, and when she resisted, he tore off her clothes, and the gospel fell to the ground. Trophime wept, stretched her hands toward heaven, and said, 'Do not let me be defiled, O Lord, for whose name I value chastity!' Immediately an angel of the Lord appeared to the youth, and he fell at the angel's feet and died . . . later she raised the lad in the name of Jesus, and all the city ran to the sight. (Gregory of Tours, *Liber de miraculis*, 23; MacDonald 1990: 282–5)

Gamble sees Trophime's possession of an *evangelium* as evidence of private reading – it is certainly evidence of private biblical piety – and it can also be seen as evidence of a kind of talismanic use of the biblical text as an amulet to ward away evil. The minute Cologne Mani Codex is perhaps the most famous example of the micro-codex, the kind of small religious book that was meant to be carried around on the person of its owner, and it is possible that this is what was meant by Trophime's *evangelium* (Gamble 1995: 236–41).

But there is another possibility which must be considered here. A Christian example of a related type is Berlin MS gr. 9096, a spell for healing and protection copied in Greek on a slip of parchment 14×8 centimetres, presumably to be carried as an amulet in a pouch or envelope by its owner. It is worth quoting the text in full for its invocation of multiple biblical texts (Ps. 91:1; John 1:1–2, Matt. 1:1, Mark 1:1, Luke 1:1, Ps. 118:6–7, Ps. 18:2, Matt. 4:23), which include the first lines of the four canonical Gospels and a cluster of well-known Psalm texts, alongside Matthew 4:23, which refers to the beginning of Jesus' career in healing and casting out demons:

> † In the name of the father and the son and the holy spirit. One who dwells in the help of the most high <will> abide in the shelter of the lord of heaven.

† In the beginning was the Word, and the Word was with <god>, and the Word was god. This was in the beginning with god.

† Book of the generation of Jesus Christ, son of David, son of Abraham.

† Beginning of the gospel of Jesus Christ, son of god.

† Since many have undertaken to compile a narrative.

† The lord is my helper, and I shall not fear. What will humankind do to me?

† The lord is my helper, and I shall look upon my enemies.

† The lord is my foundation, and my refuge, and my deliverer.

† The lord went about all Galilee, teaching in the synagogues and preaching the gospel of the kingdom and healing every disease and every infirmity.

† The body and the blood of Christ spare your servant who wears this amulet. (Meyer and Smith: 1999, 35)

In fact, Matthew 4:23 ('The lord went about all Galilee . . .') seems to have had a distinguished career as the basis for healing amulets. Another parchment amulet written in Greek, Oxyrhynchus 1077, consists entirely of a short biblical extract, Matthew 4:23–4, prefaced by the title 'Curative gospel (*evangelion*) according to Matthew'. It is entirely possible that when Gregory of Tours refers to an *evangelium* which Trophime carried with her, his Greek source in fact intended an *evangelion* similar to the Berlin and Oxyrhynchus amulets.

From these and many other instances, one can see that while the Jesus of the Gospels was understood as the predecessor and patron of latter-day Christian healers and miracle-workers, the words of the biblical text themselves were cherished in a quasi-magical sense as words of power. Hagiographical texts from the post-Constantinian period also tell us something about how the Bible was imagined as influencing those who read it. At the same time, it is clear that the figures of the apostles and evangelists have taken on a narrative life of their own.

The fifth or sixth century hagiographical romance known as the *Passion of Eugenia* offers an episode in which an aristocratic pagan heiress obtains copies of the letters of Paul and the story of Thecla. While reading during a carriage journey, she decides to follow Thecla and renounce marriage, and persuades her two eunuch chaperones to join her in fleeing to the desert, where, Eugenia having cut her hair and disguised herself as a boy, the three will join a monastery. This episode clearly bears an echo of the scene in the second-century *Acts of Paul and Thecla* in which the virgin Thecla sits at an open window and listens to the Apostle Paul preaching in the house across the street, before choosing to cut her hair and follow him, disguised as a boy. But there may also be an echo here of Acts 8, in which the Apostle Philip meets an Ethiopian eunuch, the minister of Candace, queen of the Ethiopians, while the eunuch, who is travelling by chariot, sits reading the prophet Isaiah. When Philip approaches the chariot and asks, 'Do you understand what you are reading?', the eunuch invites him to climb into the chariot and instruct him. Eventually, he stops the vehicle near water, and invites Philip to baptize him before the two return to their respective journeys. Clearly, reading and travel were linked in the imagination as methods by which an individual could be prised from the network of relationships and obligations which governed his or her actions.

By contrast, in a fourth-century Greek homily addressed to the parents of virgins, biblical study is recommended as an activity through which the girls should 'seek after Paul as Thecla did', but in this case Thecla's runaway journey with the apostle through the cities of Asia Minor as he preached is re-imagined in comparatively parent-friendly terms, as careful domestic reading of Paul's letters. This reflects, of course, a milieu in which fourth-century aristocratic ladies, many of them practitioners of household asceticism, took up biblical exegesis as the theme for discussion in their literary salons. The most famous of these circles, that of Marcella on the Aventine in Rome, cooperated closely both as patronesses and as pupils with the eminent Christian *literati* of the day – in Marcella's case with St Jerome himself, thus contributing indirectly to his work on the Vulgate, the first translation to be made into Latin directly from the original Hebrew and Aramaic rather than from the Septuagint. Another of Jerome's spiritual protégées, the teenage Eustochium, was the recipient of his famous *Letter 22* in the early 380s. In this meditation on the virtue of virginity, the young virgin is encouraged to imagine herself as the Bride of Christ through the nuptial poetry of the Song of Songs, casting herself as the Shulamite and Christ as the Beloved. To a modern sensibility, Jerome's proposal of biblical imagery as the vehicle for an erotically charged mysticism may seem prurient, but in offering a framework for the reader's imaginative participation within the biblical text, he showed himself acutely sensible to the devotional cravings of late Roman Christianity.

Other writers evidence an equal and opposite desire to dramatize the process by which familiar and beloved biblical narratives had come into being in the first place. Composed between the fifth and seventh centuries, the pseudonymous Greek *Acts of John by Prochoros* relate the miraculous process by which the evangelist himself received the inspiration to dictate his text to Prochoros, the faithful scribe who accompanied him. The dictation itself is triggered by an earth-shattering display of thunder and lightning; the narrator – Prochoros – describes how after he fainted in the face of this heavenly display, the Apostle commanded him 'to write on the paper everything you hear from my mouth. And opening his mouth, John, standing and praying up toward heaven, said, "In the beginning was the Word" ' (*Acts of John by Prochoros*, 155; Krueger 2004: 37–9). Though the reader is invited here to identify with the hapless Prochoros, most significant is the status of the Gospel itself as the miraculous instrument chosen by God to convey his Words of Power. Both writer and reader of the later text are able to capture a reflection of its glory.

Elizabeth A. Clark has argued that from the mid-fourth century, ascetic readers became expert at finding messages of sexual renunciation in the biblical text even where they had to be discovered allegorically. But this ascetic appropriation of the biblical text can be said to have back-fired if it contributed to a lay sense of exclusion from – or irrelevance of – the biblical message. We know from contemporary sermons that if the non-ascetic laity engaged in home-based biblical study, they did not do so to the satisfaction of their bishops.

Best known are the lamentations of John Chrysostom, the star-crossed bishop of Constantinople at the turn of the fifth century. When faced with the recalcitrance of his congregation in the matter of Bible study, Chrysostom challenged them: 'Who among you, if required, could recite one Psalm or any other part of divine Scriptures?

No one.' For the dearth of private reading Chrysostom had heard many excuses: a lack of leisure, a lack of books, a lack of interest, even 'I am not a monk' (Gamble 1995: 233; citing *Homilies in Matthew* 2:9, *De Lazaro* 3, *Homilies in Genesis* 21, and *Homilies in Matthew* 2, respectively).

In the West, Alan Kreider has argued that at the same period bishops were increasingly concerned that the lore and ethics of Christian community were simply not reaching the Christian membership:

> Augustine thought of the early days of the church, recorded in Acts 2, when people were 'thoroughly and perfectly' converted. Even in his day, he knew some people who sought to follow Christ, to pray for their enemies, and to distribute their goods to the needy. To their behaviour . . . the response of many baptised people was incredulous: 'Why are you acting crazy? You're going to extremes; aren't other people Christians?' (Kreider 2001: 34; citing *Sermons* 88:12–13 and 14. 4, respectively)

In Kreider's view, it was a losing battle. In his *de catechizandis rudibus*, which would be influential as a manual for clergy throughout the early Middle Ages, Augustine of Hippo (d. 430) recommended that converts who wished to be admitted to catechetical instruction be treated to a 60-minute *narratio* summarizing sacred history from the creation to Judgement Day. By the Carolingian period, Kreider suggests, the pre-catechism *narratio* was all that was left of the catechism itself, and it is not clear that non-converts – i.e. children who grew up within Christian families – received even that. Scholars have long debated whether the end of antiquity brought a decline in biblical awareness among the laity. It is certainly the case that the ascetic interest in Scripture continued to gain momentum, and that a widening gap emerged between the married and their ascetic brethren in this respect.

In his famous account (*Confessions* 3. 5) of his own first attempt to read the Scriptures as a pretentious young *rhetor*, Augustine recorded his initial disappointment at their seeming lack of eloquence. At the same time, he suggested in retrospect, it was his own inexperienced eye that had failed to see to the hidden depths. As a youth, his relationship with Scripture had foundered in the gap between two educational systems, that of Roman rhetoric – his own educational background – and that of the Christian exegete. Only in middle age – and after years of ascetic and pastoral experience – could he begin to see the seeming simplicity of Scripture as one of its strengths. Two centuries later, Gregory the Great (d. 604) would reverse the equation, casting the simultaneous transparency and mystery of Scripture in a positive light. 'Scripture', he proclaimed in the preface to his *Moralia on Job*, addressed to Leander of Seville in 591, 'is as it were a kind of river, if I may so liken it, which is both shallow and deep, wherein the lamb may find a footing and the elephant float' (Gregory, *Ad Leandrum* 4, *CCSL* 140:6). It was Gregory who, in the *Moralia* and in other exegetical writings, attempted to offer a synthesis of exegetical strategies from earlier patristic writers, integrating allegorical reading into a method for proceeding systematically through three related senses of Scripture, the historical, typical, and moral.

For Gregory, the entire system of Scripture, both Old and New Testaments, was to be understood as a unity. Irenaeus' emphasis on the ethical meaning of Scripture could and must be integrated with the reflections of learned exegesis. According to Gregory, the mystery of Scripture can, finally, only be understood in the light of the 'eye of love' that comes through the attempt to live by biblical ethics. 'Throughout Scripture God speaks to us for this purpose alone, to lead us to the love of himself and of our neighbour.' In this as in so many things, Gregory found a way to close a chapter of patristic endeavour on a note that would serve the medieval Church as a source both of wisdom and of often sorely needed encouragement.

References and Further Reading

Amand, D. and Moons, M.-C. (1953). 'Une curieuse homélie grecque inédite sur la virginité adressée aux pères de famille', *Revue Bénédictine* 63: 18–69, 211–38.

Bauer, W. ([1934] 1971). *Orthodoxy and Heresy in Earliest Christianity*, trans. and ed. Robert A. Kraft and Gerhard Krodel. Philadelphia, PA: Fortress Press.

Burton-Christie, D. (1993). *The Word in the Desert: Scripture and the Quest for Holiness in Early Christian Monasticism*. New York: Oxford University Press.

Carpenter, H. T. (1963). 'Popular Christianity and the Theologians in the Early Centuries', *Journal of Theological Studies* n.s. 14: 294–310.

Clark, E. A. (1999). *Reading Renunciation: Asceticism and Scripture in Early Christianity*. Princeton, NJ: Princeton University Press.

Cooper, K. (2005). 'Ventriloquism and the Miraculous: Conversion, Preaching, and the Martyr Exemplum in Late Antiquity', in Kate Cooper and Jeremy Gregory (eds), *Signs, Wonders, and Miracles*. Woodbridge: Boydell, pp. 22–45.

Cox Miller, P. (1993). 'The Blazing Body: Ascetic Desire in Jerome's Letter to Eustochium', *Journal of Early Christian Studies* 1: 21–45.

Dawson, D. (1992). *Allegorical Readers and Cultural Revision in Ancient Alexandria*. Berkeley, CA: University of California Press.

Gaca, K. L. (2003). *The Making of Fornication: Eros, Ethics, and Political Reform in Greek Philosophy and Early Christianity*. Berkeley, CA: University of California Press.

Gamble, H. Y. (1985). *The New Testament Canon: Its Making and Meaning*. Philadelphia, PA: Fortress Press.

Gamble, H. Y. (1995). *Books and Readers in the Early Church: A History of Early Christian Texts*. New Haven, CT: Yale University Press.

Haines-Eitzen, K. (2000). *Guardians of Letters: Literacy, Power, and the Transmitters of Early Christian Literature*. New York: Oxford University Press.

Kreider, A. (2001). 'Changing Patterns of Conversion in the West', in A. Kreider (ed.), *The Origins of Christendom*. Edinburgh: T. & T. Clark, pp. 3–46.

Krueger, D. (2004). *Writing and Holiness: The Practice of Authorship in the Early Christian East*. Philadelphia, PA: University of Pennsylvania Press.

Lamberton, R. (1986). *Homer the Theologian: Neoplatonist Allegorical Reading and the Growth of the Epic Tradition*. Berkeley, CA: University of California Press.

Lampe, G. H. W. (ed.) (1969). *The Cambridge History of the Bible*, vol. 2: *The West from the Fathers to the Reformation*. Cambridge: Cambridge University Press.

MacDonald, D. R. (1990). *The Acts of Andrew and the Acts of Andrew and Matthias in the City of the Cannibals*. Atlanta, GA: Scholars Press.

Matter, E. A. (1990). *The Voice of My Beloved: The Song of Songs in Western Medieval Christianity*. Philadelphia, PA: University of Pennsylvania Press.

Meyer, Marvin W. and Smith, Richard (1999). *Ancient Christian Magic: Coptic Texts of Ritual Power*, 2nd edn. Princeton, NJ: Princeton University Press.

Pagels, E. (1979). *The Gnostic Gospels*. New York: Random House.

Stark, R. (1996). *The Rise of Christianity: A Sociologist Reconsiders History*. Princeton, NJ: Princeton University Press.

Stark, R. and Bainbridge, W. S. (1980). 'Networks of Faith: Interpersonal Bonds and Recruitment to Cults and Sects', *American Journal of Sociology* 85: 1376–95.

Stark, R. and Lofland, J. (1965). 'Becoming a World-Saver: A Theory of Conversion to a Deviant Perspective', *American Sociological Review* 30: 862–75.

Williams, R. (1991). 'The Bible', in Ian Hazlett (ed.), *Early Christianity: Origins and Evolution to AD 600*. London: SPCK.

CHAPTER 3
The Middle Ages

Mary Dove

The anonymous writer of the Prologue to the Wycliffite Bible was an Englishman, proud of being one of the translators of the first Bible in English, completed around 1390. He addresses his Prologue to English readers, encouraging them not to be afraid 'to studie in the text of holy writ' (Forshall and Madden 1850, vol. 1: 2). Even so, when he comes to consider the problems for interpretation caused by the textual differences between the Hebrew Psalms and the Latin Psalter derived from the Greek of the Septuagint (more on this below), he calls himself and his readers 'Latyns': 'Noo book in þe eld (old) testament is hardere to vndirstonding to vs Latyns [than the Psalms], for oure lettre (our Latin text) discordiþ myche fro þe Ebreu' (ibid., vol. 1: 38). By 'Latyns' he means 'Roman Catholics', but he also means people whose 'holy writ' is the Latin Bible. His intellectual world is Latin, not English; the phrase 'vs Latyns' reminds his readers that the Latin Bible is not theirs, although the English Bible is about to be. The purpose of the Prologue to the Wycliffite Bible is to break down the longstanding barriers between Latin and English readers. For the man who wrote it, as we shall see, knowledge of the Bible is not a privilege but a right.

In early medieval Europe, only a small minority even of those literate in Latin had access to a copy of the entire Latin Bible, in spite of the fact that their culture was suffused with Christianity, and understood itself as being rooted in *sacra scriptura*, Holy Writ. Nearly half the surviving biblical manuscripts pre-800 are manuscripts of the Gospels alone. Pandects, manuscript-volumes containing all the books of the Old and New Testaments, were enormous and very rare. The oldest surviving one-volume Bible, the Codex Amiatinus, written in Northumbria around 700, has 1030 folios measuring 505 by 340 millimetres, and it weighs 34 kilos (De Hamel 2001: 33–4). The first production of Bibles on a large scale was in the early ninth century in Tours, instigated by Alcuin, Abbot of St Martin's but originally from the Cathedral School at York. Each 'Tours Bible' took about six months to make. In a poem written to accompany a presentation copy, Alcuin marvels at the fact that a single book can encompass such manifold riches: 'this manuscript contains here within one holy corpus all the great gifts of God at one and the same time' (Ganz, in Gameson 1994: 56).

The owners of 'Tours Bibles' were Cathedral Churches, religious houses and great princes; purchasing a Bible was beyond the means of the individual scholar. It was not until the late twelfth century that developments in the technology of manuscript production in France enabled Bibles of a manageable size and affordable price to be produced. From 1230 onwards, multiple copies of Bibles written in a tiny hand on ultra-thin ('uterine') vellum were sold by the Paris stationers, and spread throughout Europe (De Hamel 2001: 129–33). 'Tours Bibles' and 'Paris Bibles' could be read as well in Iceland as in Sicily, but only by the clerical class, educated in the Latin language to manage the affairs of Church or state, or to become scholars and educate others.

The arch-conservative chronicler Thomas Knighton, writing in the Benedictine Abbey at Leicester in the last decade of the fourteenth century, voices a convenient clerical supposition, that the biblical text was a divine gift to the *litterati*. Writing in Latin, Knighton says that 'Christ gave the Gospel to the clergy and doctors of the Church, so that they might administer it to laypeople'. He is only too aware, however, that the long-standing clerical prerogative is under threat:

> Master John Wyclif has translated the Gospel from Latin into the English language, which is very far from being the language of angels. As a result, because of him the content of Scripture has become more common and more open to laymen and women who can read than it customarily is to quite learned clerks of good intelligence, and thus the pearl of the gospel is scattered abroad and trodden underfoot by swine (Matt. 7:6). (Martin 1995: 242–5)

Knighton alludes ironically here to a story preserved in Bede's *Historia ecclesiastica gentis Anglorum* (Ecclesiastical History of the English People, 731 AD). Pope Gregory the Great (590–604) enquires about the origin of some good-looking lads with lovely fair hair he sees in the slave market in Rome. On being told they are *Angli* (English), Gregory replies '*bene* (very appropriate), for they look angelic, fit to be heirs of the angels in heaven' (Colgrave and Mynors 1969: 134–5). The young men who were the object of Gregory's curiosity could not have understood his pun, but Knighton (who was, like Gregory and Bede, a monk educated in Latin) appreciated it and manipulated it to his own rhetorical advantage eight centuries later – Gregory may have thought that the English look angelic, but their language is 'very far from being the language of angels'. The English language, in Knighton's view, is undoubtedly inferior to Latin. From the conversion of England to the end of the Middle Ages (and beyond), there was in effect a two-tier culture; the Latin-literate and the others. The book that was invoked as the source and justification of all authority, and informed every aspect of medieval culture, was a closed book to most men and almost all women.

The story of Gregory and the slaves does not end with the pun on Angle and angel. Gregory interprets the fact that the slaves are from Deiri (more or less coterminous with Yorkshire) as a sign that they are to be saved *de ira dei*, from the wrath of God (cf. Ps. 84:4–6, Vulgate Bible = Ps. 85:4–6, King James Bible). Since the name of their ruler is Aelle, Gregory anticipates that they are destined to sing celestial alleluias. It was this encounter, says Bede, that incited Gregory to commission Augustine (later known as Augustine of Canterbury) to bring the English into the Roman Christian Church. The story is the climax of Bede's encomium of Gregory as ecclesiast and as Christian writer *par excellence*. Bede incorporated into his *Historia ecclesiastica* Gregory's *Little Book of Answers* to Augustine's questions about Church governance and ritual purity (*Libellus responsionum*, 601 AD), and he recommended Gregory's *Regula pastoralis* (Pastoral Care), written just after Gregory was elected Pope in 590, to Egbert of York, founder of the Cathedral School where Alcuin was to study. Alcuin also held *Regula pastoralis* in high esteem, and it was cited approvingly by the canonist (ecclesiastical lawyer) Gratian in his *Decretum* (Decretals, *c*.1140).

This extremely influential work teaches that the wisdom of the ruler and the worldly well-being of the ruled go hand in hand, as God made clear to Solomon, who asked for wisdom and had worldly goods bestowed on him as well (2 Chr. 1:7–12). *Regula pastoralis* was translated into English by King Alfred, for the profit of secular as well as ecclesiastical officials (Meens, in Gameson 1999: 181). In the Preface to his translation, Alfred puts the following words into the mouths of uneducated ninth-century churchmen: 'Ure yldran . . . lufedon wisdom & ðurh ðone hie begeaton welan & us læfdon (our forefathers loved wisdom, and through it they obtained wealth and well-being, and bequeathed them to us)' (Schreiber 2002: 193). *Regula pastoralis* has an uncompromising message for illiterate or barely literate churchmen like these, who have received *welan* but will be unable to pass it on to their descendants. The words of Isaiah, which are the words of 'the voice of truth' (that is, God), condemns 'these shepherds (*pastores*) [who] have not known wisdom' (Isa. 56:11), blaming them for their ignorance (Judic et al. 1992, vol. 1: 130). Their unfortunate underlings are to be pitied. Gregory's concept of good order is uncompromisingly hierarchical; appropriately enough, he was responsible for making known to the Western Church Pseudo-Dionysius' nine orders of the celestial hierarchy (Markus 1997: 12–13).

Bede values Gregory for bringing the English into the Roman Church and for promoting cultural unity within Europe. The gigantic Codex Amiatinus, produced in Bede's Northumbria as a gift for the Pope, deliberately mimicked Italian biblical manuscripts in text and format rather than following the insular (Anglo-Saxon/Irish) models developed within the Celtic Church. The puns that make up the story of Gregory and the slaves voice Gregory's resistance to cultural difference: the boys are unnaturally fair, but therefore potential saints; they are from remote Deiri, but therefore always already recipients of God's favour. In a letter that suggests there may some historical truth behind the story (595 AD), Gregory asks one Candidus to use surplus ecclesiastical revenues in Gaul to pay for English slaves 'aged seventeen or eighteen' to be brought to Rome to be educated in monasteries – to be turned into Christians and educated in Latin (Norberg 1982: 378–9).

The nature of their education is suggested in Gregory's last work, a commentary on the first book of Kings: 'the liberal arts [non-Christian works by Greek and Roman authors] are to be studied only to the extent that knowledge of them enables divine eloquence [the Bible] to be better understood . . . God has provided this worldly knowledge (*saecularem scientiam*) as a step that ought to be able to raise us up to the lofty height of divine Scripture' (Verbraken 1963: 471–2). As R. A. Markus well says, 'the boundaries of Gregory's intellectual and imaginative worlds were', as Augustine of Hippo's had not been, 'the horizons of the Scriptures' (1997: 41). Gregory would doubtless wish to reply that those horizons are in no way limiting, since 'divine eloquence' and 'the voice of truth' (the title *Biblia*, Bible is found only from the twelfth century onwards) say everything that is worth hearing. Interpreting what is said, however, Gregory regards as the most demanding of disciplines.

Since recreation is necessary after earnest study of sacred Scripture, a monastic version of trivial pursuit was devised, the Monks' Jestbook (*Joca monachorum*), in circulation from at least the sixth century AD to the end of the Middle Ages. Gregory, Bede and Knighton may all have played it. 'Who was born once and died twice?' 'Lazarus.' 'Who gave away something he or she had never received?' 'Eve. Milk' (Dubois, in Riché and Lobrichon 1984: 268–9). Even the act of eating was not an extra-biblical event, since the educated monk was aware that Gregory (and many medieval writers following him) claim that 'scriptura sacra nobis est cibus', it is Holy Scripture that is our real food (Smith, in Gameson 1994: 227). The analogy permeates the fourteenth-century poem *Piers Plowman*.

The Book of Books is Scripture set apart, 'on a high hill' in Gregory's imagination. In the cultural imagination of the medieval West, the Bible was required to be monolithic, and yet no educated person could fail to be aware that this metaphor was illusory. In the English of the Wycliffite Bible, 'þe Lord schal telle (speak out) in þe scripturis of puplis' (*Dominus narrabit in scriptura populorum*, Ps. 86:6, Forshall and Madden 1850, vol. 3: 826) looks like a statement that the word of God is to be found in written texts in all languages. But the writer of the Prologue to the Wycliffite Bible tells his English readers that 'Jerom seiþ: hooly writ is þe scripture of puplis', written 'by autorite and confermynge of þe Hooly Goost' (ibid., vol. 1: 56). What exactly, however, was the text the Holy Spirit authorized and established, given that every word of the Latin Bible was translated from Hebrew, Greek or Aramaic?

At least three different translations of the Psalter were in circulation in the Middle Ages: a revision by Jerome of an Old Latin (that is, pre-Jerome) translation from the Greek; Jerome's second and more critical revision of the Old Latin, which came to be known as the 'Gallican Psalter' and was championed by Alcuin, and Jerome's third translation, from the Hebrew (White 1902: 874–5). It is the Gallican Psalter that reads 'þe Lord schal telle in þe scripturis of puplis'; the Hebrew Psalter's reading is 'the Lord records as he registers the peoples' (Ps. 87:6, RSV). Some medieval Bibles include parallel Hebrew and Gallican Psalters: the Wycliffite Bible does not, but the writer of the Prologue claims that he has recorded 'what þe Ebru haþ' in the margin, because the Psalms 'of alle oure bokis discordiþ most fro Ebreu' (Forshall and Madden 1850, vol. 1: 58).

The Latin Bible had entered the Middle Ages in a state of considerable textual complexity, a conglomerate of Old Latin translations, Jerome's revisions of Old Latin translations, and Jerome's translations from the Hebrew (White 1902: 873–7). Awareness of the wide variety of texts and readings preserved in biblical manuscripts and biblical commentaries resulted in several attempts at establishing a correct and consistent text. Alcuin, commissioned to do so by Charlemagne in 797, sent from Tours to York for manuscripts representing the Italo-Northumbrian branch of the biblical textual

tradition, then and now regarded very highly, but he did not have the time for intensive textual-critical work. His contemporary, Theodulf of Orleans, and the Cistercian
Stephen Harding in the middle of the twelfth century, were much more successful (ibid.,
878–9).

In spite of this, the Franciscan polymath Roger Bacon lamented in the late 1260s
that the text of 'Paris Bibles' was very poor, because of lack of knowledge of Greek
and Hebrew (Brewer 1859: 92–7). Bacon is right in saying that late-medieval Latin
Bibles characteristically include errors, inferior readings, and interpolations (Light, in
Gameson 1994: 157). Ignorance of the original languages of Scripture was, however,
beginning to be remedied. Bacon greatly admired Robert Grosseteste (Bishop of Lincoln
from 1235), who learned Greek late in life, and promoted the study of Hebrew (Smalley
1982: 343). The most significant work of biblical textual scholarship in the later Middle
Ages was the Franciscan Nicholas of Lyra's literal and moral commentary on the whole
Bible, 1322–31, informed throughout by his familiarity with the writings of Rashi
(Solomon ben Isaac of Troyes, 1045–1105) and other medieval Jewish scholars of
Scripture (Krey and Smith 2000: 1–12). Lyra's commentary strongly reinforced
Bacon's argument that biblical scholars needed to return, in the Old Testament, to the
hebraica veritas, the original Hebrew.

Because he has read Lyra, the writer of the Prologue to the Wycliffite Bible knows
that the Old Testament in the late-medieval Latin Bible diverges from the 'propre
origynals' in most books, not just in Psalms (Forshall and Madden 1850, vol. 1: 58).
The late-medieval cultural imagination pushes the text the Holy Spirit established so
far back in time that the greatest feats of linguistic scholarship are unlikely ever to
recover it completely. In his *De Veritate sacrae scripturae* (On the Truth of Holy Scripture,
1377–8), John Wyclif reacts to this by questioning whether in fact the text of Holy Writ
deserves to be called holy at all. He recalls that, while a boy at grammar school, he was
'painfully entangled in understanding and defending Scripture according to the strictly
literal, grammatical sense'. God, Wyclif says, later made it clear to him that what is
written in a Bible is in no way holy in itself; it is 'no more than the trace of a tortoise-
shell on a stone', unless it can be said to be holy 'on account of the way in which it
takes the faithful by the hand and leads them into knowledge of heavenly Scripture'
(Buddensieg 1905: 1, 114–15). The mature Wyclif's view was that Scripture should be
interpreted 'entirely according to the sense intended by its author (*pure ad sensum
autoris*)'; not its human author, but God (Forshall and Madden 1850, vol. 1: 183; Ghosh
2001: 42–5).

In his introduction to Psalms, as we have seen, the writer of the Prologue to the
Wycliffite Bible points out that the study of this book involves exceptional textual difficulties, with the result that many biblical scholars have renounced literal in favour of
spiritual interpretation (Forshall and Madden 1850, vol. 1: 38). He regards this as a
dangerous move, liable to result in 'moral fantasie', moral interpretation with no basis
in truth, as he says in his prologue to the prophetical books (ibid., vol. 3: 226). 'Wel
were him,' he exclaims, 'þat koude wel vndirstonde þe Sautir and kepe it in his lyuyng
(live according to what it says) and seie it deuoutly and conuicte (persuade) Jewis þerbi'
– persuade Jews, that is, to understand that the literal meaning of the Psalms points
to Christ, as Lyra had made clear (ibid., vol. 1: 38–9). Reading literally is something

fervently to be desired but extremely hard to accomplish in practice. In his awareness of the difficulty for everybody of reading literally and living in accordance with what is read, differences in estate and education are not an issue. It is no easier for him to read Psalms well than it is for a 'simple man of wit', a person who knows no Latin at all.

If the Bible, in medieval imagination, is a monolithic book the uncorrupted text of which is ultimately irrecoverable, it is also a monolithic book with a labile content, not all of it equally authoritative. Although Jerome specified which books of the Old Testament were canonical and could be used to determine Christian doctrine, no medieval Old Testament contains these books alone: throughout the Middle Ages, the Greek and Aramaic writings of the Christian Old Testament retained their biblical if not their canonical authority. Two of these books, however, 3 Ezra and Baruch, had a less assuredly biblical status than the rest. The writer of the Prologue to the Wycliffite Bible rightly says that Jerome 'biddeþ þat no man delite in þe dremis' of the Ezra-apocrypha (Forshall and Madden 1850, vol. 1: 2); nevertheless, medieval Bibles often include 3 Ezra (1 Esdras). The early, highly literal version of the Wycliffite Bible does, but not the later, revised version. In 'Paris Bibles' and in the Wycliffite Bible, Baruch follows Lamentations, but until 1200 Baruch was usually omitted, and, where present, it precedes Lamentations (Light, in Gameson 1994: 155). The prologue to Baruch in the Latin Bible, translated in the Wycliffite Bible, notes that Baruch is worthy of its place in the Christian Scriptures because it reveals 'many þingis of Crist and of þe laste tymes', the end of the world (Forshall and Madden 1850, vol. 3: 484).

In the New Testament, the Epistle to the Laodiceans may or may not be included: Alcuin rejected it, but Tours Bibles made in the time of his successor Fridugisus include it (Ganz, in Gameson 1994: 57). The New Testament always begins with the Gospels (usually with Matthew first and John last), but the other elements (the Pauline and Canonical Epistles, the Acts of the Apostles and Revelation) occur in a range of different orders. In the Old Testament, before 1200 the books may appear in the order derived by Jerome from the Hebrew Scriptures, with the apocryphal books added (Theoulfian Bibles have this order), or in the order broadly derived from the Septuagint (Augustine's order in *De doctrina christiana*), with the apocryphal books integrated into the canon. The 'Paris Bible' and the Wycliffite Bible have the books in the Augustinian order (De Hamel 2001: 22–4, 120–2).

Again, Wyclif responds to felt instability by questioning the significance of the underlying concept, this time the concept of higher and lower degrees of authority within the Bible. We should not think of the 'book of life' (Rev. 20:12) as being limited to the biblical canon, he says: 'it appears probable that many apocryphal books are Holy Scripture, since they are inscribed in the book of life'. As an arch-Realist, he understands the Book of Life to mean the Platonic Idea of the Christian Scriptures. He has in mind the New Testament apocrypha as well as the Old Testament apocrypha, for he specifies the Gospel of Nicodemus as well as Wisdom, Ecclesiasticus, Judith, Tobit and the Maccabees (Buddensieg 1905, vol. 1: 242).

Wyclif's idea of the Bible may be immutable, but any medieval image of the phenomenal Bible as uniform and indivisible must always be in tension with awareness of the Bible's unstable text and variable content. Moreover, it must also be in tension with awareness of the manifold ways in which the biblical text may be interpreted. An immense visual symbol of the proliferation, almost profligacy, of interpretation is the gloss (series of interpretive comments) on all the books of the Bible, compiled in northern France c.1100–30, the work that came to be known as the 'Standard Gloss', *Glossa ordinaria*. The text of the Bible together with all the interlinear and marginal glosses of the *Glossa ordinaria* could not be contained in a single manuscript, though the second volume of a massive two-volume set survives in Oxford (Bodl. Laud lat. MS 9).

One of the most heavily-glossed books of all is the Song of Songs, the gloss on which is compiled by Anselm, master of the Cathedral School at Laon, and his brother Ralph (Dove 1997: 34–6). Anselm and Ralph derive their material from many earlier commentators, but principally Bede, whose commentary is strongly influenced by Gregory, and includes as its final book a compendium of Gregory's glosses on the Song of Songs (Gregory had not written a commentary on this book, but referred to it frequently). Predictably, Gregory's glosses contribute to the Glossed Song of Songs the moral realism of a man at the centre of the institutional Church, witness his comment on 'like a lily among thorns' (2:2): 'in the Church there cannot be bad people without good people or good people without bad people; there has been no good man who has not been able to tolerate wicked men'. Other glosses have the 'thorns' as tribulation (Alcuin), heresies (Fulgentius Ruspensis) or the devil (Anselm), but for Gregory they are fellow Churchmen who enable him to practise pastoral forbearance (Dove 1997: 140–2).

Moral realism is not, however, Gregory's only mode of interpretation: there is erotic fervour, too. The saints 'glow more and more ardently the longer they yearn for the absent object of their desire' (ibid., 124). The bride is also, as she is for Origen, the soul, who turns towards her creator when she remembers that she is made in his image, and 'a certain initial sweetness from the eternal life of blessedness' encourages her to advance towards contemplation of God (ibid., 168–70). David Aers argues that the subject of the Song of Songs is 'carnal and very literal love', and that medieval Churchmen attempted to 'control the interaction between the readers' imagination and the text's diverse potentials' (Aers 1986: 63–4). Gregory, Bede and Lyra took it for granted that carnal love did not merit adult intellectual attention, and could not conceivably be the subject-matter of a book belonging to the biblical canon, but their culture did not equate the carnal with the erotic, as our culture is prone to do.

The Glossed Song of Songs invites its readers to take control of their own interaction with the text. When, for example, readers arrive at the verse 'a little bundle of myrrh is my beloved to me, he will remain between my breasts' (1:12), they may first read the marginal gloss written closest to this verse, 'the death of my beloved, which he underwent for my salvation, will always remain in my memory'. Then they may, or may not, return to the biblical verse before encountering marginal glosses that draw attention to the erotic potential of female breasts: 'in a nuptial song it was fitting to speak of *mammas*, breasts rather than *pectus*, chest', and 'it is not the breasts of chaste women but the breasts of harlots that are damaged, wrinkled with slack skin', inviting consideration of the smooth, seductive perfection of chaste women's breasts (Dove 1997: 142–6). To demand of the medieval reader, 'Are you reading these glosses literally or allegorically?' would be to attempt to control interpretation. If the Church had really wanted to exercise this kind of control (and I find no evidence for this), it should have suppressed the Glossed Song of Songs, and the *Glossa ordinaria* of which it is a part.

Medieval and Early Modern 'secular' love-literature is infused with the language of the Song of Songs. This is not because the language of the Song of Songs is carnal, and biblical scholars did not realize it, although this is just what the narrator thinks in Chaucer's Merchant's Tale (*c*.1390–5). Lecherous old January's invitation to his young wife May to join him for sex in their garden is made up of phrases from the Song of Songs:

> Rys up, my wyf, my loue, my lady free!
> The turtles voys is herd, my dowve sweete;
> The wynter is goon with alle his reynes weete.
> Com forth now, with thyne eyen columbyn!   (doves' eyes)
> How fairer been thy brestes than is wyn!
> The gardyn is enclosed al aboute
>   (*Canterbury Tales*, IV: 2138–43; S. of
>   S. 2:10–13; 4:1, 10, 12)

After these ravishing lines, the Merchant scornfully comments 'swiche olde lewed (lascivious) wordes used he' (*Canterbury Tales* IV, 2149). This put-down can be understood as the Merchant repaying in kind the habitual condescension of the cleric to the layman – but he is wrong about the Song of Songs. Secular love-literature is infused with the language of this book because in medieval imagination and culture the Song of Songs speaks at one and the same time of every dimension of human love. Only after the Enlightenment did writers begin to think it unseemly to employ erotic language to express love of God.

The writer of the Prologue to the Wycliffite Bible has little time for images of sweetness and desire. This is not because he finds them unseemly, but because he reads the Bible as a book of laws which the Church in England is intent, in his view, on breaking. Like Gregory in the *Regula pastoralis*, he draws moral lessons for the present age from the books of the Old Testament. At the end of his synopsis of the second book of Chronicles, the reader is startled by the cry 'but alas, alas, alas!' (Forshall and Madden 1850, vol. 1: 29), heralding a lengthy coda arguing that Christian lords in England, 'cristene lordis in name', that is, but with heathen characteristics (ibid., vol. 1: 30), do the opposite of the exemplary deeds of the good kings Jehoshaphat, Hezekiah and Josiah, preferring to take their (im)moral lesson from the wicked king Manasseh (2 Chr. 33:2–9) (ibid., vol. 1: 27). Rather than following Jehoshaphat's example and ensuring that God's law is taught 'opinly' to the people (2 Chr. 17:7–9), they are complicit in the offering of worthless pardons; rather than following Hezekiah's example and purifying god's house (2 Chr. 30:13–20), they 'bringin in symonient (simoniac) clerkis . . . to stoppe goddis lawe (the Bible)', and employ priests in worldly, temporal offices; rather than following Josiah's example and casting out idols from the temple (2 Chr. 34:3–5), they 'preisen and magnifien' not the Lord but the letters of friars, 'ful of disceit and leesingis (lies)'. They cruelly persecute those 'þat wolden teche treuly and freely þe lawe of god', and maintain those who preach 'fablis' and 'synful mennis tradiciouns, eiþer statutis that is canon law' while inhibiting Scripture from being preached, known and observed (Forshall and Madden 1850, vol. 1: 30).

Gregory's *Regula pastoralis* is quoted on the danger done by hypocrital and openly sinful prelates: 'noo man harmeþ more in þe chirche þan he þat doþ weiwardly and holdiþ þe name (reputation) of ordre eiþer of holynesse' (ibid., vol. 1: 32); prelates deserve to die as many deaths as they offer examples of evil-living to their underlings (ibid., vol. 1: 33). Having rejected the canon-law statutes invented by sinful men, the writer nevertheless cites eight *capitula* from the 'Rosarie', the *Rosarium super decreto* of the canon lawyer Guido de Baysio of Bologna (*c.*1300), including the whole of his demonstration that dumb prelates are idols (ibid., vol. 1: 31). The writer gestures towards the reader ignorant of canon law, explaining that Guido de Baysio is 'oon of þe famouseste doctouris of þe popis lawe', but in this passionate indictment of the contemporary Church and state he is primarily writing as a scholar to fellow-scholars, leaving English readers to cling onto his coat-tails as best they can.

Like Manasseh, the passage continues, kings and lords are idolaters, worshipping as an idol whichever mortal sin they choose, and thereby serving the devil. They are also idolaters in that they 'setten idolis in goddis hous, whanne þei maken vnworþi prelatis eiþer curatis in þe chirche . . . as god seiþ in (Zech. 11:17) to an vnable prelat: *A (O) þou schepherde and idole, forsakinge þe floc*' (Forshall and Madden 1850, vol. 1: 31). A marginal gloss in some Wycliffite Bible manuscripts identifies the shepherd as 'Antecrist', following Lyra's gloss on this verse, but here the writer is following Gregory in applying what the prophets say about shepherds to Christian pastors. Lords and prelates swear by the limbs of god and Christ and by the saints whom they make into idols, slander good men 'and clepen (call) hem lollardis, eretikis and riseris of debate and of tresoun aȝens þe king', over-tax, extort, and shed blood both in war and by refusing alms to the poor (ibid., vol. 1: 30). Manasseh in the end repented, according to 2 Chr. 33:12–16 (although he does not repent in the account of his reign in 2 Kgs. 1–18). The writer prays that God may stir lords and prelates to follow Manasseh in repenting, as they follow him in 'þese opyn synnes . . . lest oure reume (realm) be conquerid of (by) aliens eiþer heþen men' (ibid., vol. 1: 34).

According to John Foxe, this passage was the source of eight of the thirteen articles brought against one owner of a copy of the Prologue, the Lollard Richard Hunne, in 1514 (Cattley and Pratt 1853–70, vol. 4: 186). Even in the context of the Reformation, an apology was felt to be appropriate for its vehemence. In the Preface to his 1540 edition of the Prologue to the Wycliffite Bible, *The dore of holy Scripture*, John Gough says 'moste gentyl christen Reader . . . I humbly requyre you in case ye fynde ony thyng in this boke that shall offend you . . . I praye you blame not me though I haue folowed myne orygynall and olde copy in worde and sentence' (fol. Avi, r). Certainly the writer does not mince his words, but he is following Gregory in basing a pastoral discourse on Old Testament exempla, and in associating the well-being of the realm with good governance. A shockingly corrupt English Church, in his view, is likely to be the cause of foreign or even non-Christian invasion.

Happily, we no longer feel the need to be partisan about the reformist programme of the Lollards, any more than we feel the need to be partisan about Gregory's reformism.

We can see the inconsistencies, unfairnesses and excesses of this passage of the Prologue to the Wycliffite Bible without being unsympathetic to its demand for social justice
and its advocacy of Scripture in English. What is worrying, however, for anyone who
wishes Christian culture to value the works of the creative imagination is that, like
Gregory, the writer of the Prologue has a low opinion of 'fablis', fictional tales, lumping
them together with canon law as traditions deriving from men and not from God. Later
in the Prologue, he castigates the University of Oxford for attempting to introduce a
statute inhibiting students from beginning the study of Divinity until they have become
regents in Arts, a nine or ten-year process, with the result that men who go to Oxford
with little previous education, and who can afford only a short time there, will never
proceed from Arts to Divinity, and therefore 'knowe not goddis lawe to preche it gener-
aly aʒens synnes in þe reume' (Forshall and Madden 1850, vol. 1: 51–2).

Like Gregory, the writer of the Prologue to the Wycliffite Bible sees *saecularis scientia*
as having a purely instrumental role. His Prologue introduces his readers to the complete law of God in English, in order that they may keep it as their *pastores* do not. In
the previous century, Grosseteste had said that a poorly educated priest would do well,
if he knew Latin at all, to 'say over to himself during the week the naked [word-for-
word and uninterpreted] text of the Sunday Gospel', translated into English, so that his
parishioners would at least hear the whole literal narrative of the Gospel for the day in
a language they understood. The reformist bishop clearly believes that the minimum
the laity have a right to be provided with (but often are not) is the opportunity of
hearing an unglossed literal translation of some key New Testament passages. It is often
said that the laity learned their Bible from iconographic representations in wall-
paintings, stained-glass windows and the like, but the 'Bible' so learned was at best a
sequence of de-contextualized narrative moments. Grosseteste is arguing for unmedi-
ated access to the biblical text.

John Trevisa takes Grosseteste's recommendation a logical step further in his 'Dialogue Between a Lord and a Clerk' (1387), written when the Wycliffite Bible, which he
may have played some part in producing, was close to completion. If a translation of a
biblical passage is to be made for purposes of preaching, Trevisa says, then it may as
well be written down so that it will not be forgotten. If preaching in English is 'good and
neodful (necessary)', then translation is also 'good and neodfol' (Waldron 1998:
292–3). Trevisa traces the long history of translation, from the Septuagint (the translation of the Jewish Scriptures into Greek) to translations into medieval vernaculars,
and asks why the English should be deprived of a translation. Similarly, the writer of
the Prologue to the Wycliffite Bible exclaims 'Lord God, siþen at þe bigynnyng of feiþ
so manie men translatiden into Latyn, and to greet profyt of Latyn men, lat oo (one)
symple creature of God translate into English, for profyt of English men' (Forshall and
Madden 1850, vol. 1: 59), After all, Bede translated the Bible into 'Saxon', the English
vernacular of his time, and King Alfred translated 'þe bigynning of þe Sauter' (this only
partially accurate information derives from Ranulf Higden's *Polychronicon*).

One of the crucial questions in the debate about biblical translation in the last quarter
of the fourteenth century was how much of the Bible it was necessary to translate. To
us, who take for granted the Bible as book, it seems natural that a decision to translate

Holy Writ into English should have meant a decision to translate all the books of the Bible. In Wyclif's Oxford, however, it seemed natural that some books of the Bible should be translated into English and not others, for there had been a long history of highly selective translation (Shepherd, in Lampe 1969: 362–87). The Dominican Thomas Palmer argues that 'Bede did not translate Scripture beyond such things as are necessary for salvation' (c.1400) (Deanesly 1920: 435). To the argument that 'the whole law of living well [the Old and New Testaments]' needs to be available in the common tongue, Palmer replies 'not every truth is to be written in English, since many are lacking in utility' (ibid., 421).

Like Knighton, who found the English language far from angelic, Palmer feared that biblical translation would make Scripture 'open' and 'common', smudging the traditional boundaries between clergy and laity. Again, like Knighton, he recognized that in England at the end of the fourteenth century even 'quite learned clerks of good intelligence' have less access to the Gospel in Latin than literate laypeople have to the Gospel translated into English. Anxious to keep the boundaries clearly marked, Palmer argues for a better-educated clergy. Every nation needs clergy who are sufficiently learned in the language in which Scripture is preserved to be able 'to interpret Scripture to the people by way of other-than-literal explication (*per circumlocutionem*)' (Deanesly 1920: 435); that is, avoiding the simple literal sense Grosseteste had advocated, and adding various kinds of allegorical interpretation (in particular, moral interpretation).

This is necessary, in Palmer's view, because access to the 'naked text' provoked heresies in the early Church, and *a fortiori* could lead 'simple people' into error (ibid., 422). For fear of heresy, laypeople should not be allowed to read Scripture *ad libitum* even in Latin, according to the Franciscan William Butler in 1401 (ibid., 401). Another of Butler's fears is that the dissemination of translations of Scripture might result in *libri mendosi*, corrupt texts. To the inevitable argument that not all Latin Bibles are free from misreadings, either, he replies that the Church has ensured that Scripture is now taught and written in universities, so that errors can easily be corrected. He imagines the Bible being conserved within a clerical enclave to avoid contamination. As Khantik Ghosh argues, Butler's model of the relation between clergy and laity is uncompromisingly hierarchical and supervisory (2001: 93–100); in effect, Gregorian eight centuries after Gregory.

Butler's and Palmer's tracts on biblical translation both exemplify a traditional model of pedagogy, according to which there is a symbolic boundary between simple people, who understand Scripture on the literal, grammatical level, and 'those assumed to be endowed with reason and hermeneutical perspicacity (men, clergy, *litterati*)', for whom the 'higher', spiritual senses of Scripture are reserved (Copeland, in Scase et al. 1997: 138). How, given this model, could a translation of the Bible into English, without circumlocution, fail to lead the 'simple people' Palmer calls *idiote circa scriptura*, illiterate idiots as far as Scripture is concerned, astray? (Deanesly 1920: 425).

A tract advocating biblical translation (c.1400–10) argues that 'lewed curatis', men who have care of souls but little or no education in Latin, need Scripture in English to enable them to teach the people, for 'now it is fulfillid þat þe prophete seid, *the little ones looked for bread and there was no one to break it for them* (Lam. 4:4)' (Hunt 1994, vol. 2: 258–9). There are those who argue, says the tract (Butler and Palmer among them, as we know), that 'lewid peple' (laypeople) should not read the Bible because it 'haþ so manye vnderstondynges literal and spiritual þat þe lewid pepel may not vnderstonde it' (ibid., vol. 2: 262–3). The writer replies that 'þe most part' of priests 'vnderstonden not holy write ne (nor) þe gospel neiþer literalliche ne spiritualiche', in English or in Latin. Learned laypeople may understand both Latin and English better than unlearned priests do. When 'a man of lawe' quoted the law of God in the Gospel of Luke, Christ replied 'you have answered rightly' (ibid., vol. 1: 27–8); 'he seide not as men don þese dayes "who made þe borel (ignorant) clerk so hardi to rede Goddis lawe?" but he preised him for his redynge' (ibid., vol. 2: 268).

This echoes the scornful question put into the mouth of 'worldli clerkis', in other words clergy who persecute the Wycliffites, in the Prologue to the Wycliffite Bible: 'what spiryt makiþ idiotis hardi to translate now þe bible into English?' (Forshall and Madden 1850, vol. 1: 59). Certainly not, the worldly clerks imply, the Holy Spirit. The scholarly translators are accused of being 'idiotis' (illiterates) because they refuse to acknowledge that Scripture needs to be interpreted to the laity by way of *circumlocutio* rather than translated literally. The writer of the Prologue is happy with this appellation: he has, after all, contrasted the hundreds of false prophets who counselled King Ahab with the prophets Elijah and Micaiah who were in sole possession of the truth (2 Kgs. 18:22), and likened the translators' predicament to theirs:

> so now a fewe pore men and idiotis, in comparisoun of clerkis of scole, mown (may) haue þe treuþe of holy Scripture aȝens many þousinde prelatis and religiouse (members of the religious orders) þat ben ȝouen to worldli pride and coueitise (greed), symonie, ypocrisie and oþer fleschly synnes. (Forshall and Madden 1850: vol. 1: 30)

He chooses to make capital out of the role of outsider, taking up what Fiona Somerset has identified as the 'extraclergial' position characteristic of Lollard writers, who are, nevertheless, 'if anything more ostentatiously learned than the typical clerical writer' (Somerset 1998: 13).

'What spiryt makiþ idiotis hardi to translate now þe bible into English', the worldly clerics ask, 'siþen (since) þe foure greete doctouris [Ambrose, Augustine, Jerome and Gregory] dursten (dared) neuere do þis?' As the writer of the Prologue says, this is a 'lewid' (idiotic) question, no doubt introduced to enable him to remind his readers that the doctors 'ceessiden neuere til þei hadden holy writ in here modir tunge of here owne puple', Latin. He points out that the Church has approved even translations by 'open eretikis' (Jews cunningly mistranslating their own Scriptures to obscure their christo-logical content) (Forshall and Madden 1850, vol. 1: 58). Therefore, 'myche more lat þe chirche of Engelond appreue þe trewe and hool translacioun of symple men þat wolden (would wish) for no good in erþe, bi here witing (knowledge) and power, putte awei þe leste truþe, ȝea þe leste lettre eiþer title (jot or tittle) of holy writ' (Matt. 5:18).

In spite of this moving plea, the advocates of biblical translation lost the legal battle to be allowed open access to the law of God in their mother tongue in 1409, when Arch-bishop Thomas Arundel's *Constitutions* prohibited the reading of the Bible in English 'by way of a book, pamphlet or tract . . . composed in the time of John Wyclif, or since then, or that may in future be composed, in part or in whole, publicly or privately'

(Watson 1995: 822–64). The association of the English Bible with Wyclif, whom Arundel regarded as a notorious heretic, made it impossible for those in favour of translation to persuade the ecclesiastical authorities to approve it, in spite of the fact that the opponents of translation had not offered any specific criticisms of the text of the Wycliffite Bible, and in spite of the fact that the arguments put forward for Scripture in the vernacular were extremely strong.

Yet a very large number of manuscripts of the Wycliffite Bible, or portions of it, were in circulation in the fifteenth century (more than 250 survive today), and translation of the Bible into the vernacular, as James Simpson argues, 'enacts a massive transference of authority to the language itself, away from the learned languages previously reserved for arcane discourse' (2002: 466–7). Arundel's legislation could not prevent this transference of authority. For the first time, the biblical canon in its entirety was accessible to the non-Latinate English reader, but also, a fact less often recognized, the English reader literate in Latin could read the whole bible in his or her native tongue, in a translation that commanded confidence and respect as a literal and meaningful rendering of a carefully edited original. For such a reader (and Chaucer may well have been one) reading in translation would defamiliarize the well-known Latin, and sharpen awareness that the Latin was a translation, too.

The cautious Chaucer, seeing which way the wind was blowing from the early 1380s onwards, shies away from serious engagement with the Bible or ecclesiastical issues in his English poetry, although he is as ready as anyone else to satirize the friars. This is one of the great disappointments of English literary history. Langland's imagination, by contrast, is a biblical imagination. The greatest English poem of the Middle Ages, *Piers Plowman* (*c*.1367–*c*.1385), is an extremely idiosyncratic kind of commentary on the Bible, by a poet who has as little time for fiction as has Gregory or the writer of the Prologue to the Wycliffite Bible. Nevertheless, Langland's creative imagination interacts with the Bible to produce a new kind of cultural document, resisting classification as 'religious' or 'secular' and refusing to make any distinction between English readers and readers who know Latin. When the priest who tells Piers that his 'pardon' is no pardon at all condescends to the plowman with the words 'þou art lettred a litel', and suggests that an appropriate text for a sermon by the plowman would be *dixit insipiens* (the fool has spoken, Ps. 13:1), Piers tells the priest he is an ignorant good-for-nothing. If he spent more time studying the Bible he would know that Proverbs 22:10 says 'cast out the scoffers' (B. 7, 132–8).

Like Bede's *Ecclesiastical History*, *Piers Plowman* contains a story about Gregory, this time the story of a miracle attributed to him. The Emperor Trajan bursts into the poem to tell how, being a pagan, he suffered in Hell until Gregory wept and prayed over him, 'willing my soul salvation because of the truth and justice he saw in my actions' (B. 11, 146–7). The Pope's wish was granted. According to Langland, Trajan could not be saved until a Christian recognized 'soothnesse' (truth) when he saw it. 'Clergie' (knowledge of the Bible) was not enough, let alone knowledge of the liberal arts. The intensity of Gregory's passion for good governance speaks through this miracle-story and this part of *Piers Plowman*; he and Trajan both realize that 'lawe (justice and righteousness) without love' in the fullest sense of love can achieve nothing at all (B. 11, 170).

The gates of hell are broken again, by Christ, not far from the end of the poem. Just before the Harrowing of Hell, Langland transforms the Bible into a person, simply called 'Book'. Book recalls what the Gospels say about the life and death of Christ, and then promises that 'I, Book, wole be brent (burnt), but (unless) Jesus rise to lyue / In alle myghtes of man' (B. 18, 254–5). Most students reading *Piers Plowman* in the twenty-first century think that the Bible 'comes alive' when Book appears as a 'character': 'Thanne was ther a wight (creature) with two brode eighen (wide eyes) [the two testaments]; / Book highte that beaupeere (that holy father, a good fellow, was called Book), a bold man of speche' (B. 18, 229–30). This is certainly a most surprising moment, but I do not think that Langland is here bringing the Bible to life for the first time in the poem. On the contrary, the unanticipated personification shocks his readers into awareness that the Bible has been a living presence throughout *Piers Plowman*, its words quoted and their meaning debated time and time again.

When Book speaks the Bible, oral and written testimony become one and the same, and English. The idea of 'Book' giving himself to be burnt as though he were a heretic is almost painfully proleptic; this is what will soon happen to English Bibles and to some advocates of the English Bible. For Langland there is no culture without Holy Writ, and in this he is quintessentially medieval, a true heir of Gregory and Bede. The Bible is not, however, a text set apart in Langland's imagination; his God speaks out 'in þe scripturis of puplis', including his own poem. Nowhere is sacred Scripture less monolithic than it is in Langland's imagination, but everywhere in medieval culture the Bible is the slipperiest of all writings, most necessary and most difficult to know.

References and Further Reading

Aers, David (1986). *Medieval Literature: Criticism, Ideology and History*. Brighton: Harvester.

Brewer, J. S. (ed.) (1859). *Rogeri Bacon Opera Quedam Hactenus Inedita*. London: Rolls Series.

Buddensieg, Rudolf (ed.) (1905). *John Wyclif: De Veritate Sacrae Scripturae*. London: Wyclif Society.

Cattley, S. R. and Pratt, J. (eds) (1853–70). *The Acts and Monuments of John Foxe*. London.

Colgrave, Bertram and Mynors R. A. B. (eds) (1969). *Bede's Ecclesiastical History of the English People*. Oxford: Clarendon Press.

Deanesly, Margaret (1920). *The Lollard Bible and Other Medieval Biblical Versions*. Cambridge: Cambridge University Press.

De Hamel, Christopher (2001). *The Book: A History of the Bible*. London: Phaidon.

Dove, Mary (ed.) (1997). *Glossa Ordinaria in Canticum Canticorum*, Corpus Christianorum Continuatio Medievalis 170, 22. Turnhout: Brepols.

Forshall, Josiah and Madden, Frederic (eds) (1850). *The Holy Bible . . . the Earliest English Versions Made from the Latin Vulgate by John Wycliffe and his Followers* (the Wycliffite Bible), 4 vols. Oxford: Clarendon Press.

Gameson, Richard (ed.) (1994). *The Early Medieval Bible: Its Production, Decoration and Use*. Cambridge: Cambridge University Press.

Gameson, Richard (ed.) (1999). *St Augustine and the Conversion of England*. Stroud: Sutton.

Ghosh, Kantik (2001). *The Wycliffite Heresy: Authority and the Interpretation of Texts*. Cambridge: Cambridge University Press.

Hunt, Simon (ed.) (1994). 'An Edition of Tracts in Favour of Scriptural Translation and of Some Texts connected with Lollard Vernacular Biblical Scholarship', 2 vols. DPhil thesis, University of Oxford.

Judic, Bruno, Rommel, F. and Morel, C. (eds) (1992). *Grégoire le Grand: Règle Pastorale*, 2 vols. Paris: Du Cerf.

Krey, Philip D. W. and Smith, Lesley (eds) (2000). *Nicholas of Lyra: The Senses of Scripture*. Leiden: Brill.

Lampe, G. W. H. (ed.) (1969). *The Cambridge History of the Bible*, vol. 2: *The West from the Fathers to the Reformation*. Cambridge: Cambridge University Press.

Markus, R. A. (1997). *Gregory the Great and his World*. Cambridge: Cambridge University Press.

Martin, G. H. (ed.) (1995). *Knighton's Chronicle, 1337–1396*. Oxford: Clarendon Press.

Norberg, D. (ed.) (1982). *Gregorius Magnus: Registrum epistularum*, Corpus Christianorum Series Latina 140. Turnhout: Brepols.

Riché, Pierre and Lobrichon, G. (eds) (1984). *Le Moyen-Âge et la Bible*. Paris: Bible de tous les temps 4.

Scase, Wendy, Copeland, R. and Lawton, D. (eds) (1997). *New Medieval Literatures* I. Oxford: Clarendon Press.

Schreiber, Caroline (2002). *King Alfred's Old English Translation of Pope Gregory the Great's* Regula Pastoralis *and its Cultural Context*. Munich: Lang.

Simpson, James (2002). *The Oxford English Literary History*, vol. 2: *1350–1547: Reform and Cultural Revolution*. Oxford: Oxford University Press.

Smalley, Beryl (1982). *The Study of the Bible in the Middle Ages*, 3rd edn. Oxford: Clarendon Press.

Somerset, Fiona (1998). *Clerical Discourse and Lay Audience in Late Medieval England*. Cambridge: Cambridge University Press.

Verbraken, P. (ed.) (1963). *Gregorius Magnus: In librum primum Regum expositionem*, Corpus Christianorum Series Latina 144. Turnhout: Brepols.

Waldron, R. (ed.) (1998). 'Trevisa's Original Prefaces on Translation: A Critical Edition', in E. D. Kennedy, R. Waldron and J. S. Wittig (eds), *Medieval English Studies Presented to George Kane*. Woodbridge: D. S. Brewer, pp. 285–99.

Watson, Nicholas (1995). 'Censorship and Cultural Change in Late Medieval England: Vernacular Theology, the Oxford Translation Debate, and Arundel's *Constitutiones* of 1409', *Speculum* 70: 822–64.

White, H. J. (1902). 'Vulgate', in James Hastings (ed.), *A Dictionary of the Bible*, vol. 4. Edinburgh, pp. 873–90.

CHAPTER 4
The Renaissance

Ilona N. Rashkow

So securely has the English Renaissance Bible established its place in the canon of English literature that to most of its readers it *is* the Bible. I am using the term 'English Renaissance Bible' as an archetype consisting of Tyndale's New Testament (1525) and Pentateuch (1530), the Coverdale Bible (1535), the Geneva Bible (1560), the Rheims-Douay Bible (1609), and the King James Version (1611). The text is familiar because of its influence upon the growth and development of English language, literature, and culture. Yet until the sixteenth century, few Englishmen had access to the biblical text and fewer still could have read it even if they had access since it was not in the vernacular. Thus, the major impact the Bible had on Renaissance culture was its very existence in English.

Although biblical translation was favoured by humanists since it enabled them to combine their penchant for *ad fontes* with the enrichment of their native language, it was against the law. Translating the Bible could mean charges of heresy, exile, or even death. This chapter examines some of the major obstacles encountered by the translators – in particular, the politics of biblical translation.

The attitude of the Church towards biblical translation is not easy to define both because it underwent considerable modification between the tenth and the sixteenth centuries and because it always concerned the right of the laity to inquire into high and divine matters and preach without episcopal licence. Although English devotional literature flourished in the Middle Ages, it was held by the Church that the best way of knowing God was by meditation and prayer, not by reading the Bible: what knowledge of the Bible the laity acquired was through sermons. The position of the Church regarding biblical translation was determined by the status of the translator and the purpose of the translation. If the translation were made for a king or other exalted person, or by some solitary student, and remained a 'holy' but practically unused volume in a monastic or royal library, no objection was taken to the translation as such. But if the translation was used to popularize knowledge of the biblical text among lay people, prohibition followed immediately. The hardening of the Church's position regarding the *ipsissima verba* of the Vulgate arose from the political struggle between the Eastern and Western Churches when Christian missionaries made contact with the Slavs in the ninth century. In 1079, Pope Gregory VII outlawed the use of the Slavonic languages in church services. The Bible lesson was to be read in Latin, and the priest was allowed only to convey the sense of it in the vernacular. A new source of heresy was created (which led ultimately to the Reformation). From the end of the fourteenth century, however, lay people of the upper classes usually could obtain licence from their confessors to use translations of parts of the Bible, as they could obtain minor dispensations (Pollard 1974: 80). But as a rule, those who desired to obtain such dispensations were few since Bible reading was not recommended as ordinary practice for the laity.

Thus, translators were in a very difficult position. Renaissance philosophy had attempted to highlight the importance of Hebrew and Greek for the humanist scholar, and the Reformation, with its emphasis on the two founts of religion, *sola fide, sola scriptura*, emphasized it still further. If Scripture was the key to faith, as the reformers maintained, then it was necessary that an accurate Bible be in the keeping of all Christians. The humanists were able to show that some of the difficulties of the Vulgate were due to mistakes in the Latin translation. With *ad fontes* as the battle-cry of Renaissance humanism, it was necessary for biblical translators to return to the original texts and although Hebrew and Greek were not studied easily in Renaissance England, biblical translation was an important aspect of humanism. Humanist scholars, especially those associated with the Platonic Academy in Florence, were anxious to acknowledge Hebrew, Greek and Latin as the three historic languages of the West and to learn from them (Jones 1983: 20).

But translation both interprets and recreates the text it addresses. Indeed, in early English usage, the word 'interpret' was synonymous with 'translate', as the Geneva Bible translators explain in their 'Preface'. They state that their purpose in providing this new text is to shed light 'upon the dark places', passages 'so dark that by no description they could be made easy' (I have rendered all spelling into modern usage). In addition, the marginalia and annotations of the English Renaissance translations constitute a running commentary on the religious/political situation of the day and emphasize the translators' ability to shape a new text: although translators holding widely divergent world-views occasionally translated using the same words, they revealed their biases in the marginalia and annotations: often their note is related to the text only slightly, if at all. As a result, the Hebrew Bible and Greek New Testament are certainly sources of the English versions and the English versions are 'biblical', yet they do not reflect wholly the original texts. In part, this is due to the problems of translation. In greater part, however, the differences between the Hebrew and Greek texts and the English Renaissance translations are due to the conscious interpretive practices of the translators.

The Renaissance, often referred to as the 'classical' period of English biblical translations, and certainly the most political, begins with William Tyndale's translation of the New Testament (1525) and ends with the King James Version of the Bible (1611). But as discussed above, this was not an easy period for translators. Indeed, much ink – and blood – was shed on the subject.

Certainly, one of the goals of the Renaissance biblical translators was to make the text more readily accessible. However, to translate the text into the vernacular could lead to charges of heresy and death, as the controversy between Sir Thomas More and William Tyndale illustrates.

The More/Tyndale Debate

The controversy between Sir Thomas More and William Tyndale was over certain words considered heretical and therefore politically dangerous, words of high theological significance long familiar in English such as 'covenant', 'law', 'loving-kindness', 'holiness', 'judgment', 'soul', 'church', 'priest', 'grace', 'confess', 'penance', 'charity', etc. According to More, Tyndale was guilty of heresy since his translations were 'maliciously' aimed at the authoritarian structure and sacramental system of the Catholic church. And, no doubt, Tyndale intended to challenge the established ecclesiastical order with his own understanding and interpretation of the texts. Although the theology is not debated in this chapter, the details of their controversy, as contained in More's *Dialogue Concerning Heresies* (More 1976), Tyndale's *Answer to More* (Duffield 1965), and More's *Confutation of Tyndale's Answer* (More 1976) are significant since they crystallize and synthesize the relationship of Bible and culture during the Renaissance.

The More/Tyndale dispute began with Tyndale's translation of Erasmus' *Enchiridion militis Christiani* (*The Christian Soldier's Handbook*), one of the principal themes of which is that Christians have the individual responsibility to study the Bible. Tyndale, realizing the importance of the translator, acknowledges that through biblical translation potentially he can affect both the mighty civic and religious leaders (as well as the laity) by eradicating ignorance of the source texts. A first-hand account of Tyndale's career at this time, which John Foxe later incorporated in his *Acts and Monuments*, reports Tyndale's position:

> Not long after, Tyndale happened to be in company of a certain divine, and in disputing with him he pressed him so hard that the doctor burst out into these blasphemous words: 'We were better to be without God's law than the pope's.' Tyndale, full of godly zeal, replied: 'I defy the Pope and all his laws'; and added, that if God spared him his life, 'ere many years, he would cause a boy that drives the plough shall know more of the Scripture than he did'. (Foxe 1877: 169)

However, the prohibition of the 1408 Council at Oxford, which forbade the possession of any English version of the Bible without licence from a bishop, was still in effect, and only by the permission of a bishop could a translation be prepared. Tyndale encountered opposition not so much because his work was unauthorized, but because his prefaces, notes, and choice of ecclesiastical words were politically unacceptable to the Church – and he refused to compromise on these matters. As a result, in 1528, More, as the councillor and Chancellor of Henry VIII, published a volume of more than 150 pages officially entitled: '*A dialogue of Sir Thomas More knight . . . wherein be treated diverse matters, as of the veneration and worship of images and relics, praying to saints and going on pilgrimage, with many other things touching the pestilent sect of Luther and Tyndale, by the tone begun in Saxony, and by the other labored to be brought into England.'*

Although in the title of the *Dialogue* Luther's name stands before Tyndale's and the last of its four books is directed against him, nevertheless the chief antagonist throughout is Tyndale. The 'many other things' include the subject of biblical translations (to which he devotes the sixteenth chapter of the third book). He refers here to the edict of the Council of Oxford where Archbishop Arundel had forbidden biblical translation or the reading of any such translation made in the time of John Wycliffe (1380) or since. In this connection, More touches upon the subject of Wycliffe's Bible and the attitude of the Church towards translations in his day. But the matter with which he is most concerned is Tyndale's translation.

More's approach is interesting. He casts his work in the form of the dialogue (the form of his *Utopia* and of his earlier Latin translations of Lucian), and constructs his defense of the status quo in four conversations between himself and an emissary from a friend, who, exposed to and perplexed by heretical doctrine, wishes to have More's views on certain points. In using this literary form, More not only provides more lively reading than in a straightforward treatise, but also makes it easier to state his enemy's case in a way that suits himself. More secures entire freedom of speech by making his interlocutor 'merely' the messenger of a friend, one who reports everything he hears without taking any responsibility for it. By representing the interaction of two divergent personalities and viewpoints, More rhetorically attempts to move his readers into agreement with the traditional position through humanistic persuasion rather than dogmatic coercion.

The character of the Messenger is that of a promising young student, inclined towards the ideas of 'New Learning' and ready to agree with the plausible arguments of the 'man in the street'. Though not himself a Lutheran, he *acts* as the spokesman of that party and protests that they are being treated harshly. He professes to set forth the thoughts of 'reasonable' men of limited education, attracted by some of the new teaching, or at least considering heretics unfairly persecuted. In the *Dialogue*, the Messenger reports that he, as well as the 'man in the street', think the Bible ought to be accessible in English. And, to some extent, More agrees. More emphatically disassociates himself from those members of the clergy who refuse to allow a vernacular translation of the Bible on the basis that seditious people would do more harm with such a translation than honest men would benefit: 'For else if the abuse of a good thing should cause the taking away thereof from other that would use it well, Christ should himself never have been born, nor brought his faith into the world' (More 1976: 332).

More even expresses amazement that God had not provided a satisfactory English Bible already. The 'lewdness and folly' of those who might misuse an English Bible 'were not in my mind a sufficient cause to exclude the translation' (ibid.: 338). The description of the Messenger's personal attitude to the scriptures is significant. 'Some men believe,' he says, 'that Tyndale's New Testament was burned at St. Paul's Cross, not because of the faults declared to be found in it, but to disguise the fact that none such were found' (ibid.: 109). The Messenger explains that he (as well as the 'man in the street') believes that the clergy keep the scriptures from the laity. More, however, is scholar enough to be able to quote the provincial Council of Oxford in support of his contention that they do not do so – totally. He devotes three chapters to the instruction of the Messenger on the subject of biblical translations, the first to explain the enactment of the Council in 1408, the others to show that the laity may use such translations under certain restrictions. 'Here was no constitution,' says More, 'which positively forbade the people to have any scripture translated' (ibid.: 224–6, 233–47). More explains that translations have been allowed from the earliest days of the Church and that he would favour their being allowed now – under proper supervision.

More claims that unsupervised biblical translation is tantamount to heresy, a crime for which the punishment was death. His *Dialogue* leaves no doubt that he regards deviation from the established Church, deviation from the accepted ideas of biblical translation (and thus deviation from the status quo) a crime against God, conscience, and society. Certain that the offender's soul will burn, it matters little to More that the body should burn first. According to Mozley, his rise to the chancellorship made him a 'theological zealot [who] sat in the seat of secular power' (1937: 217), and his *Dialogue* became a particularly powerful tool. He accuses Tyndale of wilful perversion of the text to suit the ends of his political goals: the Reformation. Tyndale's translation, he says in the *Dialogue*, is not the Bible at all: 'for so had Tyndale, after Luther's counsel, corrupted and changed it from the good and wholesome doctrine of Christ to the devilish heresies of their own, that it was a clean contrary thing' (More 1976: 111).

Again and again he makes the claim that the official church could not err, but that Tyndale had – by virtue and manner of translating the Bible. To say that More so bitterly opposed Tyndale's version because it was unauthorized merely forces the question back a step. From a purely humanist position, it would seem natural that the English bishops, several friends of More and Erasmus among them, would welcome a translation at once so readable, scholarly, and humanistic in its devotion to *ad fontes*. But Tyndale's work was viewed as part of the Lutheran movement. The translation contained both in its text and in the apparatus of notes and prefaces matter which was unquestionably intended to promote reform along Lutheran lines. In sixteenth-century England, religious reform meant civil action; it is virtually impossible to separate biblical translation, historic changes, and the religious/political background which accompanied them both.

While More's sweeping accusation of heresy was based both on Tyndale's interpretations and word choice, More focused on Tyndale's power to choose words laden with what he considered 'politically dangerous' overtones. He argues in the *Dialogue* that the translation was unauthorized and unorthodox, and thus Tyndale was a heretic. Tyndale responds to More's calumnies in *An Answer unto Sir Thomas Mores Dialogue* which put More on the defensive, as demonstrated by his *Confutation of Tyndale's Answer*. Tyndale's opposition brought out the absolutist in More. No longer content merely to 'refute', he now sought to 'confute' Tyndale.

More's charge of heresy was based on Tyndale's translation of certain fundamental words (see Table 4.1). While it is beyond the scope of this chapter to examine Tyndale's translation of the Christian New Testament entirely, a few comments on these key words as debated in the three tracts of More and Tyndale are important in order to put the Bible and culture in the Renaissance into perspective (for a more detailed analysis, see Rashkow 1990).

Table 4.1 Comparison of translations of biblical words

Greek text	Vulgate	More	Tyndale
ekklesia	congregatio	church	congregation
presbuter	senior/presbyter	priest	senior
metanoeite	penitentiam agite	do penance	repent
homologeo	confiteor	confess	acknowledge
charis	gratia	grace	favour
agape	caritas	charity	love

In the *Dialogue*, More does not consider the contexts in which these words were used in the original Greek New Testament, only in the Vulgate. However, even the Vulgate does not always support More's accusation of heresy. Tyndale's translation of *ekklesia*, for example, was the first of his 'heretical' acts. In Greek, it was used to denote a 'body of select or called-out counsellors' and came to signify a 'properly constituted assembly' for which 'congregation' appears to be a good word choice. The Greek word for 'church' (*kyriakon*) did not come into use until the third century CE and was used to describe that which was 'pertaining to the Lord' (from *kyrios*, lord). Thus, the original meaning of 'church' was 'a *place* of worship', not a '*gathering* of worshippers' (*Oxford English Dictionary* 1978, 2:403). The term was appropriated by early Catholic authorities for the organized body of the clergy, the meaning which More attaches to 'church' in the *Dialogue*. Tyndale, in his *Answer to More*, finds support in the use of *ekklesia* in the Septuagint for a Hebrew religious assembly (*qahal*). Inconsistently, More had approved Erasmus' use of *congregatio* in Latin while accusing Tyndale of heresy for his use of 'congregation' in English. The difference, however, is that Erasmus did not make the same inflammatory marginal comments as Tyndale did regarding the established hierarchy of the Church. Tyndale, acting as an interpreter for his readers, states that he wishes to guard them from being 'misled by common usage' since the clergy had consolidated themselves at the expense of the laity.

In objecting to the 'malicious' purpose of 'senior' for *presbyter*, More regards the Latin borrowing an intrusion, and asks why Tyndale four times retains 'priest' for leaders in the synagogue, thus robbing only the Christians of their 'true' title. Tyndale replies in his *Answer* that on these occasions he was translating Greek *hiereus* ('sacrificer'), a member of the tribe of Levi. Again, More shows an inconsistency in his argument since Jerome and Erasmus, More's proclaimed references, translate the word by 'senior' or 'presbyter' and never by the proper Latin word for priest (*sacerdos*) which they regularly use to signify the Levites. When Tyndale raises this point in his *Answer* and asks how it is that Jerome and the apostles never call the Christian leaders 'priests' (*sacerdos* or *hiereus*), More, instead of grappling with the question, slides out of it, saying that he has never spoken with these old writers, and therefore has been unable to ask them. In fact, the word 'presbyter' was not in English usage until Hooker first used it in 1597. Wycliffe used 'senior' as a synonym for 'elder' in Revelation 7:2.

Tyndale's next offence, according to More, was his use of 'repent' instead of 'do penance'. According to More, John the Baptist told the people to 'do penance, for the kingdom of heaven is at hand', and accuses Tyndale of maliciously using the word 'repent' in order to banish all 'penance' from the Bible. Of course, the word 'penance' and its relation to indulgences were extremely significant during the Reformation, a point which Tyndale knew and exploited.

Similarly, More criticized Tyndale's use of 'love' rather than 'charity' (Latin *caritas*). More claims in his *Dialogue* that 'charity' means not every kind of love, but a good love, a Christian love, to which Tyndale replies in his *Answer* that if 'love' has more than one meaning, so also has 'charity'. The Greek word, he argues, is general and neutral, and should be translated by the broad English word 'love'. He appeals to common usage also: in practice, we speak of our 'love' *of* God, not our 'charity' *to* God. Finally, he claims the advantage for 'love' on the linguistic ground that it can be used, like the Greek word, as a verb as well as a noun, but 'charity' is only a noun, and one cannot 'charity' God or 'charity' a neighbour. Here, too, Tyndale cites Jerome and Erasmus who use *dilectio* ('love') rather than *caritas* when signifying the Greek *agape*, the former occasionally and the latter more frequently.

In examining More's charges, Tyndale notes in several places that it is inconsistent to label him a heretic for his word choice and to tolerate the same words in Erasmus' Latin version. More responds to this criticism by saying that in Erasmus he found no 'malicious intent,' as he did in Tyndale's version. Thus, it was not the *translation* but the *translator* and his political views to which More really objected. Tyndale was taken into custody by imperial representatives in Antwerp and, after 16 months of imprisonment, was tried. On 6 October 1536, he was strangled and burned at the stake.

It is often implied, if not stated in so many words, that Tyndale died for daring to give Englishmen a Bible which they could understand. Tyndale's emphatic assertion that 'neither was help with English of any that had interpreted the same' led Alfred Pollard to conclude that he had made no use of Wycliffe's version (1974: xiii). Yet their almost identical translation of numerous passages would argue a strong relationship between the two versions, and thus Lollardy, a movement both politically and theologically repugnant to More, would certainly have been an influence on Tyndale, causing More to view him as a heretic. Even more heretical to More was Luther's influence on Tyndale: 'For so had Tyndale after Luther's counsel corrupted and changed it [the New Testament] from the good and wholesome doctrine of Christ to the devilish heresies of their own' (More 1976: 8).

Regardless of the veracity of the charge of Lutheranism, Henry VIII believed the charges against Tyndale to be valid, and wrote:

> [Tyndale] fell in device with one or two lewd persons both in this our realm for the trans-
> lating of the New Testament into English, as well with many corruptions of that holy text,
> as certain prefaces and other pestilent glosses in the margents for the advancement and
> setting forth of his abominable heresies. (Pollard 1974: 118)

It is more than a little ironic that Sir Thomas More, who successfully persecuted William Tyndale as a heretic, also suffered death for the sake of his conscience. The issue, biblical translation, was one in which the lives of men were *literally* at 'stake'. And the translators involved were not minor literary figures, but the leading humanists and patrons of the 'New Learning'. More and Tyndale had many friends and colleagues in common (Erasmus, for example), and were it not for the highly charged atmosphere and character of the translation involved, it is likely that More would have appreciated the cultural and scholastic value of Tyndale's work. But Tyndale's theology was reflected in his translation. Tyndale's text reproduced his 'world-view', and was thus ideologically and politically marked. 'Tyndale's New Testament', said More, was not '*the* New Testament at all; it was a cunning counterfeit, so perverted in the interests of heresy . . . that it was not worthy to be called Christ's testament, but either Tyndale's own testament or the testament of his master Antichrist' (More 1976: 9). To search for errors in it was like 'searching for water in the sea; it was so bad that it could not be mended . . . for it is easier to make a web of new cloth than it is to sew up every hole in a net' (ibid.: 9). Thus, according to More, there is *the* New Testament and Tyndale's. Despite the fact that Tyndale's New Testament (according to Tyndale as well as contemporary scholars) is not very different from that of Erasmus, it was banned. For More, the Vulgate and Erasmus' versions were sanctified, while Tyndale's version was heretical, a version to be burned along with its translator.

More's diatribe notwithstanding, Tyndale began work on a translation of the Pentateuch (the first five books of the Hebrew Bible) which was published in 1530. He was particularly enthusiastic about this translation, having asserted in the Preface to *The Obedience of a Christian Man* that Hebrew can be translated far more easily into English than into Latin. Those who claim that the original text of the Hebrew Bible cannot be rendered into English because it is such a 'rude' language are branded 'false liars' for

> the properties . . . agree a thousand times more with the English than with the Latin. The manner of speaking is both one . . . when thou must seek a compass in the Latin, and yet shall have much work to translate it well-favouredly, so that it have the same grace and sweetness, sense and pure understanding with it in the Latin as it hath in the Hebrew. A thousand parts better may it be translated into the English than into the Latin. (Duffield 1965: 104)

According to Tyndale, the need for a translation is clear: 'ecclesiastical students are armed with false principles, with which they are clean shut out of the understanding of Scripture . . . which is locked up with false expositions and with false principles of natural philosophy' (Demaus 1871: 22).

In the 'Prologue to Genesis', Tyndale lists the reasons given by the Church against vernacular translation, including the impossibility of the task, the illegality, the risk of increasing the number of heretics, and the potential for civil rebellion. However, he claims that the real reason is:

> to drive you from the knowledge of the scripture, & that you shall not have the text thereof in the mother tongue, and to keep the world still in darkness, to the intent they might sit in the consciences of the people, throw vain superstition and false doctrine, to satisfy their filthy lusts, their proud ambition, and insatiable covetousness, and to exalt their own honor above king & emperor, yea & above God himself.

Tyndale's Pentateuch was provocative. His marginal glosses and Prefaces to the five books emphasize his perceived contradiction between 'official church practice' and the 'laws of God'. His translations in general (and his marginalia in particular) are subjective in outlook and as a result, it became politically impossible for the bishops not to condemn his work. Indeed, it has been argued that Tyndale wished to hold bishops up to 'opprobrium as murderers', and that 'his works . . . [were] intended to produce an ecclesiastical and social revolution, of a highly dangerous character, aided by mistranslations of Holy Writ and sophistical glosses in the margin . . . there is a perverse and bitter spirit running through the whole design' (Gairdner 1908: 1/228; 2/367).

Times were very different by the time Coverdale began translating. In December 1534, the Synod of Canterbury, under the leadership of Archbishop Thomas Cranmer, petitioned Henry VIII 'to decree that the holy scripture shall be translated into the vulgar English tongue by certain upright and learned men to be named by the said most illustrious king' (Pollard 1974: 177). In 1535 (the year Henry broke with the Church of Rome), encouraged by Cranmer and Cromwell, Miles Coverdale translated the entire Bible without formal authority, but with a dedication to Henry VIII and the 'most virtuous Princess, queen Anne'. (In 1535, Anne Boleyn was Henry's Queen. But by the time the sheets reached the printer, the 'virtuous princess' had been executed. Change had to be made: in the British Museum copy 'Anne' has been altered with a pen into 'JAne'.) In the dedication Coverdale markedly emphasizes how scripture teaches the pre-eminence of the temporal sword, and the king in his realm is 'under God the chief head of all the congregation and church of the same'. He outlines Henry's defence of the faith against Rome and speaks critically of the Pope whom he compares to Caiaphas. Henry, according to Coverdale's dedication, has proven himself a worthier Defender of the Faith than even the Pope had imagined:

> And the truth of our Balaam's prophecy is, your grace in very deed should defend the Faith, yea even the true faith of Christ, no dreams, no fables, no heresy, no papistical inventions, but the incorrupt faith of God's most holy word, which to set forth (praised be the goodness of God, and increase your gracious purpose) your highness with your most honourable council apply all his study and endeavour.

Coverdale claims that his translation is actually a result of the king's *own* wishes: 'Josias commanded straightly (as your grace doth) that the law of God should be read and taught unto all the people' (cf. 2 Kgs 23:1–3).

Having received Henry's permission to translate, Coverdale asserts that the new text is wholly English. He accomplishes his goal in two ways. The first (and more obvious) is marked by a significant bibliographical fact. The original title-page, printed in the same type as the Bible, reads 'faithfully and truly translated out of Dutch [i.e. German] and Latin into English'. However, the use of 'Dutch' was a dangerous confession of Lutheran heresy. Later copies merely stated 'faithfully translated into English'.

Coverdale's second method, using as 'text' the wood-cut on the title page, conforms to the sixth-century directive of Gregory the Great: '. . . in the same thing [i.e., 'picture'] they read (the truth) who do not understand the letters. Whence and especially to the (common) people the picture is in place of reading' (King 1982: 40). At the top of the woodcut, appearing in a burst of heavenly light, is the Tetragrammaton, symbolizing the direct revelation of the Word to the sovereign. Lower on the page, Henry VIII is depicted on his throne distributing Bibles to the kneeling bishops, with various crowned heads admiring his action. To emphasize further the appropriate role and power of the king, figures of harp-playing David and sword-bearing Paul, representing the Old and New Testaments, flank Henry, who is armed with the Sword and the Book, a personification of the Reformation ideal of evangelical kingship at the moment of transition from Old Law to New Law.

The Geneva Bible and the Rheims-Douay Bible

The direct politics of producing a new biblical text in the vernacular is most apparent in the case of the two exilic versions, the Geneva Bible and the Rheims-Douay. With the accession of Catholic Queen Mary in 1553, the printing of Protestant vernacular Bibles in England came to an abrupt stop. No official use of the English Bible was allowed and no printers were allowed to print English versions. Henry's proclamation that 'Bibles . . . be fixed and set up openly' was repealed, and those already 'set up' were burned. The works of Coverdale and Tyndale were specifically forbidden by the 'Proclamation for restraining books and writings against the Pope' issued in 1555. Protestants in England were in a precarious position, particularly those who had urged biblical translation, and as a result, colonies of English exiles were established in Germany and Switzerland.

In April 1560, the Protestant exiles in Geneva published one of the most overtly political English translations of the Bible and the only English translation to appear during the reign of Queen Mary. In fact, in the Preface, the translators comment that 'the time then was most dangerous and the persecution sharp and furious'.

The key feature of the Geneva Bible that distinguishes it from all other Bibles of its time and made it so popular was the extensive marginal notes that were included to explain and interpret the scriptures for the common people. For example, 'the sun, the moon and the stars falling from the heavens' (Mark 13:24) was interpreted as meaning that the religious leaders of the latter days would be discredited. These notes run to approximately 300,000 words, or one-third the length of the text of the Bible itself! However, in addition to being the reason for its popularity, the marginal notes of the Geneva Bible were also the reason for its demise. Indeed, the notes so infuriated King James I that he considered it 'seditious' and made its ownership a felony. James I was particularly worried about marginal notes such as the one for Exodus 1:19, which allowed disobedience to kings. Significantly, the translators do not identify themselves anywhere in the text, the Prologue, or the Dedication. One explanation for the anonymity is offered by Westcott, that they were 'several and perhaps not the same during the whole time' (1992: 91). Perhaps a better explanation is that the notes of the Geneva Bible are so outspokenly anti-Roman and blatantly Calvinistic in doctrine that it was dangerous to advertise authorship and these translators chose anonymity. As stated above, in 1644, the Geneva Bible was printed for the last time.

Despite the 1408 prohibition of vernacular translation, there were some Catholic humanists such as Erasmus who urged biblical translation for the lay-reader, writing:

> I totally dissent from those who are unwilling that the sacred Scriptures, translated into the vulgar tongue, should be read by the unlearned, as if Christ had taught such subtle doctrines that they can with difficulty be understood by a very few theologians, or as if the strength of the Christian religion lay in men's ignorance of it. The mysteries of Kings at war perhaps better to conceal, but Christ wishes his mysteries to be published as widely as possible. I could wish even all women to read the Gospels and the Epistles of St. Paul . . . that the farmer may sing parts of them at his plow and the weaver at his shuttle, that the traveler with their stories beguile the weariness of the journey. (Erasmus 1970: 205)

Erasmus' views notwithstanding, as late as 1546 the Council of Trent declared the Vulgate 'only of all other translations to be authentic' (*Canons* 19). Yet a Catholic vernacular translation was made, and for purely political reasons: Queen Elizabeth, a staunch Protestant, ascended to the throne in 1558 and just as the Geneva Bible was the result of political exile, so too the Rheims-Douay.

Catholics felt no safer in England during the reign of Elizabeth than had Protestants during the reign of Mary. As a result, Catholic English colonies were established on the Continent where William Allen, Fellow of Oriel College, Oxford, founded the English College at Douay in 1568, after refusing 'to acquiesce in the Elizabethan religious settlement' (Bruce 19878: 114). In a major break from tradition and theology, Cardinal William Allen, in a letter to Dr Vendeville, Regius Professor of Canon Law at Douay, explained how Catholic preachers were at a disadvantage compared with the Protestants who were familiar with English biblical translations and were therefore not required to translate extemporaneously from the Vulgate when preaching to a popular audience:

> On every Sunday and festival English sermons are preached by the more advanced students on the gospel, epistle or subject proper to the day . . . We preach in English, in order to acquire greater power and grace in the use of the vulgar tongue . . . In this respect the heretics, however ignorant they may be in other points, have the advantage over many of the more learned Catholics, who having been educated in the universities and the schools do not commonly have at command the text of Scripture or quote it except in Latin. Hence when they are preaching to the unlearned and are obliged on the spur of the moment to translate some passage which they have quoted into the vulgar tongue, they often do it inaccurately and with unpleasant hesitation, because either there is no English version of the words or it does not then and there occur to them. Our adversaries on the other hand have at their fingers' ends all those passages of Scripture which seem to make for them and by a certain deceptive adaptation and alteration of the sacred words produce the effect of appearing to say nothing but what comes from the bible. This evil might be remedied if we too had some catholic version of the bible, for all the English versions are most corrupt. I do not know what kind you have in Belgium. But certainly we on our part, if his Holiness shall think it proper, will undertake to produce a faithful, pure and genuine version of the bible in accordance with the edition approved by the Church, for we already have men most fitted for the work. (Allen 1882: 64–5)

His letter makes the motives for a translation clear: although *theologically* it would be better not to translate, *politically* the Catholic cause was suffering by not having an English Bible. Thus, the power of language was a sufficient cause to overrule the traditional objections to vernacular versions. Gregory Martin, a former fellow of St. John's College, Oxford, lecturer in Hebrew and Holy Scripture at the Rheims-Douay College, began work on a Catholic English Bible.

Martin had previously authored a scathing treatise: '*A Discovery of the manifold Corruptions of the Holy Scriptures by the Heretics of our Days, especially the English Sectaries, and of their foul dealing herein, by partial and false translations to the advantage of their heresies, in their English Bibles used and authorized since the schism*'. The main contention of the Discoverie is that 'the English heretics' purposely mistranslate the text in favour of their 'own erroneous teachings', and that the doctrinal claims of the Protestants rest on a 'deliberately' false translation of the original. In other words, the Protestant translators have power and know it.

The Catholic translation was published in 1609 and as the Preface states, this translation was deemed necessary by the circulation of many 'false translations' by Protestants who corrupted the truth, 'adding, detracting, altering, transposing, pointing, and all other guileful means: especially where it serves for the advantage of their private opinions'. Continuing Martin's diatribe against the insidious translation practices of the Protestants, the argument becomes *ad hominem* and links the Protestants with other 'syncretisantes': 'Protestants having no lawful generation, but proceeding of bastards race, upstarts of unknown progeny, are no less at discord among themselves, only agreeing against Catholics, like syncretisantes against their common enemies, or Herod, Pilate, and the Jews against Christ.'

According to the translators themselves, the appearance of an English Bible for Catholics may be required by political exigencies, but does not imply that Scripture *must* be available in the vernacular and certainly not available to *all* readers. The translators are quite clear on this point: 'We must not imagine [putting] the translated Bibles in the vulgar tongues into the hands of every husband-man, artificer, apprentice, boys, girls, mistress, maid, man: that they were sung, played, alleged, of every tinker, taverner, rhymer, minstrel: that they were for table talk, for ale benches, for boats and barges, and for every profane person and company'. Their point is emphasized by the new text itself: the translators make a statement by keeping much of it in Latin, effectively preventing it from reaching the hands of 'profane person(s) and company'.

One issue which had led to the Catholic prohibition of biblical translation centred on the translator as interpreter and his role in determining whether the actual *words* of the original were so full of significance that they had to be rendered (as far as possible) literally, or whether the subject matter was to take precedence and the translator was to express the *idea*. The role of tradition and doctrinal significance became enmeshed in the theoretical controversy. While biblical translation was viewed by the Reformers as an opportunity for confronting the theologian, and ultimately the state, afresh, Catholics viewed biblical translation as an opportunity to be guided and ruled by the theologian, thus reinforcing the status quo. Of course, this controversy was not a Renaissance phenomenon; it had occurred in the fourth century between Jerome and Augustine over the different methods with which to approach biblical translation and had established the basic dichotomy between philological and inspirational/literal translation (Schwarz 1970: 26–43). Philologists (such as Jerome and later, the Reformers) viewed the text as a medium of information which had to be transmitted through an accurate, yet contemporary equivalent in the new language. The philologists viewed the translator as inspired, but not an instrument merely used by God to write down the single words and sentences. Instead, the translator was allowed to make 'additions' to the original for stylistic reasons. As Erasmus describes: 'It is one thing to be a prophet and another to be a translator; in one case the Spirit foretells future events, in the other sentences are understood and translated by erudition and command of language' (*Erasmus' Prefaces* 1970: 52).

The Catholic translators wrote that their translators were inspired by God and thus errors were not made. The Rheims-Douay translators, quoting Augustine, write that God adapted his Word to man's damaged understanding, speaking to him by inspiring the human authors of the books of the Bible to write down his Word in a form intelligible to 'fallen man'. According to the Catholic translators, the Bible has 'modes' of speaking and its usage is different from common usage (*communis locutio*) and daily usage (*quotidiana loquendi consuetedo*). In the 'Preface to the Reader', the Rheims-Douay translators, referring to Augustine again, emphasize the authority of the Vulgate, and point out that they are at a loss to understand how anything could be found in the Hebrew or Greek texts that had escaped the attention of all the earlier and very learned translators: 'If the text is obscure, you too will probably be mistaken; if it is clear, it is incredible that the earlier translators were mistaken.'

It should be noted that the Rheims-Douay Bible was equipped with a very full apparatus of annotations, some intended to resolve any difficulties of a non-theological character, but most of which had the sole purpose of interpreting the text in conformity with the faith as the editors understood it (specifically in conformity with the pronouncements of the Council of Trent) and to rebut arguments of the Reformers. As a result, the apparatus is as controversial and outspoken as the Tyndale and Geneva translations.

The King James Version

By 1604, vernacular translation no longer involved legality but rather quality. As a result, King James actually welcomed the project:

> I profess, I could never yet see a Bible well translated in English; but I think, that of all, that of Geneva is the worst. I wish some special pains were taken for an uniform translation; which should be done by the best-learned men in both Universities, then reviewed by the Bishops, presented to the Privy Council, lastly *ratified by Royal authority*, to be read in the whole church, and none other. (Pope 1952: 308; emphasis added)

Forty-seven men divided into six panels undertook the project. Two of the panels met at Oxford, two at Cambridge, and two at Westminster. When the panels completed their work, the draft translation of the whole work was reviewed by a smaller group of twelve men, two from each panel, and then the text was sent to the printer. Miles Smith, Canon of Hereford (who ultimately became Bishop of Gloucester) and Thomas Bilson, Bishop of Westminster, shepherded it through the publication process. Ironically, the translation of the biblical text itself was drawn largely from the Geneva Bible.

The rules which guided the translators were sanctioned (if not indeed written) by James himself. Old ecclesiastical words were to be kept (for example, 'church' and not 'congregation'). Unlike the politically inflammatory Tyndale and Geneva Bibles, marginal notes were to be used only to explain Hebrew and Greek words and to draw attention to parallel passages. The translators' dedication of their work was 'to the most high and mighty prince James,' language the king must have found flattering in contrast to the language of some of his Scottish churchmen such as Andrew Melville who called him 'God's silly vassal', and reminded him that although he was king in the kingdom of Scotland, he was only an ordinary member in the kingdom of Christ (Bruce 1978: 100).

Interestingly, from a political perspective, this text was considered to be a 'revision' rather than a 'translation,' and therefore was not entered on the Stationers' Register. Thus, the overt political power of the translators was subjugated to the less direct, the 'hidden' – the translators being anonymous and the volume not immediately well publicized.

C. S. Lewis notes that in considering the power of the translator, there is Homer's Homer, Chapman's Homer, and Pope's Homer. 'Chapman's is always teaching lessons of civil and domestic prudence which never crossed the real Homer's mind' (1954: 517). This is the basic premise of all Renaissance biblical translation, and it is on this issue that the power of biblical translation hinges. The Renaissance biblical translator exercised his power in his word choice, his style of translation, and his decision as to what needed further elucidation and comment. The choices were made with great deliberation and with political acuity, in recognition of the significant impact of and on the politics of the day. During the Renaissance the 'politics of the day' entailed the relationship between the monarchy and the Church and thus it is impossible to read Renaissance biblical translations outside of the cultural context, that is to say, outside of the concern for royal authority and Church matters.

This view of the biblical translator as a powerful figure was generally accepted in Renaissance England since the translator made a conscious decision to wield his pen either for or against the establishment – Church *and* State – attempting to rally support for his political position. The translator's 'view of the world' was reflected to such an extent that some biblical translators were put to death because of specific word choice, and other interpretive practices held to be not only political, but also heretical, monarchist, or anti-monarchical. For those readers of the English Renaissance Bible who do not read Hebrew or Greek, the English texts have become canonized and are now the accepted reading. As John Lowes notes, biblical phraseology has become 'part and parcel of our common tongue – bone of its bone and flesh of its flesh' (1967: 3). 'Bible and Culture' during the Renaissance – they are inseparable.

References

Allen, W. C. (1882). *Letters and Memorials (1532–1594)*, ed. T. Knox. London: Nutt.
Bruce, F. F. (1978). *History of the Bible in English: From the Earliest Versions*. New York: Oxford University Press.

The Canon and Decrees of the Sacred and Ecumenical Council of Trent: Celebrated Under the Sovereign Pontiffs, Paul III, Julius III and Pius IV (n.d.). Trans. J. Waterworth. Chicago: Christian Symbolic Publication Society.

Coverdale, M. (1975). *Coverdale Bible: 1535*. Folkestone: Dawson.

Demaus, R. (1871). *William Tyndale*. London: Religious Tract Society.

The Douay Bible: The Holie Bible Faithfully Translated: A Facsimile of the 1609 Edition in 2 Vol (1975). London: Scholar Press.

Duffield, G. (1965). *The Works of William Tyndale*. Philadelphia, PA: Fortress Press.

Erasmus' Prefaces: 1505–36 (1970). Ed. and trans. R. Peter. Menton: no publisher

Foxe, J. (1877). *Acts and Monuments*, 4, ed. S. Cattley. London: J. Pratt.

Gairdner, J. (1908). *Lollardy and the Reformation in England*. London: Macmillan.

The Geneva Bible: A Facsimile of the 1560 Edition (1969). Madison, WI: University of Wisconsin Press.

Jones, G. L. (1983). *The Discovery of Hebrew in Tudor England: A Third Language*. Manchester: Manchester University Press.

King, J. N. (1982). *English Reformation Literature: The Tudor Origins of the Protestant Tradition*. Princeton, NJ: Princeton University Press.

Lewis, C. (1954). *English Literature in the Sixteenth Century*. Oxford: Oxford University Press.

Lowes, J. L. (1967). 'The Noblest Monument of English Prose', in *Essays in Appreciation*. Port Washington, DC: Kennikat Press, pp. 3–31.

More, T. (1976). *The Complete Works of St Thomas More*, various eds. New Haven, CT: Yale University Press.

Mozley, J. (1937). *William Tyndale*. New York: Macmillan.

Oxford English Dictionary (1978). Oxford: Clarendon Press.

Pollard, A. W. (1974). *Records of the English Bible: Documents Relating to the Translation and Publication of the Bible in English, 1525–1611*. Folkestone: Dawson.

Pope, H. (1952). *English Versions of the Bible*. St Louis, MO: Herder.

Rashkow, I. N. (1990). *Upon the Dark Places: Sexism and Anti-Semitism in English Renaissance Biblical Translation*. Sheffield: Sheffield Academic Press.

Schwarz, W. (1970). *Principles and Problems and Biblical Translation: Some Reformation Controversies and Their Background*. Cambridge: Cambridge University Press.

Tyndale, W. (1967). *Five Books of Moses Called The Pentateuch: Being a Verbatim Reprint of the Edition of M.CCCCC.XXX*, ed. J. Mombert. Carbondale, IL: Southern Illinois University Press.

Westcott, B. (1972). *A General View of the History of the English Bible*. London, Macmillan.

CHAPTER 5
The Reformation

Peter Matheson

The Bible burst on the sixteenth century with the force of a revelation. In recent decades we have become much more sharply aware of the dominance of eschatological and apocalyptic perspectives in the reception of Scripture. The very proliferation of translations into new languages was taken as a sign that the end was at hand. The Word of God was experienced as a hurricane, turning the world's values upside down, heralding the Last Day, which was close at hand – a promise as much as a threat. In these 'last times', the Church, the ship of faith, had to batten down, dispose of all unnecessary cargo, and head for harbour. For Protestants, the exclusivity of Scripture (*sola Scriptura*) actually functioned as a code for the imminence of Christ's Kingdom. As the world became senile (*natura senescit*), the reliance on institutions and doctrines based on human wisdom instead of God's word had led to a flood of vice and endangered our very salvation. Scripture's message therefore had immediate and desperately urgent implications for everything from the most intimate of personal concerns to the entire ordering of society.

There was nothing subtle, then, about the impact of the Bible on the early modern mind, nothing resembling the pluralist filter through which biblical values, ideas, narratives trickle into Western culture today. We are entering a very different world. In the early modern period Scripture's authority had become so massive, so unquestioned and unquestionable that its proponents had no need to be self-consciously authoritarian. There was no Enlightenment heritage to be countered, no secularist ideology. Renaissance humanism was an ally of the Scriptural revival. Yet the influence of Holy Scripture on sixteenth-century European society was nothing if not complex. Understandings of it varied extraordinarily widely, and eclectic combinations of legalist, humanist, sapiential, apocalyptical, and mystical readings were frequent. Some read it quite simplistically as divine law. Those in the Erasmian, humanist mode dreamed of a gentle diffusion of its wisdom, proverbial, psalmic and evangelical, into school and home and work. Others found in Scripture a dramatic message of catastrophe and crisis, of redemption for a world in chaos, while in some streams of radical

Protestantism and Catholicism, the Bible was interpreted in profoundly mystical categories. Common to virtually all these different approaches was an awesome seriousness.

Moreover, the manner of its impact varied enormously, depending on whether its message was being embraced by individuals and consensual groupings, or by governments that adapted its message to promote their nationalist or state-building agendas. Equally critical was the relationship between Scripture and Church, or rather Churches. The latter sought to ensure, though with varying degrees of success, that Scripture was read through the lenses of their approved theologians, preachers and teachers, their catechisms, liturgies, councils, and credal confessions.

Enthusiastic advocacy of the supremacy of Scripture by both humanists and Protestant reformers met with considerable suspicion from the Old Church, and was soon modified even within the Protestant camp by concerns at the rash of divergent readings of the Bible. Initially, the Catholic opposition was driven by a traditionalist defence of existing thought and practice. Deeper concerns, however, soon surfaced about safeguarding the apostolicity and catholicity of the Church, and balancing the claims of Scripture with the unwritten rule of faith as preserved in ecumenical councils, and by the magisterial authority of the Church. What one party saw as the Scriptural renewal of the Church and its Sacraments was viewed by other as their comprehensive ruin.

As the religious divisions hardened along national or state lines, they were reinforced by the development of state bureaucracies and centralization. The pervasiveness of confessionalization, that alliance of the ecclesiastical and secular elites to channel the reception of Scripture, is hotly debated in contemporary scholarship. There is considerable evidence, however, that decrees and reforms which came down from on high and which were not integrated with local piety and praxis only gained limited and nominal adherence. The instrumentalization of Scripture for political ends is at best only part of the story. Side be side with it was the genuine concern to be churches 'under the Word'. Scripture was never a mere tool in the hands of the modernizing state.

We must seek explanations elsewhere for its enthusiastic reception. When the Bible burst on laypeople it was first and foremost by courtesy of an extraordinary revival in preaching. Moreover, by 1500, it was evident that a new actor had swept onto the stage, the printing press, that innovative replicator of identical and readable copies, for Luther the 'latest and greatest gift of God'. From Wittenberg alone, some 100,000 copies of the New Testament had poured out by Luther's death in 1546. Alongside these foot-soldiers of the biblical army ranged the light cavalry of innumerable pamphlets and tracts, while behind them boomed the big guns of countless biblical commentaries. Rulers now had to contend with that virtually uncontrollable beast: the Fourth Estate, or public opinion. It has been estimated that more than 80 pocket-sized editions of the New Testament appeared between 1522 and 1545 in the Netherlands alone, though for most of that time they were illegal. Anna Bijns commented sarcastically on Luther's 'miracles':

> Scriptures are read in the taverns,
> In the one hand the gospel, in the other the stein,
> They are all drunken fools; nevertheless by these
> Are learned preachers ridiculed.

Such versions of the Bible constituted a radical empowerment of ordinary people, providing them with an unchallengeable authority to back their awkward and probing questions. In the early years of the Reformation 'printing, preaching and singing', were perceived as inseparable allies in the broadcasting of the Scriptural message. It was sung into people's hearts by the new hymns, and proclaimed from pulpits or tavern tables, while printing had the allure of globalization. It took the message out, as the fiery radical, Thomas Müntzer said, 'for the whole world to see' (Matheson 1988: 68, 77, 133). The naked text was then 'studied' in the privacy of people's homes with breath-taking ardour. The Catholic controversialist Cochlaeus complained that the New Testament was so commonly available 'that even tailors and cobblers, even women and other simple folk, who had only learnt to read a little German in their lives, were reading it with great enthusiasm as though it were the fount of all truth, while others carried it around, pressed to their bosom, and learned it by heart'.

Woodcuts, etchings, illustrated broadsheets, paintings, poems, ballads, folk songs and inflammatory or devotional pamphlets, often in dialogue form, salted and peppered the scriptural message. The old images of the saints might be disappearing in many places, but new images replaced them: of Adam's Fall and Christ's Ascension, of Jeremiah's fiery cauldron warning of disaster, of a world divided down the middle between light and dark, grace and law: a new Jerusalem, the imminent dawn of a new age. The text of Scripture was also read side by side with the happenings which were shaping their lives, 'texts' of communal rituals, events, confrontations (Scribner 1981). This synergy of the communal and the personal was hardly new, but the printed word gave it a new edge and a new edginess. The biblical message landed in a heady mix of past frustrations and soaring hopes.

The Bible was different things to different people, of course. On one level it was a book like any other, full of stories and images to stir the heart, striking woodcuts often playing an important role. But it was also an 'inner book', its contents being interiorized and collated by believers into their own personal 'canons'; people read Scripture highly selectively. As William Tyndale, the greatest of the early English translators of Scripture put it, the only way to 'understand the scripture unto our salvation' was to search it for God's personal covenant with us in our baptism. But this had not only personal but class and gender connotations: as Miriam Chrisman has demonstrated the Christ of the peasant or artisan was very different from that of the patrician or the nobility (Chrisman 1996).

Many city dwellers had the opportunity, through formally staged civic disputations, to weigh up for themselves divergent 'readings' of Scripture, the magistrates putting a new gloss on the old tradition of the sacred city by acting as judges between the advocates of the tradition and their evangelical opponents. Others pondered what they had heard in discussions in the tavern or challenges from the pulpit. Scripture was controverted and controversial as never before. What lay people read in the privacy of their own homes, or with little groups of trusted friends, might conflict with the sermons they heard, or the public worship in which they participated. Sermons were often interrupted. Angry French and Scottish women were known to hurl their stools at the preacher when provoked.

The potential for private judgement on the mysteries of divine revelation was a *novum* with explosive consequences. Martin Luther's audacity in claiming ultimate privilege for his conscience at the 1521 Diet of Worms spawned consequences he could never have dreamt of, and he was soon to deplore all manner of 'heavenly prophets' who seemed to think they had swallowed the Holy Ghost, feathers and all! When he attempted to rein in the discussion, this led in turn to his denunciation as the 'new Pope'.

Households and individuals poring over Scripture without supervision from the clergy could come to socially alarming and theologically unorthodox conclusions. Radicals such as Valentin Ickelshamer, himself no mean grammarian, encouraged ordinary Christians to read and interpret Scripture for themselves. Magistrates and princes such as the dukes of Bavaria were quick to see the threat this posed to social cohesion. Archbishop Whitgift found it necessary to clamp down hard on independent ideas; Queen Elizabeth's dislike of Puritan 'prophesyings' is well known.

The exponential growth in the prestige of Scripture, however, provided laypeople with clear norms by which conventional beliefs and practices could be measured. Everything from celibacy to usury, from hoarding goods during a famine to the authority of the pope came under scrutiny. This had momentous consequences for a society in which Church and society were virtually coterminous. Apart from a tiny minority of radicals, after all, the concept of Christendom remained unchallenged. Hence when the Bible was championed as the supreme authority for faith and life, this not only made the reform of the church inevitable – as its magisterial, legal, pedagogical, sacramental and pastoral practices came under scrutiny – but potentially threatened every single custom and social institution in 'secular' society. Family life, gender norms, Church–state relations, all had to be revisited. Scriptural blueprints loomed large in the popular as well as the scholarly imagination.

'Ah, what a joy it is when the spirit of God teaches us and gives us understanding, flitting from one text to the next – God be praised – so that I came to see the true, genuine light shining out' (Matheson 1995: 86). The young Bavarian mother who penned these lines in 1523, Argula von Grumbach, stood for countless others. Where she was unique was that she had climbed into print and challenged the theologians of her day to a debate in German. For her, Scripture was the source of light, joy and illumination as the Spirit of God swept her on from one text to the next. The biblical preaching she had heard, and the pamphlets from Wittenberg which she had devoured had spurred her to a disciplined 'study' of Scripture which revolutionized her life totally. The wall of separation between private and public collapsed. 'Dr Martin' had opened up for her with his translation of Scripture a quite new understanding of God, Church and society. As 'a mere woman' she proceeded to launch a frontal challenge on the Old Church, starting with the prestigious theology faculty in Ingolstadt. She launched a swingeing critique of Bavaria's legal, educational, and patronage systems and questioned both the traditional understanding of women and the mores of her own class, the nobility. What gave her a voice was the printing press. What made her audience sit up and listen was her mastery of Scripture. Her best-selling pamphlets, headed by flamboyant woodcuts, were in large part catenae of biblical quotations.

This is but one example of the subversive and programmatic impact of Scripture. One wonders whether any book has ever had an impact remotely comparable with that of the Bible in the early modern period. As Christopher Hill, the superb Marxist historian of seventeenth-century England put it, the Bible was 'accepted as the ultimate authority on economics and politics no less than on religion and morals' (Hill 1993: 31). Virtually every issue in heaven and earth could be settled by reference to it.

All this was, to put it mildly, surprising. The language, thought, and cultural presuppositions of the Hebrew Bible and the New Testament could hardly have been rivalled for obscurity and remoteness. Its holiness codes, convoluted patriarchal narratives and the intricacies of its Pauline thought were inconceivably alien to sixteenth-century Europeans. One could scarcely imagine any book less likely to become a household possession! Yet it was precisely at this time that the Bible was 'laïcized'. For Luther, the father of a household, which included servants and guests, was effectively its bishop, with the right and duty to read and explain Scripture. In Scotland, John Knox bound the reading of Scripture at home closely to common prayer and to 'exhorting'. Behind such advocacy lurked the belief that the message of Scripture was plain, unitary, and clear.

The Bible became the reading primer in schools. People carved biblical texts about their doorways. In 1579, the dedication to the Scottish reprinting of the Geneva Bible claimed that 'almaist in euerie priuate house the buike of Gods law is red and understand in oure vulgaire language'.

Availability and accessibility were important presuppositions. One recalls Henry VIII's legislation of 1541 stipulating that a copy of the Great Bible should be available in every parish church. But enthusiasm for Scripture could not 'trickle down' from above. Its strength lay in its grassroots popularity. The scene in the obscure Saxon town of Allstedt in 1523–4, when a little group gathered around their preacher, Thomas Müntzer, in the 'upper room', to read Scripture and to pray, could be replicated across Europe. Instruction in the faith, he sighs, is not to be achieved in a day (Matheson 1988: 104). Werner Packull has demonstrated how little groups of radical lay people constituted their own hermeneutic circles, developed their own contextualized interpretations, and gathered collections of key inter-connected texts which. provided artisans, villagers, women with their own stepping stones through Scripture (1995: 16–32). Such groups saw the schools of the prophets, the first followers of Jesus, the primitive Christian Church as their models. Biblical worship was the training ground which steeled them for a disciplined, communal life and not seldom for martyrdom.

We have to guard against exaggerations when assessing the impact of Scripture. In the German countryside, for example, literacy will seldom have been as high as 5 per cent and the folio-sized volumes initially produced were well beyond the pockets of all but a privileged few. Even the New Testament would have cost an artisan a week's wages. Many, however, would have had Scripture read to them by others, at the mill, the inn, the market-place, the back of the church. People read aloud as a rule, anyway, so a reader would have an instant audience. The new print culture often reinforced oral culture.

Many would have had to be content, however, with the poor folks' Bible, which meant being drilled by the pastor in the catechism, on a sleepy Sunday afternoon! In Poland, Lithuania, and Rumania, vernacular catechisms long preceded translations of Scripture. Protestant and Catholic writers alike used the simple 'echo' technique, in which the question foreshadowed the answer, to inculcate the biblical message. However pocket-sized editions of the Geneva Bible, with its clear Roman type, and reasonable price, soon became highly popular, not least in England and in Scotland. It boasted punctuation and clear paragraphs and by 1553 numbered verses. To commercially minded printers a standard work such as the Bible was a godsend, returning high profits. Perhaps a million versions of the Scriptures and of the New Testament circulated in England between the Reformation and 1640. Humble folk clubbed together to buy a New Testament, gathering together to read it and hear the 'glad and sweet tidings of the gospel'.

How are we to explain this hunger for Scripture, since the sheer number of Bibles in circulation explains very little? One key factor must have been the confidence that the code of Scripture had been cracked, in Gadamer's terms that there had been a 'fusing of the horizons'. As Christopher de Hamel points out, the title page of the 1534 Wittenberg Bible depicted it 'as a physical object distributed from the court of Heaven' (2001: 235). This was no mere book. It offered wisdom for life. It unlocked salvation. It offered a map to eternity.

In most instances, no doubt, Scripture first came alive through the mediation of some 'earnest' or learned preacher. Unofficial or peripatetic 'hedge preachers' were common, as were laypeople, including women. The reverse is also true. A preacher suspected of being the arm of an alien court or magistracy would get short shrift. This was, of course, not entirely new. In Renaissance Italy, for example, as Peter Howard has argued in a recent lecture, it was widely recognized that worthy preachers and a reference to local, living experience were required to 'reactivate' the text. Such preachers combined the roles of today's social and political commentators, journalists, talk-back personalities, counsellors, as well as being exegetes and spiritual leaders. In Scotland, John Knox, a fervent advocate of the teaching of Scripture 'by tong and livelye voyce', influenced social and political life quite as much as that of the Church.

Another reason for the enthusiasm for Scripture was the widespread conviction, voiced by Luther, Müntzer and many other reformers, that, after generations when it had been hidden away from sight, concealed 'beneath the bench', or under a 'cover', reserved for the eyes of the privileged few, a prey to dust and moths, it had been dramatically rediscovered and brought back to the light of day. This is puzzling, of course, because Scripture had been fundamental to medieval theology and piety. Gregory the Great had based his eleventh-century programme of pastoral reform on 'the pages of the prophets and the Gospels'. The Psalms had been the backbone to the whole Benedictine tradition of monastic worship, in all its myriad permutations. There was a vigorous revival of preaching in the latter decades of the fifteenth century and a careful study of printed sermons demonstrates that some 76 per cent of the preachers' quotations were taken from the Bible (Taylor 1992: 74). The stories of Noah and Moses, Daniel and John the Baptist, the life and death and resurrection of Jesus, were etched on the stone carvings of the churches, danced out of the stained glass windows, shimmered on the great tapestries which hung on the walls of the wealthy, leapt out of the manuals of personal devotion. At a popular level, the carved figures of the Hebrew prophets, of Jesus and his disciples were interwoven into the liturgical and domestic life of great and small, in a thousand homely variations. Hardly a town was without a carved figure of Jesus mounted on a donkey, which was wheeled through the streets on Palm Sunday.

Yet for reformers, Catholic and Protestant, it was as if the wild animal that was the Word of God had previously been tied up, shackled, domesticated, and as if God himself had thereby been censored and tamed. The reference in Luke 11 to the lawyers hiding away the key of knowledge was endlessly repeated by advocates of the vernacular versions. Harmony between tradition and Scripture, between the authority of the Church hierarchy and the message of the Gospel, between pious devotion and biblical faith, even between the devotional paintings on the walls and the sermon, was no longer assumed. Too often in the past, it was felt, biblical texts had been used simply to back up arguments arrived at elsewhere, from university teachers or Canon Law. The two Testaments had been seen as the breasts of the Church for infants in the faith, but the more mature were to move on to solider food. The witness of lay schismatic groups from the eleventh century on, and of Wyclif and Hus in the fourteenth and fifteenth centuries had, of course, never been wholly forgotten. The Brethren of the Common Life had called for a return to apostolic simplicity. The extraordinary achievement of Reformers such as Luther and Zwingli, however, was to identify a Gospel of liberation as the central and unifying core message of Scripture. Now the Word could 'run free', unshackled. Scripture could be quoted against tradition, against academic theology, against the Pope. As Argula von Grumbach admonished the Regensburg City Council in 1524: 'Do not be led astray by old customs and traditional ways. The Lord says: "I am the way, the truth, and the life." John 14. He does not say: "I am what is customary"' (Matheson 1995: 157). Or as George Hakewell put it, books which had formerly been imprisoned in the libraries of the monasteries 'were redeemed from bondage, obtained their enlargement, and freely walked about in the light' (Hill: 1993, 7).

This sense of the 'liberation' of Scripture was intimately connected with the élan of Renaissance humanism. Humanists such as Erasmus had argued, more inductively than deductively, for the absolute priority of Scripture, although seldom challenging the authority of the Church in principle. Their concern was for the removal of abuses. The Hebrew and Greek scriptures offered, they felt, the only reliable path back into the pristine world of the apostles and the early Church, just as classical literature and philosophy had re-opened the portals to good grammar and rhetoric, to cultured conversation, to the literary and philosophical excellence. The younger generation of 'poets', historians, and linguists embraced Scripture ardently as part of an insurrection of the young and intelligent against 'barbarism' and superstition. This indignant rejection of a clericalized Scripture has similarities to the excitement and controversies generated in post-Enlightenment Europe two hundred years later, when critical biblical scholarship challenged the reigning orthodoxies and pieties.

Thus, the defence of intellectual freedom, and the autonomy of scholarly enquiry, rapidly emerged as the by-products of biblical scholarship. From 1509 onwards, the outstanding Hebraist, Johannes Reuchlin, found himself defending the right of biblical scholars to study Rabbinic texts and deploy Hebrew philology and grammar. When this was bitterly opposed by the Dominicans of Cologne, their obscurantism became the butt of humanist derision throughout Germany and beyond in the *Letters of Obscure Men*. This affair, however, challenged the assumption of the Church, as articulated by outstanding theologians such as Aquinas and Bonaventura, that Scripture had to be read in accordance with the consensus of the Church's teachers down the centuries and that only the hierarchy could judge on how Scripture could be interpreted. The large illustrated bibles which emerged in France and Italy towards the end of the eleventh century were seen as splendid visual symbols of the authority of the church. The humanists' enthusiasm for Scripture was seen as intrusive, unprecedented and one-sided, 'putting the sickle into another man's crop' and something of a turf war developed, the scholastic theologians in the universities sensing that their prerogatives were being threatened (Rummel 1995: 85). Matters were made much worse as it became clear that the thousand-year reign of the Vulgate, the authoritative text of Scripture for worship and doctrine, was also being challenged.

The biblical humanists were part of a new generation of lay professionals, in law, diplomacy, and government. In their concern to recover the authentic text of Scripture they produced a new generation of dictionaries, grammars, commentaries, companions to Scripture. Giant steps were taken to recover and foster the knowledge of Hebrew and Aramaic and Greek, often in collaboration with Jewish scholars, and to enhance the prestige and status of the ancient languages. Since early Church Fathers such as Origen, Jerome and Augustine were particularly valued as reliable exegetes new editions and translations of their works poured out. Literary and historical skills were honed. John Colet, the Dean of London, for example, came to see that the letters of Paul had been written at particular times to particular people and places; their message, as we would say today, had to be contextualized. This encouraged attention to a historical approach to the text and an awareness of the different literary genres of poetry, songs, love lyrics, historical accounts, legal codes contained within the Bible.

Such biblical humanism tended to cluster around the royal and princely courts, the reforming monasteries, and the arts faculties of the universities. It tapped new sources of financial support, the patronage of the nobility and of wealthy patricians, for example. Lay sodalities emerged in the cities of Italy and Germany, and individual scholars and groups kept in touch by letter-writing. Networks began to stretch right across Europe, including women such as Caritas Pirckheimer in Nuremberg and Giulia Gonzaga in Fondi. The scholarly links which developed between Spain and Italy, England and the Netherlands, Scotland and France, Germany and Switzerland were to prove crucial for the future. Erasmus, as has often been noted, was the first truly European scholar.

Thus, the fascination with Scripture, its languages, discourse, and message, had encouraged the formation of new informal groupings. The sodalities, while open to clergy, had a strong lay ethos, and were relatively free from church or university control. Their members frequently bonded closely together as friends, though as always among intellectuals, rivalries crackled and grievances, real and imaginary, were freely aired, not seldom in the heady new medium of print. These networks were held together by travel, hospitality, the exchange of books and flattery, and developing their own forms of corporate life. At times, they almost appeared to be a para-church. They cooperated closely with the printing press, producing new editions of the Fathers and of Scripture itself. Cardinal Ximines, *Quintuplex Psalter*, or Erasmus' 1516 edition of the New Testament, the *Novum Instrumentum*, were among the most famous. Erasmus, is often pictured as studying in the workshop of the Basel printer Froben. This stream of editions set new parameters for scholarly discussion, and challenged the traditional theological curriculum in the universities. As whole new 'libraries' of hitherto unavailable texts became available, space and freedom opened up for a new 'discursive field', for quite different patterns of religious and cultural reflection and discussion.

The defence of their own personal intellectual freedom, therefore, was not the only concern of the humanist groups which gathered around More, Colet and Erasmus in England, around Bishop Briconnet at Meaux, or around Valdes at Naples. They were crusaders, if gentle ones. A purified Scripture would open the way, they believed, to a reformed Church and society. They hoped to achieve their objectives by example, education, and not least humour, by training up a new generation which would gradually purify the existing institutions in Church and society. Authentic texts of Scripture would replace 'superstitious' relics or objects of adoration such as the 'authentic' depiction of the Virgin Mary by Luke the Evangelist, such as that in Santa Maria del Popolo in Rome, copied all over Europe and famously displayed in the Regensburg pilgrimage church to which hundreds of thousands flocked for healing around 1520.

Insensibly, then, the scholarly study of Scripture by individuals was transmogrified into a movement to renew the Church and, indeed, the whole of society. Education, rather than sacramental piety, was identified as the true path towards personal and social redemption. Dynastic wars were pilloried, the pomp and ignorance of clergy deplored. In all this, Scripture was absolutely central. It was the norm by which the special pleading of clerics or monastics or predatory rulers was to be side-stepped, and godly patterns devised for the future. Outward religiosity was less important than inward faith, ascetic withdrawal from the world was less important than obedience to God in one's secular vocation, in home and work and civil life. Scriptural ideas and models were used to commend a more earthy brand of holiness.

Such views attracted magistrates and reforming courts keen to assert their authority over ecclesiastical jurisdictions and immunities, over hospitals, for example, or preaching positions in the cities. Simultaneously Scripture was eyed by artisans and villagers as providing a charter for the rights of lay people. Pressure mounted for more learned preachers who could expound Scripture properly, and for a pruning of mass priests and 'useless' monastics, who did not foster lay education. Nor did criticism stop at the theologians, whose fanciful doctrines, based on philosophical speculation seemed to have little foundation in the simple gospel of the first followers of Jesus. In other words, the growing enthusiasm for Scripture was often wedded to anticlericalism, or, put more positively, to a reinvention of society along the lines of lay interests.

Virtually all the later reformers, including of course Luther himself, Catholic reformers such as Cochlaeus or Seripando, and radicals such as Thomas Müntzer began with the vision of the biblical humanists, or at least incorporated it in their thinking. They were first, and foremost exegetes, not reformers. Erasmus himself had characterized previous scholarship as a stagnant lagoon, which needed to be renewed by going up river to the sparkling sources of the true faith, back to Scripture and the Fathers. *Ad fontes!* Truth lay in the beginning of things. Conversely, the progressive corruption of the Church was attributed to pious and well-meaning people departing from the original revelation.

Early Reformers such as Zwingli, Luther, Tyndale stood in this tradition. Yet they also introduced a forward-looking, eschatological perspective and their commitment to painstaking scholarly team-work in philology, grammar and history – 'The devil loves bad grammar', as Luther loved to say – was combined with a flair for vernacular translation. They had a remarkable ability to commute between different worlds of discourse. Their combination of linguistic skills in the original languages with a rhetorical flair for the vernacular has been described as a 'stroke of strategic genius' (de Hamel 2001: 218). Some of the best linguists of the time teamed together as translators of Scripture. They were able to swing, imaginatively, from one world to another, to catch not only the nuances of meaning, but the 'grace and sweetness' of the original, as Tyndale put it, mastering the rhythms and cadences of the original biblical language as well as those of their own mother tongue. Tyndale was so at home in Hebrew and Greek grammar and syntax that he could say with conviction that both were much closer to English than to Latin. This gave additional warrant to the side-lining of the Latin Vulgate.

The case for vernacular translations was argued on many counts, historical and pastoral. Thomas Müntzer, who produced for his parishioners the first German Mass in the little Saxon town of Allstedt, argued that when Germans were first missionized, their language was as yet unformed, so it was

> quite understandable that they used Latin for the services. But it would be a bizarre matter indeed if there were never to be any progress beyond that point. From day to day there is a drive for improvement in all man's worldly undertakings; and are we to regard God as so impotent that he cannot progress further in this matter?

Papal mumbo jumbo had to be replaced by an intelligent understanding (Matheson 1988: 167, 181). Humanists such as Sir David Lindsay in Scotland made the obvious point that when God wrote the Law for Moses, 'in Tablis hard of stone' it was in his own 'vulgare language of Hebrew' and that if Jerome, the author of the Latin Vulgate, had been a Scot, living in Argyle, he would have rendered it into the 'Yrische toung' (Wright 1988: 166).

In his marvellous 1522 New Testament, Luther rendered its message into the direct, everyday language of life. Scripture was to become again the possession of the ordinary people to whom it was originally addressed. The resentment at Latin could also swell into nationalist pride. The vernacular bibles were, *inter alia*, indicators of a more self-assertive nationalism.

The transition from a largely visual, celebratory culture to one more focused on the word is one of the main influences of the new centrality given to Scripture. The pulpit, the rostrum, moved to the centre of attention, though, of course, it is a mistake to think of this in too institutional or pedagogic terms. In this period oral and literary culture reinforced one another, and the rostrum would often have been the kitchen table. In theological terms Luther's emphasis that Scripture was less a book than a 'crying out of the Gospel' underlined this. Erasmus had a vivid sense that all language was address; yet in a quite particular way, God, he believed, had condescended to reach down to the human race in Scripture, and spoke to us in a discourse that we could understand. This awareness of God's linguistic accommodation to our condition was to be taken up later by Calvin and others. It complemented a popular, and even populist confidence in the transparency of the Word.

The Scriptural movement also certainly promoted that quest for interiority which is often seen as one of the marks of modernity. '[A]n outward testimony cannot create inward reality', as Thomas Müntzer said (Matheson 1988: 223). Karl Holl, at the beginning of last century, famously described Lutheranism as a religion of the conscience. It is impossible, reading an early reformer such as Andreas Karlstadt, to miss the intimate link between Scripture, the cultivation of interiority and the empowerment of laypeople. This is true of Catholic evangelicals as much as Protestants, both of them latching on to Augustinian and mystical traditions. The Bible enabled a personal voyage of discovery and self-discovery, not least through the Psalms. The remarkable fascination with the Pauline corpus also indicates a willingness to plumb the depths of doubt and despair in the quest for liberation from sin, fear, and death. The evangelical Catholic reformer, Jacques Lefevre, insisted that the only access to the world of the Bible was by imaginative, empathetic prayerfulness. For all his emphasis on the need for attention to the exteriority of Scripture, Martin Luther was also quite adamant that it was only the Spirit which could open up the meaning of the text, the inner word.

Likewise a new pattern of pastoral theology and praxis developed, centred less on the sacraments and the traditional codes of penitence, and more on person-to-person counselling. Thomas Müntzer, and in not dissimilar ways Juan Valdes in Catholic Naples, practised what we today would call spiritual direction, inculcating a form of popular mysticism. Müntzer's theology of the Spirit valorized the personal experience of the biblical prophets and apostles, but insisted that our calling was not to parrot or slavishly follow them, but to see them as catalysts to plumb the abyss of the soul for oneself.

The whole understanding of the Church was also radically altered for Protestants. In the classic definition of the Lutheran Augsburg Confession, the Church was defined as the people of God gathered around the preaching of the Word and the administration of the sacraments. Luther's *Appeal to the German Nobility* of 1520, probably the single most influential writing in the entire Reformation, argued that canon-law definitions of the Church, already profoundly shaken by anticlerical attacks, were to be replaced by a Pauline model of participatory leadership and based on the priesthood of all believers. Others, including the Calvinist and Anabaptist traditions, interpreted the apostolic models rather differently, and the seed for many future and bitter conflicts was sown. In Lutheranism itself one notes a steady retreat from such participatory models of governance as a result of these conflicts.

So far, we have been talking about the transformation of the Church. Given the pervasiveness of that institution in the early modern period that is of massive importance. The influence of the Bible went far beyond piety, theology and the Church, however. The whole relationship between sacred and secular space was revisited. The Mosaic law, the covenants, the Davidic monarchy, the prophetic call for justice, together with the evangelical and apostolic models for community life, provided new paradigms for social relationships and political life throughout the early modern period. Centralizing rulers, patrician republicans, Lutheran preachers and Reformed noblemen, not to mention the Anabaptists, all modelled themselves on Scripture, drawing of course extraordinarily divergent conclusions from the same texts.

Henry VIII complained to Parliament in 1546 that the Bible was 'disputed, rhymed, sung and jangled in every alehouse and tavern'. William Tyndale, on the other hand, mocked the 'holy prelates' who fear that God's word 'causeth insurrection and teacheth the people to disobey . . . and moveth them to rise against their princes, and to make all common, and to make havoc of other men's goods'.

Control and manipulation of the versions and exegesis of Scripture became a crucial concern of governments. As Alistair McGrath comments:

> The title page of the Great Bible (1540) is to be seen as a classic example of image-making. The image projected is that of a unified nation, united under the monarch and the Bible . . . It is an icon of a godly state and church under their supreme head. The social ordering of England was thus affirmed every time the Great Bible was opened on a church lectern. (2001: 95)

Authorized collections of biblical homilies, often inculcating obedience, were a key weapon in the enculturation of the Reformation in England. One of James I's main motivations for sponsoring the Authorized Version in 1611 was his profound aversion to the marginal notes of the popular Geneva Bible, with their potential for social and political radicalism.

Urban republics drew heavily on the Pastoral Epistles, criticizing aristocratic and feudal features in society, such as conspicuous consumption, the whole culture of 'magnificence'. In Nuremberg, the shoe-maker poet Hans Sachs was an indefatigable advocate of a civic ethic which commended the 'common good', whatever was useful to one's neighbour. Biblical values are here accommodated to the patriarchal values of the middling classes, the skill-based guild culture, to a mercantile and professional ethos.

A more radical edge emerged in the communal reformation, whose concerns for divine justice, based in part on the Old Testament, phased into the Peasants' War of 1524–5. The latter spawned an impressive number of egalitarian utopias with biblical undergirding. Recent research has demonstrated the intimate link between Anabaptists' concerns for the common ownership of goods with a close study of Acts 2 and other biblical texts. In the ill-fated apocalyptic Münster experiment of 1534–5, hopes centred on recreating the sacred city of Jerusalem in theocratic form.

With its greater confidence in the Law, the Calvinist tradition also went further than Luther in seeing the Bible as a blueprint for all aspects of social and cultural life. Theologies of history were developed which drew on God's ancient covenants with his people to justify resistance to tyrannical governments. There was an impressive determination, often at the expense of individual liberties, to promote education and to rebuild society along godly lines. For Knox, Scripture was the 'tuchstone to try the rycht from the wrang'. The Scottish Book of Discipline of 1560 saw the Bible as providing a pattern not only for church polity, but for the provision of poor relief and education in every parish.

The ascetic or puritanical elements associated with this biblical understanding of worship and discipleship often had a deleterious effect on the variety, colour and communal character of religious and cultural life. However, we can be too precious about popular pieties based on reverence for often absurd saints, for example. The Reformation's alliance with humanism released countless new energies, including a healthy ongoing tension between laity and clergy. Artists such as Cranach and Dürer worked closely with the Reformation. Protestant house art included broadsheets, almanacs or 'painted cloths' which would often portray biblical themes. The woodcuts and etchings in Bibles recalled familiar images in stained, glass, paintings and carvings and provided people with a 'reassuring anchor' for their faith. Popular hymns and metrical versions of the Psalms flourished, and, as in the *Gude and Godlie Ballatis* of the 1540s in Scotland, poetry and theatre were used to propagate biblical ideas:

> My New Testament, plaine und gude,
> For quilk I sched my precious blude

In the Low Countries guild plays deployed vivid costumes and bawdy humour, to contrast the 'clear gospel' with the depredations and cruelty of the clergy. The allegorical figure of Amsterdam complained that the clergy have given Scripture a wax nose, which they twist to suit their interests. Sometimes straight biblical plays were presented, such as *The Acts of the Apostles*, in which 'False Prophet' is made to wonder: 'What? Is God so ignorant as to send his Spirit to lay people?' (Waite 2000: 93, 131ff.).

The great biblical themes of freedom and liberation became popular currency and had an incalculable effect in firing the public imagination. References abound in sermons and pamphlets to Genesis 1, setting out the just order of creation, to Daniel defying Nebuchadrezzar, to the humble, undaunted Jesus of the Gospels. One cannot begin to imagine reforming Strasburg or Zürich or Geneva without the vision of a godly Jerusalem. Where would Luther have been without his evocation of the 'captivity of Babylon' or without Lucas Cranach's apocalyptic images of the monstrous 'whore of Babylon'? The flags the peasants fought under during the Peasants' War, the rainbows they saw in the sky, the articles they drew up for their negotiations with the authorities all testify to the biblical themes of creation, divine justice, redemption. Pamphlets, broadsheets, woodcuts and thousands of sermons contrasted zealous prophets with tyrannous kings, Jesus with the religious establishment of his day, or presented John the Baptist preaching in the 'wilderness of men's hearts'. The biblical images of light and darkness, of leaking cisterns and wells of living water, of God's Word as hammer and fire, recur in endless, kaleidoscopic variations. Biblical women, such as Deborah, Jael, Judith, Esther, Mary, the daughters of Philip, were hailed as exemplars for a new age. Such images and models walked right out of Scripture, invaded people's dreams, instigated their actions, accompanied them on the way to the stake.

Finally, the influence of the translations of Scripture on the development of Europe's vernacular languages was incalculable. The Latinate monopoly of theology and worship was rejected in Protestant worship, and with it the assumptions of 'diglossality', the use of Latin for the sacred, but the vernacular for daily life and work and popular piety.

This was more than a mere linguistic shift for it emphasized the holistic nature of reality. The availability of the sources of revelation in the vernacular meant that preachers and theologians now found themselves much more accountable. Although the vernacularization of the liturgy was not the primary concern of Luther, and services in Latin continued – Calvin was much more rigorous in rejecting it – the astounding success of his biblical translation accelerated the move to a more standardized German, building on the language of the Saxon chancellery, which combined central and Eastern German dialects.

We should not romanticize the process of translation, as one of the best connoisseurs of Luther's language, Birgit Stolt, has warned. It was sweat and blood and tears. The struggle to find the exact German equivalent to a Latin term proved extraordinarily exacting. The insistence that pastors be trained in the original languages proved a corrective to any absolutization of a vernacular culture. The new translations of Scripture were, however, truly pioneering, vastly extending the linguistic range of the vernacular languages, and combining earthiness with dignity and a sacral style. Linguistically, Europe emerged from its adolescence. Hebraic, Greek and Latin terms enriched the vernacular, together with a host of idioms we take for granted such as 'licking the dust', and like a 'lamb to the slaughter'. Only Shakespeare's influence on the English language can begin to rival that of the Authorized Version of the Bible. Most of its contributors came from the South East, so the English language was effectively standardized. It appears that biblical translations even saved some languages such as Welsh from extinction. As Isaac Thomas, speaking of the 1588 translation, argues: 'Without this Welsh Bible the Welsh language would gradually but surely have disappeared from the churches, the parishes and the land. The Wales of the last four centuries would have been a very different Wales without William Morgan's Bible.'

The heroic attempt to transplant biblical values to early modern society had significant limitations. The communal reformation had little to show for its dream of bringing divine law to bear on injustice, and the spirited attempts of some individuals to extend the priesthood of all believers to women ran against the contemporary tide. One has to be cautious about exaggerating the impact of any body of ideas, biblical or otherwise, on the culture and society of early modern Europe. Biblical ideas tended to be factored in only where they forged creative alliances with other factors, social, economic and political.

This brief chapter has only been able to very selectively sketch some of the emergent issues. For some fleeting moments of time, it might have appeared as if Scripture might sweep away everything in its path, forging a wholly 'biblical culture'. This was neither a real option, nor a desirable one. Oberman has pointed to the 'disguised' nature of the impact of the biblical movement, even in its robust Calvinist form. It had to work against the grain of its own explicit concern to resist all innovation (Oberman 1994: 201–20).

In the end, there were many Bibles. Erasmus found the unity of Scripture in the Gospels, Luther focused on the covenantal theme of grace, as recapitulated by Jesus and Paul. A radical theologian, such as Müntzer, blended together texts from Genesis and the Gospel of John, from Jeremiah and Paul in his mystical and apocalyptic reading of divine and human reality. And we may end with Argula von Grumbach, for whom the prophets and apostles became contemporaries, living companions on her own journey. No aspect of her life remained untouched by Scripture, yet she remained quintessentially herself, a child of her day and age. Properly so.

References

Bradshaw, Christopher (1996). 'David or Josiah? Old Testament Kings as Exemplars in Edwardian Religious Polemic', in Bruce Gordon (ed.), *Protestant History and Identity in Sixteenth-Century Europe*. Aldershot: Scolar Press, pp. 77–90.

Chrisman, M. U. (1996). *Conflicting Visions of Reform: German Lay Propaganda Pamphlets 1519–1530*. Atlantic Highlands, NJ: Humanities Press.

Daniell, David (ed.) (1989). *Tyndale's New Testament*. New Haven, CT: Yale University Press.

De Hamel, Christopher (2001). *The Book: A History of the Bible*. London: Phaidon.

Duffy, Eamon (1992). *The Stripping of the Altars: Traditional Religion in England c. 1400–c. 1580*. New Haven, CT: Yale University Press.

Flood, John L. (2001). 'Martin Luther's Bible Translation in its German and European Context', in Richard Griffiths (ed.), *The Bible in the Renaissance: Essays on Biblical Commentary and Translation in the Fifteenth and Sixteenth Centuries*. Aldershot: Ashgate.

Fox, Adam (2000). *Oral and Literary Culture in England 1500–1700*. Oxford: Clarendon.

Hill, Christopher (1993). *The English Bible and the Seventeenth-Century Revolution*. London: Allen Lane.

Mackenzie, Cameron (2002). *The Battle for the Bible in England 1557–1582*. Berne: Peter Lang.

Matheson, Peter (1995). *Argula von Grumbach: A Woman's Voice in the Reformation*. Edinburgh: T. & T. Clark.

Matheson, Peter (ed.) (1988). *The Collected Works of Thomas Müntzer*. Edinburgh: T. & T. Clark.

Matheson, Peter (2000). *The Imaginative World of the Reformation*. Edinburgh: T. & T. Clark.

McGrath, Alistair (2001). *In the Beginning: The Story of the King James Bible and How It Changed a Nation, a Language and a Culture*. New York: Anchor.

Oberman, Heiko (1994). *The Reformation: Roots and Ramifications*. Edinburgh: T. & T. Clark.

Oberman, Heiko and Dykema, Peter (eds) (1993). *Anticlericalism in Late Medieval and Early Modern Europe*. Leiden: Brill.

Packull, Werner (1995). *Hutterite Beginnings: Communitarian Experiments during the Reformation*. Baltimore, MD: Johns Hopkins University Press.

Rummel, Erika (1995). *The Humanist–Scholastic Debate in the Renaissance and Reformation*. Cambridge, MA: Harvard University Press.

Scribner, R. W. (1981). *For the Sake of Common Folk: Propaganda for the German Reformation*. Cambridge: Cambridge University Press.

Stayer, James (1991). *The German Peasants' War and Anabaptist Community of Goods*. Montreal: McGill-Queen's University Press.

Stolt, Birgit (2000). *Martin Luthers Rhetorik des Herzens*. Tübingen: Mohr Siebeck.

Taylor, Larissa (1992). *Soldiers of Christ: Preaching in Late Medieval and Reformation France*. Oxford: Oxford University Press.

Trinkaus, Charles and Oberman, Heiko (eds) (1974). *The Pursuit of Holiness in Late Medieval and Renaissance Religion*. Leiden: Brill.

Waite, Gary K. (2000). *Reformers on Stage: Popular Drama and Religious Propaganda in the Low Countries of Charles V 1515–1556*. Toronto: University of Toronto Press.

Watson, Timothy (2002). 'Preaching, Printing, Psalm-Singing: The Making and Unmaking of the Reformed Church in Lyon, 1550–1572', in Raymond A. Mentzer and Andrew Spicer (eds), *Society and Culture in the Huguenot World 1559–1685*. Cambridge: Cambridge University Press, pp. 10–28.

Wright, David (1988) '"The Commoun Buke of the Kirke": The Bible in the Scottish Reformation', in David Wright (ed.), *The Bible in Scottish Life and Literature*. Edinburgh: St Andrew Press.

CHAPTER 6
The Counter-Reformation

Euan Cameron

The Historical Background

The story of the Roman Catholic Church in the early modern period is riddled with historiographical puzzles and disputes. One of the most persistent concerns the name to
be assigned to this period in Catholic history and the movements for change and development that occurred within it. The most durable description, and the one canonized
in many reference works, is the unwieldy description favoured by Hubert Jedin, of
'Catholic Reform/Counter-Reformation' (Jedin, in Luebke 1999: 21–45). The broad
outlines of the story were established as early as the middle of the nineteenth century
by Leopold von Ranke, and most subsequent narratives have been to some extent variations on his themes (Ranke 1834–7; cf. Hsia 1998; Bireley 1999; O'Malley 2000;
Mullett 1999). By the second half of the fifteenth century, the papacy had largely
weathered the storms of the Great Schism of 1378–1417 and the conciliar agitation
that supported the claims of the Fathers of the Councils of Constance (1414–18) and
Basle (1431–49). The Hussite challenge in Bohemia was contained, and its surviving
remnants were negotiated into a largely manageable and moderate form. The papacy
successfully accommodated the desires of secular governments for control (or at least
veto) over decisions affecting the Church in their territories – the movement sometimes
misleadingly called ecclesiastical nationalism – by a series of concordats. These were
highly favourable to stronger monarchs and much less so to weaker ones, such as the
German emperor. Across Western Europe diocesan bishops made essays in the holding
of reforming synods, aspiring to lead their clergy by example. Meanwhile the ordinary
people of Europe gave extravagant evidence of their endorsement of Catholic Christianity. Churches and cathedrals were embellished and rebuilt in many regions. Believers of quite modest means invested in increasing quantities of masses for the souls of
the departed, turning the support of those in purgatory into a major concern of the
Church (Galpern 1976; Chiffoleau 1980). Spontaneous cults and devotions dating
from the fourteenth centuries, such as the miraculous bleeding hosts of Wilsnack, in

Germany, attracted crowds of pilgrims and equivocal responses from the religious establishment (Damerau 1976; Lichte 1990; Bynum 2004).

In these circumstances the political leadership of the Roman Church, perhaps understandably, turned its attention to more immediately pressing concerns than strengthening its hold on a Church that seemed already well under control. From 1494 to 1559 armies from northern Europe repeatedly invaded the Italian peninsula in pursuit of dynastic claims to Milan and Naples. The popes, as lords of the papal patrimony stretching across the middle of Italy from Ostia to the Adriatic, needed great political dexterity to steer their state through the ensuing crises. Moreover, several of the dynasties that held the papal throne in this period, most notably the Medici and the Farnese, had territorial concerns and ambitions of their own within Italy. Notwithstanding the political turmoil of the period, Christian religious culture saw some creative achievements in the first decades of the sixteenth century. The most obvious and best known of these achievements are the artistic and architectural works of the high Renaissance, increasingly devoted to religious subjects as well as classical mythology. Just as important was the rise of new devotional styles, less formal and more personal, under the impact of so-called 'Christian humanism'. These movements were initially confined to small elite discussion-groups of the relatively wealthy and mostly leisured, lay and religious alike, in a few centres in Germany, France, Italy and Spain (Bataillon 1937; Spitz 1963; Veissière 1986; Firpo 1990). Erasmus of Rotterdam (c.1467–1536) though publishing exclusively in Latin, worked hard to publicize and encourage a style of devotion and piety that was more personal, less materially grounded, and based on more intimate contact with Scripture than was the prevailing practice in most churches. The scholarly vogue for the 'complete text' characteristic of Renaissance philology began to have a real impact on biblical scholarship and ultimately on theology itself. For the first time in several centuries a real need was widely felt to reach beyond scholastic exposition of the Latin Vulgate text to the Hebrew and Greek originals.

The Reformation came upon Catholic Europe as an unexpected and initially incomprehensible shock. It seems fairly clear that when Martin Luther (1483–1546) raised his protests first against the application of indulgences to the souls of the dead (1517) and then to a whole range of ritual, legal and institutional aspects of the Church up to 1520, most people understood him initially to be another rather more trenchant advocate for ideas already expressed. To Erasmian humanists he was a bolder critic of materialistic religion. In the eyes of German ecclesiastical nationalists, he denounced, a little more emphatically than most, the long-resented plundering of the German Church by the papal curia through canon law and papal provision. To laypeople exasperated with the abuse of clerical legal and fiscal privilege, he affirmed the rights of the community to take these matters in hand. As a consequence, at first only an elite of Catholic theologians, such as Jakob von Hochstraten of Cologne or John Fisher, Bishop of Rochester, accurately perceived that Luther's challenge was at heart driven by theological insights regarding divine grace and human salvation (Ozment 1971: 148–52; cf. Rex 1991: 110–28).

The problems for theologians who remained loyal to the Roman obedience and traditional theology were multiple. Luther's theology of justification touched an area where no definitive doctrinal decree had been made, or thought necessary, by popes or councils in the past. Ockhamists and neo-Augustinians had argued fairly freely about the relative roles of divine grace and human co-operation (Cameron 1991: 83–7). It was clear that Luther's claims implied or required attacks on agreed rites and customs (auricular confession, sacrificial private masses, monastic vows) that were well entrenched in the Church. The theological premises on which these rites and customs were to be defended were less clear. In particular, Luther had called into question the relative status of different and (in the traditional view) mutually supportive sources of authority. Very broadly, two attitudes towards the relationship between Scripture and Church tradition can be identified in late medieval thought, though these were nothing like two distinct 'schools', and not all scholars agree on the distinction. Some theologians argued that Scripture alone formed the basis for all doctrines and practices in the Church. However, they also agreed that the exegesis of Scripture was the collective responsibility of what would later be called the *magisterium*: in other words, Scripture could not be invoked to testify against the custom and collective view of the Church. Secondly, another group of theologians argued that certain teachings, customs and practices which were not explicitly laid down in Scripture (say, the rite of confirmation, or aspects of the doctrine of the Virgin Mary) could be deemed to have been handed down as unwritten verities guaranteed by apostolic tradition.[1] In all of this there was also room for the extremes of Scriptural or hierarchical positivism. One of the first and least adroit responders to Luther, Silvestro Mazzolini of Priero, argued in his *Dialogue on the Power of the Pope* (1517) that the 'doctrine of the Roman Church and the Roman Pontiff [was] an infallible rule of faith, from which even Holy Scripture takes its force and authority' and that any who dissented from that doctrine was a heretic (Kidd 1911: 31–2; see also Tavard 1959: 116–17).

Between *c.*1525 and *c.*1545, Catholic Europe struggled to define an acceptable response to the Reformation crisis, while also dealing with other quite autonomous ongoing developments. There was considerable diversity in reactions, particularly in Italy and Germany. The best theological minds tended to take a mediating stance. Moderate Catholic theologians such as Julius Pflug and Johann Gropper, or Italian curialists such as Gasparo Contarini, sought a theological position that would reconcile elements in the Lutheran message and somehow knit up the unity of the Church once more (Braunisch 1974; Gleason 1993; Lexutt 1996). However, one should not construct an artificially rigid axis of liberals versus conservatives, let alone crypto-reformers against would-be inquisitors.[2] There were many devout, serious and sophisticated thinkers whose theologies could not readily be classified in either camp. The Cassinese Benedictines, in particular, maintained throughout the Reformation era a subtle and independent position, resisting categorization either as crypto-reformers or traditionalist Catholics (Collett 1985). Through the work of a Cassinese monk, Benedetto da Mantova, this perspective helped to inform one of the most perplexing religious tracts of the pre-Trent era in Italy, the *Beneficio di Cristo* of 1543.[3]

It had been assumed from early in the Reformation debates that the eventual outcome would be a General Council of the Church, with the hope, expressed at least in the early stages of the crisis, that an agreed resolution could be reached. By the time that Pope Paul III issued a summons to a council in Mantua in 1537, it was already clear that, for the Protestants, matters had gone too far for a solution to be negotiated consistent with papal monarchy and the sovereignty of continuous tradition. When the Council finally opened on 13 December 1545 at Trent, in the foothills of the Alps symbolically mid-way between Roman and Habsburg Austrian influence, the position of the reformed communions was of less importance than the centuries-old power struggle between the papacy and the empire. Charles V of Habsburg, after many years of deferring the religious issue in order to address other concerns, aimed to impose a religious settlement acceptable to moderate Lutherans as well as Catholics. Paul III regarded the emperor's ambitions with great suspicion, and might have preferred to see the Habsburg emperor weakened, even if that meant greater freedom for the German heretics.

In the end, the Council Fathers at Trent seem to have acquired a dynamic and priorities of their own independent of either pope or emperor. Despite the leadership of several prominent moderates among the papal representatives, the critical decrees set the tone for a resolutely traditionalist response. Perhaps the most important of the early decrees were those 'on the canonical Scriptures' and 'concerning the edition and use of the sacred books' passed in the fourth session on 8 April 1546 (see below) (Tanner 1990, vol. 2: 663–5). In effect these decrees pre-judged the rest of the Council's deliberations, since they bound the Church to a resolution consistent with its continuous tradition and hierarchically guided ministry. The remaining decrees grouped into two types, each debated and issued interleaved and intermingled with the other. First, there were decrees on doctrine. These provided for the first time a consistent and authoritative theological underpinning for many of the mandatory liturgical and devotional practices of Catholic Christianity. There was, however, much fine print to be resolved, since late medieval Christianity had been anything but homogeneous, and the rival views of the followers of Aquinas, Scotus and Ockham had to be tested and compared. Secondly, there were disciplinary decrees for 'reforming' – in truth, reaffirming and tightening discipline over – the clergy and laity in those parts of Europe that remained obedient. These decrees have often been seen as the glory of the Council, since they committed the Church to make an everyday reality of the ideals that had been remote aspirations in much of the Middle Ages. The reforming decrees, however conservative their intentions, did somewhat reorder the balance of power within Catholicism. Priests won out over laypeople, since it was resolved that priests should henceforth be educated in strictly regulated vocational seminaries and thereby rise to a level of skill and knowledge exceeding that of all but the most learned of their congregants. Bishops won out over heads of religious orders and other formerly exempt bodies, since the clear sense of the Council was that diocesan pastoral visitations and synods should have unrestrained oversight over all dioceses. Finally, the popes won guarantees against all potential threats to their authority. Pius IV ensured that at all costs his and his successors' authority was to remain untouched, and the popes were to interpret and implement the workings-out of the decrees (Tanner 1990, vol. 2: 796). After Trent, no General Council met until the First Vatican Council opened on 8 December 1869.

One important outcome of this consolidation and clarification of Catholic teaching was the establishment of a large body of codifying and standardizing texts for Catholic worship and teaching. A profession of faith summarizing the decrees of Trent was issued in 1564, to which laypeople as well as clergy could be required to subscribe. The Roman Catechism appeared in 1566, an ample manual of instruction to compare with medieval and Protestant *summae*, destined to last until its major revision in 1994.[4] The *Roman Ritual* acquired definitive form under Paul V in 1614, amalgamating multiple earlier editions into a single manual of all major liturgical texts; it remained substantially unaltered until a revision in 1952.[5] The revising of the Latin Vulgate text of the Bible (see below) in the last decades of the sixteenth century should therefore be seen against this background of codification and consolidation elsewhere in the Church's core documents.

Despite increasingly focused guidance from the centre, the Counter-Reformation witnessed many spontaneous initiatives in Catholic Christianity from the body of the Church. Most conspicuous was the rise of a multiplicity of new religious orders. Often these orders somehow devoted themselves to education, mission, and to bringing to the laity a more effective, informed and emotive religious life. The largest and most influential was the Society of Jesus, incorporated in 1540 though active informally before that date. An important recent insight into the Society of Jesus suggests that its members, at least in the first generation, were largely detached from the waves of 'Counter-Reformation' thought, with its focus on doctrinal definition, administrative control, and militant re-conquest of lost regions of Europe. The first Jesuits sought 'the good of souls' through pastoral preaching and teaching, including missions abroad, and were not specially concerned either with theology or government (O'Malley 1993). However, circumstances soon conspired to deflect the Jesuits somewhat from their original intent. In the *Spiritual Exercises* St Ignatius Loyola advised his readers to think loyally towards the Church in all respects, where disputed doctrines and practices were concerned.[6] Because of their masterly programme of education for their novices, the Jesuits' colleges rapidly fulfilled the role that had originally been envisaged for diocesan seminaries, giving them a preponderant influence on the training of many future priests. Jesuit educators became prolific authors of educational texts (Scaglione 1986; cf. Cesareo 1993). Finally, by the middle of the seventeenth century Jesuit confessors found themselves in places of influence as spiritual advisers to many of the most important Catholic rulers in Europe. As a consequence, they became uniquely placed to observe, comment on and even to seek to guide the confessional politics of Europe (see especially Bireley 2003).

The tenor of lay religious life changed considerably as a consequence of the Counter-Reformation, though it is not always easy to evaluate the consequences of those changes for the place of the Bible in culture. From something collective, physically grounded and cult-based, and deeply rooted in the rhythms of the agricultural year, Catholic Christianity became in the early modern period significantly more individualistic, emotive, and based on the intermittent personal relationship between confessor and penitent. The confessional box, popularized by St Carlo Borromeo of Milan, made sense in a world in which confession was a constant individual activity, now detached from the community experience of Lent (Myers 1996). Religious art presented less of a coded narrative of sometimes esoteric patron saints, and more of the great dramas of the lives of Jesus and the Virgin Mary. It would be hard to sustain the argument that Scripture played the sort of decisive, foreground role in Catholicism that it did in Lutheranism or among English puritans in the seventeenth century. Nevertheless, in a different, more mediated way the Bible and the issues it raised were omnipresent.

'Catholic Reform' and 'Sacred Philology'

Scholars from the Catholic tradition have long argued, and correctly so, that stirrings of innovation and creativity were discernible in the Church long before Luther. In the areas of administrative and disciplinary reform, the case for 'pre-reform' is problematic: it ultimately becomes difficult to tell where the religious vigour and energy characteristic of the Middle Ages ends and the 'pre-reform' of the early modern period begins. In the area of biblical scholarship, however, there are some fairly clear boundary marks. In the fifteenth and early sixteenth centuries in Western Europe scholars learned to use the original languages of the biblical texts, together with several of the ancient languages of the Christian East, to a significantly greater degree than before. Naturally enough, Greek was the first and the most widely revived: Greek was the language not only of the New Testament but of the great philosophers, rhetoricians and historians of Greek antiquity. (Coincidentally, the contrast between learned classical and Patristic Greek and the language of the New Testament would awaken Western scholars to the fact that the biblical texts were originally written in a homely, simple, relatively unsophisticated lingua franca.) A handful of travelling teachers instilled an awareness of Greek in a learned elite from the early decades of the fifteenth century onwards (Renaudet 1953). By the 1490s, it was commercially realistic for the Venetian printer-publisher Aldus Manutius to concentrate his efforts on issuing relatively expensive small-format editions of Greek classics for the Italian humanist market (Lowry 1979; see also Pelikan 1996: 3–22). Knowledge of Hebrew grew more slowly, but once again its currency can be demonstrated by events in the publishing business. In 1506, Johannes Reuchlin issued the first edition of his *On the Rudiments of Hebrew*, thereby providing western scholars with a guide to the language written substantially in Latin. It became feasible to publish editions of texts in Hebrew shortly after. In 1516, an Antwerp-born publisher named Daniel Bomberg was given a papal privilege to publish Hebrew books: he began by issuing a Hebrew Bible with rabbinic commentaries edited by a convert from Judaism, Felix of Prato. There had already been small-scale ventures in publishing Hebrew texts for the Jewish market, which Bomberg would also supply.[7]

The study of languages acquired a particular tone under the influence of Renaissance humanism, which the scepticism expressed towards philology by some later Catholic theologians could never entirely efface. Renaissance humanists had originally taken an interest in texts in order to understand the inner structure and rhetorical logic of a language: how it should sound, how persuasive and elegant arguments might be framed in it. Once acquired, such skills had a reflexive effect on the critique of texts. One could readily test texts by other texts; by establishing grammatical and rhetorical rules, one could evaluate conflicting readings and emend corrupt or questionable versions of a text.[8] This process led initially to two important and, in some sense, contrary developments in pre-Reformation Catholicism. First, new editions were prepared of biblical texts in their original languages. Secondly, new translations were prepared in accordance with the new philological discoveries, sometimes incorporated with textual editions. The earliest new printings of biblical texts issued in the West were not necessarily intended for Latin Christian use, as, for instance, the Greek Septuagint Psalter issued by Aldus as early as c.1496, directed at Greek Orthodox Christians.[9] In 1516, Desiderius Erasmus issued, with revisions in 1519, 1522, 1527, and 1535, an enormously influential edition of the Greek New Testament accompanied by his own new Latin translation.[10] Although it was much the most influential and widely used of these early Greek Bibles, Erasmus's edition did not quite have the market to itself. The house of Aldus Manutius issued the first complete Greek Bible, comprising the Septuagint translation of the Old Testament and the original of the New Testament, in 1518.[11] A little later the printing house of the scholar–publisher Robert Estienne issued an epoch-defining Greek New Testament under the protection of the Most Christian King Henri II at Paris in 1550, just before the publisher-printer decamped to Calvin's Geneva.[12] The following year, Estienne would produce his parallel-column Greek and Latin New Testament, and while so doing inaugurate the system of numbered verses for biblical references, which was almost immediately taken up across Western Europe.[13]

For Catholic Europe, however, the most important textual editions of the Bible in the original languages were the scholarly polyglot editions. The most famous and copious polyglot of the early period was that printed at Alcalá de Henares between 1514 and 1517. It was edited by Diego López de Zúñiga with Demetrios Ducas, Elio Antonio de Nebrija, Fernando Nuñez de Guzman, Juan and Pedro de Vergara, and three converts from Judaism, Alfonso de Zamora, Alfonso de Alcalá, and Pablo Coronel. The work was begun under the patronage of Cardinal Francisco Ximénez de Cisneros, Archbishop of Toledo (1436–1517).[14] The 'Complutensian Polyglot' was an astounding achievement both in scholarship and in printing technology. However, there is a grim historical irony in that this monument to the scholarship achievable in the Semitic languages in the Iberian peninsula was produced under the patronage of Ximénez de Cisneros. It was Ximénez who had done the most, through forced conversions and militant Catholic evangelizing, to bring the medieval coexistence of the Jewish, Muslim and Christian worlds of Iberia to a brutal end (Hillgarth 1976–8, vol. 2: 470–83). The subsequent climate in Spain did little to encourage the full development of the potential for critical evaluation of the texts afforded by the great polyglot Bible. However, the Complutensian Polyglot had an important successor in the 'Antwerp Polyglot' or 'King's Bible' prepared by the publisher–printer Christophe Plantin and published in Plantin's workshop in Antwerp between 1569 and 1573 at the behest of Philip II of Spain. The chief editor of this work was the Andalusian, Benito Arias Montano (1527–98), though he worked from some of the earlier translations of Santi Pagnini (1470–1541).[15] This work tends to be celebrated more as an event in the history of typography than of biblical scholarship. It became notorious because of the appalling financial effects on Christophe Plantin of King Philip II's chronic untrustworthiness as a sponsor and paymaster for the project. It comprised the complete text of the Bible in Hebrew and Greek, in ancient Aramaic and Syriac versions, together with the Vulgate, followed by three volumes of Apparatus.

The great polyglot bibles were not unique in developing the potentialities of print for compiling comparative editions of biblical texts. In France, Jacques Lefèvre d'Étaples edited at St-Germain-des-Prés and published in 1509 the first edition of his *Fivefold Psalter*, a comparative edition of four ancient versions of the Latin Psalter and the editor's own modern version, accompanied by liberal references to the Greek and Hebrew editions.[16] More ambitious still was the 'Genoa Psalter', Agostino Giustiniani's edition of the Psalms in eight columns including versions in Hebrew, Greek, Arabic, and Aramaic as well as Latin translations of several of these versions.[17] A logical corollary of this work was to present the Scriptures in new individual translations, in part or in whole. Erasmus, Lefèvre d'Étaples, Santi Pagnini, and the Cassinese Benedictine Isidoro Chiari all issued new Latin translations to convey to the learned the nuances of textual insight gleaned from the new scriptural philology.[18] Erasmus also largely invented the genre of the prose paraphrase of the New Testament: between 1517 and 1525 he produced paraphrases on the entire New Testament except for Revelation.[19] In parallel to his work of editing and translating, Erasmus issued multiple editions of his *Annotations on the New Testament*, based on notes written but never published by Lorenzo Valla under the title *Collatio Novi Testamenti*, from 1505 onwards.[20] Before the Reformation there was, however, a weak connection between the sacred philologists and the translators into the vernacular. With the exception of English (where an extreme allergy to biblical translations existed since the days of the Lollard Bible), all the major languages of Europe saw multiple editions of the Bible before 1520 (Delumeau 1973: 71, n. 2). However, these early vernacular translations usually rendered the Vulgate with little effort at either subtlety or doctrinal precision; sometimes moralizing or allegorizing commentary was inserted directly into the text itself. In the early decades of the Reformation era it would be the reformers who devoted most energy to lively, modern Scriptural translations in the vernacular.

Medieval orthodoxy taught that Scripture and tradition must be mutually coherent. It was unthinkable that Scripture could legitimately be invoked against the custom, practice and authority of the Church. However, in the early decades of early modern Catholicism certain key issues ranged one biblical commentator against another. One of the most notorious was the controversy that erupted between Erasmus and Edward Lee in the wake of the former's publication of the *Novum Instrumentum* in 1516. Despite the best efforts of their friends to restrain and moderate the controversies, each published their biblical annotations against the other in 1519 (Rex 1991, 52–3 and nn. 18–32). Even more significant for biblical exegesis (and modern feminist thought) was the controversy sparked off by the pamphlet *On Mary Magdalen* published by the great French humanist scholar Lefèvre d'Étaples in 1517/18. Lefèvre argued that the three figures traditionally conflated into the Mary Magdalen of medieval legend were in fact three entirely separate persons: (1) Mary of Magdala; (2) Mary of Bethany, the sister of Martha; and (3) the nameless woman taken in adultery and saved by Jesus. This provoked a minor and short-lived storm of controversy, in which various biblical scholars weighed in on either side of the controversy. Ultimately it was overwhelmed by the greater questions over the cult of saints aroused in the Reformation (Rex 1991: 65–77 and nn. 1–12).

The First Response to the Protestant Reformation

It would be easy and convenient to treat the mature responses of the Catholic tradition to the Reformation, as exemplified in the Council of Trent and the documents issuing from it and its aftermath, as though those were the sum total of the Catholic response to Protestantism in the sixteenth century. However, that will not do, not least because Trent itself emerged out of a complex sequence of historical developments. In the immediate wake of the Lutheran movement and the spread of the Reformation across central Europe, a whole range of responses were evoked among those who remained loyal to the Catholic principle and the papal primacy. Indeed, even among prominent Catholic apologists for Trent, it has become traditional to describe the Council as bringing Catholic order and clarity out of a situation where there had been disorder and confusion, even among those who called themselves Catholic (Tavard 1959).

Martin Luther did not challenge the Catholic Church in a systematic, moderate, methodical way, over Scripture any more than over any other head of doctrine. Rather, his challenge grew out of the passionate fervour to which his discovery of the Reformation doctrine of justification roused him at the end of the 1510s. The Church had lost sight of the Gospel: instead of the free grace proclaimed in the New Testament and discernible in the best of the Fathers, it had elevated a whole edifice of 'human works' to make the believer purer and therefore more acceptable to God. It was almost a by-product of this argument to insist that such things – priestly celibacy, monasticism, the sacrificial mass, the cult of saints – were unknown to the early Church and (above all) neither found in Scripture nor required by God. Such soon became the standard position of Protestant apologetics (Cameron 1991: 121–35).

Luther's earliest Catholic antagonists responded equally instinctively at first, and only gradually with greater prudence and temperateness. Reading some of the arguments one senses that it was the outrageousness of Luther's denial of authority to sources putatively 'outside' Scripture – the Councils, the Fathers, the tradition of the Church, the papal primacy – that provoked them to respond before their positions had been at all carefully thought out. Some of Luther's early antagonists, like Silvestro Mazzolini of Priero, wrote as outright papal positivists. Mazzolini argued that the Church was prior and superior to Scripture, and that the papacy as head of the Church was in effect and in fact lord over Scripture (see above). However, such extremism was somewhat exceptional. More typical was the response of Luther's subtle antagonist from the Leipzig disputation, Johannes Maier von Eck. Eck argued initially that Scripture and Church cohered together, each depending on the other. Scripture held an authority clearly superior to that of Councils and popes; but Scripture could only be correctly interpreted with the assistance of the continuing tradition of the Church, above all as expressed in the exegetical work of the early Fathers (Tavard 1959: 118–19). However, Eck also gave considerable space to the notion that Christ had taught some things to the apostles that were not recorded in Scripture, and must therefore be received as tradition. Moreover, where Scripture was unclear or insufficient to resolve controversies, it was necessary to resort to the continuing Spirit-led voice of the Church, which at times looked very much like the institutional hierarchy. In some of his later controversial works Eck appeared to magnify the voice of the Church as the authoritative interpreter of Scripture, even as an apparent second source, to an even greater degree (ibid.: 120–4). In a similar way, Johannes Cochlaeus, a persistent, long-lived and prolific opponent of the reformers, insisted on the two cardinal points of Catholic controversy: (1) that it is the necessary role of the Church to discern the Word of God within Scripture by interpreting it; and (2) the Spirit, which speaks through Scripture, can most easily and reliably be discerned in the voice of the visible Church (ibid.: 124–30). Both these controversialists ended up by insisting that things absolutely invisible in Scripture must nevertheless be accepted by the faithful as articles of faith.

Within this broad range of early Catholic responses various themes recurred, one of the most potent of which was the insistence that Christ had said many things not recorded in the written Scriptures (John 21:25); and that he had promised that the Holy Spirit would guide his followers into all truth regarding those things on which he had not been explicit (John 16:12–13). By this means, the testimony of Scripture was invoked, paradoxically perhaps, to bear witness to its own incompleteness. The visible expression of this guidance by the Spirit was found in the customs and traditions of the Church: in certain circumstances these might have a force alongside with or even prior to Scripture. Many of these early controversialists quoted with approval Augustine's aphorism when responding to the Manichaeans, that 'I should not believe the gospel except as moved by the authority of the Catholic Church . . . it was at the command of the Catholics that I believed the gospel'.[21] The basic argument for the indivisible mutual coherence of Scripture and the witness of the Spirit-led Church reappeared in authors as diverse as Jacobus Latomus of Louvain, John Fisher, Bishop of Rochester, and Josse Clichtove. However, the argument for 'mutual coherence' was open-ended. It could be used to chain theology effectively to the Word of Scripture; but it could also be used to extend Scriptural authority outwards and onwards, to envisage an almost infinitely extendable Scripture which consisted of the continuing witness of the Church (Tavard 1959: 163ff., 173ff.; Bagchi 1991: 163–8).

The problem with these early Catholic responses to the claims of the reformers was that they denied, ex hypothesi, what was rapidly becoming a core working principle of Protestant thought. The reformers insisted that Scripture possessed independent authority by itself and of itself. Scriptural exegesis could not be conducted 'in cold blood': all the reformers acknowledged that it required the intervention and the guidance of the Holy Spirit. However, they also argued that Scripture could and must be legitimately invoked against the errors of the Church: that it was not only possible, but necessary, to cite Scripture to prove that the Church had erred. So, for example, Luther could encourage the faithful to cite 1 Tim. 4:1–3 as proof against the Church's laws on priestly celibacy and dietary abstinences (Pelikan and Lehmann 1955–86, vol. 51: 79–80). For the first generation of Catholic antagonists (and many of their successors since) this procedure opened the way to unbridled subjectivism. Those who renounced the faith of the true Church could not, by definition, interpret its Holy Scriptures correctly. The rebuttal of the reformers therefore rested on a profoundly circular, self-reinforcing argument.

The Council of Trent

The historiography of the Council of Trent's response to questions about Scripture has been somewhat bedevilled by the partisan scholarship of different confessional positions. An earlier generation of Protestant scholarship was at times casually dismissive of the Catholic stress on 'unwritten traditions'. A learned, but also somewhat defensive, Catholic academy faulted the Protestants for failing to appreciate the theological subtleties involved in a dynamic analysis of the relationship between Bible and Church. Part of the problem lies in the fact that it suits both confessions, for different reasons, to treat the Council of Trent as representing the definitive majority view of the Catholic tradition then and since. Such an impression belies the historical progress of the council: its outcomes were by no means foreordained, and indeed occasioned real surprise in Rome when they were made public.

Issues regarding Scripture constituted some of the first substantive theological problems to be tackled in the early months of 1546 after the Council of Trent began its business. The first problem arose over the Canon. Jerome had questioned the status of some of the books conventionally transmitted in Latin Bibles, those regarded as deutero-canonical in the Catholic tradition (principally Tobit, Judith, Wisdom of Solomon, Ecclesiasticus, Baruch, and the first two Books of Maccabees). There was lively debate in the Council as to how to rank these works, and some of the other marginal books and additions to books. In the end the Council cut short the discussion by adopting in its entirety and without amendment the formula of the Canon decided more than a century earlier in the Council of Florence in its 11th Session on 4 February 1442, in which a Bull of Union with the Coptic Churches was promulgated. In this the most broadly accepted of the 'apocryphal' or deuterocanonical Old Testament books were included in a sequence interleaved with the undisputed books. This order in turn largely followed that of the Septuagint (Jedin 1961, vol. 2: 55–8). The status of some of the lesser deutero-canonical books and additions (for instance, 3 and 4 Esdras and 3 and 4 Maccabees) was thus not discussed and left unclear. This tendency to pass over difficult issues in silence would reappear in others of the council's decrees.

Much more troublesome and contested was the issue of the relative authority to be assigned to Scripture and tradition. In the first place, 'traditions' could mean a range of things, from dogmas required to be believed even though not stated explicitly in Scripture, to disciplinary rules binding on good Catholics even though of post-apostolic origin. In a perfect world, the delegates to the Council might perhaps have discussed the whole issue as a sort of theological prolegomenon, an epistemology for analysing comprehensively the place of Scripture within the Catholic scheme of knowing: and some wanted this to happen. The problem with this approach was that the views represented at the Council were so diverse and even mutually hostile. There were extreme clerical positivists like Alfonso de Castro on the one hand, and vocal defenders of the unique status of Scripture in the form of Giacomo Nacchianti, Bishop of Chioggia or Agostino Bonuccio, General of the Servites, on the other. A working party produced a draft decree which stated that the Council embraced the 'apostolic traditions' (what these were no-one was willing to specify, however) alongside Scripture as sources of authority. In its first form, this draft used the notorious expression '*partim . . . partim*', implying that Christian revelation was found *partly* in Scripture and *partly* in tradition. The decree was subsequently edited to read that:

> this truth and discipline are contained in the written books, and the unwritten traditions which, received by the Apostles from the mouth of Christ himself, or from the Apostles themselves, the Holy Ghost dictating, have come down even unto us . . . [the Synod] following the examples of the orthodox Fathers, receives and venerates with an equal affection of piety (*pari pietatis affectu*) and reverence, all the books both of the Old and of the New Testament – seeing that one God is the author of both – as also the said traditions.

It was passed by a majority vote. A significant minority wanted the traditions to be ranked below Scripture (Jedin 1961, vol. 2: 58–64, 74–8, 82, 86–7; Tanner 1990: 663).

The Council of Trent also addressed the issue of the languages in which Scripture was to be conserved and regarded as authoritative. Broadly speaking, there were three essential questions: (1) the status of the Latin Vulgate; (2) the posture of the Council regarding the Scriptures in their original languages; and (3) the Council's attitude towards vernacular translations of the Bible. On each of these issues there were all sorts of diverse views. First, some scholars believed the Vulgate Latin to be so seriously corrupt and so diverse in its current versions as to need drastic editing and amendment; others thought it needed only minor typographical corrections. Some must have heard ringing in their ears Erasmus's withering satire, in his *Letter to Martin Dorp* of 1515, of those 'Vulgate only' theologians who wished to preserve cumulative scribal errors and mistranslations as though they were holy writ (Erasmus 1971: 247).There was also disagreement as to how far the current Vulgate was actually Jerome's own translation; and some awareness of the diversity between the commonly circulating versions (Jedin 1961, vol. 2: 84). In the end, as on other topics, potentially endless discussion was circumvented by a decree which stated that 'the said old and vulgate edition, which, by the lengthened usage of so many years, has been approved of in the Church, be, in public lectures, disputations, sermons and expositions, held as authentic'. It was antiquity and long usage rather than any other reason that made the case for the Vulgate. All other versions were simply passed over in silence (Jedin 1961, vol. 2: 85; Tanner 1990: 664–5). There was much enthusiasm and much discussion about the possibility of issuing an amended and corrected version of the Vulgate, and in fact – some decades later – such a revised edition would be issued. However, the Council of Trent did not in fact decree this revision: it simply required 'that, henceforth, the sacred Scripture, and especially the said old and vulgate edition, be printed in the most correct manner possible' (*quam emendatissime imprimatur*) and that it be subject to the supervision and censure of the bishops.[22] This was an attempt to prevent unlicensed editions, not a sponsorship of critical scholarship.

As a result of this decree, the other versions of the Bible then current, including the new Latin translations described earlier, were so to speak left high and dry. They were not, at least at this point, explicitly condemned; but they were clearly deemed inferior to the Vulgate. Similar was the situation regarding the Scriptures in the original texts.

Many of the best minds in the Council of Trent, such as Girolamo Seripando, Cristoforo Madruzzo, and Reginald Pole, favoured issuing authorized versions of Scripture in the original Greek and Hebrew; but the lack of agreement forestalled any decision to this effect (Jedin 1961, vol. 2: 85–6). If the more liberal were disappointed by the lack of explicit provision for the original languages, the rigorists and conservatives may well have been disappointed by the lack of a specific reference to the Scriptures in the vernacular. There had, of course, been printed vernacular Bibles for decades. However, the advent of specifically Protestant translations, above all Luther's German Bible completed in 1534, as well as Olivétan's French Bible in the following year, gave urgency to the Council's discussions. One response was to issue alternate vernacular translations from a Catholic standpoint: this policy was followed by German anti-Lutherans such as Emser, Eck, and Dietenberger, and would be followed for the English language by the Rheims-Douay Bibles of the late sixteenth century. However, several leading figures in the Council favoured an absolute prohibition on the publishing of the Scriptures in the vernacular. Such prohibitions already existed in Spain and in France, though not (given the political fragmentation of these territories) in Italy or the Empire (Jedin 1961, vol. 2: 67–8). On 3 April 1546, Pedro Pacheco, Cardinal-bishop of Jaen, argued that all translations other than the Vulgate, even the Septuagint, must be forbidden (ibid., vol. 2: 83–4). In the end, this issue, like others, was simply passed over in silence. Vernacular Scripture was not explicitly forbidden, but the primacy of the Latin was asserted over all other versions for all purposes, whether scholarly, liturgical or devotional. Underlying all this was a long-standing Latin prejudice against the Greek texts, based on the fear – not entirely unwarranted – that the Greek versions then in circulation were as corrupt or more so than the Latin versions, and that the Greek versions might have been amended over time to serve the dogmatic claims of the Eastern churches against those of the West. On the other hand, there was a real and growing conviction that if laypeople were given the Scriptures in the vernacular, their unguided and uncontrolled reading would lure them into heresy. The same fear would inspire Henry VIII of England's extraordinary piece of legislation in 1543 that forbade reading of his own authorized Bible by commoners and women (Ryrie 2003: 15, 18, 28–9).

The most startling aspect to the story lies in the astonished reaction of the Roman Curia to the decrees promulgated by the Council of Trent in its formal session on 8 April 1546. The Council had revealed itself as far more conservative than many prominent figures in Rome itself. In particular, the curia took for granted that the Vulgate needed radical revision – possibly in consultation with the original texts – and was dismayed by the possible inference from the decree that the Vulgate text as then received was inerrant. Despite this unease the decree was not amended, and the revision of the Vulgate was deferred for many years (Jedin 1961, vol. 2: 94–8).

After Trent

The Council of Trent enshrined the position that Scripture was the authoritative source of Christian revelation, but that the correct interpretation of Scripture was that which concurred with the continuing witness and traditions of the Church. A visible embodiment of this approach can be seen in the way in which Scripture was handled in the *Roman Catechism* of 1566. This text was authorized by Pius V under the original title of *Catechismus ad Parochos*; it was subsequently more commonly known as either the *Catechismus Romanus* or as the 'Tridentine Catechism', since it was commissioned by one of the last sessions of the Council of Trent on 4 December 1563 (Tanner 1990: 797). First, the Catechism made clear that the primary use of Scripture was to be in the preaching offered by priests to their parishioners. Moreover, it envisaged that the preaching of a text should be regulated according to the subdivisions of the Catechism. The four principal parts of the Roman Catechism were the Apostles' Creed, the Seven Sacraments, the Ten Commandments, and the Lord's Prayer. Priests were specifically instructed to order and organize their exposition of Scriptural passages under one or other of these four primary divisions (*Catechism* 1923: 9–10).

Secondly, the Catechism exemplified what one might term the proof-text approach to the confirmation of Catholic doctrine. References to Scriptural passages in support are numerous in this work, comparable to some of its Protestant counterparts. In a handful of instances there are separate short paragraphs entitled something like 'proofs from scripture' for particularly important doctrines: the resurrection of the body, the nature of a sacrament, the matter of baptism, the real presence of Christ in the Eucharist, the transubstantiation of the elements, the sacrificial nature of the mass (*Catechism* 1923: 121–2, 144, 164, 229, 236–7, 257–8; cf. Bradley 1990). However, the special distinction given to these short sections is less important than the texture of biblical reference that suffused the entire work. However, the principles of 'equal affection of piety' and the complementarity of Scripture and tradition are likewise seen at work in the Catechism. Proofs from Scripture rarely stand alone: they are reinforced by the exegetical tradition. The Fathers of the Church, the Councils (including Trent, just then completed) and even Reason are invoked alongside Scripture, both as supporting proofs in themselves, and as guides to the proper understanding of the biblical texts.

In comparison with the energy displayed over the Catechism, the revision of the Vulgate proceeded quite slowly. For the first decades after Trent the putatively 'official' edition of the Vulgate was that first published in Louvain in November 1547 edited by Johannes Henten and published by Barthélemy de Grave. This edition was sponsored by Charles V and was not a product of the Council of Trent (Jedin 1961, vol. 2: 97). It derived largely from Robert Estienne's Bible of 1538–40, incorporating some of the latter's apparatus. There matters rested until the first appearance of the Vulgate edition of Pope Sixtus V in 1590. The Sixtine Vulgate was based, according to some authorities, more heavily on the 1540 Estienne edition than Henten's had been. However, it is also claimed that the *Codex Amiatinus*, one of the finest early manuscripts of the Vulgate, originally copied in Anglo-Saxon Northumbria at the command of Abbot Ceolfrid of Wearmouth-Jarrow, was used in the editorial process.[23] In any event, the outcome was initially something of a disaster. Sixtus V introduced his own idiosyncratic system of verse numbering, and interfered inexpertly in the process of textual editing. Many last-minute editorial emendations appeared in the first printed copies, either as corrections in ink or pasted-on pieces of printed paper. Sixtus V died just as this seriously defective edition was ready. A new editorial commission appointed in 1591 under Cardinal Marco Antonio Colonna contrived, allegedly at the prompting of Robert

Bellarmine, to prevent the Sixtine Vulgate from circulating widely. Sixtus's successor Clement VIII ordered the withdrawal of the 1590 edition early in 1592, and a new revised Vulgate was hastily prepared. Robert Bellarmine reputedly wrote the explanatory preface, which stated that because of various typographical errors it was necessary to prepare this new edition.[24] The 1592 Vulgate was closer to Henten's Louvain edition than its predecessor. It restored the by now conventional Estienne 1551 versifications. It thus became the definitive version, even though some Catholic scholars have since disputed some of its 'hasty' amendments. Everything was done to make the typography and layout of the 1592 edition as close as possible to the 1590 version. The 1592 Bible circulated under the names of both Sixtus V and Clement VIII, sparing both the popes and the Church as a whole the embarrassment of this editorial debacle. The names of both popes were commemorated on the title pages of all subsequent editions. The Clementine Vulgate remained – and to some extent remains – the definitive Catholic Latin Bible. In 1907 a revision, the *Nova Vulgata*, was commissioned under Pope Pius X, to take account of new textual discoveries. However, the basic assumption on which the alleged primacy of the Vulgate was based, namely that Jerome must have had access to Greek and Hebrew originals older than and superior to any that now survive and are available, has persisted.

Conclusion

The Roman Catholic Church found itself by the beginning of the seventeenth century equipped with an array of key documents for the mission field both within and beyond Europe. The keynote of this period was mission: the Church sought to win souls, whether they were Polish, French or English nobility and gentry, Incas, south Indians or Japanese, or even ordinary peasant folk in an otherwise neglected corner of Europe, through aggressive evangelism. Such campaigns required that clergy as well as laity be kept relentlessly 'on message'. For a Church in this condition the uniformity represented by a Roman Catechism, a Tridentine Profession of Faith, a body of Conciliar Decrees on doctrine and discipline, a revised and near-uniform liturgy, and an unchallenged and authorized edition of Scripture, constituted vital equipment. All these documents cohered together and reinforced each other. Doctrine and message could be presented with a uniformity and articulation that could resist the blandishments of Protestantism and look pityingly on the internal disputes that divided Lutherans from Calvinists and everyone from the sects. However, it is impossible not to feel that the excitement of discovery evinced in the 'sacred philology' of the Renaissance had been lost. Doctrinal ambiguity, the questing after elusive textual accuracy amid the chaos of variant readings, were perhaps dangerous luxuries when the wholeness of the Church and the salvation of souls were perceived to be at stake. Nevertheless, the Roman Catholic tradition left the search *ad fontes*, the quest for the most ancient and original readings of the texts of the Christian faith, very largely to its Protestant critics and rivals until the nineteenth century. It consolidated, in a work such as Baronius's *Ecclesiastical Annals*, a view of the Church's history that insisted *a priori* that the growth and spread of the Christian religion had led naturally and inevitably towards a Roman papacy and a Tridentine conception of doctrine, discipline and order as the one true and correct form of Christianity. The Catholic Church's encounter with modernity would be dominated by its struggles with that legacy.

Notes

1 On the complex and contested issue of Scripture and tradition in the Middle Ages, see Oberman (1981: 53–120); McGrath (1987: 140–51); Pelikan (1984: 118–26).

2 Cf. the antithesis drawn between 'spirituali' and 'zelanti' in Fenlon (1972). See also the works of Massimo Firpo, e.g. *'Disputar di cose pertinente alla fede': studi sulla vita religiosa del Cinquecento italiano* (2003).

3 Collett (1985) is crucial in reconstructing the role played by the author of the first draft of the *Beneficio*, Benedetto da Mantova. Cf. Flaminio (1996).

4 *Catechismus, ex decreto Concilii Tridentini, ad parochos, Pii Quinti Pont. Max. iussu editus* (Romae: In ædibus Populi Romani, apud Paulum Manutium, 1566).

5 *Rituale Romanum Pauli V. Pont. Max. iussu editum* (Venetiis: Apud Juntas, 1614).

6 See the final section in Ignatius Loyola's *Spiritual Exercises*, which is entitled 'To have the true sentiment which we ought to have in the Church Militant'.

7 Johann Reuchlin, *De Rudimentis Hebraicis* (Phorce: in aedib. Tho. Anshelmi, 1506); *Rabbinic Bible of Daniel Bomberg*, 4 vols in 3 (Venice: Bomberg, 1516–17).

8 On the methods of textual criticism in the Renaissance, see especially Grafton (1991).

9 *Psalterium Graecum*, ed. Justinus Decadyus (Venice: Aldus Manutius, 1496?); see http://www.smu.edu/bridwell/publications/ryrie_catalog/5_1.htm.

10 Erasmus (ed.), *Novum Instrumentum* (Basel: Joannes Frobenius, 1516). Cf. Halkin (1993: 104–11).

11 *Biblia* (Venice: House of Aldus Manutius and of Andrea [of Asola (Andrea Torresani)], February 1518); see http://www.smu.edu/bridwell/publications/ryrie_catalog/5_3.htm.

12 *Novum Testamentum* (Paris: Robert Estienne, 15 June 1550); see http://www.smu.edu/bridwell/publications/ryrie_catalog/5_6.htm.

13 *Novum Testamentum* (Geneva: Robert Estienne, 1551); see http://www.smu.edu/bridwell/publications/ryrie_catalog/xi_3.htm.

14 *Biblia Polyglotta*. 6 vols (Alcalá de Henares: Arnaldo Guillén de Brocar, printed 1514–17, published 1521–22).

15 In *Biblia Sacra*, 8 vols (AntuerpiæAntwerp: Christoph Plantinus excud., 1569–73); see Museum Plantin-Moretus, *De Polyglot-Bijbel: de geschiedenis van een reuzenonderneming, 14 Juli–30 September 1972* (Antwerp: Musée Plantin-Moretus, 1972).

16 Jacques Lefèvre d'Étaples (ed.), *Quincuplex Psalterium* (Paris: Henricus Stephanus, 1509).

17 Agostino Giustiniani (ed.), *Psalterium* (Genoa: Pietro Paolo Porro, 16 November 1516).

18 Besides Erasmus's *Novum Instrumentum* (see above, note 10), see e.g. Jacques Lefèvre d'Étaples (ed.), *Epistolae Diui Pauli* (Paris: Gormontius, 1531); Santi Pagnini (trans.), *Biblia* (Lyon: Antonius du Ry, 1528); and Isidoro Chiari, *Vulgata æditio*, 3 vols (Venice: P. Schoeffer, 1542).

19 Erasmus, *Paraphrases* (Basileae Basel: Apvd Hieronymvm Frobenivm et Nicolavm Episcopivm, 1548). The paraphrases are becoming available in English in *The Collected Works of Erasmus*, vols 42–50 (1984–2003); cf. Rex (1991: 52, n. 13).

20 For modern editions, see Erasmus, *Annotations on the New Testament* (1986); Anne Reeve and M. A. Screech (eds), *Erasmus' Annotations on the New Testament* (Studies in the History

of Christian Thought; vol. 42) (1990); and Anne Reeve (ed.), *Erasmus' Annotations on the New Testament: Galatians to the Apocalypse* (Studies in the History of Christian Thought, vol. 52) (1993).

21 Augustine, *Against the Epistle of Manichaeus Called Fundamental*, Chapter 5 in P. Schaff et al. (1956), vol. iv, p. 131.

22 Norman Tanner's (1990) translation of this phrase, 'after a thorough revision', seems to strain the Latin with the benefit of hindsight.

23 See 'Vulgate, Revision of', in Herbermann et al. (eds) (1907–12) or at http://www.newadvent.org/cathen/15515b.htm.

24 See 'Bellarmine, St. Robert', in Herbermann et al. (eds) (1907–12), or at http://www.newadvent.org/cathen/02411d.htm; see also the article 'Vulgate' in the *International Standard Bible Encyclopedia*, edited by Geoffrey W. Bromiley and others, vol. 4.

References

Bagchi, David V. N. (1991). *Luther's Earliest Opponents: Catholic Controversialists, 1518–1525.* Minneapolis, MN: Fortress Press.

Bataillon, Marcel (1937). *Érasme et l'Espagne: recherches sur l'histoire spirituelle du XVIe siècle.* Paris: E. Droz.

Bireley, Robert (1999). *The Refashioning of Catholicism, 1450–1700: A Reassessment of the Counter Reformation.* Washington, DC: Catholic University of America Press.

Bireley, Robert (2003). *The Jesuits and the Thirty Years War.* Cambridge: Cambridge University Press.

Bradley, Robert I. (1990). *The Roman Catechism in the Catechetical Tradition of the Church: The Structure of the Roman Catechism as Illustrative of the 'Classic Catechesis'.* Lanham, MD: University Press of America.

Braunisch, R. (1974). *Die Theologie der Rechtfertigung im 'Enchiridion' (1538) des Johannes Gropper: sein kritischer Dialog mit Philipp Melanchthon.* Münster: Aschendorff.

Bromiley, Geoffrey W. et al. (1988). *International Standard Bible Encyclopedia*, vol. 4. Grand Rapids, MI: William B. Eerdmans.

Bynum, Caroline W. (2004). 'Bleeding Hosts and their Contact Relics in Late Medieval Northern Germany', *Medieval History Journal* 7(2): 227–41.

Cameron, Euan (1991). *The European Reformation.* Oxford: Clarendon Press.

Catechism of the Council of Trent for Parish Priests, Issued by Order of Pope Pius V (1923) trans. with notes, John A. McHugh, O. P., and Charles, J. Callan, O. P. New York: Joseph F. Wagner; London: B. Herder.

Cesareo, F. (1993). 'Quest for Identity: The Ideals of Jesuit Education in the Sixteenth Century', in Christopher Chapple (ed.), *The Jesuit Tradition in Education and Missions: A 450-Year Perspective.* Toronto: University of Toronto Press.

Chiffoleau, Jacques (1980). *La comptabilité de l'au-delà: les hommes, la mort et la religion dans la région d'Avignon à la fin du Moyen Age, vers 1320–vers 1480.* Rome: École française de Rome; Paris: Diffusion de Boccard.

Collett, Barry (1985) *Italian Benedictine Scholars and the Reformation: The Congregation of Santa Giustina of Padua.* Oxford: Clarendon Press.

Damerau, Rudolf (1976). *Das Gutachten der Theologischen Fakultät Erfurt 1452 über 'Das heilige Blut von Wilsnak'*, Studien zu den Grundlagen der Reformation, vol. 13. Marburg: im Selbstverlag.

Delumeau, Jean (1973). *Naissance et affirmation de la Réforme*, 3rd edn. Paris: Presses Universitaires de France.

Erasmus (1971). *Praise of Folly: and, Letter to Martin Dorp, 1515*, trans. Betty Radice, with introduction and notes by A. H. T. Levi. Harmondsworth: Penguin.

Erasmus (1984–2003). *The Collected Works of Erasmus*. Toronto: University of Toronto Press.

Erasmus (1986). *Annotations on the New Testament*, ed. Anne Reeve with introduction by M. A. Screech. London: Duckworth.

Fenlon, Dermot (1972). *Heresy and Obedience in Tridentine Italy: Cardinal Pole and the Counter Reformation*. London: Cambridge University Press.

Firpo, Massimo (1990). *Tra alumbrados e 'spirituali': studi su Juan de Valdes e il valdesianesimo nella crisi religiosa del '500 italiano*. Florence: Olschki.

Firpo, Massimo (2003). *'Disputar di cose pertinente alla fede': studi sulla vita religiosa del Cinquecento italiano*. Milan: Unicopli.

Flaminio, Marcantonio (1996). *Apologia del Beneficio di Christo e altri scritti inediti*, ed. Dario Marcatto. Florence: L. S. Olschki.

Galpern, J. N. (1976). *The Religions of the People in Sixteenth-Century Champagne*. Cambridge, MA: Harvard University Press.

Gleason, Elisabeth G. (1993). *Gasparo Contarini: Venice, Rome, and Reform*. Berkeley, CA: University of California Press.

Grafton, Anthony (1991). *Defenders of the Text: The Traditions of Scholarship in an Age of Science, 1450–1800*. Cambridge, MA: Harvard University Press.

Halkin, Léon-E. (1993). *Erasmus: A Critical Biography*, trans. John Tonkin. Oxford: Blackwell.

Herbermann, Charles G., Pace, Edward A., Pallen, Condé B., Shahan, Thomas J. and Wynne, John J. (eds) (1907–12). *The Catholic Encyclopedia*, 15 vols. New York: Robert Appleton Co. Available at http://www.newadvent.org/cathen/15515b.htm

Hillgarth, J. N. (1976–8). *The Spanish Kingdoms, 1250–1516*, 2 vols. Oxford: Clarendon Press.

Hsia, R. Po-Chia (1998). *The World of Catholic Renewal, 1540–1770*. Cambridge: Cambridge University Press.

Jedin, Hubert ([1949–75] 1961). *Geschichte des Konzils von Trient*, 4 vols in 5. Freiburg: Herder. Trans. Dom Ernest Graf as *A History of the Council of Trent*, 2 vols. London: Nelson.

Jedin, Hubert (1999). 'Catholic Reformation or Counter-Reformation?' in David M. Luebke (ed.), *The Counter-Reformation: The Essential Readings*. Malden, MA: Blackwell, pp. 21–45.

Kidd, B. J. (ed.) (1911). *Documents Illustrative of the Continental Reformation*. Oxford: Oxford University Press.

Lexutt, Athina (1996). *Rechtfertigung im Gespräch: Das Rechtfertigungsverständnis in den Religions - gesprächen von Hagenau, Worms und Regensburg 1540/41*. Forschungen zur Kirchen- und Dogmengeschichte, vol. 64, Göttingen: Vandenhoeck and Ruprecht.

Lichte, Claudia (1990). *Die Inszenierung einer Wallfahrt: der Lettner im Havelberger Dom und das Wilsnacker Wunderblut*. Worms: Wernersche Verlagsgesellschaft.

Lowry, Martin (1979). *The World of Aldus Manutius: Business and Scholarship in Renaissance Venice*. Oxford: Blackwell.

Luebke, David M. (ed.) (1999). *The Counter-Reformation: The Essential Readings*. Malden, MA: Blackwell.

McGrath, Alister (1987). *The Intellectual Origins of the European Reformation*. Oxford: Blackwell, pp. 140–51.

Mullett, Michael A. (1999). *The Catholic Reformation*. London: Routledge.

Myers, W. David (1996). *'Poor, Sinning Folk': Confession and Conscience in Counter-Reformation Germany*. Ithaca, NY: Cornell University Press.

Oberman, Heiko Augustinus (1981). *Forerunners of the Reformation: The Shape of Late Medieval Thought*. Philadelphia, PA: Fortress Press, pp. 53–120.

O'Malley, John W. (1993). *The First Jesuits*. Cambridge, MA: Harvard University Press.

O'Malley, John W. (2000). *Trent and All That: Renaming Catholicism in the Early Modern Era*. Cambridge, MA: Harvard University Press.

Ozment, Steven (1971). 'Homo Viator: Luther and Late Medieval Theology', in Steven E. Ozment (ed.), *The Reformation in Medieval Perspective*. Chicago: Quadrangle Books, pp. 148–52.

Pelikan, Jaroslav (1984). *The Christian Tradition: A History of the Development of Doctrine*, vol. 4: *Reformation of Church and Dogma (1300–1700)*. Chicago: University of Chicago Press, pp. 118–26.

Pelikan, Jaroslav, with Hotchkiss, Valerie R. and Price, David (1996). *The Reformation of the Bible/The Bible of the Reformation*. New Haven, CT: Yale University Press.

Pelikan, Jaroslav and Lehmann, H. T. (eds) (1955–86). *Luther's Works*, 55 vols. St Louis, MO: Concordia; Philadelphia, PA: Fortress Press.

Ranke, Leopold [von] ([1834–7] 1901). *Die römischen Päpste, ihre Kirche und ihr Staat im sechzehnten und siebzehnten Jahrhundert*, 3 vols. Berlin. Trans. E. Fowler as *History of the Popes: Their Church and State*. New York: Colonial Press.

Reeve, Anne (ed.) (1993). *Erasmus' Annotations on the New Testament: Galatians to the Apocalypse: Facsimile of the Final Latin Text with All Earlier Variants*; introduction by M. A. Screech (Studies in the History of Christian Thought, vol. 52). Leiden: Brill.

Reeve, Anne and Screech, M. A. (eds) (1990) *Erasmus' Annotations on the New Testament* (Studies in the History of Christian Thought; vol. 42). Leiden: Brill.

Renaudet, Augustin (1953). *Préréforme et humanisme à Paris pendant les premières guerres d'Italie, 1494–1517*, 2nd edn. Paris: Librairie d'Argences.

Rex, Richard (1991). *The Theology of John Fisher*. Cambridge: Cambridge University Press.

Ryrie, Alec (2003). *The Gospel and Henry VIII: Evangelicals in the Early English Reformation*. Cambridge: Cambridge University Press.

Scaglione, Aldo (1986). *The Liberal Arts and the Jesuit College System*. Amsterdam: Benjamins.

Schaff, P. et al. (eds) (1956). *A Select Library of the Nicene and Post-Nicene Fathers*, 1st series, vol. iv. Grand Rapids, MI: Eerdmans, p. 131.

Spitz, Lewis W. (1963). *The Religious Renaissance of the German Humanists*. Cambridge, MA: Harvard University Press.

Tanner, Norman P. (ed.) (1990). *Decrees of the Ecumenical Councils*, 2 vols. London: Sheed and Ward; Washington, DC: Georgetown University Press.

Tavard, George H. (1959). *Holy Writ or Holy Church: The Crisis of the Protestant Reformation*. London: Burns and Oates.

Veissière, Michel (1986). *L'Évêque Guillaume Briçonnet (1470–1534): contribution à la connaissance de la réforme catholique à la veille du Concile de Trente*. Provins: Société d'Histoire et d'Archéologie.

CHAPTER 7

The Modern World

John W. Rogerson

Modernity is a relative term. The temptation to regard the present time as the culmination of a process that has led to a 'coming of age' has assailed more than one generation. At the time of the Renaissance and of the Enlightenment, it was easy to think that a modern age had begun, superseding that which had gone before. 'Modernity' is also relative to different spheres of culture. What is 'modern' in art, music and architecture has been viewed in quite different ways within those areas; and it must never be forgotten that the division of the past into periods such as the Renaissance, the Enlightenment and 'modernity' (however understood) is the subjective 'looking back' of a generation over a stream of events with a view to giving that undifferentiated past a form which can be grasped in the present.

In this chapter, the notion of 'modernity' will be adopted which has been developed by Jürgen Habermas from Max Weber (Habermas 1981: 444–63). This sees the main characteristic of 'modernity' as the growing apart, and the increasing specialization, of the once-connected spheres of science (empirical knowledge), ethics (the moral realm) and aesthetics (the artistic realm in the broad sense). This growing apart has been accompanied by a changing relationship between these increasingly specialized spheres and a general public that is largely ignorant of the developments, but which is affected by them. Habermas deals mainly with art criticism, and the tensions that arise between 'art for art's sake' and the reactions of a general viewing public that may be alienated by what it sees. In the realm of biblical studies, the problem has taken a different form, which will now be stated as setting out the programme for the chapter.

At the beginning of the 'modern' era of biblical studies, it was recognized that the Bible related mainly to the moral and aesthetic spheres of human experience rather than to the scientific. However, among the general public and many church leaders the belief persisted that it was the scientific realm to which the Bible contributed most. This belief led to a rift between theology and the increasingly specialized and successful natural sciences in the nineteenth century, a rift that fed back into biblical scholarship and prevented its development as a discipline more closely related to ethics and aesthetics. At the same time, the critical results of biblical scholarship alienated many 'ordinary believers'. Such results were held to undermine traditional Christian beliefs and doctrines. The gap between biblical scholarship as a specialized discipline and ordinary churchgoers and the distress it caused – a gap that still remains largely unbridged – provided further ammunition for those who continued to fight for the Bible as a source for scientific knowledge (including history). Only in comparatively recent times (from the late 1960s) has it been finally recognized that biblical studies belongs fundamentally to the area of moral and aesthetic concerns.

To argue that any one person is the inaugurator of the 'modern' period of biblical studies is perilous, and invites criticism and refutation. However, I have suggested elsewhere that that role can be attributed to the German scholar W. M. L. de Wette (1780–1849), and I intend to maintain the position here, because it accords with the understanding of 'modernity' and the Bible's relation to it which are fundamental to this chapter (see Rogerson 1984: 28–49; 1992). De Wette was the first scholar to use the results of biblical criticism in order to maintain that the actual history of Israelite religion and sacrifice differed radically from the story presented in the Old Testament itself. That story made Moses the founder of Israelite sacrifice and priesthood at an early and formulative stage of the people's history. De Wette argued that the institutions attributed to Moses were, in fact, a late development in Israel's religious history. For the purpose of the present chapter, the evidence on which de Wette based his reconstruction is less important than the underlying reasons why he proceeded as he did. He had come to believe that the Bible's importance lay in its relationship to morality and aesthetics, not in its relationship to science, including history.

When he became a student at the University of Jena in 1798, de Wette found himself in an atmosphere of thought that was particularly influenced by two philosophers, Immanuel Kant and F. W. J. Schelling. Kant's essay *Der Streit der Fakultäten* (The Conflict of the Faculties), published in 1797, had given classical expression to the view that only truths derived from human reason were universal, that is, valid for all times and circumstances. Truths derived from historical sources were essentially contingent, that is, of validity only for particular times and circumstances. The implications of this for the Bible was that few, if any, universal truths could be found in its pages, given the historical and culturally specific nature of its contents. Those universal truths that it did contain were truths that accorded with, and could be established by, human reason. De Wette fully accepted this position, but he supplemented it with ideas gained from Schelling, and other contemporary writers about art (see Rogerson 1992: 33–9). Whereas Kantian philosophy left de Wette feeling empty, the contemplation of art (in its broadest sense) gave to de Wette profound apprehensions of divine reality manifesting itself in human experience. These aesthetic experiences in turn became the criterion by which truth could be sought in religion and in the Bible. 'O holy art', wrote de Wette in an essay in 1802, 'you bring down to us from heaven the divine in earthly form, and bringing it into our view you move the cold and narrow heart to accept feelings that are divine and mediate harmony' (De Wette 1802; translation in Rogerson 1992: 38). Some years later, de Wette would anchor his beliefs in the philosophical system of J. F. Fries, a Kantian philosopher who argued that religion belonged properly to the sphere of aesthetic experience; the next step is to see how de Wette's beliefs translated into his epoch-making biblical scholarship.

In 1805, de Wette wrote two works: his *Aufforderung zum Studium der hebräischen Sprache und Literatur* (Invitation to Study Hebrew Language and Literature) and a book on the Pentateuch that would appear as the second volume of his *Beiträge* (Contributions to Old Testament Introduction) that was published in 1807. What was common to the two works was a radical attack on the view that the primary value of the Old Testament was as a source for the history and religion of Israel. What the biblical texts gave access to was not history but religion, the religious beliefs held in Israel at different periods of its history. These religious beliefs were to be understood with the help of art, and especially a study of the way in which the mythologies of ancient peoples were the poetical expressions of their apprehensions of the divine. De Wette thus argued that much of the Pentateuch was mythical, by which he did not mean that it was false, but that it contained poetic expressions of apprehensions of the divine, in story-like form. For all that he down-graded the importance of history as of concern to biblical studies and theology, de Wette was also a formidable historical critic, and it was in this role that he proposed a radical re-writing of the actual history of Israelite religion, a re-writing that would become central to Old Testament criticism in the late 1870s. But behind de Wette's work as an historical critic was his conviction that it was aesthetic experience that enabled the Old Testament to be most adequately understood, and therein lay his greatest contribution to the study of the Bible in 'modernity'.

It was hardly surprising that such a radical approach to the Bible, one that made a virtue of being sceptical about the historical information in the Bible, in order to emphasize its theological importance, should have found little acceptance both professionally and in wider circles. Because the Bible was regarded as a prime source of empirical knowledge, including science and history, de Wette's position was widely regarded as an attack upon its authority. In Germany, it was assailed from two quarters. The first was located in a neo-orthodox and Pietist movement which emphasized the centrality of traditional Confessional statements of Christian faith for understanding the Bible, and in particular the Augsburg Confession of 1530, whose three-hundredth anniversary in 1830 brought it into prominence (Rogerson 1984: 79–81). Any attack upon the historical information contained in the Bible was seen as an attack upon its witness to truth, and to the Reformation doctrines that were proved by reference to the Bible.

The other attack upon the position of de Wette and those sympathetic to him came from a new general interest in history within the humanities, history being seen as an organic whole being providentially guided, by which the human race was ascending from savagery to ever higher stages of intellectual and cultural achievement. This movement took two forms. In the hands of the Göttingen Orientalist, Heinrich Ewald, the Bible was studied critically in order to enable those parts of the history of mankind that it covered, to be reconstructed so as to indicate how God had guided it (Rogerson 1984: 91–103). This meant abandoning a literal reading of biblical history in favour of a critically reconstructed one; but Ewald's resultant picture was much closer to the Bible's own account than was de Wette's reconstruction, and it enabled critical scholars to practise what was called a positive criticism as opposed to de Wette's negative criticism. The second form of the concern with history was exemplified by

J. C. K. von Hofmann, who saw the history in the Bible as *Heilsgeschichte*, that is, as the inspired account of special divine intervention in the affairs of mankind, culminating in the life, death and resurrection of Jesus (Rogerson 1984: 104–11). Because it was the history of God's special intervention in human affairs, the Bible's history was unassailable by criticism – a view obviously diametrically opposed to the position of de Wette. Indeed, von Hofmann's approach was a sophisticated version of the view of the proponents of the priority of the Augsburg Confession, namely, that the interpretation of the Bible must be regulated by theological premises that ruled out any radical historical criticism.

The influence of those who opposed de Wette's position was such that it was largely ignored in Germany for nearly 50 years, and when it was 'rediscovered', it was de Wette's 'negative' historical results rather than his aesthetic-moral approach to the Bible that came to prominence. In Britain, in the nineteenth century, a completely different set of events unfolded, dominated not by a concern with history but a concern with science. The climate of thought in Britain was very different from that in Germany. Whereas the latter was characterized by the idealist philosophies of Kant, Schelling and Hegel, the British scene was heir to the empirical philosophies stemming from Locke and Hume. These were concerned with the evaluation of evidence gained from the physical world, not with speculations derived from reflection on modes of human experience. Above all, theology in Britain owed much to William Paley's evidences, a type of natural theology which argued from the evidence of design in the world of nature that there must have been a designer, i.e. God (Addinall 1991: 35–55). The science which was implied in Paley's system affirmed the fixity of species, a doctrine that would be challenged by Darwin's theory of evolution. That would not be until 1859. In the earlier part of the nineteenth century, biblical scholarship had to come to terms with the geological researches of Charles Lyell, which indicated that the world was much older than the nearly 6,000 years indicated in the Bible, according to the influential reckonings of James Ussher in 1685.

The challenge posed to a literal reading of the early chapters of Genesis by the newly-emerging natural sciences was partly met by the Bridgewater Treatises – a series of publications in the 1830s financed by the will of the Earl of Bridgewater, whose purpose was to reconcile the scientific claims held to be made in the Bible with the findings of the natural sciences (Addinall 1991: 87–107). The publication of Darwin's *Origin of the Species* in 1859 moved the discussions to a higher plane, and although the belief that it was the signal for the outbreak of a war between science and religion has been exaggerated (Moore 1979), it certainly polarized learned circles into those who believed that science should be an autonomous sphere unfettered by traditional biblical and ecclesiastical doctrines, and those who clung to the hope of proving that what the Bible claimed about science and history could be shown to be in accord with the latest scientific discoveries.

A concrete example of the lengths to which the latter would go is provided by Christopher Wordsworth's 'Notes' on Genesis and Exodus, first published in 1865 (Wordsworth 1866, 2nd edn). Wordsworth reconciled the findings of geology with the first chapter of Genesis by arguing that the words 'without form and void' referred to the work of an agency hostile to God, which had somehow distorted an original creation which, as geology showed, was of great antiquity. The account of God creating the world in six days had to do with the *recreation* of the original world which had been corrupted. Wordsworth was less accommodating to Darwin's theories. The human race had not progressed from a savage to a civilized stage. Barbarism and cannibalism were *contrary* to nature and corruptions of it. It was necessary to affirm that the whole human race was descended from one pair, Adam and Eve, otherwise the Christian beliefs were destroyed that mankind was made in the image of God, and that Christ had restored the image that had been lost in the Fall. Wordsworth also gave short shrift to the idea that scientific discoveries brought into question the miracles that were related in the Bible. A main principle was that miracles accepted by Jesus and his disciples must have happened. Thus Jesus confirmed the story of Jonah being swallowed by a whale (Matt. 12:40) and St Peter the incident of Balaam's talking ass (2 Pet. 2:16, cf. Num. 22:28).

Wordsworth was no fool. He was an extremely competent and intelligent man, who would be Bishop of Lincoln from 1869 to 1895 and thus representing his conservative and traditional views from a prominent position in the establishment until almost the end of the nineteenth century. Of a totally different character and spirit was J. W. Colenso (1814–83), Bishop of Natal, in the British South African colony of that name. Colenso is best known – and to this day still often misrepresented – as a simplistic biblical critic who poured scorn on the historical accuracy of the story of the Israelite crossing of the Red Sea. Less well known is his attitude to 'modernity', to the emerging independence of the natural sciences and the implications of this for biblical studies and theology. In May 1865, during one of his visits to Britain to defend himself against attempts to 'depose' him from his bishopric, Colenso delivered a lecture to the Marylebone Literary Institution entitled 'On Missions to the Zulus in Natal and Zululand' (Colenso 1982: 205–33). The purpose of the lecture was to defend Christian missions against the view, derived from but not sanctioned by Darwin, that missions were a vain attempt to interfere with the process of natural selection, whereby 'higher' races would survive and 'lower' races would disappear as human history progressed. Unlike Wordsworth, Colenso did not reject Darwin's theories out of hand, but was prepared to allow that they might be correct. On the other hand, he had reservations about the theory of evolution because he believed that the human race had had a plural origin rather than being descended from a single pair of humans, and he could not see how Darwin's theory could account for that. His reservations were, however, based upon reason and not, as in the case of Wordsworth, upon an interpretation of Genesis 1:27.

Colenso was broad-minded enough to allow that science might one day prove that humans had developed from animals; and in any case, he accepted that the history of the human race was one of progress from lower to higher moral and cultural achievements. How, then, did he reconcile this with the Bible and theology? His first answer was pragmatic. His work with the Zulus (he had pioneered the study of the Zulu language and had composed a Zulu grammar) had convinced him that even peoples at a 'savage' state of human existence compared with modern Western Europeans were capable of feelings of affection, loyalty and sorrow, and that they had rudimentary ideas of an afterlife. Colenso was convinced, on the basis of his success in training Zulu converts to become preachers and catechists, that Christian moral teaching could raise the whole nation to greater moral and cultural levels, and he quoted in the lecture examples of such achievements. This experience, however, led to his views on the Bible and how it should be used. On the one hand, the Bible's teaching about the one-ness of the human race and of God's care and love for it allayed any fears that might arise from science proving that humans were descended from animals. Such findings would not disprove that there was a common brotherhood under the Fatherhood of God. On the other hand, Colenso was sharply critical of the idea that his converts should be required to accept material in the Bible that science showed to be false, such as that the world was only 6,000 years old and that there had been a universal flood. Colenso was particularly critical about biblical teaching on witchcraft, and how this had affected 'cultured' societies to even recent times.

'How is it possible?' asked Colenso, 'to teach the Zulu to cast off their superstitious belief in witchcraft, if they are required to believe that all the stories of sorcery and demonology which they find in the Bible . . . are infallibly and divinely true? He continued: 'The time is come, through the revelations of modern science, when, thanks to God, the traditionary belief in the divine infallibility of Scripture can, with a clear conscience, be abandoned – can, in fact, be no longer maintained' (Colenso 1982: 232).

But Colenso also denied that he was taking the Bible away from believers:

> We seek to establish your faith – not, indeed, in the mere Book, but in the Living Word which speaks in the Book, and speaks also by the lips of apostles and prophets in all ages, of all good men and true, whose heart God's Spirit has quickened to be the bearers of His messages of truth to their fellow-men. (ibid.: 233)

In view of the foregoing, there is no need here to detail Colenso's contributions to biblical criticism, which spanned the period 1862 to 1878 and ran to over 3,000 pages (see Rogerson 1984: 220–37). Suffice it to say that Colenso pointed out many literary and historical difficulties in the Old Testament which needed critical explanation, and that in some regards, his own solutions anticipated those of modern critical scholarship. He was, however, far ahead of his time within the British context. Despite a ruling of the Judicial Committee of the Privy Council (the highest judicial body in Britain) in Colenso's favour, Colenso was 'deposed' from his bishopric and a rival bishop was consecrated to take his place. Further, in order to combat his views on the Bible, a series entitled *The Speaker's Commentary* was organized, named after the Speaker of the House of Commons, a prominent layman. But there can be little doubt that, within the British scene Colenso was one of the first, if not the first, prominent churchman to recognize 'modernity' and to work out its consequences for the Bible. He was not entirely alone, for in 1860, two years before the appearance of the first volume of his *The Pentateuch and Joshua*, a volume entitled *Essays and Reviews* also alerted the general public to the changing world in which they were living (Rogerson 1984: 209–19). Far less radical than Colenso's work, *Essays and Reviews*, written by prominent churchmen and laymen, nonetheless provoked fierce opposition because of its embrace of scientific advances, and its advocacy of a poetic rather than a literal interpretation of the account of the creation of the universe in Genesis 1. Its claim that if the Bible was studied 'like any other book' believers would gain rather than lose, was scornfully dismissed by opponents on the grounds that the Bible was *not* like any other book. A volume entitled *Aids to Faith* was produced, which aimed to refute and/or correct each of the chapters in *Essays and Reviews*.

However, the tide of 'modernity' could no longer be held back, and the next British biblical scholar to suffer for recognizing this was a young Scot, William Robertson Smith. Smith and Colenso had two things in common: both were deeply committed Christian believers, which gives the lie to the supposition that biblical criticism was a rationalistic exercise designed to discredit the Bible. Colenso was an Anglican missionary bishop, Smith a Minister of the Free Church of Scotland, and professor at his church's college in Aberdeen. The other thing they had in common was acquaintance with the Dutch biblical scholar Abraham Kuenen. Colenso corresponded regularly with Kuenen both from Natal and Britain, and was influential in shaping Kuenen's emerging critical views (see Rogerson 1993: 91–104; 1995: 190–223). Smith began by being hostile to what he at first regarded as the anti-supernaturalism of the Leiden School, but later came to regard Kuenen highly, and to receive the latter's support when accused of heresy and facing dismissal from his post in Aberdeen.

The mention of Kuenen and Smith makes it imperative to return for the moment to Germany, and to one of the most famous names in the history of biblical scholarship, that of Julius Wellhausen. It was noted earlier that the radical views proposed at the beginning of the nineteenth century by de Wette had been ignored or forgotten. From the 1860s, researches by scholars such as Colenso, Kuenen, Hermann Hupfeld and Karl Heinrich Graf led to the gradual 'rediscovery' of the essentials of the de Wette position, namely, that the actual history of Israelite sacrifice and priesthood differed from that given in the Bible itself, and that this had implications for how the date and mode of composition of much of the Old Testament were regarded (Rogerson 1984: 257–72). It was Wellhausen who gave classic expression to the de Wette view, albeit an expression much refined and altered by subsequent researches. This was in 1878 in his *Geschichte Israels* (History of Israel) of which a second edition entitled *Prolegomena zur Geschichte Israels* appeared in 1883. The genius of Wellhausen's exposition lay in the way in which it correlated three main stages of Israelite religion with three literary complexes. A first stage in the early monarchy (tenth to eighth century BCE), that of a spontaneous 'patriarchal' religion with no fixed priesthood or rituals, was reflected in parts of Genesis and especially in parts of Joshua, Judges and Samuel. Underlying these parts were a southern source of traditions J (so called because they predominantly used the divine name Jahweh) and a northern source E (using predominantly *Elohim*, God(s) in Hebrew). The second stage, that of the centralization of the cult in Jerusalem in the late seventh century, was reflected in D (Deuteronomy). The third stage, after the exile (sixth to fifth centuries BCE) was characterized by concern for ritual and atoning sacrifices carried out by a centralized priesthood. This was reflected in the Priestly traditions in parts of Exodus, Numbers and Leviticus, which were the latest parts of the Pentateuch to be written.

Robertson Smith followed the latest developments in German critical scholarship closely, and became convinced that these developments, far from undermining the authority of the Bible or threatening Christian faith, were in fact a continuation of what had been begun at the Reformation. Then, the power of the Bible had been rediscovered by being freed from the constraints of mediaeval theology. Now, it needed to be freed from prejudices that tried to protect it from modern knowledge. Perhaps it is significant that Smith could have followed an academic career in Mathematics or Physics as well as in Hebrew and Old Testament studies (Black and Chrystal 1912: 106–9), and that he accepted the autonomy of the natural sciences. As a young man who fully appreciated the challenges to Christian faith presented by late Victorian Britain, Smith believed that the discoveries of biblical criticism provided the churches with the wherewithal to formulate an intellectually coherent account of Christianity that would appeal to his age. Basically, his position was that it had become possible to reconstruct a history of how the hand of God had guided the human race to the present day, and how the ideal towards which human effort should strive was summed up in the biblical notion of the kingdom of God. The Bible, studied critically, was the chief witness to this divine process.

Like Colenso, Smith was too far ahead of his time as far as his church was concerned. Two of his articles in the ninth edition of the *Encyclopaedia Britannica* (of which Smith was the editor – an indication of his 'modernity'!) were regarded as heretical by certain members of his church, and Smith was charged with heresy and tried by the General Assembly of the Free Church in 1880. He was admonished and allowed to retain his post in Aberdeen. However, the appearance of two articles that had been in press at the time of the first trial led to renewed charges and a second trial that resulted in his dismissal. In the period between the renewal of the charges and his second trial, Smith gave a series of public lectures in Glasgow and Edinburgh in the early part of 1881, which were published under the title *The Old Testament in the Jewish Church*. They remain arguably the best presentation in English of what has been misleadingly called the Graf–Wellhausen hypothesis – misleadingly, because others such as Kuenen and August Kayser contributed to it, and because Smith had arrived at the same conclusions without slavishly following Wellhausen. The 'hypothesis' was as described above in connection with Wellhausen, with a central role being given to the prophets of the Old Testament as the inspired originators of the ethical monotheism of the Old Testament. One of the central planks of Smith's position was that only divine inspiration had enabled the tiny Israelite and Judahite communities to achieve that (i.e. ethical monotheism) which had eluded the far more culturally advanced civilizations of Egypt and Mesopotamia, and which would also elude all the philosophical learning of Greece. Following his dismissal in 1881, Smith moved to Cambridge, where he later became Professor of Arabic and devoted his prodigious learning to three series of Burnett Lectures, delivered in Aberdeen towards the end of his all-too-brief life. He was only 47 when he died in 1894. These *Lectures on the Religion of the Semites* sought to show how the religion of the Old Testament could only have arisen from the general matrix of 'Semitic heathenism' through divine guidance. At the same time, Smith's analyses of the social contexts in which Semitic religions had functioned broke new ground and led to him being described as a founder of the sociological study of religion.

Smith played a decisive role in persuading some of the leading thinkers in the churches that biblical criticism could not be ignored, and that it had a vital role to play in making the Bible credible in an emerging scientific age. Two years after Smith's dismissal from Aberdeen, a sermon was given in St Mary's, Oxford, by the newly-appointed

Regius Professor of Hebrew, S. R. Driver, on the theme 'Evolution compatible with faith' (Driver 1892: 1–27). Driver followed this up with a commentary on Genesis (Driver 1904) which accepted the latest findings both of biblical criticism and natural science. Driver's insistence that these did nothing to undermine the spiritual message of the Bible, and that they enabled it to be read for what it was – a collection of texts concerned with religion and not science – marked a coming of age so far as the modern study of the Bible was concerned in Britain, except for a recognition of its aesthetic dimension. This did not come until after the Second World War. It has been claimed that Driver's commentary saved the faith of a generation of believers.

This chapter has so far concentrated on the Old Testament. What of the New? If we go back to de Wette and his time as a student in Jena, we learn that he attended the lectures of the rationalist H. E. G. Paulus, and listened with admiration to the way in which Paulus explained the miraculous elements in the gospels in natural ways (Rogerson 1992: 31). For example, at the Feeding of the Five Thousand, the example of the lad who gave up his five loaves and two fishes shamed the rest of the company into producing their own food and sharing it with those who had none. Jesus was presented as a kind of Kantian moral teacher. At this stage, there was no radical questioning of the shape of the story of Jesus as presented in the gospels. Only its supernatural elements were questioned, and given rational explanations. The study of the gospels was conducted according to the theory of another of de Wette's teachers, J. J. Griesbach, according to which there were two eye-witness gospels, those of Matthew and John (for what follows, see generally Kümmel 1973). Mark and Luke were not the work of eye-witnesses, and Mark was an abbreviation of Matthew (a theory that went back at least to the time of Augustine, fifth century CE). D. F. Strauss's *Life of Jesus*, published in German in 1835, attacked the credibility of John's Gospel as a source for the life of Jesus, and, as the century progressed, the view gained ground that Mark was the earliest gospel to have been written and that it had been used by Matthew and Luke. Material common to Matthew and Luke but not found in Mark had come from a collection of sayings of Jesus.

The most radical attack on the traditional view of the origin of Christianity and the composition of the New Testament came from F. C. Baur (1792–1860) between 1831 and 1853. Baur argued that there had been fierce opposition in the earliest church between Jewish Christians and Gentile Christians. This had led eventually to a compromise which was represented in the New Testament as we had it. An implication of this was that the New Testament books were dated much later by Baur than was usually held to be the case. Only four letters of Paul, those to the Corinthians, Romans and Galatians were held to be genuine. The remainder of the New Testament letters and the Acts of the Apostles were composed in the second century CE as part of the compromise between Jewish and Gentile Christianity. John's Gospel was dated by Baur as late as 170 CE.

There was certainly an element of truth in Baur's contention that early Christianity had been affected by a clash between Jewish and Greek Christian communities, and that Paul had played a decisive role in shaping the outcome. Other aspects of his position were grossly exaggerated, and no one today would advocate such late datings for the composition of the books of the New Testament. However, his work stimulated research, if only to refute him, and placed the study of Christian origins on a firmer footing.

One important aspect in which 'modernity' affected biblical studies was the development of comparative religion, in the sense of the study of the religions of Israel's neighbours, not in order to denigrate them so as to claim superiority for the Bible, but in order to understand more fully the religious backgrounds from which Old Testament and Jewish (including Christian) faith had emerged. Robertson Smith's work on 'Semitic heathenism' has already been mentioned, but this was based upon an evolutionary view of how religions had developed, a view which enabled Smith to use Greek, Latin and Arabic sources much *later* than the Old Testament in order to reconstruct primitive Semitic religion. The justification for this lay in the view that these later sources retained evidence of 'primitive' stages of religion which the ancient Hebrews had once passed through on their way to 'higher' stages.

The newer study of Israel's neighbours was based upon the decipherment of Egyptian hieroglyphs and Mesopotamian cuneiform, and the discovery, through excavations in countries such as what is now Iraq, which revealed thousands of original texts concerning the history, religion and culture of ancient Babylonia and Assyria. In the 1870s, Babylonian versions of the story of the flood and of the creation of the world were discovered and published, versions which were similar in some respects to the biblical accounts. In 1901, a version of the laws of Hammurabi, an eighteenth-century BCE king of Babylon were discovered. The laws resembled some of those in Exodus 21–3. These discoveries made it clear that the biblical writers had drawn upon legal and 'mythic' traditions that were well known outside of Israel, and that the background from which the Bible had emerged could not be ignored. A group of scholars in Göttingen founded what became known as the 'history of religions' school, particularly concerned to investigate the religious backgrounds to the Bible. One of its effects on New Testament scholarship was to focus attention upon Jewish apocalyptic traditions, that is, traditions which took a pessimistic view of the present state of the world as under the domain of evil powers, and which looked forward to decisive interventions of God to inaugurate a new age. The influence of Zoroastrianism could be detected here, the religion of the empire of which Judah was part from 540 to 330 BCE.

Interest in apocalyptic traditions affected the understanding of the mission and message of Jesus. Whereas the so-called liberal theology of the late nineteenth century saw him as a moral teacher of this-worldly values, the history of religions approach saw him more as an eschatological prophet warning his generation about the imminent end of human history and the arrival of the Kingdom of God. This view was given classic expression in 1906 in Albert Schweitzer's *The Quest of the Historical Jesus*. According to this view, the form that Christianity took owed much to the non-fulfilment of the expectations raised by Jesus, that the end of the age was imminent. Some British scholars gave a cautious welcome to the interpretation advocated by Schweitzer. The general tendency in Britain, however, was to believe that Mark's Gospel was a reliable guide to the mission and message of Jesus, and that with the help of a mild criticism, a non-ecclesiastical Jesus could be recovered who could become a moral figure to be admired and followed, especially in religious instruction in schools. The radical theories of Rudolf Bultmann, as set out in his *History of the Synoptic Tradition* of 1922 found little acceptance in Britain until after the Second World War. Bultmann's method, which among other things involved disregarding the order of events in the gospels and treating individual stories as instances of particular genres such as disputation stories, was likened to cutting the string of a necklace that held the beads together.

A survey of all the developments in biblical studies in the twentieth century would demand far more space than is allowed in this chapter. It will therefore conclude by considering two aspects of 'modernity' in the twentieth century germane to a volume on the Bible and culture: the German Church struggle and the rise of so-called post-modernism.

One of the paradoxes of the Enlightenment project is that it should have spawned the two totalitarian regimes that cast such ghastly shadows over the history of the twentieth century: Stalinist communism and Nazi fascism. In the form of instrumental reason, the Enlightenment project learned to dominate and control the natural world, and came to believe that history was something to be made and fashioned by humans, not something to which they were helplessly subject. In themselves these ideas were not objectionable, and had the potential to do much good. In the hands of ruthless dictators they became instruments of mass murder and total wars.

In Nazi Germany the churches were put under great pressure by so-called German Christians (who belonged to movements through which the National Socialist Party sought to control the churches) to abandon the Old Testament because of its Jewish origins and associations (see Zabel 1976). If the Old Testament had any value, it was because it showed how disobedient and self-willed the Jewish people had been throughout its history. A milder, more theological, but more insidious version of the same idea presented the Judaism of the Old Testament as a foil to the Christianity of the New, demonstrating the great superiority of the latter. That Jesus had been a Jew was a difficulty for some, and serious academic attempts were made to question the Jewishness of Jesus. It is still possible to see a portrayal of Jesus as a blue-eyed, fair-haired man in the triptych behind the communion table in the Lutheran church in Wasserburg-am-Bodensee, executed by a Munich artist in the late 1930s. That Jesus had died as a passive, suffering, victim was also an embarrassment to 'German Christians', who demanded a Jesus cast in their heroic image as one who had fought bravely against overwhelming odds.

One of the outcomes of the attack on the Old Testament at this time was a return to its theological significance on the part of some of those who opposed National Socialism. So far from using the Old Testament simply as a foil for the New Testament, they saw the Old as an anticipation of the New, which contained the Gospel, or even implicit references to Jesus Christ. While this last point was an over-exaggeration, the Nazi era gave birth to some profound thinking about Old Testament theology which endured well into the post-war period and received classic expression in the work of Gerhard von Rad (1901–71).

The post-war period has been characterized by an explosion of methods in biblical studies stimulated by contacts with developments in the humanities including linguistics, various forms of structuralism, literary new criticism, deconstruction, reader-response criticism, feminism, ideological criticism and cultural studies. A development within theology, liberation theology has also profoundly affected the discipline. The explosion of methods has meant that traditional historical criticism, concerned to investigate the origin of the oral and literary sources underlying the Bible, and to recon- struct both its literary and religious history, has lost its pre-eminence in biblical studies. An era of what has become almost 'anything goes' has been linked to so-called post- modernism: a tendency to discard grand explanatory theories in favour of many com- peting theories and approaches, none of which can claim any priority or superiority over the others.

Two examples of how this has affected biblical studies can be given, which relate to the figure of Jesus. Whereas more traditional academic study of the figure of Jesus has argued about whether he was a Jewish miracle worker, a political revolutionary, a wisdom teacher, or a roving philosopher on the model of the Greek cynics, liberation theologians have largely accepted the gospels as reliable, but have read them in order to emphasize Jesus' empathy for the poor and oppressed and his opposition to all forms of state and religious-dominated power. On the other hand, those feminists who accept that the Bible is redeemable for feminist readers have emphasized Jesus' enlightened attitude to women, while also making the point that Jesus must be seen as working with the men and women who made up his entourage (see Soelle and Schottroff 2002). The search for the individual male hero is regarded as a throwback to 'patriarchal' ways of approaching the Bible.

Biblical studies have changed unrecognizably in the past two hundred years since de Wette first glimpsed the implications of 'modernity' for the interpretation of the Bible. As in the world of technology, the changes have advanced at ever-increasing speed, especially with the explosion of methods and approaches in the past 20 years. It says much for the content and enduring value of the Bible that it has managed to retain its fascination for practitioners of an increasing number of specialisms. Those who sought to protect it from the implications of 'modernity' underestimated its intrin- sic power.

References

Addinall, Peter (1991). *Philosophy and Biblical Interpretation: A Study in Nineteenth-Century Con- flict*. Cambridge: Cambridge University Press.

Black, J. S. and Chrystal, G. W. (1912). *The Life of William Robertson Smith*. London: Adam and Charles Black.

Colenso J. W. (1982). 'On Missions to the Zulus in Natal and Zululand', in Ruth Edgecombe (ed.), *Bringing Forth Light: Five Tracts on Bishop Colenso's Zulu Mission*. Pietermaritzburg and Durban: Killie Campbell Africana Library.

Driver, S. R. (1892). 'Evolution Compatible with Faith', in *Sermons on Subjects Connected with the Old Testament*. London, pp. 1–27.

Driver, S. R. (1904). *The Book of Genesis with Introduction and Notes*. London: Methuen & Co.

Habermas, Jürgen (1981). 'Die Moderne – ein unvollendetes Projekt', in *Kleine Politische Schriften*, vols I–IV. Frankfurt-am-Main: Suhrkampf Verlag, pp. 444–63.

Kümmel, W. G. (1973). *The New Testament: The History of the Investigation of its Problems*. London: SCM Press.

Moore, James R. (1979). *The Post-Darwinian Controversies: A Study of the Protestant Struggle to Come to Terms with Darwinism in Great Britain and America 1870–1900*. Cambridge: Cambridge University Press.

Rogerson, J. W. (1984). *Old Testament Criticism in the Nineteenth Century: England and Germany*. London: SPCK.

Rogerson, J. W. (1992). *W.M.L. de Wette: Founder of Modern Biblical Criticism: An Intellectual Biography*. Sheffield: Sheffield Academic Press.

Rogerson, J. W. (1993). 'British Responses to Kuenen's Pentateuchal Studies', in P. B. Dirksen and A. van der Kooij (eds), *Abraham Kuenen (1828–1891): His Major Contributions to the Study of the Old Testament*. Leiden: E. J. Brill, pp. 91–104.

Rogerson, J. W. (1995). 'J. W. Colenso's Correspondence with Abraham Kuenen, 1863–1878', in W. P. Stephens (ed.), *The Bible, the Reformation and the Church: Essays in Honour of James Atkinson*. Sheffield: Sheffield Academic Press, pp. 190–223.

Soelle, Dorothee and Schottroff, Luise (2002). *Jesus of Nazareth*. London: SPCK.

Wordsworth, Christopher (1866). *Genesis and Exodus; with Notes and Introductions*, 2nd edn. London.

Zabel, James A. (1976). *Nazism and the Pastors: A Study of the Ideas of Three Deutsche Christen Groups*. Missoula: Scholars Press.

PART II
The Nomadic Text

Part II

The Nomadic Text

CHAPTER 8
Judaism

Edward Kessler

In a work where the 'nomadic text' is considered in its global context, a study of the role of the Bible in Judaism must begin by noting two important differences between the Bible in Judaism and the Bible in Christianity. First, the Hebrew Bible of Judaism is not the same thing as the Christian Old Testament. Clearly, the two sacred texts have much in common, but they are not the same. The arrangement of the books is significantly different: in the Christian Old Testament, the Prophets come at the end and are inseparable from the New Testament, while the books of the Hebrew Bible are arranged in order of decreasing legal authority and liturgical importance, the Torah at the beginning, followed by the 'Prophets', and the other books known as the 'Writings'. The books of Ruth and Daniel appear among the Writings in the Hebrew Bible, while in Christian tradition they both have a more significant position, Ruth between Judges and Samuel, and Daniel alongside Ezekiel with the status of a Major Prophet.

The contents of the two sacred texts are also different. The apocryphal books of Ecclesiasticus (or the Wisdom of Jesus ben Sira), the Wisdom of Solomon, Judith, Tobit and Maccabees, which are for most Christians integral parts of the Old Testament, are not in the Hebrew Bible. They are Jewish texts and are occasionally referred to in Jewish literature, but they never had a role in Jewish worship or education as parts of Scripture, while they figure regularly in Christian lectionaries. A third difference between the Hebrew Bible and the Old Testament is a linguistic one. The Bible in virtually every Jewish synagogue is read and studied in the original Hebrew, at least by some of the community, while all but a very few Christians read the Old Testament in translation, from the Greek versions already current in New Testament times down to the vernacular translations available in every part of the world today. The priority of the Hebrew text over any translation, however successful and however official, has been a fundamental tenet of Jewish belief down the ages, one which has frequently hindered communication between Jewish and Christian biblical experts.

One other essential distinction between the Bible in Judaism and the Bible in Christianity, is that in Judaism written Scripture does not have a separate existence from the oral tradition. The Oral Torah (*Torah she-be'al peh*) is believed to have been revealed to Moses at Sinai at the same time as the Written Torah, handed down from generation to generation (Mishnah Avot 1:1), and has the same authority as the Written Torah. Indeed it is said more than once in the rabbinic literature that where there is disagreement between the Written and the Oral traditions, the Oral is to be preferred. This is mainly because the Oral Torah, eventually collected and written down in the Mishnah, Talmud and Midrash, is vastly more detailed and contains infinitely more examples and arguments than the Bible. It is true that the Christian Bible rarely if every stood on its own, unaccompanied by official Church pronouncements and interpretations, despite the efforts of the Reformers to disentangle *sola scriptura* from Catholic tradition. But the situation in Judaism has always been more radical in this respect and traditional Jewish education concentrates as much on the study of the Talmud as on the Hebrew Bible, if not more so. This means that in a study of the Bible in Judaism, we must take as much account of the rabbis' interpretations of Scripture as of Hebrew Scripture itself, if not more. As a way into this vast subject we shall be using as a kind of case study the story of Abraham's near-sacrifice of his son Isaac, known in Jewish tradition as the *Akedah*, and our discussion will range far beyond the eighteen short verses of the original biblical version of the story in Genesis 22.

'For the Sake of Heaven'

Jewish exegetes, ancient, mediaeval and modern, are concerned with interpreting revelation, not just with understanding the origin and meaning of the biblical text. As the rabbis put it, Jewish study of the Bible is carried out for 'the sake of heaven'. For them there is extra meaning to be uncovered in every detail of Scripture. They fill in the gaps in the biblical account. For example, they were interested in what might have occurred during Abraham and Isaac's three-day journey to Moriah (Gen. 22:4). The commentators suggest that the three-day journey enabled Abraham to ponder the divine command and forced him to endure the torture of considering what lay ahead. According to the rabbis, Satan appeared and increased Abraham's torment further by placing obstacles on the journey to prevent them from reaching the place of sacrifice. He attempted to persuade Abraham not to sacrifice his son. These interpretations have a literary function in filling out the biblical story which is so compressed and so lacking in detail, but their main purpose is to exalt the obedience of Abraham, and set the story in a wider theological or religious context.

According to Jewish tradition, the very act of reading a sacred text is of religious significance. The rabbis created the following prayer for those who participate in study: 'We praise you, O Lord our God, King of the Universe, who enjoins us to busy ourselves in your Torah.' Biblical study is associated with prayer and is found in a liturgical setting. Many of the traditional rabbinic interpretations, which are read today, were originally synagogue sermons. The reading of the *Akedah* was prescribed to be read in synagogues on Rosh ha-Shana, the first day of the Jewish New Year. This marks the beginning of a period of ten days known as the Days of Awe which come to their climax on Yom Kippur, the Day of Atonement, and prayers for mercy contain references to the *Akedah*: 'O Merciful One, remember for our sake the covenant of Isaac, the bound one', to which the congregation replies, 'For his sake, let Him forgive.'

An important part of the interpreting process in Judaism is the attempt to allow the biblical text 'to speak for today', especially when it appears ambiguous or irrelevant to contemporary life. In the words of Deuteronomy, '[the Torah] is not an empty thing for you: it is your very life' (32:47). This is interpreted by Rabbi Akiva (*c*.40–135 CE) and others to mean that, if a text appears to have no meaning, it is your fault, it is because you have not studied it enough (Genesis Rabbah 1:14). From ancient times the rabbis devised methods of interpretation designed to ensure that every detail of the biblical text could be understood and made relevant to contemporary life. A well-known example is the law prohibiting the boiling of a kid in its mother's milk. The rabbis asked why this law is repeated verbatim three times in the Torah (Exod. 23:19; 34:26; Deut. 14:21). One answer was that it is intended to apply to cattle, goats and sheep, not just goats; another that it refers not only to cooking it but also to eating it and benefiting from it in any way. It is incidentally on this thrice-repeated law that one of the chief Jewish dietary regulations, the prohibition of having meat and milk products at the same meal, is based. To the question what does the reference to the 'mother' signify, one answer was that it explicitly excludes chicken and other fowl from the prohibition.

In the ongoing life of a synagogue, everyone is encouraged to study Hebrew and attempt to understand Scripture, familiarizing themselves both with the biblical text itself and with the traditional rabbinic and mediaeval exegetical literature. Indeed, this is indicated in two of the commonest terms for synagogue as a place of education: the ancient Hebrew *bet midrash* 'study centre' and modern Yiddish *shul* 'school'. In the Mishnah, it is recommended that Scripture and other religious texts are better understood when studied in groups: 'Provide yourself with a teacher and get a partner' (Mishnah Avot 1:6).

Studying the Bible and Talmud in pairs (*sugim*) has always been encouraged and this makes the use of dialogue particularly appropriate. Not only does it provide a literary form in which different points of view can be effectively expressed and debated, as in the Book of Job, for example, or Aesop's fables. It also captures the freshness and variety of oral tradition as can be seen in the Talmud, most of which is actually in the form of discussions and debates among the rabbis. Dialogue is often used to expand or elaborate a biblical narrative as for example in the following *midrash* on a verse from the *Akedah* (Gen. 22:3):

God said to Abraham: 'Please take your son.'
Abraham said: 'I have two sons, which one?'
God: 'Your only son.'
Abraham: 'The one is the only son of his mother and the other is the only son of his mother.'
God: 'Whom you love.'
Abraham: 'I love this one and I love that one.'
God: 'Isaac.' (Genesis Rabbah 55:7)

The use of dialogue here offers a number of benefits, both literary and theological. It heightens the suspense of the narrative, but it also implies that Abraham, perhaps in sheer disbelief and bewilderment, either deliberately misunderstood the divine command or attempted to delay its implementation.

Since each generation attempts to make sense of the Bible for its own contemporary situation, each interpretation becomes part of the general development of the biblical tradition. Thus, the Bible becomes part of an ongoing process, involving hundreds if not thousands of interpretations, from all kinds of different contexts, down the centuries to the present day. The Rabbinic Bible, known as the *Mikra'ot Gedolot*, first published in Venice in 1516 by the Christian printer Daniel Bomberg, contains the Targum, an ancient Aramaic version of the Bible, and the commentaries of the great medieval scholars Rashi (1040–1105), Ibn Ezra (1092–1167) and Nahmanides (1194–1270), together with super-commentaries on them and other material, ranged around the biblical text. Regarded as a celebration of an ongoing debate about the meaning of the text and its relevance for each generation, and reprinted many times, it remains to this day the standard text on which most Jewish biblical study is based.

'A Hammer that Shatters a Rock'

The willingness to see a multitude of different possible meanings, rather than one single 'authentic' or 'original' meaning, is the key to understanding the relationship between Jews and the Bible. This is beautifully expressed in the following passage from the Babylonian Talmud:

> In the School of Rabbi Ishmael it is taught: 'See, My word is like fire, an oracle of the Eternal, and like a hammer that shatters a rock' (Jeremiah 23:29). Just as a hammer divides into several sparks so too every scriptural verse yields several meanings. (Sanhedrin 34a)

This recognition that texts have a variety of different meanings, each of which claims validity in its own right, is an insight shared, not only by postmodernists, but also by the rabbis' Christian contemporaries, the Church Fathers such as Origen and Augustine. Both distinguished between the plain meaning of the text (Hebrew *peshat*) and other meanings including allegorical, typological or the like, known collectively as the *sensus plenior* 'the fuller meaning' (Hebrew *derash*). Several writers in the period, both Jewish and Christian, make it clear that they believe the latter to be often more important theologically and pedagogically than the former.

Scholem Aleichem's character, Tevye the Milkman, nicely exemplifies this plurality of interpretation. In the stories which later became immortalized in *Fiddler on the Roof*, Tevye regularly turns heavenward when he struggles to make a decision, particularly about the marriage of his daughter, saying, 'on the one hand . . . but on the other hand'. An example from the *Akedah* concerns the age of Isaac. According to one tradition he was '37 years of age when he was offered upon the altar' (Genesis Rabbah 55:4); another interpretation gives his age as 26 years (Genesis Rabbah 56:8) and a third makes him 36 (Targum Pseudo Jonathan). None of these interpretations is given primacy but each is granted validity within its own context, each worthy of consideration in its own right.

This approach has a number of benefits, not least of which is that it offers an intrinsic means of tackling biblical texts, which appear to run contrary to what we regard as the fundamental values of our tradition or which may be read as a licence for violence or bigotry. Since God's word cannot conceivably run contrary to the highest contemporary values at any given period, texts which have been used to maintain slavery or to hold women in subjugation to men can be re-interpreted so as to conform to those values. In this way Judaism keeps open the doors of interpretation. To justify such a process, even when it means going against earlier tradition, the rabbis would cite the following biblical authority:

> If any case arises requiring decision between one kind of homicide and another, one kind of legal right and another, or one kind of assault and another, any case within your towns which is too difficult for you, then you shall arise and go up to the place which the LORD your God will choose, and coming to the Levitical priests, and to the judge who is in office in those days, you shall consult them, and they shall declare to you the decision. Then you shall do according to what they declare to you from that place which the LORD will choose; and you shall be careful to do according to all that they direct you; according to the instructions which they give you, and according to the decision which they pronounce to you, you shall do; you shall not turn aside from the verdict which they declare to you, either to the right hand or to the left. (Deut. 17:7–10)

Since the phrase, 'in those days', is seemingly redundant, the rabbis interpret it to mean that the judge in your day is the one to consult and his judgment is to be accepted, even if he is less eminent than those of previous generations. For example, the law about the stubborn and rebellious son who is to be stoned to death (Deut. 21 18–21), was turned into a purely hypothetical exercise and the command restricted by so many conditions that it could never be applied. Similarly the notorious 'eye for an eye' law in Exodus 21:24 was viewed as an artificial construct for addressing the legal problem of compensation for damages. The rabbinic view is explained succinctly by Rashi: 'If one blinded the eye of his fellow, he pays him the equivalent of the decrease of his value if he were sold in the marketplace; and similarly in all the other cases, where it does not mean the taking of an actual part of the body.' Relevant to this argument is the Hebrew term, *pikkuah nefesh* 'the preservation of life', that is to say, the commandment or sacred duty to preserve life normally takes precedence over other commandments. In an exegetical context this means that, according to the rabbinic reading of Leviticus 18:5, when human life is at stake, the biblical text needs reinterpretation.

Occasionally, there are inherent ambiguities within the biblical text itself. Consider the following translations of Job 13:15, in which the modern Revised Standard Version (1952) has the exact opposite of the King James Version (1611):

> Behold, he will slay me; I have no hope (RSV)
> Though he slay me, yet will I trust in him (KJV)

The reason for the difference is a variation in the written and spoken forms of the Hebrew text, both recorded in the printed Hebrew Bibles commonly in use today. The first version follows the written, probably more ancient, consonantal text (*Ketiv*) which gives Job no hope, while the second version follows the traditional spoken reading (*Qere*) in which Job has hope. The Mishnah acknowledges the ambiguity in the biblical text and recognizes that both readings are possible: 'the matter is undecided (whether it means) "I trust in Him" or "I do not trust"' (Sotah 5:5). In fact, we could say the contradiction makes good sense as an expression of the tension of one who is torn between hope and doubt: the very tension that inhabits our mind when we read the Bible today. Job's words appear to signify *simultaneously* hope and hopelessness.

Reading the Bible Today

Ambiguity and tension characterize many of the interpretations of the bible in response to the two major events in the history of twentieth-century Judaism, the Shoah and the creation of the state of Israel. In general, Jewish responses to the Shoah tend to fall into two categories, both of which impact upon Jewish reading of the Bible. The first response is to view events between 1933 and 1945 as one would persecution and oppression during other periods of extreme Jewish suffering. Jewish scholars such as Jacob Neusner, Eliezer Berkovits, Eugene Borowitz and Michael Wyschogrod represent this view. In the words of Wyschogrod: 'the voices of the prophets speak more loudly than did Hitler'; that is to say, traditional biblical interpretation provides the means by which to come to terms with the Shoah. The second is represented by figures such as the philosopher, Emil Fackenheim, the theologian, Richard Rubenstein and the novelist Elie Wiesel. According to them, the Shoah resulted in a 'rupture' in the relationship between Jews and God and a consequent Jewish distancing from Scripture. Rubenstein, for instance, in his 'death of God' theology, offered what is in effect the reaction of an atheist. In *After Auschwitz* (1966), he stated that the Shoah had buried any possibility of continued belief in a covenantal God of history and that instead of interpreting the Bible in traditional terms, Jews should consider it simply in terms of an earthly existence.

Emil Fackenheim calls for a struggle with the biblical text and if need be, a fight against it. The biblical text is accepted as a primary text but is viewed as 'naked', and Jews are impelled to tackle the biblical text because they too are 'naked':

> After the Holocaust Jews cannot read, as they once did, of a God who sleeps and slumbers not; so enormous are the events of recent history . . . that the Jewish Bible . . . must be struggled with, if necessary fought against. (Fackenheim 1990: vii–viii)

In the same work, Fackenheim goes on to argue that:

> Enormous events have occurred between then and now. This 'generation' knows. It cannot *but* know. But it has begun to understand. Some do understand. If these open the Jewish Bible they are more than 'vexed' and 'defiant': the Book fills them with outrage; yet, too,

more than merely 'preoccupied' with it, they clutch it as if for survival. So new, so paradoxical a relation is coming into being between the Book, then and there, and the 'generation' here and now. This is because of two events both referred to by names of places. One
is Auschwitz, the other, Jerusalem. (ibid.: 16–17)

Fackenheim suggests that it is essential to take seriously the biblical account that possession of the land of Israel was an indispensable condition of self-fulfilment both in
terms of the individual as well as the community. Dispossession was associated with
powerlessness and divine disapproval. Jews (and also Christians but for different
reasons) believed that the exile and consequent powerlessness, which befell Israel after
70 CE, occurred partly as a result of divine punishment. The rabbis explained that the
Temple was destroyed because of the 'senseless hatred of one Jew for another' and that
God has no patience with Jews fighting each other. However, the Bible also expressed
both the hope of divine restoration and the more mystical idea that God's Presence
(shekinah) was also exiled with His people. According to the rabbis, the Diaspora
also had the positive consequence of ensuring that Jewish teaching could be spread
far and wide.

Modern Zionism, beginning in the 1870s, drew on earlier messianic hope and
longing for 'Zion', the land of Israel and, in particular, the city of Jerusalem. Yet at the
same time those Jews who joined the Zionist enterprise took their destiny into their own
hands and stopped waiting for a divine solution to their predicament. This was a dramatic break with the Diaspora strategy of survival, which had advocated endurance of
the status quo as part of the covenant with God. Indeed, some scholars have frequently
described Zionism as a form of secular messianism in which political, social, and cultural concerns transformed the relationship between Jews, Israel and the Bible. Many
view the Jewish State as more than a geographical entity like any other country, and
believe its establishment to be their best hope not only for survival but also for their religious and cultural fulfilment.

Martin Buber explained the Jewish historical attachment to the Land of Israel in a
letter to Mahatma Gandhi, written in response to Gandhi's November 1938 declaration, which was critical of Zionist aspirations. Gandhi had recommended that Jews
remain in Germany and pursue satyagraha 'holding on to truth' even unto death, which
was the basis for his own non-violent resistance to British rule. Buber forcefully rejected
this argument and explained the connection between the Jewish people and the land
as follows:

> You say, Mahatma Gandhi, that a sanction is 'sought in the Bible' to support the cry for a
> national home, which 'does not make much appeal to you'. No, this is not so. We do not
> open the Bible and seek sanction there. The opposite is true: the promises of return, of
> reestablishment, which have nourished the yearning hope of hundreds of generations,
> give those of today an elementary stimulus, recognised by few in its full meaning but effec-
> tive also in the lives of many who do not believe in the message of the Bible. (Glatzer and
> Mendes-Flohr 1991: 479–80)

Nevertheless, the majority of Jews are intensely aware, as Gandhi was, of the inherent
danger in the use of the fulfilment of biblical prophecy as the sole basis for Jewish

attachment to the Land of Israel. What happened a hundred years ago to the Jews outside of Israel is considered by some as historically remote compared to biblical events, which are viewed as almost contemporary. The present becomes transformed into biblical language and geography, which leads to the danger of giving metaphysical meaning to geographical places. Indeed, the fundamentalist Jew in Israel, citing Scripture, interprets the ownership of the Land of Israel as a divine gift, a very dangerous belief bound to make international relations difficult for the State of Israel. Another problem is that the biblical promises do not always define the same borders, and by choosing the widest ones the fundamentalist abuses the whole idea of a divine promise to the Jews. This use of the Bible by Jewish fundamentalists has incidentally resulted in a major theological crisis for the Palestinian Church since the establishment of the State of Israel. Naim Ateek goes so far as to argue that 'since the creation of the state . . . some Jewish and Christian interpreters have read the Old Testament largely as a Zionist text to such an extent that it has become almost repugnant to Palestinian Christians' (1989: 77).

It is true that most Christians have found it hard to understand Jewish attachment to the land, and the American biblical theologian Walter Brueggemann argues that the subject of land should move to the centre of Christian theology. He suggests that Christians cannot engage in serious dialogue with Jews unless they acknowledge the theological significance of land (Brueggemann 1977). Similarly, Alice Eckardt points to the contrast between Christian willingness to tackle anti-Semitism and the Shoah, on the one hand, and Christian reticence on the subject of Israel, on the other. She argues that this is because the Shoah accords with the traditional stereotype of Jews as a suffering and persecuted minority, while the establishment of the State of Israel challenges this assumption, and for the first time in 2000 years, transforms the victim into a victor (Eckardt 1992). In the words of the Jewish theologian, David Hartman, 'the rebirth of the State of Israel has shattered the Christian theological claim of God's rejection of the Jewish people as witnessed by their endless suffering and wandering' (1985: 284).

Many writers in this post-Holocaust era have turned to the *Akedah* in their attempt to address the challenge to faith posed by the Holocaust and the State of Israel. Berkovits, for example, making reference to Søren Kierkegaard's famous study of Genesis 22 in *Fear and Trembling* (1843), rejects the view that Abraham makes a leap of faith. Grappling with the contradiction between God's promise of a son and his command to sacrifice the son, Berkovits argues that the very essence of trust consists not in 'leaping' but in standing firm. For him, the *Akedah* is a story of the monumental faithfulness of a man who retains his faith in the covenant with God, and a story that mirrors the faithfulness of those who retained their faith even in the ghettoes and concentration camps of Nazi Europe.

For Elie Wiesel, Isaac is the 'first survivor'. Wiesel is acutely aware that there exists a gulf between the biblical narrative and the experience of the Holocaust:

> We have known Jews who, like Abraham witnessed the death of their children; who like Isaac lived the Akedah in their flesh; and some who went mad when they saw their father disappearing on the altar, in a blazing fire whose flames reached the highest heavens. (1976: 95)

But the story does not end on Moriah. Isaac, 'the survivor', remained defiant. He defied death and survived, and consequently the *Akedah* has something to say to the Jewish survivors of the Holocaust, including Wiesel himself.

The *Akedah* has been an important text for Israeli poets as well (Abramson 1990). For example, the poet Amir Gilboa, who emigrated to Israel before World War II and for the rest of his life carried feelings of guilt for the deaths of those he left behind, portrays Isaac as a child who naïvely protests against the impending sacrifice only to learn that it is his father that has been slaughtered, not him. The poem expresses the impotence of the father, too weak to withstand God's command, and the guilt of the son who feels responsible for the destruction of his father's tradition (Carmi 1981: 560). Others have viewed the *Akedah* as a metaphor for the sacrifice by fathers of their children to ensure the survival of Israel. In stories and poems that deal with the wars following Israel's independence, fathers are depicted as sending out their sons to fight and thus sacrificing them on the altar of Zionism. Eli Alon, for instance, complains that 'the sons pay for their father's deeds', and protests that Israelis are forced into the sacrificial role of an eternal Isaac (Abramson 1990: 109).

Yehuda Amichai also touched on this subject in his poem, *The True Hero of the Akedah*, composed shortly after the 1982 Lebanon War (1994: 345). Amichai's condemnation of the disregard of suffering in the context of war is reminiscent of First World War poetry and especially of Wilfred Owen's famous poem *The Parable of the Old Man and the Young* (Owen 1963). According to Owen, when the angel called out to Abraham to stop the sacrifice, 'the old man would not so, but slew his son – and half the seed of Europe, one by one'. Amichai identifies the ram as the true hero of the biblical story because it is the only figure in the biblical narrative that dies, and portrays the other characters in the story as indifferent witnesses to its suffering on the altar.

The Bible in Art

Until now, we have been considering biblical interpretation purely from a literary perspective. We turn now briefly to the Jewish Bible in art, in particular to some illustrations of the *Akedah* (Kessler 2002). There is of course in the Decalogue biblical authority for the prohibition of every form of figurative visual representation:

> You shall not make for yourself a graven image, or any likeness of anything that is in the heaven above, or that is in the earth beneath, or that is in the water under the earth; you shall not bow down to them or serve them; for I the Lord your God am a jealous God. (Exod. 20:3 ff.)

In the first century of the Common Era, Josephus was clearly hostile to images. Tacitus, Pliny and others remarked on the absence of statues and images in Jewish cities and synagogues, and to this day elaborate works of art like the Chagall windows at the Hadassah hospital in Jerusalem, are exceptional in synagogue architecture. But this does not mean that there was no Jewish art in ancient synagogues. As far as the rabbis were concerned, there were, as so often, differing views. There is the well-known story about Rabban Gamaliel II (*c*.80–115), who was criticized for going into a bath-house which boasted a statue of Aphrodite. Yet many rabbinic passages make reference to the existence of Jewish figurative art. According to Targum Pseudo-Jonathan, for instance, figurative art in synagogues was approved as long as it was not used for idolatrous purposes but only for decoration:

> You shall not set up a figured stone in your land, to bow down to it, but a mosaic pavement of designs and forms you may set in the floor of your places of worship, so long as you do not do obeisance to it. (Targum Pseudo-Jonathan on Leviticus 26:11)

Figurative art certainly seems to have fulfilled an important function in everyday life in ancient Jewish communities. Images have been found on glass, jewellery, amulets, seals and even ivory, and a good number of ancient synagogues have now been excavated with decorative mosaics, stone reliefs or frescoes, such as those at Capernaum, En Gedi, Beth Shean, Beth Alpha, Gaza and Dura Europos.

We shall conclude our brief study of the Bible in Judaism with a look at two of these, one in the Diaspora (Dura Europos) and one in the land of Israel (Beit Alpha). Both are examples of the artistic interpretation of the *Akedah*, one of a small number of popular biblical images which also included Noah, Daniel in the lion's den and King David, each character suggesting the promise of deliverance. To understand them, we must be aware of a number of significant developments in the interpretation of the *Akedah* in the rabbinic writings. In the first place, Isaac becomes a central character and is no longer a passive victim: for the rabbis he is a grown man and joins Abraham and God as a principal actor, allowing himself to be offered upon the altar, and thus becoming the paradigm of martyrdom. Such is his stature that he is able to 'view the perfection of the heavens'.

Second, the *Akedah* was linked to the Passover as well as to Rosh ha-Shana. In the Targums and the Mekhilta, for example, Isaac is placed on the same theological level as the Passover lamb. 'By a lamb Isaac was redeemed; by a lamb Israel was redeemed.' According to a comment in the Mekhilta on Exod. 12:13 ('And when I see the blood [of the Passover lamb], I will pass over you'), the blood is the blood of Isaac's *Akedah* (Spiegel 1967: 57–8). The association with Rosh ha-Shana eventually triumphed and the *Akedah* became part of the New Year liturgy. But it remains closely associated with the concept of human atonement and divine forgiveness, e.g. whenever the children of Israel ask for forgiveness, God remembers the *Akedah* and when he remembers he forgives (Genesis Rabbah 65.10).

Another very important part of the rabbinic interpretation is that, even though Isaac was not actually sacrificed, the *Akedah* is regarded by the rabbis as a true sacrifice and wholly acceptable to God. In the words of the rabbis, 'although the deed was not carried out He accepted it as though it had been completed' (Tanhumah Toledot 7, 46a). Hence the references in Jewish prayer to the 'blood of Isaac' and even in a few instances the 'ashes of Isaac' (Spiegel 1967). Finally, it must be remembered that Mount Moriah, where the *Akedah* takes place, is one of the names for the hill where Solomon built the Temple (2 Chron. 3:1). So for Josephus and the rabbis, the site of the *Akedah* was none other than the site of the Temple at Jerusalem.

Dura Europos

The synagogue at Dura Europos, a frontier town on the River Euphrates in eastern Syria, contains the earliest known cycle of biblical images, painted probably around the middle of the third century CE. Externally, the building was modest, being located in a private house, but its uniqueness lay in the interior where its wall decorations were second to none. They consist of more than thirty scenes covering the four walls of a room approximately 10 m × 5 m.

The Ezekiel cycle will serve to illustrate the nature of these remarkable paintings (Figure 8.1). The painting, based on Ezekiel 37, depicts the resurrection of the dead. Ezekiel appears three times as he receives the threefold divine commission to 'prophesy to these bones' (v.4) . . . to prophesy to the wind (*ruah*) (v.9) . . . to prophesy to the house of Israel' (v.12). At his feet lie numerous body parts (not the bones mentioned in the biblical text), and beside him a mountain has split in two with an olive tree on each peak. To the right is a fallen house, illustrating perhaps the earthquake accompanying the resurrection. To the right of one of the two mountains stands Ezekiel, his right hand raised towards the hand of God, his left hand pointing to three lifeless bodies beside which stands a female figure probably representing the *pneuma* 'spirit' that provides the breath of life to revive the dead. Further right stands Ezekiel again pointing to the three

Figure 8.1   The Ezekiel cycle. Dura Europos. Kraeling 1956.

psychai 'souls' that bring new life to the dead bodies. In addition to the sheer richness of the painting, it is interesting to note that Ezekiel's palm is turned outward, the second and third fingers extended while the thumb, fourth and fifth fingers are bent back against the palm, an image perhaps influenced by the Christian gesture of benediction (Kessler 2004: 165).

The image of the *Akedah* (Figure 8.2) is found over the opening for the ark, one of the most prominent features of ancient synagogue architecture, always built on the Jerusalem orientated wall. Our eye moves from left to right, focusing first on the menorah (candelabra), palm branch, (*lulav*) and citron (*etrog*) on the left, next on the Temple in the centre, and then, on the right, on the *Akedah*. The symbols of the Festival of *Sukkot* 'Tabernacles' and the Temple perhaps suggest the vision of a future feast to be celebrated in Jerusalem by all nations as described in Zechariah 14. The Temple may also be viewed as much in terms of the future as the past, and might represent the new Temple to be built on the site of the Temple destroyed in 70 CE.

Let us examine the characters of the *Akedah* in more detail. A primitively drawn Abraham, knife in hand, stands resolutely with his back to the onlooker. The little bundle of Isaac, clearly a child and apparently unbound, lies on the altar. In the distance in front of a tent, stands a tiny figure. The figure appears to be wearing a man's clothing and is therefore unlikely to be Sarah as some have suggested. He is not wearing the same clothes as Abraham and therefore unlikely to be Abraham himself, while the

Figure 8.2   The Menorah, Temple and *Akedah*. Dura Europos. Kraeling 1956.

traditions concerning hostility between Isaac and Ishmael rule out Ishmael. Most likely it is Isaac, a reference to Genesis 24:67 where he takes Rebecca into his mother's tent and becomes her husband. 'So Isaac was comforted after his mother's death.' According to Genesis 23:1, his own mother Sarah died immediately after the *Akedah* (Kessler 2004: 166). Beside the tent is the open hand of God, symbolizing the *bat kol* 'a voice from heaven', a frequent rabbinic expression of divine intervention. This is the earliest surviving representation of the hand of God in Jewish art.

Although there are some differences, notably the fact that Isaac is unbound, the representation of the *Akedah* at Dura Europos remains close to the biblical text in other respects. The ram is behind Abraham and apparently tethered to a tree as the text says (Gen. 22:13). The mention of a 'ram tied to a tree' in the fourth-century Coptic Bible may indicate the existence of a Jewish interpretation which survives in art but not in the literature. This suggestion is supported by evidence from elsewhere, both Jewish and Christian, which depicts the ram tied to a tree (Kessler 2004: 169).

Perhaps the most significant difference between the Dura Europos *Akedah* and the Genesis story is the prominent location of the ram in the foreground of the picture. This feature of the picture agrees with later rabbinic literature, such as the eighth-century *Pirke de Rabbi Eliezer*, where the ram is given a far more colourful and significant role than he has in the Bible. According to rabbinic tradition, the ram had been created on the sixth day of creation and was waiting since then for its moment of destiny. It was the first sacrifice on the altar at Jerusalem. Its skin provided the strings for David's lyre. Its horn provided the shophar, which they blow on Rosh ha Shanah and when they blow on it, 'they are remembered before the Holy One who forgives them' (Genesis Rabbah 56.9). It seems likely that this development in the literature was influenced by artistic interpretations such as those at Dura Europos and Beit Alpha (Weiss and Netzer 1996: 30–1; Kessler 2004: 171).

Beit Alpha

In 1929 an excavation in the eastern Jezreel valley, just south of Galilee, unearthed the mosaic floor of a sixth-century synagogue. A sequence of three scenes, the *Akedah*, the zodiac and the ark, bordered like a carpet, makes its way to the Torah located in a wall orientated towards Jerusalem (Figure 8.3). The narrative plane (Figure 8.4) moves from left to right, from the ass to the ram to Isaac; from the accompanying youths to Abraham. By contrast, the Hebrew writing naturally moves from right to left, identifying Isaac, Abraham, the command accompanying the appearance of the hand of God and the ram caught by one horn and tied to a tree. Abraham, with a large knife in his hand, is throwing his son on to the altar fire, while the hand of God prevents the sacrifice. As at Dura Europos the prominence of the ram, which is even bigger than the tree and placed right in the centre of the picture, is in contrast to the earliest Jewish literary traditions which rarely refer to the role of ram.

In the mosaic, two servants, one of whom has a whip in his hand, hold the ass which has a bell around its neck. Above, the hand of God extends from a dark area which could be a cloud or perhaps the end of a sleeve. The most remarkable figure is

Figure 8.3   The *Zodiac* mosaic. Beit Alpha. Sukenik 1932.

Figure 8.4   The *Akedah*. Beit Alpha. Sukenik 1932.

the child Isaac, floating beyond Abraham's fingertips, his arms crossed but not bound, swinging precariously between his obedient father and the flames of the sacrifice. The trial is still Abraham's, but not unequivocally for we focus on the helpless, dangling figure of the son. The ambiguity of the mosaic raises the question of Isaac's willingness to offer himself as a sacrifice. As mentioned earlier, the literary tradition emphasizes Isaac's voluntary obedience by describing him as an adult, while the artistic portrayal of Isaac as a child, both here and at Dura Europos, suggests that he has little active role in the sacrifice. The artists of these and other graphic interpretations of the story, should thus be viewed as exegetes in their own right, no more or less bound to the biblical text than their literary counterparts, though as we have seen, subject to different cultural and artistic influences.

References and Further Reading

Abramson, G. (1990). 'The Reinterpretation of the Akedah in Modern Hebrew Poetry', *Journal of Jewish Studies* 41: 101–14.

Amichai, Yehuda (1994). *A Life of Poetry, 1948–1994*, New York: HarperCollins.

Ateek, N. (1989). *Justice and Only Justice: A Palestinian Theology of Liberation*. Maryknoll, NY: Orbis.

Berkovits, E. (1976). *Crisis and Faith*. New York: Sanhedrin Press.

Bowker, J. (1969). *The Targums and Rabbinic Literature: An Introduction to the Jewish Interpretations of Scripture*. Cambridge: Cambridge University Press.

Brueggemann, W. (1977). *The Land*. Philadelphia, PA: Fortress Press.

Carmi, T. (1981). *The Penguin Book of Hebrew Verse*. London: Allen Lane.

Eckardt, Alice (1992). 'The Place of the Jewish State in Christian-Jewish Relations', *European Judaism* 25: 3–9.

Fackenheim, E. (1990). *The Jewish Bible after the Holocaust*. Manchester: Manchester University Press.

Fishbane, M. (1985). *Biblical Interpretation in Ancient Israel*. Oxford: Clarendon Press.

Ginzberg, L. (1909–55). *The Legends of the Jews*. Philadelphia, PA: Jewish Publication Society.

Glatzer, N. N. and Mendes-Flohr, P. (1991). *The Letters of Martin Buber*. New York: Schocken Books.

Hartman, D. (1985). *A Living Covenant*. New York: Macmillan.

Hirshman, M. G. (1996). *A Rivalry of Genius: Jewish and Christian Biblical Interpretation*. Albany, NY: State University of New York Press.

Horbury, W. (1998). *Jews and Christians in Contact and Controversy*. Edinburgh: T. & T. Clark.

Jacobs, I. (1995). *The Midrashic Process: Tradition and Interpretation in Rabbinic Judaism*. Cambridge: Cambridge University Press.

Kartun-Blum, R. (1988). 'Where Does this Wood in My Hand Come from?: The Binding of Isaac in Modern Hebrew Poetry', *Prooftexts* 8(3): 293–310.

Kessler, E. (2002). 'The Sacrifice of Isaac (The Akedah) in Christian and Jewish Tradition: Artistic Representations', in M. O'Kane (ed.), *Borders, Boundaries and the Bible*. London: Sheffield Academic Press, pp. 74–98.

Kessler, E. (2004). *Bound by the Bible: Jews, Christians and the Sacrifice of Isaac*. Cambridge: Cambridge University Press.

Kierkegaard, S. (1985). *Fear and Trembling*. London: Penguin.

Kraeling, C. H. (1956). *The Synagogue: The Excavations of Dura-Europos Final Report VIII, Part I.* New Haven: Yale University Press.

Kugel, J. L. (1998). *Traditions of the Bible: A Guide to the Bible as It Was at the Start of the Common Era.* Cambridge, MA: Harvard University Press.

Levenson, J. D. (1993). *The Death and Resurrection of the Beloved Son: The Transformation of Child Sacrifice in Judaism and Christianity.* New Haven, CT: Yale University Press.

Maccoby, H. (1993). *Judaism on Trial: Jewish-Christian Disputations in the Middle Ages.* London: Littman Library of Jewish Civilization.

Milgrom, J. (1988). *The Binding of Isaac: The Akedah, a Primary Symbol in Jewish Thought and Art.* Berkeley, CA: Bibal Press.

Mulder, J. (1988). *Mikra: Text, Translation and Interpretation of the Hebrew Bible in Ancient Judaism and Early Christianity.* Assen: Van Gorcum.

Owen, W. (1963). *The Collected Poems of Wilfred Owen.* London: Chatto and Windus.

Rubenstein, R. (1966). *After Auschwitz: Radical Theology and Contemporary Judaism.* Indianapolis, IN: Bobbs Merrill.

Saebo, M. (ed.) (1996). *Hebrew Bible/Old Testament: The History of its Interpretation.* Göttingen: Vandenhoeck & Ruprecht.

Spiegel, S. (1967). *The Last Trial: On the Legends and Lore of the Command to Abraham to Offer Isaac as a Sacrifice: The Akedah.* New York: Schocken Books.

Sukenik, E. L. (1932). *The Ancient Synagogue of Beith Alpha.* Jerusalem: Hebrew University, Oxford: Oxford University Press.

Targum Pseudo-Jonathan (1984). Eds E. G. Clarke, W. E. Aufrecht et al., Hoboken, NJ: Ktav.

Urbach, E. E. (1975). *The Sages: The World and Wisdom of the Rabbis of the Talmud.* Cambridge, MA: Harvard University Press.

Vermes, G. (1961). *Scripture and Tradition in Judaism.* Leiden: Brill.

Weiss, Z. and Netzer, E. (1996). *Promise and Redemption: A Synagogue Mosaic from Sepphoris.* Jerusalem: The Israel Museum.

Wiesel, E. (1976). *Messengers of God: Biblical Portraits and Legends.* New York: Random House.

CHAPTER 9
Islam

Stephen N. Lambden

In the context of current anti-Islamic reverberations and the 'clash' (to be loose and imprecise) between the Jewish-Christian-Western and the Islamic-Eastern 'civilizations', few subjects can today be regarded as of greater significance than an empathetic, balanced consideration of the positive, symbiotic and intertextual relationships between the Bible and the Qur'ān, the foundational scriptural books of Judaism, Christianity, Islam and a plethora of associated religious and spiritual movements. For more than a millennium and a half, the alleged differences, contradictions and idiosyncratic dimensions of the Bible and the Qur'ān have been vociferously and voluminously mouthed and penned by triumphalist Muslim polemicists and Islamophobic Western missionaries and orientalists. A consciousness and appreciation of the oneness of humankind and the legitimacy and interrelated beauty of its multi-faceted religiosity and scriptural legacy should today lead towards a renewed respect for the moral and inspirational value of both the Bible and the Qur'ān. Both these sacred texts claim to be divinely inspired and each has generated a massive amount of expository literature over hundreds of years. Each should be taken seriously in a spirit of humble fellowship, and new pathways to mutual appreciation be assiduously explored.

A twenty-first-century global scriptural perspective can attempt to redress aspects of the aforementioned age-old prejudices and imbalances by focusing upon respected and established modern perspectives about the Bible and the Qur'ān as well as complementary insights generated by past exegetes. Academic perspectives and theological methodologies incorporating new, non-prejudiced, intertextual and related hermeneutics must be allowed to speak out in the arena of dialogue and mutual understanding (Hary 2000; McAuliffe et al. 2001–5, 2003; Reeves 2004). We know far more about the Bible and the Qur'ān and their centuries of transmission, translation and interpretation today than was ever possible in the past. The modern editing and study of ignored and newly discovered scriptural and related texts and mss. in a plethora of languages (including Hebrew, Aramaic, Greek, Ethiopic, Syriac and Arabic) reveal data that were unimagined by past scholars and exegetes. Methodological approaches and historico-critical tools have been developed and refined over the past few centuries that today permit a more balanced and open-minded, potentially insightful evaluation of these many new materials and the light they throw upon issues in biblical and the related field of Qur'ānic studies. Qur'ānic studies and Muslim dialogue would be enriched by a greater awareness of modern biblical studies and associated academic disciplines.

The study of the 'Dead Sea Scrolls' discovered from 1947, along with the numerous other biblical and related finds from the Judaean desert, has revolutionized biblical studies and thrown much suggestive light upon Qur'ānic studies (Tov 2002, in Herbert and Tov 2002; Rabin [1957] 2001), as has the study of the fourth-century CE Nag Hammadi codices discovered in Upper Egypt in 1945, and other Hermetic and Gnostic writings. Recent research on Jewish and Christian pseudepigraphical writings, as evidenced in the *Journal for the Study of the Pseudepigrapha* (Issue 1 1987) and the massive work of DiTommaso, *A Bibliography of Pseudepigrapha Research* (2001), has thrown new light on elements in the Qur'ān, Tafsīr (Commentary), Ḥadīth (Tradition) and related literatures. The Qur'ānic Solomon narratives (Q. 21:82, 34:12–14), for example, are illuminated by select passages within the evolving *Testament of Solomon* cycle (*c*. second–ninth century CE?), not unknown in Syriac and Arabic versions also (Harding and Alexander 1999). The discovery of early (first–third century AH) Qur'ān codices (*maṣāḥif*), 'manuscripts' and other fragments in Ṣan'ā' in 1972 (Puin, in Wild 1996; Leehmuis, 'Codices of the Qur'ān', in E-Q 1:347–51) should also be mentioned at this point, especially since the study of early Qur'ān texts and their paleographical dating, variant readings and transmission history has taken major leaps forward in the past decade (Déroche, 'Manuscripts of the Qur'ān', E-Q 3:253–75).

Despite such discoveries which have opened up new vistas and challenges within both biblical and Qur'anic studies, medieval and pre-twentieth-century attitudes still dominate much of the Jewish-Christian-Muslim debate and dialogue. Muslim scholars, for instance, seldom refer to the modern findings of western biblical scholars, often reprinting anti-biblical material based on dated and inaccurate medieval polemic. Attitudes considered quintessentially biblical or Qur'ānic-Islamic need reappraisal in the light of the above-mentioned finds and related advances in Semitic scriptural research. Many essential doctrinal, textual and hermeneutical ideas need rethinking and rearticulation at both the academic and theological level, if the true relationship between Jewish, Islamic and Christian traditions is to be properly understood and appreciated.

The Bible and the Qur'ān

Though not simply a new Bible, there is little doubt that the Qur'ān is in various ways neo-biblical. Its opening ordering of the sūrahs ('sections'), as a cluster of 'seven long sūrahs', reflects the initial gravitas of a five-fold Pentateuch (or Torah) and a four-fold Gospel mode of scriptural commencement. Frolov in this connection translates the following ḥadīth of the Prophet, 'I was given the seven long surahs instead of the Torah, the surahs of a hundred verses instead of the Gospel . . .' (Frolov 2002: 194). Although echoes of the Bible permeate the Qur'an, very little Jewish or Christian scripture is directly cited or straightforwardly alluded to, a fact reflected in the Islamic doctrine that the Qur'an both expounds and supersedes past sacred books as 'Archetypal Scripture' (*umm al-kitāb*, 'Mother Book'; Q.13:39; 43:4, etc.). The Qur'ān can thus be viewed as an Arabic intertextual yet metatextual or supratextual universe which both interacts with and transcends the Bible. It would be difficult to adequately fathom its historical and scriptural depths outside of a knowledge of its biblical substrate. Though the Qur'ān transcends the Bible, this and related sacred books remain hauntingly omnipresent within it.

Though the Jewish and Christian Bibles were known at least orally to Muhammad and his contemporaries, they were largely bypassed. Most scholars today affirm the Arabian prophet's considerable awareness of oral channels of biblical and post-biblical religious tradition, but hold back from affirming the contemporary availability of an Arabic Bible. Transcending the limitations of biblical Scripture, the Qur'ān presents itself as a revealed (*waḥy*) text communicated piecemeal in history to Muhammad between *c.*610 and 632 CE. It is a collection of divine revelations in Arabic, new and pre-eminently 'clear' (*mubīn*), which abrogate biblical Scripture and claim a miraculous inimitability (*i'jāz*).

The Islamic Bible as sanctioned in the Qur'ān includes four bodies of biblically related scripture:

(1)   Antediluvian and later Ṣuḥuf ('scriptural pages', Q. 20:133; 53:37; 74:52; 87:8–19).

Muslims believe in pre-Mosaic divine revelations to numerous prophets who lived between the time of Adam (prophet and the first man in Islam) and the biblical-qur'ānic Moses. In the Qur'ān and elsewhere, such writings are several times referred to as (pl.) ṣuḥuf (sing. ṣaḥīfah), loosely, scriptural 'leaves', 'pages' or 'scrolls'). This is succinctly expressed in the 'History of Prophets and Kings' of al-Ṭabārī (d. 923):

> It is said that the leaves [ṣuḥuf] which God revealed to Abraham were ten in number. I heard this [related] from . . . Abū Dharr al-Ghifārī: I asked, 'O Messenger of God! How many books [*kitāb*] did God reveal?' He said, 'One hundred and four books. To Adam he revealed ten leaves [ṣaḥā'if], to Seth fifty leaves, and to Enoch thirty leaves. To Abraham he revealed ten leaves [ṣaḥā'if] and also the Torah, the Injīl, the Zabūr, and the Furqān.' I said, 'O Messenger of God! What were the leaves of Abraham?' He answered, 'They were all proverbs . . . And they included parables.' (Ṭabarī, Tārīkh [1997] I:187; trans. Brinner, History II:130–1)

Numerous other Islamic sources register similar traditions which have something of a basis in the vast Jewish, Christian, Gnostic pseudepigraphical literature ascribed to pre-Mosaic figures. These include, for example, writings such as an Apocalypse and Testament of Adam, three or more books of Enoch and writings ascribed to Noah (the Sepher ha-Razim, 'Book of Mysteries') and Abraham (Sepher Yetsirah, 'Book of Formation'). Islamic literatures ascribe many Arabic texts to these and other antediluvian figures as well as later sages and prophets. Most await translation and study.

(2)   The Tawrāt ('Torah', 'Pentateuch', 'Hebrew Bible') of Moses.

In the Qur'ān, the term *Tawrāt* (18 times) often indicates ancient scripture sacred to Jews. In the *Tawrāt* the advent of Muhammad as *al-nabī al-ummī* 'the Gentile-unlettered prophet' is predicted (Q. 7:156) and many attempts have been made to identify this reference. The *Tawrāt* is only a few times loosely cited: for example, Exodus 21:25–6 at Q. 5:45a ('hand' and 'foot' replace 'nose' and 'ear'), and Genesis 32:33 (25) where Jacob–Israel is said to have allowed 'all food' to the 'children of Israel' except what Israel (Jacob) 'forbade unto himself' (cf. Q. 3:87). It has been recently been suggested that the Prophet introduced a revised form of the Ten Commandments (Exod. 20:1–17; Deut. 5:6–21) in Qur'ān 17:22–39 and 6:151–3 though this has no clear Islamic precedent (Brinner 1986; Lewinstein, E-Q 1:365–7). Muhammad, it might be suggested, could have been made aware of the *Tawrāt* through his companion Zayd ibn Thābit (d. 655 or 675/6) who had received instruction in Hebrew (and Syriac) at a Jewish school (*midrās*).

Post-qur'ānic Islamic literatures contain many thousands of *Tawrāt* quotations, many of which are not to be found either in the Pentateuch or any other biblical text. An example of this is to be found the *Kitāb al-Jalāl wa'l-jamāl* 'Book of the Divine Majesty and Beauty' of Muhyī al-Dīn Ibn al-'Arabī (d.1240). Commenting upon Q. 51:56, he quotes the following extra-qur'ānic revelation (*hadīth qudsī*) allegedly contained in 'His [God's] Torah' (*tawrāt*)':

> God . . . revealed in his *tawrāt*, 'O Son of Adam, I created everything for thy sake and I created thee for My sake. So do not subjugate what I created for My sake to that which I created for thine own sake.' (Ibn al-'Arabī, *Rasā'il*, 15)

Note the use here of the biblical phrase *yā ibn ādam* ('O Son of Man'). Ibn al-'Arabī does not appear to cite the canonical Bible but often quotes non-canonical Islamo-biblical citations from pre-Islamic prophets.

The Q. also refers to divine revelations to Moses as *alwāh* (sing. *lawh*) scriptural 'Tablets' (Q. 7:145–51 cf. Exod. 24:12), *kitāb* 'the Book' and *al-Furqān* 'the Criterion' (Q. 21:49). Muslim commentators have given rich interpretations to the 'Tablets' given to Moses on Sinai. The wide-ranging *Fihrist* 'Bibliographical Compendium' of the probably Persian Shī'ī, Baghdadī book dealer, Abū'l-Faraj Ishāq b. Warrāq al-Nadīm (d. 990) records a great deal relating to the Bible and related traditions including the fact that a certain Ahmad had it that the *alwāh* 'tablets' revealed to Moses on Sinai were 'green' in colour with the writing on them 'red like the rays of the sun' (Fihrist, 38/Dodge, 43). In his seminal *al-Insān al-kāmil . . .* 'The Perfect Man . . .', the Shī'īte Sufi 'Abd al-Karīm al-Jīlī (d. *c*.1428) writes: 'God sent down the *Tawrāt* unto Moses on nine *alwāh* (cf. Q. 17:101), and commanded him to communicate seven of them and abandon two . . . The [seven] *alwāh* contained the sciences ('*ulūm*) of the ancients and moderns.' In view of the description of the Tawrāt in Q. 5:46, al-Jīlī also has it that the first two *alwāh* were characterized by 'Light' and 'Guidance' (Insān, 1:114). Elsewhere, it is said that God sent down to Moses 'nine Tablets' but commanded him to divulge only seven of them. Two were made of 'Light', the *lawh al-rubūbiyya* 'the tablet of Lordship' and the lawḥ al-qadr 'the tablet of Destiny', and were set aside. The other seven were made of marble, each exemplifying a divine quality, save the seventh which had to do with guidance on the religious path:

Tablet 1 = *al-nūr* (Light)
Tablet 2 = *al-hudā* (Guidance) (cf. Q. 5:44)
Tablet 3 = *al-ḥikma* (Wisdom)
Tablet 4 = *al-taqwā* (Piety – the Fear of God)
Tablet 5 = *al-ḥukm* (Justice)
Tablet 6 = *al-ʾubūdiyya* (Servitude)
Tablet 7 = 'The explication of the way of felicity as opposed to the way of misfortune [distress] and the clarification of what is foremost' (1:114–15).

This, al-Jīlī asserts, is the substance of what God commanded Moses to instruct the people.

The huge and widely respected early nineteenth-century commentary of the 'Alīd Sunnī Abū al-Thanā', Shihāb al-Dīn al-Ālūsī (d. 1854) also provides detailed comments upon the tablets which God gave to Moses on Sinai. Expounding the words, 'And We wrote for him [Moses] upon the Tablets something of everything (Q. 7:145a), Ālūsī records various opinions as to the number of tablets, their substance, their scope and their writer:

> [Regarding] their number, it is said that there were ten and [also that there were] seven or two . . . the tablets were [made of] green emerald. The Lord . . . commanded Gabriel and he brought them from [the Garden of] Eden . . . Others say that they were [made] of ruby . . . I say that they were of emerald . . . It is related from the Prophet, 'The Tablets which were sent down unto Moses were from the Lote-Tree of Paradise (*sidr al-jannat*) and the length of the Tablet(s) was twelve cubits. (*Rūḥ al-maʿānī* V:55)

(3) The Zabūr ('Psalter', 'Psalms').

The term *zabūr* designates the revealed book of 150 (or so) 'Psalms', attributed to David (alone) in Islamic literatures (Q. 4:161; 17:57; 21:105). It may reflect the Hebrew term *mizmôr* ('Psalm') or be a popular general designation for this Davidic part of scripture (Jeffery 1938: 148–9). The plural *zubur* means 'scripture' in general (Q. 26:196 etc.). Psalm 37:29a (cf. 37:9b, 11a) as a citation from the *Zabūr* is quoted at Qur'ān 21:105b, 'My righteous servants who shall inherit the earth'. This stands out as the only fairly literal biblical citation in the Qur'ān. During the first Islamic centuries, versions of the Psalms were much cherished by Muslim philosophers, ascetics, Sufis and others. *Zabūr* texts were early translated, even recreated into Arabic (Schippers, 'Psalms', E-Q 4:314–18), most notably perhaps by Wahb ibn Munabbih (d. 728 or later) who composed a still extant and variously entitled *Kitāb Zabūr Dāwūd* (Khoury 1972: 258f. and EI² article). As with the *Tawrāt*, Islamic literature contains large numbers of *Zabūr* citations often with no identifiable relationship to the biblical Psalms. In his commentary on the Shī'ī ḥadīth compendia of Kulaynī, Ṣadra al-Dīn Shīrāzī (d. 1640) cites the *Zabūr* with the following introduction:

> And as for the *Zabūr*, God (exalted be He), said [therein], 'O David! Say unto the learned [Rabbis] of the children of Israel and their monks: "Address such people as are God-fearing. And if you do not find among them the fear of God, then converse with the learned ones. And if you do not find it with them, converse with the wise. The fear of God, knowledge and wisdom are three realities which exhibit a degree of oneness such that if but one of them is absent in any one of My creatures, I have desired his destruction."' (Sh-Kafi 1992, vol. 3: 99–100)

Illustrative of a developed Islamic view of the *Zabūr* are the following statements of 'Abd al-Karīm al-Jīlī. For him, *Zabūr* is a Syriac term meaning 'book'. It was sent down for David, as the most sensitive of the people and one especially good and virtuous. A recluse, hardly appearing before his people, he only made the *Zabūr* known to a select group. It mostly consisted of religious exhortations and praises of God. It is without a religious law (*sharī'a*) save for a few specified verses (al-Insān, 1:121–4).

(4)   The Injīl ('Evangel', Gospel[s]) of Jesus.

Twelve times used in the Qur'ān, the qur'ānic Arabic *Injīl* translates the Greek *evangelion* 'good news', 'gospel' (cf. the Ethiopic cognate *wangĕl*, 'Evangel', Jeffery 1938: 71–2). It evidently signifies the original *kerygma* of Jesus as well as the Scripture of Christians at the time of the Prophet. Though now lost, an Arabic Injīl probably existed around or just after the time of the Prophet (EI[2] *Indjīl*). Muhammad may have had some exposure to New Testament concepts through Waraqah b. Nawfal, the biblically learned cousin of his first wife, Khadījah bint al-Khuwaylid (d. *c*.619 CE) (Ibn Isḥaq-Guillaume, 83). From Wahb ibn Munabbih (d. *c*.732) and Ibn Isḥaq (d. 765) to the polymath Abū Rayḥān al-Bīrūnī (d. 1051) and the mystically inclined 'Abd al-Ḥamīd al-Ghazzālī (d. 1111) among many others, Muslim thinkers throughout the centuries have cited the New Testament in biblical or Islamo-biblical forms. Thousands of texts ascribed to Jesus or the Injīl exist in the Islamic sources. They often express Islamic perspectives rather than anything Jesus might have uttered, but must still be viewed as important expressions of Islamic spirituality. Sayings of Jesus or sayings from the Injīl are especially significant in Islamic mysticism and Shī'ī gnosis (Asín Palacios 1919, 1926; Ayoub 1976; Khalidi 2001).

A one-time disciple of the unworldly 'Umayyad preacher Abū Sa'īd Ḥasan al-Baṣrī (d. 728), the important early Iraqi preacher and moralist Abū Yaḥyā Mālik b. Dīnār (d. *c*.747) frequently cited Jewish sources and was greatly influenced by Christianity (Pellat EI[2] VI:266–7). Known as the *Rāhib* (monk-ascetic) of the Arabs, he is presented by Tor Andrae as the Muslim originator of the Islamo-biblical version of the following story of Jesus, the disciples and the dead dog:

> Jesus and his disciples walked past a dead dog. The disciples said: 'How disgustingly he stinks!' But Jesus said: 'How white his teeth are!' In this manner he exhorted them not to speak ill of anyone. (Isfahani, Ḥilyā 2:283 trans. Andrae [1947] 1987:17)

Versions of this story are found in the writings of various Persian poets including the *mathnawī* poem entitled *Bustān* ('Orchard') of Shaykh 'Abū 'Abd Allāh Sa'dī of Shīrāz (d. *c.*1292). A poetical version is also found in the *Khamsah* of Niẓāmī: 'Even pearls are dark before the whiteness of his [the dead dog's] teeth!' (trans. Alger, Poetry of the Orient: 70; Khalidi 2001: 127).

The deeply spiritual and intellectual mystic Ibn al-'Arabī (d. 1240) quite frequently cited the Injīl, though rarely, if ever, the canonical Bible. He claimed mystic intercourse with the celestial Jesus which evidently made concrete biblical consultation and citation unnecessary. Jesus, the fountainhead of the Injīl, converted him, taught him and ever watched over this deeply qur'ānocentric mystic (Futuhat vol. III: 341; vol. II: 49; Addas 2000: 25–6). Islamo-biblical pericopae relating to Jesus or the Injīl are found in the writings of many Shī'ī sages, philosophers and theologians. Ṣadr al-Dīn Shīrāzī (d. 1640) attributes the following words to Jesus, which obviously say more about Mullā Ṣadrā or his source than anything Jesus himself might have uttered:

> Out of the community of Muhammad . . . are the '*ulamā*' (the learned), *ḥukamā*' (the wise, philosophers). In view of (their) [legal] comprehension (*fiqh*) they are even as prophets (*anbiyā*'). They will be made content by God with but little of providence (*al-rizq*) and God will be satisfied with them through a mere token of their action. They will assuredly enter Paradise through [their uttering] 'There is no God but God'. (Sh-Kafi 3:100)

For many disciples of Ibn al-'Arabī in particular, both the Tawrāt and the Injīl anticipate the Qur'ān. They become quintessentially proto-qur'ānic writings mystically registered in the Qur'ān, just as the whole Qur'ān was thought to have been registered in the *basmalah*, its first letter 'b' or its dot as the alphabetic locus of created Reality and the divine Word. 'Abd al-Raḥman Jāmī (d. 1492), like other Sufīs of the school of Ibn al-'Arabī including al-Jīlī (d. *c.*1428: *al-Insān*, 1:111–14), expressed this in the 28th section of his composite Arabic-Persian *Naqd al-nuṣūṣ* (The Deliverance of the Texts), which comments upon aspects of Ibn al-'Arabī's *Naqsh al-fuṣūṣ* (The Imprint of the Bezels). Focusing upon the mysteries of the 'bezel' relative to 'the peerless wisdom in the Muhammadan Word', the Qur'ān is equated with the Logos-like *nafs* ('Self') and *ḥaqīqa* (Reality) of Muhammad seen as

> a singular expression of the combination of the entirety of the divine books. He said, 'God revealed one hundred and four books from heaven.' Then he deposited the knowledge of these one hundred in these four; that is, the *Tawrāt*, the *Injīl*, the *Zabūr* and the *Furqān* 'Criterion' (= the Qur'ān). Then he deposited the knowledge of these four in the Qur'ān. He then deposited the knowledge of the Qur'ān in the substance of its [114] sūrahs. Then he deposited the substance of its surahs into *al-Fātiḥa* 'the opening Sura'. Whoso has a knowledge of the commentary (*tafsīr*) on has a knowledge of the commentary upon all the revealed books of God. Whosoever recited it (*al-Fātiḥa*) it is as if he had recited the *Tawrat*, the *Injīl*, the *Zabūr* and the *Furqān*. (Jāmi', *Naqd*: 275)

Jāmī's mystical conflation of all the revealed books in this way, so that the substance of the Bible as contained in the *Tawrāt, Zabūr* and *Injīl* is spiritually subsumed within the essence of the Qur'ān, to some degree, rendered biblical citation and knowledge secondary or unnecessary. It also highlights the essential 'oneness' of Abrahamic, biblical-qur'ānic sacred writ (Lambden 2002).

Aside from the Sufi mystical appropriation of the Injīl and other pre-Islamic scriptures, Shī'ī ḥadīth collections include texts that establish a close connection between pre-Islamic scripture and the authoritative Being of various (Twelver Shī'ī) Imams as loci of Islamic authority and persons truly biblically aware. The Imams and especially the twelfth messianic Qā'im ('Ariser') or Mahdī inherit the real pre-Islamic scripture and Abrahamic-Isrā'īliyyāt traditions as well as the secrets of future events either in oral, mystical ways or in the form of varieties of an inscribed, though 'unwritten', scroll known as the Jafr (lit. inscribed cow-hide) ('Ali, Kitab al-jafr; al-Bursi, Mashariq, 94; Mulla Sadra, Sh-Kafi 2: 85–9; Majlisi, Bihar² 1: 238f.; 47:270ff.). The future messianic Qā'im is expected to appear in possession of varieties of this Jafr, including divinatory dimensions of the 'ilm al-ḥurūf, the qabbalistic 'science of letters' or gematric prognostication. According to Imam Ja'far al-Ṣādiq (d. c.765) and others, there were two types of Jafr: (1) al-jafr al-abyaḍ 'the white jafr' with pure recensions of the Ṣuḥuf of Abraham, the Tawrāt of Moses, the Zabūr of David and the Injīl of Jesus as well as the muṣhaf (Scroll) of Fāṭimah; and (2) al-jafr al-aḥmar 'the red jafr', a bag containing the weaponry of the prophet Muhammad or of the messianic Qā'im as the bearer of the sword.

'Abd al-Karīm al-Jīlī's consideration of the Injīl also includes the following interesting passage,

> God sent down the Injīl unto Jesus in the Syriac language and it is recited in seventeen languages. The beginning of the Injīl is 'In the Name and the Father and the Mother and the Son' like the beginning of the Qur'ān, 'In the Name of God, the Merciful, the Compassionate'. His community takes this utterance (al-kalām) according to its outer sense. They suppose that the Father and the Mother and the Son are tantamount to the Spirit, Mary and Jesus. Thus they say: 'God is the third of three (Q. 5:73) and they do not realize that the intention of 'the Father' is the name Allāh (God). And the 'Mother' is His Being, the Divine Essence which is expressive thereof through the substance of Reality. And in the 'Son' is the 'Book' which is indicative of absolute existence for he is the subsidiary and outcome of the substance of His Being. Hence God, exalted be He, says, 'and with Him is the Archetypal Book (umm al-kitāb)' (Q. 13:39b). (al-Jīlī, al-Insān 1: 143–4)

The real Injīl is here painted in distinctly proto-qur'ānic terms. The true Gospel must be expressive of Islamic perspectives and be in the language of Jesus, assumed to be Syriac-Aramaic as it is in several other medieval and some later Islamic sources. The original Injīl was thought to have been written in Hebrew or Syriac (Aramaic) being replaced by inadequate Greek Gospels, or texts in other languages. Such a viewpoint was expressed, for example, by numerous medieval and later writers, including al-Jāḥiẓ (d. 869), 'Abd al-Jabbār (d. 1025), and al-Shahrastānī (d. 1153). Established New Testament scholarship affirms that the four canonical Gospels were originally written in Greek though the existence of earlier Aramaic or Hebrew texts has been voiced since the first Christian centuries and is today fundamental to those 'criteria for authenticity' surrounding the scholarly quest for the genuine, Aramaic kerygma or logia of Jesus (Casey 1998, 2002; Peterson 1989). As indicated in the above passage, it was following and developing qur'ānic polemic that Muslim scholars contested Christian doctrines, including the Trinity, Incarnation, Sonship, Atonement, Crucifixion and Resurrection, etc. Existing New Testament texts were often viewed as not being proto-Islamic enough as well as textually corrupt, indirect representations of the original Injīl.

The always singular qur'ānic Injīl (Gospel – not Gospels) may refer to a unified original Gospel. Such a text is believed by Muslims to have been revealed to Jesus though he is not known to have written or personally directed the writing of anything (cf. though Rev. 1:1f.). The Injīl may have something of a prototype in Tatian's (d. 185 CE) *Diatessaron*, a conflation of the four gospels into a continuous narrative, written around the year 170 CE, and widely used in Syriac-speaking churches until the adoption of the four separate Gospels probably in the fifth century CE (see Peterson 2001). The Injīl of the Qur'ān is assumed to be identical to the Gospel in the hands of the Prophet's Christian contemporaries (Q. 5:47).

Statements are attributed to the Shī'ī Imams which are interesting in the above connection. The first, sixth, seventh and eighth Shī'ī Imams are presented in various Shī'ī sources including the Iḥtijāj (Religious Disputation) compilations of al-Ṭabarsī (d. *c*.1153) and Majlisī (*Bihar*[2] vols 9–10) as having an impressive knowledge of the Bible and of the Jewish and Christian religions. In Ibn Bābūya al-Qummī's (d. 901) *Kitāb al-Tawḥīd* ('Book of the Divine Unity', *c*.950), there is an account of the conversion of the (now unknown) Christian Patriarch Bārīha by the eighth Imam Mūsā al-Kāẓim (d. 799) and the Shī'ī theologian Hishām b. al-Ḥakam (d. 796). The Imam is presented as having an unsurpassed knowledge of *al-kitāb* 'the Book' (Bible, New Testament) and its *ta'wīl* 'exegesis'. He is said to have recited the Injīl/Gospel in Christ-like fashion and explained to the astounded Bārīha that 'We [the Imams] have the [Abrahamic] books as a legacy from them. We recite them as they did, and pronounce them as they did' (*Tawhid*, 275; trans. Thomas 1988: 54ff., 60). In a debate with the (Armenian) Patriarch (*al-jāthilīq*), the Jewish Exilarch (*rā'is al-jālūt*) and others (Ibn Bābūya, Tawhid, 417), Imam 'Alī al-Riḍā' (d. 818) is said to have shown his expertise in all past sacred scriptures in their original languages (Hebrew, Persian, Greek, etc.). He exhibited a perfect knowledge of biblical prophecies fulfilled in Islam, for example, and stunned the Jewish Exilarch by reciting verses of the Torah and a conflation of Isaiah 21:7 with parts of Psalm 149 (*Tawhīd*, trans. Thomas, 1988: 73 n.53, 77). When asked by the Christian Patriarch to explain how 'the first Gospel' had been lost, rediscovered and reached its present form, he replied that the Gospel was lost for a day, then rediscovered when John and Matthew communicated it. Claiming a greater knowledge of Gospel origins than the Patriarch, Imam al-Riḍā' explained:

> I know that when the first Gospel was lost the Christians met together with their experts and said to them: 'Jesus, son of Mary, has been killed and we have lost the Gospel. You are the experts, so what can you do?' Luke and Mark said to them: 'The Gospel is in our hearts and we will produce it for you book by book, every one . . . we will recite it to you, each and every book, until we have brought it together for you completely.' So Luke, Mark, John and Matthew sat down and wrote for you this Gospel after you had lost the first Gospel. But these four were disciples of the first disciples. (Ibn Bābuyā, *Tawhid*, 425–6 trans. Thomas, 74 cf. *Bihar*[2] 10: 306f.)

In this text the Imam understands that the extant Gospels are not first-hand, eye-witness accounts and acknowledges the fourfold origins of the canonical Gospels. Though an alleged first Gospel (= the qur'ānic Injīl) had been lost, it was recovered by 'disciples of disciples'. This Imam does not accuse Christians of *taḥrīf* 'falsification' and in fact quite frequently cites canonical Bible texts. Others, however, perhaps a majority of Muslims, have not been so favourably disposed.

Accusations of Scriptural *Taḥrīf* 'Falsification' and *Tabdīl* 'Alteration'

Accusations of tampering with biblical Scripture for polemical or selfish reasons were common within all varieties of Judaism and Christianity from the early centuries CE. Recent careful textual analysis suggests that biblical texts were somewhat malleable in Antiquity, even leaving room for the occasional 'orthodox' rewriting ('corruption') of Scripture (Ehrman 1993; Kannaday 2004: 5ff.). From pre-Christian times Jews accused their Samaritan neighbours and various Christian groups of tampering with sacred writ (Tov 2001: 80ff., 94–6, Lowry 1977). Justin Martyr (d. *c.*165 CE) objected to Jews who contested the veracity of the Greek (LXX) version of Isaiah 7:14, accusing them of 'imprudent and selfish thinking' (Hengel 2002: 29ff.). The second-century Christian ascetic Marcion of Sinope (d. *c.*160 CE) affirmed only the partial veracity of select letters within the 'corrupted' Pauline corpus and the Gospel of Luke and considered the Hebrew Bible the aberrant production of the false God of this world, not the benign 'Father of Jesus Christ'.

Accusations along these lines are to be found in the Qur'an though the veracity of the whole Bible is not contested:

> a section of them [the Jews] heard the word of God and then, having understood, they deliberately falsified it (*yuḥarrifūna*) (Q. 2:75b) . . . some among the Jews distort the words out of their context (*yuḥarrifūna*). (Q. 4:46a)

Following a few qur'ānic verses primarily directed towards Jews (e.g. 2:75b; 4:46a; 5:13a; 5:41b, cf. 4:48, 5:16), and exaggerating and extrapolating for apologetic or polemical reasons, Muslim writers from early on in the evolution of Islam condemned both Jews and Christians for indulging in the *taḥrīf* 'scriptural falsification' or *tabdīl* 'textual alteration' of the biblical text. Dialogue has never recovered from such attacks despite the fact that the Qur'ān itself does not support radically negative views of biblical Scripture, as both learned Muslims and Western scholars have frequently pointed out (Montgomery Watt: 1991: 30; Ayoub 1986: 3). The qur'ānic use of the imperfect active form *yuḥarrifūna* 'they falsify' does not support the post-qur'anic theory of the corruption of the whole Bible, although belief in the *taḥrīf* ('falsification') of the Bible became widespread in the Muslim world. Muslim Bible study and quotation were outlawed or inhibited, and to this day Jewish-Christian-Muslim dialogue about the Bible remains difficult in the light of issues surrounding accusations of *taḥrīf*.

Insufficient attention has been given to those great Islamic thinkers who distinguished between *taḥrīf al-naṣṣ* 'textual falsification' and *taḥrīf al-ma'nā* 'falsification of meaning' in Jewish and Christian Bible exegesis. Despite prejudices born of exaggerated notions of biblical *taḥrīf*, there were a fair number of apologists, thinkers and philosophers, both Sunnī and Shī'ī, who cited the Bible with confidence and apologetic acumen. Aside from the Shī'ī historians al-Ya'qūbī (d. c.905) and al-Mas'ūdī (d. 956), who cited and gave weight to the integrity of biblical Scripture, a distinguished example is the Iranian (possibly Ismā'īlī) thinker Muhammad ibn 'Abd al-Karīm al-Shahrastānī (d. 1153), best known for his *Kitāb al-milal wa'l-niḥal* 'The Book of Religious and Philosophical Creeds', which is recognized today as the first history of religion text in world literature (Wasserstrom 1997: 128). Aside from his positive view and knowledge of the Bible evident in his *Kitāb al-milal*, almost no attention has been paids to the prologue to his incomplete Persian *Tafsīr* work *Mafātīḥ al-asrār wa maṣābiḥ al-abrār* 'Keys of the Mysteries and Lamps of the Pious'. Therein, it is stated that despite some Jewish twisting of scriptural word(s) out of context (Q. 4:46), there existed a single recension (*naskh*) of the *Tawrāt*, representative of the *alwāḥ* 'Tablets' given to Moses and entrusted to the safekeeping of the sons of Aaron. The *Tawrāt* did not lose its status as an honourable expression of the 'Word of God' *(kalām Allāh)*. This is clear from the qur'ānic reference to it as 'a guidance and a light' (Q.5:44a). The *Injīl* 'Gospels' are likewise the 'Book of God' (*Kitāb Allāh*) although existing in four differing recensions with innumerable differences deriving from their four authors. The extant Gospels are thus not wholly the 'Word of God' but contain portions of the true Gospel, just as the Qur'an is not wholly present in the commentaries of the Islamic commentators. That there is *wahy* ('divine inspiration') in the existing Gospels is also apparent from the Qur'ān which states that the Injīl confirms previous scripture (Q. 3:3, 50) (Shahrastanī 1997: 122–3).

Even the far-sighted and brilliant Muslim historian Ibn Khaldūn (d. 1406), who pioneered the philosophy and sociology of history and is well known for his rejection of polemical views of biblical *taḥrīf*, upholds the genuineness of the Bible with reference to Q. 5:43[7] and in view of a tradition handed down from Ibn 'Abbās to the effect that a religious community is unable to wholly, materially corrupt their sacred book (Fischel 1958, 1967). In his famous, though still uncritically edited *Muqaddimah* (Prolegomenon), he argues for the authenticity of the Bible: 'the statement concerning the alteration (of the Torah by the Jews) is unacceptable to thorough scholars and cannot be understood in its plain meaning' (*Muqaddimah*, trans. Rosenthal 1: 20–1). Most Muslim editions of this work, including the very recent Beirut 2004 edition, omit the paragraph about the falsity of the Muslim accusation of biblical *taḥrīf* ('corruption') though it is almost certainly authentic (cf. Lazarus-Yafeh 1992: 48).

In the nineteenth-century Muslim world there was a recrudescence of polemical, anti-biblical writing in response to evangelical Orientalism and Christian missionary propaganda. The widely distributed Orientalist, anti-Islamic *Mīzān al-Ḥaqq* 'The Balance of Truth' by the German Protestant missionary Carl Gottleib Pfander (1803–65), early published in Armenian (1831), Persian (1835) and Arabic (1865), sparked off many anti-biblical Muslim responses. The most famous of these, focused mainly on the issue of biblical *taḥrīf*, was the *Iẓhār al-ḥaqq* (The Manifestation of the Truth) of the learned Indian Shī'ī Muslim writer Raḥmat-Allāh ibn Khalīl al-'Uthmānī al-Kairānawī [al-Hindī] (d. Mecca, 1891). Born out of a debate with Pfander held in

Agra (British India) in 1854, Kairānawī sought to underline the magnitude of biblical *taḥrīf* with a detailed critique of biblical texts. His work stands out as one which took some account of the 'folly' of ancient and mid-nineteenth-century ideas about the biblical text (Powell 1976: 53). It is based on now-dated Western biblical scholarship, including the massive *Introduction to the Critical Study and Knowledge of the Holy Scriptures* by the English theologian and bibliographer Thomas Horne (1780–1862), and contains highly selective presentations of medieval Islamic anti-Bible materials. Kairānawī, for example, accurately records Horne's denial of the Davidic authorship of the biblical Psalms and rejoices in Patristic and mid-nineteenth-century Western 'confusion' about the authorship of the *Zabūr* (Psalms) (Iẓhar, 1:138, referring to Horne 1828, 4: 102–3). The *Iẓhār al-ḥaqq*, first published in two volumes in 1867 and then in subsequent translations into French (1888) and English (1989–90 and 2003), was an effective response and is still highly regarded in the biblically uneducated Muslim world. No detailed and up-to-date Western analysis of the contents of the *Iẓhār al-ḥaqq* in the light of contemporary biblical scholarship seems to have been attempted. This and a fresh study of *taḥrīf* in the same light remain something of an academic and theological desideratum (Schirrmacher 1992).

Finally, in this connection mention should be made of the zealous evangelical missionary Henry Martyn (d. Tokat 1812) whose missionary propaganda precipitated more than a dozen Persian and Arabic treatises, several of which dwell upon biblical *taḥrīf*. Martyn not only translated the Hebrew Psalms and Greek New Testament into Persian, but his preaching and literary activities in and around Shiraz in 1811–12 led Shī'ī mullas and mujtahids to pen detailed treatises. Of these, several were published in nineteenth-century Iran and a few others were summarized by the Oxford Semitic scholar Samuel Lee (1783–1852), himself the author of a response to accusations of biblical *taḥrīf* (falsification) (Lee 1824). Other responses to Henry Martyn, which frequently exhibit a high level of biblical knowledge, include the leading mujtahid of Shiraz Mīrzā Ibrāhīm Fasā'ī, Mullā Aḥmad Narāqī (d. *c*.1829), and the Ni'matallāhī Sufi Mullā Muhammad Riḍā' Hamadānī (d. 1841) whose erudite writings raised *taḥrīf* issues in such great detail (Lee 1824: 161–450) that Samuel Lee was moved to write the above mentioned defence published in his *Controversial Tracts* (Lee 1824: 451–584).

Negative Islamic *taḥrīf* doctrines propagated from medieval times by Ibn Ḥazm and others, inhibited Muslim Bible study and acted as a barrier to adequate awareness of Western biblical scholarship. Very few Muslim commentaries upon biblical texts exist, though notable exceptions include learned Persian Shī'ī scholars of the Safavid and Qajar periods including Sayyid Aḥmad ibn Zayn al-'Ābidīn al-'Alawī (d. *c*.1650), author of four volumes ('Alawi 1995; Corbin, EIr. 1: 644) and Muhammad Bāqir ibn Ismā'īl Ḥusaynī Khātūnābādī, (d. 1715), who wrote a recently published Persian commentary upon the four Gospels, the *Tarjumah-yi anājīl-i arba'ih* (ed. Ja'fariyan, 1996). A relative of his was involved in the biblical translation project of Nādir Shāh Afshār (r. 1688–1747) (Netzer, EIr. IV: 298).

Shī'ī-Shaykhī contributions generated by disciples of Shaykh Aḥmad al-Aḥsā'ī (d. 1826) and Sayyid Kāẓim Rashtī (d. 1843) to the debate with western evangelical Christianity, notably those of the polymathic and anti-Bābī third Shaykhī leader Karīm Khān Kirmānī (d. 1871) and his followers, have yet to be studied (Kirmani, Nusrat).

But it can be confidently stated that it was the quasi-Shaykhī-rooted Bābī-Bahā'ī religions which successfully made the transition from Islamic Shī'sm to biblically affirmative post-Islamic religiosity (Lambden 2002). Bahā'ī leaders and their zealous disciples embraced and made good use of the Bible in their attempt to convert their hearers, including missionaries and others who themselves had largely failed to make converts in the Muslim world.

Islamic Bible Citations

By about the middle of the eighth century, biblical quotations began to become numerous in a wide range of Islamic literatures. They may be loosely divided into five categories, none of which need be regarded as aberrant or 'false'. First, the number of *literal, accurate* Bible citations increased markedly in the second and third centuries of the Islamic era, though it was not until the circulation of printed Arabic, Persian and Turkish Bibles from the sixteenth century CE, that segments of the literate Islamic world had direct access to the complete text of the Bible. Early examples of straightforward Arabic Bible citation, including verses from Genesis 1 and New Testament texts, are found for example in statements attributed to the (Twelver) Shī'ī Imams, and certain of the writings of 'Abd-Allāh Ibn Qutayba (d. 889), whose accurate knowledge of the New Testament is evidenced in his reference to three sets of fourteen generations (Heb. David = D + W + D = 4 + 6 + 4 = 14) separating Abraham and Jesus (*K. al-Ma'ārif*, 34) in line with Matthew 1:17. An interesting juxtaposition of a literally conveyed biblical logion of Jesus, and an Islamo-biblical version is found in the *Ḥilyat al-awliyā'* of Abū Nu'aym al-Iṣfahānī:

> Jesus walked past a woman who said, 'Happy, happy is the womb that carried you, and the breasts that suckled you' (Luke 11:27–8). But Jesus [the proto-Muslim] said, 'No, happy is the one who reads the Qur'ān and keeps that which is written therein.' (Ḥilyā IV: 119, trans. Tor Andrae [1947] 1987: 27)

Other examples are Matthew 6:21 (= Luke 12:34) cited, for example, by Aḥmad ibn Ḥanbal (d. 241/855), Kitāb al-zuhd (The Book of Asceticism) and Ibn al-'Arabī, al-Futūḥāt al-makkiyya (The Meccan Disclosures) 2:812: Jesus said, 'Place your treasures in heaven, for the heart of man is where his treasure is' (cf. Khalidi 2001: 71). The negative form of the 'golden rule' ascribed to Jesus (Matt. 7:12/Luke 6:31; Matt. 5:39b/Luke 6:29) is cited by the sixth Shī'ī Imam Ja'far al-Ṣādiq (d. c.145/760): 'Whatsoever you do not wish to be done to yourself, do not do the same to anyone else. And if anyone should strike you on the right cheek, then let him strike the left one also' (cited Majlisī, Biḥār[2] 14:287).

A second category may be defined *as interpretive, paraphrastic or extended citations containing elements of textual divergence or apologetic rewriting.* Recreated citations of Deuteronomy 33:2 ('The Lord came from Sinai'), for example, are found in numerous Islamic sources including the writings of 'Alī al-Ṭabarī (fl. mid-ninth cent CE) and Abū Rayḥān al-Bīrūnī (d. 1051). The opening words are sometimes extensively rewritten to avoid anthropomorphism, while other parts of this text are interpreted to express an Islamic view of salvation history fulfilled in Muhammad and Islam. A beautiful example appears in the Shiʻi prayer *Duʿā al-simāt* (Supplication of the Signs) ascribed to Muhammad al-Bāqir (d. 126/743):

> I beseech Thee, O my God! by Thy Glory through which Thou did converse with Thy servant and Thy messenger Moses son of ʻImrān in the sanctified [Sinaitic] regions beyond the ken of the cherubim above the clouds of Light beyond the Ark of the Testament (*al-tābūt al-shahāda*) within the Pillars of Light; in Mount Sinai and Mount Horeb in the sanctified vale in the blessed spot in the direction of the Mount [Sinai] situated at the right-hand side of the [Sinaitic] Bush [Tree]. (cited al-Kafʻamī, al-Miṣbāḥ, 561)

Another example is the interpretive citation of John 16:7f. as a messianic prediction of the advent of Muhammad as the Fāraqlīṭ (Paraclete = ʻComforter') who will communicate all mysteries:

> The Son of Man (Ibn al-bashar) [= Jesus] is going and Fāraqlīṭ (Paraclete) [= Muhammad] will come after him. He will communicate the secrets unto you and expound all things. He will bear witness unto me just as I have borne witness unto him. I, verily, have come unto you with parables but he will come unto you with [clear] exegesis (bi'l-taʾwīl). (Majlisī, Ḥaqq al-yaqīn, cited al-Aḥsāʾī, al-Kashkūl, mss, 2: 538–9)

A third category contains *citations exhibiting significant textual 'rewriting' and interpretation*, particularly to highlight cases of scriptural fulfilment in Muhammad and Islamic history. Expansions or conflations of Isaiah 42:1f. are cited by several authors in this way as intimations of the person of Muhammad in the Tawrāt (Torah = Hebrew Bible). Ismāʻīl al-Bukhārī's (d. 870) provides a good example:

> He [God] said in the Tawrāt, ʻO thou Prophet! We assuredly sent you as a witness, a herald of good-tidings (*mubashshir*) and a protector of those [Arab] unlettered ones. You are my Servant and my messenger (cf. Isa. 42:1). I have named you al-Mutawakkil (ʻThe Trusting [in God]'), one neither given to hard-heartedness nor crudity: not shouting out in the streets (cf. Isa. 42:2a–3). He will not requite evil for evil, but shall pardon and forgive. God will never withhold his grasp upon him until through him he straightens a twisted [Arab] community such that they exclaim ʻThere is no God but God', thereby opening the eyes of the blind, the ears of the deaf and the uncircumcised [hardened] hearts (cf. Isa. 42:6–7). (Bukharī, *Sahīh, Kitab al-tafsīr* on Q. 48:8)

Another example is the rewritten, Islamo-biblical form of the ʻLord's Prayer' (Matt. 6:10–13; Luke 11:3–5) attributed to Muhammad as found in the *Sunan* of Abū Dāwūd al-Sijistānī (d. 888):

> Our Lord God, which art in heaven, hallowed be Thy Name; Thy kingdom [is] in heaven and on earth; as Thy mercy is in heaven, so show Thy mercy on earth; forgive us our debts and our sins. Thou art the Lord of the good; send down mercy from Thy mercy and healing from Thy healing on this pain, that it may be healed. (Abū Dawud, *Sunan* I, cited in Goldziher, trans. Stern 1971 (Muslim Studies) II: 350)

There is a tradition that, just prior to this prayer, Muhammad said that 'if anyone suffers or his brother suffers' he should recite it (ibid.).

A fourth category consists of Islamo-biblical texts which *echo, conflate and/or transcend biblical text(s) in expressing a distinctly Islamic perspective with minimal or unclear biblical precedent.* To this category belong certain Islamic Merkabah ('Throne mysticism') and related texts (cf. Q. 2:255), found in Tafsīr works and mystical literature, and rooted in Ezekiel 1:1ff. and Revelation 4:6b–9. The possibly Zaydī (Shīʿī) commentator Muqātil b. Sulaymān al-Khurāsānī (d. Basra, 767) relays the following tradition from Wahb ibn Munabbih via the *ahl al-kitāb* ('possessors of scripture'):

> Four angels bear the [divine] Throne [Seat] (*kursī*), every angel having four faces. Their legs are situated beneath the [foundational] Rock which lies beneath the lowest earth extending [for the distance of] a 500-year journey; and between all [of the seven] earth[s] is a 500-year journey! (1) [There is] an angel whose face has the appearance of a man [human form] which is the archetype of forms. Of God he requests sustenance for the progeny of Adam. (2) [There is] an angel whose face has the appearance of the exemplar of cattle which is the Ox. Of God he requests sustenance for the cattle [animals]. (3) [There is] an angel whose face has the appearance of the exemplar of the birds which is the Eagle [Vulture]. Of God he requests sustenance for the birds. (4) [There is] an angel whose face has the appearance of the exemplar of beasts of prey which is the Lion. Of God he requests sustenance for the beasts of prey. (Muqātil, *Tafsir* I: 213 on Q. 2:255b cf. V:222)

The qur'ānic image of the celestial Throne of God was of central cosmological and mystical importance as evidenced by the qur'ānic 'Throne verse' (Q. 2:255). This text was given a variety of symbolic and esoteric interpretations by the twelver Imāms and by numerous Sufi and other exponents of the *ʿulūm al-ghayb* (Islamic esoterica). While Ezekiel 1:10 mentions 'the four faces of the four creatures which he visioned', the Ezekiel Targum understands this to signify four multi-faceted faces (4 × 16) equalling 64 faces. The above tradition reflects such traditions.

A final category would include Islamic *pseudepigraphical texts and writings* (sometimes) with biblical-qur'ānic ascription but often exhibiting little or no concrete biblical basis or substrate. Examples of this category are the many pseudepigraphical texts ascribed to Adam, Abraham, Moses, David, Daniel and others including, for example, the *ṣuḥuf* (sing. *saḥīfa*) 'scriptural leaves' attributed to Idris, i.e. Enoch. These are paraphrased and set out in the *Saʿd al-suʿūd li'l-nufūs manḍūd* ('The Felicity of Good Fortune for Blanketed Souls') of Ibn Ṭāwūs (d. 1226) and the *Biḥar al-anwār* (Oceans of Lights) of Muhammad Baqir Majlisī (d. 1699/1700) which cites no less than 29 titled, pre-Islamic pericopes ascribed to Idrīs–Enoch (*Biḥar²*, vol. 95: 453–72; cf. 11: 269).

There are also Islamicate recreations or versions of the *Zabūr* or *Mazamir* (Psalms) and the Book of Daniel such as the *Kitāb al-malāḥim li Dāniyāl* (The Book of the Conflagration of Daniel) existing in a number of Shīʿī recensions. According to one of these, knowledge of the cryptic predictions in the *Malhamat Dāniyāl* enabled the Sunnī Caliphs Abū Bakr and ʾUmar to gain successorship after the passing of Muhammad (Fodor 1974: 85ff.; Kohlberg 1992: 143). Then there are the extra-qur'ānic 'divine sayings' (*ḥadīth qudsī*) attributed to biblical figures as transmitted by the Prophet Muhammad or the Shī'ī Imams. These include a great deal of Islamo-biblical material, even whole pseudepigraphical books. According to some traditions the Prophet and the Imams were heir to pure forms of pre-Islamic sacred writ either orally or through secret and guarded channels. The well-known Sufi theological disclosure which commences, 'I [God] was a hidden treasure' is believed to have been revealed to the biblical-qur'anic David, while the following remarkable prayer for blessings upon all the prophets is attributed to his mother:

> O my God! Blessings be upon [1] Hābīl (Abel), [2] Shīth (Seth), [3] Idrīs (Enoch), [4] Nūḥ (Noah), [5] Hūd, [6] Ṣāliḥ [7] Ibrāhīm (Abraham), [8] Ismā'īl (Ishmael) and [9] Isḥāq (Isaac), [10] Ya'qūb (Jacob), [11] Yūsuf (Joseph), [12] and the tribes [of Israel] (al-asbāt), [13] Lūṭ (Lot), [14] Shu'ayb, [15] 'Ayyūb (Job), [16] Mūsā (Moses), [17] Hārūn (Aaron), [18] Yūsha' (Joshua), [19] Mīshā (?), [20] Khiḍr, [21] Dhū-l-Qarnayn ('Double-horned' [Alexander the Great]), [22] Yūnūs (Jonah), [23] Ilyās (Elijah), [24] Alyasa' (Elias), [25] Dhu'l-Kifl, [26] Ṭālūt (Goliath), [27] Dā'wūd (David), [28] Sulaymān (Solomon), [29] Zakā'riyya (Zachariah), [30] Yaḥyā (John [the Baptist]), [31] T-W-R-KH (= Turkh = Turk?), [32] Mattā (Matthew), [33] Irmīyā (Jeremiah) [34] Hayaqoq (Habbakuk), [35] Danyāl (Daniel) [36] 'Azīz ('Mighty'), [37] 'Īsā (Jesus), [38] Shimūn (Simon [Peter]), [39] Jirjīs (St. George), [40] the Disciples [of Jesus] (al-ḥawariyyīn), [41] the (secondary) 'Followers' [of Jesus] (al-Atbā'), [42] Khālid [b Sinān al-'Absī]), [43] Ḥanẓalah [ibn Ṣafwān] and [44] (the sage) Luqmān. (Majlisī, Biḥār² 11:59).

This prophetological supplication is among very many devotional pieces which are attributed to pre-Islamic figures in Shī'ī literature. It lists over 40 messengers and related figures, in a loose and sometimes eccentric chronological order, and perhaps suggests Islamic devotion to some Israelite and related prophets, largely unmentioned in the Qur'ān.

These apologetic and interpretive Islamo-biblical citations which translate and make the biblical Hebrew text meaningful for succeeding generations, are in that sense no more 'false' than Jewish or Christian pseudepigraphical writings, recreations and re-translations of biblical texts. Islamic works in this category were considered important enough to be ascribed to such past sages and prophet figures as Adam, Enoch, Hermes, Moses, Solomon, Daniel, Jesus and others. Other examples include a proto-qur'anic Munājāt Mūsā ('Supplications of Moses'), Islamic recreations of the Zabūr of David sometimes reflecting the biblical Psalms (Schippers, 'Psalms' E-Q 4:314–18) and even an Islamic Tawrāt ('Torah') divided, like the Qur'ān, into sūrahs! These Islamo-biblical recreations with the many texts in Islamic sources ascribed to pre-Islamic scripture can be viewed as the fruits of a creative scriptural symbiosis among diverse 'people of the Book', and need not be dismissively or derisively ignored as a pseudo-biblical phenomenon.

Though genuine manuscripts representative of early Arabic Bible translations are few, Islamic pseudepigraphical texts and writings are numerous. Some Muslims claim to have rediscovered or creatively invented allegedly 'genuine' texts or portions of the Tawrāt (Pentateuch) of Moses, the Zabūr ('Psalter') of David, the original Injīl (Gospel) of Jesus as well as other books ascribed to pre-Islamic prophets. A modern example is the so-called 'Gospel of Barnabas'. This is a work of 222 chapters (200+ pages) ascribed to a Christian companion of Paul originally named Joses then Barnabas (fl. first century CE, Acts 4:36, chapters 11–15), but it is essentially a sixteenth-century Islamic-created Gospel harmony, extant in only a few sixteenth–seventeenth-century mss of Spanish and Italian Morisco (Crypto-Muslim) provenance. It has been frequently reprinted and translated in the Muslim world (Arabic, 1908; Urdu, 1916, etc.) from the 1907 English translation of Lonsdale and Laura Ragg, though without their critical introduction in which it was exposed as a medieval 'forgery'. Muhammad is mentioned by name in the 'Gospel of Barnabas' and many Muslims today view this as the only remaining authentic Gospel despite the fact that western scholarship has for long remained unconvinced of its veracity (Ragg 1907; Sox 1984; Slomp http://www. chrislages.de/barnarom.htm). A massive literature now surrounds the debate over this and related issues of scriptural preservation, transmission, falsification and veracity. Abrahamic religionists have long accused each other of tampering with sacred writ and of misquoting established scripture to suit selfish or polemical purposes.

The Bible, Islamo-biblica and Isrā'īliyyāt ('Israelitica')

By the tenth to eleventh centuries CE many, though by no means, all Muslims came to regard the Bible as largely or wholly 'corrupted'. They repeated versions of a tradition banning qur'ānic-Islamic exposition through biblically related traditions known as Isrā'īliyyāt ('Israelitica'), and played down prophetic traditions which advocated the opposite. The Arabic plural isrā'īliyyāt 'Israelitica' is derived from the biblical and qur'ānic figure Israel, also known as Jacob, father of the twelve tribes (Gen. 32:28, 35:10; cf. Qur'ān 3:87, etc.). In use from the early Islamic centuries in Tafsīr (qur'ānic exegesis) and other oral and literary connections (Khoury 1972: 227ff.; EI² XI: 34a), the term is indicative of data and traditions thought to have been transmitted by or derived from the Jews or 'children of Israel' (banī Isrā'īl), although its uses in a multitude of ancient and modern Islamic sources presuppose that Isrā'īliyyāt material can indicate a very wide range of Abrahamic-Israelite, biblical and associated scripture and tradition. Early on, this type of material was communicated by such Muslim believers and converts as 'Abd-Allāh ibn 'Abbās, the Father of Islamic Tafsīr, Rabbi of the Arabs and cousin of the Prophet (d. c.687), and Abū 'Abd Allāh Wahb ibn Munabbih (d. c.728) perhaps the most important Muslim transmitter of Isrā'īliyyāt.

The term Isrā'īliyyāt initially had purely descriptive and neutral connotations (Adang 1996: 9, n. 49), but in some circles in later centuries it came to be used pejoratively though this negative use of Isrā'īliyyāt was not and never has been adopted universally in the Muslim world. Isrā'īliyyāt can indicate the biblical heritage and related Islamo-biblical materials transmitted in a wide range of Islamic literatures often by Jewish converts to Islam. A wide-ranging trajectory of 20 or more key categories of Islamic literatures rich in Isrā'īliyyāt traditions containing biblical and/or Islamo-biblical materials could today be confidently set down (cf. Lambden 2002 and forthcoming). This massive, symbiotic Islamic heritage bears eloquent testimony to the creative Islamic engagement, occasional remythologization and exegesis-eisegesis of Abrahamic and related scripture and tradition.

Without attempting a full overview, Islamic literatures containing Isrā'īliyyāt would include Islamic pseudepigraphical texts and biblically ascribed writings of the kind mentioned below (Sadan 1986). Significant in this respect are numerous *Tafsīr* (exegetical) and related literatures of Qur'ān commentary along with works of exegesis-eisegesis and hermeneutics (Newby 1979). In addition to *Ḥadīth* compendia of prophetic and other authoritative traditions where multitudes of Isrā'iliyyāt-related texts can be found, such materials are likewise fundamental to many *Qiṣaṣ al-anbiyā'* (Stories of the Prophets) and related literatures such as works of *Mubtadā'* ('Beginnings'), *Awā'il* ('Originations') and *Mu'ammarūn* (the 'Long-Lived'). Works associated with *Nubuwwa* ('Prophetology') such as the *Dalā'il al-nubuwwa* ('Proofs of Prophethood') texts as well as volumes of Islamic *Sīrāh* ('Biography') and *Tārīkh* (History writing) often exhibit considerable biblical influence and the presence of Islamo-biblica or modes of Isrā'īliyyāt. Sufi and related literatures such as Persian poetry also contain thousands of biblical, Islamo-biblical and Isrā'ilīyyāt motifs, texts and narratives as do Islamic *adab* (*belles lettres*) works, Wisdom literatures and those associated with religious disputation, dialogue and world religions. Finally, but not exhaustively, mention should be made of Islamic devotional literatures and works representative of messianism and apocalyptic eschatology which often contain a good deal that is biblically related or Isrā'īliyyāt informed.

Writings and literary remnants of emergent Islam and diverse orthodox-heterodox factions which proliferated throughout Islamic history, including Imamī Shī'īsm (Wasserstrom, bib. Modarressi 2003), various *ghulāt* ('extremist') groups, Zaydism and (proto-)Ismā'īlism, are replete with echoes of biblical and Isrā'īliyyāt traditions. So too are many of the little-studied literatures representative of the *'ulūm al-ghayb* (Islamic esoterica), including *Jafr* (gematric divination), *Sihr* (varieties of Magic), *Kimiyā'* (Alchemy) and dream-vision interpretation.

Only a few specific further examples of Islamo-biblica or Isrā'īliyyāt can be spelled out here which illustrate that widespread Muslim notions of *taḥrīf* failed to eclipse the wonderfully creative Islamic reaffirmation of the pre-Islamic scriptural heritage of humankind. Biblical and extra-biblically generated ideas, texts and motifs remained very much alive in the Islamic intertextual universe of discourse. A probable example of Isrā'īliyyāt is found in the occurrence of the Arabic loan word هورقليا H-W-R-Q-L-Y-A (pointing uncertain as *hurqalyā* or *havaqalyā*) in the *Ḥikmat al-ishrāq* of Shihāb al-Dīn Yaḥyā Suhrawardī (d. 1191) when understood as originating from a somewhat garbled Arabic rendering of the Hebrew הָרָקִיעַ ha-raqī'a (= AV 'the firmament', Gen. 1:5–7, etc.), interpreted as a cosmogonic and mystical interworld. Another Shī'ī example would be the Arabic 'I am' type logion as translating ἐγώ εἰμι ... ἡ ἀλήθεια ('I am the Truth') allegedly uttered by Imam 'Alī (d. 40/661) in his arcane and possibly *ghuluww* ('extremist') *Khuṭba al-ṭutunjiyya* ('Sermon of the Gulf') (cited al-Bursī, *Mashariq*: 176).

Conclusion

This survey of the relatioinship between Islam and the Bible has in no way been motivated by an orientalist-type attempt to source-critically account for Islamic doctrines and perspectives by dismissively registering their biblical roots or origins. The Islamic assimilation of the Bible in no way devalues the creative genius of Islam and its founder prophet. Sadly, the post-qur'ānic assertion of the total loss or textual falsification of the Jewish and Christian Bible is without doubt the greatest barrier to dialogue and mutual appreciation among Abrahamic religionists or 'peoples of the Book'. Along with those Safavid works relating to biblical texts which have been mentioned above, the two mid-nineteenth-century volumes comprising *The Mohomedan Commentary on the Holy Bible* (1862, 1865) by the Indian Muslim modernist Sir Sayyid Aḥmad Khān (d. 1898) remain virtually unique. Modern Muslim engagement with the Bible and biblical scholarship largely awaits balanced and unprejudiced realization. This is hardly surprising given the orientalist venom which pollutes much pre-modern evangelical and missionary discourse and the volume of triumphalist, ill-informed, sometimes anti-Semitic and anti-biblical-Isrā'īliyyāt propaganda which blackens the face of Islam. Hopefully the rise of a globally less prejudiced scholarship and an increasing awareness of the religious interdependence of all humanity, will remain fundamental and ultimately succeed.

References

Adang, C. (1996). *Muslim Writers on Judaism and the Hebrew Bible from Ibn Rabban to Ibn Hazm*. Leiden: E. J. Brill.

Addas, Claude (2000). *The Voyage of No Return*, trans. D. Streight. Cambridge: Islamic Texts Society.

al-Aḥsā'ī, Shaykh Ahmad (no date). *al-Kashkul*, 2 vols. Unpublished manuscript.

al-'Alawī, Sayyid Aḥmad b. Zayn al-'Ābidīn ['Āmilī, Iṣfahānī] (1995). Misqal = Miṣqāl-i ṣafā dār tajliyya-yi ā'īnah-yi ḥaqq-namā ed. Najī Iṣfāhānī, Qumm: 1415/1373 Sh.

Alger, William (1883). *The Poetry of the Orient*. Boston: Roberts Brothers.

'Alī b. Abī Ṭālib (1987). *Kitāb al-jafr al-jāmi' wa al-nūr al-lawāmi'*. Beirut: Dār al-Maktaba al-Tarbiyya.

'Alī b. Abī Ṭālib (1978). al-Khuṭbah al-ṭutunjijyyah [taṭanjiyyah] ('The Sermon of the Gulf') in al-Bursī, *Mashāriq anwār al-yaqīn*. . . . Beirut: Dār al-Andalus, pp. 168–71.

al-Ālūsī, Shihāb al-Dīn Abū al-Thanā' (1870). Rūḥ al-ma'ānī fī tafsīr al-qur'ān al-'aẓīm. Cairo: al-Maṭba'at al-Amīrah. CD-ROM rep.

Andrae, Tor (1987). *In the Garden of Myrtles: Studies in Early Islamic Mysticism*, trans. Birgitta Sharpe. Albany, NY: State University of New York Press.

Asín Palacios, Miguel (1919). Logia = 'Logia et Agrapha Domini Jesu apud moslemicos scriptores, asceticos praesertim, usitata', *Patrologia Orientalis* XIII(iii): 335–431; see also XIX(iv) (1926): 531–624.

Ayoub, Mahmud (1976). 'Towards an Islamic Christology: An Image of Jesus in Early Shī'ī Muslim Literature', *MW* 66: 163–87.

Brinner, William M. (1986). 'An Islamic Decalogue', in William M. Brinner and S. D. Ricks (eds), *Studies in Islamic and Judaic Traditions*. Atlanta, GA: Scholars Press, pp. 67–84.

al-Bukhārī, Abī 'Abd-Allāh Muhammad ibn Ismā'īl. *Kitāb al-tafsīr* (on Q. 48:8) within his Ṣaḥīḥ ('Sound' Ḥadīth compilation), ed. Muhammad Nizar Tamīm and Haytham Nizar Tamīm. Beirut: Dār al-Arkam ibn Abī al-Arkam.

al-Bursī, Rajab, al-Ḥāfiẓ (1978). Mashariq = *Mashāriq anwār al-yaqīn fī asrār Amīr al-Mu'minīn*. Beirut: Dār al-Andalus.

Casey. M. (1998). *Aramaic Sources of Mark's Gospel*. Cambridge: Cambridge University Press.

Casey. M. (2002). *An Aramaic Approach to Q, Sources for the Gospels of Matthew and Luke*. Cambridge: Cambridge University Press.

Déroche, François (2001–5). 'Manuscripts of the Qurān', in Jane Dammen McAuliffe et al. (eds), *Encyclopedia of the Qur'ān*, vol. 3. Leiden: Brill, pp. 253–75.

DiTommaso, Lorenzo (2001). *A Bibliography of Pseudepigrapha Research 1850–1999* (= *Journal for the Study of the Pseudepigrapha*, supplement series 39). Sheffield: Sheffield Academic Press.

Ehrman, Bart D. (1993). *The Orthodox Corruption of Scripture: The Effect of Early Christological Controversies on the Text of the New Testament*. Oxford: Oxford University Press.

EI² = ([1960] 2003). *Encyclopedia of Islam*, new edn, ed. H. A. R. Gibb et al.; WebCD, 2003. Leiden: E. J. Brill.

E.Ir. (1982). *Encyclopedia Iranica*, ed. Ehsan Yarshater. Costa Mesa, CA: Mazda Publishers.

Fischel, W. J. (1958). 'Ibn Khaldun on the Bible, Judaism and the Jews', in S. Lowinger et al. (eds), *Ignace Goldziher Memorial Volume*. Budapest, Jerusalem: no publisher, pp. 147–71.

Fischel, W. J. (1967). *Ibn Khaldūn in Egypt, His Public Functions and His Historical Research, 1382–1406: A Study in Islamic Historiography*. Berkeley, CA: University of California Press.

Fodor, A. (1974). 'Malhamat Daniyal', in G. Kaldy-Nagy (ed.), *The Muslim East, Studies in Honour of Julius Germanus*. Budapest: Loránd Eötvös University, pp. 85–133, plus 26 pages of reproduction of the anonymous Najaf (n.d.) edn of Malḥamat Danīyal.

Frolov, Dmitry (2002). 'The Problem of the "Seven Long" Surahs', in S. Leder et al. (eds), *Studies in Arabic and Islam: Proceedings of the 19th Congress, Union Européenne des Arabisants et Islamisants, Halle 1998* (= Orientalia Louvaniensia Analecta 108). Paris-Sterling, VA: Uitgeveru Peeters, pp. 193–203.

Goldziher, I. (1850–1921). 'Über muhammadanische Polemik gegen Ahl al-kitāb' *ZDMG* 32: 341–87.

Goldziher, I. ([1888–90] 1967–71) [MS] *Muhammedanische Studien*, 2 vols. Halle: Max Niemayer, 1888–90. Trans. S. M. Stern and C. R. Barber as *Muslim Studies*, 2 vols. London: George Allen and Unwin.

Goldziher, I. (1902). 'Mélanges judae-arabes: isra'iliyyāt', *REJ* XLIV: 63–6.

Harding, James and Loveday, Alexander (1999). 'Dating the Testament of Solomon' = http://www.st-andrews.ac.uk/~www_sd/date_tsol.html

Hary, Benjamin H., Hayes, John L. and Astren, Fred (eds) (2000). *Judaism and Islam: Boundaries, Communication and Interaction: Essays in Honor of William M. Brinner*. Leiden: Brill.

Hengel, Martin (2002). *The Septuagint as Christian Scripture: Its Prehistory and the Problem of Its Canon*. Grand Rapids, MI: Baker Academic.

Herbert, Edward D. and Tov, Emanuel (2002). *The Bible as Book: The Hebrew Bible and the Judaean Desert Discoveries*. London: British Library and Oak Knoll Press.

Horne, Thomas H. ([1818] 1828). *An Introduction to the Critical Study and Knowledge of the Holy Scriptures*, 6th edn, vol. IV. London: A. & R. Spottiswoode.

Ibn al-'Arabī, Muḥyī al-Dīn (n.d., 1968 = Cairo edn 1911). *Futuhat = al-Futūḥāt al-Makkiyya*, 4 vols. Beirut: Dār Ṣādir.

Ibn al-'Arabī, Muḥyī al-Dīn (n.d.). *Rasā'il Ibn al-'Arabī*, ed. Affifi, Abul Ela, reprint. Beirut: Dār Ihyā al-turuth al-'arabī.

Ibn Bābūya [Bābawayh], Abū Ja'far Muhammad. b. 'Alī, [al-Ṣadūq] (n.d.). *Tawḥīd = Kitāb al-tawḥīd*. Beirut: Dar al-Ma'rifa.

Ibn Isḥāq, Muhammad ['Abd al-Malik ibn Hishām] (1858–60). *Sira = Sīrat Rasūl Allah*, ed. Ferdinand Wüstenfeld (*Das Leben Muhammeds*), 2 vols. Göttingen: Dieterichsche Universitäts-Buchhandlung. Trans. Alfred Guillaume as *The Life of Muhammad: A Translation of Ibn Ishaq's Sirat Rasul Allah*. Oxford: Oxford University Press, 1955.

Ibn Khaldūn ([1958] 1986). *The Muqaddimah*. Trans. Franz Rosenthal, 3 vols. London: Routledge & Kegan Paul.

Ibn Khaldūn (2004). *al-Muqaddimah*. Beirut: Dār al-Kitāb al-Lubnānī.

Ibn Qutayba, 'Abd-Allāh ibn Muslim (1969). *Ma'arif = K. al-ma'ārif*, ed. Thawat Ukāsha. Cairo: Dār al-ma'arif.

Jāmī, 'Abd al-Raḥman (1977). *Naqd = Naqd al-nuṣūṣ fī sharḥ naqsh al-fuṣūṣ*, ed. W. C. Chittick. Tehran: Imp. Iranian Academy of Philosophy.

Jeffery, Arthur ([1938] 1977). *The Foreign Vocabulary of the Koran*. Lahore: al-Biruni.

al-Jīlī, 'Abd al-Karīm ibn Ibrāhīm ([1375] 1956). *Insan = al-Insān al-kāmil fī ma'rifat al-awākhir wa'l-awā'il*, 2 vols in 1. Cairo: Muṣṭāfa al-Bābī al-Ḥalabī.

al-Kaf'āmī, Taqī al-Dīn ([1414] 1994). *Miṣbah = al-Misbāḥ*. Beirut: al-A'lamī Library.

al-Kairānawī, Raḥmat-Allāh ibn Khalīl al-Raḥmān al-'Uthmānī al-Hindī ([1410] 1989). *Izhar = Iẓhār al-ḥaqq . . .* ('The Demonstration of the Truth'), 4 vols, ed. Muhammad Aḥmad Muhammad 'Abd al-Qadir Khalīl Malkāwī, Kingdom of Saudi Arabia.

al-Kairānawī, Raḥmat-Allāh ibn Khalīl al-Raḥmān al-Uthmānī al-Hindī (2003). Izhar-ul-haq (*Basic Teachings*), 3 vols in 1. London: Ta-Ha Publishers.

Kannaday, W. C. (2004). *Apologetic Discourse and the Scribal Tradition: Evidence of the Influence of Apologetic Interests on the Text of the Canonical Gospels*. Leiden: Brill.

Khalidi, Tarif (ed. and trans.) (2001). *The Muslim Jesus: Sayings and Stories in Islamic Literature*. Cambridge, MA: Harvard University Press.

Khātūnābādī, Muhammad Bāqir ibn Ismā'īl Ḥusaynī ([1375] 1996). *Tarjāmīh-yi anājil-i arba'ah*, ed. Rasūl Jā'faryān (= Persian Literature and Linguistics 10). Tehran: Nuqṭih Press.

Khoury, R. G. (2000). 'Wahb b. Munabbih, Abū 'Abd Allāh'. *EI²*, vol. XI: 34a–35b.

Khoury, R. G. (1972). *Wahb b. Munabbih*, vol. 1: *Der Heidelberger Papyrus PSR Heid Arab 23*, Leben und Werkes Dichters, 2 vols. Wiesbaden: O Harrassowitz.

Kirmānī, Ḥajjī Mīrzā Muhammad Karīm Khān (n.d.). *Nusrat = Kitab. Nuṣrat al-dīn*. Kirmān: Sa'ādat.

Kister, M. J. (1972). 'Ḥaddithū 'an banī isra'ila we-la haraja: A Study of an Early Tradition', *IOS* 2: 215–39.

Kohlberg, Etan (1992). *A Medieval Muslim Scholar at Work: Ibn Tāwūs and His Library*. (Islamic Philosophy, Theology and Science: Texts and Studies 12). Leiden: E. J. Brill.

Kulīnī [= Kulaynī], Abū Ja'far Muhammad ([1405] 1985). *al-Uṣṣūl min al Kāfī*, vols 1 and 2, ed. A. A. Ghafārī. Beirut: Dār al Aḍwā.

Kulīnī [= Kulaynī], Abū Ja'far Muhammad ([1405] 1961). *al Furū' min al-Kāfi*, vols 3 and 7, ed. A. A. Ghafārī. Beirut: Dār al Aḍwā.

Lambden, Stephen N. (2002). 'Some Aspects of Isrā'īliyyāt and the Emergence of the Bābī-Bahā'ī Interpretation of the Bible', unpublished PhD thesis, University of Newcastle upon Tyne.

Lambden, Stephen N. (forthcoming). *Islamo-Biblica: Some Aspects of the Isrā'īliyyāt (Israelitica) Phenomenon and the Islamo-Biblical Tradition*. Oxford: OneWorld.

Lazarus-Yafeh, Hava (1992). *Intertwined Worlds: Medieval Islam and Bible Criticism*. Princeton, NJ: Princeton University Press.

Leder, S. et al. (eds) (2002). *Studies in Arabic and Islam: Proceedings of the 19th Congress, Union Européenne des Arabisants et Islamisants, Halle 1998* (= Orientalia Louvaniensia Analecta 108). Paris-Sterling, VA: Uitgeveru Peeters.

Lee, Samuel (1824). *Controversial Tracts on Christianity and Mohammedanism by the Late Rev. Henry Martyn, B.D. . . . and Some of the Most Eminent Writers of Persia Translated and Explained*. Cambridge: J. Smith.

Leehmuis, Frederick (2001–5). 'Codices of the Qurān', in Jane Dammen McAuliffe et al. (eds), *Encyclopedia of the Qur'ān*, vol. 1. Leiden: Brill, pp. 347–51.

Lewinstein, Keith (2001–5). 'Commandments', in Jane Dammen McAuliffe et al. (eds), *Encyclopedia of the Qur'ān*, vol. 1. Leiden: Brill, pp. 365–7.

Lowry, S. (1977). *The Principles of Samaritan Bible Exegesis*. Leiden: Brill.

Majlisī, Muhammad Bāqir ([1376–94] 1956–74 and [1403] 1983). *Bihar²* = *Biḥār al-anwār*, 2nd edn, 110 vols. Beirut: Dār al-Iḥyāʾ al-Turāth al-ʿArabī.

McAuliffe, Jane Dammen (1998). 'Assessing the Isrāʾīliyyāt: An Exegetical Conundrum', in S. Leder et al. (eds), (2002) *Studies in Arabic and Islam, Proceedings of the 19th Congress, Union Européenne des Arabisants et Islamisants, Halle 1998* (= Orientalia Louvaniensia Analecta 108). Paris-Sterling, VA: Uitgeveru Peeters, pp. 345–69.

McAuliffe, Jane Dammen et al. (eds) (2001–5). (= E-Q) *Encyclopedia of the Qur'ān*, vols 1–5. Leiden: Brill.

McAuliffe, Jane Dammen et al. (eds) (2003). *With Reverence for the Word: Medieval Scriptural Exegesis in Judaism, Christianity, and Islam*. Oxford: Oxford University Press.

Modarressi, Hossein (2003) *Tradition and Survival: A Bibliographical Survey of Early Shīʿite Literature*, vol. 1. Oxford: Oneworld.

Montgomery Watt, W. (1990). *Muslim-Christian Encounters: Perceptions and Misperceptions*. London: Routledge.

Muqātil ibn Sulaymān (1979–88). *Tafsīr Muqātil b. Sulaymān*, ed. ʿAbd Allāh Maḥmud Shaiḥata, 4 + 1 vols. Cairo: no publisher.

Newby, Gordon (1979). 'Tafsīr Isrāʾīliyyāt', *Journal of the American Academy of Religion* (Thematic Issue S) 47: 694–5.

Petersen, W. L. (ed.) (1989). *Gospel Traditions in the Second Century: Origins, Recensions, Text and Transmission*. Notre Dame, IN: University of Notre Dame Press.

Petersen, W. L. (2001). 'The Diatessaron of Tatian', in Bart D. Ehrman and Michael W. Holmes (eds), *The Text of the New Testament in Contemporary Research: Essays on the Status Quaestionis*. Eugene, OR: Wipf and Stock Publishers, pp. 77–96.

Pfander, Carl Gottlieb (1866, 1867). *Mizan Ul Haqq; or Balance of Truth*, trans. R. H. Weakley London: Church Missionary House.

Pfander, Carl Gottlieb (1874, 1888). *Kitāb Mīzān al-ḥaqq*. Leipzig: F. A. Brockhaus.

Powell, Ann Avril (1976). 'Maulānā Rahmat Allāh Kairānawī and Muslim-Christian Controversy in India in the mid 19th Century', *JRAS* 20: 42–63.

Puin, Gerd R. (1996). 'Observations on Early Quran Manuscripts in Sanʿāʾ', in Stefan Wild (ed.), *The Qur'an as Text*. Leiden: E. J. Brill, pp. 107–12.

Rabin, Chaim ([1957] 2001). 'Islam and the Qumran Sect', *Qumran Studies* (= Scripta Judaica 2). New York: Oxford University Press, pp. 112–30.

Ragg, Lonsdale and Ragg, Laura (eds and trans.) (1907). *The Gospel of Barnabas*. Oxford: Clarendon Press.

Reeves, John. C. (ed.) (1994). *Tracing the Threads: Studies in the Vitality of Jewish Pseudepigrapha*. Atlanta, GA: Scholars Press.

Reeves, John. C. (ed.) (2004). *Bible and Quran: Essays in Scriptural Intertextuality*. Leiden: Brill Academic.

Rosenthal, F. (1962). 'The Influence of the Biblical Tradition on Muslim Historiography', in B. Lewis (ed.), *Historians of the Middle East*. pp. 33–45.

Rosenthal, F. (1968). *A History of Muslim Historiography*, rev. 2nd edn. Leiden: Brill.

Rosenthal, F. (1989). 'General Introduction', in al-Ṭabarī, Muhammad b. Jarīr, English trans. = *The History of al-Ṭabarī*, trans. various, general ed. E. Yarshater, vol. 1. Albany, NY: State University of New York Press, pp. 5–154.

Sadan, J. (1986). 'Some Literary Problems Concerning Judaism and Jewry in Medieval Arabic Sources', in Moshe Sharon (ed.), *Studies in Islamic History and Civilization in Honour of Professor David Ayalon*. Jerusalem: Cana, pp. 353–94.

Ṣadr al-Dīn al-Shīrāzī (= Mullā Ṣadrā) ([1370Sh.] 1992). *Sh.-Kafi. = Sharḥ uṣūl al-kāfī*, 3 vols. Teheran: Intishārāt 'Ilmī va Farhang.

Schippers, Arie (2004). 'Psalms', in Jane Dammen McAuliffe et al. (eds), *Encyclopedia of the Qur'ān*, vol. 4. Leiden: Brill, pp. 314–18.

Schirrmacher, Christine (1992). *Mit den Waffen des Gegners: christlich-muslimische Kontroversen im 19. und 20. Jahrhundert, dargestellt am Beispiel der Auseinandersetzung um Karl Gottlieb Pfanders 'Mizân al-ḥaqq' und Raḥmatullâh ibn H̲alîl al-'Uṯmânî al-Kairânawîs 'Iẓhâr al-ḥaqq' und der Diskussion über das Barnabasevangelium* (= Islamkundliche Untersuchungen, Band 162). Berlin: Klaus Schwartz Verlag.

al-Shahrastānī, Muhammad ibn 'Abd al-Karīm (1997) *Mafatih = Mafātīḥ al-asrār wa maṣābīḥ al-abrār* (Keys of the Mysteries and Lamps of the Pious). ed. Muhammad 'Alī Adharshab, Tehran: Iḥyā-yi Kitāb, Daftar-i Nashr-i Miras-i Maktūb.

Sharon, Moshe (ed.) (1986). *Studies in Islamic History and Civilization in Honour of Professor David Ayalon*. Jerusalem: Cana.

Slomp, Jan (1997) 'The "Gospel of Barnabas" in recent research', http://www.chrislages.de/barnarom.htm

Sox, David (1984). *The Gospel of Barnabas*. London: George Allen & Unwin.

Stone, Michael E. and Bergen, Theodore A. (eds) (1998). *Biblical Figures outside the Bible*. Harrisburg, PA: Trinity Press International.

al-Ṭabarī, Muhammad b. Jarīr (1985–98). English trans. = *The History of al-Ṭabarī*, trans. various, general ed. E. Yarshater, 37 + 1 vols. Albany, NY: State University of New York Press.

al-Ṭabarī, Muhammad b. Jarīr ([1408] 1988). *Tarikh = Ta'rīkh al-rusul wa'l-mulūk*, 15 vols. Dār al-Fikr.

al-Ṭabarsī, Abū 'Alī ([1403] 1983). Ihtijaj = *al-Iḥtijāj*. 2 vols in 1. Beirut: Mu'assat al-A'lamī.

Thomas, David (1988). 'Two Muslim Christian Debates from the Early Shī'ite Tradition', *JSS* 38: 53–80.

Tov, Emanuel (2001). *Textual Criticism of the Hebrew Bible*, 2nd edn. Minneapolis, MN: Fortress Press; Maastricht: Van Gorcum.

Tov, Emanuel (2002). 'The Biblical Texts from the Judaean Desert: An Overview and Analysis of the Published Texts', in Edward D. Herbert and Emanuel Tov, *The Bible as Book: The Hebrew Bible and the Judaean Desert Discoveries*. London: British Library and Oak Knoll Press, pp. 139–66.

Vajda, G. (1981). 'De quelques empreints d'origine juive dans le ḥadīth Shi'ite', in *Studies in Judaism and Islam*. Presented to D. Goitein (eds.), pp. 45–53.

Wild, Stefan (ed.) (1996). *The Qur'an as Text*. Leiden: E. J. Brill.

CHAPTER 10
Asia

Choan-Seng Song

'The history of Christianity in Asia during the nineteenth century and much of the twentieth was dominated by the growth of missionary activity' (McManners 1990: 488). But one must remember that Christianity in Asia is as old as Christianity itself. 'It is too often forgotten that the faith moved across Asia as early as it moved into Europe . . . It was a Christianity that has remained for centuries unashamedly Asian' (Moffett 1992: xiii). That 'Christianity remained for centuries unashamedly Asian' may be true for West Asia in the early centuries, but is an overstatement as far as East Asia, South Asia and South-east Asia are concerned. In the past two centuries in particular, development of Christianity in these regions of Asia has been largely shaped by the expansion of the churches in Europe and North America, by missionary efforts 'at one extreme . . . to save souls . . . producing conversions . . . [and] at the other extreme . . . aiming at Christianization of society as a whole through humanitarian ideas' (McManners 1990: 488).

The fact of the matter is that these regions of Asia have not been 'Christianized'. To this day Christians in these parts of Asia have remained less than 5 per cent of the total population of Asia. In spite of the fact that Christianity is a minority religion in East Asia, South Asia and South-east Asia, the extremes mentioned above still prevail today in this first decade of the twenty-first century. The Bible for most churches and Christians in these three regions of Asia continues to be a sacred book with the divine imprint, not to be contaminated by Asian cultures alien to Christianity.

Things have changed dramatically in recent years. Freed from Western missionary Christianity and the theology of mission it represented, the increasing numbers of indigenous Christians and theologians in these regions of Asia have taken steps to engage the Bible with local cultures. Interaction between the Bible and culture in this way is bringing about important changes in the understanding both of the Bible and of cultures quite unrelated to it. One may dismiss such efforts as too little too late, but there is no doubt that a very different 'Christian era' is beginning to dawn in these parts of Asia, different both from centuries-old theological traditions in the West, and from the self-contained and self-sufficient Christian ethos deeply rooted in the mindset of those Christians who live a double life as members of the Christian Church and as members of the society in which they were born.

The purpose of this chapter is to show how some of these theological efforts are slowly but steadily making inroads into the religious worlds of South Asia, South-east Asia and East Asia, making it possible for people to engage one another in matters of life and faith on Asian terms and not on terms prescribed by the faith, theology and Christian ethos developed in the West. These relatively recent theological developments are as diverse and complex as the peoples and cultures of those parts of Asia. And how diverse and complex they are! Asia is the largest continent in the world, both in area and in population. As many as three-fifths of the world's population live there. How could cultures, religions and ways of life, lived and practised in this vast continent of the planet Earth, not be diverse and complex? In South Asia alone we are talking about a third of the population of Asia and a fifth of all the people in the world; in East Asia about 43 per cent of the population of Asia and a quarter of all people in the world; and in South-east Asia as many as 400 million people, that is, 14 per cent of all Asians. One cannot but wonder whether those Christians both in the West and in Asia itself have realized this immense diversity and enormous complexity of the world they have tried to evangelize and Christianize.

In the midst of such great diversity and complexity, some major theological trends have emerged to chart a new course for Christianity in parts of East Asia including Hong Kong, Taiwan, China, Korea and Japan, in the nations of South-east Asia including Indonesia, Malaysia and the Philippines, and among the nations of South Asia particularly India and Sri Lanka. It is these trends that this article will try to highlight. The nations just mentioned will not be treated separately. Instead, they will be discussed under each major trend in order to show what has been happening there and how new theological directions are emerging in East Asia, South Asia and South-east Asia as a whole.

A Bible Freed from Doctrinal Premises

Almost from the beginning of its history the Christian Church has revered the Bible as God's revealed word, containing the categorical will and final purpose of God for human salvation and destiny. The birth of 'Christian' Europe gave credibility to Christianity's claim to a 'unique' relationship with God and God's saving activity in the world. The Bible was 'de-cultured', unhinged from its cultural matrix among the people of ancient Israel and the cultural world of Jesus' life and ministry. Then it was 'de-historicized', detached from the historical particularities of Christian believers in the West, and when this happened, inevitably the faith, theology and ethos represented by Christianity claimed universal validity and application. What was true in the West was equally true in Asia; what was regarded as valid in matters of faith and morals in the Western world had to be equally valid in the world of Asia. What has emerged is Christian centrism, not only subsuming Judaism under its doctrinal premises but rejecting other cultures, religions, even ways of life, as incompatible with Christianity. To this day

Christianity in Asia is still perceived by the majority of people to be a Western religion foreign to Asian soil. Basically, it has to do with the Bible, especially how the Bible is used as a doctrinal blue-print for Christians and churches. This approach to the Bible, with the doctrinal premises that have prevailed in the West for centuries, has underlain and still underlies the faith and theology of the majority of Christians in East Asia, South Asia and South-east Asia.

But a very different approach has emerged in recent years, and most prominent in the new effort to free the Bible from traditional doctrinal premises were Asian women. The 'Voices' from the workshop held in Seoul, Korea in 1990 declared that:

> involvement in serious Bible study happens everywhere . . . and the trend is very strong here among Asian women doing theology from our own context. We see our context basically as a double structure – one of women and the other of certain nationalities in the third world structure . . . The biblical passages were written, inspired by the Holy Spirit, in a certain context to give readers meaning and encouragement in the situations they were facing. Their purpose is for readers to be uplifted, and wisdom in life to be cultivated. (*Women of Courage* 1992)

Instead of beginning with 'God who Acts' and 'Christ and Salvation History', for example, staple Western theological norms, the 'contextual hermeneutical methods' (ibid.) have liberated theological efforts in Asia from the grip of Western theological premises and enabled not only women but men in diverse and complex situations of Asia to interact with biblical messages and draw implications for their life and faith.

In India, 'the contextual hermeneutical methods' give rise to 'two distinct questions among other questions: (1) the sociological question: to what extent is the biblical narrative intelligible in terms of class and class struggle? (2) the hermeneutical question: how far does one's class culture determine one's reading of the biblical text?' (Soares-Prabhu 1991: 148). These questions throw doubt on the legitimacy of the interpretation of the Bible solely in reference to the Western social, religious and cultural backgrounds in a country such as India, a country entirely different from the West socially, religiously and culturally. Thus, 'dialogue with Neo-Hindu religious and cultural movements' prompts theology in India to wrestle with 'the anthropological basis of national politics but also . . . the exploration of an Indian theology of Christ, church, and Christian mission' (Thomas 1994: 160).

India is defined by the age-old caste system that has divided people socially, religiously and culturally strictly on the basis of their birth, creating a majority of people who are economically poor and oppressed as the untouchables. Reading the Bible from the predicaments of the untouchables makes irrelevant the distinction between the Christians who are privileged to God's salvation and the Hindus who are excluded from such privilege. It relates them at once to the poor and the oppressed who, Jesus said, belong to the kingdom of God.

'The contextual hermeneutical methods' also have far-reaching implications for who Jesus is and what he means for people in Asia today. Essentially, it is the question of what constitutes 'the centre of the Gospel'. The question is particularly acute for some Christians in Korea in the days when they sided with the socially, politically and economically oppressed people (*minjung* in Korean) against the military dictatorship.

Because we have been enslaved by the Christology of Kerygma even when we read the synoptics, we focused our attention on Jesus as the Christ and considered him to be the center of the Gospel . . . However, as we began to read the synoptics again with more skeptical eyes, the features of Jesus turned out to be quite different. (Byung Mu Ahn 1993: 167)

'Enslaved' is a strong word here, but it describes in a pointed way how Christianity in Asia has been subjected to 'enslavement' by Western Christianity. The enslavement is especially severe and intense in Christology. Images of Jesus as 'the Son of God, the Messiah, the pre-existent Being, the exalted Christ sitting on the throne and the coming Christ who will be the Judge on the last day' (ibid.: 167) are firmly implanted in the faith and theology of Christian churches in Asia. In the place of these images of Christ, a very different picture of Jesus emerges as people (minjung) with their han (unrequited injustice that brings about suffering) are identified as the centre of Jesus' gospel. This inevitably leads to the assertion that 'where there is Jesus, there is the Minjung. And where there is the Minjung, there is Jesus' (ibid.: 167). Freed from the church's doctrinal assertions about the person of Jesus Christ, this Jesus of people (minjung) can be construed from the Gospels.

Theological enterprise in China is a relatively recent undertaking. Throughout most of its history China has been a turbulent nation buffeted by social and political storms. Emerged from the Great Cultural Revolution (1966–76) that completely isolated China from the outside world for a decade, Christian theology has been making a belated entry into a very different theological world. Even to this day one has to read between the lines the theological writings from China. It seems evident that what theology encounters within the Christian church in China is a tenacious reluctance to deal with the Bible in relation to Chinese culture, be it traditional or socialist. There is, for instance, the insistence that 'we must remember that we are supported spiritually and materially by Christians in China. To be true to native sons and daughters is the glory of our theologians . . . We meet them where they are in ways they can accept. We do not impose on them anything they are not ready for' (Ting 1989: 182–3). But almost in the same breath it is also pointed out: 'Religious commitment and spirituality – whatever the theology – cannot really remain untouched by social and political stance, although in many cases the changes are just 'touches' and nothing dramatic. It is for theologians to be sensitive to these touches and to reflect them honestly and reverently in their work' (ibid.: 183). To be sensitive to those 'touches' and reflect them 'honestly and reverently' should enable theology in China to be freed from the doctrinal premises imposed on them from outside and to wrestle with the consequences of the relation between the Bible and Chinese culture. This leads to the following admission: 'some say that there is an internal development in the Bible . . . we have no reason to oppose such a view' (Wickeri and Wickeri 2002: 109). The Bible, in other words, is not the divine oracle set in stone once for all. This is a cautious admission, to be sure, but it suggests, however vaguely, the intention of theology in China to begin to appreciate the importance of Chinese culture for the Bible.

This trend of the Bible to be set free from traditional doctrinal premises is not an option for doing theology in Asia. On the contrary, it is a mandate: the Bible and culture must interact one with the other so that the biblical message may speak to the people of Asia. In short,

> our understanding of Asia must take into consideration the changing history and culture of the people. On the one hand, we cannot simply look back nostalgically to the past, as if Asia is always ancient, traditional, and unchanging. On the other hand, we must reclaim and reaffirm the national identity and cultural autonomy of the Asian people, so that we see ourselves through our own eyes. (Kwok Pui-lan 1995: 20)

How to see the Bible through Asian eyes and to reconstruct Christian theology is a tall order. But the work has begun.

The programme called 'Reading the Bible with New Eyes', promoted by the Christian Conference of Asia, adopted and implemented by the Presbyterian Church in Taiwan, is an earnest effort to read the Bible informed and challenged by a particular situation. It is based on the faith that 'God is still speaking today. God is speaking to us through the Bible today. The reader's life situations are closely related to the interpretation of the Bible. In the course of interpreting the Bible, the world of the reader and the world of the Bible interact with each other' (Chen Nan-Chou 2000: 13). The world of the reader includes, of course, his/her history, culture, society, even ideology. Reading the Bible is, then, a 'dialogue between the biblical texts and the realities of our life situations' (ibid.: 13). This means that biblical and theological developments in Taiwan have to become closely related to 'cultures in Taiwan, enabling the struggle of the people of Taiwan to be part of the world-wide struggle for human integrity' (Wang Hsien-Chih 1990: 88).

Bible, Culture and People

For most Christians in Asia the Bible not only contains the word of God, it *is* the word of God. It is God who speaks in the Bible, who makes God's will known to people, who tells them what is going to happen to them and to the world. Readers of the Bible are merely a passive audience. They are not to question the authority of the Bible because to question it would be to question the authority of God. This is still a widely held view about the Bible throughout the region. But things have begun to change. It is a fact that people play an active role in their daily lives, in the history of their nation, in their relation to God. It is people and their power that put an end to dictatorship and bring about democratization. The active involvement of the people in the history of their nation has made people realize they are 'subjects' of history rather than 'objects' of it. This active sense of history has deeply affected Christian theology in Asia with a new emphasis on 'people as the subjects of history', in, for instance, the theology of people in Korea called *minjung* theology.

History is of course not just what happens to people at a certain time in a certain place. Whether it is a personal history, the history of a family, a clan, a tribe or a nation, history is inseparably bound with culture. If people are subjects of history, they are also 'subjects of religious and cultural life' (Kim Yong Bok 1995: 23). People 'are cultural

actors . . . singers of songs, poets, painters and actors of dramas . . . the original cre-
ators and sustainers of cultures and religions' (ibid.: 30–1). The rediscovery of people
as subjects of history, culture and religion, the central thrust of people's theology
(*minjung* theology), is also the foundation on which theology in other Asian countries
is constructed. A typical example of such people's theology is what is called 'the theology of struggle' in the Philippines. It is the theology that

> works for justice not only from the pulpit or in words but also in solidarity with other men
> and women of goodwill engaged in a struggle to pave the way for more just and humane
> structures in society . . . through mass actions in the streets, through organizing farmers,
> fisherfolk, tribal Filipinos, youth and women in their communities and the laborers in the
> factories. (*Witness and Hope amid Struggle* 1991: 5)

It is this theology charged with people's power that drove out President Marcos in 1986.
The impact of such theology on how to read the Bible is profound. Reading the Bible
'is not complete without . . . bearing in one's mind and heart the socio-political [and
religious-cultural] realities of the Filipino people' (ibid.: 33).

Does not this also suggest that the Bible must be read in relation to the social-
political and religious cultural realities of the people who appeared on the stages of the
Bible? The Bible cannot be read behind their back. Theological efforts in Asia will be
more and more premised on the reading of the Bible informed and challenged by the
people in the ordinary walks of life both in the Bible and in Asia. Faith and theology
that emerge and develop from this basic biblical and theological premise, promises to
be very different from the faith and theology Asia inherited from the West which still
prevails in most churches in Asia today.

Theology in Asia has shifted its focus from the doctrine of God to the life of people
who play the dominant role in the history of their nation. If Korean *minjung* theology
exploited this people's theology to the full during the time when Korea was under dic-
tatorial rule, what is now known as *Dalit* theology in India has been developing it with
similar exciting results. The word *dalit* 'literally means "oppressed" . . . the untouchables, the so-called "*harijans*" of India' (Wilfred 1993: 79–80). 'Numbering
160 million, 19% of the population . . . along with "scheduled castes" and "scheduled
tribes," "other backward classes," and minority groups such as Muslims and Sikhs . . .
[they] constitute 85% of Indians' (Kim 2002: 5). This is a theology developed from the
liberation movements of the religiously, culturally and socially oppressed people against
the powers that have dominated them for centuries. It is emphasized that

> the people who fight for freedom and struggle for justice are the subjects of theology. It is
> they that call it into being . . . People are already theological, and are the doers of theol-
> ogy, interpreting the Divine to the world in terms of freedom and justice, and making it
> possible for the Divine to take hold of the Earth, and for the Reign of God to become a social
> reality. Professional theologians and experts may not manipulate people's experience; they
> may not pose as owners of theology. (Rayan 1993: 201)

Dalit theology, the people's theology, turns the traditional concept and practice of Christian theology upside down. When people, especially the oppressed such as the *Dalits* in

India, become the subjects of theology, not only its methodology, but its content will have to change. How they experience Jesus in the midst of their pain and suffering, how they perceive God to be in the light of the miserable fate imposed on them, and how they develop the community of men, women and children in their efforts to redress their suffering and build a new life with hope and future, will break down the walls of religions that have separated them and bring about inter-cultural and inter-religious communities.

What *dalits* are to India is what *burakumin* are to Japan. *Burakumin* in Japan are despised, like *eta* 'much filth':

> [Their] outcast status and social codes of untouchability were set during the medieval period, reflecting a complex network of economic, political and religious conditions. It was in the rigid stratification of society under the Tokugawa Shogunate, beginning in 1600 CE that the degraded outcast status of those practicing 'defiled' jobs [jobs that dealt with blood and death] was formally established. The lowest status of the outcasts were called the *Hinin*, or 'non-people', a heterogeneous group made up of beggars, prostitutes, entertainers, mediums, diviners, religious wanderers, executioners, tomb watchers, and fugitives. (Kuribayashi 1995: 90–1)

Implications for Christian theology with *burakumin* as its focus are very critical. The faith and theology that 'speak much about the Cross of Christ using "Jesus died for all" language,' are challenged as a 'false theology of the Cross' that hides the suffering of the *burakumin*. In the place of 'the false theology of the Cross' stands the theology of 'the crown of thorns', another striking example of how awareness of one's religious, cultural and social realities leads to a reinterpretation of the Bible and the construction of a theology dramatically different from what had been held before:

> It is the oppressed *Burakumin* themselves, and not the church theologians and biblical scholars in Japan, who have rightly recovered the radical meaning of Jesus' crown of thorns . . . when interpreted in the eyes of the Japanese outcasts, Jesus' crown of thorns has become a symbol representing, in an oppressive world, the Kingdom of freedom and justice to come . . . Recovered through the eyes of the *Burakumin*, the symbol of the crown of thorns confirms Christian faith as the faith in the liberating work of God for the outcasts in the world. (Kuribayashi 1995: 103)

In Taiwan, the discovery of people as subject of history and culture, especially politically, socially and culturally oppressed people, has led to the development of 'homeland theology'. What homeland theology 'seeks to do, inspired by biblical faith, is to strive towards the future of Taiwan and to build the identity of Taiwanese people on the foundation of faith' (Chen Nan-Chou 2001: 83). Identity here refers to people's political identity as a nation different from China. It also refers to their cultural identity as a people distinct from the people of China. Because of the political and ideological tension and conflict between Taiwan and China, the emphasis on the identity of the people of Taiwan inspires hope as well anticipates suffering. Homeland theology is to grow out of the hope the people of Taiwan long for and the suffering they undergo as they strive for their nationhood and for their place in the international community of nations and peoples.

Bible and Religions Illuminated by Life

In Asia, culture and religion are hardly distinguishable. Almost all cultural practices are fraught with religious meanings and almost all religious beliefs are expressed in cultural forms. What prevails in Asia is religious cultures in an almost infinite variety of forms, from ancestor rites to religious festivals to institutionalized rituals and practices. Such is the rich and complex world of religious cultures into which Christianity has entered.

Christianity has not, however, been able to deal with the critical issue of the relationship between Christianity and Asian religions. 'While it is encouraging that a number of churches are beginning to take note of this important fact, many still continue to focus purely on the numerical growth of the church, thus ignoring the harmony of Asian society' (*CCANews* 2002: 5). The emphasis on converting people of other faiths to Christianity continues to be the main preoccupation of the churches in Asia. Only recently has Christian theology begun to learn that to ignore the pluralistic religious cultures of Asia only contributes to its theological poverty. Theology has not been able, on the whole, to avail itself of the rich resources of Asian religious cultures. Christianity has not been able to shed its foreignness and has continued to maintain its aloofness from the rest of society. Even in the Philippines, which enjoys the dubious reputation of being the only Christian country in Asia, largely as a result of more than 200 years of Spanish rule, and in Confucian and Buddhist South Korea, where a quarter of the population are said to be Christian, initially as a consequence of the exodus of Christians from the Communist North during the Korean War of 1950–53, Christianity is still largely held at arm's length as an outsiders' religion.

But the religious conflicts that irrupted in January 1999 in the Moluccas, Indonesia, for example, gave the impetus to some communities in that country to change their attitude towards other religions and people of other faiths, particularly when it was realized that the conflicts were often instigated by 'the political elites who use religion as a means to achieve their [political] ends' (Sapulete 2002: 18). It was reported that 'during October 1999, in Ambon [the capital of the Moluccas] women from all sides of the conflict, Protestant, Catholic and Muslim, came together to work for peace and "close the gap" that had grown between them' (*CCANews* 2002: 6).

What took place in Ambon is not an isolated case. Something similar also happened in Sri Lanka which has been devastated by religious and ethnic conflicts. Sri Lanka is a land of four major religions: Buddhism 67 per cent, Hinduism 18 per cent, Islam 8 per cent, Christianity 7 per cent. It is also a land where the majority of Sinhalese are Buddhists and the minority of Hindus Tamils, while Christians come from both these ethnic groups (Balasuriya 1994: 239). In August 2002, 21 Sri Lankan Hindu, Buddhist, Christian (both Protestant and Catholic) and Muslim young people gathered at Kandy, Sri Lanka, for the Young Ambassadors for Peace Program organized, at the Sri Lankans' request, by the Uniting Church in Australia. A common focus on the shared concern for peace led to the study and discussion of religious differences, language differences and the three cultures (Muslim, Tamil and Buddhist) in an atmosphere of friendship and respect (*CCANews* 2002: 5). Most people, whether Christian, Buddhist, Hindu or Muslim, are grieved by the enormous cost of the conflict and have grown tired of it. It is definitely a sign of hope that young people from different ethnic and religious backgrounds are able to get together to study each other's religious culture with the common aspiration for peace.

What has been happening among the people who bear the brunt of religious conflict is bound to affect Christian theology in Asia. It will reverse its orientation from a predominantly Western theology to a truly Asian theology. In the light of the religious and ethnic conflicts in which 'ten thousand people have been killed in the past four years, and over one thousand persons since the Indo-Sri Lankan peace accord' (Balasuriya 1994: 249), those engaged in Christian theology have to think again:

> If the Buddha and Jesus were to meet today, they would not engage in a debate as to who is the greatest but rather would tend to serve each other . . . We have therefore a call to cure ourselves of the arrogance implicit in our exclusivist positions. It is arrogance that makes Christianity closed to others and limiting to themselves. (ibid.: 247)

The urgent reconstruction of theology is now on the agenda as never before. It lies at the heart of Christian faith and theology and the practice of Christian mission. If this is true in all countries of Asia in which Christianity is a late comer and has remained a minority religion, it is even more urgent in a country such as India in which 'religious fundamentalism and communalism' increases, 'very often instilled, inflated, manipulated and abused by all the political parties to gain political power' (Pathil 1994: 56). This of course is not new. What is new is that absolute claims for one's religion bring about endless cycles of violence and loss of life, quite contrary to everything religion, including Christianity, should stand for. What is called for is a 'new positive approach to other religions that accepts them as legitimate "ways of salvation" . . . a radical change in the history of Christianity' (ibid.: 59). Biblical support for this new approach to other religions can be found in the story of creation in Genesis 1:1–2:3 that points to 'one God who is the creator of all', in the Book of Jonah, 'a beautiful parable of universal salvation', or by 'the Kingdom of God Jesus proclaimed and inaugurated not limited to Israel and church' (ibid.: 60–1).

A theology based on God the creator of all and on universal salvation shifts Christianity away from its claim to exclusiveness and absolutism. It results in a radical shift in other fundamental Christian concerns as well, such as the person and work of Jesus, the activity of God as Spirit, the ministry and mission of the Christian church, and the theology and practice of the Eucharist. Theological efforts in these areas promise to be a liberating, albeit at times laborious, process. A theology derived from God as universal creator will set the stage for alternative theological directions in Asia.

Who Do You Say That Jesus Is?

In some religions there is a central figure who inspires visions of the future, shapes faith and morals, and is engaged in efforts to change people and their community. For

Buddhism that central figure is Gautama the Buddha, for Islam, Muhammad, and for Christianity, Jesus. As far as Christianity is concerned, the question that has to be asked in Asia is the question Jesus asked his disciples on their way to the villages of Caesarea Philippi: 'Who do you say that I am?' (Mark 8:29; par. Matt. 16:15; Luke 18:22). In wrestling with this perennial question, central to the Christian faith, the approach of Asian theology is bound to be quite different from that of Western theology.

> Whereas Euro-American christological reflections insist on logic, internal coherence, and precise theories of knowledge, prefer to discover Jesus on the pages of the written text, and place him in a social, political and religious environment, Asian understandings of Jesus rely on impulses and assortments of ideas and contextual needs. They take him out of his milieu and place him with the peoples of Asia and with other venerated sages like Buddha, Krishna and Confucius. They try to take Jesus out of the study into the dusty streets of Asia and let him mingle with other seers and saviors. (Sugirtharajah 1993b: xi)

What theology must pursue is the 'Unbound Christ' (Samartha 1974), 'unbound', that is, from Western theological incarceration and set free to live a new life among the peoples of Asia.

Such an approach is on the whole legitimate, stressing as it does the distinctiveness of Asian theology over against Western theology, but one has to be careful not to over-simplify the differences. This is especially important today when we consider how many of the boundaries between West and East have been broken down by economic global-ization. One has also to bear in mind that liberation theology and feminist theology, both of which emerged out of the heart of Western theology, undoubtedly crossed East–West boundaries to inform and inspire Asian theology. Furthermore, while it is true that the engagement of Asian theology with the search for Jesus spills more and more over into streets and marketplaces where masses of people are engaged in the business of life, 'the written text' still plays an important role in the search. As a matter of fact, the search for Jesus among the people has inspired Asian theology to go back to the Gospels and rediscover how and why Jesus associated himself with the people of his day, particularly people estranged from the religious institutions and hierarchies of their time. In the quest for Jesus in Asia, there is thus an increasingly greater appre-ciation of how and why the oppressed peoples of Asia are intrinsically related to the oppressed people in Jesus' company, and why the oppressed people in Jesus' company are internally related to the suffering masses in Asia.

What has been noted above enables us to grasp the meaning of what has been said in Sri Lanka about the search for Jesus: 'our desperate search for the Asian Face of Christ can find fulfillment only if we participate in Asia's own search for it in the unfath-omable abyss where religion and poverty seem to have the same common source: God, who has declared Mammon the enemy' (Pieris 1982: 175–6). This 'desperate [or better, earnest] search for the Asian Face of Jesus' has a huge obstacle to overcome:

> both the exclusivist and the inclusivist theories of religions end up asserting the supremacy of the Buddha over the Christ, and vice versa . . . This is the impasse that any 'dialogical' theology of religions, even in its most inclusivist form, runs into. (Pieris 1993: 55)

This is not only the impasse facing the religious communities in Sri Lanka but in many other countries in Asia as well. It is common knowledge that religious fundamentalism, including Christian fundamentalism, is on the rise in Asia today.

What has led to this 'christological' impasse or 'blind alley', in the midst of religious tensions in Sri Lanka, 'is their [theologians'] obsession with the 'uniqueness' of Christ' comprehended 'in terms of 'absoluteness' that Christians indicate with titles like Christ, Son of God, and the like' (ibid.: 55). Such 'christological obsession' continues to prevail not only in the Christian Church in Sri Lanka but in most churches in Asia. What will become increasingly apparent is that to answer the question, 'Who do you say that Jesus is?' the Christian Churches in Asia will become deeply polarized. On the one hand, the majority of the Christian churches will put even more stress on the uniqueness and absoluteness of Christ in confrontation with other religions, while, on the other, a minority of them will tone down, if not do away with totally, the assertion about the uniqueness and absoluteness of Christ.

Christianity in Japan, which accounts for only 1 per cent of the population, is a minority religion in a society shaped by Buddhism, Confucianism and the nationalistic religion of Shintoism. Holding the uniqueness and absoluteness of Christ to be not negotiable in such a situation, Christianity in Japan tends to isolate itself from the rest of the society culturally. But the movement known as the 'Mu-kyokai,' or Non-church, developed at the turn of the twentieth century, looked for 'a way to believe in Christ as a Japanese . . . that led to a clash with missionaries and to estrangement from the established churches' (Dohi 1997: 18–19). The movement, founded by the charismatic Christian leader Kanzo Uchimura (1861–1930), advocated that Christians in Japan should 'live in two "J's", that is, Jesus and Japan.' It also believed that 'love of Jesus purified love of Japan, and that love of Japan clarified the love of Jesus and also gave people a goal in life' (ibid.: 19). Some active members of the movement protested against the Japanese invasion of China in the 1930s and later against the Pacific War of 1937–45, while the established churches gave a tacit or not so tacit support to the military government. They were persecuted and imprisoned for the firm stance they took against the war Japan waged on China and on the countries in South-east Asia.

Over against the mainstream theology of the Church in Japan, there is now an awareness on the part of those actively engaged in theological dialogue with Japanese Buddhism, of 'the relativity of Christianity'. This has led to the affirmation by, for example, the New Testament scholar Seiichi Yagi, that 'the basis of Christianity [is] not in the death, resurrection, and atonement of Jesus Christ, but in the Logos which worked everywhere to actualize religious experience' (1997: 99). Obviously, understanding Jesus as the Logos will link up theology in Japan with the theology developed in the early centuries of Christianity strongly influenced by Greek philosophy. But more importantly, such an affirmation has profound ramifications not only for Christology but especially for the doctrine of God. The question, 'Who do you say that Jesus is?' would then turn into the question, 'Who do you say that God is?' 'Theology [in Japan] *before* 1970 is christologically oriented, then theology *after* 1970 is a theology centered on the doctrine of God' (Odagaki 1997: 116).

In contrast to the rather academic theological and christological discourse characteristic of theology in Japan, a very different kind of theology has emerged within the same Japan to grasp the meaning of Jesus in relation to the life of the oppressed people. In this theological effort Jesus' crown of thorns takes centre stage. Reference has already been made to the theology of the crown of thorns.

> The crown of thorns put on to Jesus' head was a symbol of becoming valueless and powerless in comparison with the powerful ruling class. The situation of Jesus on the cross is like the *Buraku* people's in terms of the negation of their existence because of discrimination and oppression. The crown of thorns is the Christian symbol most closely related to the suffering and humiliation of Jesus during the trial. (Hatakeyama 2002: 55–6)

Theology in Japan has not yet resonated with the increasingly loud theological voices in the rest of Asia, but with the emergence of the theology of the crown of thorns, which tries to come to grips with the meaning of the life and ministry of Jesus for oppressed people, it has begun to echo the cries of the people heard throughout Asia.

The theology of the crown of thorns finds a strong echo, for instance, in 'the Paraiyar of South India, a major and specific community of *Dalits* (the untouchables or outcasts of India)' (Clarke 1999: 2). Christ's presence was and is encountered by the Paraiyar of South India through the drum (ibid.: 197). 'The drum' mentioned here is the musical instrument used by the Paraiyar on many occasions including religious festivals, a symbol of the culture of people in which the dramas of life take place. This is another example of theological efforts in Asia to take with all seriousness 'the influence of our culture, religious framework and communal experience of the Divine . . . on any interpretation of Jesus' (ibid.: 197). In this way the Bible and culture interact with each other in tension and creativity, contributing to the construction of a theology for Asia.

Further confirmation of the radical change in Asian approaches to the christological question: 'Who do you say that Jesus is?', comes from the theological creativity of women in Korea concerning the influence of Korean culture on the meaning of Immanuel, incarnation, and the divinity and humanity of Jesus. In Korea 'special persons having done special things in a lifetime, become gods after death' (Lee Oo Chung 1987: 230).

> In this cultural framework Christology from above (God become human) is difficult to understand for the ordinary masses of people (*minjung*), especially laborers. Conceptual and abstract images of God in Christian theology, such as 'totally other,' 'unmoved mover,' and as 'immutable, impassable, unchangeable God,' do not make much sense to Korean people. (Chung Hyun Kyung 1993: 231)

In a theological assertion such as this, we hear the reverberations of a statement of *minjung* theology in the early stage of its history: 'Wherever Jesus went, many nameless crowds followed him. The crowds surrounding Jesus were the shadow which demonstrated that Jesus was not an abstract figure but a historical being with a particular existence' (Suh Nam Dong 1981: 159). This is a striking example of how the central assertion of Christian faith within a culture different from the cultures within which traditional christological dogma was formed, can be reformulated.

Doing Theology with Bible and Asian Resources in Asia

In 1983, the Programme for Theology and Cultures in Asia (PTCA) was started with 'the vision and determination to make a concentrated effort to foster the formation of living theology in Asia'. During the ensuing ten years seminar-workshops, attended by more than 300 young theological teachers and church leaders from all over Asia, were held in many cities in Asia such as Hong Kong, Kyoto, Yogyakarta, Seoul, Manila, Chiang Mai (Thailand) and Manila. The seminar workshops explored such areas as folk literature, people's movements, living faiths of world religions, Asian cultures, people's symbols and images and God's purpose for all of Asia. The basis that underlay these theological explorations was 'biblical resources, along with the insights of Asian writings . . . fully drawn on . . . for the construction of innovative theologies which may do justice to God's presence' in Asia (England 1993: 40). It was further stressed that 'we continuously maintain the centrality of the Biblical revelation in our common endeavor', recognizing at the same time that 'most creative theological formulation is a product of the encounter between the Biblical revelation and the experience of people in a particular cultural, social and historical context' (Takenaka 1993: 3).

The Programme for Theology and Cultures in Asia clearly charted the future course of theological developments in Asia. In its theological experiments with almost unlimited resources in Asia, it came to this conclusion: 'Bringing both the biblical text and our Asian text into contact will provide a perspective from which to interpret one in relation to the other. The Asian text can be read critically and the biblical text can be interpreted cross-culturally' (Lee 1994: 3). This is a step beyond 'the contextualizing theology' promoted by Shoki Coe, a Taiwanese theologian, during his tenure as the executive secretary and later director of the Theological Education Fund of the World Council of Churches between 1965 and 1979 (Coe 1976). It has to be said that he and his contemporaries such as D. T. Niles, an eminent Sri Lankan theologian and ecumenical church leader, continued to be under the strong influence of Karl Barth in stressing the Christian Gospel as the text to be 'contextualized' in Asian contexts.

The interaction between the Bible and cultures in Asia as a biblical and theological method, opens an exciting theological era in Asia. An excellent example is a study on the biblical story of creation and the Chinese creation stories of *P'an Ku* and *Nu Kua* conducted in Hong Kong. The study concludes:

> For us Chinese and for this matter, Asians in general, with ancient cultures [including] creation myths, the key issue of biblical hermeneutics is not merely how to understand the Judeo-Christian tradition mainly from the western Christian perspective, but the question of having to deal seriously with two texts, our own cultural-religious text, both in oral and written form, and the biblical text. The old approach of leaving aside our presumed pagan cultural-religious text in order to be truly converted to Christianity does not provide living theology and meaning of life. (Lee 1994: 231)

This hermeneutical method, still needing to be refined and developed, is bound to yield fresh theological insights that enable Christianity to make an 'indigenous' contribution to the religious cultures of the countries in Asia.

In India, the *Dalit* theology exemplifies the strenuous but promising theological journey that lies ahead for Asian theologians. It will increasingly

> play a role in raising the consciousness of the Church/Christian Community as a whole. The current traditional theologies have been playing a role which has forced the Church to maintain the status quo or existing orders of political, economic, social, religious, cultural, including caste based divisions, not only outside, but within the Church also. So it is the *Dalit* theology which can challenge the Church to change her stand . . . In this way the *Dalit* theology will help the Church to become an instrument of change. (Massey 2002: 850)

There is now a realization among churches in Indonesia as well that

> the expressions of Christian religion, whether in the forms of doctrines, worship, or the whole structure with its leadership, are limited . . . The churches are helped by other faiths, religions and different cultures to understand and to live out better the gospel and the mystery of Christ. Hence, we can speak here about dialogue as openness to God and mutual evangelization. From this point of view one can take a step to understand the dialogue of life. (Widyatmadja 1992: 63)

Dialogue of life! This is what doing theology with Asian resources is about. Theology is the dialogue of life, and not comparison of doctrines and claims to truth. It is theology as dialogue and practice, which will enable churches in Asia to break out of isolation from their cultural environment to become part of the people in Asia in their search for the meaning of life. In Taiwan, theology takes place also in dialogue with the history of Taiwan, as is evident in the following statement:

> From the standpoint of church history and local history, engagement with the indigenous theology of history in Taiwan must be derived from involvement and participation in the history of Taiwanese society. Thus the first step is to collect resources of history indigenous to Taiwan. (Cheng Yang-en 2001: 48)

As theology becomes engaged with the realities of life, reading the Bible enables the churches and Christians in the Philippines to see in

> the people's movements . . . the unknowing bearers of God's liberating grace – movements of God's Spirit in our lands . . . the acts of identification [with people] . . . could very well be the locus where a new eruption of the liberating and transformative power of Christ could take place. (Oracion 1991: 144)

The task of theology in Asia is thus not to dictate what people must believe and do, but to discern what God is doing with the people and their resources and to articulate it in the language with which people can identify. This will not only be the case with the Philippines but also with other Asian countries. Theology in Asia will grow out of the people who struggle to live in the midst of social-political and religious-cultural ferments.

The affirmation of life as an essential part of faith and theology in Asia is a critical part of the Confession of Faith made by the Presbyterian Church in Taiwan in 1986. The Confession grew out of three statements published by the Church to declare its position regarding Taiwan's political, social and cultural situations, namely, 'Statement Concerning Our National Fate' (1971), 'Our Appeal' (1971), and 'Declaration on Human Rights' (1977). The Confession says in part: 'We believe that God has given human beings dignity, talents and a homeland, so that they may share in God's creation, and have responsibility with God for taking care of the world.' The Confession sounds as if it is an innocuous statement, but read in the light of the people of Taiwan struggling to be free from the external powers that colonized and ruled them with brute force for centuries, the Confession of Faith expresses what resonates deeply in the hearts of the majority of the people of Taiwan. It sums up the theological efforts in Taiwan to develop a perception of God 'in a non-Christian context,' the self-understanding of the church based on 'the experiences of suffering and hope,' and the re-conception of mission derived from 'the church's experience of the context of Taiwan' (Po Ho Huang 2002: 86). In such a theological effort the tribal cultures of the native people of Taiwan will play a crucial role. 'The traditional faith of the tribal people,' it is emphasized, 'contributes to the understanding of Christian faith . . . Without experiences of the traditional faith of the tribal people, Christian mission would not have borne fruits among them' (Pu Shin Ta Li 2003: 14). This is another example showing why theological developments in Asia have to grow out of creative interactions between Jesus and diverse cultures of Asia.

What is the theological dynamic that moves theology in Japan closer to theological efforts in the rest of Asia? Besides the *burakumin* theology already mentioned, feminist theology in Japan has begun to play an important role. Christian women in Japan have begun to reconstruct theology, out of the long tradition of discrimination against women in Japanese society, in the light of their reading of the Bible. Doing theology with the marginalized people such as women in Japan, 'must first take women's experience seriously, second, take a critical look at the society that has given rise to the marginalization of women, and third, re-interpret the Bible and the traditions of the church.' Doing theology in this way will, it is hoped, lead to the overturning of Japanese patriarchal society and the emperor system that has developed from the patriarchal tradition (Kinukawa 1993: 32–5).

In Korea, now that dictatorship has long gone and democracy has been firmly established, the *minjung* theology has also been going through transformation.

> [Even] the meaning of *minjung* has changed. Its denotation has been extended. Many *minjung* congregations developed their own special fields of commitment such as mission for the 'disabled' ('differently abled'), mission for teenagers, foreign workers' mission, living community for homeless teenagers, and the environment mission . . . *Minjung* pastors have rediscovered the importance of the 'faith' and the Bible. (Hong Eyoul Hwang 2000: 117)

This transformation from a city-based and working-class-based theology to a more broadly based meaning of *minjung*, who face vastly different kinds of problems and difficulties, will play an important role in theological development in Korea.

In China too the question addressed today is 'how is the essence of Christianity and its combination with China's new culture to be understood. This concerns the vitality of the Christian faith and the effectiveness of its message' (Zhao Zhien 2001: 133). Once theology in China begins to deal with this basic issue, it will find itself faced with the tension and conflict with the traditional understanding of, for example, God, Spirit, Church, Mission. It remains to be seen what form 'a pluralistic and multi-layered theology with Chinese characteristics' will take and how it 'will prosper in the Church in China' (ibid.: 139).

In conclusion, theology in Asia is on the move. There are forces that seek to slow down its movement, even to stop it, but both the external and internal forces that set it in motion will press forward, demanding that the Bible be open to the realities of Asia and to the experiences of Asian people in very different cultural situations. The Bible and Asian resources, historical, social, political, cultural and religious, will interact with each other and illuminate each other, enabling Christians to perceive at a deeper level how God has been present and active in Asia, not only in the past two centuries through Western missionary efforts but in centuries past, present and future through countless Asian humanity.

References

Balasuriya, T. (1994). 'Ethnic Conflict in Sri Lanka and the Responsibility of the Theologian', in R. S. Sugirtharajah (ed.), *Frontiers of Asian Christian Theology: Emerging Trends*. Maryknoll, NY: Orbis, pp. 236–51.

Byung Mu Ahn (1993). 'Jesus and People (*Minjung*)', in R. S. Sugirtharajah (ed.), *Asian Faces of Jesus*. Maryknoll, NY: Orbis, pp. 163–72.

CCANews (2002). 37 (4 December). Hong Kong: Christian Conference of Asia.

Chen Nan-Chou (2000). 'Reading the Bible with New Eyes', in *Manual for Reading the Bible with New Eyes*. Tainan: Taiwan Church Press, pp. 10–18 (in Chinese).

Chen Nan-Chou (2001). 'Theology of [People's] Identity: Constructing Indigenous Theology in Taiwan Contexts', *Tao: A Bimonthly Theological Journal* 5 (December): 77–89.

Cheng Yang-en (2001). 'Towards the Future of an Indigenous Theology of History in Taiwan', *Tao: A Bi-Monthly Theological Journal* 2 (June): 40–9 (in Chinese).

Chung Hyun Kyung (1993). 'Who Is Jesus for Asian Women?', in R. S. Sugirtharajah (ed.), *Asian Faces of Jesus*. Maryknoll, NY: Orbis, pp. 223–46.

Clarke, S. (1999). *Dalits and Christianity: Subaltern Religion and Liberation Theology in India*. New Delhi: Oxford University Press.

Coe, Shoki (1976). 'Contextualizing Theology', in Gerald H. Anderson and Thomas F. Stransky (eds), *Mission Trends No. 3: Third World Theologies*. New York: Paulist Press, pp. 19–24.

Dohi, Akio (1997). 'The First Generation: Christian Leaders in the First Period', in Yasuo Furuya (ed. and trans.), *A History of Japanese Theology*. Grand Rapids, MI: William B. Eerdmans, pp. 11–42.

Doing Theology with Asian Resources (1993). *Ten Years in the Formation of Living Theology in Asia: The Programme for Theology and Cultures in Asia 1983–1993*. Auckland: Pace Publishing.

England, J. C. (ed.) (1982). *Living Theology in Asia*. Maryknoll, NY: Orbis.

England, J. C. (1993). 'A Theological Overview of the Programme's Work', in *Doing Theology with Asian Resources*. Auckland: Pace Publishing, pp. 36–45.

Fabella, V., Lee, P. K. H. and Suh, D. K. (eds) (1992). *Asian Christian Spirituality*. Maryknoll, NY: Orbis.

Furuya, Yasuo (ed. and trans.) (1997). *A History of Japanese Theology*. Grand Rapids, MI: William B. Eerdmans.

God, Christ and God's People in Asia (1995). As seen by the participants of the Consultation on the Theme 'Through a New Vision of God towards the New Humanity in Christ', Kyoto, 1994. Hong Kong: Christian Conference of Asia.

Hatakeyama, Y. (2002). 'The Liberation Grace of God: The Task of the Japanese Church for the Liberation of the Discriminated People called *"Hisabetsu-Burakumin"* ', in *CTC (Theological Concerns) Bulletin* XVII(2): 47–56.

Hong Eyoul Hwang (2000). 'The Legacy of the *Minjung* Congregation Movement in South Korea 1983–1997', in W. Ustorf and T. Murayama (eds), *Identity and Marginality: Rethinking Christianity in North East Asia*. Frankfurt am Main: Peter Lang, pp. 113–19.

Kim, Marion (2002). 'Special Feature: India's Dalit People', *Sangsaeng: Living Together, Helping Each Other: A Quarterly Journal* (Autumn): 4–8.

Kim Yong Bok (ed.) (1981). *Minjung Theology, People as the Subjects of History*. Singapore: The Commission on Theological Concerns; The Christian Conference of Asia.

Kim Yong Bok (1995). 'Jesus Christ among *Minjung*', in *God, Christ and God's People in Asia*. Hong Kong: Christian Conference of Asia, pp. 11–46.

Kinukawa, H. (1993). 'Overturning the Patriarchal System', in *Directions and Tasks of Japanese Theology*. Tokyo: Sinkyo Publishing Company, pp. 32–5 (in Japanese).

Kuribayashi, T. (1995). 'The Story of the *Buraku* People of Japan', in *God, Christ and God's People in Asia*. Tokyo: Hsin Kyo Shut-Pan Sha, pp. 90–114.

Kwok Pui-lan (1995). *Discovering the Bible in the Non-Biblical World*. Maryknoll, NY: Orbis.

Lee, A. C. C. (1994). 'Towards the Year 2000: Christian Theological Endeavor in Asia', *PTCA Bulletin* 7(1): 2–4.

Lee Oo Chung (1987). 'Korean Cultural and Feminist Theology', in *God's Image (Journal of Asian Women's Resource Center for Culture and Theology)* September, quoted in Chung Hyun Kyung, 'Who Is Jesus for Asian Women?', in R. S. Sugirtharajah (ed.), *Asian Faces of Jesus*. Maryknoll, NY: Orbis pp. 223–46.

Massey, J. (2002). 'Movements of Liberation: Theological Roots and Vision of *Dalit* Theology', *CTC Bulletin* XVLI(2): 76–86.

McManners, J. (ed.) (1990). *The Oxford Illustrated History of Christianity*. Oxford: Oxford University Press.

Moffett, S. H. (1992). *A History of Christianity in Asia*, vol. 1: *Beginning to 1500*. San Francisco: Harper.

Odagaki, M. (1997). 'Theology after 1970', in Yasuo Furuya (ed. and trans.), *A History of Japanese Theology*. Grand Rapids, MI: William B. Eerdmans, pp. 113–40.

Oracion, L. B. (1991). 'God's Dialectic of Liberation', in *Doing Theology with the Spirit's Movement in Asia* (Occasional Paper No. 11). Singapore: Association of Theological Education in South East Asia, pp. 136–44.

Pathil, K. (1994). *Indian Churches at the Crossroads*. Bangalore: Center for Indian and Interreligious Studies.

Pieris, A. (1982). 'The Asian Sense in Theology', in J. C. England (ed.), *Living Theology in Asia*. Maryknoll, NY: Orbis, pp. 171–6.

Pieris, A. (1993). 'The Buddha and the Christ: Mediators of Liberation', in R. S. Sugirtharajah (ed.), *Asian Faces of Jesus*. Maryknoll, NY: Orbis, pp. 46–61.

Po Ho Huang (2002). 'Retrospect and Prospect of Doing Contextual Theology in Taiwan', *Journal of Theologies and Cultures in Asia* 1(February): 79–92.

Pu Shin Ta Li (2003). 'Creative Mission Dynamic of Aboriginal People in Taiwan', *Taiwan Church News* 2659 (February 16): 14.

Samartha, S. J. (1974). *The Hindu Response to the Unbound Christ*. Madras: Christian Literature Society.

Sapulete, H. L. (2002). 'Some Thoughts on the Riots in the Moluccas', *Asia Journal of Theology* 16(1): 17–28.

Soares-Prabhu, G. M. (1991). 'Class in the Bible: The Biblical Poor a Social Class?', in R. S. Sugirtharajah (ed.), *Voices from the Margin: Interpreting the Bible in the Third World*. Maryknoll, NY: Orbis, pp. 147–71.

Sugirtharajah, R. S. (ed.) (1991). *Voices from the Margin: Interpreting the Bible in the Third World*. Maryknoll, NY: Orbis.

Sugirtharajah, R. S. (ed.) (1993a). 'Prologue and Perspective', in R. S. Sugirtharajah (ed.), *Asian Faces of Jesus*. Maryknoll, NY: Orbis, pp. viii–xii.

Sugirtharajah, R. S. (ed.) (1993b). *Asian Faces of Jesus*. Maryknoll, NY: Orbis.

Sugirtharajah, R. S. (ed.) (1994). *Frontiers of Asian Christian Theology: Emerging Trends*. Maryknoll, NY: Orbis.

Suh Nam Dong (1981). 'Historical References for a Theology of *Minjung*', in Kim Yong Bock (ed.), *Minjung Theology, People as the Subjects of History*. Singapore: The Commission on Theological Concerns; The Christian Conference of Asia, pp. 155–84.

Takenaka, M. (1993). 'Preface: Toward the Formation of Living Theology in Asia: The Basic Perspective of PTCA', in *Doing Theology with Asian Resources*. Auckland: Pace Publishing.

Thomas, M. M. (1994). 'My Pilgrimage in Mission', in R. S. Sugirtharajah (ed.), *Frontiers of Asian Christian Theology: Emerging Trends*. Maryknoll, NY: Orbis, pp. 156–60.

Ting, K. H. (1989). *No Longer Strangers: Selected Writings*. Maryknoll, NY: Orbis.

Ustorf, W. and Murayama, T. (eds) (2000). *Identity and Marginality: Rethinking Christianity in North East Asia*. Frankfurt am Main: Peter Lang.

Wang Hsien-Chih (1990). 'Taiwanese Culture: Redemption, Identity and Responsibility', *Theology and Church* 18(1/2): 79–93 (in Chinese).

Wickeri, J. and Wickeri, P. (eds) (2002). *A Chinese Contribution to Ecumenical Theology: Selected Writings of Bishop K. H. Ting*. Geneva: World Council of Churches.

Widyatmadja, J. O. (1992). 'A Spirituality of Liberation: An Indonesian Contribution', in Lee Fabella and Kwang-sun Suh (eds), *Asian Christian Spirituality*. Maryknoll, NY: Orbis, pp. 49–63.

Wilfred, F. (1993). *Beyond Settled Foundations: The Journey of Indian Theology*. Madras: University of Madras, Department of Christian Studies.

Witness and Hope amid Struggle (1991). *Towards a Theology and Spirituality of Struggle*, Book II. Manila: Forum for Interdisciplinary Endeavors and Studies.

Women of Courage (1992). *Asian Women Reading the Bible*, ed. Asian Women's Resource Center for Culture and Theology. Seoul.

Yagi, S. (1997). 'The Third Generation: 1945–1970', in Yasuo Furuya, *History of Japanese Theology*. Grand Rapids, MI: William B. Eerdmans, pp. 83–111.

Yayan, S. ([1992] 1993). 'People's Theology', *Jeevadhara* 22: 201, quoted in F. Wilfred, *Beyond Settled Foundations: The Journey of Indian Theology*. Madras: University of Madras, Department of Christian Studies, pp. 85–6.

Zhao Zhien (2001). 'Fifty Years of Theological Transformation in Chinese Christianity', *Asia Journal of Theology* 15(1): 133–9.

CHAPTER 11

Africa

Jonathan A. Draper

Africa is a vast continent, diverse in language, culture and geography. To generalize about such diversity and to synthesize it into a generic 'Africanness', is likely to be dangerous and misleading, even for a well-informed and sympathetic observer like John S. Mbiti (1969, 1979), who has contributed so much to the recovery of African culture. It would be even more problematic for a white South African male like me to undertake such a task. Some African scholars would argue that studies by white male scholars of black agency are a species of 'fake' discourse designed to serve as a 'pretext for the exoneration of White and male guilt' (Maluleke and Nadar 2004: 16). This study is offered in the hope, however, that an 'etic' perspective of a participant observer can add something to the 'emic' discourse of black African scholars and thus enlarge and enrich the 'universe of human discourse' (Geertz 1973: 14). The diversity in the African experience of the Bible (see the great variety of interpretations in West and Dube 2000) is not just geographical and cultural but also historical. If North Africa and Ethiopia are included in a general survey, for instance, then African Christianity and African readings of the Bible are nearly as old as Christianity itself, and show signs of re-asserting themselves and their cultural appropriation of Christianity in Africa (de Gruchy 2001: 24–39; Loubser 2000: 103–26). On the other hand, Christianity reached Africa south of the Sahara during the period of Western imperialism and colonialism, and is indelibly marked by issues of cultural conflict, hegemony and intrusion. The Bible has been inextricably linked to this process of struggle, both as a tool of oppression and as a resource for liberation.

Despite the diversity, there are commonalities of culture among African Christians, especially south of the Sahara. At the heart of these is the sense of the intrinsic value of community in constituting humanity, 'We are human through other human beings'. The saying in Zulu 'Umuntu uwumuntu ngabantu', is found in multiple forms throughout Africa. This continuity and the centrality of human community are not broken by death, but rather cemented by it (Setiloane 1986: 9–16, 41–2). The departed remain in fellowship with and dependence on the living, as protectors, healers, sources of power and guarantors of ethical conduct. Often there is a connection between the ancestors and the land, reinforcing belonging and guaranteeing the fertility of land and people. The positive interconnectedness of all these things produces a sense of 'well-being' similar to the Old Testament concept of *shalom* (Adamo 1997: 99–111; Kinoti and Waliggo 1997: 112–23). The concept of a high God may or may not be present – the matter is much debated – but there is a strong sense of the immanence of spirit as a general force, as well as in specific localized forms of power. There is no separation between the world of the spirit and the world of everyday material concerns; life is experienced as a unity:

> Because traditional religions permeate all the departments of life, there is no formal distinction between the sacred and the secular, between the religious and the non-religious, between the spiritual and the material areas of life. Wherever the African is, there is his religion. (Mbiti [1969] 1989: 1; cf. Setiloane 1986: 37–42; Bujo 1992: 18–32)

Likewise, despite great differences between Christians in Africa, which derive from the missionary bodies that evangelized them, there are commonalities in attitude towards the Bible. African Catholics and Protestants may have received very different doctrinal teaching, but may well use the Bible in ways closer to each other than they are to Western Catholics and Protestants. Its influence on ordinary people is far stronger than is customary elsewhere in the Christian world (in 'township language' it is often called *incwadi yabantu* or 'the people's book', since it is found in nearly every home even if it is rarely read):

> The Bible is central to African Christianity. It is the most widely translated, and the most widely read book in tropical Africa. The Bible is the most widely available book in both rural and urban areas. It can be regarded as the most influential book in Africa. (Mugambe 1995: 142)

The understanding of the Bible as the 'Word of God' is pervasive (e.g. Mbiti 1979: 90; Bediako 1995: 116–25), a perspective which is vigorously critiqued by Mosala (1989: 175–99) and Maluleke (1996: 10–12; 1997: 14–16).

While such generalizations may set the scene for a study of the relationship between Bible and culture in Africa, this study will approach the topic ethnographically, examining the emergence of the relationship and its evolution in the microcosm of Zulu culture. In this, I am drawing on the theory of culture advocated by Clifford Geertz:

> The aim is to draw large conclusions from small, very densely textured facts; to support broad assertions about the role of culture in the construction of collective life by engaging them exactly with complex specifics. (1973: 28)

This is partly because of a sense of the danger of generalization and partly out of a sense that the general is best understood from the perspective of the local.

The Bible and Conversion

In a fascinating narrative account of her conversion to Christianity, Unomguqo Khulumani Dlamini (*c*.1857–1942) describes her call in terms of a night vision in which the Bible is offered to her by a white person (*omhlophe*) and proscribed by a black person (*omnyama*):

> The reason for my conversion in the house of Gert van Rooyen where *Inkosi* came to me, in a dream and said: 'Paulina, get up! Take the Book and teach my people in the east. Indeed, receive the book, the Bible, and the book for instructing children and of hymns. Taking the book, you shall teach my people in the east. This was at Hlimbitwa where van Rooyen lives.' That person who spoke the words was dazzling white like one sent. And the person was wearing white clothes. The person spoke before me.

> My sister Miriam was also there. We slept there in the house of van Rooyen where he ate. But the book was given to me. I was not a believer, I was a person on the outside.

> When I had received the book, there came a tall black person to me, clothed in black garments, who said, 'Do not open the book. You will die if you open it.' The person left who was sent who gave me the book. I got up. I was afraid. I saw a great flame of fire. I cried out. I woke van Rooyen. He got up quickly, he kindled the lamp. I narrated the matter of the book. He took the Bible and laid it on the table. He opened what was written. I was comforted by what it said: 'Look, this one is sent by the *Inkosi*. It is the *Inkosi* who gives you the book.' I replied, 'I am not a believer. How can I read it without being a believer?' He said, 'The *Inkosi* will show you what you must do. The *Inkosi* does not deceive.' Gert spoke these words to me. He said, 'It is Satan who throws away the book. Do not fear if the word comes to you again.' Van Rooyen knelt and prayed. He said, 'Go and sleep. If the word (voice) comes again, you must come and tell me.'

> We slept that night. During the very early hours of the morning of the second night the white person with the book came again and said: 'Paulina, do not lose that book, you are going to use to teach my people.' But her form was that of a girl and she said again, 'Do not be afraid if that person comes.' Again that person came and said: 'Do not open that book, you will die.' We said, 'The person with the book is back again.' Van Rooyen said: 'It is the *Inkosi* not a person who gives you the book.' 'Oh, being an non-believer what am I to do?!' Van Rooyen then said: 'The *Inkosi* knows what he will do through you.' And so it was.

> It was a Monday when this first happened. On Wednesday van Rooyen saddled his horse and went to report this matter to the members of his community. Yes, van Rooyen went. He reported the matter. They then decided on a day to meet in van Rooyen's house. They then met the following Wednesday for a prayer. The prayer was to thank the word that a sent one was seen in van Rooyen's house. Thanksgiving was made. After the prayer I was called to be questioned. I was questioned by Botha the leading member that time. But he was a Methodist. He then questioned me for some time. I said: 'Seeing that I am not a believer, what am I to do?' They then said: 'You must pray to *Inkosi*.'

> I then did not know what to do. After that van Rooyen went to Minister Johannes Reibeling in the *veld*. He said van Rooyen must bring me to see him. Then another girl had to come up and take my place so that I could go. I studied for three months and was

then baptised. Honoured ministers, Haccisius and Harms came. I was baptised by the most Reverend Haccius (*sic*). There were five of us being baptised. I learnt very fast. The minister Manqashaza Reibeling related my story to the honoured ministers. One honoured minister took a photo of me. A big meeting of the Germans took place, all the ministers were present. I was afraid. When I was being baptised it felt like I was dying.

Well, that's the end of the story about my baptism. The Minister Reibeling took me to stay with him. Minister Reibeling asked for the story of my conversion and wrote it down. (My translation from Filter's pencil transcription of an interview in Zulu, assisted by Thandeka Tshazi; cf. the translation from German in Bourquin and Filter 1986: 83–5)

This account is significant for a number of reasons (Draper 2002). In the first place, it happens to a young Zulu woman of royal Swazi descent who had been a member of King Cetschwayo's *isigodlo* or royal harem of wives. The Zulu War of 1879, instigated by the British settlers to facilitate the annexation of Zulu land, was followed by the deliberate destruction of the Zulu kingdom and a prolonged period of disastrous civil war fomented by British colonial policy (see Guy 2001, for an excellent account). The *isigodlo* was disbanded and the royal princess, after a period of flight, danger and starvation, becomes a domestic worker on an Afrikaner farm, sleeping on the kitchen floor at night, when she has this vision.

Second, Unomguqo is illiterate and deeply rooted in the rich oral culture of her people, as her verbatim recital of many beautiful traditional songs and stories, recorded in this book, shows. The Bible is not a written text for her, but an icon mediating the numinous power of the whites whose guns had destroyed her people's independence (cf. Ukpong 2000b: 587, who refers to the 'magical dimensions' of the Bible in popular African culture; also West 2003: 41–55). Indeed, the connection between the Bible and the gun is frequently made in the Xhosa praise poetry cited by Jeff Opland (1999: 90–110), as in this example he gives from Nontsizi Mgqwetho in the 1920s:

> They clapped shackles on Africa
> With Bible and gun they brought her down;
> Africa wails its laments.
> Where's that Bible now, O Christians?

Dlamini's vision unconsciously highlights this by the opposition of the shining white man and the tall black man (Bourquin and Filter use 'dark' for *omnyama* and miss the point) who warns her that the book will kill her. While white and black are important symbolic opposites in Zulu *iphupho* dreams (Berglund 1976: 140–4), with white closely associated with the ancestors, this dream is fraught with ambiguity. She herself reconstructs her own life story in retrospect as positioned 'between the service of two kings', Cetschwayo and Jesus, so that one could imagine that the opposition to the Bible in the vision comes from the tall handsome black figure of Cetshwayo, last independent king of the Zulu, whom she admired and continues to show ambivalence towards in her narrative, despite her choice of Jesus as her new (white) king.

Third, Unomguqo does, in a certain sense, die, as the black figure had warned, since now the mission-educated Paulina regards her people's culture as demonic, 'beliefs and customs which only lead people into darkness and distract their minds from the love and omnipotence of God' (Bourquin and Filter 1986: 106). At the heart of Zulu culture is a profound belief in the continuity of life, between the living and the departed, so that the ancestors continue to live with, protect and empower their living descendants. Hence the ancestors are invoked for healing and protection, but Dlamini sees this as 'using demons to cast out demons' (Mark 3: 23). Sharing in the food or drink which has been offered in honour of the ancestors is eating 'at the table of the devils' (1 Cor. 10: 21) (ibid.: 94–7). Yet she recognizes that the ancestral spirits can cure disease, since 'even Satan can perform miracles' (ibid.: 101). She retains a certain ambivalence, 'We Zulus have many customs [imvelo] which make it difficult for a Christian to decide whether they are objectionable heathen customs, or whether they are innocuous and compatible with life in a Christian congregation' (ibid.: 105). Some of this ambivalence in the text may be the result of missionary editing of the oral narration, but it is not uncharacteristic of the new African converts. The Bible as 'Word of God' in the missionary era was regarded as the opposite to a demonic and savage indigenous oral culture, but many African Christians from 'mainline' churches continued to visit the traditional healers and diviners 'after dark'. After independence and the resurgence of indigenous culture, however, enormous energy has been expended by African scholars in the attempt to recover and legitimize African culture by means of exegesis of the Bible, to discover its 'cultural continuity' with Africa.

Fourth, the fact that her conversion is the result of a dream at night is not accidental, but deeply rooted in African culture, where dreams (amaphupha) are associated with the ancestors who provide guidance in times of crisis (Guma 1997: 12–31). Important events are often associated with dreams and visions. The world of spirits and the world of everyday reality interpenetrate each other in a holistic way alien to Western modes of thinking and being, and this is particularly true of dreams and visions:

> Among abaNguni [the Zulu people are one branch of this grouping], dreams are understood as a meeting of subjective and objective reality. It is where the spiritual dimension of reality unites with the social and material conditions of Nguni existence. (ibid.: 13)

As the Bible passes into the common cultural heritage of Africa, it plays an important role in dreams, feeding the symbolism of dream and in turn providing new perspectives on the interpretation of texts, especially in the umbono dreams understood to be prophetic in Zionist churches (ibid.: 16). The many accounts in the Bible of divine guidance in dreams and visions are read as confirmation of the African cultural practice. So, for instance, Dlamini's oral account of her conversion is clearly influenced in its form and even wording by the story of the call of Samuel and the response of Eli in 1 Samuel 3. She gets up and goes to her employer van Rooyen who shows her a Bible, prays and says, 'Go back to sleep, but call me, if you hear the Voice again'. The dream is repeated and is duly understood as a call from God to an agency role of reconstruction of the people of the Zulu kingdom or 'the east', in which Dlamini is to play a leadership role as an 'apostle' like Paul, hence her new name, Pauline (Bourquin and Filter 1986: 82–3). In Zulu culture, women play important roles as izangoma or mediums for the ancestors, and Dlamini certainly does not accept the kind of subordinate role commonly assigned to women by the missionaries.

Fifth, conversion was necessarily followed by a period of three months spent at a mission school learning not just about the Christian faith, but also to read and write. Indeed, she spends between one and two years living at the mission. Becoming a Christian all through Africa, was associated with a transition from an oral culture to a literate, mission school influenced culture (cf. Scribner and Cole 1973; Goody 1987: 139–47, for the impact of Western schooling). Yet, while Dlamini learns to read and write, she does not leave the world of orality nor does the Bible become a 'text' in the Western sense. It is more a source of story, symbol and power. When she begins preaching to heathen Zulu, they spread the word that she is secretly entrapping people to be sent away to slavery overseas, until she demonstrates the opposite by confronting a white Afrikaner farmer, 'who behaved like a Pharaoh' and was renowned for his harsh labour conditions and violent temper (Bourquin and Filter 1986: 86). She turned the Bible against him by pointing out that he was breaking the Ten Commandments because he had his labourers working on the Sunday. Her rebuke led to his conversion and 'from then onwards he never again made his workers toil like animals'. This is understood as the power of the Word: 'When the people realised what effect the word of God had had in converting a violent person into a reasonable human being, they stopped defaming me by saying that I was misleading them. They actually began to refer to me as *umPhositoli* [the Apostle]' (ibid.: 87).

Sixth, this oral narrative is taken down in handwritten notes in Zulu by the missionary Heinrich Filter, typed up in modified form, and then re-organized and re-written again in German into a linear Western-style literary life history. The notes indicate that the narration is episodic and 'circular' in its structure: details radiate outwards from events considered significant. The text is then rewritten as a narrative in German, and while it is still charming and faithful in many respects to Dlamini, it becomes an archetypal 'mission apologetic'. The German narrative was subsequently published in English translation, made with minimal reference to the original Zulu transcript. The various phases of production are preserved in the Killie Campbell Archives in Durban and make fascinating reading. At the end of it, Dlamini's voice is only been heard in a foreign language, with foreign intonations and imputed meaning, like thousands of early indigenous vernacular accounts and writings in missionary archives around the world waiting to be rediscovered and appropriated by African theologians and Bible scholars (Tshehla 2004: 19–33).

Translation is a complex linguistic negotiation, in which meaning is 'slippery' and open to multiple interpretations between the parties. This is characteristic not only of this narration of Dlamini, but even more so of the presence of the Bible among the African people. The voice of difference and 'impropriety' found in the vernacular response is muted, though never quite erased.

The Bible and Vernacular Translation

Translation of the Bible into the vernacular was a central aspect of the Western missionary effort from the beginning. In a context of largely oral cultures, where there were no dictionaries or grammars, translation of even the most basic things presented the missionaries with problems. In the early mission to the Zulu people as so often in Africa, the name of God presented a particular problem. The first choice was the KhoiKhoi word *uThixo* used by the missionaries to the Xhosa, or the loan words *uYehova* or *uDio*, none of which meant anything in Zulu and had no previous associations. However, Bishop John William Colenso (1814–83), who was greatly influenced by Coleridge's Enlightenment theology, believed deeply in the universality of religious experience and human ethics and gave Zulu culture a positive valuation. He rightly perceived that 'no genuine communication between the missionary teacher and the heathen pupil' was possible without a thorough knowledge of the vernacular in conversation and Bible translation (Guy 2001: 65; cf. Tshehla 2003: 29–41). In his translation of the Bible, he spent enormous amounts of time in discussion with his Zulu interlocutors, both mastering the language and discussing with them the meaning of the text. He insisted on the use of the normative vernacular Zulu names for the high God, *uNkulunkulu* or *uMvelinqangi* and succeeded in establishing this against spirited opposition. In other words, he argued that the creator God whom the Zulu already worshipped was the same as the God of Jesus Christ. He also insisted in his *Zulu Dictionary* (1861) on the use of *ukuthemba* for the Greek word *pistis*, which means 'to believe' in the sense of trusting that a thing is so, even when one does not yet see it, rather than *ukukholwa*, which means 'to believe' in the sense of experiencing and knowing already that something is true. Furthermore, he translates the Greek word *ephanerosen* by *kuhlalukiswa* as a 'continuously progressing manifestation' and comments in his *Commentary on Romans*: 'The recognition of the Eternal Power and Deity of our glorious Maker involves a natural and necessary consequence, the duty of fearing, loving, trusting, and obeying Him, in proportion to the Light He gives us' ([1861] 2003: 42). These seemingly simple decisions of translation open the way for an appropriation of the Christian gospel in terms of Zulu religion and culture, and his converts were not slow to grasp this (Draper 2004b: 57–82).

Magema kaMagwaza Fuze (c.844–1923) was one of Colenso's first pupils at his school at Ekukhanyeni, and baptized by him only after he had obtained the permission of his non-Christian parents by making Fuze read the Ten Commandments in Zulu to them from the Bible without commentary (Fuze [1922] 1979: iii). He was an accomplished typesetter with his own business in Pietermaritzburg and was later tutor to the children of King Dinizulu. He responded to Colenso (Draper 2003a: 414–54) by writing the first book in Zulu by a Zulu person, *Abantu Abamnyama Lapa Bavela Ngakona* (1922) or *The Black People and Whence They Came* (1979). Fuze sees no contradiction between Zulu culture and the Bible, but rather warns his people against abandoning their culture and running after European civilization:

> ceasing to observe our own ways and respectful customs, and grasping those of the foreigners and then finding that we had been abandoned by the One above from whom we originated. I now warn you to abandon all this pretence because it is of no benefit whatever. Adhere strictly to your own. It does not mean to say that because you see civilized people and wish to become like them, that you should discard your own which is good. It may happen that in seeking to do so, you may suddenly find yourselves being cast into a bottomless pit. The creator did not create us foolishly, but wisely, and there can be no doubt

that if we love and acknowledge Him, He will uplift us like all the nations; but if we treat Him with disdain, and do not acknowledge Him, He will forsake us for ever. (Fuze 1922: viii)

Fuze takes his bearings from creation, in which Zulu culture has an equal place with European culture, so that for Zulus to adopt the latter is a rejection of the creator God and brings disaster on the nation.

Thus the vernacular translation of the Bible in Africa, which was often largely carried out by indigenous mission assistants, was frequently a (hidden or 'off stage' in the sense of James Scott 1990) site of resistance to missionary domination. Some modern African scholars (e.g. Sanneh 1989, 1993; Bediako 1992, 1995) have argued for translation as a hermeneutical device in Africa. The insistence of the missionaries that Africans read the Bible in their own language did more than explore the semantic potential of the text, since the word slips from the control of the missionaries in the process of translation. This results in a dynamic and creative interaction between the semantic signifiers in the biblical text and African culture at its deepest level. Hence it is not just the Bible but Christianity itself, which is essentially translatable: 'in so far as Christianity has successfully penetrated African societies, this is largely because it has been assimilated into local idiom' (Sanneh 1993: 16, quoted in Maluleke 1996: 5). This attempt to uncouple Christianity from the colonialism which introduced it in Sub-Saharan Africa has been strongly critiqued by Maluleke (1996: 3–19) as a 'hollow triumphalism', which does not take the material reality of Western economic and cultural domination, nor the way in which the Bible has served gender oppression:

> Translation is, by its very nature, a fragile human process. By its very nature translation could be a lot more messy and disagreeable than the proponents of agency are willing to come to terms with. some vernacular translations could militate against transformative agency. The vernacular Bible could function in ways that both strengthen and weaken the Christian church. Translatability is an interesting notion but it is no panacea for the problems of lack of voice for the marginalized and oppressed. (Maluleke and Nadar 2004: 14)

Bearing in mind these important reservations, there is no doubt that the drive to translate both the Bible and the Christian faith into vernacular categories has played and continues to play an important dialogical role in the relationship between the Bible and culture, especially in those African cultures which were orally mediated before the advent of Christianity.

The Bible and Cultural Continuity

The missionaries who brought Christianity to Africa were unaware of the extent to which their understanding of the Bible was culturally conditioned. They assumed the superiority of European culture and saw African cultural practices, such as polygamy and *ilobolo*, ritual sacrifice and veneration of the ancestors, as evil and barbaric. Let us take as an example, the question of polygamy and *lobola*, which the American Board of

Commissioners for Foreign Missions, one of the earliest entries into the field of Zulu mission, described as 'the twin pillars of heathenism' and prohibited. However, when their converts began to hear, read and study the Bible for themselves, they understood it differently to the missionaries. To the dismay and disconcertion of their teachers, they found an essential 'cultural continuity' with the Bible, especially the Old Testament but also the New Testament which presupposed the Old (Dickson 1984: 141–84). The London Missionary Society missionaries persuaded King Sechele of the Bastwana that becoming a Christian meant putting away his wives, but when he learnt to read the Bible for himself, he could not see why he should not imitate David and Solomon (Nkomazana 2000: 223–35).

Breakaway Independent Church Movements could claim scriptural warrant far more easily than the missionaries, as they recast their Christian faith in an African cultural mode. An interesting example can be seen in the *AmaNazaretha* church begun by Isaiah Shembe (1870–1935). He is able, for example, to permit and regulate polygamy and *lobola* with biblical authority in his *Imilando Nemithetho*, as edited and translated by Liz Gunner (2002: 65–7; cf. 74–5):

> This is the law I set out for believers who wish to marry. If a man asks his wife permission to take a second wife and she agrees, she should go to the elders of the church and say, 'I wish my husband to take another wife.' The church is not in a position to refuse if it happens in this way. But if the wife does not agree to her husband's marrying again, the man must go to the elders himself three times.

> He must separate out the times when he approaches them as follows: he may go back to the elders after six months; he should have proof that, 'Yes I have spoken to my wife three times, begging her to agree to my taking another wife. I do not find fault with her over anything, I simply wish to take another wife.'

> The elders will reply, 'What evidence have you that there were people who heard you when you asked your wife on three occasions and she refused?' If he replies, 'I have evidence,' the elders should call both the witnesses and the wife. If the witnesses agree that the wife did indeed refuse three times, the elders are obliged to wait and ask the wife whether the husband treated her just as well after the three people had given witness, as he had before? If the wife replies, 'Yes.' They should say, 'Does he still treat you well today?'

> If she replies, 'Yes he does,' the elders say, 'Well, why should he start mistreating you today then? Surely it's not as if you are saying, "My husband wants to remarry and is ill-treating me?" ' If that were the case, we would refuse permission because when he was married a second time he really would treat you badly, seeing that he is already doing so'. (Genesis 16:4–6)

> A man may marry but he must not take the *lobolo* cattle from the beasts already at the homestead (Genesis 21:8–11). He must take cattle that have been farmed out and are elsewhere. Once the bride price has been paid he should not take the [new] wife into the homestead, but build her home somewhere else.

The practice of taking multiple wives was a deep-rooted aspect of Zulu culture. A man wishing to marry a certain woman would have to approach his father and negotiations would begin between the two families on the question of *ilobola* or the payment of cattle to the woman's family. This was never seen as 'buying' a wife, but was a means of ensuring the viability and stability of the marriage and of protecting the woman from abuse, since the cattle are lodged with her father. A man might take as many wives as he could afford, the requirement of cattle ensuring that he did not go beyond his means. Usually each wife would have her own kraal in which she lived with her children, unless the man were particularly poor. The first missionaries argued that such unions were not really marriages but concubinage, and that converts must put away all but one wife before baptism (Maclean 2003: 265–92; Ngewu 2003: 266–305).

The cruelty and social dislocation this occasioned to wives and children are rightly attacked by Bishop Colenso in his remarkable *Letter to his Grace the Archbishop of Canterbury upon the Question of the Proper Treatment of Cases of Polygamy as found Already Existing in Converts from Heathenism* (1862). Colenso points out that polygamy was practised by 'eminently pious men' in the Old Testament 'without a single word of reproof, or intimation of God's displeasure being addressed to them on account of it', and that it was only 'indirectly' forbidden in the New Testament (ibid.: 4–7). On the other hand, Jesus teaches that putting one's wife away is tantamount to committing adultery against her (ibid.:16–17; cf. Dwane 1989: 115–27), so that putting away wives in polygamous marriages breaks Christ's command. For scriptural legitimation, Colenso's missionary opponents turned to the story of Abraham, who had been a polygamist in Ur, but had left there with only one wife, Sarah, and had, moreover, put away Hagar in accordance with God's will (ibid.: 8–9).

Shembe's 'halakic' reading of Genesis 16:4–6 and 21:8–11, given above, is thus directed at the missionary reading of the same texts. He finds that, far from supporting a ban on polygamy, they legitimate it. Abraham takes another wife, Hagar, only because Sarah requests him to. Further, he notes that the problem between Sarah and Hagar arises out of the question of inheritance. Thus, Shembe's position in 'cultural continuity' with the text of Genesis enables him to use the story to regulate the practice of polygamy in his community in a creative way (cf. Mbuwayesango 1997: 27–36, who nevertheless critiques the male patriarchy inherent in such interpretations). He acknowledges the potential problems in the practice where there is arbitrary behaviour by the husband and no agreement from the other wife or wives. Therefore he requires that the request for a man to take a new wife must come from the earlier wife/wives or else she/they must be given fair chance to object over a six-month period of testing. Sarah's protest to Abraham about the contempt shown her by Hagar is used as the basis for the regulation. The husband has to prove his ability to continue to relate well to the first wife by his good treatment of her during the probationary period. Second, the question of *ilobola* is also addressed from the story, taking up Sarah's jealousy about the possibility of Hagar's son inheriting what should belong to her son Isaac. Shembe's ruling forbids the husband to use his existing cattle in the homestead, which are deemed to belong to the first wife's children, to be used to pay *ilobola* for a new wife, potentially disinheriting them. Instead he must use cattle at his disposal from elsewhere. Moreover, as Hagar and her son were driven out because of Sarah's jealousy and yet God gave them their own place, so the new wife must not live in the same homestead, but be given her own place elsewhere. Elsewhere, Shembe limits the number of wives a man may take to six, on the basis of Deuteronomy 17:15–19 (Gunner 2002: 106–7).

In this example, which can be replicated in indigenous interpretations of the Bible on other issues, the proximity of the culture of Israel to Zulu culture enables a very direct appropriation of its meaning in a way not possible for modern Western readers whose culture is very different. Colenso, who considered monogamy to be forbidden 'directly in the spirit of Christianity, as not being in accordance with the Mind of the Creator' despite his impassioned defence of existing polygamous marriages, argued that converts should take no new wives if already married and hold to one wife where possible. However, his own converts overruled him on this, and their entry into polygamous marriages subverted his attempts to create an indigenous clergy!

The Bible and Creative Cultural Adaptation

While Shembe may have felt cultural continuity with regard to the Bible and polygamy in African culture, his response to the place of the ancestors is far more nuanced or ambivalent. While his biographers (Vilakazi et al. 1986: 76) argue that 'he has given a place to the Zulu ancestral spirits in his system of theology', there is no mention of the *amadlozi* explicitly in his hymns and laws. Significantly, they give no references to substantiate their assertion, and a somewhat polemical study by Kitshoff (1996: 23–36) provides contrary evidence, that Shembe rejected the ancestor cult, *per se*. The ancestors are probably the central feature of African religious culture across the continent, regarded as the source of social cohesion, healing and power. This is certainly so among the Zulu people (Berglund 1976: 78–245; cf. Setilonae 1986: 21–8; Mafico 2000: 481–9). Tied to the veneration of the ancestors (and gods who were originally ancestors in some cultures) in virtually all African cultures is the practice of sacrifice, whereby the blood of animals and ritually prepared beer is poured out onto the ground in libation (for the practice in Zulu culture, see Berglund 1976: 197–245). Hence sacrifice in the Bible and especially the human sacrifice of Jesus by his Father play a pivotal role in African cultural appropriations of the Bible (Ubruhe 1996: 13–22; Dickson 1984: 185–19). Nevertheless, the process of reconciling the ancestors to the mediatory role of Jesus is especially complex, despite the efforts of some African interpreters to see Jesus as the universal human ancestor figure:

> Christ was the perfect victim; by his death he merits, to use an African image, to be looked upon as Ancestor, the greatest of ancestors, who never ceases to be one of the 'living-dead', because there always will be people alive who *knew* him, whose lives were irreversibly affected by his life and work. He becomes the one with whom the African Christian lives intimately (as well as with the other living dead), on whom he calls, and to whom he offers prayer. (Dickson 1984: 197–8; cf. Bediako 1995: 85; Bujo 1992: 75–92)

The problem is that the ancestors are very closely associated with biological kinship and family (e.g. the Zulu word for ancestors, *amadlozi*, means sperm in Xhosa), tied to the local and particular, so that such a universalizing of the ancestors has not met with much enthusiasm, even among those who stress the continued importance of the ancestors.

Many African interpreters prefer to stress the similarity between Jesus' healing and acts of power with the practice of the mediums of the ancestors in African culture: the *ngaka* among the Batswana and Basotho (Ntloedibe 2000: 498–510; Masoga 2003: 217–25) or the *isangoma* among the Zulu:

> In this post-colonial era, it is just and right that some of us who are undeniably both African and Christian read for ourselves from both religious testaments – from both African Traditional Religion and the Bible. (Ntloedibe 2000: 310)

However, for others, such as Shembe, the place of the ancestors as mediators has been taken by angels. The worship sites of the *amaNazaretha* are holy because they are 'the entrance for God's angels who keep watch over the community;' so that improper sexual conduct or impurity in this space will cause the angels to 'turn their backs on that community' (Gunner 2002: 90–1; cf. Muller 1999: 66–7). Angels also play an important role in Shembe iconography, since the prophet is portrayed in photographs with angels over his head (Muller 1999: 120) or hovering over the people during pilgrimage to Nhlangakazi (Gunner 2002: Plate 8). This seems a common move among those African Independent Churches which reject the veneration of the ancestors and in African Christian piety. It is a creative substitution of angels for ancestors as mediators of visions, protection and healing. It also provides a hermeneutical key for the re-reading of the Bible.

A particularly interesting movement in this regard is the *iBandla Labangcwele* of George Khambule (1884–1949), a prophet from Nqutu in rural Zululand (Draper 2003a: 57–89; 2004: 250–74; cf. Sundkler 1976: 119–60). After serving in the South African Native Labour Corps on the Western Front in World War I, Khambule has a 'near death experience' while working as a captain in the mine police in 1918, in which he goes to heaven and sees himself condemned to hell. His dead sister, Agrineth, intercedes with God on his behalf and he is sent back to earth to preach repentance. This same dead sister remains with him and mediates the word of God to him. The book of Revelation becomes the central point of Khambule's understanding and organization of the church. He has a vision of the Ark of the Covenant in Revelation 11: 19 being entrusted to the community, which necessitates the setting apart of virgins to form the royal harem (*isigodlo*) of King Jesus, as for the Zulu king:

> *Priest*:   On the 20 of June 1922 a word of God came to St. Nazar [George Khambule] saying, 'You are lucky because the ark which used to be handled by the Cherubim is going to be handed to you.'
> *Congregation*:   The angel said to St. Nazar you are lucky because you are going to be given power.
> *Priest*:   The Ark of the Covenant is going to be given to the virgins (*isigodlo*) of your house. Therefore, set them apart.
> *Congregation*:   The Ark of the Covenant is going to be given to the virgins of your house.
> *Priest*:   It repeated for many times indeed saying, It is good that you set them aside because they are going to be given power.
> *Congregation*:   Indeed, it is good that you set them apart because they are going to be given power.

Priest: By that time St. Nazar told them that it is good that they set them apart because the Ark of the Covenant is to be given to them.
Congregation: St. Nazar said to the women . . .
Priest: It really happened when they set them apart, there was a great commotion but they finally set them apart.
Congregation: They did as the angel have told them, all that was gain to them they count as loss. (*Diary* 3: 118–22; texts transcribed and translated by me and a team including M. B. Mkhize, B. Maseko, M. K. Ntuli and M. Ndawondi)

All the members of the community are required to enter the 'marriage of the Lamb' which has 'come down to earth' (*Diary* 3: 96) and live a celibate life of holiness, refusing both sexual relations with their spouses and food which is tainted by 'idolatry' (Rev. 2: 14) through being offering to the ancestors. The angels are present in the community, since the setting up of this community marks the coming down of Jerusalem and the throne of God to earth:

Priest: We thank the holy ones (*abangcwele*, i.e. angels) of the Church.
Yes, they cannot be seen.
Let peace be among you.
This is the new throne which was established
When we wrote the papers . . .

Congregation: The throne of kingship which settled.
The throne (*isihlalo*)is established on earth
Through the victory of the Lord the Judge (*Inkosi Umahluli*) [George Khambule].
Yes, Amen! We thank you Lord God for ever! (*Liturgy* 3: 3–4)

Judgement now flows out from the community at the service of the Seven Candlesticks (*Diary* 1: 21A). Members of the community wage ceaseless warfare against Satan to bring healing to the sick and oppressed with demons, with the holy stones (weapons or *izikhali*) they carry.

Central to this re-interpretation of Revelation is a creative adaptation of the Zulu cultural understanding of the ancestors, since the angels not only mediate the Word of God but also become united to particular members of the community through the marriage of the Lamb. Joanna Ndlovu, Khambule's 'General of the Lord and Prosecutor' or 'Captenis' is possessed by, or becomes the fleshly incarnation of, his dead sister, Agrineth:

It is no longer said, 'Joanah.' It is now said, 'Agreneth Hlazile.' So it is with Joanah in the heavens, say the scriptures, that she will come by means of a person. This is quite clear. This is now Agreneth. It is now so, say the great ones in truth. We did not know this. It is so . . . This marriage is very great! (*Diary* 1: 13A, 14A)

Khambule himself is possessed by the Spirit of Jesus, so that what is said of Jesus in Revelation can be said of him:

Priest: One of his seven angels . . . [said], 'I am coming to tell St. Nazar that God (*uTixo*) Jesus has come upon you. The angel repeated twice swearing and said, 'I have come upon

St. Nazar. Today you would be going home [to heaven] if you had told all the people why you are here. All the witnesses agreed, those of the Cross and the elders said, 'Indeed it is so,' and Substatno [Fakazi] said, 'Yes it is so.'

Congregation: If you conquer, I will grant you to sit on the throne of Kingship, like myself.

Priest: I have conquered and I sit together with my Father on the throne. Amen. (*Liturgy* 3: 6–7)

Indeed, each of the members of the community 'becomes an angel' in some sense after being purified of their sins and entering the marriage of the Lamb:

The word which comes from Jehovah.

The Judge.

Take another stole and it shall be written thus, The righteousness of the Saints, This name was never given to any angel except for the Lord who was called the righteousness of the saints. The angels left here with sins and went were tried [in court]. They then received the nature of angels (*zabutata ubungelosi*), but none was called the Righteousness of the Saints like it is said to you. This is said to you, Your doing is very much like it. It is wonderful. Who am I? says the Lord. It shall be written and everyone shall see it for themselves clearly. It is really, really great. There will be written on that notice board the very same thing, We praise God, it shall say, *Ibandhla laBancwele*. There has been appointed over it a female chief steward, *uMpathi Ark* (the Bearer of the Ark). She is not greater than the chief steward of the four corners of the earth; she is only the bearer of the Ark; but the real chief steward is the one that is God's interpreter (*humusha*). So indeed, Captenis is the bearer of the Angel. I praise the God. The seclusion (*umgonqo*, ritual for girls reaching puberty) will start on Monday, says Jehovah. (*Diary* 1: 15A–16A)

The implicit understanding found in *iBandla LamaNazaretha* becomes explicit in Khambule's movement: angels have taken over the role of the ancestors as mediators and sources of God's numinous presence and power. It is not blasphemous for Khambule to say that he is Jesus, since he is not claiming to have replaced him or to be greater than him, but only to be possessed by the spirit of Jesus, in the same way as an *isangoma* is possessed by a particular spirit of the ancestors. A similar dynamic probably lies behind the role that Shembe plays for his church, taking the place of Jesus as mediator figure without denying Jesus and his teaching. The way in which what is heavenly becomes what is earthly and immediate is, in some ways, characteristic of indigenous church movements in Africa. The Bible can then be directly appropriated by the community here and now as applying to them.

The Bible and the Land

Just as the New Jerusalem is frequently located on earth in African indigenous interpretations of the Bible, so has the land of Israel and its covenant relationship with Yahweh. This derives in part from the link between the land and the ancestors, which was widely held to be a sacred bond, particularly in terms of burial sites, but also in terms of 'where the umbilical cord is buried' (the *inkaba* in Zulu). The ancestral cult centres around sacrifices and communion meals in which 'eating together seals the continuing bond with the dead, while also strengthening the bond between the living' (Bujo 1992: 25). Place is important and ancestor cults usually have shrines to the ancestors connected in some way (at least originally) to their place of burial, e.g. the *msamo* or far interior of the chief hut in Zulu culture, where offerings may be made, is connected with the interior of the *isibaya* or cattle kraal, where sacrifices are made. The departed are ritually 'brought back' to the homestead in Zulu culture (*ukubuyisa*), wherever they may have died, even if the body is buried in a city cemetery rather than in the cattle kraal (Berglund 1976: 102–23). This gives land and place a sacral value in African culture.

Living contrary to the customs and values of the ancestors was believed to bring drought and other natural disasters, while living in accordance with the traditions and values of ancestors by honouring the ancestors in ritual and sacrifice brought blessings and fertility (Berglund 1976: 112–13; cf. Dickson 1984: 160–6). Land in Zulu tradition is communally owned, allocated by the chief as representative of the people and held in trust by the individual. In South Africa the cultural affinity between biblical covenantal theology of the land was sharpened and centralized by the theft of land by white settlers, not only in the early colonial period but also in the disastrous relocation policy of the apartheid government. As we have seen, it is no accident that Unomguqo Dlamini heard her call to take up the Bible and become an apostle to her people in the wake of the theft of land from the Zulu Kingdom by the settlers in Natal. Subsequently, however, black people have felt that it was the Bible itself which robbed them of their land, as expressed in a popular anecdote:

> When the white man came to our country he had the Bible and we had the land. The white man said to us 'let us pray'. After the prayer, the white man had the land and we had the Bible. (Mofokeng 1988: 34)

The understanding that it was not just guns but also the Bible that dispossessed them runs strongly through the Xhosa *izimbongi* recorded and discussed by Jeff Opland (1999: 90–110). Stories like the Exodus of Israel and their entry into the promised land and also the theft of Naboth's Vineyard play an important role in the resistance mythology of many South African communities as they struggled to come to grips with dispossession and relocation (James and Nkadimeng 2003: 111–31). Furthermore, independent church movements have often invested heavily to buy land to establish their vision of the New Jerusalem, which is then sacralized in terms of biblical myths of Exodus and Zion coming down out of heaven from God. George Khambule's community, after its expulsion from its holy mountain at Telezini, understands its temporary residences as 'Elim', until they purchase a farm with other *Amakholwa* (Westernized Christian Africans) near Dundee to build the new Jerusalem. The land has more than symbolic meaning in such communities, since it is also farmed and served as a way of resisting dispossession and incorporation as cheap labour into the capitalist economy by white settlers. Another interesting example of this process of 'resacralization' of the land as communal inheritance is provided by the vision of Shembe, who also bought land to secure his Zion, as the glorious figure of Daniel 10:4–7 having three portions of land (Gunner 2002: 154–5).

The question of an understanding of the land and its relationship to the Bible has become an important issue in the rebuilding of South Africa after the democratic elections of 1994 (see the collections of papers edited by Guma and Milton 1997 and by Philpott 1998). Takatso Mofokeng, for instance, takes up Mosala's repeated insistence on the need to take sides in the conflict *inside* the biblical text between royal Davidic theology of land and the popular prophetic egalitarian theology of the oppressed. He argues for a new synthesis between the ancestral connection with the land and the egalitarian view of land as a gift of God in the latter strand in the Bible, commenting:

> I would rather opt for a synthesis of the egalitarian theology of land with the African theology of the centrality of the African household and the God givenness of the land of the household and its inalienability. It should be clear that when we say that land belongs to the ancestors, that we critically believe in the equality of ancestors who won the land. It should also be clear then, when we confess that God gave our land inalienably to the ancestors, that we confess that God gave our land inalienably to the ancestors, that we believe in the light of our understanding of the redemptive life and death of Jesus Christ and his propagation of the concept of the kingdom of God, the land of our ancestors is an equal inheritance to all African people. Jesus Christ is on their side, condemning the sin of the theft of the land of the African poor. (1997: 55)

The Bible and African Women

In the face of assertions of the kind of 'cultural continuity with the Bible' claimed by many African interpreters, women have faced a particular challenge as they come to appropriate the Bible in Africa. African culture is in many respects patriarchal in nature and has contributed to a marginalization of women in society and academy, as well as a marginalization in terms of leadership roles in the Church:

> This is where the tasks lie for those of us reading the Bible from those cultures that closely mirror the times and practices similar to those in the Bible. We can quickly rush to justify our behaviour simply because we think we are in good company with the biblical culture. (Phiri et al 2002: 10)

While most African women do not wish to reject or demonize African culture, but rather to affirm the importance of enculturation in interpreting the Bible in Africa, they are beginning to insist on the importance of their own experience in religion and culture. This means that the experiences of African women illuminated the interpretation of the Bible and that, conversely, the reading of the Bible 'poses questions to communities in Africa' (ibid.: 11).

This process is being driven by a highly significant common purpose developed in the Circle of African Women Theologians, which includes women of other faith as well as Christian, but has a strong focus on readings of the Bible (Kanyoro 2002b: 15–38). Because of the complexity of the issue of patriarchy and culture in *both* the culture of the Bible and their own African culture, the writings of women are becoming increasingly fertile and creative in the study of the Bible and culture (see e.g. the collections of papers in Oduyoye and Kanyoro 1990; Ackermann et al. 1991; Oduyoye and Kanyoro 1992; Oduyoye 1995; Phiri 1997: 68–70; Akoto 2000: 260–77; Dube 2000; Okure 2000; Njoroge and Dube 2001; Kanyoro 2002a; Phiri et al. 2003; Masenya 2004). Teresa Okure (2000: 199), for instance, argues that life and the experience come before 'the Book', so that neither the original context and meaning of the biblical texts nor subsequent interpretations of them, which are rooted in specific cultures, can 'become automatically normative for all time'. Likewise, Mercy Oduyoye (2001: 124) sees women's experience as 'a cardinal part of a heritage to be appropriated', without rejecting African culture or making men 'the enemy'.

Many African women draw on the African cultural tradition of the 'hearth-hold' (ibid.: 122) with its rich tradition of proverbs (Kinoti 1998: 55–78; Masenya 2004a) and story telling, in order to 're-tell biblical stories so that they tell the untold stories of women' (Dube 2001: 22–3; cf. Masenya 2004b: 46–59). The stories of women in the Bible provides a fertile ground for creative telling and re-telling against the pervasive background of African cultural tradition in a way which critiques both the Bible and African culture without rejecting either.

Conclusion

Obviously, this short study has been uneven in its treatment. It is skewed towards Southern Africa, and has left many areas untouched. In particular, the way the Bible has served in resistance to colonialism and in the struggle for liberation deserves further treatment, since it springs from the holistic African cultural understanding of the inseparability of the spiritual and the material (the debate over the Bible and liberation is a long and fascinating one; e.g. Boesak 1984; Mofokeng 1988; Mosala 1989; West [1991] 1995; Maluleke 1996). This aspect has been taken up again in 'reconstruction' theology (Mugambe 1995; Farisani 2003). Another important area of cultural interaction between Africa and the Bible lies in the area of healing, which runs through main line churches and independent church movements alike (Bate 1995), and in which the Bible and Jesus as healer play a central role. The richness of the cultural interaction between the Bible and African culture can be seen in the proliferation of written studies which continue to flow from all corners of the continent, often on local presses with very localized distribution (see the bibliography provided by LeMarquand 2000: 633–800).

What is clear is that the Bible has taken deep roots in Africa, and that the interaction of the Bible with African culture has, from the beginning been a rich and complex one. African biblical scholars today continue to emphasize and privilege the centrality of their own cultural locatedness in their reading of the Bible (Ukpong 1995: 3–14). One of the first converts to Christianity among the Xhosa people was Ntsikana kaGabha (*c*.1780–1821). He was illiterate when he was converted by hearing the Bible preached by unknown missionaries, and gathered a group of followers around him independent of any white church. His deeply influential hymns are still sung all over South Africa, and show a deep interaction between African religion and culture and biblical themes that are already characteristic of later developments. It would be a fitting way to complete this brief perspective on the Bible and African culture with his *Great Hymn*:

> He is the Great God, who is in heaven;
> Thou art Thou, shield of truth.
> Thou art Thou, stronghold of truth.
> Thou are Thou, thicket of truth.
> Thou art Thou, who dwellest in the highest.
> He, who created life below, created life above.
> That creator who created, created heaven.
> That maker of stars, and the Pleiades.
> A star flashed forth, it was telling us.
> Maker of the blind, does he not make them on purpose?
> The trumpet sounded, it has called us,
> As for his chase, he hunts for souls.
> He, who amalgamates flocks rejecting each other.
> He, the leader, who has led us.
> He, the great blanket, which we put on.
> Those hands of thine, they are wounded.
> Those feet of thine, they are wounded.
> Thy blood, why is it streaming?
> Thy blood, it was shed for us.
> This great price, have we called for it?
> This home of thine, have we called for it?
>
> (Opland 1992: 111–12)

References and Further Reading

Adamo, D. T. (1997). 'Peace in the Old Testament and in the African Heritage', in H. W. Kinoti and J. M. Waliggo (eds), *The Bible in African Christianity: Essays in Biblical Theology*. Nairobi: Acton., pp. 99–111.

Akoto, D. B. E. A. (2000). 'The Mother of the Ewe and Firstborn Daughter as the 'Good Shepherd' in the Cultural Context of the Ewe Peoples: A Liberating Approach', in G. O. West and M. W. Dube (eds), *The Bible in Africa: Transactions, Trajectories and Trends*. Leiden: Brill, pp. 260–77.

Bate, S. (1995). *Inculturation and Healing: Coping-Healing in South African Christianity*. Pietermaritzburg: Cluster.

Bediako, K. (1992). *Theology and Identity: The Impact of Culture upon Christian Thought in the Second Century and Modern Africa*. Edinburgh: Edinburgh University Press.

Bediako, K. (1995). *Christianity in Africa: The Renewal of a Non-Western Religion*. Edinburgh: Edinburgh University Press.

Berglund, A.-I. (1976). *Zulu Thought-Patterns and Symbolism*. (Studia Missionalia Upsaliensia 22). Bloomington, IN: Indiana University Press.

Boesak, A. (1984). *Black and Reformed: Apartheid, Liberation and the Calvinist Tradition*. Johannesburg: Skotaville.

Bourquin, S. and Filter, H. (1986). *Paulina Dlamini: Servant of Two Kings*. Durban: Killie Campbell Africana Library.

Bujo, B. (1992). *African Theology in its Social Context* (Faith and Culture Series). Maryknoll, NY: Orbis.

De Gruchy, J. W. (1997). 'From Cairo to the Cape: The Significance of Coptic Orthodoxy for African Christianity', *Journal of Theology for Southern Africa* 99: 24–39.

De Gruchy, J. W. (2001). *Christianity, Art and Transformatiion: Theological Aesthetics in the Struggle for Justice*. Cambridge: Cambridge University Press.

Dickson, K. A. (1984). *Theology in Africa*. Maryknoll, NY: Orbis.

Draper, J. A. (2000). 'The Bishop and the Bricoleur: Bishop John William Colenso's *Commentary on Romans* and Magema kaMagwaza Fuze's *The Black People and Whence They Came*', in G. O. West and M. W. Dube (eds), *The Bible in Africa: Transactions, Trajectories and Trends*. Leiden: Brill, pp. 415–54.

Draper, J. A. (2002). 'The Bible as Poison Onion, Icon and Oracle: Reception of the Printed Sacred Text in Oral and Residual Oral South Africa', *Journal of Theology for Southern Africa* 112: 39–56.

Draper, J. A. (ed.) (2003a). *Orality, Literacy and Colonialism in Southern Africa*. Atlanta, GA: Society of Biblical Literature; Leiden: Brill; Pietermaritzburg: Cluster.

Draper, J. A. (2003b). 'The Closed Text and the Heavenly Telephone: The Role of the *Bricoleur* in Oral Mediation of Sacred Text in the Case of George Khambule and the Gospel of John', in *Orality, Literacy and Colonialism in Southern Africa*. Atlanta, GA: Society of Biblical Literature; Leiden: Brill; Pietermaritzburg: Cluster, pp. 57–89.

Draper, J. A. (ed.) (2003c). *The Eye of the Storm: Bishop John William Colenso and the Crisis of Biblical Inspiration* (JSOTSS 386). London: T. & T. Clark International; Pietermaritzburg: Cluster.

Draper, J. A. (2004a). 'George Khambule and the Book of Revelation: Prophet of the Open Heaven', *Neotestamentica* 38: 250–74.

Draper, J. A. (2004b). 'A 'Frontier' Reading of Romans: The Case of Bishop John William Colenso (1814–1883)', in Y. Khiok-Khng (ed.), *Navigating Romans through Cultures: Challenging Readings by Charting a New Course*. New York: T. & T. Clark International, pp. 57–82.

Dube, M. W. (2000). *Postcolonial Feminist Interpretation of the Bible*. St Louis, MO: Chalice.

Dube, M. W. (2001). 'Introduction: "Little Girl, Get Up!"', in N. J. Njoroge and M. W. Dube (eds), *Talitha Cumi! Theologies of African Women*. Pietermaritzburg: Cluster, pp. 3–24.

Dube, M. W. and Kanyoro, M. (eds) (2004). *Grant Me Justice! HIV/AIDS and Gender Readings of the Bible*. Pietermaritzburg: Cluster; Maryknoll, NY: Orbis.

Dwane, S. (1989). *Issues in the South African Theological Debate: Essays and Addresses in Honour of the Late James Matta Dwane*. Johannesburg: Skotaville.

Fuze, M. M. (1922). *Abantu Abamnyama Lapa Bavela Ngakona*. Pietermaritzburg: University of Natal Press.

Fuze, M. M. (1979). *The Black People and Whence They Came*. Durban: Killie Campbell; Pietermaritzburg: University of Natal Press.

Geertz, C. (1973). *The Interpretation of Cultures: Selected Essays*. New York: Basic Books.

Goody, J. (1987). *The Interface between the Written and the Oral*. Cambridge: Cambridge University Press.

Guma, M. P. (1997). 'Ithongo Dream Narratives', in M. Guma and L. Milton (eds), *An African Challenge to the Church in the 21st Century*. Cape Town: SACC; Salty Print, pp. 12–31.

Guma, M. P. and Milton, L. (eds) (1997). *An African Challenge to the Church in the 21st Century*. Cape Town: SACC, Salty Print.

Gunner, E. (2002). *The Man of Heaven and the Beautiful Ones of God: Umuntu Wasezulwini Nabantu Abahle Bakankulunkulu: Writings from Ibandla lamaNazaretha, a South African Church*. Leiden: Brill.

Guy, J. (2001). *The View across the River: Harriete Colenso and the Zulu Struggle against Imperialism*. Cape Town: David Philip.

James, D. and Nkadimeng, G. M. (2003). 'The Land and the Word: Missions, African Christians, and the Claiming of Land in South Africa', in J. A. Draper (ed.), *Orality, Literacy and Colonialism in Southern Africa*. Atlanta, GA: Society of Biblical Literature; Leiden: Brill; Pietermaritzburg: Cluster, pp. 111–31.

Kanyoro, M. R. A. (2002a). *Introducing Feminist Cultural Hermeneutics: An African Perspective* (Introductions in Feminist Theology 9). Sheffield: Sheffield Academic Press.

Kanyoro, M. R. A. (2002b). 'Beads and Strands: Threading More Beads in the Story of the Circle', in I. A. Phiri, D. B. Govinden and S. Nadar (eds), *Her-Stories: Hidden Histories of Women of Faith in Africa*. Pietermaritzburg: Cluster, pp. 15–38.

Kinoti, H. W. (1996). 'Well-Being in African Society and in the Bible', in H. W. Kinoti and J. M. Waliggo (eds), (1997) *The Bible in African Christianity: Essays in Biblical Theology*. Nairobi: Acton, pp. 112–23.

Kinoti, H. W. (1998). 'Proverbs in African Spirituality', in M. N. Gitui (ed.), *Theological Method and Aspects of Worship African Christianity* (African Christianity Series). Nairobi: Acton, pp. 55–78.

Kinoti, H. W. and Waliggo, J. M. (eds) (1997). *The Bible in African Christianity: Essays in Biblical Theology*. Nairobi: Acton.

Kitshoff, M. (1996). 'Isaiah Shembe's Views on the Ancestors: A Biblical Perspective', *Journal of Theology for Southern Africa* 95: 23–36.

LeMarquand, G. (2000). 'A Bibliography of the Bible in Africa', in G. O. West and M. W. Dube (eds), *The Bible in Africa: Transactions, Trajectories and Trends*. Leiden: Brill, pp. 633–800.

Loubser, J. A. (2000). 'How Al-Mokattam Mountain was Moved: The Coptic Imagination and the Christian Bible', in G. O. West and M. W. Dube (eds), *The Bible in Africa: Transactions, Trajectories and Trends*. Leiden: Brill, pp. 103–26.

Maclean, I. S. (2003). ' "The Twin Pillars of Heathenism": American Missionaries, Bishop Colenso and Converts in Conflict – Polygamy and *Ukulobola* in Nineteenth-Century Natal and Zululand, South Africa', in J. A. Draper (ed.), *The Eye of the Storm: Bishop John William Colenso and the Crisis of Biblical Inspiration* (JSOTSS 386). London: T. & T. Clark International; Pietermaritzburg: Cluster, pp. 265–92.

Mafico, T. L. J. (2000). 'The Biblical God of the Fathers and the African Ancestors', in G. O. West and M. W. Dube (eds), *The Bible in Africa: Transactions, Trajectories and Trends*. Leiden: Brill, pp. 481–9.

Maluleke, T. S. (1996). 'Black and African Theologies in the New World Order: A Time to Drink from our Own Wells', *Journal of Theology for Southern Africa* 96: 3–19.

Maluleke, T. S. (1997). 'Half a Century of African Christian Theologies: Elements of the Emerging Agenda for the Twenty-First Century', *Journal of Theology for Southern Africa* 99: 4–23.

Maluleke, T. S. and Nadar, S. (2004). 'Alien Fraudsters in the White Academy: Agency in Gendered Colour', *Journal of Theology for Southern Africa* 120: 5–17.

Masenya, M. (nhwana' Mphahlele) (2004a). *How Worthy is the Woman of Worth? Rereading Proverbs 31:10–13 in African-South Africa*. New York: Peter Lang.

Masenya, M. (nhawana' Mphahlele) (2004b). 'Struggling with Poverty/Emptiness: Rereading the Naomi-Ruth Story in African-South Africa', *Journal of Theology for Southern Africa* 120: 46–59.

Masoga, M. A. (2003). 'Becoming *Ngaka*: Coming to Terms with Oral Narrative Discourses', in J. A. Draper (ed.) *Orality, Literacy, and Colonialism in Southern Africa* (*Semeia* Studies 46). Atlanta, GA: Scholars Press; Leiden: Brill, pp. 217–25.

Mbiti, J. S. ([1969] 1989). *African Religions and Philosophy*, 2nd edn. London: Heinemann.

Mbiti, J. S. (1979). *Concepts of God in Africa*. London: SPCK.

Mbuwayesango, D. R. (1997). 'Childlessness and Woman-to-Woman Relationships in Genesis and in African Patriarchal Society: Sarah and Hagar from a Zimbabwean Woman's Perspective (Gen. 16:1–16; 21:8–21)', in P. A. Bird (ed.), *Reading the Bible as Women: Perspectives from Africa, Asia, and Latin America* (*Semeia* 78). Atlanta, GA: Scholars Press, pp. 27–36.

Mofokeng, T. (1988). 'Black Christians, the Bible and Liberation', *Journal of Black Theology in South Africa* 2: 34–9.

Mofokeng, T. (1997). 'Land is our Mother: A Black Theology of Land', in M. P. Guma and L. Milton (eds), *An African Challenge to the Church in the 21st Century*. Cape Town: SACC; Salty Print, pp. 42–56.

Mosala, I. J. (1989). *Biblical Hermeneutics and Black Theology in South Africa*. Grand Rapids, MI: Eerdmans.

Mugambe, J. N. K. (1995). *From Liberation to Reconstruction: African Christian Theology after the Cold War*. Nairobi: East African Educational Publishers.

Mugambe, J. N. K. (1998). 'Theological Method in African Christianity', in M. N. Getui (ed.), *Theological Method and Aspects of Worship in African Christianity* (African Christianity Series). Nairobi: Acton, pp. 5–40.

Muller, C. A. (1999). *Rituals of Fertility and the Sacrifice of Desire: Nazarite Women's Performance in South Africa*. Chicago: University of Chicago Press.

Ngewu, L. L. (2003) 'John William Colenso adn the Enigma of Polygamy', in J. A. Draper (ed.), *The Eye of the Storm: Bishop John William Colenso and the Crisis of Biblical Inspiration* (JSOTSS 386). London: T. & T. Clark International; Pietermaritzburg: Cluster, pp. 293–305.

Njoroge, N. J. and Dube, M. W. (eds) (2001). *Talitha Cumi! Theologies of African Women*. Pietermaritzburg: Cluster.

Nkomazana, F. (2000). 'Earliest Southern African Biblical Interpretation: The Case of the *Bakwena*, *Kakolo* and *Bangwato*', in G. O. West and M. W. Dube (eds), *The Bible in Africa: Transactions, Trajectories and Trends*. Leiden: Brill, pp. 223–35.

Ntloedibe, G. S. (2000). '*Ngaka* and Jesus as Liberators: A Comparative Reading', in G. O. West and M. W. Dube (eds), *The Bible in Africa: Transactions, Trajectories and Trends*. Leiden: Brill, pp. 498–510.

Oduyoye, M. A. (1995). *Daughters of Anowa: African Women and Patriarchy*. Maryknoll, NY: Orbis.

Oduyoye, M. A. (2001). *Introducing African Women's Theology* (Introductions in Feminist Theology 6). Sheffield: Sheffield Academic Press.

Oduyoye, M. A. and Kanyoro, M. R. A. (eds) (1992). *The Will to Arise: Women, Tradition and the Church in Africa*. Maryknoll, NY: Orbis.

Okure, T. (2000). 'First Was the Life, Not the Book', in T. Okure (ed.), *To Cast Fire Upon the Earth: Bible and Mission Collaborating in Today's Multicultural Global Context*. Pietermaritzburg: Cluster, pp. 194–214.

Opland, J. (ed.) (1992). *Words that Circle Words: A Choice of South African Oral Poetry*. Johannesburg: A. D. Donker.

Opland, J. (1999). 'The Image of the Book in Xhosa Oral Poetry', in D. Brown (ed.), *Oral Literature and Performance in Southern Africa*. Cape Town: David Philip, pp. 90–110.

Philpott, G. (ed.) (1998). 'Church and Land', *Bulletin for Contextual Theology* 5(3).

Phiri, I. A. (1997). 'Doing Theology in Community: The Case of African Women Theologians in the 1990s', *Journal of Theology for Southern Africa* 99: 68–76.

Phiri, I. A., Govinden, D. B. and Nadar, S. (eds) (2002). *Her Stories: Hidden Histories of Women of Faith in Africa*. Pietermaritzburg: Cluster.

Phiri, I. A., Haddad, B. and Masenya, M. (eds) (2003). *African Women, HIV/AIDS and Faith Communities*. Pietermaritzburg: Cluster.

Sanneh, L. (1989). *Translating the Message: The Missionary Impact on Culture*. Maryknoll, NY: Orbis.

Sanneh, L. (1993). *Encountering the West: Christianity and the Global Cultural Process*. Maryknoll, NY: Orbis.

Scott, J. (1990). *Domination and the Arts of Resistance: Hidden Transcripts*. New Haven, CT: Yale University Press.

Scribner, S. and Cole, M. (1973). 'Cognitive Consequences of Formal and Informal Education', *Science* 1823: 553–9.

Scribner, S. and Cole, M. (1981). *The Psychology of Literacy*. Cambridge, MA: Harvard University Press.

Setiloane, G. M. (1986). *African Theology: An Introduction*. Johannesburg: Skotaville.

Sundkler, B. (1976). *Zulu Zion and Some Swazi Zionists*. Oxford: Oxford University Press.

Tshehla, M. S. (2003). 'Colenso, John 1.1–18 and the Politics of Insider- and Outsider-Translating', in J. A. Draper (ed.), *The Eye of the Storm: Bishop John William Colenso and the Crisis of Biblical Inspiration* (JSOTSS 386). London: T. & T. Clark International; Pietermaritzburg: Cluster, pp. 29–41.

Tshehla, M. S. (2004). 'A Plea for Indigenous Written Sources in South African Theological Discourse: Basotho as Test Case', *Journal of Theology for Southern Africa* 120: 19–33.

Ubruhe, J. A. (1996). 'Traditional Sacrifice: A Key to the Heart of the Christian Message', *Journal of Theology for Southern Africa* 95: 13–22.

Ukpong, J. S. (1995). 'Rereading the Bible with African Eyes: Inculturation and Hermeneutics', *Journal of Theology for Southern Africa* 91: 3–14.

Ukpong, J. S. (2000a). 'Development in Biblical Interpretation in Africa: Historical and Hermeneutical Directions', in G. O. West and M. W. Dube (eds), *The Bible in Africa: Transactions, Trajectories and Trends*. Leiden: Brill,, pp. 11–28.

Ukpong, J. S. (2000b). 'Popular Readings of the Bible in Africa and Implications for Academic Readings', in G. O. West and M. W. Dube (eds), *The Bible in Africa: Transactions, Trajectories and Trends*. Leiden: Brill, pp. 582–94.

Vilakazi, A., with Mthethwa, B. and Mpanza, M. (1986). *Shembe: The Revilatization of African Society*. Johannesburg: Skotaville.

West, G. O. ([1991] 1995). *Biblical Hermeneutics of Liberation: Modes of Reading the Bible in the South African Context*. Pietermaritzburg: Cluster; Maryknoll, NY: Orbis.

West, G. O. (2003). 'The Bible as *Bola* to Biblical Interpretation as *Marabi*: Tlhaping Transactions with the Bible', in J. A. Draper (ed.), *The Eye of the Storm: Bishop John William Colenso and the Crisis of Biblical Inspiration* (JSOTSS 386). London: T. & T. Clark International; Pietermaritzburg: Cluster, pp. 582–94.

West, G. O. and Dube, M. W. (eds) (2000). *The Bible in Africa: Transactions, Trajectories and Trends*. Leiden: Brill.

CHAPTER 12
North America

Scott M. Langston

Scholars working in the fields of biblical studies and American history and culture have well chronicled many of the various aspects of the relationship between the Bible and American culture. The influence of the Bible within the American context is undeniable. According to Nathan O. Hatch and Mark A. Noll, two prominent American historians, the Bible is 'nearly omnipresent' in American history, and American cultural history is 'unthinkable' without the Bible. At the same time, they recognize that American uses of the Bible have been complex and ambiguous (Hatch and Noll 1982: 4, 6). Indeed, one must be careful not to generalize too much about the Bible and American culture for a variety of reasons. American culture itself is difficult to define, especially in light of the diverse populations residing within its borders. It might be more helpful to think in terms of American cultures. As the various population groups have interacted with each other, beginning with contact between native populations who had a long history in the land and Africans and Europeans who were newcomers, the Bible played an important role. Furthermore, these cultures have made varying responses to and uses of the Bible which has in turn led to disputes over the role and meaning of the Bible in American life. Yet these disputes themselves reflect the Bible's significance as Americans have almost constantly contended with its presence and appropriation. While Hatch and Noll's characterization of the uses of the Bible in America as complex and ambiguous is fitting, one might also add contested. The contesting of the Bible and its interpretations represents a common characteristic throughout the American experience. Although certain understandings of biblical texts have proven more powerful than others and therefore have become entrenched across a broad section of American life, they have not been uncontested. The Bible in American culture thus represents a struggle for and reaction to particular understandings of it. This struggle in itself reflects the cultural authority of the Bible as Americans of all sorts, even those who do not recognize its religious authority, have dealt with the reverberations created by its presence in American culture. As Robert Alter has observed, 'However skeptical a secular observer may choose to be, the

imperative presence of the Bible remains something serious to conjure with in contemporary American life' (1985: 45).

Prominent among such conflicts has been the belief that God has chosen America
for a special purpose. The Bible fuelled this idea, and many Americans have thought of
their country as a 'light to the nations', either serving as a model to the world or as an
agent for spreading and preserving American values beyond its borders (Cherry 1998:
1, 11, 20). From the earliest discoveries of the 'new' lands, Europeans endeavoured to
incorporate them into their world-views, often using the Bible to shape their understandings. For example, Christian readings of the Bible helped motivate Spanish exploration, as well as frame their colonization efforts. In the early sixteenth century, the
Spanish geographer Martín Fernández de Encisco argued that these lands had been
given to Spain in the same way that Canaan had been given to the Jews, thereby justifying the treatment of the indigenous populations in the same manner Joshua had dealt
with Jericho (Thomas 1993: 59, 71–2). The French explorer, Jacques Cartier, read the
opening verses of the Gospel of John, as well as Chapters 18 and 19, to Huron Indians
he encountered in 1535 near modern-day Montreal. He hoped that the mere reading
of these passages might help bring them the knowledge of Christianity (Morison 1971:
414). These brief examples represent a larger, biblically inspired understanding of the
Americas as a land intended by God for the establishment of Christianity. This concept,
with its biblical underpinnings, however bore both noble and sinister implications for
others, especially since Christianity and European culture(s) typically were viewed as
being synonymous.

Of course, Europeans themselves did not agree on Christianity's true expression. At
the heart of these disagreements were varied interpretations of the Bible, many of
which were brought to America. So, for instance, the Puritans left Europe for the
Promised Land of America, hoping to establish a Christian society based on the Bible's
truth (Cherry 1998: 26–7). Yet, as Lisa M. Gordis has shown, the Puritans did not have
a biblical culture characterized by closed-mindedness, but one that produced 'both a
flowering of richly intertextual literature and a series of divisive interpretive controversies' (2003: 2). Puritans, as well as a host of other Christians, may have agreed that
America was a 'light to the nations' and God's New Israel, but they often did not agree
on the specific social manifestations of the Bible. These debates, however, were not confined to Europeans because as they introduced (and applied) the Bible to Native Americans and Africans, the latter in turn used the Bible to contest and shape the notion of
'America'.

The Bible and Racial Struggles

'Jesus was an Indian'

The Bible has been a traditional tool for gaining, maintaining, and overthrowing power
in America as various groups have deployed it in support of their cause and in opposition to others. This is not unique to the American context, but it does reflect the use
and authority of the Bible in American struggles for power, especially those between

ethnic groups. Europeans brought the Bible with them as they explored and colonized the North American continent. In their encounters with Native Americans, the Bible proved useful in justifying the domination and subordination of the various tribes. Europeans transmitted the Bible through the filters of religion (Roman Catholicism or Protestantism) and nationalism, and employed it in the debate over the nature and treatment of Native Americans. In their arguments over the status of Native Americans, the Bible became one of the lenses through which Europeans understood and related to them. Drawing on biblical and nationalistic categories, Europeans often described Native Americans as idol worshippers and uncivilized barbarians, descriptions that reflected their status as non-Christians and non-Europeans and that continued to be applied to them for centuries. During the sixteenth century, the Bible played a central role in the Spanish debates over the status and treatment of the native populations. Spaniards such as Gonzalo Fernández de Oviedo y Valdéz, Juan Ginès de Sepúlveda, and Bartolomé de las Casas deployed the Bible abundantly in their debates. Many contended that the rejection of Christianity and the Bible by the indigenous peoples indicated their inferior status and thus justified their domination by European Christians. Some doubted that Native Americans could be Christianized, while others invoked the example of Joshua and the conquering Israelites and urged that they be forced by military means if necessary to convert. These conclusions, however, did not go uncontested. Las Casas, for example, combined Matthew 28:18, Romans 10:16, and Exodus 10:3 in order to argue that non-Christians who were not subjects of a Christian ruler could not be punished by Christians or the Church (1992: 55–6; Hanke 1974: 34–45, 82, 95–9).

Within an English context, the Bible was used similarly to categorize and deal with the native populations. In seeking to win Indian converts, the Puritan missionary John Eliot (1604–90) had translated the Bible into Algonquian (Calloway 2004: 88). Around 1671, he created a series of dialogues between Indians who had converted to Christianity and those who had not; the dialogues were intended for use in training missionaries to deal with unconverted Indians. One conversation took place between Piumbukhou, who had converted, and his non-Christian relatives. Reflecting Native objections, his relatives argued that the biblical stories and teachings could be the invention of Englishmen for the purpose of subduing them. Piumbukhou asserted that the Bible 'is the holy law of God himself' and no invention of the English. Just as the English had searched it for the 'knowledge of God', Native Americans had the same freedom to do so. Eliot then had Piumbukhou espouse the great things the English, under God's guidance, had done for the Indians. Having 'heard of us, and of our country, and of our nakedness, ignorance of God, and wild condition', the English sailed to America. In addition to loving them and purchasing their land, according to Piumbukhou:

> God put it in the heart of one of their ministers (as you all know) to teach us the knowledge of God, by the word of God, and hath translated the holy Book of God into our language, so that we can perfectly know the mind and counsel of God. And out of this book have I learned all that I say unto you, and therefore you need no more doubt of the truth of it, then (*sic*) you have cause to doubt that the heaven is over our head, the sun shineth,

the earth is under our feet, we walk and live upon it, and breathe in the air. (Calloway 1994: 46–9)

Although not a historical event, this dialogue reflected objections that Eliot had encountered and revealed attitudes held by Native Americans and the English toward the Bible. Indians suspected that the biblical text was being employed in order to awe them into submission. The English held out to them the promise of the true knowledge of God if they accepted it by converting to Christianity. Yet Eliot's dialogue made clear the indebtedness Native Americans would incur by accepting the Bible and Christianity. The power of the Bible and the importance of controlling its interpretation are evident. By possessing and controlling the biblical text, the English could exercise dominion over the meaning of their actions. Rather than appearing as those who were stealing the land from Native Americans, they used the Bible to cast their actions as expressions of their love of God and humanity. Coming to North America and gaining possession of Native American lands thus reflected their efforts to teach 'the good knowledge of God' that came through the biblical text. Native acceptance of the Bible and Christianity, however, implied acceptance of English dominance.

The Bible, therefore, from America's earliest days became an arena in which conflicts between and within cultures were played out. Playing a prominent role in contact between Europeans and Native Americans, the Bible served as the basis for the religious ideas communicated to native inhabitants and came to symbolize the authority of whites. This textual source of authority differed from that of Native Americans who often found non-textual sources such as dreams to be authoritative. One mid-eighteenth-century Indian recounted to Moravian missionaries in Pennsylvania a vision in which God revealed that he had made both 'brown and white people', and had given sacrifice to the Indians as a means of divine encounter, while the whites had received the Bible, or the Book. Although they shared the same creator, they had been given different religious traditions. The Book, therefore, became the symbol of white religion and authority. As Indians better understood biblical ideas, they used it to challenge whites by pointing out their failure to live up to biblical standards (Merritt 2003: 90, 124–7). Some white Americans, such as Roger Williams and William Penn, also used the Bible to contest the treatment of Indians. While the response of Native Americans to the Bible and Christianity ranged from outright rejection to almost complete acceptance of whites' interpretations, the use of the Bible to resist and reject the religion, culture, and actions of the whites reflected Native appropriations of biblical authority.

In 1916, Charles Eastman, a Wahpeton Dakota (Sioux) Indian who served as a field organizer for the Young Men's Christian Association (YMCA), described the reaction he received from an older Indian man after Eastman conducted several Bible studies on the life of Jesus. According to Eastman, the man said:

> I have come to the conclusion that this Jesus was an Indian. He was opposed to material acquirement and to great possessions. He was inclined to peace. He was as unpractical as any Indian and set no price upon his labor of love. These are not the principles upon which the white man has founded his civilization. (Hoxie 2001: 76–7)

This individual had used the Bible, without necessarily accepting its religious authority, to repudiate whites and their religion. To him, the Bible vindicated rather than denounced Native American religion and values. This cultural conflict can also be seen in hearings held in 1918 by the United States Congress on the legality of use of the peyote cactus in Native American rituals, a centuries-old practice that had recently spread among other tribes. One Congressman asked a chief of the Osage Indians to explain 'to this committee where you get any authority from the Bible for the use of this bean in worship'. The chief replied that he did not understand the Bible, nor did he know if the Bible gave any authority for its use, but his people had a tradition of peyote usage (Hoxie 2001: 85–6). This exchange reflected the division over the Bible, its use, and authority. While the Congressman used it as his basis for evaluating and denouncing this Native American practice, the chief openly admitted that in essence the Bible was irrelevant for him. As the century progressed, however, the use of the Bible in this cultural conflict changed. The Bible ceased to be put forth by government representatives as an argument against the use of peyote, but ironically some Native Americans appropriated it to support their practice. The Native American Church, a loose confederation of congregations or chapters organized in 1918 in an effort to provide legal protection for the practice, paralleled the use of peyote to the Eucharist. Biblical passages have even come to be used in rituals related to the ingestion of peyote (Gill 2003: 19–20). The fact that some Native Americans incorporated it into their defence and ritual reflects at least a tacit recognition by them of the authoritative influence of the Bible in American culture. Even though the Bible was no longer explicitly being deployed against them, Native Americans understood its cultural value and sought to contain its threat to them by appropriating it. They have been somewhat successful in gaining legal acceptance for the use of peyote. In 1994 the US Congress passed the American Indian Religious Freedom Act Amendments that allowed the use of peyote by Native Americans for traditional religious purposes. The Bible was nowhere mentioned, but it had played an important role in the efforts of Native Americans to retain their cultural traditions and to adapt to foreign cultural elements.

'One dark like me'

The Bible has continued to be an important element in managing relationships between the various American cultures. As with Native Americans, the Bible originally was a foreign element used by whites to understand and dominate blacks, but as African Americans became familiar with it, they employed it to challenge this domination. It also supplied a common ground from which some whites and African Americans could join together. Before and during the Civil War, whites commonly made biblical arguments for and against the enslavement of blacks. Pro-slavery advocates made claims like that in an article appearing in the September 1850 *De Bow's Review*: 'To any man, who admits that the Bible is given by inspiration from God, they prove that, in buying, selling, holding and using slaves, there is no moral guilt' (Finkelman 2003: 113). On the other hand, abolitionists made arguments similar to that put forth by Theodore Dwight Weld who asserted, 'The advocates of slavery are always at their wit's end when they try to press the Bible into their service' (Weld 2000: 55). African Americans also appropriated the biblical text to sustain themselves through the brutality of slavery and to challenge white hegemony. Frederick Douglass pointed out:

> He who proclaims it a religious duty to read the Bible denies me the right of learning to read the name of the God who made me . . . We have men sold to build churches, women sold to support the gospel, and babes sold to purchase Bibles for the *poor heathen! all for the glory of God and the good of souls!* (Douglass 1988: 156)

Abraham Lincoln recognized the ambiguity of northern and southern biblical usage when in his second inaugural address he said, 'Both read the same Bible, and pray to the same God; and each invokes His aid against the other' (Lincoln 1989: 687). This ambiguity reflected the recognition by all of the Bible's cultural power and the need to align one's position with it. Both the author of the *De Bow's* article and Weld, in seeking to build support for their actions, had appealed to differing applications of the biblical text. Douglass used it to denounce the effort of pro-slavery advocates to control access to the Bible and ultimately its interpretation. He also employed it to discredit one of the South's most important institutions. In the American debate over slavery, the Bible provided one of the contexts within which Americans engaged each other and struggled for control.

Despite the disagreements among white Americans over slavery, few whites supported racial equality. Emancipation and abolition of slavery did not bring equality for African Americans. That struggle continued throughout the nineteenth and twentieth centuries. African Americans employed the cultural power and authority of the Bible to challenge white discrimination. Langston Hughes, a prominent literary figure of the twentieth century, frequently incorporated biblical themes in his poetry. At times he subtly combined the biblical text with racial issues. In his poem, *Carol of the Brown King*, he noted that one of the wise men who humbly worshipped Jesus in the manger was 'a brown man', 'one dark like me'. While he made no racially charged statements, the point was clear – a person of colour participated in the Nativity. The inclusion of the brown king in the birth story of Jesus affirmed the value of African Americans within a context where typically they were degraded (Hughes 2001: 232). At other times, Hughes could be provocative. The poem, *Christ in Alabama*, used the shocking language of 'Christ is a nigger, beaten and black.' It then beckoned Mary as 'Mammy of the South' to be silent and petitioned God, the 'White Master above', to bestow his love on the 'Nigger Christ'. By associating Jesus with a 'nigger', Hughes confronted the white South with the atrocities it was committing against African Americans. By referring to God as the 'White Master', he highlighted the power of white southerners to stop the violence. His encoding of the African American experience into the biblical crucifixion spoke to southerners in a language they would find familiar, but with an application that would shock and enrage many. Combining the holy and secular helped confront white southerners with the horror of their treatment of blacks and the contradiction of their actions when compared with the biblical story. He made a similar point in his poem, *Bible Belt*, a term first coined by H. L. Mencken in the 1920s to refer to areas of the nation, primarily identified with the South, that contained high concentrations of fundamentalist Christians who advocated the literal, inerrant nature of the Bible.

The poem addresses segregation by considering what would happen if Jesus came back as a black man. It concludes that Jesus himself would not be allowed to pray in many churches because these churches glorified 'race, not religion'. Yet it also concludes that the one who points out this discrepancy does so at the risk of being crucified by Christians who claim to be most faithful to the Bible (Hughes 2001: 155–6). Again, Hughes had identified the African-American experience with that of Jesus. Just as Native Americans found the Bible a useful conduit to engage and challenge whites, so did African Americans. Read from their perspective, the Bible proved useful in bolstering hope, affirming African Americans' sense of value, and confronting racism.

The Bible also helped inspire and provide models for whites and blacks involved in the Civil Rights movement. Chief among the biblical models was the prophetic paradigm (especially Amos, Isaiah, and Jeremiah). This tradition viewed humanity and its institutions as essentially sinful and corrupt. With little hope of reform, they stood in need of fundamental change. The prophet then challenged people to change their sinful ways. Applied to the Civil Rights movement, the sin that drew the ire of modern prophets was segregation. Just as the biblical prophets encountered fierce resistance, so their American counterparts anticipated and received the same treatment. Convinced of divine sanction for their cause, African Americans persevered (Chappell 2004: 3–4; West 2003: 1037–49). Martin Luther King, Jr. in his 1958 book, *Stride Toward Freedom*, highlighted the need for at least some ministers to take up the role of the prophet. He praised the few Southern rabbis and Christian ministers who had already done so and who 'stood unflinchingly before threats and intimidations, inconvenience and unpopularity, even at times in physical danger, to declare the doctrine of the Fatherhood of God and the brotherhood of man' (Washington 1986: 481). The prophetic model not only encouraged African Americans to challenge southern segregation, but it also provided a conduit through which some whites joined them. Southern rabbis in particular stood with African Americans. The Fatherhood of God and brotherhood of humanity were key concepts in Reform Judaism that manifested itself in the Civil Rights movement. Rabbis such as Bernard Wax of Memphis, Tennessee, applied the prophetic example to the fight against racial inequality. Wax, who was especially influenced by the prophet Amos, played an important role in the struggle for civil rights in Memphis especially during the 1968 sanitation workers strike (LaPointe 1997: 153, 160–5). Some whites, therefore, found the biblical text to be a stimulus for crossing racial barriers.

Ironically, many Southern whites who supported segregation made little use of the Bible to support their views. Historian David L. Chappell has demonstrated that mainstream religious leaders who embraced segregation argued at most that the Bible did not explicitly prohibit segregation (2004: 109–17). They, however, did not or could not produce a bevy of scripture as their antebellum counterparts had done in arguing for slavery. In contrast, African Americans, as well as sympathetic whites, continued to use Scripture to confront white hegemony, just as their antebellum counterparts had. The discontinuance of biblical arguments by whites in spite of continued use by African Americans paralleled the same development in relations between whites and Native Americans. What this lessened use of the Bible by whites means is not entirely clear. Did it represent an effort by whites to disengage Native Americans and

African Americans on a biblical or religious level? Did it suggest that whites themselves doubted the biblical strength of their position? Or, did it represent an erosion of whites' power as they abdicated use of the Bible? On the other hand, perhaps whites felt strong enough to no longer put forth biblical arguments. The answers to these questions are difficult to discern, but the change in usage reflects a greater dependence on governmental power to maintain whites' dominance rather than a co-dependence with the Bible's cultural power. Native and African Americans, however, had little governmental power from which to engage whites. Their use of the Bible, therefore, represented one of their most effective tools. So when whites largely discontinued their widespread utilization of the Bible, they perhaps unintentionally neutralized or at least lessened the impact of the Bible in the relationships between whites and Native and African Americans. This muted the debate over the meaning, application, and control of the Bible. Indians and blacks, nonetheless, continued to employ the Bible as an effective tool in their efforts to engage whites.

The use of the Bible by Americans of various ethnic backgrounds illustrates its contested nature. Understandings of the Bible spring out of diverse cultural contexts and engage each other in a number of issues. Americans cannot escape the Bible, but they do contest it and its appropriations. Debate over the control and use of the Bible is a mainstay of American culture. This makes it a key tool for gaining, maintaining, and overthrowing power among the races. Representatives of these groups have articulated their understandings and critiques of others, as well as their values and hopes in biblical terms even when they did not accept the religious authority of the Bible. The Bible also has inspired some to cross boundaries established by their own race. Native and African Americans who embraced the biblical message, or whites who were motivated by the biblical message to embrace Native and African-American causes did so at great peril to themselves. Challenging an entrenched racial understanding that is wrapped in biblical arguments has always been risky in America.

The Bible and the Struggle over Social Issues

The Bible has throughout American history played an integral role in the debates over social issues that did not have race as the primary focus. It has inspired Americans to become involved in the political process in order to insure that their particular biblical understanding is applied to social issues, and it has become a favourite tool in the struggle to gain the necessary power to implement this view. Even though America was not founded on a particular understanding of the Bible, Americans have nonetheless sought to apply diverse biblical interpretations in their efforts to deal with social issues. Often those attempting to do so have considered their application of the biblical text to be the only correct appropriation, as well as the one envisioned by America's founders. These claims have sparked disagreement and further illustrate the contested nature of the Bible. Again, the contesting of the Bible with regard to social issues is not a uniquely American experience, but it does reflect the diversity of opinion among Americans, as well as the importance of the Bible in shaping social discourse and inspiring social action. Americans frequently have had to come to grips with biblically informed social ideas even when they did not accept the Bible or the idea as authoritative. The debates spawned by this environment arise in part from the fact that the nation's founding documents do not give the government the responsibility for promoting religious values, even though many of the founders believed that the nation's welfare depended on its citizens' morality and that religion played a key role in developing this morality (Foster 2002: 9). In other words, no public office or institution in the United States holds the power to determine the meaning and application of the Bible. In fact, diversity, not uniformity, of opinion on biblical meanings has been considered a necessary element in American culture and society.

The founders certainly did not envision that a single understanding would gain governmental sanction, and they expressed great concern over protecting the rights of individuals and minorities against the will of the majority. They understood that uniformity of opinion on virtually any topic was impossible, that various factions inevitably would arise, and that the possibility of the majority oppressing the minority would always be a threat. Furthermore, they recognized that religion was particularly inclined to oppress dissenting opinions. The founders repudiated the propensity of religious sects to consider their expression of religion to be the only true one and, therefore, to establish it by law, while excluding other expressions. To them the presence of various parties or factions in a republic was necessary for insuring that a tyranny of the majority, or what James Madison called 'a majority of the whole number in an unjust pursuit', was not perpetrated against the minority. Madison argued, 'Religion flourishes in greater purity, without than with the aid of Govt', and in *Federalist No. 10*, he explained, 'A religious sect, may degenerate into a political faction in part of the Confederacy; but the variety of sects dispersed over the entire face of it, must secure the national Councils against any danger from that source' (*Federalist No. 10*, in Bailyn 1993: 404–11; James Madison to Thomas Jefferson, 24 October 1787; and Madison to Edward Livingston, 10 July 1822 in Madison 1999: 148–52, 789; Thomas Jefferson to Dr Benjamin Rush, 23 September 1800; Jefferson to Revd Samuel Miller, 23 January 1808; and Jefferson to Dr Thomas Cooper, 2 November 1822, in Jefferson 1984: 1080–2, 1186–7, 1463–5). The nation's founders understood the inevitability of religious disputes occurring and the importance of the presence of diverse opinions for insuring that one view did not attain governmental sanction even when the majority of Americans might support that view. The American cultural and social environment encouraged the contesting of biblical meaning and its appropriation. Many Americans, however, brought their biblically informed ideas of morality into the public arena, and in contradiction to the designs of the founders, sought to establish by law their particular biblical understandings. The debates engendered by such efforts became in part struggles over which biblical interpretation would prevail or have the greatest impact on American culture. The attempt to establish one particular interpretation made the stakes quite high as some sought to use public power to insure its hegemony. These efforts also tended to identify the Bible, or a certain interpretation of it, with true American identity. The Bible, therefore, took on tremendous symbolic significance and became associated with certain perspectives. Once these perspectives were equated with the Bible, those who took issue with them were put in the difficult position of being portrayed as anti-Bible and anti-American. In the private realm such assertions were not unexpected, but in the public sphere these could prove quite destructive. From the perspective of America's founders, the debates were not undesirable, but the effort to establish the public hegemony of a certain biblical understanding was.

Seeking to install a particular understanding of the Bible rather than having diverse understandings inform the viewpoints and actions of individuals meant subjecting the Bible to majority rule. Instead of acting as an influence on a person's conscience and behaviour, the Bible became a political tool and object in the shaping of public policies. As the line between the two uses blurred, governmental power rather than private persuasion became the prized possession in seeking to ensure a particular biblical application. Rather than persuading people of the merits of a biblical interpretation, governmental power compelled acceptance. The Bible came to be the focus of many public debates which some cast in terms of a struggle between good and evil. The Bible, or rather, a particular understanding of it, did not merely act as a tool to critique some public matter, but it became the point of debate, the object of power. The object of the public debate often slid from a particular issue to the enshrinement of a certain understanding of the Bible as a national expression of devotion to God.

The Bible 'was the sheet anchor'

This dynamic can be seen throughout American history. During the antebellum period, evangelicals were particularly active in efforts to gain political support for their views. One heated debate involved the reading of the King James Version of the Bible in public schools in communities throughout the nation. Catholics objected and sought to have these practices changed by either eliminating these readings or allowing Catholic children to read from the Douay Version. Hostilities flared in a number of communities, but the struggle took on national ramifications as reflected in the comments of one evangelical that the Bible 'was the sheet-anchor of *American* as well as *Christian* hopes' (Carwardine 1997: 81–5). In this case, the Bible had become the locus for religious hostilities that were being vented in the public realm. Protestant evangelicals could not understand objections to the reading of the King James Version because they equated it with true Christianity and true American identity. Defenders of this practice, therefore, viewed themselves as defending God and the nation, and cast anti-Christian and anti-American aspersions on opponents. The King James Bible had taken on great symbolic significance as a mark of devotion to God and America, but as such it devalued the expressions of devotion made by groups like Catholics and Jews.

During the antebellum period, organized attempts to secure a biblically based public morality typically used moral suasion, personal liberty, and legislation at the state level to attain their goals. Beginning with the Civil War, however, these efforts began to employ federal power. Reformers reasoned that if the abolition of slavery could be secured through the Emancipation Proclamation and the Thirteenth Amendment to the Constitution, then other matters of morality could be similarly regulated on the national level. These encompassed a large number of issues including the delivery of mail on Sundays, Sabbath observance, prizefighting, drinking, gambling, divorce, and prostitution. An attempt was even made to amend the Constitution to include an acknowledgment of God, Christ, and the Bible. By the early twentieth century, attention focused on the conflict between modernists and fundamentalists, most clearly expressed in the debate over evolution (Foster 2002: 1–7, 223). The Bible was at the centre of this disagreement.

Harry Emerson Fosdick, who taught at Union Theological Seminary in New York and also served as a pastor, understood that the introduction of historical criticism to biblical studies changed the way people read and used the Bible. In his 1924 book, *The Modern Use of the Bible*, he divided the appropriation of the Bible between the 'older methods of employing Scripture', which took the Bible at face value, and the 'modern study of Scripture', which sought to understand the Bible in light of literary, historical, and scientific discoveries (Fosdick 1945: 4–6). This dichotomy split over whether or not the truths discovered by modern research should be understood in light of the ancient standards and concepts found in the biblical text, or the truths of the biblical text should be understood in light of the standards and concepts employed by the modern world. The debate over evolution highlighted this dichotomy. Opponents of evolution connected the veracity of the biblical text with ancient biblical cosmology, and some sought to protect it through legislation. This resulted in legal challenges, the most famous of which was the 1925 Scopes trial.

The trial occurred in Dayton, Tennessee, when a high school teacher, John Scopes, was found guilty for having violated a recently enacted law that forbade the teaching of evolution in Tennessee's public schools. Known as the Butler Bill, it specifically banned the teaching of 'any theory that denies the story of the Divine creation of man as taught in the Bible, and to teach instead that man has descended from a lower order of animals'. This reflected attempts by fundamentalist Christians to counteract the threats raised by modernism to the literal interpretation of the Bible. Clarence Darrow, the nation's leading criminal defence attorney, led the defence and argued that the Bible was not a book of biology, geology, or science, but one of religion and morals. He also asserted that with at least 500 or more different sects in America, great disagreement existed over the Bible's views on many topics. This difference of opinion reflected the great difficulty involved in any government discerning and enforcing what the Bible taught. William Jennings Bryan, a three-time Democratic presidential nominee, assisted the prosecution and reflected the views of many fundamentalists (Moran 2002: 8–24, 90–1).

Fundamentalists typically linked their understanding of the Bible with the nation's well-being. Bryan himself had linked national greatness with the same biblical principles that bound individuals. What applied to one person applied just as much to those who corporately acted as a nation (Bryan 1905: 250–1). With this logic, the biblical principles used to inform and constrain an individual's morality would be the same for the nation. This understanding of the Bible helped collapse the divisions between public and private morality and asserted that even though the Scopes trial was being argued at the state level, the challenge that evolution raised to the literal interpretation of the Bible ultimately threatened the nation's welfare. On the fifth day of the trial as the prosecution objected to Darrow's ultimately unsuccessful efforts to introduce expert testimony on the Bible and science, Bryan argued that evolution denied the miracles of the Bible, including the virgin birth and resurrection of Jesus, and removed 'every moral standard that the Bible gives us'. Furthermore, he asserted that 'Bible experts' were unnecessary for the trial because 'every member of the jury is as good an expert on the Bible', and no expert is needed for a person to understand the Christian message of the Bible (Moran 2002: 123–5). For fundamentalist Christians, teaching evolution had tremendous ramifications for their religious and national aspirations.

When Bryan argued that the people of Tennessee had decided that evolution contradicted the Bible and should not be taught, he appealed to majority rule as the manner for determining what the Bible says. Majority rule is a common way of determining biblical meaning and application in America. This combination of Protestant tradition and democratic ideals creates an environment whereby biblical interpretive authority emanates from the majority rather than an institution, although the institution retains an important role. When this is combined with a belief that the literal interpretation of the Bible is integral to the national well-being, then gaining control of the legislative mechanism becomes a particularly important and powerful means for implementing this interpretive slant. Gaining the high ground of biblical interpretation by offering a clear, simple, and often literal interpretation and traditional application of the Bible to a social issue makes an effective weapon in obtaining the support of a majority. This represents a combining of the tactics of moral suasion and governmental power to give a certain biblical understanding the force of law. Moral suasion is necessary to gain a majority, but then becomes less important in the maintenance of a particular biblical understanding once it is translated into law. Those who find themselves in the minority (especially non-Christians) often must deal with accusations of not believing the Bible or being un-American, and then must find other means of counteracting or accommodating any governmental actions that enshrine particular biblical interpretations.

This use of the Bible continues to manifest itself in the contemporary period. In the aftermath of the Scopes trial, those opposed to evolution sought to enshrine creationism (the literal interpretation of Genesis) through the state and local levels. Linking the literal interpretation of the creation accounts found in Genesis 1–2 with a literal reading of the flood account in Genesis 6–9, creationists buttressed their understanding with passages such as Nehemiah 9:6, Psalm 104:24, and 2 Timothy 4:4. Boards of education became the focus of their efforts to ban the teaching of evolution. In 1968, however, the US Supreme Court ruled that Arkansas' anti-evolution law, passed in 1928 by a popular vote, violated the First Amendment. In 1987 it ruled that teaching creationism amounted to the teaching of religion (Moran 2002: 51–5). Advocates of a literal interpretation have subsequently sought to challenge evolution by having Intelligent Design, a theory that posits an intelligent force behind creation, taught in public schools. In 1999, the Kansas Board of Education voted to drop questions about evolution from its standardized testing which in essence gave local districts freedom to choose not to teach evolution. Two years later, the board rescinded this action ('Kansas Restores'), although there is discussion about restoring it. In 2002, the Cobb County, Georgia Board of Education approved a policy requiring stickers be placed on tenth grade biology textbooks warning students that evolution is 'a theory, not a fact' and encouraging them to approach the topic with an 'open mind'. Six parents of students filed suit alleging that the stickers were thinly veiled efforts to teach creationism ('Cobb

Evolution'). In January 2005, a Federal District Court judge ruled that the stickers must be removed, noting that 'an informed, reasonable observer would understand the School Board to be endorsing the viewpoint of Christian fundamentalists and creationists' regarding evolution (*Selman, et al. v. Cobb County*: 33)'. The Dover, Pennsylvania school board in 2004 became the first in the nation to mandate the teaching of Intelligent Design. Opponents have filed a lawsuit, arguing that this too is an attempt to teach creationism. From the opposite perspective, one local pastor asserted, 'If the Bible is right, God created us. If God did it, it's history and it's also science' ('School Board'; 'Evolution Shares'). The contesting of the Bible has developed into a struggle that in essence seeks governmental power rather than moral suasion to maintain and protect a certain understanding of the Bible. As fundamentalist Christians continue to blur the distinctions between the Bible and interpretations of it, and to embrace the use of public power to enforce an interpretation on the masses rather than moral suasion to convince individuals, the struggle over biblical meaning remains a public process in America. By equating the literal interpretation of the Bible with the Bible, fundamentalist Christians perceive the teaching of evolution to be a use of public power to attack simultaneously their religious beliefs and the Bible; science and religion are rooted in the same source – the Bible – and cannot be separated. Thus, their efforts at gaining public power become for them an act of self preservation, as well as an act of faithfulness by standing up for God and his Word. For those who are not Christian fundamentalists, the reading and application of the Bible is a more private affair against which the public sphere must be protected from any efforts to impose a particular understanding. The meaning and use of the Bible in America inevitably become public matters.

'The favor and guidance of almighty God'

The use of the Ten Commandments also illustrates the place of the Bible in American culture as a contested symbol. During the twentieth century individuals and communities often displayed depictions of the Decalogue as a way of expressing devotion to God. While Cecil B. De Mille was involved with the remake of his 1923 movie, *The Ten Commandments* (which was released in 1956), he participated with the Fraternal Order of Eagles to place monuments bearing the Ten Commandments in communities throughout the United States. The presence of these and similar monuments in public spaces has generated numerous challenges on the basis that they violate the separation of church and state. Federal courts have given mixed rulings regarding the use of the Decalogue in public places. In general, the contexts in which the monuments are placed are determining factors as courts recognize that biblical law has influenced the Western legal tradition. The contexts for these public monuments must be historical and secular. The Supreme Court, however, ruled in 1980 (*Stone v. Graham*; 449 US 39) that the Decalogue represented a religious text.

A recent dispute over the display of the Ten Commandments originated in Alabama in 2001 when the newly elected Chief Justice of the State Supreme Court, Roy Moore, installed in the rotunda of the state judicial building a two and one-half ton monument bearing the Decalogue (using the Protestant translation found in the King James Version of the Bible). The Commandments were surrounded by quotes from various sources including the Constitution, the Declaration of Independence, and some of the nation's founders. A lawsuit was filed in federal court, and Moore was ordered to remove the monument. He refused to comply and was subsequently removed from his position as Chief Justice.

Moore argued that by displaying the Ten Commandments he was merely upholding a requirement established by the Alabama Constitution when it invoked 'the favor and guidance of Almighty God'. Furthermore, by ordering the monument's removal, the federal judge had continued a practice of judges who sought to impose their will on the people rather than interpret the law. According to Moore (2003), 'For half a century the fanciful tailors of revisionist jurisprudence have been working to strip the public sector naked of every vestige of God and morality.' He cast his refusal to comply as part of a struggle for freedom of thought and belief (ibid.). He also asserted that he was only 'acknowledging God', and lamented 'that someone can become a hero (among Christians) simply for acknowledging the God upon which the nation and our laws are founded' (Kirkpatrick 2004). Moore and other fundamentalists have portrayed themselves as victims of anti-religious and anti-Bible sentiment and have used freedom of belief as a shield to gain public establishment of their biblical interpretations. At the same time, they have characterized the alleged anti-Bible sentiment as a departure from the views of the nation's founders; Moore himself dubbed the Ten Commandments as the 'moral foundation of our law' (Gettleman, 28 August 2003). By equating their interpretation of the Bible with the Bible, they have parlayed a powerful tool in the effort to gain public support. Those who do not share their interpretive view have attempted to rebut it, often pointing out that even the translation and organization of the Decalogue are matters of interpretation. Yet the cultural impact of the Bible, in general, and the Ten Commandments, in particular, is so strong that the nuances drawn by Moore's opponents are often overshadowed. Moore employed this power by running for election as the 'Ten Commandments judge'. In the words of one University of Alabama political science professor, 'He strikes a chord with the masses and it would be a huge risk for someone to be remembered as the one who voted against the Ten Commandments judge' (Gettleman, 13 November 2003). Commenting on the courage of the Alabama Supreme Court in removing Moore as Chief Justice, a *Washington Post* editorial said, 'A large sector of the American electorate, after all, has yet to reconcile itself to the notion of a public square that does not elevate particular religious traditions over others or elevate religious belief over skepticism' ('No More Justice Moore').

This struggle over biblical meaning manifested itself in measures taken at the federal level. Not long after the Moore decision, the US House of Representatives passed a measure that would withhold any funds used in the enforcement of it. About the same time in 2003 a Congressman from Alabama, Robert Aderholt, introduced the Ten Commandments Defense Act which sought to protect the authority of states to display the Commandments in public places. According to Aderholt, 'This legislation simply recognizes that Biblical principles inspired our founding fathers . . . No one can deny the fact that the founding fathers used scripture such as the Ten Commandments as foundations for our government' ('Congressman Aderholt' 2003). These actions fail to recognize or regard the diversity of opinion that Americans have on texts such as the Ten Commandments, and resort to the Bible's cultural and political power in order to establish an essentially Protestant and fundamentalist understanding. Proponents believe that these actions are necessary in order to ensure the well-being of the nation. When Judge Ashley McKathan, a Covington County, Alabama Circuit judge appeared in his courtroom in December 2004 with the Ten Commandments embroidered on his robe, he explained, 'I see the Ten Commandments as a connection to the truth' (Marus 2004). The truth, the Bible, and true American identity have been woven into a single entity and turned into a political tool. Practitioners of this understanding typically describe themselves as 'Bible-believing', giving the implication that those who do not support their views do not believe the Bible. This fundamentalist creation has aided them in gaining political influence, while the power of such labels and implications has been used by the Republican Party to gain the support of 'Bible-believing' Christians. Ronald Reagan and George W. Bush have been particularly effective in using the Bible in this manner. Both regularly inserted biblical references and allusions into their speeches and contributed to the public establishment of a particular biblical understanding (Lienesch 1993: 14–15; Micklethwait and Wooldridge 2004: 144–50).

In addition to the debates over biblical meaning and public morality that have manifested themselves in the evolution and Ten Commandments disputes, Americans have deployed conflicting understandings of the Bible in relation to a host of other social issues. Examples of these and the biblical texts that commonly accompany them include homosexuality (Gen. 2:24–5; 19; Lev. 18:22; 20:13; Rom. 1:26–7; Heb. 13:4), abortion (Gen. 1:27; 9:6; Ps. 139:13–16; Jer. 1:5), and capital punishment (Gen. 1:27; 4:11–15; 9:6; Exod. 20:13; 22:20; Lev. 20:9–16; Rom. 13:1–4). Gun control advocates have used passages such as Exodus 22:2–3, 22–4, Psalm 68:5, and 1 Timothy 5:8 to argue that 'godly' people have a right and responsibility to defend others, and that using firearms is one way to fulfil this duty. They note that biblical heroes used force to rescue their families (Gen. 14; 1 Sam. 30), and that the New Testament condones self-defence (Luke 22:36) (Pratt 1999; 'Is Gun Control' 2001). Often Americans who are opposed to homosexuality, abortion, and gun control support capital punishment and affirm the literal interpretation and unchanging nature of the Bible. Like their predecessors in the Social Gospel movement (Rauschenbusch 1912 and Matthews 1928), Christians today who embrace an opposing view typically appeal to the example and teachings of Jesus, especially the Sermon on the Mount (see Matt. 5:7, 38–48) (Fox 2004: 322–8; Washington 1986: 14–15, 50–1, 253–8, 491–517). Although Christians in both groups appropriate both testaments, the teachings of Jesus generally are problematic for the former, while Old Testament passages pose obstacles for the latter. The troublesome passages necessitate their being fashioned and contextualized in a way that supports their respective positions. In the process, selected portions of the Bible shape one's understanding of the issue, while one's understanding of the issue often acts as the glue that binds together and harmonizes disparate passages of the Bible. The mixture of biblical texts and contemporary beliefs that have developed from a variety of sources come together to form what many Americans call 'the Bible'. The distinction between the ancient books of the Bible and American cultural ideas often is blurred into a single entity. Americans use the same biblical language and concepts, but in different combinations and cultural understandings. This, practically speaking, forms the American Bible (or perhaps more appropriately, Bibles).

Recent debates over the Bible in American life, therefore, have essentially become struggles over its interpretation and use in the public sphere. The Bible has always been a source of religious inspiration and consternation, influencing personal and corporate expressions of piety, morality, and belief. It acts as a prism through which many Americans view and relate to themselves, others, and ultimately the world. It, however, is not a prism in and of itself, but is one among many components through which Americans make sense of their lives. Even those who do not accept the Bible's authority must deal with the repercussions created by those who do. The Bible does not stand outside of a monolithic American culture and critique it, but instead interacts with and contributes to the formation of various American cultures. It can act as a bridge or a barrier to the various expressions of American culture, but these are not always constructed easily as Americans constantly debate the meaning and significance of the Bible.

The authority of the Bible in American culture is nonetheless reflected by its ubiquity, but the struggle over efforts to apply it in the public realm raises the issue of the certainty with which it is often deployed. While many Americans affirm the importance of the Bible, they disagree on its contemporary meaning and relevance. 'The Bible' usually becomes code for a person or group's particular understanding, and often is accompanied by the certainty that one's interpretation is right, while that of others is wrong. This is not an unexpected or unnatural conclusion, but it can develop into a myopic effort to appropriate biblical cultural authority that is antithetical to American concepts of freedom. Americans' attempts to hold together the Bible's authority and the faithful implementation of their varying understandings of it inevitably create conflict. This is exacerbated by the passion and certainty that accompany these understandings. How contemporary Americans attempt to regulate the volatile mix of passion, authority, and certainty with the recognition of and respect for variant expressions of passion, authority, and certainty remains to be seen. The nation's founders sought to confine these expressions to the private realm and depended on divergent viewpoints to keep the public sphere free from one understanding gaining hegemony. More contemporary efforts have depended on the courts to referee the debates. Coming to terms with biblical cultural authority, confidence in one's interpretation, and the willingness to admit that one's interpretations and the Bible are not equivalent will not be an easy task because individuals and groups are often reluctant to give up the power associated with equating one's position with the Bible. Finding a workable relationship between the confidence inherent in applying 'the Bible' and the attendant humility and even uncertainty in recognizing one's view as an interpretation looms as a major challenge to Americans as they confront the Bible's cultural impact. It, however, is a struggle that has not only characterized American culture from its outset, but has been necessary to maintain American ideas of freedom. The American tradition of biblical cultural authority, therefore, remains dependent on the presence of diverse and conflicting understandings of the Bible rather than the triumph of a single understanding.

References and Further Reading

Alter, Robert (1985). 'Scripture and Culture', *Commentary* 80(2): 42–8.

Bailyn, Bernard (ed.) (1993). *The Debate on the Constitution*, Part I. Washington, DC: Library of America.

Barr, David L. and Piediscalzi, Nicholas (eds) (1982). *The Bible in American Education*. Atlanta, GA: Scholars Press.

Bryan, William Jennings (1905). *Under Other Flags: Travels, Lectures, Speeches*. Lincoln, NE: Woodruff-Collins Printing.

Calloway, Colin G. (ed.) (1994). *The World Turned Upside Down: Indian Voices from Early America*. Boston: Bedford/St Martin's.

Calloway, Colin G. (ed.) (2004). *First Peoples: A Documentary Survey of American Indian History*. Boston: Bedford/St Martin's.

Carwardine, Richard J. (1997). *Evangelicals and Politics in Antebellum America*. Knoxville, TN: University of Tennessee Press.

Chappell, David L. (2004). *A Stone of Hope: Prophetic Religion and the Death of Jim Crow*. Chapel Hill, NC: University of North Carolina Press.

Cherry, Conrad (ed.) (1998). *God's New Israel: Religious Interpretations of American Destiny*, rev. edn. Chapel Hill, NC: University of North Carolina Press.

'Cobb Evolution Stickers Face Court Challenge', WSBRadio. http://wsbradio.com/news/110804evolutiondebate3a.html Accessed 29 December 2004.

'Congressman Aderholt Introduces Ten Commandments Defense Act', 14 May 2003. News release from Congressman Robert B. Aderholt. http://aderholt.house.gov/HoR/AL04/Newsroom/News+Releases/2003/05-14-03+Congressma+Aderholt+Introduces+Ten+Commandments+Defense+Act.htm Accessed 30 December 2004.

Douglass, Frederick (1988). *Narrative of the Life of Frederick Douglass, an American Slave Written by Himself*, ed. Benjamin Quarles. Cambridge, MA: Belknap Press.

'Evolution Shares a Desk With "Intelligent Design"', 26 December 2004. http://www.washingtonpost.com/ac2/wp-dyn/A25961-2004Dec25?language=printer Accessed 30 December 2004.

Finkelman, Paul (2003). *Defending Slavery: Proslavery Thought in the Old South: A Brief History with Documents*. Boston: Bedford/St Martin's.

Fosdick, Harry Emerson (1945). *The Modern Use of the Bible*. New York: Macmillan.

Foster, Gaines M. (2002). *Moral Reconstruction: Christian Lobbyists and the Federal Legislation of Morality, 1865–1920*. Chapel Hill, NC: University of North Carolina Press.

Fox, Richard Wightman (2004). *Jesus in America: Personal Savior, Cultural Hero, National Obsession*. New York: HarperSanFrancisco.

Frerichs, Ernest S. (ed.) (1988). *The Bible and Bibles in America*. Atlanta, GA: Scholars Press.

Gettleman, Jeffrey (2003a). 'Monument is Now Out of Sight, but Not Out of Mind', *New York Times*, 28 August.

Gettleman, Jeffrey (2003b). 'Court Orders Alabama's Chief Justice Removed from Bench', *New York Times*, 13 November.

Gill, Sam (2003). 'Native Americans and Their Religions', in Jacob Neusner (ed.), *World Religions in America*, 3rd edn. Louisville, KY: Westminster/John Knox Press.

Gordis, Lisa (2003). *Opening Scripture: Bible Reading and Interpretive Authority in Puritan New England*. Chicago: University of Chicago Press.

Gunn, Giles (ed.) (1983). *The Bible and American Arts and Letters*. Philadelphia, PA: Fortress Press.

Hanke, Lewis (1974). *All Mankind is One*. DeKalb, IL: Northern Illinois University Press.

Hatch, Nathan O. and Noll, Mark A. (eds) (1982). *The Bible in America: Essays in Cultural History*. New York: Oxford University Press.

Hoxie, Frederick E. (ed.) (2001). *Talking Back to Civilization: Indian Voices from the Progressive Era*. Boston: Bedford/St Martin's.

Hughes, Langston (2001). *The Collected Works of Langston Hughes*, vol. 3: *The Poems: 1951–1967*, ed. Arnold Rampersad. Columbia, MO: University of Missouri Press.

Jefferson, Thomas (1984). *Writings*, ed. Merrill D. Peterson. Washington, DC: Library of America.

Johnson, James Turner (ed.) (1985). *The Bible in American Law, Politics, and Political Rhetoric*. Philadelphia, PA: Fortress Press.

'Kansas Restores Evolution Standards for Science Classes', 14 February 2001. http://archives. cnn.com/2001/US/02/14/kansas.evolution.02/ Accessed 30 December 2004.

Kirkpatrick, David D. (2004). 'A Former Justice with the Law, and God, as His Guide', *New York Times*, 7 March.

LaPointe, Patricia M. (1997). 'The Prophetic Voice: Rabbi James A. Wax', in Mark K. Bauman and Berkley Kalin (eds), *The Quiet Voices: Southern Rabbis and Black Civil Rights, 1880s to 1960s*. Tuscaloosa, AL: University of Alabama Press.

Larson, Edward J. (1997). *Summer for the Gods: The Scopes Trial and America's Continuing Debate over Science and Religion*. Cambridge, MA: Harvard University Press.

Las Casas, Bartolomé de (1992). *In Defense of the Indians*, trans. Stafford Poole. DeKalb, IL: Northern Illinois University Press.

Lienesch, Michael (1993). *Redeeming America: Piety and Politics in the New Christian Right*. Chapel Hill, NC: University of North Carolina Press.

Lincoln, Abraham (1989). *Lincoln: Speeches and Writings, 1859–1865*, ed. Don E. Fehrenbacher. Washington, DC: Library of America.

Madison, James (1999). *Writings*, ed. Jack N. Rakove. Washington, DC: Library of America.

Marus, Robert (2004). 'Another Alabama Judge Stirs Controversy over Display of Ten Commandments', *Associated Baptist Press*, 16 December. http://www.abpnews.com/news /news_detail.cfm?NEWS_ID=412 Accessed 30 December 2004.

Merritt, Jane T. (2003). *At the Crossroads: Indians and Empires on a Mid-Atlantic Frontier, 1700–1763*. Chapel Hill, NC: University of North Carolina Press.

Micklethwait, John and Wooldridge, Adrian (2004). *The Right Nation: Conservative Power in America*. New York: Penguin Press.

Moore, Roy S. (2003). 'In God I Trust', *Wall Street Journal*, 25 August.

Moran, Jeffrey P. (2002). *The Scopes Trial: A Brief History with Documents*. Boston: Bedford/St Martin's.

Morison, Samuel Eliot (1971). *The European Discovery of America: The Northern Voyages A.D. 500–1600*. New York: Oxford University Press.

Noll, Mark A. (1998). 'The Bible and Slavery', in Randall M. Miller, Harry S. Stout and Charles Reagan Wilson (eds), *Religion and the American Civil War*. New York: Oxford University Press.

'No More Justice Moore' (2003). *Washington Post*, 16 November.

Phy, Allene Stuart (ed.) (1985). *The Bible and Popular Culture in America*. Philadelphia, PA: Fortress Press.

Pratt, Larry (1999). 'What Does the Bible Say about Gun Control?' Gun Owners of America, http://www.gunowners.org/fs9902.htm Accessed 3 January 2005.

Raboteau, Albert J. (2001). *Canaan Land: A Religious History of African Americans*. New York: Oxford University Press.

Sandeen, Ernest R. (ed.) (1982). *The Bible and Social Reform*. Philadelphia, PA: Fortress Press.

'School Board OKs Challenges to Evolution'. 12 November 2004. http://www.msnbc. msn.com/id/6470259 Accessed 30 December 2004.

Selman, et al. v. Cobb County School District and Board of Education 1 02-CV-2325-CC, 13 January 2005. United States District Court for the Northern District of Georgia. http://www.gand. uscourts.gov/documents/02cv2325ord.pdf Accessed 14 January 2005.

Thomas, Hugh (1993). *Conquest: Montezuma, Cortés, and the Fall of Old Mexico*. New York: Simon & Schuster.

Washington, James M. (ed.) (1986). *A Testament of Hope: The Essential Writings and Speeches of Martin Luther King, Jr.* New York: HarperSanFrancisco.

Weld, Theodore Dwight ([1837] 2000). *The Bible against Slavery*, in Mason Lowance (ed.), *Against Slavery: An Abolitionist Reader*. New York: Penguin.

West, Cornel (2003). 'The Prophetic Tradition in Afro-America', in Cornel West and Eddie S. Glaude, Jr. (eds), *African American Religious Thought: An Anthology*. Louisville, KY: Westminster/John Knox Press.

Wright, Melanie J. (2003). *Moses in America: The Cultural Uses of Biblical Narrative*. New York: Oxford University Press.

CHAPTER 13
Latin America

Erhard S. Gerstenberger

The Discovery of the Bible

The Christian Bible of course had been present in Latin America from colonial beginnings in the sixteenth century. Over the centuries, however, it had served, along with
the cross in the conquerors' other fist, as outward symbol of power, demanding the submission of all indigenous peoples. Sensing the potential dynamic of biblical knowledge
among the underprivileged, the ruling classes at times even banned access to the Latin
language to prevent reading of the Scriptures, vernacular translations not yet being
available (Prien 1978: 250). Despite the republican revolutions of the early nineteenth
century which achieved some freedom for the top layers of society, the old power structures nevertheless persisted in regard to the larger, dependent parts of the population.
For the plain reader the Bible stayed out of reach. All the more significant is the emergence of a powerful biblical movement after the Second World War which had repercussions in almost part of Latin American society. We might even say that, on a
thoroughly Catholic continent, the Bible for a short time became a cultural and political force as never before since the Protestant revolution in the sixteenth century.

What were the reasons, at the time, for this unpredictable development? How did it
unfold and to what avail? To understand the role played by biblical testimonies in Latin
America's tormented and teeming history over the past half-century, we have to consider an intricate bundle of factors and motivations, analysed by scores of researchers
in the political and social sciences. But one thing is clear, and gives us a firm point of
departure. The Bible was discovered by the so-called base communities (*comunidades de
base*), often also called 'grassroots congregations'. We may put it the other way round:
the Bible frequently was the focal point of reading and debating groups (*círculos biblicos*), transforming them into active base communities, fermented with old ideas of
justice, peace and social reconstruction. Of course, the rapid formation of thousands
of 'revolutionary' congregations using biblical ideas and models to articulate their
political and spiritual longings, did not occur by chance. There were other national and

international factors in the situation which we must briefly consider (cf. Cook 1985; Shaull 1984; Núñez 1985).

In the first place, the process of socio-economic transformation in Latin America was accelerated by enforced industrialization, burgeoning cities and the impoverishment of ever larger segments of the population. Property and capital owners flourished in the post-war boom, but millions of people lost their livelihood, especially in rural areas. Ancient, feudalistic power structures persisted, even under the rule of moderately democratic constitutions (cf. Medellin 1968). Furthermore the war of the Western Allies against Nazism and fascism had brought to mind, world-wide, the awareness that the highest principles of our cultures are freedom, human dignity and justice without prejudice and discrimination. These 'Western values' had touched the conscience of the underprivileged as well as of those middle and upper classes who still nourished a sense of solidarity, and from whom revolutionary leaders, since times immemorial, have come.

Within the Christian Churches, there came about, as a result of war, scientific and technical progress, industrialization and economic exploitation, a growing awareness that the deterioration of human welfare around the globe was due, not to some inescapable divine prescription, but to human irresponsibility. A first official signal had been sounded as early as 1891 by the Vatican's encyclical 'Rerum Novarum'. Protestant inter-denominational associations, such as, for example, ISAL (Iglesia y Sociedad en América Latina), had taken up the social question early in the twentieth century, and with the establishment of the World Council of Churches (WCC) in 1948, delegates and commissions tackled concerns about global social justice. Of prime importance for Latin America were the Second Vatican Council (1962–65) and the ensuing conference of Latin American bishops at Medellin, Columbia, in 1968. Now all the liberalizing and modernizing tendencies already existent in the Church came into the open. Focusing on the social conditions of the poor and, with biblical authority, siding with them, the official Church now gave its support to the growing movement for a just world and a renewed Church (Medellin 1968; Bonino 1977).

As many Latin American thinkers have pointed out, there were also diverse intellectual and theological influences from Old Europe and the United States at work in one way or another in the Latin American 'awakening'. Liberal Marxist philosophers, openminded theologians (including the 'God is dead' school), resistance fighters against Hitler, worker-priests, and all those who participated in the intense post-war debates on how to construct a peaceful and just new world, all had an influence on this great continent which had always cultivated close cultural ties with Europe, especially with Spain, Portugal and France (Croatto 1984).

The most important impetus, however, in the creation of 'comunidades de base' was undoubtedly the personal involvement of countless Christians, of both sexes, from all walks of life and from many different denominational or ethnic backgrounds (Cook 1985; Gerstenberger 1992b). Someone, be it lay-person or clergy, mostly in a milieu of social need or oppression, would take the initiative and gather friends and neighbours either to discuss the burning issues of immediate concern, or to conduct acts of devotion. In both cases, the Bible entered the scene almost as a matter of course. Why? Because 'The Book' had rapidly gained the reputation of being on the side of the underprivileged. Here was the voice of God who heeded the forlorn, who sided with the down-trodden, who was determined to realize a programme of justice and dignity for all humans. All governmental institutions and the whole of organized political and economic society were looked upon with suspicion as of little help in social matters, being, on the contrary, oppressive, exploiting and cynical, especially in Latin America at a time when most countries were passing through phases of dictatorship. The Word of God, by contrast, was really trustworthy. Did a Protestant principle come in at that point, combined with an urgent quest for the autonomy of lay-members of the congregation? In fact, this was a suspicion of the Vatican Congregation on Faith which denounced base communities as 'Protestant' and 'Marxist' (Vatican 1984).

There was a climate of deep satisfaction in the meetings of base communities, of solidarity, strength, and joy. Ernesto Cardenal (1976) gives a vivid impression of how such conversations over the Bible developed in a devotional context. Solentiname is a group of little islands in the Great Lake of Nicaragua. The participants, fishermen, farm-hands, housewives, all with very little formal education, in a remarkable spirit of equality, voice their ideas about a given text. They immediately identify with the suffering protagonists and the divine promises made to them. Central to these talks are social justice and personal guilt, but also – astonishingly for people in apparently hopeless situations – emerging change to the better and the dynamic of God's new reign. The learned theologian, in this case Cardenal himself, is but one member of the group, sought after in matters of historical understanding or difficult wording, but integrated into the 'people of God', communicating with each other over biblical testimony in matters of faith and ethos. This levelling down of the priest's sacred office was another concern for the conservative hierarchy. The Bible from the very beginnings of liberation theology among the marginalized, proved to be a spiritual and social power in Latin America, a disturbing development for those in authority.

Slowly, as the years went by, reflection began on the underlying 'Hermeneutics of Freedom' (Croatto 1973). Severino Croatto, a laïcised priest, working at ISEDET (Instituto Superior Evangélico de Estudios Teológicos) in Buenos Aires, was a high-level interpreter of the Scriptures. He drew on Paul Ricoeur's hermeneutical philosophy and methodology, adapting it to the Latin American situation of glaring social inequalities and to the challenges of parish work. Bible interpretation for him is a constant going back and forth between the present-day interpreter and the ancient witnesses. In this process the 'surplus meaning' of texts is creatively brought to the surface. Another great name in Latin American biblical exegesis is that of Carlos Mesters (1971; 1980). For decades he was the leader of the 'Centro de Estudios Bíblicos', now in Belo Horizonte, Minas Gerais (cf. Schürger 1995). In his courses at grassroots level he starts out with his famous triangle: (1) understanding the Bible occurs under the auspices of the Spirit; (2) looking at the texts from our real social, cultural, ideological situation; and (3) going to the ancient testimony of the texts. We have to transport the message from the past to the present in order to achieve God's creative designs in our own worlds. Other important biblical thinkers in Latin America are George Pixley (Nicaragua; cf. Fricke 1997), Milton Schwantes (1987a, 1987b), Leonardo Boff (1972), Elsa Tamez (1979; 1989), Johan Konings, Gilberto Gorgulho, Nancy Cardoso Pereira, Fernando Segovia, René Krüger and a host of others. Many of them consciously do biblical theology in the aftermath of the basic experiences of faith among ordinary people. They are, so to speak, students of that particular Latin American ecclesiogenesis, which was initiated by the discovery of the Bible in the 1950s and 1960s.

Needless to say, the biblical movement created adverse reactions, as has already been hinted at, among traditionalists in the Churches as well as from the military governments. In fact, the traditionalists stayed in the majority as far as most ruling ecclesiastic bodies are concerned, from the local level to regional and national institutions. There was never a majority of liberation theologians either in the Conference of Catholic Bishops in Brazil (CNBB = Conferência Nacional dos Bispos do Brasil) with about 250 members, or in the larger Episcopal Council which covered all of Latin America (CELAM = Consejo Episcopal Latinoamericano; cf. Prien 1978: 890–92). The rule of the thumb for the most liberal aggregation, the Brazilian hierarchy, at the movement's high point was this: one-third liberationists, one-third conservative, and one-third could be swayed one way or the other. The conservative majority, in any case, included an aggressive reactionary wing which eventually even went along with the government in subduing the liberalizing movement at the bases. The Cardinal Bishop of Porto Alegre, for example, would not help arrested liberation theologians, as Frei Betto reports in a moving account of his imprisonment ('Batismo de Sangue', 'Baptized in Blood', 1982); and Bishop Pedro Casaldaliga of São Felix do Araguaia, victim of several assassination attempts, was denounced by his own colleague, the Archbishop of Diamantine, in national newspaper ads, as a communist who should (as a foreigner) be banned from Brazil by the government. Parts of his diary of persecution have been published (Casaldaliga 1978).

Schools of theology of all denominations, on the other hand, most of them church-owned seminaries, across the continent tended to be more open to the grass-roots Bible movement. Many theological teachers, especially in the field of biblical literature, most of them Catholic priests and/or members of some monastic order (Franciscans, Jesuits, Carmelites) picked up the message of the base communities. Even although they remained in minority positions at their respective schools, they would captivate the attention of growing numbers of students who in their turn contributed to the spread of the movement. It was helped also by the great efforts of many churches to educate the poor by literacy programmes and the reading of the Bible (as well as political and theological literature!). Some experts maintain that the educational thrust (in Brazil MEB = Movimento de Educação de Base) was the main force in the whole affair. A prime example of this is Paulo Freire (1975) who used the medium of educational dialogues to revive self-esteem among the de-humanized masses. Most, if not all, of these humanitarian and emancipating efforts were considered subversive by the military governments, and Paulo Freire himself, who had been working in the national literacy campaign since 1963, was imprisoned and banned from Brazil in 1964, immediately after the coup by the generals.

Twenty Years of Opposition (1965–85)

As long as the 'Cold War' between the communist and capitalist alliances held sway, military governments, as long as they proved to be anti-communist, were looked upon as strongholds of civilization by Western democracies. *Coups d'état* against Marxist governments (Chile 1973) were even supported and subsequent massive violations of human rights in the name of 'freedom' and 'capitalism', were considered inevitable or at the most as 'collateral damage' by the self-styled 'Free World' leaders. Latin American base communities, inspired by their new reading of the Bible, and their middle-class supporters, found themselves in diametrical, antagonistic opposition to the ruling forces of their day. The Bible, according to their reading of it, announced the ideal of God's reign of justice and peace, with special emphasis on the liberation of people as enslaved and poor as they found themselves to be (Boff 1972; Gotay 1981; Shaull 1984). The Exodus motif of the Old Testament became an important object of study, both in its Mosaic and its Deutero-Isaianic form (Pixley, in Fricke 1997). Also, the social preachings of the prophets and the truly evangelical life and actions of Jesus of Nazareth contrasted fundamentally with the reality of modern, capitalist societies.

The rest of the Bible was studied primarily in the light of the same tormenting questions, dictated by present misery: Who are the oppressors in a given text? Which mechanisms of subjugation do they use? How do the exploited survive? With whom can we identify ourselves? What are the promises of God to improve the situation and bring about His true reign? (cf. Mesters 1980). The whole testimony of the Old and New Testaments seemed to contradict ongoing economic and political machinations with their concomitant deprivation of countless lives of the marginalized. Since there happened to be available also Marxist analyses of this corrupt world which also purported to pave the way towards a just and peaceful world, many liberation theologians did not hesitate to use the terminology of class struggle and victorious socialism to articulate their vision. Cuba, Allende's Chile, and the Nicaragua of the Sandinistas showed positive examples of progressive justice in this world. There should be no doubt, however, that Christian opposition in Latin America against predominant, de-humanizing economic and social conditions did not arise from communist but from biblical inspiration, as is true also of much of the thinking of Karl Marx. Both systems converged in a semi-eschatological reconstruction of existing social systems, implying at the same time a renovation of the human heart and spirit (cf. Jer. 31:31–4; Ezek. 36:26–7). Thorough corruption cries out for a completely new creation: that is what the Bible seems to be demanding as a matter of urgency under existing circumstances (Mesters 1971; Tamez 1979; Schwantes 1987b).

The base communities compared their actual social and ideological situation with the liberating proclamations of the Bible, and realized that the reign of God had already begun in their own experiences of hope, solidarity, and new life. Grassroots congregations constituted the real seeds of a better future (Camara 1980). Human dignity, still so much betrayed and debased, had started to be respected in their immediate context. The law of the survival of the fittest was broken by Christian forbearance and love for one another. Countless martyrs of the new movement, as in the early days of Christianity, gave powerful witness to the presence of the biblical God, who in the image of Christ became a co-sufferer on behalf of a forlorn humankind. Militarization and campaigns of hate, which were characteristic of the old mentalities of dominance, would eventually be replaced by lasting peace and harmony. Not that readers of the Bible as a rule were pacifists: in fact, many cautiously accepted the use of force as the last resort and the only possible means to overcome the evil of this rotten world. Camilo Torres, Columbian priest and scholar (1929–66) and, in a way also Dietrich Bonhoeffer, became icons of Christian militants who had sacrificed their lives in active resistance to tyranny. In later years, ecological concerns and the struggle for female emancipation entered the scene, also fostered partly by intensive, new readings of the Bible (Pobee and Wartenberg-Potter 1986; Tamez 1989).

The base communities and their discovery of revolutionary action in the Bible originated as small local groups. They soon felt the need to link up to similar neighbouring congregations in order to exchange experiences and pursue common goals within the same city. A whole range of connections and common projects soon arose. Staging joint feasts and acts of worship, but also uniting in joint campaigns and demonstrations, increased the feeling of unity and common strength. Local, regional, national, even inter-Latin American ties were created by grassroots congregations of Bible-oriented Christians. The 'Centro de Estudios Bíblicos', for example, mentioned above, became a well-known, nationwide and very effective biblical educational institution. Regional centres, as well as the national centre in Belo Horizonte, ran courses for members and leaders of base communities. The literary output, from these centres, particularly of exegetical tools for laypeople, was and still is enormous. The work of CEBI reached Europe, where it has inspired biblical study groups to use and adapt its methods of Bible interpretation.

Countless periodicals, mostly produced cheaply on simple writing and copying machines, were distributed in several countries in Latin America. The first volume of the *Bibliografia Bíblica Latino-Americana* (1988) lists 171 periodicals where Bible-oriented essays cited in that edition had been published. Among the titles are *Aconteceu no Mundo Evangélico* ('Events in the Protestant World') and *Amanecer* ('Dawn') from the Ecumenical Centres of Rio de Janeiro and Managua, respectively. Two theological quarterlies come from the largest Protestant faculties in Latin America, ISEDET in Buenos Aires (*Cuadernos de Teologia*) and São Leopoldo, Brazil (*Estudios Teológicos*). The Methodist Faculty of Theology published its *Mosaico*, a bulletin of information, and the Protestant seminary of Costa Rica *Vida y Pensamiento* ('Life and Thought'). Typically, a preacher's annual handbook entitled *Proclamar Libertação* ('To Proclaim Liberation') was published by the Faculdade de Teologia of the originally German Lutheran church at São Leopoldo (IECLB): 30 volumes appeared from 1976 to 2005. In Lima, Peru, there came out the *Fichas de Formación Bíblica* ('Leaflets for Biblical Education'). The 'Ecumenical Centre for Education' at Santiago, Chile, published its *Biblito*, and the headquarters of base communities in the Caribbean at Santo Domingo its *Encuentro*. The renowned ecumenical institution at San José in Costa Rica had its journal *Pasos*. CEBI at Belo Horizonte called its biblical monthly *Por trás da Palavra* ('Behind the Word'). Another ecumenical centre at São Paulo chose the name *Povo faz Caminho* ('The people leads the way') and another at Rio de Janeiro *Tempo e Presença* ('Presence in Time'). Some projects in the biblical field were national and some were oriented towards the whole of Latin America, bridging language barriers between Spanish and Portuguese zones. These include *Estudios Bíblicos de Petrópolis*, Brazil, the bibliographies *Bibliografia Teologica Comentada* and *Bibliografia Bíblica*, and the important *Comentário Bíblico (Ecumênico) 1985* and the *Revista de Interpretação Bíblica Latino-Americana*. Milton

Schwantes presents the general ideas underlying the *Bibliografía Bíblica Latino-Americana* (1988):

> The Bible has had a heavy impact in all of Latin-America and in the Caribbean. It contains the life-essence of the base communities. It exemplifies the churches' experiences. It comes to the fore in popular movements. The bibliography is designed to make possible an exchange of experiences and ideas across the whole, vast continent. Focal point is the popular interpretation ('leitura popular'). But this is not the only reading existing in society. The new Latin-American interpretation is being worked out in the context of other modes of reading the Bible which are applied within the churches, and quite influentially so. Therefore, it was our understanding from the beginning, that we should not limit ourselves to the new readings, that is, not exclude other hermeneutical approaches. Consequently, we try to be comprehensive. (1988: 10, 11)

All these attempts to unite the powers of the biblical liberation movement, however, were not meant to create a powerful structure able to resist the forces of military regimes. Here and there, it is true, public opinion and the official ranks of the Christian Churches (bishops, synods, monastic orders) would raise their voices in protest against state persecution and the abuse of power. But on the whole, all those prophetic believers who opposed the government and big business as incarnations of evil, were, politically speaking, on the loser's side (Betto 1982; Casaldaliga 1978). They would never be able to implement their biblical, utopian ideas, and there can be a very profound, intrinsic reason for this. Biblical visions of the reign of God, both in the Old and New Testaments, grew out of precise ancient life situations which no longer exist in the same form today. Moreover biblical attitudes towards society at large, and the notion of hoped-for righteousness came from small-scale communities, built on intimate personal values, that is, I–You relationships. The same holds true for Latin American base communities. Their theology and ethos are closely tied to the small local congregations and intimate, personal relationships throughout. Both the ancient biblical and the modern grassroots communities suffered from anonymous large-scale societies and their exploitative institutions, and are perfectly right to protest against all possible abuses of power. But they were and are in no condition to present detailed models for a just society at large. How should big companies, huge state administrations, legislation and jurisdiction, commerce and social security systems, function in order to meet God's will for justice and peace? Never being in a position to take over responsibility for the large, national social body or for international capital markets, biblical liberationists could venture only vague demands for equity and love, which are certainly justified, but do not provide blueprints for a harmonious world. So the inherent weakness of believers in God's coming reign of justice and peace is their limited social responsibility and political experience, in biblical times as well as today. Latin American Christians, the Bible in their hands, waged a heroic fight against the evils in their countries and the whole continent. They suffered arrest, torture, martyrdom, the best known of which are the assassinations of Bishop Romero in his own cathedral in 1980, and of a group of six Jesuits in the same city, San Salvador, in 1989. Pater Ellacuria, head of the department they had been working in, had returned from a journey to Europe a few days earlier; Jon Sobrino was travelling at the time of the massacre.

Thousands more have died because of their firm stand against tyranny and violations of human rights, and in suffering, like some of the biblical figures and early Christians under Roman persecution, they kept alive the contours of a utopian, yet utterly desirable life without oppression, and a deep longing for the reign of God.

The Bible in Traditional Churches

We should not deceive ourselves by assuming that the discovery of revolutionary thrusts in the Bible was the only possible approach to Scripture in Latin America. Sure enough, the liberationist movement captured most attention outside the continent. Indeed, the biblical protests against oppressive structures were practically the only part of the picture to be reported abroad. Traditional attitudes, however, to the Bible, Church and society permeated probably 60–80 per cent of the ecclesiastic hierarchy and membership, and this larger part of Christianity, mostly Catholic, but also Protestant, and some non-Christian religions also rediscovered the Bible. The difference was that their aim was to stabilize the existing regimes, and to make the faithful obedient citizens or even turn them into militant opponents of communism and the biblical liberationists.

During colonial times, the rulers of Latin America tried hard to keep the whole continent exclusively Catholic. Roman Catholicism was a kind of state religion. After the wars of independence in the early nineteenth century, the Catholic dominance remained unbroken, but here and there Protestants from the USA, Britain, the Netherlands and Germany sneaked in, mostly through commercial and cultural contacts, but some as settlers and industrial pioneers. The Protestant influence made itself felt especially through foreign, clandestine missionaries trying to distribute Bibles in the vernacular (Prien 1978: 742–7). The Church had long ruled that the people should not read the Scriptures by themselves, but learn it only through the mediation of official representatives. Protestants, for their part, trusted that the 'Holy Word' in itself would testify against Catholic doctrine and thus prepare Latin Americans for conversion to evangelical denominations. Occasionally, this kind of missionary activity caused problems with the hierarchy and in 1836 Pope Gregory XVI banned protestant Bible missions. In 1844, Bibles were confiscated and in 1836 they were publicly burnt in Uruguay (ibid.: 440).

It was only in the twentieth century that the Roman Catholic Church accepted and promoted Bible translations in the vernacular, together with Bible reading in the congregations, and critical biblical scholarship. In particular, the encyclical 'Divino afflante Spiritu' of 1943 paved the way to a freer handling of established hierarchic rules and biblical movements began to stir within the Catholic Church. But in Latin America it was due to the pioneering efforts of Protestants to spread the Sacred Book that the wave of Bible enthusiasm became particularly strong, and in due course, reading the Bible turned into an interdenominational activity in Christian communities across the continent.

Bible festivals were celebrated in traditional as well as in liberation communities. Bible monuments were erected like that of Londrina, Paraná, a towering 10 m concrete structure of four columns merging heavenwards. Quite often political leaders took part and in Brazil, as well as in other countries, an official day of commemoration was established for the 'Holy Book' on the second Sunday of December. On 9 December 2004, for example, the event was celebrated also in Parliament with João Mendes de Jesus, economist and theologian, present. In Nicaragua, the day of the Bible is the last Sunday in September.

Marathon bible readings, from the first to the last page, were staged in public. Bible competitions were held, and Bible literature – the Book itself as well as exegetical works at all levels – was in high demand. Bible expositions and museums were sponsored, and the biblical message was expounded in scores of TV broadcasts (many religious groups bought their own stations) and in mass rallies using stadiums, factory halls and marquees. Biblical pamphleteering and the free distribution of the Bible became fashionable: in 2004, the Brazilian Bible Society alone distributed 50,000 free Bibles. Sometimes it was rumoured that conservative churches had their free Bible distribution programmes financed by foreign secret services. Inside a free New Testament one might find a photo of the ruling military president, and a reading guide leading to biblical admonitions to trust in the Lord, hope for the resurrection from the dead and be obedient to the God-given government.

It was, to a large degree, patriotism that propelled conservative protestants to side even with military governments. The Brazilian *Sociedade Bíblica* ('Bible Society', SBB) was founded in 1948 under the motto: *Dar a Biblia à Patria* ('To give the Bible to the Fatherland'). A strong missionary drive was intimately connected with this endeavour. The founders of the Society wanted 'to distribute the Bible to everyone and to all social groups, as an instrument of spiritual and social transformation, and to strengthen ethical values and cultural development'. The actual SBB website proudly announces the establishment of a modern printing plant for Bibles in Tamboré, San Paolo, a successful mission of Bible carrying boats up the Amazon, and the production of 4.2 million Bibles or sections of the Bible in the year 2002. The ostentatious patriotism of Protestant Bible distributors often corresponds to a conservative or a-political stance against god-given rulers, Romans 13:1–2 being taken as an absolute command; but it was also a necessary move to legitimize themselves over against Catholicism and the ruling powers. Small wonder, then, that the latter did not hesitate to recognize them and rely on them for support. In 1967, for example, the Brazilian military government conferred on the above-mentioned Bible Society, the rights of a *Entidade de Utilidade Pública* ('Corporation of Public Utility').

Generally speaking, support for the military governments, often upheld by vehement denials of human rights violations, was strongest among fundamentalist, Bible-based Pentecostalist groups. With their dogmatic insistence that every word of Scripture constitutes eternal truth to be revered and obeyed, and their physical presence in the ever-growing slum areas of Latin America, they attracted much attention among the poor and became the fastest-growing churches on the continent. Belief in the infallible Word of God thus spread through large sections of the population. Nor was it only Pentecostals who were caught up in the mystification of the Bible. Those Protestant denominations, which had their roots in Bible-oriented American mother churches like the Baptists, Presbyterians, some Methodists and Lutherans, all joined in the apotheosis of the Word. So did conservative Catholics in their particular way. They maintained their doctrinal stand on the primacy of the magisterial office and its authoritative interpretation, but they were also concerned to promote the correct knowledge of biblical facts among the believers. The old days of keeping Scripture in safe seclusion are definitely gone. A good example of conservative projects of this kind are the Brazilian periodicals *Revista de Cultura Bíblica*, a mainly Jesuit publication from Recife, edited by João Evangelista Martins Terra, and *Revista Bíblica Brasileira* from Fortaleza, which for many years was edited and written almost single-handedly by Caetano Minette de Tillesse. Both these erudite biblical scholars were dedicated to sound biblical scholarship, the dissemination of accurate factual information about the Bible, and the maintenance of church control over Bible interpretation.

What we notice, then, is the ambivalence of biblical interpretation in a continental society marked, from colonial beginnings to our own post-modern age, by terrible dichotomies in the areas of welfare, social status, economic and political participation, and cultural and religious identity. The Bible is a motivating force in more than one of the various ideological camps. What has impressed the outside world, especially in the decades of the 1960s to the 1980s was the unbelievable force of political and cultural change which resulted from intense, popular readings of the Bible. But what about the developments since 1985?

Twenty Years of Adaptation (1985–2005)

The year 1985 marks a kind of dividing line, heralding the demise of the military dictatorships. Argentina and Uruguay had shed their military regimes. Chile was to follow in 1990. Bolivia experienced some internal reforms. Paraguay overcame the dictator J. Stroessner in 1989. But 1985 was the year in which the largest country in Latin America, Brazil, for the first time since 1964, elected a new president by a democratic vote. The circumstances were dramatic. Millions had demonstrated for 'elections now!' Tancredo Neves won the race, but died in mysterious circumstances before he could take office. His designated vice-president took over, and despite being close to the armed forces, initiated a period of civil government which has lasted until today. Along with other countries Brazil chose the road to formal democracy. Analysts well know that foreign pressure regarding economic free market ideas and motivated by ideological reservations against military dictatorships, had been instrumental in these political changes in Latin America. But a deep change had taken place within Latin America itself, politically, economically and in terms of ideology, and a few years later, the socialist system collapsed, an event which made world history go backwards.

One of the first to address the ensuing problems of this capsizing of the world order in regard to liberation theology and biblical exegesis, was Pablo Richard of Chile, working mainly in Costa Rica. Being an experienced liberation theologian, he was familiar with the notion that every interpretative discourse is strictly tied to the interpreter's own context. He or she is always conditioned by personal experience and cultural and social parameters. Hadn't Carlos Mesters been saying all those years, 'We are looking at the Bible through our own coloured glasses, always?' So to acknowledge that the world had radically changed, to take up a dialogue now with the new situation, seemed natural. Pablo Richard (1991), among others, gave his voice to a new chapter in the history of liberation exegesis. The frame of reference for liberation exegesis, he said, that is to say, oppression by military dictatorships and exploitation by other brutal forces, had vanished. But social conditions had stayed the same: they had even worsened. Instead of marginalizing the poor, the new capitalist economies, no longer hampered by socialist competition, now completely excluded the surplus population from their productive and consumptive system. The more the rich pushed the poor out beyond the margins of participative society, the higher profits would rise. There was no need to keep so many 'lazy crocodiles on welfare bonuses', as a US Senator in Florida was reported to have put it.

Pablo Richard concluded that biblical liberation theology has every right to continue to fight for the cause of the lost ones of this earth; but the articulation of these legitimate concerns has to be different. The terminology of class struggle does not fit an open society, in which everyone is co-responsible for existing conditions. Society as a whole is culpable for any grave distortions of justice, equity and the existing social abyss. To unmask culprits may still be necessary, but not in a confrontation between social classes. The former discourse of class struggle is no longer used nor understood in a democratic environment. Pablo Richard's latest book, presented at the 14th Book Fair of Havana, Cuba, is appropriately entitled *The Ethical and spiritual Force of Liberation Theology*.

The revolutionary reading of the Bible has all but disappeared in these past two decades. Instead, an evolutionary, for the most part educative, reading has taken place. The enthusiasm, or even at times ecstasy, at the possibility of rapidly changing the world for the better according to biblical visions, has all but disappeared. Milton Schwantes, in a lecture given in 1993, compared biblical interpretation to planting little trees, instead of shooting arrows against enemies. Jung Mo Sung, a Brazilian of Korean descent, draws on biblical concepts in his analysis of the suicidal dimensions of modern economy and economic theory. Economy is the great and – for one-third or more of world population – destructive power, the real anti-divine system. Yet, we cannot blame its monstrosity on specific individuals. Biblical witnesses had realized the dangers of rampant economic dominance (Ezek. 27). Our theological and exegetical task is to carefully analyse all the ramifications of the human condition, look for the deep faults in our economic systems, and then slowly repair them by patient education (Assmann and Sung 2000). Education is the main emphasis, just as it was for Paulo Freire (1975). Of course, this is quite a different approach to Scripture from what had gone before. The hermeneutics of revolution has given way to a hermeneutics of evolution. But the underlying zeal is still the same: to improve the situation of the poor, to create humane living conditions for all, and to prevent the destruction of our planet.

The Bible is still very important in progressive as well as traditional and fundamentalist parishes and church groups. Bible study goes on; biblical preaching is still (after 2500 years!) uncontested as the basic form of divine communication with humans. A great deal of Jewish and Christian social ethics is rooted in ancient Scripture. All the Latin American denominations, from the still dominant Catholic Church down to the smallest confessional groups, both within the Christian tradition and beyond into hetero-confessional, syncretistic religious bodies, all of them hold the Bible in very high esteem. Latin America, by and large, is a religiously teeming continent, with Brazil probably leading the way by the sheer intensity and variety of its religious faith, a faith which never really suffered any secularist, enlightened screening. The Bible is still almost universally recognized as 'The Word of God'. Bible schools, academic institutions dedicated to Bible research, streams of publications to this day continue the early post-war period of effervescent biblical euphoria. A new ecumenical association of biblical scholars in Brazil was founded in September 2004 at a congress in Goiânia. Nowadays, work and dialogue with the Bible are calmer, more reflective and perhaps dedicated to different texts in the canon. Whereas Exodus, the Prophets, the gospels loomed large formerly, in revolutionary times, now there is a major focus on instructions and regulations, on the Wisdom literature and Psalms, on restoration as well as organization of the communities of old. It would be interesting to investigate these shifting themes in relation to parochial activities, academic teaching and lists of publications.

Conclusion

Having briefly surveyed the role of the Bible in Latin America after the Second World War, we conclude by considering the continuing significance of this period for the inhabitants of the southern hemisphere and for people in other parts of the world. Since revolutions are rather rare in the mainstream history of Christianity after 325 CE, we should be attentive to that special upheaval caused by the Bible on the Latin American continent in the decades up to 1985, and its repercussions down to the present day. The way the Scriptures came to life in that period, opposing power structures, is remarkable. Its counterpart, the Bible fortifying and stabilizing traditional systems, is much more common in the history of Christianity, but it may also have its significance.

   Millions of people have been studying biblical texts over the past decades in countries where the rate of literacy has traditionally been low, because of the predominance of oral cultures and relatively poor educational facilities. To handle texts, ancient ones at that, requires a hermeneutical understanding of what reading and interpreting written testimonies is like. The degree of insight into these processes certainly will vary from reader to reader and from congregation to congregation. But there is no doubt that the very experience of encountering the biblical text over all these years has promoted the skills required to deal with writings from the past, and to tackle the basic problems of human life expressed in them. This process in itself is essential to human education and ethical learning in a world which desperately needs sober and wise judgements. Both popular wisdom and academic teaching have grown considerably in depth and fullness along with the various Bible movements. A certain soberness can sometimes be observed, transforming the Bible, the medium of a mysterious or miraculous revelation, into a trustworthy companion in a life-long journey.

   A second consequence of the Bible movements in Latin America is the astonishing ecumenicity which has evolved from the serious reading of the Scriptures. The base communities, as a rule, did not ask participants in communion services or bible study groups for their denominational or religious affiliations. Everyone was accepted as a full member of the community. Joint reading of the Bible under-girded that ecumenical attitude. In fact, the Scriptures do contain much diversity in faith. As José Comblin, one of the main editors of the *Comentário Bíblico* (1985), puts it: 'The Bible no longer separates Christians from each other; rather, it is beginning to unite them . . . because the Bible is the heritage of all Christians' (General Introduction 1985: 10). Today, twenty years later, he might plainly say 'the heritage of all humankind'.

Last but not least, we should remember that Latin American base communities, along with others in Africa, Asia and a few also in Europe and the USA, with their Bible reading and their praxis of solidarity, emphasize in a unique way common ancient theological concerns about all fellow beings. Jewish, Muslim and Christian faiths agree on this point: there is no way of claiming knowledge of and trust in the One God, creator of heaven and earth, while at the same time letting millions of people starve on this planet. Equally, there is no way of reconciling faith in One God with actively engaging in the destruction of his creation. The Bible, translated into modern living conditions, does not give us a licence to postpone salvation to future life or to a mere spiritual existence. Christian responsibility is with the present state of affairs, with society and nature, as they exist here and now. Latin American readers of the Bible tell everybody on this earth that a joint effort on the part of all human beings is required to take care of this beautiful world, threatened by human ignorance and selfishness. In the words of a biblical prophet central to Latin American biblical life: 'Let justice roll down like waters, and righteousness like an ever-flowing stream' (Amos 5:24).

References and Further Reading

Alves, Rubem (1972). *Tomorrow's Child: Imagination, Creativity, and the Rebirth of Culture*. New York: Harper & Row.

Assmann, H. and Sung, J. M. (2000). *Competência e sensibilidade solidária: Educar para a esperança*. Petrópolis: Editora Vozes.

Betto, Frei (1982). *Batismo de Sangue: Os dominicanos e a morte de Carlos Marighella*, 2nd edn. Rio de Janeiro: Civilização Brasileira.

Bibliografia Bíblica Latino-Americana (1988–). São Bernardo do Campo: Programa Ecumênico de Pós-Graduação em Ciências da Religião, Faculdade de Teologia da Igreja Metodista.

Bibliografia Teológica Comentada del Area Iberoamericana (1973–96). 24 vols. Buenos Aires: ISEDET.

Boff, L. (1972). *Jesus Cristo Libertador*. Petrópolis: Editora Vozes.

Bonino, J. M. (1977). *La fe en busca de eficacia: Una interpretación de la reflexión teológica latinoamericana de liberación*. Salamanca: Ediciones Sígueme.

Camara, Helder (1980). *Mille raisons pour vivre*. Paris: Editions du Seuil.

Cardenal, E. (1976). *El Evangelio en Solentiname*. Salamanca: Ediciones Sígueme. Trans. D. D. Walsh (1977) as *Love in Practice: The Gospel in Solentiname*. London: Search Press.

Casaldaliga, P. (1978). *Creio na justiça e na esperança*. Rio de Janeiro: Civilização brasileira.

Centro de Estudos Bíblicos, various publications, e.g. *Por trás da palavra* (1980–). Angra dos Reis and Belo Horizonte: CEBI.

Comentário Bíblico (1985–). Petrópolis: Editora Vozes.

Cook, G. (1985). *The Expectation of the Poor: Latin American Base Communities in Protestant Perspective*. Maryknoll, NY: Orbis.

Croatto, J. S. (1973). *Liberación y libertad: Pautas hermenéuticas*. Buenos Aires: Mundo Nuevo. Trans. S. Attanasio (1981) as *Exodus: A Hermeneutics of Freedom*. Maryknoll, NY: Orbis.

Croatto, J. S. (1984). *Hermenéutica bíblica*. Buenos Aires: La Aurora. Trans. R. R. Barr (1987) as *Biblical Hermeneutics: Toward a Theory of Reading as the Production of Meaning*. Maryknoll, NY: Orbis.

Croatto, J. S. (1997). *Exílio y sobrevivência: Tradiciones contraculturales en el Pentateuco*. Buenos Aires: Editorial Lumen.

Croatto, J. S. (2002). *Hermenéutica práctica: Los principios de la hermenéutica bíblica en ejemplos*. Quito: Centro Bíblico Verbo Divino.

Estudos Bíblicos (1984–). Petrópolis: Editora Vozes.

Freire, P. (1975). *Pedagogia do Oprimido*, 2nd edn. Rio de Janeiro: Paz e Terra.

Fricke, M. (1997). *Bibelauslegung in Nicaragua: Jorge Pixley im Spannungsfeld von Befreiungstheologie, historisch-kritischer Exegese und baptistischer Tradition*. Münster: Lit-Verlag.

Gerstenberger, E. S. (1992a). 'Lieder von Freiheit und Leben: Die Psalmen in den Basisgemeinden Lateinamerikas', *Bibel und Kirche* 47: 214–19.

Gerstenberger, E. S. (1992b). 'Theologie der Befreiung: Der Aufbruch der Kirchen in Lateinamerika', *Braunschweiger Beiträge* 62: 5–19.

Gerstenberger, E. S. (1993). 'Exegesis Biblica en America Latina y en Europa', *Revista Teologica Limense* 27: 242–52.

Gerstenberger, E. S. (1994). 'Befreiungstheologien im Wandel: Das alttestamentliche Zeugnis und der Weg lateinamerikanischer Christen nach der "Wende"', in W. Kurz, R. Lächele and G. Schmalenberg (eds), *Krisen und Umbrüche in der Geschichte des Christentums*. Giessen: Verlag des Fachbereichs 07 der Justus-Liebig Universität, pp. 157–77.

Gerstenberger, E. S. (1995). '"Exodus" als Leitmotiv der Befreiungstheologie', *Braunschweiger Beiträge* 71: 49–56.

Gerstenberger, E. S. (1997). 'Bibel und Befreiung: Von den Wurzeln und der Wirkung der lateinamerikanischen Befreiungstheologie', *Weltmission heute* 31: 67–86.

Gotay, S. S. (1981). 'Origem e desenvolvimento do pensamento christão revolucionário a partir da radicalização da doutrina socialista nas décadas de 1960 e 1970', in E. Dussel (ed.), *História da teologia na América Latina*. São Paulo: Edições Paulinas, pp. 133–64.

Gutiérrez, G. (1973). *A Theology of Liberation: History, Politics and Salvation*. Maryknoll, NY: Orbis.

Gutiérrez, G. (1986). *On Job: God-Talk and the Suffering of the Innocent*. Maryknoll, NY: Orbis.

Medellin Document (1968). *Resolutions of the General Assembly of Latin American Bishops, Aug. 24 to Sept. 6, 1968*. Medellin, in *The Church in the Present-Day Transformation of Latin America in the Light of the Council* (1970). Washington, DC: CELAM.

Meissner, D. (2004). *Die 'Kirche der Armen' in El Salvador*. Neuendettelsau: Erlanger Verlag für Mission und Ökumene.

Mesters, C. (1971). *Deus, onde estás?* Belo Horizonte: Editora Vega. Trans. J. Drury and F. McDonagh (1995) as *God, Where Are You?* Maryknoll, NY: Orbis.

Mesters, C. (1980). *Círculos Biblicos*. Petrópolis: Editora Vozes.

Miranda, J. P. (1974). *Marx and the Bible: A Critique of the Philosophy of Oppression*. Maryknoll, NY: Orbis.

Núñez, E. A. (1985). *Liberation Theology*. Chicago: Moody Press.

Pobee, J. S. and Wartenberg-Potter, B. von (1986). *New Eyes for Reading: Biblical and Theological Reflections by Women from the Third World*. Geneva: World Council of Churches.

Prien, H.-J. (1978). *Die Geschichte des Christentums in Lateinamerika*. Göttingen: Vandenhoeck & Ruprecht.

Revista de Interpretação Bíblica Latino-Americana (1988–). São Paulo: Imprensa Metodista.

Richard, P. (1991). 'A Teologia da Libertação na Nova Conjuntura: Temas e Novos Desafios para a Década de Noventa', *Estudos Teológicos* 31: 206–20.

Schürger, W. (1995). *Theologie auf dem Weg der Befreiung. Geschichte und Methode des Zentrums für Bibelstudien: CEBI in Brasilien.* Erlangen: Verlag der Ev. Lutherischen Mission.

Schwantes, Milton (1987a). *Amós: Meditações e estudos.* São Leopoldo: Editora Sinodal.

Schwantes, Milton (1987b). *Sofrimento e esperança no exílio.* São Leopoldo: Editora Sinodal.

Schwantes, Milton et al. (eds) (1988). *Bibliografia Bíblica Latino-Americana,* vol. 1. São Bernardo do Campo: Programa Ecumênico de Pós-Graduação em Ciências da Religião, Faculdade de Teologia da Igreja Metodista.

Shaull, R. (1984). *Heralds of a New Reformation: The Poor of South and North America.* Maryknoll NY Orbis.

Tamez, E. (1979). *La Bíblia de los oprimidos: La opresión en la teologia bíblica.* San José (Costa Rica): Departamento Ecuménico de Investigaciones. Trans. M. J. O'Connell (1982) as *Bible of the Oppressed.* Maryknoll, NY: Orbis.

Tamez, E. (ed.) (1989). *Through Her Eyes: Women's Theology from Latin America.* Maryknoll, NY: Orbis.

Vatican (1984, 1986). *Instructions of the Congregation of Faith,* 24 August 1984 and 22 March 1986.

CHAPTER 14
Australasia

Roland Boer and Ibrahim Abraham

Jon Frum, Ned Kelly and Bashir Baraki: three names that mark the extraordinary realm of subcultural appropriations, twistings and representations of a Bible that hardly seems familiar any more in the Antipodes. Once put into the subcultural mill – which here includes apocalyptic cargo cults from Melanesia, active engagements with Christian missions and Australian pop culture among Australian Aborigines, and video interviews of Jesus' close associates that bring together gay subculture and exploratory art – the Bible reappears, now in the volcano jungles of Vanuatu, the red desert at Australia's heart and on the small video screens of a gay artist, as a very different text, decked out in homemade American military uniforms (Jon Frum), a suit of armour (Ned Kelly), or with a video camera in its hands (Bashir Baraki).

In other words, we cannot emphasize enough that *the Bible becomes an object and a political symbol as much as a text* in these three situations. In the Jon Frum cult, the Bible must be resisted as a symbol of Western Christian imperialism. Among the Aborigines of northern Australia, the Bible is appropriated in extraordinarily creative moments of exegesis in which it becomes part of a much larger mythical collection. And then in the queer subculture of immigrant art, the Bible moves across media to take on a much more intimate feel with Bashir Baraki. Each moment in our discussion is concerned with a subcultural appropriation of the Bible, as text, symbol and object with deep political resonances.

In what follows we are less interested in offering an overarching theory that will make sense, in some fashion or other, of our trio than in how the intersections of the aesthetic and religious work themselves out in a political direction. The candidates whose hands are up most eagerly for a theoretical say would have to be globalization and regional culture, although we don't intend to make another weighty contribution to that already overblown debate – just a few comments that will situate our chapter. Agency and hybridity, stalwarts of much postcolonial theory, are also keen to have a say, but our take on these is just as much indebted to that old Marxist space cadet Ernst Bloch, searching for the wary, critical and mocking appropriation-as-resistance that we find in cargo cults, Australian Aboriginal and queer approaches to the Bible (Bloch 1972, especially pp. 15–24, 38–58; see also 1995). Another eager hand is that of the theory of subculture itself, for which the primary reference remains Dick Hebdige's (1987) classic; it is a term that has in many respects replaced the older modernist division between high and low culture. While this division has collapsed, as Fredric Jameson has argued on a number of occasions (see especially Jameson 1991), in the context of the explosion of interest groups, identity and micro-politics in the postmodern cultural terrain, the terms culture and subculture have, albeit uneasily, come into service. And of course there will be an underlying Marxist interest, as is our wont, but it will manifest itself less in direct Marxist theory than in the political implications of the three exhibits.

Local and/or General[1] and/or Subculture and/or the Bible

Literature on the relationship between the global and the local, or globalization and regionalism is, like the phenomenon itself, massive, although our preferred angle follows that of Appadurai (1990) and Hardt and Negri (2000). For Appadurai, those who favour the hypothesis of a homogenization of culture – usually in terms of Americanization or commoditization – ignore that fact that 'at least as rapidly as forces from various metropolises are brought into new societies they tend to become indigenized in one or another way' (Appadurai 1990: 295). In what is now a famous essay, and a response to Jameson's equally famous 'Postmodernism, or, the Cultural Logic of Late Capitalism' (Jameson 1984), Appadurai seeks – through the five neologisms of ethnoscapes, mediascapes, technoscapes, finanscapes and ideoscapes – to reshape the Marxist narrative in order to pay closer attention to global fragmentation, uncertainty and difference. Similarly, for Hannerz (1990), global culture in fact means a fluid network of diversity, of the interconnectedness of local cultures and those that have no anchorage in any one territory. And on this matter Hardt and Negri agree, pointing to the increasing flows of peoples and cultures across the globe, which they read as the source of a new strength. Yet, on the issue of globalization and regionalism Hardt and Negri equivocate, or rather want to move past this old divide, for then we fall into the debate as to whether globalization generates the new regionalisms, or whether those regionalisms are in fact genuine and alternative responses to globalization, the source of possible resistance. For Hardt and Negri, any possibility of resistance must come from an equally global movement, which they see in all its diversity as the multitude, or rather multitudes.

All of this – we refer to the work of Appadurai, Hannerz and Hardt and Negri – means that whereas we can't be sure of what 'Australasia' is, where it starts or finishes or even whether it exists at all, we can examine it as a series of highly interactive and disjointed cultures that have had to react and incorporate imperial culture(s), including the Bible, into their own cultures. And always with a distinct wariness and surprisingly innocent mockery that would make Ernst Bloch smile. For instance, 'why would a people on a remote island north of New Guinea want Lyndon B. Johnson as their leader?' (Billings 2002: 3). To mock its neo-colonial Australian administrators, argues Billings. It was, in other words, political performance. So, if we don't view 'Australasia' as a series of inter-connected subcultures – think of the overlapping circles of Venn diagrams – then we will end up talking about 'civilization' (Sandall 2001, especially pp. 151–77). 'Australasian' civilization, as with Huntington's 'clash of civilizations,' will lead to ridiculous over-simplifications, insulting generalizations and incorrect homogenizations. So it is preferable to say that there are some diverse cultures that have, for our purposes, engaged in similar processes of resistance and (not uncritical) appropriations of the imposed meta-texts of the Bible.

As far as subcultures are concerned, the writing has been overwhelmingly Western and urban and suburban, yet often redeploying old-school anthropological approaches. Thus, there is much about mods and goths and working-class kids from the 'burbs, but little consideration of colonized peoples such as the Johnson cult of New Guinea or, more to the point for this essay, the Tannese of Vanuatu or the Aborigines of northern Australia. The standard text is still Dick Hebdige's *Subculture: The Meaning of Style* (Hebdige 1987), which has enough Althusser and Williams and Marx and Lévi-Strauss to keep Roland happy, and more than enough mods, punks, skinheads and Jean Genet to satisfy Ibrahim. Pretty much everything written on subcultures since begins with this classic (see, for instance, Gelder and Thornton 1997), but it is the material on bricolage, heavily indebted to Lévi-Strauss, that most interests us for all three characters we consider in this study, for are not Jon Frum, Ned Kelly as saviour and video interviews with Christ's followers not prime examples of excessive bricolage? Indeed, if anything unites our exhibits, it is their use of bricolage, the apparently haphazard and uninformed, but in fact highly conscious and deliberative collation of disparate materials in order to construct a new scale of meaning.

Thus far, we have written enough on culture and subculture to set the context for our romp through Vanuatu (Jon Frum), outback Australia (Ned Kelly) and suburban Melbourne (Bashir Baraki), but what of the Bible itself? As we suggested a little earlier, we take the Bible very much as a meta-text in this chapter, one that not merely has selected texts we can interpret (the favoured mode of biblical scholarship), but is an object of power itself with a host of hangers-on, such as a distinct religious system, culture, politics, assumed social system, and so on. It is an object of worship in its own right, 'cargo' brought by the Western missionaries, and a mocked or rejected symbol of white imperialism. This mixture of mockery and feared reverence – characteristic of so many appropriations all the way from cargo cults to queer appropriations – is a tension-filled response that acknowledges the Bible's enduring power to kill. Finally, the nagging question – flagged elsewhere (Boer 2001a; 2001b; 2005) – is whether inventive (mis)appropriations, whether deliberate or not, actually move much further than futile responses to an overwhelming force, whether, in other words, it is little different to reaction. For the problem is, we suspect, that there is less knowing mockery, too few winks of resistance, and far too much earnest belief in the inherent power of the responses that can all too often become merely other modes of acquiescence.

Jon[2] Frum: Apocalyptic Pentecostalism and 'Cargo'

We have been waiting only 60 years for Jon Frum to come back. Christians have been waiting 2000 years for Jesus Christ. Why are we the ones who are thought of as strange? (Roial Kilma, quoted in DiManno 1999)

The Bible says you must sweat to receive. You cannot expect things to fall from the sky. People still hope the riches will come, but maybe they have been delivered. John and Jesus speak the same message. Perhaps they are the same person. (Maliwan Taruayi, quoted in Dutter 2001)

The Story of John Frum, could all its chapters and verses be collated, would outweigh a Bible. (Lindstrom 1993: 73)

We are by no means the first to be enticed by the sheer exoticism – no, the right word is 'wackiness' – of the religion of Jon Frum (Jon From America, Jon From Jesus Christ, Jon Broom who will sweep away Europeans, Jon Brown of anti-slavery fame in the USA – who knows?). Indeed, we follow a host of others, from tourist books to adventure travellers like Paul Theroux and Michael Krieger (Krieger 1994: 118–28) and theorists of religion such as Mircea Eliade. For Eliade he is the 'the celebrated John Frum' (Eliade 1965: 136), while Theroux, paddling his way from island to island in the Pacific, desperately desired to visit Tanna, Jon Frum's home, since he 'had heard that a cargo cult, the Jon Frum Movement, flourished on the island' (Theroux 1993: 187). Not to be outdone, both the *South Pacific Handbook* (Stanley 2000: 784) and *Lonely Planet Vanuatu* (O'Brien 1999: 154–6) also trot out the story of Jon Frum. And so we arrive, not in a canoe, nor even with an anthropologist's notebook and pencil, but with a few strokes on a keyboard (see http://www.enzo.gen.nz/jonfrum).

Just when we think that we can delve into the whole realm of 'cargo cult' we find that anthropologists have been shying away from the term for more than three decades, particularly the crudeness with which it has been applied across many Pacific Islands (see Cochrane 1970; Eves 1998; Lindstrom 1993; Worsley 1968). And yet it has a life of its own, well beyond anthropological research and literature and will not disappear without a fight. What intrigues us about the Jon Frum movement is the way it simultaneously rejects the Bible and all that trails along behind this 'sacred text,' while at the same time it bounces off Christianity, providing, if you will, the obverse of the same coin.

But first, who and what is Jon Frum and what is his gospel? After the first wave of Presbyterian missions in the mid-nineteenth century, when conversions seemed to secure for the Presbyterian Church the island of Tanna in the southern part of the archipelago of what was then called the New Hebrides (by the colonial administrators), a sizeable part of the population apparently rejected Christianity in favour of Jon Frum, probably in the 1930s. His name first appeared in written form in the reports of the colonial District Agent James M. Nicol in 1940, of the Presbyterian missionary H. M. (Jock) Bell in 1941 and in the police reports of the local police officer Joe Nalpin in the same year (see Lindstrom 1993: 74). When the administrators and missionaries ended their writing upon independence in 1980, journalists and travel writers took over, joining the anthropologists who had become enamoured since the beginning of the 1950s. In fact, there seem to be more followers of Jon Frum outside the island of Tanna than on the island itself.

As for Jon himself, he appears in the 1930s at times as a small white man, at others as huge black man, depending which story you read (but that is of course part of the appeal), telling the villagers to discard the Bible of the Presbyterian missionaries in favour of Tannese 'kastum' – kava drinking, singing, dancing, magic stones, and so on. By 1943, with the massive presence of American troops in the Pacific War, Jon becomes an American, responsible for the arrival of planes, ships, cigarettes, machinery, food and refrigerators (for some reason the refrigerators keep reappearing in the stories). All this took place despite American efforts to persuade them that Jon Frum was a false messiah, a message belied by American 'generosity' as the Tannese provided much needed labour (Krieger 1994: 123). Then too the Red Cross symbol becomes that of the (new) religion and of Jon Frum himself. Most writers point out, suffering momentary amnesia over its origins, that this is not a Christian cross. For quite a few decades the paraphernalia of the US armed forces enter into the beliefs and practices of the Frum followers: the Stars and Stripes, homemade military uniforms, spears or sticks in place of rifles, makeshift jetties, airstrips and radios. Although these have faded, the core belief is that Jon Frum will return, bringing plenty, which boils down to the endless commodities of late capitalism, including refrigerators. Having come once, he will no doubt return in glory. Worship involves weekly gatherings on Friday, with visions of Jon delivered by 'prophets', singing, dancing, guitar playing and kava drinking, all customs that Jon encouraged them to continue when rejecting the Bible. And then the annual festival on 15 February includes combat drill, a long procession carrying a large red cross up the slopes of the active volcano Mount Yafur to be placed on the edge of the crater (for one of Jon's abodes is in fact the volcano itself), much kava drinking, along with intoxicated music and dance throughout the night.

Now, we can follow a number of tracks through the jungle at this point, the one that runs past poor and derelict villages with wheezy old chiefs who claim theirs fathers met Jon Frum (Theroux 1993), or another that listens to the villager who claims that in many respects Jon Frum has delivered, for the island itself now has an airport near the capital on Lanakel, planes, ships, cars, cigarettes, Coca-Cola and, yes, refrigerators (Dutter 2001), or yet another, more educated voice, that of a school teacher, who suggests that Jon Frum, should he actually have existed, was the manifestation an old Tannese spirit in a new form (Theroux 1993), or, finally, the path to Frum prosperity, peace and tourism (Krieger 1994). But we want to follow another path, one that does not mean we need to 'cross a volcanic plain, ford a lake and endure a bone-rattling ride down a pot-holed track' (Dutter 2001) to the village of Sulphur Bay, the spiritual home of the Jon Frum movement. Or rather, we need to travel out from Sulphur Bay and not to it. And when we come out into the wider reaches of Tanna and Vanuatu as a whole, we find that the islanders have been and continue to be a somewhat political, if not militant bunch.

Colonial administrators remained interested in the group from the 1930s to independence in 1980 not only because they seemed odd, but because they regarded the movement as subversive, a front for an independence movement. Thus, the colonial administrator Nicol jailed almost 100 Frummers in 1940, some of whom served up to 11 years in jail (Krieger 1994: 121). The administrators didn't have to look far for evidence to support such an opinion, since the overt militarization of the movement included not merely the uniforms and dreams of American goods, especially boats, planes, wharves and military vehicles, but also the forming of a regiment in the 1940s and daily military drills. And the carrying of sticks or spears instead of guns was hardly the result of lack of opportunity to acquire guns, but due to the ban on weapons by the administrators. All of this came to a head when the drive for independence from the British and French grew stronger in the 1970s. The election of 1979 saw a coalition of the dominant Modérés Party in the rest of Vanuatu over against the secessionist Nagriamel movement on the island of Santo, the custom group called Kapiel on Tanna, and of course the Frummers. Spurred on by a close defeat in the election by only 2 per cent, and alleging electoral fraud, the Tannese followed the Nagriamel group on Santo and rebelled, seizing two British government administrators. Police subsequently freed the prisoners and arrested many of the rebels. On the verge of civil war, 300 Tannese – Frummers and the 'kastom' group Kapiel – attacked the town of Isangel on 10 June 1980, in order to free those arrested. One of the coup leaders was shot, many others were arrested and the rebellion died down. That the Jon Frum movement won a seat in parliament in the early days of the new millennium indicates that its political aspirations are far from over.

Now, this is hardly the work of an isolated and ignorant group with a weird religious system. In this light, the earlier rejection of the Presbyterian missionaries and the adoption of Jon Frum begins to look distinctly more political. This was symbolized in Jon Frum's advice – so the story goes – to throw out their Bibles. Here the meta-text takes on a distinctly political nature, for the rejection of the Bible is a rejection of a text that kills, specifically custom and belief, but also as part of the whole colonial machinery that brought the plagues through which so many died. Indeed, another of Jon Frum's promises was that disease would fade away when all the Europeans left.

As we write, the Bible is again at the centre of conflict, now in terms of the return of Christianity and the conversion of many Tannese away from Jon Frum. For in the first years of the zeros the Presbyterians have been drawing the young people back to the church. Roman Catholics and Seventh Day Adventists are also after their share, so much so that the shrine at the centre of the movement, in Sulphur Bay, has been moved a kilometre away to the village of Lamakara (see Dutter 2001). Given the highly political nature of the movement, it comes as no surprise that Chief James Thru has endorsed the return of the Presbyterian Church, appointing his great nephew to undertake theological training, whereas Chief Wan watches the developments with alarm. In a curious reversal of the rejection of Christianity in the 1930s, the tension came to a head in April 2004, when a battle involving Jon Frummers on one side and Christians led by 'prophet' Fred Nasse on the other left 25 injured by axes, slingshots, and bows and arrows, along with some torched houses and a church building (see Squires 2004). Order came with the police from Port Vila and an uneasy truce was endorsed by all the chiefs of the island.

It is not merely that the Bible stands in as a conflictual symbol for a range of other interests, such as inter-chief conflict, militant politics, traditional customs versus imperial inroads, but that as a meta-text it provides both the context, or world-view and terms within which such conflicts take place. At this level, the Jon Frum movement's identity is determined by its rejection of a dangerous and feared text. But this point only removes the upper layer of the problem and we need to burrow further. For it is not so much the case that the Bible provides the world-view in which conflict manifests itself: rather, the Bible both transforms and is transformed by the wider Melanesian cultural and economic milieu. And that milieu is determined by the conjunction of wealth – the possession of objects – and prestige, except that whereas the underlying drive of capitalism is the accumulation of wealth through profit and thereby the gaining of prestige, in Melanesian society prestige is achieved through the giving of the objects of wealth. In a crucial passage, Deborah Bird Rose points out that a 'great deal of evidence from Papua New Guinea suggests that where wealth is an important measure of personal and group esteem, displays of unmatchable and unshared wealth induce those with less to query their own adequacy, to seek the causes of inequality, and to search for means whereby an equitable distribution of wealth and power can be enjoined' (Rose 1994). Thus, faced with the vast discrepancy of objects that the colonial powers displayed, and especially the American armed forces during World War II, cargo becomes a distinct effort to deal with the disparity, both in terms of gaining the objects that should have been given in exchange and in order to acquire adequate items for exchange and therefore prestige.

This argument is, to our mind, a more nuanced way of understanding cargo, at least in economic and social terms, than the oft-repeated point that cargo is but the mirror of a capitalism shorn of its work ethic and built on immediate gratification, whether through credit or lottery. The mirror of cargo, it would seem, is distorted and blurred, for the co-ordinates are appropriated and rearranged. So also with the Bible: in their apparent rejection, the Jon Frum movement and many others like it simultaneously pick up the Bible and transform it. Millenarian, apocalyptic, often charismatic and pentecostal, it reflects back a wavy and altered image that is both alien and yet oddly familiar. The same may be said of appropriations of the Bible by Aboriginal Australians, except that the pattern of engaging with the Bible is markedly different from the Melanesians. To a couple of examples of such engagements we now turn.

'Ned Kelly Died for Our Sins'[3]

> Ned once visited Wave Hill station long before any whitefellows had come into the Victoria River District. There he taught people how to make tea and cook damper. Although there was only one billy of tea, and one little damper, everybody got fed. (Rose 1994)

The allusion, in case you missed it, is of course to the miraculous feeding stories in Matthew 14:13–21, 15:29–39, Mark 6:32–44, 8:1–10, Luke 9:11–17 and John 6:5–13. In fact, we would argue that the replication of the stories themselves throughout all the gospels is a formal multiplication of the content; it is as though the loaves and fish multiply to feed a multitude of readers. But now we move from the Pacific Island of Tanna in Vanuatu to northern Australia, and what we find is a *Bible interpreted and appropriated in ways that are entirely unexpected*. It is incorporated into a mythological field where it becomes part of a much greater whole.

The full flavour of that greater whole comes out in the preceding quotation. Thus, the billy of tea and damper – a loaf of bread cooked in the fire's coals or in a heavy iron pot – are themselves European foods appropriated as staples by many Aborigines, as the story makes clear. And Victoria River Downs, one of the largest cattle stations on earth in the Northern Territory of Australia, sits hard by Wave Hill Station in the home of the Yarralin and Lingara peoples – the source of this story. Apart from this wholesale appropriation of Ned Kelly, note that he precedes other whites and is, above all, a positive figure in this story.

But *Ned Kelly?* For those outside Australia, Ned Kelly is one of the heroic figures of Australian (and by that we mean both indigenous and non-indigenous) mythology: turning from grinding rural poverty and continual police harassment in mid-nineteenth century south-eastern Australia, he and his mates took to the bush and waged a small insurrection that included holding up remote stations and stage-coaches, until in the final battle at the village of Glenrowan (in the south-eastern state of Victoria) he was wounded and captured soon afterwards. Irish, rural poor, decked in home-made armour to protect him from bullets,[4] author of the famous Jerilderie Letter, explicitly targeting the police and wealthy landowners, setting out to avenge the wrongs done to his single mother, uttering the final words 'Such is life' before he was hanged, Ned Kelly has of course become the figure of the underdog who fights a losing battle against corrupt power.

Obviously he is also a positive figure in these Aboriginal stories, unlike Captain Cook:

> You, Captain Cook . . . You kill my people. You been look around, see the land now. People been here, really got their own culture. All around Australia . . . We remember for you. I know. Why didn't you look after London and Big England? Why didn't you stop your government, Captain Cook? You're the one been bring him out now, all your government from Big England. You been bring that law. (Hobbles Danayari, quoted in Rose 1994)

Captain Cook as the immoral and reprehensible European turns up throughout the northern half of Australia, from the Kimberley Ranges in Western Australia, across the Top End (Arnhem Land in the Northern Territory) to Queensland in the east.

Before we consider this, one more narrative that brings together Ned Kelly, Captain Cook and, of course, the Bible. This time, Rose quotes Big Mick Kankinang:

> Miki? Early day people might be see him. This world been salt water before, every way, every land. This world been covered up. All the salt water every way. Two men came down from sky. Ned Kelly and Angelo. Come down, get a boat, travel round that sea, salt water. Can't findem any bank. Those fellows travelling. This leaf been fall down. 'Hello! Green leaf here!' Twofellow still travelling la boat. They hit a high ridge. 'Hello! Pull up here.' Put em anchor. Go down [out of the boat] and stand up. 'What me and you gotta do?' 'We'll have to do something.' They been makem river, and salt water been go right back. That's for Ned Kelly and Angelo. Dry now, every way. Twofellow just walking now. Some bush blackfellow been go longa business [doing ceremony]. They come down. 'Hello! Some blackfellows there!' Blackfellows been talk, 'What's this fellow here?' The blackfellows understand English. Twofellow travelling now, longa dry land. Walking. Go longa Wyndham. Wyndham people look those two whitefellows: 'Oh, really different men. Different to we. We'll have to get em

policemen.' Four policemen been come. Had a bit of a row longa twofellow. Twofellow get a gun and shoot four policemen la Wyndham. And travel back, go back this way.

Captain Cook been come down to Mendora [beach, in Darwin], gotta boat, from England they been come. Captain Cook come longa this land, longa Sydney Harbour. Good country him been look. Captain Cook shot and broke a leg for one fellow belonging to that country Sydney Harbour. Get a boat and going back again. Bring longa this country now horse and cattle. Captain Cook got a revolver. Photo there all around Daguragu, he's holding a revolver. Where that breed up bullock and horse, that's where the Ned Kelly going back to England, Ned Kelly by himself now, he lose his mate. Ned Kelly got his throat cut. They bury him. Leave him. Sun go down, little bit dark now, he left this world. BOOOOOOOMMMMM! Go longa top. This world shaking. All the white men been shaking. They all been frightened!

This miki been working for blackfellows, making gutters [to drain off the salt water]. Right la Crawford Knob there, some blackfellows there, that miki been come out there. He's not here now. He's finished from that salt water time. Him blackfellow, first blackfellow. That Dreaming been come up, and that blackfellow got law now. That miki been finished altogether. (Rose, 1994)

We want to stay with this text for a while, for what interests us is not so much the desire for the positive image of a European – what Rose calls the moral European – as the appropriation of the Bible. What we want to do then, is offer an exegesis of this particular exegesis presented in the story that Big Mick Kankinang passes on. To begin with, or rather in the beginning we find Noah as Ned Kelly, and the creation narrative begins – in a perceptive *tour de force* that implicitly recognizes the narrative of Genesis 6–9 as another creation story – with the flood. Various items are recognisable from the Genesis story: the boat on which they travel around (Gen. 7:17–18); the absence of dry land, or rather the covering over of this world (Gen. 7:19–20); the leaf (Gen. 8:11); hitting the high ridge (Gen. 8:4); the recession of the waters (Gen. 8:1–6, 13–14 – here the tensions in the flood narrative show up); and then it is 'Dry now, everyway' (Gen. 8:13–14). But the differences are also quite notable. The story begins with the whole earth covered with salt water and Noah and Angelo (in some other versions it is a 'mob' of angels) descend from the sky and find a boat in which to travel around. The leaf falls rather than being found by a dove, and, apart from the omission of whole range of details concerning Ned/Noah's family (it is just Angelo or the angels) and the animals on board the boat, once on dry land they set out to walk the country.

These variations are enough to locate Ned Kelly squarely within Dreaming: he is, in other words a Dreaming figure who descends from the sky, before human beings or animals or plants or even landforms. He has a creative role in which both the Jewish and Christian creator God appears – he separates dry land from water in an echo of the second creative act of Genesis 1:6–8 – and the role of the Dreaming Being. But from the moment he and Angelo set out on foot they are those Beings in their creative walk through country. After making a river they walk until they meet some blackfellas in ceremony: land, human beings and the crucial role of ritual were first established in the Dreaming, as well as (omitted here), the various plants and animals. And in the last paragraph he is also responsible for law.

Like the Dreaming Beings, he also disappears at some point, although in this story his mode of disappearance comes via another appropriation, this time from the passion narratives in the Gospels. Before we peer more closely at the passion of Ned Kelly, a comment concerning the shooting of the policeman. Here of course the other Ned Kelly comes to the surface, the rebel who was at odds – like so many Aborigines – with the police. When the whitefellas see Ned and Angelo in the centre of white civilization, Wyndham, they call the police who are duly shot by Ned and Angelo. Not only does this come out the story of Ned Kelly himself, albeit further south in Victoria, it is also still part of the Dreaming narrative, for after disposing of the police, they continue their journey through the country: they 'travel back, go back this way'. Note that whereas the blackfellows understand English, the whitefellas in Wyndham see Ned and Angelo as distinctly different.

So far we have Noah and the Dreaming linked through the figure of Ned Kelly, but what of Ned's own passion narrative? Let us quote the relevant text again:

> Ned Kelly got his throat cut. They bury him. Leave him. Sun go down, little bit dark now, he left this world. BOOOOOOOMMMMM! Go longa top. This world shaking. All the white men been shaking. They all been frightened! (Rose 1994)

To make an obvious comment, this version is somewhat shorter than the passion and resurrection narratives in Matthew 26–8, Mark 14–16, Luke 22–4 and John 13–21. But even in this short passage what does appear is intriguing: the earthquake and dark-ness happen after his burial and not during the crucifixion (Matt. 27:45 and 51; Mark 15:33 and perhaps 38; Luke 23:44–5). If anything, the text that resonates most strongly is that of Matthew. Mark and Luke merely have the curtain in the temple tearing in two, but Matthew's is much more exciting, full of earthquakes and the dead rising:

> And behold, the curtain of the temple was town in two, from top to bottom; and the earth shook, and the rocks were split; the tombs also were opened and many bodies of the saints who had fallen asleep were raised, and coming out of the tombs after his resurrection they went into the holy city and appeared to many. (Matt. 27:51–3)

In Big Mick Kankinang's version, the earthquake is part of the resurrection – 'he left this world. BOOOOOOOMMMMM! Go longa top' – or is that the return of a Dreaming figure to the sky? The overlay is, as expected, crucial. Matthew's narrative resonates closely with the Dreaming, particularly in terms of the significance of natural events such as the earthquake. As Rose points out, Big Mick found this the most amusing part of the story, for despite the obvious meaning of the earthquake in terms of Dreaming, Europeans fail to see its significance. This is their own Dreaming and yet they don't understand it: how thick can you be! Here the white men echo the dense disciples in the synoptic gospels, who just don't seem to get it.[5]

We don't want to spend an inordinate amount of time on the remainder of this story. There are obvious differences, such as Ned Kelly getting his throat cut in England, and Captain Cook is a distinctly unsavoury character, bringing pain, weapons, and the bullocks and horses that overrun the country. But we do need to make a few comments about Dreaming since it pervades not only this story by Big Mick Kankinang but is the world-view through which the Bible is appropriated and rearranged (see Swain 1993). To speak of it as a creative time before ordinary time is only partially correct, for the Dreaming endures, is with us now in a way that can only inadequately be described as synchronic in the sense that eternity itself is synchronic. While there is a distinction between the ordinary and ephemeral and the Dreaming, and while there is a sense that what was fluid in Dreaming has now become fixed, the overarching sense is a synchronous eternity. Everything in the Dreaming exists at the same time, yet the determination of people and events takes place in terms of space. Thus, while Ned Kelly, Angelo, Captain Cook, Noah, Jesus, the blackfellas and whitefellas all interact on the same temporal plane, Ned works at Crawford Nob among the Aborigines (where he also becomes the 'first blackfellow'), goes to Wyndham and then England. Or, to put it in terms of the distinction between ordinary time and Dreaming, whereas one deals with the everyday rhythms of eating, sleeping, sex, the phases of life and so on, and while the other provides a synchronous perspective on a much vaster arena, both are anchored on earth, understood in terms of specific and identifiable places. Of course, the distinctions we have all too briefly outlined begin to leak into each other, synchrony becomes diachrony (subject to the demands of narrative itself), for events do take place in sequence in the Dreaming narratives – the flood precedes the dry land, walking around, Ned's death and resurrection (of course, on one level such a sequence is also the requirement of narrative itself). The sequence may in fact shuffle around, as the last paragraph in Big Mick's story indicates, but there is a tendency for time to be drawn into space. The key lies in the complexity and detail of space as story after story indicates: the creation, identification and fixation of each identifiable landmark, ritual site, type of animal and plant sets the spatial coordinates of local space.

Thus, in other Yarralin stories, we find that emergence of life from holes in the ground, including sun, moon, stars and rainbow, all of which walked around at first in human shape. As they walked, they created the social, cultural, judicial and economic system by which human beings were to live: they brought ceremonies, languages and customs to different, named and created places. Once this was done, once places were fixed, the fluidity of identity passed, and animals, plants, humans and celestial bodies also became fixed as we know them now. But they are still very much part of the Dreaming.

It is into this context that the story of Ned Kelly fits, as also the narratives of the biblical flood and the death and resurrection of Jesus. Yet it is a vastly different appropriation of the Bible than with Melanesian cargo cults. The question then is: why is Jon Frum so different from Ned Kelly? If Jon Frum exhibits the effort to deal with a vast inequality of the objects of wealth and prestige – an inequality that rules out the process of offering gifts as a mark of prestige – in terms of a belief system, responding to the Bible as a meta-text, that would set such a system back on even keel, then Ned Kelly reveals a very different effort in terms of the metaphysics of Dreaming. These narratives exhibit, as Rose argues, an effort at accommodation between groups of people. The result is that these people, whether Noah or Jesus or Ned Kelly or Captain Cook, enter the narratives with Aborigines, along with the whole natural and social order in an extraordinary imaginative effort at accommodation. But it also manifests itself in terms of marriage, trade, allocation of rights to food sources and also by means of exchanges of knowledge, or rather of myths, rituals and certain objects. It is in these patterns of exchange, showing up most markedly in stories such as the one we quoted above, that we find the effort to locate a shared social, cultural, economic and even metaphysical realm. This takes places not merely in terms of an appropriation of the Bible *into* Aboriginal world-views, but the offer, by means of the Bible, of a transformed world-view *for others*.

Bashir Baraki: Vox Unpopuli

And so we move to a third space, from Tanna in the Pacific through the deserts of northern Australia to Melbourne, southern cosmopolitan city that was the home of Bashir Baraki. We have reproduced here stills from a series of videos on the life of Christ made by Baraki in the last few years before his death from cancer in 1998. Jesus never appears in them, apparently tied up with other business: rather, they are a series of non-scripted interviews with various characters in the gospel narratives. In this last section we are going to stay close to these videos, exegeting the videos themselves but particularly, because they are here and seen rather than buried in the video vaults of a few art gallery collections in Australia, the stills themselves: Judas, Mary, Mary Magdalene, and Lazarus.

But who is Bashir Baraki? Even to Australians, except for the few in the art network and a slightly wider group in Melbourne, he is not particularly well known. And the chances of seeing his work are predicated on landing in an Australian city when one of his brief shows were on – no mean feat even from within Australia, let alone outside it – or managing to slip away from the incessant pressures of the knowledge factory in order to find a moment or two of furtive peace in the quiet of a university art gallery such as the one at Monash where he was working ever so slowly towards his PhD. He died at 55, having lived in Australia for over 20 years. Brought up as a Roman Catholic, his father's family were Muslim, while his mother converted to Judaism later in life. Now, while you may imagine that Baha'i would be the obvious solution to such an interesting mix, Bashir was also gay, overtly gay, particularly through his art. And Baha'is have a distinct problem with gays, still holding that it is possible to be cured, with God's help, from this aberration.

But what is significant about all of this is that although he had no firm or embedded Christian background, he chose to make use of Christian, indeed 'High' European Christian imagery. Baraki is, or rather was, the non-Christian and non-European existing in a space colonized by both, so we might want to ask what *his* status is? What is the status of the outsider coming into the inculturated colonial local? Further: like the indigenous people of Australasia at the time of colonization, Baraki had no personal connection to Christianity, and yet he took a similar approach to biblical narratives and images as the indigenous peoples we considered above. Here we find comparable acts of appropriation and resistance, albeit chronologically and spatially diverse. The question then becomes why Baraki, coming in from the outside (whether as an immigrant or local, social outsider) acts not to colonize, as the previous influx of outsiders did, but to resist?

As an artist, Baraki showed as much versatility as his religious background, making most of his controversial impact with innovative usage of the Canon Laser Copier in the early to mid-1990s, but moving across a range of technologies including photography, computer generated imagery, traditional paint, live installations (as with the dance of Lazarus that we will discuss in a moment) and of course video. And it is the lure of technique that most of the relatively scarce commentary on Baraki's work can barely resist (Scene 1996; Kirker 1992; Storey 1999). We have no desire to pretend that we are art critics, although their tendency to draw on feminism, Marxism, psychoanalysis and so forth, along with the traditional notions of art history does make them seem curiously like biblical critics. The allure of Baraki's work for us is somewhat different, for we are seduced by his double inscription within Australian subcultures *and* his intriguing reshaping of the Bible from that context. To begin with, As Storey (1999) points out, the category of the gay artist, and of queer art as such, are 'patronised as the cultural off cuts of a complaining minority'. The centre ground is occupied by straight boys who stagger into their studios each morning, existentially facing paint, brush and canvas in a moment of pure individuality, all the while entertaining odd moments of queer representation such as drag queens with their silk dresses billowing against the backdrop of the red desert, or boys and girls flaunting it at the Mardi Gras in Sydney, or poignant images of HIV/AIDS sufferers. The catch with someone like Baraki is that with the various ways in which he lived out his homosexuality in his work, he was locked into that narrow category of the gay, quietly political artist.

If that is not enough of a subculture, overlapping with that of artists themselves, then Baraki dared to deal with that leaden weight of religious art. Not just religion in a broad and somewhat spiritual, eclectic New-Agey sense, but the central images of Christian art. For all the efforts of the annual Blake Prize in Religious Art in Australia, or the Religion, Literature and the Arts conferences (drawing a large slab of priests and educators in religious schools), or the occasional controversy that Andres Serrano's 'Piss Christ' photograph generated in Australia in the late 1990s, religious art is not the topic of critical discussions of art in Australia. In fact, for all Melbourne's vaunted cosmopolitanism, 'Piss Christ' was smashed in 1999 when on exhibit in that very same city. Religious art, it seems, really has no place to go but stained glass windows in churches, and they're all taken. Even the increasingly commodified status of Aboriginal art reinforces this point, for although such art, particularly in more traditional forms, incorporates significant religious (often Christian) content, it is not really recognized as such. Religious art is, then, more about the form than the content, and this is where Baraki's play with form while drawing on very conventional Christian content gives his work extra bite.

Yet religion, or rather Christianity, or even more specifically the Bible, was one of the mainstays of Baraki's work. Perhaps his best-known image is *Australian Football and Giotto's 'The Lamentation of Christ'* in which a newspaper clipping of an injured player from an Australian Rules football game is juxtaposed with a print of Giotto's pious and haloed fresco of the wounded, reclining Christ. The Aussie Rules player's pose, as he is being placed on a stretcher by medical staff in the top panel, echoes that of Christ in the lower panel. Impossible to find and reproduce, we have to content ourselves with a brief description before passing on to *The Interview Series*.

Unlike the Australian Football piece, produced on a laser copier, Christ is absent from the videos. All we get, in the stark contrasts of black and white, are non-scripted interviews with Judas, Mary, Mary Magdalene and Lazarus, consciously anachronistic efforts at *cinéma vérité*. Actually Lazarus is not 'exactly' interviewed: he performs a silent dance as he extracts himself from the grave clothes. In Baraki's own words, these interviews are not so much an exercise in film but 'painting with a video camera, with a focus on texture, light and shade and positive and negative images' (quoted in Scene 1996).

The stills reproduced in Figures 14.1–14.4 come from four of the videos. As for Mary, she appears middle-aged, wearing cheap glasses, pearls around her neck, her hands moving about (those that touched Jesus so often?). The lines and sags on her face are

Figure 14.1   Judas Iscariot, video still from *The Interview Series*

Figure 14.2   Mary, video still from *The Interview Series*

Figure 14.3   Mary Magdalene, video still from *The Interview Series*

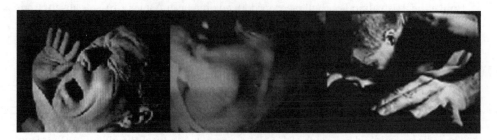

Figure 14.4   Lazarus, video still from *The Interview Series*

prominent, rather than the smooth-skinned small-breasted virgin of traditional representations. Of course – we realize – *if* Jesus died at 33, then Mary would have had to
have been in her forties. The questions to Mary, coming from an unidentified interviewer, ask her about mother–son relationships, how they really got on, and the grief
of losing a child. Here Baraki's cuts close to the psychological bone, for the woman who
acts Mary's part had lost her own son and so the issues become blurred as her grief
begins to show through. The other Mary, the Magdalene, does not have the close-
cropped presentation of Jesus' mother. This Mary is younger, set back in a context of
more shadow and darkness than the open whiteness of Jesus' mother's face. While
more flattering, it also leaves the Magdalene a more enigmatic figure, even though the
questions now ask about her relationship with Jesus, why he never married, whether
they ever fought, whether they loved each other.

Rather than the feel of a press conference, these interviews are informal, chatty, personal; except for Lazarus, who dances his way out of death and funeral cloths. But there
is no music, just the sound of Lazarus's breathing. The Lazarus dance was also a live
installation for a time when the videos first appeared. Bony back, splayed hands, the
grimace of a face (is that the pain of coming back to life just when he was at peace or
the gasp of the first breath of a new life, or . . . ?), a body in intimate touch with the
ground (does he kiss the ground or is he pushing himself off it?) – all of these, along
with the stark black and white, play on the fine line between corpse and living body,
death and life.

But we have left Judas until last: for as he begins to answer questions – was their jealousy between the disciples? How did they get on? Was he on the outer? What about the
money? What happened to the money? And, most importantly for Baraki, how did the
men bond with each other, giving that they lived and worked so closely with each other?
– then we learn that Judas himself was the interviewer of the others, chatting with
them over deeply personal and intimate details concerning their relationship with
Jesus. We're not sure what to make of Judas here: the half-face in shadow, the large
earring, the blank eyes, the pursed lips and stubble on his face suggest an outsider, one
who may well have cooked the books a little for his own benefit, ready to do a deal with
the authorities for a bit of extra cash. But this reading has much to do with the biblical narrative and the expectations it sets up. Judas's appeal for us is quite different, for

the earring, slightly hooded eye, sensuous lips and long stubble . . . all of these drip sensuality, and a decidedly queer sensuality at that. And so we begin to wonder about the close-knit group of disciples, the intimacy of Jesus and Judas (Matt. 26:23; Mark 14:20; Luke 22:21) and his desire to interview the others.

Conclusion

What are we to make of *The Interview Series?* Obviously there are the big questions of everyday life and death, and Baraki gives full scope to these, in contrast, say, to the hilarious high camp of *Jesus Christ: Vampire Hunter* (directed by Lee Demarbre and launched in 2001, its premise is the need to bring Jesus back to life in order to crack down on a ring of lesbian vampires whose leader is, of course, the local priest). But our question actually hinges on the relationship, if any, with the Jon Frum movement and Aboriginal appropriations of the Bible through Ned Kelly. On one level, there is little direct engagement with the Bible or with specific texts. But that is the case with the others as well, although the Ned Kelly story came closest. So we will invoke again the category of Bible as meta-text, one that moves beyond the page of the written text itself and runs through a whole series of after-lives, interacting with and in many cases constructing the world-views within which it is appropriated. The distinctly subcultural influences come through as well, particularly the various media of an exploratory artist, and an immigrant, non-Western, non-Christian gay artist at that. Here these videos touch on, albeit tangentially, the biblical scholarship concerning the homosociality, homoeroticism if not outright gay identity of Jesus, no matter how anachronistic such a concept might be.

Yet, it is on the question of anachronism that the difference becomes sharpest between this engagement with the Bible by Baraki and those of the Tannese Islanders and Yarralin people. If the cargo cult of Jon Frum seeks to address the imbalance of an exchange economy through a distinctly political millenarian cult, and if the story of Ned Kelly attempts an incorporation and mutual transformation of cultures and their stories, then Baraki's work displays the continued and vibrant desire to delve into the past in order to find out who Jesus really was. It is, in the end, a distinctly historical question that continues to bedevil a significant slab of New Testament scholarship, let alone a wider Western culture obsessed with the past as an originating moment. But if this was all that Baraki was doing, then his work would hardly be any different from that chunk of culture that attempts to keep its vast bulk somewhere in a middling position that then passes itself off as 'mainstream' (which is really just an excuse for crap to dominate other forms of culture). Baraki's subcultural take is then anachronistic, consciously so – *of course you can't* interview Jesus's intimate friends after his death. Yet, given the urge to look into history in order to re-orient urgent questions of today, these interviews give a quietly queer edge to big questions of human relationships. We can put this in two ways. Firstly, all that the past reveals in all its apparently stark reality (hence *cinéma vérité*) is a series of layers of hearsay, recollections, emotional responses, chatty reconstructions, gossip or just the movement of a body without words. Second, we take Baraki's interviews as an effort to come up with an alternative history, or rather *story*, that may possibly lead to an alternative present and future, and a queer present and future – with a distinctly Australian inflection (Altman 1994) – at that.

But the specificity of Baraki – queer, non-Western, non-Christian, immigrant, in Melbourne, of all places – shows up the difficulty of over-arching categories, the fragmentation, uncertainty and difference that Appadurai seeks to account for. For how can Jon Frum, the Aboriginal stories of Ned Kelly and Bashir Baraki's art represent any coherent connection with each other? The paradox here is that while, like REM, we proclaim that 'withdrawal in disgust is not the same as defeat', this inability at coming up with even regional unifying categories is part of the very logic of that most unrepresentable and unimaginable of categories, global capitalism.

Notes

1 With thanks to the Indy Oz Rock band from the 1980s, The Models, who had a hit with the same title.
2 We have opted for the slightly more common 'Jon', but 'John' also appears frequently in quotations.
3 The subtitle for this section comes from an extraordinary article by Deborah Bird Rose, which we openly acknowledge has heavily influenced our reading here.
4 Readers might like to think back to the film *Ned Kelly* in which Mick Jagger (of course!) starred, resplendent in home-made armour.
5 'He said, in subsequent discussions of the story, that when Ned Kelly rose up to the sky, there was such a great shaking of the earth that all the buildings in Darwin trembled and all the Europeans cowered in fear and wondered what was happening. He found this to be very funny' (Rose 1994).

References

Altman, D. (1994). 'Homosexuality', in R. Nile (ed.), *Australian Civilisation*. Melbourne: Oxford University Press Australia, pp. 110–24.
Appadurai, A. (1990). 'Disjuncture and Difference in the Global Cultural Economy', *Theory, Culture & Society* 7: 295–310.
Billings, D. K. (2002). *Cargo Cult as Theater: Political Performance in the Pacific?* Lanham, MD: Lexington Books.
Bloch, E. (1972). *Atheism in Christianity: The Religion of the Exodus and the Kingdom*, trans. J. T. Swann. Munich: Herder and Herder.
Bloch, E. (1995). *The Principle of Hope*, trans. N. Plaice, S. Plaice and P. Knight. 3 vols. Cambridge MA: MIT Press.
Boer, R. (2001a). *Last Stop before Antarctica: The Bible and Postcolonialism in Australia*. Sheffield: Sheffield Academic Press.
Boer, R. (2001b). 'Introduction: Vanishing Mediators'. *Semeia* 88: 1–12.
Boer, R. (2005). 'Marx, Postcolonialism and the Bible', in S. Moore and F. Segovia (eds), *Postcolonial Biblical Criticism: Interdisciplinary Intersections*. London: T. & T. Clark International.
Cochrane, G. (1970). *Big Men and Cargo Cults*. Oxford: Clarendon Press.

DiManno, R. (1999). 'The Believers', *Toronto Star*, 28 December.

Dutter, B. (2001). 'John Frum Is Given His Marching Orders', *Daily Telegraph*, 7 July.

Eliade, M. (1965). *Mephistocles and the Androgyne: Studies in Religious Myth and Symbol*. New York: Sheed and Ward.

Eves, R. (1998). *The Magical Body: Power, Fame and Meaning in Melanesian Society*. Amsterdam: Harwood Academic Publishers.

Gelder, K. and Thornton, S. (eds) (1997). *The Subcultures Reader*. London: Routledge.

Hannerz, U. (1990). 'Cosmopolitans and Locals in World Culture', *Theory, Culture & Society* 7: 237–51.

Hardt, M. and Negri, A. (2000). *Empire*. Cambridge, MA: Harvard University Press.

Hebdige, D. (1987). *Subculture: The Meaning of Style*. London: Routledge.

Jameson, F. (1984). 'Postmodernism, or, the Cultural Logic of Late Capitalism', *New Left Review* 146: 53–92.

Jameson, F. (1991). *Postmodernism, or, the Cultural Logic of Late Capitalism*. Durham, NC: Duke University Press.

Kirker, A. (1992). 'Bashir Baraki and Patt Hoffie: Extending the Vernacular of Prints', *Continuum* 8: 240–7.

Krieger, M. (1994). *Conversations with the Cannibals: The End of the Old South Pacific*. Hopwell, NJ: Ecco Press.

Lindstrom, L. (1993). *Cargo Cult: Strange Stories of Desire from Melanesia and Beyond*. Honolulu: University of Hawaii Press.

O'Brien, D. (1999). *Lonely Planet Vanuatu*, 3rd edn. Footscray, Australia: Lonely Planet.

Rose, D. B. (1994). 'Ned Kelly Died for Our Sins', *Oceania* 65. http://static.highbeam.com/o/oceania/december011994/nedkellydiedforoursinsaboriginalhistoriesaborigina/ Accessed 23 August 2004.

Sandall, R. (2001). *The Culture Cult: Designer Tribalism and Other Essays*. Boulder, CO: Westview Press.

Scene (1996). 'JC in 3D', in www.monash.edu.au/pubs/scene/scene1.96/jcin3d.html Accessed 25 August 2004.

Squires, N. (2004). 'Culture Clash in the South Pacific', in BBC News World Edition, 20 May. http://news.bbc.co.uk/2/hi/programmes/from_our_own_correspondent/3729715.stm Accessed 26 August 2004.

Stanley, D. (2000). *The South Pacific Handbook*, 7th edn. Emeryville, CA: Moon Travel Publications.

Storey, J. (1999). 'Baraki's High Wire Act: Images of Christ and the Blessed Virgin on Video', *Metro Magazine Online* 127–8. www.photography.rmit.edu.au/arts/postgrad/jr_bashir.html Accessed 26 August 2004.

Swain, T. (1993). *A Place for Strangers: Towards a History of Aboriginal Australian Being*. Cambridge: Cambridge University Press.

Theroux, P. (1993). *The Happy Isles of Oceania: Paddling the Pacific*. New York: Ballantine Books.

Worsley, P. (1968). *The Trumpet Shall Sound*. London: Macgibbon and Kee.

PART III
The Bible and the Senses

CHAPTER 15
Literature

Jo Carruthers

> [T]hat the Bible holds a unique status in the religious history of the Western world is obvious enough; what is less obvious, but no less true, is that it holds an equally unique status in literary history and even what might be called our collective cultural psyche. To begin with, we owe to it much of our notion of what constitutes a 'book'. (Jasper and Prickett 1999: 2)

The influence of the Bible on Western literature is incalculably powerful and diffuse, not least because, as Jasper and Prickett note, the Bible is the archetypal literary text. It has been written and rewritten, interpreted and 'misinterpreted', revised and supplemented, in innumerable poems, plays, novels, stories and essays from the Anglo-Saxon period to postmodernism. As David Lyle Jeffries' (1992) encyclopaedic *Dictionary of Biblical Tradition in English Literature* shows, literature is saturated with biblical inter-textualities. But this is hardly surprising, considering that the very institution of Western 'Literature' – the creation and reverential study of great books – owes its existence to the Bible. Our sense of what literature is has long been derived from what the Bible is and does; literary study meanwhile is our modern secular version of biblical hermeneutics. The debates about the canon that have so divided modern literary scholars are variations on centuries-old attempts to separate sacred text from apocryphal and heretical writings. Literary scholars, like their biblical counterparts, are engaged constantly with the task of separating the canonical from the non-canonical, the valuable, timeless and 'sacred' from dispensable ephemera and shallow trivia. The literary canon, therefore, emerges as the secular equivalent of the biblical canon, a body of texts endowed with unique authority and power, and worthy of the attention of generations of scholarly experts.

If the flourishing state of literary studies is a veiled tribute to the power and authority of the Bible and biblical studies, however, we have now entered an era in which the Bible itself has been subsumed by the very intellectual traditions and cultural categories that it gave rise to. In short, the Bible has shifted from being the archetypal *book* – the greatest source-book of language, imagery and narrative – to being simply a *text* like any other. In an age in which the authority of the Bible is no longer sacrosanct and in which its cultural power is fading, the study of literature's biblical inheritance may therefore appear of interest only to religious historians. However, it would be a gross act of cultural amnesia to suppress the biblical presence in our literary tradition, a tradition that continues to shape the present. The Bible persists as a presence that haunts supposedly secular, postmodern writing and the emergent literature of decolonizing nations in strange and unexpected ways.

The Bible has always been the central, indispensable and ubiquitous artefact of Western culture. Its place in the recent past of England is a case in point. The number of Bibles published in England between the Reformation and 1640 has been estimated at over a million (Hill 1993: 18). At this time, most children learnt to read through the Bible, the only readily available text (ibid.: 39). As the main, or often sole, book readily available in the early modern period, the Bible became synonymous with literature and even affected the ways in which reading was conceptualized and practised. Christopher Hill points to the changes that the vernacularization of the Bible had on the new early modern reading culture that at this time took precedence over earlier common forms of leisure activity: 'Private reading replaced community or family singing – a momentous change – just as it replaced reading aloud or repetition of sermons followed by family or group discussions – both frowned upon by the ecclesiastical hierarchy' (ibid.: 339). The Bible was thus a household item at the point when England was forming into a modern nation and when the English language was becoming stabilized through print. Whereas medieval literature was undeniably 'biblical' – one has only to think of Dante's vision of hell or the medieval mystery plays with Everyman's journey to salvation in Christ – literature in the early modern period, with its Caesars and Tamburlaines, Cleopatras and Fausts, is less biblical to the modern eye. But as scholars such as Christopher Hill have shown, the Bible permeates the literature of this period at every level. Its saturation in English culture means its influence reached far beyond strictly religious or theological boundaries. The Bible was significant, as Hill insists, in 'its use for political and other purposes, and its unforeseen effects on literature, political theory, social relations, agriculture and colonization, among other matters' (ibid.: 18), matters that he goes on to trace out in his book, *The Bible and the Seventeenth-Century Revolution*. The language we now use, its cadence and its phrases, are all indebted to the diffusion of biblical language and idiom in early modern England. Faithfulness to the Hebrew style by influential translators such as Tyndale – to what Gerald Hammond specifies as 'its variations in word order, its uses of verbal redundancies, and its readiness to hang verbless clauses on the end of poetic statements' – helped to make the English language what it is today (1992: 20). Contemporary language abounds in biblical phrases: David Daniell's list includes 'The salt of the earth' (Matt. 5), 'They made light of it' (Matt. 22), 'Eat, drink and be merry' (Luke 12), 'A law unto themselves' (Rom. 2) and 'Filthy lucre' (1 Tim. 3) (1989: x). In the most casual idioms of conversation, we quote the Bible without knowing it.

Many early modern writers will have assumed a biblically literate audience – after all, many people knew not merely verses, but entire passages by heart. Readers with little or no knowledge of the Bible will miss allusions that are crucial to the plot. Marlowe's *Dr Faustus*, for instance, is the infamous sixteenth-century story of an ambitious man who sells his soul to the devil in exchange for great powers. In literary critical terms, the play has prompted much debate regarding its relationship to Christianity: does it undermine orthodoxy and belief or further its dogma? As the play opens, Faustus contemplates the limitations of worldly knowledge, disparaging the arts of logic, medicine, law, and theology. Is this an early expression of disenchantment with religion and conventional systems, or the rantings of a sinful man? Quoting from 'Jerome's Bible', Faust 'exposes' the harshness of biblical doctrine: 'The reward of sin is death: that's hard [. . .] If we say that we have no sin, we deceive ourselves, and there's no truth in us. Why, then, belike we must sin, and so consequently die.' His conclusion is final: 'What doctrine call you this? *Che sarà, sarà:* / What will be, shall be! Divinity, adieu!'. The arguments Faust presents here seem convincing: Christianity is too harsh and demanding. However, Marlowe would have known that his biblically literate audience of the late sixteenth century would have been aware of his partial quoting of the Bible. The two verses quoted (Rom. 6:23 and 1 John 1:8) each contain a further clause that changes the significance of the elements that Faustus cites. The bipartite structure is a rhetorical device to emphasize grace; Faustus is therefore offering a misquotation which would have been recognized as such by Marlowe's contemporaries. Tyndale's translation of 1534 renders the verses:

> For the reward of sin is death: but eternal life is the gift of God, through Jesus Christ our Lord.

> If we say that we have no sin, we deceive ourselves, and truth is not in us. If we knowledge our sins, he is faithful and just, to forgive our sins, and to cleanse us from all unrighteousness.

Recognition of this 'misquotation' undermines the validity of Faustus's choice and sets the audience in a specific attitude of distrust towards him: a reading that promotes a negative interpretation of Faustus's fall from grace. Faustus has either deliberately misused the evidence of the Bible against Protestantism or has misunderstood the simplest of Protestant doctrines. Either way, in the eyes of the audience his authority is undermined and his move towards the magic arts becomes marred by miscalculation. The play implicitly challenges its audience to display a more secure grasp of the Bible than its hero. If we fail to notice the gaps in Faustus's biblical knowledge, then we are in a sense reproducing the arrogant superficiality of his own display of learning.

For at this time, the Bible was a matter of life and death. It was a text bought at a high price – to use a biblical metaphor. Early translators were martyred for bringing the vernacular to the people: Tyndale, perhaps the most influential of early Bible translators was burned at the stake. The Bible was no longer merely an elite text: the vernacularization of the Bible was perhaps most notably a popularist event. Thought of as an act of subversion and potential anarchy, the Bible's rendition in English (and elsewhere in other European vernaculars) was feared by monarchs and elites for its rendering of an authoritative text into the populace's hands. It was therefore a text whose language as much as its content was to influence those who read it so fervently.

The contemporary West is shaped by a heritage in which the Bible was all-pervasive, making the Bible a text that, as Harold Fisch notes, 'the Western imagination cannot escape' (1998: viii). As the death of God was proclaimed by an increasingly secular culture, the Bible continued to haunt the Western world. Further, while the Bible was indeed an authority for some, it was no longer unquestionably so. As Fisch goes on to state, the Western imagination cannot escape it 'but neither can it accept it unaltered' (ibid.: viii). There emerged an uneasiness with the Bible that reveals the everyday struggles individuals had with all or parts of this 'authoritative' text, a wrestling even sanctified for devout rewriters in figuration of the biblical character Jacob's transformation into Israel – the one who wrestled 'until the breaking of the day', but also the one whose new name valorizes his wrestling with God: 'And he said, Thy name shall be called no more Jacob, but Israel: for as a prince hast thou power with God and with men, and hast prevailed' (Gen. 32:28).

Many interactions with the Bible emerge from this 'uneasiness', from a crisis of faith, or in order to battle with a heritage. The fact that Fisch is speaking about the novel makes his words all the more apt. The genre that emerged in the rationalist eighteenth century – the century of revolutions and of secularist nationalism – is, according to Mikhail Bakhtin, a dialogical form: it represents discussions, dialogues, and multiple perspectives that inherently undermine dogmatism. If Bakhtin is right, then the very form of the novel is resistant to the Bible as the monologic voice of unquestionable transcendent authority. As Harold Fisch maintains in his *New Stories for Old: Biblical Patterns in the Novel* (1998), the history of response to Scripture in the novel 'has been profoundly antithetical'. Thus Jeanette Winterson's novel *Oranges Are Not the Only Fruit* (1985) rails against evangelical Protestantism in its form as well as its content. By naming the chapters after books of the Bible, Winterson overwrites the Genesis narrative with her protagonist's beginnings, and, in her chapter 'Ruth', evokes Ruth and Naomi's relationship with reference to her protagonist's lesbian relationship. Jim Crace's recent *Quarantine* (1998a) rewrites Christ's 40 days in the desert in such a way as to present Jesus as a naïve youth who does not fully understand his place on earth, thereby strongly emphasizing his humanity. Crace has explicitly positioned his rewriting in a confrontational framework. In an article introducing his work, he states: 'Quarantine with Science as its sword would kill Christ after only thirty days in the wilderness. There'd be no Ministry or Crucifixion. The novel would erase two thousand years of Christianity. This would be my party-pooper for the Millennium' (1998b).

These contemporary rewritings of the Bible are not mere pilferings of biblical images and phrases, but are actively involved in a fight over meaning with the biblical text itself. Winterson's novel demands the right to overwrite the Bible, to create a new Genesis for her character Jess. The novel's biblically inspired form rails, with its protagonist, against an authority that, as Fisch has so deftly put it, 'The Western imagination cannot escape.' Crace's novel is similarly combative. However, the effects that Crace's novel has had on readers' sense of the Bible are perhaps not those that Crace had expected. Christian responses have returned to the biblical narrative of Christ with fresh eyes, drawn to the humanity emphasized in Crace's account, countering an over-emphasis upon Christ's divinity that had been more prominent in Christian theology historically (Tate 2005). Thus, although Crace may not be able to 'erase two thousand years of

Christianity', Christians nevertheless negotiate their view of the Bible in the light of his interpretation. Rather than closing off the Bible, Crace's novel illuminates a hitherto neglected facet of it.

The Bible may be only a ghostly presence in contemporary Western literature, but because Jasper's and Prickett's emphasis is confined to the Western world, it leaves open the question of the different cultural histories – and different cultural psyches – of the non-Western world. As Alan Jacobs insists in *The Oxford Companion to the Bible*, the new home of biblical influence is outside of Western society, in places such as South America and Africa in which Protestant Christianity – and thus the Bible – has a stronger influence than in the secular, 'post-religious' West. Alan Jacobs points to Alan Paton's *Cry, the Beloved Country* (1948) and the novelist, Peter Abrahams' self-proclaimed learning of biblical prose style and vocabulary of 'justice and injustice, power and oppression' from the King James Bible. The influence of evangelicalism in Africa, due to nineteenth-century missionary fervour, has not been able to shake off its allegiance to imperialism and for novelists such as Barbara Kingsolver the Bible represents a troubling instance of colonial imposition. In contemporary fiction such as Kingsolver's *The Poisonwood Bible* (1998), the Bible is less an influence than a subject and character within her fiction, to be scrutinized and laid bare. Kingsolver laments the cultural imposition of Western interpretations of the Bible and aggressive missionary work. Her title refers to the Reverend Price's bumbling mispronunciation of 'Bible' leading him to signify a feared poisonwood tree instead of holy scripture, fatally – and at his very beginning – undermining his missionary quest. This linguistic mistake represents cultural insensitivity, ignorance and imposition in Kingsolver's narrative in which the Bible is a prime agent in the colonialist venture. In her epigraph to Book One, she quotes Genesis 1:28 in which God commands Adam and Eve to 'replenish the earth, and subdue it: and have dominion over the fish of the sea, and over the fowl of the air, and over every living thing that moveth upon the earth', making an implicit link between the Bible and colonial domination in Africa.

However, even in this novel, the Bible is not monologic but is revealed to be open to alternative readings. A rigid and narrow view of Scripture is expressed by the Reverend Price but is contested by the alternative multiple perspectives of the reverend's wife and four daughters who narrate the story. The novel in its very form thus privileges multiple and marginal perspectives. The claustrophobic, biblically-sanctified world created by the reverend is questioned by his daughter, Adah, who offers alternative interpretations that reveal the bias inherent in the reverend's reading. Her contrary interpretations reflect those offered by feminist biblical critics. Her father preaches on Susannah, who, whilst bathing in her garden, is approached by her husband's advisors who demand she sleeps with them or they will bear false witness against her. The reverend's hero is Daniel, who intervenes and exposes the advisors' duplicity. Adah, however, asks completely different questions of the story: 'Were we not supposed to wonder what kind of husband was this Joakim, who would kill his own lovely wife rather than listen to her side of the story?' (1998: 82). Demolishing Daniel as hero, she instead questions the cultural system in which Susannah could be so vulnerable.

A more heterogeneous representation of the place of the Bible in African society is represented in Chinua Achebe's novel, *Things Fall Apart* (1958). In this novel, the Bible's arrival may be contingent with the break-up of African indigeneous society – perhaps revealing its centrality to Western identity – but it is revealed as being not inextricable from that identity. Although depicting the destruction that missionaries wreak upon the protagonist's village, Achebe nevertheless pits two types of missionary against each other, each with a representative approach to the Bible. The Reverend Brown converses on an equal level with the great men in the village in everyday language. He 'preached against' 'excess of zeal' and 'came to be respected even by the clan, because he trod softly on his faith' (2001: 130). While orthodox in his views and approach, Mr Brown is distanced from his successor, the Reverend James Smith, and Brown's over-zealous translator, Mr Kiaga, who disparages Brown's dialogue with the villagers. In their hands the Bible becomes Kingsolver's weapon of colonialism. The narrative soon echoes Mr Smith's bibliophilism: 'He spoke in his sermons about sheep and goats and about wheat and tares. He believed in slaying the prophets of Baal . . . Mr Brown had thought of nothing but numbers . . . Narrow is the way and few the number' (2001: 134). The harshness of biblical weaponry shows in the Reverend Brown's over-zealous interpreter who responds to the protagonist's son, Nwoye's desire to leave his father to join the church with a sinister, heartless biblicism that Nwoye doesn't even comprehend:

> Mr Kiaga's joy was very great. 'Blessed is he who forsakes his father and mother for my sake', he intoned. 'Those who hear my words are my father and my mother.'
>
> Nwoye did not fully understand. But he was happy to leave his father. (2001: 112)

Jasper and Prickett's notion of the 'Western cultural psyche' also suggests a cultural homogeneity that postcolonial critics have worked hard to undermine. Thus, in Sam Selvon's *The Lonely Londoners* ([1956] 2003), the Bible becomes a site of a shared cultural resource that crosses West/non-West boundaries. It is a novel that explicitly links itself to West Indian culture by its use of what Selvon calls 'dialect' and Kamau Braithwaite has termed 'nation language', the representation of Caribbean English in its phonetic specificity, differentiating it from standard, Received Pronunciation English. His naming of his protagonist Moses – the great Patriarch – endows the novel with what Roydon Salick describes as 'a life of exile, hardship, not belonging, wandering, power and privilege', in which London becomes the promised land that Moses will never, and can never, fully participate in (2001, 127–8). Although the use of 'nation language' evokes the Caribbean culture that Selvon's characters have hailed from, this biblical figure of exile, Moses, is a shared trope that has been used by the English but never completely owned by them. The use of the Bible in this literary text can thus act as a stabilized shared ground upon which the communication of exile may be achieved.

The inherent orality of Selvon's *The Lonely Londoners* also gestures towards the differing cultural positioning and functioning of the Bible in difference cultures. Much writing on the Bible and literature sees the Bible as a literary exemplar. Its translation into the vernacular in England, both in the fifteenth and sixteenth centuries, is often heralded as a literary revolution, while its translation into non-English vernaculars by the Bible Society in the nineteenth century has produced a sense of the Bible as linked intimately with vernacularization and the consolidation of written language. However, to presume this is the case is to ignore other experiences, and the place of the Bible in non-Western, non-literary cultures challenges these assumptions. Linton Kwesi Johnson, the Jamaica-born dub poet, who has lived in Britain since the age of 11, speaks of the influence of the Bible on his own poetry and its special oral status in the Caribbean:

> When I began to write verse, a lot of it was full of 'thou' and thee' and 'thy' and stuff because, as I said, my primary literary influence was the Bible. I say literary but, of course, in the Caribbean the Bible is part of the oral tradition; there are people who are illiterate who can recite and quote entire sections of the Bible by heart, so as far as the Bible is concerned it has become a part of the oral tradition in the Caribbean. (1996: 65)

As the literary depictions of the Bible in Kingsolver's and Achebe's novels show, the Bible is not easy to pin down as a collaborator in imperial aggression. In Henry Rider Haggard's *King Solomon's Mines*, the Bible is anything but a weapon of imperialism. In this story of three Englishmen's adventures in Africa, it disrupts colonial, Western discourse. White, patriarchal, monarchical identity is shored up in the novel constantly through the differentiation between 'whites' and 'blacks', and where 'blacks' subvert this order, it is only in order to support monarchical hierarchies – the noble king is validated because of his naturalized monarchical character, as are his people the Kukuanas, an especially 'noble' race of Zulus, considered the aristocracy of the South African races in the nineteenth century. Within a secure ordering of races and nations, the allusion to the Book of Ruth by the Kukuana girl Foulata disrupts this seemingly neat narrative. A romantic attachment has been established between one of the white heroes of the adventure narrative, Captain Good, and Foulata in which she declares to him: 'whither thou goest, there will I go also' (1991: 261), echoing Ruth's attachment to her mother-in-law Naomi in Ruth 1:16. Despite Foulata's later death-statement, 'I know that he cannot cumber his life with such as me, for the sun cannot mate with the darkness, nor the white with the black' (1991: 281), this quotation from the Ruth narrative evokes the story of a racial outsider – a Moabitess – who marries into Naomi's family and who becomes the ancestor of the venerated King David. As a narrative that advocates miscegenation, the Book of Ruth disrupts the apparently anti-miscegenation text of *King Solomon's Mines*.

An attentive reading of the biblical presence in colonial and postcolonial literature therefore challenges any easy conceptions of the Bible as suited to the cultural imperialist ends that it is often associated with. Indeed, the Bible is notably difficult to recruit or enlist in the service of narrow, ideological agendas. The Bible is not a monolithic text and literature's interactions with it are never free from complexity or ambiguity. The use made by creative writers of the Bible provides an excellent illustration of Valentine Cunningham's assertion that 'all reading is re-reading'. Cunningham goes on to say that 'all reading is in some measure abusive' (2000: 78) and the history of biblical intertextuality in literature might be seen as a long history of use and abuse.

It is precisely this mutual influence, of biblical text upon literary rewriting, and of literary rewriting upon biblical text, that has provoked much theoretical debate in recent years. To produce a viable theoretical model for this two-way exchange between the Bible and its literary progeny is both difficult and necessary. Many critics have embraced the concept of midrash – the Hebrew term for the Jewish practice of retelling biblical tales in such a way as to extract more profound meanings from gaps or insignificant details – in order to recognize the symbiotic relationship between the Bible and its rewritings. Harold Fisch describes novelistic rewritings as midrash precisely because he sees them as 'not extravagant notions but the elaboration of meanings which the text seems to authorize and even invite'. He concludes that 'the result is something between interpretation and a new invention, for biblical narratives, by virtue of their polyphonic character, as well as their pregnant silences, are peculiarly suited to beget other narratives' (1998: 18). His view of rewriting reflects the concept that the rewriter is expressing in writing the process that all readers necessarily go through: the activity of filling in the gaps of what is not said in any narrative.

The rewriter thus expresses the tension between creativity and dependence inherent in every act of reading, a tension expressed in Wolfgang Iser's (1980) concept of the active reader. Iser refers to a process of reading in which the reader is guided through the gaps in the text by what is explicit within it. Reading gleans the implicit from the text, which constantly has to be negotiated with the explicit in the text. Or as Zotlán Swáb puts it: 'reading is a conversation between the text and the reader that is (at least partly) led by the text' (2003: 171). Many creative rewritings of biblical tales and tropes can therefore be understood as similar to the relationship between commentary and biblical text in the teasing out of implicit significances alongside the often too obvious insertion of the reader's perspective. The insistence on both sides of this process – the creative aspect is often heralded at the expense of the coercive nature of the text – is important if the power of texts is not to be ignored. The creative thus sits alongside the derivative: 'If midrash . . . gives the reader a more creative role in the interpretive process, it also paradoxically places him under greater constraints . . . he is responsible to, coerced by, a source text which cannot be ignored or set aside' (Fisch 1998: 20). As the participant in a dialogue, the Bible cannot easily be 'silenced', as though it is overwritten by the reading process: it continues to jar, to interrupt and clash with reading strategies and presumptions. Like any text, the Bible must be studied in the context of what Edward Said terms its 'configurations of power' (1995: 5).

Iser's notion that rewriting reflects back upon and impacts the originary text is hard to deny in a world in which literature is in fact so replete with repetitions and rewritings of biblical stories that it even overwhelms the Bible. Few people, even today in our supposedly post-Christian, secular, world come to the Bible without preconceptions of the stories of Adam and Eve, Noah, Jonah, or Jesus. We experience what Fredric Jameson has described as reading the 'always-already-read'. He explains: 'We apprehend [texts] through sedimented layers of previous interpretations, or – if the text is brand-new – through the sedimented reading habits and categories developed by those inherited interpretive traditions' (1986: 9).

In reading the biblical story of Adam and Eve's sin and expulsion from the garden of Eden, images from literature and popular culture come to mind: the eating of the apple; the shameful covering of nakedness with hands; the complicity of Eve above Adam; the sexual nature of Eve's tempting of Adam with the apple. In fact, all of these factors are not explicit in the biblical account, but occur prominently in famous rewritings or have simply diffused into popular culture. The reading of Eve's greater implication in the fall follows a theological trend evident from the first few centuries of the Christian Church in the writings of the Church Fathers onwards.

The Anglo-Saxon poem *Genesis B*, from the ninth century is perhaps the first English rendition of this inclusion of theology into literature that has passed through John Milton's rendering of Eve to the present cultural imagination. In *Genesis B*, the poet explains that 'God had granted her a weaker mind (*wacran hige*)'. David C. Fowler explains:

> In allegorical readings of the temptation, the senses are represented by the serpent, who insinuates himself into the confidence of the lower reason (Eve), which in turn corrupts the higher reason (Adam), resulting in the Fall. This was understood to be the psychological process that results in sin, a process that repeats itself in the life of every individual. (1977: 108)

The persistence of allegory in the early Church promoted this reading of Eve and resulted in the rewritings of the Bible being dominated by such culturally resonant theological readings. John Milton's version of the story in *Paradise Lost* is perhaps the most well-known rendition of the Genesis story of Adam and Eve. It may not have been read by many, but its poetic retelling has survived in the Western imagination more substantially than the biblical account. Hence, Milton has Eve alone approached by the serpent, he makes Eve particularly responsible for the sin, and he has Adam and Eve jumping lustily into a bush as soon as they eat the apple. When teaching *Paradise Lost* to English Studies undergraduates, they are often surprised by the Genesis account because it differs so greatly from their preconceptions. In our current culture, people's familiarity with stories will more often come from childhood tales than from the pages of the Bible itself.

This reciprocity of the Bible and its rewritings even affects our very mode of reading. Hence, students are surprised when they read the Genesis narrative because they already have expectations of what the narrative should and shouldn't contain. Jameson suggests that this experience of the 'always-already-read' – of approaching a text through a mist of preconceptions and contesting narratives – engenders a specific method of reading which he calls the 'metacommentary'. For this, 'our object of study is less the text itself than the interpretations through which we attempt to confront and to appropriate it' (1986, 9–10). Therefore, as I have done above with the story of Adam and Eve, the reader's preconceptions can be understood as a consequence of having to wade through a sea of interpretations on the way to the Bible. As with this example, the rewriting can often take precedence over the biblical text itself. This can be seen in the infamous Romantic response to the figure of Satan, not based upon the biblical text, but again, on Milton's rewriting. William Blake's contention that Milton was 'of the Devil's party without knowing it' responds to the depiction of the Devil and God in *Paradise Lost* in which rebellious energy is pitted against oppressive limitation, a battle that the former must ultimately win in the Romantic context (Blake in Wu 1994: 80). This representation leads Shelley in his *Defence of Poetry* (Shelley in Wu 1994: 962) to marvel at Satan's 'energy and magnificence', which 'nothing can exceed'. Because Milton's God is tyrannical and his Satan a personification of the Romantic characteristics of perseverance against adversity, Shelley logically concludes that this Devil is a 'moral being' 'far superior to his God', a reading that sets Milton's poem far from his explicit intention to 'assert Eternal Providence,/ And justifie the wayes of God to men' (2000, I: 24–5). The Romantic response to Satan therefore makes sense only through the 'always-already-read' in which Milton's rewriting imposes a specific reading. The biblical Satan is simply not substantial enough to provoke such a response.

The metacommentary stems from a recognition of the historical positioning of authors, texts and readers: that we must recognize the 'situatedness' of any reading experience, a situatedness that can perhaps best be traced through the reception histories of individual biblical books or tropes. This interest has engendered exciting new impulses in biblical studies such as Margarita Stocker's analysis of the cultural history of the Judith story in *Judith: Sexual Warrior* as well as Yvonne Sherwood's *A Text and Its Afterlives: The Survival of Jonah in Western Culture* as well as Blackwell's new series of biblical commentaries that focus on impact history. Tracing reception, or impact, histories has been massively influenced by reader-response criticism, such as Iser's, in its emphasis upon readings of a text – what happens to a text beyond the reach of its author. However, in reception histories a major focus of investigation has to be the author – and more specifically the reading author. When surveying rewritings and responses to a specific biblical text, we come across individual writers who offer a reading of that text at the same time as offering a new piece of writing: within the writing is also a reading.

Jauss – a figure now commonly associated with the concept of reception history or *Rezeptionsaesthetik* – is helpful in this attempt to understand the relationship between rewriting author and text. A key element of Jauss's work is his emphasis upon the historical positioning of the writing and writer, a recovery of the author that is not a return to the impossible task of recovering the consciousness of the author. Rather, historical positioning recognizes the social construction of meaning, literature's 'social character' as well as its aesthetic character (1982: 76). He explains: 'Just as there is no act of verbal communication that is not related to a general, socially or situationally conditioned norm or convention, it is also unimaginable that a literary work set itself into an informational vacuum, without indicating a specific situation of understanding' (ibid.: 79). Texts – and authors – work within a field in which there are always a set of conventions, what Jauss calls 'horizons of expectations', ' "rules of the game" to orient the reader's (public's) understanding and to enable a qualifying reception' (ibid.: 79). Although not claiming to understand what the author 'thought' as he or she wrote, Jauss is insisting that authors, working within a set of conventions, manipulate these purposefully. Of course, even here there are limits as to how an author's manipulation of convention can be traced. Derrida does warn after all that 'the writer writes *in* a language and *in a* logic whose proper system, laws, and life his discourse by definition cannot dominate absolutely'. There is always, necessarily, therefore a tension between 'what he commands and what he does not command of the patterns of the language that he uses' (1998: 158). Despite its limitations, the recognition of literature's inherently social nature does nonetheless allow the tracing of historically specific meaning.

What is interesting about rewritings of the Bible is the dialogue that they set up with the biblical book. In Jauss's terms, it is the 'answering character' of works of past art that enables an understanding of the positioning and specificity of both elements of the dialogue: both Bible and rewriting (ibid.: 108). What we are seeking from the appropriation is the question to which it thought it was providing an answer (ibid.: 113). Of course, rewritings of the Bible point towards its cultural primacy, but the reasons why a certain text is rewritten at a particular time suggests that specific answers are being promoted to culturally specific problems. Jameson insists that 'the aesthetic act is itself ideological and the production of aesthetic or narrative form is to be seen as an ideological act in its own right, with the function of inventing imaginary or formal "solutions" to unresolveable social contradictions' (1986: 79).

One of the most famous Anglo-Saxon poems is *Judith*, a retelling of this apocryphal tale. The fact that this marginal text should be rewritten at such a time points towards its relevance to wider cultural issues. That the poem contains a long description of the battle between the Israelites and Assyrians, an event briefly summarized in the biblical rendering, suggests, as David C. Fowler contends, that the poem is not simply a 'reflection of the poet's barbaric absorption in bloodshed', but that 'Judith's outstanding virtue', of 'courage in the face of overwhelming odds' is perhaps a response to the 'threat to England represented by Danish invaders'. He concludes that 'the courage of Judith may have been intended as a model for Englishmen . . . Indeed, some students of Old English believed that the poet may have based his characterization of Judith on a Saxon heroine, Aethelflaed, daughter of King Alfred' (Fowler 1977: 122). Literature viewed in such a way becomes an enduring record of the anxieties and preoccupations of an otherwise opaque age.

Thus, a dramatic, poetic or novelistic rewriting, or partial appropriation of a biblical text, can be approached in a similar manner to the way in which a commentary would be approached: the manner of interpretation – the prejudices, assumptions and questions that the reader brings to the text – can be teased out of the weave of the commentary. Therefore, despite her resistance to identifying the Book of Jonah as an 'originary text', Yvonne Sherwood can conclude that early Christian readings of the book offer a 'force of resistance to recalcitrant elements in Jonah the text, and Jonah the character' (2000: 20). To be able to distinguish between texts and the forces they expend (between the resisting text and the recalcitrant text, for example) is to acknowledge a degree of autonomy (even if that is a small degree) that moves beyond the idea that a reading is pure invention.

By emphasizing the historical, reception histories are not therefore a simple matter of seeking only historically typical appropriations of a biblical book, for example, *the* Victorian interpretation of Jonah or *the* Renaissance Protestant version of the Book of Ruth. Because of the perception of the biblical text as the ultimate authority at specific times and places, it is not unlikely that there will be dominant readings of biblical texts at certain periods. However, this approach wrongly presupposes the homogeneity of any culture and reading public. More interestingly, the analysis of specific interpretations can do precisely the opposite: it can reveal the intricacies and nuances of antagonistic and surprising cultural expressions, assumptions and norms. In this study, attention to the canon only would be inappropriate. 'Literature' in its widest sense needs to be the object of study. For example, allusion to the Book of Esther within the pamphlet, *Ester Hath Hang'd Haman* (1617) by Ester Sowernam reveals a surprisingly radical approach to the nature and role of women in the early modern period (Carruthers 2003). This pamphlet in its title points to Esther as a woman who has hanged Haman and who acts as a model – along with many other citations of warlike women – of woman's nature as a combatant of evil. Sowernam even turns to Eve in her pamphlet, usually depicted in the early modern period as equally to blame alongside the evil Serpent in the fall of Adam, and argues instead that because of the 'inseparable hatred and enmitie put betwixt the woman and the Serpent' (1617: 15), it is woman, and not man, who is most suitable for fighting evil. Many critics of this pamphlet reproduce a very conventional view of the Book of Esther and its interpretation in the early modern period. One critic's explanation for the allusion to Esther in this pamphlet, for example, is that 'as well as being the saviour of her people [Esther] was also supposed to be famously beautiful and seductive' (Purkiss 1992: 86). Assumptions that Esther is a basic fairytale story in which a beautiful woman influences her husband to save her people is undermined by the representations of her in literature. This may, indeed, be the dominant reading of the story as evidenced in sermons and commentaries from this period. However, Sowernam's and others' readings point towards an alternative strand of interpretation in which Esther's violent qualities are made prominent.

Francis Quarles's poetic rewriting of the Esther story has a similar – although sinisterly different – portrayal of Esther as violent. Considering Esther's request to kill the enemies of the Jews at the end of the biblical story, Quarles claims that her 'lips did ouer flow/ With streames of blood' (1621, sig. L6). This bloodthirsty image of Esther is not the valorizing one that Sowernam presents, but merely adds to the demonization of Esther that Quarles effects throughout his poetic rewriting. This image of the Jewish Esther as revengeful was one that had great cultural currency in the early modern period. Her bloody *lips* depict the Jews as cannibals, a belief expressed in the so-called blood libel legend according to which Jews killed Christian children in order to drink their blood. That Quarles is also presenting a culturally resonant view of women in general as being particularly revengeful, is evident in his comment that he thinks it is unreasonable for God to 'slake the vengeance of a woman's mind,/ With flowing riuers of thy subjects blood' (1621, sig. L6). Although verging upon the blasphemous in his questioning of God's motives, this attitude demonizes both Esther and women in general as inherently untrustworthy.

Our reading of the Book of Esther has to be challenged by its reception history. It is not a simple fairytale and contains elements that appear more sinister or threatening after a reading of Sowernam or Quarles. Even if we dispute Sowernam's and Quarles's version of Esther as wishful thinking or misogynistic or anti-Semitic – they cannot all be right – there is a sense in which they have made their mark upon the biblical text. These readings bring interpretive possibilities that cannot then be denied, potentials in the text that might otherwise be glossed over. The challenge that literature offers students and readers of the Bible is therefore one of defamiliarization that compels us to re-think our previous interpretations of well-known texts.

If the history of the Bible's reception in literature has been one of re-writing, supplementation or defamiliarization, then one might expect this process to reach a high point in the literature of postmodernism, which thrives on the practices of playful re-writing, pastiche, imitation and intertextuality. However, in our secular age, which Jean-François Lyotard has famously characterized as the era of the demise of the grand narrative, the Bible, one of the grandest narratives of all, may seem a redundant text, a relic of an obsolete belief system. In the light of the theories of Lyotard and others, however, it now becomes possible to think in terms of a 'postmodern bible': that is, a set of heterogeneous, conflicting voices and stories rather than a monologic voice of unquestionable divine authority. The possibilities for thinking of the Bible as a set of *petits récits* have already been opened up in such notable postmodern texts as Julian Barnes's *History of the World in 10½ Chapters* (1989), which begins with a mischievous rewriting of the story of Noah from the perspective of a woodworm. Barnes's 10½ chapters give a consciously fragmentary, incomplete, multi-voiced account of world history in a way that invites us to contemplate the Bible as a text that shares some of the same qualities. Of course to describe the Bible as fragmentary, incomplete and multi-voiced might seem to play into hands of a postmodern relativism that denies any possibility of faith or revealed truth. But in a sense these qualities are precisely those that one might expect to find in a text designed, as Prickett puts it, to convey 'the numinous, the holy, the "otherness" of religious experience' (1986: 32).

Acknowledgements

I am grateful to those colleagues who read and advised me on this chapter, especially Dr Michael Greaney for his help with the final editing. I am also indebted to the Leverhulme Trust and St Deiniol's Library for their support. Thank you also to Professor Gerald Hammond who first inspired me to work in the area of the Bible and literature.

References and Further Reading

Achebe, Chinua ([1958] 2001). *Things Fall Apart*. London: Penguin.
Alter, Robert (1992). *The World of Biblical Literature*. London: SPCK.
Alter, Robert (2000). *Canon and Creativity: Modern Writing and the Authority of Scripture*. New Haven, CT: Yale University Press.
Alter, Robert and Kermode, Frank (eds) (1989). *The Literary Guide to the Bible*. London: Fontana.
Barnes, Julian (1989). *The History of the World in 10½ Chapters*. London: Picador.
Blake, William (1994). 'The Marriage of Heaven and Hell', in Duncan Wu (ed.), *Romanticism: An Anthology*. Oxford: Blackwell, pp. 84–94.
Braithwaite, Kamau (1984). *History of the Voice: The Development of Nation Language in Anglophone Caribbean Poetry*. London: Beacon Press.
Carruthers, Jo (2003). ' "Neither Maide, Wife or Widow": Ester Sowernam and the Book of Esther', *Prose Studies* 26: 321–43.
Crace, Jim (1998a). *Quarantine*. London: Penguin.
Crace, Jim (1998b). 'Crace on Quarantine'. Available at: www.jim-crace.com
Cunningham, Valentine (2000). 'The Best Stories in the Best Order? Canons, Apocryphas, and (Post) Modern Reading', *Literature and Theology* 14(1): 69–80.
Daniell, David (ed.) ([1534] 1989). *Tyndale's New Testament*. New Haven, CT: Yale University Press.

Derrida, Jacques ([1976] 1998). *Of Grammatology*, trans. Gayatri Chakravorty Spivak. Baltimore, MD: Johns Hopkins University Press.

Fisch, Harold (1971). *Hamlet and the Word: The Covenant Pattern in Shakespeare*. New York: Frederick Ungar Publishing Co.

Fisch, Harold (1998). *New Stories for Old: Biblical Patterns in the Novel*. Basingstoke: Macmillan.

Fisch, Harold (1999). *The Biblical Presence in Shakespeare, Milton and Blake: A Comparative Study*. Oxford: Clarendon Press.

Fowler, David C. (1977). *The Bible in Early English Literature*. London: Sheldon Press.

Fowler, David C. (1984). *The Bible in Middle English Literature*. Seattle, WA: University of Washington Press.

Haggard, Henry Rider (1991). *King Solomon's Mines*. Oxford: Oxford University Press.

Hammond, Gerald (1992). *The Making of the English Bible*. Manchester: Carcanet New Press.

Hastings, Adrian (1997). *The Construction of Nationhood: Ethnicity, Religion and Nationalism* (the 1996 Wiles Lectures given at the Queen's University of Belfast). Cambridge: Cambridge University Press.

Hill, Christopher (1993). *The English Bible and the Seventeenth-Century Revolution*. Harmondsworth: Allen Lane.

Iser, Wolfgang (1980). *The Act of Reading: A Theory of Aesthetic Response*. Baltimore, MD: Johns Hopkins University Press.

Jameson, Fredric (1986). *The Political Unconscious: Narrative as a Socially Symbolic Act*. London: Routledge.

Jasper, David and Prickett, Stephen, assisted by Andrew Hass (1999). *The Bible and Literature: A Reader*. Oxford: Blackwell.

Jauss, Hans Robert (1982). *Toward an Aesthetic of Reception*, trans. Timothy Bahti. Brighton: The Harvester Press.

Jeffries, David Lyle (1992). *A Dictionary of Biblical Tradition in English Literature*. Grand Rapids, MI: William B. Eerdmans Publishing Co.

Jobling, David (2001). 'Methods of Modern Literary Criticism', in Leo G. Perdue (ed.), *The Blackwell Companion to the Hebrew Bible*. Oxford: Blackwell, pp. 19–31.

Johnson, Linton Kwesi (1996). 'Linton Kwesi Johnson talks to Burt Caesar at Sparkside Studios, Brixton, London, 11 June 1996', *Critical Quarterly* 38(4): 64–77.

Kermode, Frank (1979). *The Genesis of Secrecy*. Cambridge, MA: Harvard University Press.

Kingsolver, Barbara (1998). *The Poisonwood Bible*. London: Faber and Faber.

Marlowe, Christopher ([c.1604] 1990). *Doctor Faustus*, ed. John D. Jump. Manchester: Manchester University Press.

McClintock, Anne (1995). *Imperial Leather: Race, Gender and Sexuality in the Colonial Context*. London: Routledge.

Metzger, Bruce M. and Coogan Michael D. (1993). *The Oxford Companion to the Bible*. Oxford: Oxford University Press.

Milton, John (2000). *The Poetical Works of John Milton*, ed. Helen Darbishire. Oxford: Clarendon Press.

Paton, Alan ([1948] 2000). *Cry, the Beloved Country*. London: Penguin.

Prickett, Stephen (1986). *Words and the Word: Language, Poetics and Biblical Interpretation*. Cambridge: Cambridge University Press.

Prickett, Stephen (1996). *Origins of Narrative: The Romantic Appropriation of the Bible*. Cambridge: Cambridge University Press.

Purkiss, Diane (1992). 'Material Girls: The Seventeenth-Century Woman Debate', in Clare Brant and Diane Purkiss (eds), *Women, Texts and Histories 1575–1760*. London: Routledge, pp. 69–101.

Quarles, Francis (1621). *Hadassa: Or the Historie of Queene Ester. With Meditations Thereupon, Divine and Morall*. London.

Said, Edward ([1978] 1995). *Orientalism*. London: Penguin.

Salick, Roydon (2001). *The Novels of Sam Selvon: A Critical Study*. Westpoint, CT: Greenwood Press.

Sawyer, John F. A. (2005). 'The Role of Reception Theory, Reader-Response Criticism an/or Impact History in the Study of the Bible: Definition and Evaluation'. Available at: www. bbibcomm.net

Selvon, Sam ([1956] 2003). *The Lonely Londoners*. New York: Longman.

Shelley, Percy (1994). 'A Defence of Poetry; or, Remarks Suggested by an Essay Entitled "The Four Ages of Poetry" ', in Duncan Wu (ed.), *Romanticism: An Anthology*. Oxford: Blackwell, pp. 944–56.

Sherwood, Yvonne (2000). *A Biblical Text and its Afterlives: The Survival of Jonah in Western Culture*. Cambridge: Cambridge University Press.

Sowernam, Ester (1617). *Ester Hath Hang'd Haman: or an Ansvvere to a lewd Pamphlet, entituled, The Arraignment of Women: With the Arraignment of Lewd, Idle and Froward, and Vnconstant men and Hvsbands*. London.

Stocker, Margarita (1998). *Judith: Sexual Warrior Women and Power in Western Culture*. New Haven, CT: Yale University Press.

Swáb, Zoltán (2003). 'Mind the Gap: The Impact of Wolfgang Iser's Reader-Response Criticism on Biblical Studies – A Critical Assessment', *Literature and Theology* 17(2): 170–81.

Tate, Andrew (2005). ' "So, Here, Be Well Again": The Human/Divine Body of Jesus in Crace's *Quarantine*', in Andrew Dix and Jonathan Taylor (eds), *Figures of Heresy: Radical Theology in English and American Literature, 1830–2000*. Sussex: Sussex Academic Press, pp. 141–56.

Winterson, Jeanette (1984). *Oranges Are Not the Only Fruit*. London: Pandora.

Wu, Duncan (ed.) (1994). *Romanticism: An Anthology*. Oxford: Blackwell.

CHAPTER 16
Film

Alice Bach

For the Roman soldiers at Christ's preaching in Jerusalem, I had to think of the *Celere*; for Herod's soldiers before the Massacre of the Innocents I had to think of the Fascist mob; Joseph and the Madonna as refugees were suggested to me by refugees in my analogous tragedies in the modern word, for example, Algeria. (Pier Paolo Pasolini)

Many of the films about the Christ-figure or the metaphoric Suffering Servant tell us as much about the culture of the filmmakers and their expectations of religion as they do about their personal faith. Films claimed by critics to be prophetic, to enforce Christian values or Christian narratives, from the Assumption to the Resurrection, or to embody the imprint of the Christ figure, may be transformative for the critic, or the spectator who shares the same interpretive vision, but too often they become mired in their Christ figure interpretations. When one is teaching a course on various aspects of religion and film, the temptation to build totems out of celluloid is enormous. Reading and analyzing films, I have built such totems that I am now prepared to topple. How many of us have pointed students toward women as Christ-figures in Federico Fellini's *La Strada* and *Nights of Cabiria*, Gabriel Axel's *Babette's Feast*, Percy Adlon's *Baghdad Café*, and Tim Robbins's *Dead Man Walking*? Each of the films yields different pieces of the Christ story – the salvation of Zamparo and the suffering of Cabiria, the offering of self that Babette gives to the small Lutheran community, the life-giving healing of Jasmin, and Sister Helen Prejean's participation in the suffering of the killer and the families of the victims.

But there is a caveat when reading film, to treat the splices, cuts, and fades as though they were the gaps in a textual narrative. Another caveat is to read the director with suspicion; the camera eye may not be the director's eye. With the exception of Mel Gibson who has compulsively publicized his religiosity, many directors have used Old Testament narratives and the Gospels as sure-bet crowd pleasers, not as statements of faith. As Pasolini commented to journalist Oswald Stack, 'I, a nonbeliever, was telling the story (*Il Vangelo*) through the eyes of a believer. The mixture at the narrative level produced the mixture stylistically.' On further probing of the music and paintings in the film that gave it a feeling of unity to most spectators, Pasolini added, 'I probably do believe after all. The stylistic unity is only my own unconscious religiousness, which came out and gave the film its unity' (Stack 1969: 86–7). The eye of the spectator is not the eye of the director.

Jesus Christ, Celluloid Superstar

Talk about a slippery slope. Jesus films are fraught with theology, ideology, sentimentality, pageantry, and sophistry. I am certain that it is a losing battle to talk about favourite or most effective Jesus films, sometimes called biopics, especially among scholars who are still wrestling with images of the historical Jesus. So much has been written about Mel Gibson's *The Passion of the Christ* (2004), from the US Catholic Bishops to the American Anti-Defamation League, from biblical scholars to irate film critics, that I have chosen not to write about the film here. In a recent book (Bach 2004), I have examined the marketing of the film, as the selling of the greatest story ever told is important to the mutual influence of bible and popular culture.

Not surprisingly, one's favourite Jesus film often tells us a great deal more about the spectator than the film itself. One person's faith is another person's fantasy. For instance I have a colleague who thinks Monty Python's *Life of Brian* is as profound as Proust, another who hums along with *The Greatest Story Ever Told*. Full of self-revelation, I am willing to admit my own strong connection to Martin Scorsese's *The Last Temptation of Christ* (1988). Lest you think you have me typed, dear reader, I also love some of the great pious films such as Robert Bresson's *The Diary of a Country Priest* (1954), Henry King's *The Song of Bernadette* (1943) and a film that defies category, Franco Zeffirelli's *Brother Sun, Sister Moon* (1972). I treasure these films for their traditional religiosity and also for their gentle view of life. Often showing these films to students without secondary analysis can result in meatier discussions than offering other critics' analyses. Of course, one's hand is already tipped when the title of the class is Religion and Film, necessitating a rigorous emphasis upon secular readings of the cinematic narratives to balance the Christology in the room.

Alas, this chapter is as tipped as my course titles. Once again I am reflecting upon the complicated patterns resulting from the nexus of religion *and* film. I can hope only that readers will read this text with suspicion, and glower when they do not agree with my tinted interpretations. For many years my favourite Jesus film has been Martin Scorsese's *The Last Temptation of Christ* (1988): I value the movie even more now because it has made me appreciate the work of Pasolini. The greatest example of how film can illuminate and extend the Gospels is in my opinion, *Il Vangelo secondo Matteo* ('The Gospel According to Matthew') directed by Pier Paolo Pasolini (1964). The original Italian film title did not include the term 'Saint', although St Matthew is the way the English translation of the title consistently appears. While this film is the major connection most contemporary Biblicists have with Pasolini, it is not what he is primarily remembered for in his native Italy. Known as a poet and public intellectual throughout his short life, Pasolini was a constant irritant to the powers and principalities. He was a tangle of contradictions: Communist and Catholic, artist and ideologue, celebrity and outcast, homosexual and rigid traditionalist. One of his early poems, 'The Ashes of Gramsci' (1954) presents his paradoxical public persona:

> The scandal, of contradicting myself, of being
> With you and against you; with you in my heart,
> In light, but against you in the dark viscera.

Pasolini might have been speaking of Scorsese, another troubadour of the streets, who is not so extreme as Pasolini, not so dedicated to the mythification of the underclass. A practising Catholic, and lifelong New Yorker, in many of his more violent films, Scorsese comes close to a similar style of mean street life as metaphor for the tension of good and evil. Scorsese's work lacks the tart irony and rage that one finds in Pasolini.

Pasolini walked a fragile line between his Marxist and Catholic beliefs, both of which were rooted in his distaste for industrialization and consumerism. There is a tough, gritty unsentimental quality that distinguishes Pasolini from other neo-Realists, even when he is adapting 'great works'. Two of his other films of that period, *Medea* and *Oedipo Re*, reflect Pasolini's desire to reinterpret the text, to challenge and reinscribe the narrative for his contemporary Italian society. Post-war Italy reflected the social leveling and political centrism that Pasolini loathed. He saw film as a cultural medium that would retrieve the poor from being pushed to the edge of social and cultural oblivion. Using most of the original texts, Pasolini kept what he wished, and stretched their episodic narration to insert linkages to his own society and culture. Pasolini was the real thing: he lived among the rootless underclass of Southern Italian peasants. By using the familiar narratives of the Greek epics, and later, the short narratives from Boccaccio, Chaucer, and the Arabian Nights, Pasolini brought the world of *I ragazzi di vita*, the cut-throat ethics of the street tempered with the naïve ways of the countryside, into whatever he wrote about or committed to film. Perhaps his most artistic creation was his own life, ending in his murder in 1975, apparently by a teenage male prostitute.

Pasolini did not feel bound to the original geographical locations of Greek islands or the ancient Holy Land for the films of this period. Pasolini was disappointed by Israel as a movie set. After his arrival at Tel Aviv airport, 'there appeared reforestation works, modern agriculture, light industry. Israel is too modern to play its ancient self. And not only was its built world disappointing. So were the people. I realized it was all no use – that was after only a few hours driving' (*Sopraluoghi in Palestina* 1964). Returning home to Rome, he shot *Il Vangelo* in southern Italy, where he found the landscapes of the humble and the powerful. His Bethlehem was a village in Apulia, where people were still living in caves; Jerusalem was really the crumbling part of Matera. The castles were Norman castles near Apulia and Lucania. The desert where Christ walks with the apostles is actually in Calabria. And Capernaum is a pastiche of towns close to the seaside.

My own view of Pasolini's well-regarded film is shared by Lloyd Baugh, whose analysis 'The Masterpiece: The Gospel According to Saint Matthew' (Baugh 1997: 94–108) provides both excellent background on Pasolini as a creative artist and a crisp analysis of the Italian filmmaker's portrait of Jesus. A professor at the Pontifical Gregorian University in Rome, Baugh focuses on Pasolini's representation of the Matthean Jesus as a human rather than a divine hero, but one who is much more distant from the people and his disciples than the Matthean figure. Cutting to the bone, Baugh argues that Pasolini sees an irritable Jesus, one not well integrated into human society. 'Solitary, aloof, he is a kind of biblical intellectual, who despite an intense desire to be organically linked to the people, cannot breach the immeasurable gap between them' (ibid.: 104). Baugh argues, and I think rightly, that Pasolini's Jesus is an extreme figure, who discomforts many interpreters of the film, but that the severity of the film's interpretation is in keeping with the radical nature of the Gospel. Pasolini's broken-faced peasants are much closer to a Gospel peasantry, I suspect, than the bland Hollywood peasants or even the Bronx-voiced disciples of Scorsese. Baugh also notes the nuances of Pasolini's Jesus:

> When Jesus heals the leper, there is a marvelous warm exchange of smiles between him and the man; and when Jesus cures the cripple, he smiles at him and later he even speaks gently and reasonably to the Pharisees. During his triumphal entrance into Jerusalem, Jesus is anything but solemn. He is clearly enjoying himself and participating in his popular manifestation. (ibid.: 103)

There is something so fitting in the hollow-cheeked, slight, Mediterranean Jesus that Pasolini envisions that resonates with my own internal portrait. After seeing one of these Jesus films, particularly the Pasolini or the Scorsese film, one never reads the Gospels in quite the same way again. Both Scorsese and Pasolini rejected the cinemascopic vistas and grandiose palaces of the usual biblical epics. Instead of faithful historical reconstructions, both films are analogic rereadings.

One proof of the power of the spectator in interpreting film is that the so-called New York accents found in the Scorsese film sounded normal to me (a native New Yorker), and the tough guy Judas played by Harvey Keitel finally gave me a 'henchman/betrayer' figure who was simultaneously intimate and inimical, one who brought depth and complexity to Judas that I had never understood. Scorsese considered the look of Jesus fundamental to his production:

> The moment I saw Willem Dafoe, I felt very comfortable with his face. When Christ changes after returning from the desert, or at the moment when He takes His heart out – which refers to the Catholic Sacred Heart motif – He becomes the Jesus we are familiar with in the Aryan Christian tradition. Oddly enough, all the guys we considered for the part were blue-eyed. (Scorsese 1989: 126)

Sting was originally cast as Scorsese's Pilate, but he could not make the shooting schedule. So Scorsese settled upon David Bowie, an intriguing parallel, pale, diffident, and not easily compared with the dark menacing Pilates from the epic Jesus pictures. Similar to Sting, a composer, musician, and actor, Bowie's accent put him outside the harsh New Yorky voices of Jesus and most of the disciples. Aside from the dialogue Scorsese was careful to avoid either musical or visual cues that might hint at epic for his mostly American audience. One should note that casting familiar actors in roles pushes the spectator to certain conclusions about the character's identity. Bowie is playing against type physically, but is known by the audience for 'bad-boy' antics, providing a cinematic wink from the boy who fell to earth to many of his fans. His Pilate seems bored with Jesus. His most memorable line to the doomed Dafoe is delivered without affect, 'Unfortunately for you, we don't want things changed.'

For Pasolini, faces are critical. He was not interested in the mask faces of actors:

> The only time I am interested in an actor is when I use an actor to act an actor. For example, I never use extras in my films because they are just hacks. Their faces are brutalized by living all their life at Cinecitta, surrounded by whores who are always hanging around there. When I was shooting Il Vangelo I went round and chose all the extras myself, one by one from among the peasants and the people in the villages round where we were shooting. I used real extras. (Stack 1969: 40)

In *Sopraluoghi*, a hastily cobbled together film about the scouting of locations for *Il Vangelo*, Pasolini explained that in 1963 the southern Italian peasants, the non-actors who played most of the characters in the film, are 'still living in a magical culture, where miracles are real, like the culture in which Matthew wrote'. In choosing Welles to play the director in *La Ricotta*, Pasolini had perfect pitch. Welles was perfectly cast as the director, after all, he was a director. Fat and forbidding in a black coat, with dark rings under his eyes, Welles chomped on a large cigar throughout his time on screen and his manner was haughty and languid. He bellowed directions a few times in the film, but his most extended dialogue with an unctuous journalist was a dead-on parody of overwrought intellectualized cant. Whether Welles is Fellini, Pasolini, or himself – or all of them at once – is for each viewer to determine.

The scoring of *Il Vangelo* is startling and unique. Using the recently composed Congolese Missa Luba at the final scene is a triumph. The pounding drums and joyful cries of the women pick up the ultimate triumph as they approach the tomb. The drumbeat reflects the same urgency as the Gospel, as death is silenced by the fierce and harsh music of the victory of the risen Christ. And what better visual interpretation of the triumph of the embattled Matthean community than Italian peasants, sure-footed on rocky terrain, in a fight against hostile forces?

In an interview while he was working on *Il Vangelo*, Pasolini reflected on the tension in his creative vision: 'In the world in which I live I am rather the sheep in the midst of wolves. And it's been shown by what has happened in these years – I've been literally torn to pieces.' A sheep amid wolves also defines the *ragazzi di vita*, who were cast in Pasolini's films, filled his fantasies, and eventually left him dead, bloodied, beaten, face down in the sand of Ostia.

La Ricotta

Filled with satiric element, including a belly-dancing Magdalene, a talking dog, and an insufferable film director who seems stuck in his chair throughout the film, *La Ricotta* is very funny as well as being the most provocative religious film made by Pasolini. Pasolini filmed *La Ricotta* in the autumn of 1962, on a hilly ridge in the countryside near the gates of Rome, between the Via Appia Nuova and the Via Appia Antica, near the Acqua Santa aqueduct, where pimps, hookers, *ragazzi di vita*, and other subprole-tarian folk lived. The film was suppressed for many years due to its combination of irony, tragedy, and a focus on filming the Crucifixion, rather than the suffering of Jesus on the Cross. *La Ricotta* starts with a brief note from Pasolini proclaiming his devotion to Catholicism, although there is nothing in the film to support that notion.

The 35-minute, low-budget film, part of *RoGoPaG*, a compilation title created from the initials of the directors of the four short films, Rosselini, Godard, Pasolini and Ugo Gregoretti, is a distillation of Pasolini's anger against the well-fed hierarchy of the Church, the bourgeois consumer society, and evil capitalists. Pasolini anticipated the almost unanimously negative reaction to his film with a note at the beginning of the picture. 'However one takes *La Ricotta*, the story of the Passion is for me the greatest story ever told and the texts which recount that story the most sublime ever written.' Lest the audience get lulled into a sense of smarmy bliss, Pasolini then cuts fast to two men dancing the twist in front of the site of the Crucifixion set in jewel-toned Technicolor. In the early Sixties in Italy as in the US the twist was considered shock-ing to the middle class, certainly not a dance! The twist music echoes throughout the movie.

La Ricotta was shot mostly in black and white, with brief colour sequences carefully composed to recall the paintings of Rosso Fiorentino or Jacopo Pontormo (such as 'Descent from the Cross' from the Church of Santa Felicità in Florence). There is a similarity between Pasolini's scathing commentary on film, art and religion in *La Ricotta*, and Denys Arcand's *Jesus of Montreal*, in which Arcand uses the Passion Play to subvert and criticize the culture of modern French Canada. Of course satirizing one of the holiest and most familiar narratives in Western culture sounds more taboo than it has been in actuality. The Monty Python troupe's unforgettable 'Look on the Bright Side', reflects just how easy that playfulness is to produce and to be accepted by audiences.

La Ricotta is blatantly self-referential. In one scene Orson Welles, who plays the film's director in English, dubbed by Giorgio Bassani, recites lines from a Pasolini poem. A copy of the script for Pasolini's earlier film *Mamma Roma* is prominently displayed next to the director's chair. Welles's character is perhaps an alter ego for Pasolini and allows the director to spout some rather inflammatory remarks concerning Italy's *petit bourgeois*, the Church's 'profound, secret, archaic Catholicism', and Italians in general ('the most illiterate masses . . . in Europe'). The actors in the production are mockeries of their religious namesakes, e.g., Magdalene dances a vulgar striptease, the Madonna is portrayed as an arrogant prima donna, and the Christ actor is a bit of a sleazy beatnik. Hints of homoeroticism and sexual undercurrents abound in the film.

Viewed in its most august light, Pasolini has created in *La Ricotta* a visual poem through images evoking class, hunger, poverty, desire. At the same time it is a movie about the foolishness of intellectual cineastes intent on shooting an opulent Passion, as glossy as a Cardinal's robe, as far from the hungry people of God as the satins and silks of the privileged. The cinema as *mise en abîme*, filmmaking caught in its own trappings, a film about film, it also uses references to Renaissance paintings of the Crucifixion and the Deposition.

The dialogue is as tempting to the audience as the great wheel of ricotta is to the starving peasant Stracci, the extra who plays the crucified thief to the left of Jesus on Golgotha: 'Get those crucified characters out of there . . . bring up the crosses . . . leave them nailed up there . . . cuckolds . . . silence . . .!' Then there is the sheer crassness of the actress Magdalene who dances a voluptuous cha-cha-cha (the censors cut the striptease) in front of the laden crosses; and of Stracci, 'poor Stracci' ('Rags' in Italian), the doomed peasant, who gobbles so much ricotta during the lunch break that he gets a severe attack of indigestion. Uncomplaining he staggers back to the set, climbs the ladder to his Cross, and, while the crew is concentrating on angles and shots and close-ups of the central figures, Stracci literally dies, tied to the cross under the broiling sun. Stracci's death goes unnoticed until the director calls the next break. 'Poor Stracci, he had to die,' reflects the director (Welles); 'it was his only way of telling us he was alive.' In the actual shooting script found among papers published long after Pasolini's death, the director's line before the censors deleted it, read 'Poor Stracci. Dropping dead was his only way of making revolution.'

A word must be said about the ricotta, the object of Stracci's desire as well as the instrument of his death. Ricotta is simple unadorned peasant fare, the food that Stracci stuffs into his mouth, sitting in the mouth of a cave. This scene is contrasted with the long table laden with elegantly prepared technicolor food for luncheon provided for the producer and his guests. The formally appointed table, looking like a possible set piece for the Last Supper, forms a frame for the long shots, when the actors are mounting and climbing down from the Crosses. Unadorned, lacking subtlety in both form and flavour, the ricotta reflects the purity and simplicity of the poor, the followers of Jesus. In sharp contrast to the squatting Stracci gnawing at the cheese in the stone cave, Pasolini intercuts the tricked-out set and theatrical nibblers of the finer food, a metaphor for the moneychangers in the temple, as well as the hierarchy of the Church. As none on Pasolini's movie set could see Stracci dying, none of the bourgeoisie can see the true church through the lavish sets and costumes of consumerist, industrialized life.

La Ricotta did not stand a chance in the heat of a huge angry response to almost every shot. Intellectuals on the left and intellectuals on the right were offended by the comments about the stupidity of the bourgeoisie and the emptiness of contemporary Italian culture. The Church did not take kindly to the film, particularly to the comments by the Welles character, directing the most sacred scene in Christianity. 'Get that Crown of Thorns,' shouted and relayed multiple times from one crew member to another, did not delight the faithful. Movie audiences were understandably perplexed about the film as well, unsure how to interpret Welles's declaration to the journalist that the average man was 'a monster, a dangerous criminal. . .a mediocrity.' For 'insulting the religion of the state' with this short film, Pasolini was prosecuted and sentenced to prison (his conviction was later overturned). Ironically, his next film, which garnered favourable critic and public approval, was an actual passion play about Christ, *The Gospel According to St Matthew*. Once again, although with less fury and rancour, Pasolini demanded that the Church live up to the promise of Christianity.

Not Gibson's *Passion*

While 2004 may be the year of Passion filmmaker Mel Gibson's martyrdom or villainy, depending on your point of view, there is another recent Jesus film that has gone almost unnoticed. Overshadowed by *The Passion* is British director Philip Saville's *The Gospel of John* (2003) a film whose text is the Gospel of John, word for word from The *Good News Bible* translation by the American Bible Society. Using the biblical text is where the similarity to the grittier Pasolini work ends. Jesus is played by the Shakespearean actor Henry Ian Cusick, whose edgy performance gives great depth to the Johannine scenes in which Jesus tells the crowds that the way to eternal life is to follow him. Under Saville's direction, the shock and disbelief of the Romans and the traditional Jewish leaders seem justified when they hear such extraordinary claims. Perhaps it is the skill of the actors in this interpretation of the Gospel, but Jesus' words to his followers and the audience of the film, present more challenges and nuances than the words of the actors of the son of God in earlier biopics. When Daniel Kash's Peter denies Jesus three times, the spectator can feel how difficult belief is for even the most ardent of Jesus' followers. The film is narrated by Christopher Plummer, whose authoritative voice makes the text sound like gospel. I suspect that the film has not ignited the passions of critics because its emphasis is upon the teachings and ministry of Jesus, rather than the intense violence and suffering that is the focus of Mel Gibson's Passion play. The stentorian tones of Plummer's narration add to the cinematic quality and help to distance the audience from the characters. Thus, one is always a spectator of the Saville *Gospel of John* since the film does not cut into one's passions in the way that the Gibson film threatens one's emotions as it flays the flesh of Jesus.

Shadows of the Bible in Film

Most of the early black films with a religious theme emphasized the great theological antimonies through folkloric symbols and narratives. Right and wrong are played out in all their standard heart-wrenching forms: sin and redemption, seduction and salvation. Spencer Williams was one of the most prolific filmmakers of the 1940s, making nine black-subject films in the decade. His early films were based on religious themes and pious sentiments: *Brother Martin: Servant of Jesus* (1942), *Marchin' On* (1943), *Go Down Death* (1944), *Of One Blood* (1945). There was a variety of similar 1930s films made expressly for a black market, most of which have disappeared from the archives (a few are available in the African-American film heritage video series), such as *Moon over Harlem*, *Lying Lips*, *The Girl from Chicago*, and *The Scar of Shame*. These films were distributed to African-American 'ghetto theaters', but never succeeded on general release. According to film historian Donald Bogle, these early examples of black films may seem naïve or dated today, but were very important to the black audiences for whom they were a source of great pride.

Of particular interest to readers of this collection will be *Blood of Jesus*, written and directed by Spencer Williams in 1941. This fantasy is rooted in the soil of the

African-American South, filled with the sounds of gospel singing and baptisms in the river. Briefly, it relates the story of a wicked crap-shooting fellow who accidentally shoots his newly baptized wife with his hunting rifle. Just after their marriage, Martha asks her husband Raz, 'Why don't you pray and try to get religion? We could be so much happier if you did.' This wish of the young pious woman becomes the soul of the movie. After being shot, lying inert on the bed, Martha is escorted by an angel away from the cabin, away from reality into a somewhat clumsily photographed out-of-body experience. However, dark reality follows Martha in the form of zoot-suited fancy-talking Judas Green, a slick Satan who tempts Martha with fancy clothes and hot 'city life'. Predictably bad turns to worse, water to whiskey and things look very dire indeed for Martha.

The redemption scene at the foot of the Cross glitters with goodness. After being chased out of the juke joint by a bunch of rowdy wicked drink-soaked men, Martha is about to be killed by them on the dusty road between town and cabin. Standing under a crude road sign that points the way to Hell or Zion, Martha and the men hear God's voice: 'He who is without sin, cast the first stone at her!' The crossroads sign dissolves into the Cross of Jesus. Frightened by the spectacle, and presumably by the presence of God, the men run away. Drops of the Precious Blood fall on Martha, and miraculously she is returned alive and awake to her bed in the small cabin . . . Was Martha truly dead? Did prayer actually bring her back to life? The cast includes Cathryn Caviness, Spencer Williams, and Juanita Riley – and has enough sin and redemption for all.

Block that Metaphor!

Another interpretive current, neither culturally nor ethnically interpreting biblical or Christological figures, has been formed by a wave of biblicists and scholars of that broader epithet 'religious studies', using biblical tropes as heuristic tools in analyzing films. While I understand Owens's claim that allegory in a postmodern sense exists 'in the gap between a present and a past (Owens 1992: 68), I have trouble reconciling my own readerly location in this gap between sign and meaning with the biblical texts, where sign and meaning overlap. Too often the comparisons between contemporary films and biblical tropes in recent collections attempt such a false unity, one that bridges an unbridgeable gap. For me, this situation calls for the firmest cry of 'Block that metaphor!' I find McLemore's attempt to trace this connection between filmic and social representation in David Lynch's surrealistic film *Blue Velvet* compelling on a theoretical level, that is, where she presents the various contemporary concepts of allegory, as well as the reactions to Lynch's complex and elusive work. However, I do not think she presents as sophisticated an understanding of the codes in the biblical narratives in her discussion of the possible allegorical interpretation of *Blue Velvet* as 'Christian typology, replete with Jeffrey as the angelic choirboy, Adam in the garden, and Sandy as his Eve' (McLemore 1995: 136). Nowhere does she admit to the 'over the top' quality of such an interpretation.

In an earlier version of this piece, I used biblicist Bernard Scott's *Hollywood Dreams & Biblical Stories* (1994) as a parade example of tropic hermeneutics. Scott's Table of

Contents provided a clue to the matrix of his vision, especially titles such as 'From Graven Image to Dream Factory', 'The Poor You Always Have with You', and 'Loss of Innocence'. My biggest difficulty with Scott's argument is that I got bogged down in the vast unexplored territory that separates the biblical world from which he draws his trope, and the film in which he finds the trope. All of Western culture and knowledge is situated in that world. Try as I might, I could not find the road that Scott had used to lead from Jerusalem to Hollywood, from graven image to dream factory, though it does seem fair to suggest that Hollywood is a world of graven images, of icons, of gods erupting from celluloid, and that the Bible is a dream factory, one that may have been in business longer than any other in the Western world.

In my view Scott's most successful chapter is 'From the Destruction of the Temple to *Mad Max*', a discussion of biblical apocalypticism, particularly in Matthew and Mark, and science-fiction imagery. While I think some of his film analyses are cursory at best, especially *Metropolis* (1926), with its tempting Eve/Eden motifs, and *Blade Runner* (1982), the chapter illustrates the real plus to a cinematic reading by a biblical scholar. Scott gives a credible reading to *Mad Max Beyond Thunderdome* (1985), connecting it, as a part of the sci-fi genre dedication, to global destruction, doom and dewy-damp rebirth. He also gives a marvellous thumbnail of recent New Testament criticism focusing upon the dark warnings from the Gospels. I may well be missing Scott's intentions, but I long for a genuine connection, of character, of plot, something more than proclamations of doom two thousand years apart.

Scott is certainly not the only biblical scholar to hitch his Bible to the Hollywood sign. Nor is he the only moviegoer who seeks to transform the celluloid Prince of Darkness into the Prince of Peace. The books of Holloway, Kreitzer, May, and Miles all climb similar scaffolding, that is, either biblical echoes in contemporary films, or a reading of the appropriation of a biblical narrative into a biblical epic film. Kreitzer's two books (1993, 1994) are the weakest, mere retelling of the filmic plots, pointing out where they differ from the written biblical narratives. Miles (1996) gives a strong theoretical grounding, with a focus on the desirability of cultural readings, but most of her readings seem vague to me, putting the films into the service of some meta-topic of 'religious thought'. I would recommend her book for students to get a sense of how one might think about film in a religious studies context.

The use of the biblical narrative by the 1950s dream-spinners had much more to do with the end of World War II, and the pre-eminence of the USA and the Soviet Union in the Cold War, than with the quest for religion on the big screen. The American 1950s of homemaking and prosperity was yoked to the fear of Communism that pervaded both domestic politics and foreign policy. The somewhat heavy-handed triumph of good over evil was easily achieved through the familiar biblical narrative tradition. Like an unwrapped box of rich chocolates, sword and sandal films have sorely tempted the vast majority of religious studies readers/spectators of film. I do not exempt myself from waves of feeling obliged to find fragments of Jesus or biblical morality behind every camera lens. A shift away from Christological to cultural understandings would, in my opinion, move our analyses away from New Critical symbolic patterning. It might (or not?) be more enlightening to uncover the cultural engines that spit out Bible movies, one stiffly secular, the other so certain about right and honour and God on our side.

In spite of, or perhaps because of the stringent Production Code that has maintained stringent control over Hollywood productions since 1934, a group of religious Protestants and Catholics censored films to make sure they were 'clean family entertainment'. For more than three decades these men tried to incorporate their theological values into the very marrow of movie-making. And what could reflect righteous purity more than the Bible itself? And what could be more protective for the assimilationist Jews of Hollywood, who produced much of Hollywood's American myth (see below), than the Christianized biblical epics, where the theology was more America as God's chosen people in God's chosen land than any biblical version of chosenness? Delighted with celluloid Scripture, the Hays Commission overlooked the half-naked stars, suggestive dancing, and frequent passionate embraces in the sword and sandal films, after all, that was how people, especially pagans, behaved in those days.

At the time of the great sword and sandal productions, the American film industry was operated by Eastern European Jews who themselves seemed to be anything but the quintessence of America. The Jewish moguls envisioned behind the barricades of gentile gentility the respectability and status that they envied. The movies were to become the bridge into the American dream, for the dream makers as well as the other European minorities who shared their dream and aspirations. For the white immigrant working class, the picture palace was a view into American royalty.

Most of these films were produced for the 1950s American culture by Hollywood power-brokers who created other America-first-and-best myths too. Hollywood was under siege by the anti-Communist madness, a time when accusations without proof were immediately granted the status of truth, when guilt was assumed, and innocence had to be documented. Of all cultural scholars looking at the biblical epics of the 1950s, surely the power of the right-wing politicians to give or withhold 'clearance [of accused actors, directors, writers]. . .repudiating all liberal opinions and associations, former Communists were required to perform a humiliating public ritual of expiation by naming names of other Hollywood Communists' (Sklar 1994: 266). In a time when any ideas outside the picket-fence norm were being challenged, what could be safer than the certainty of the Bible? The iconoclasm of the class comedies of the 1930s, and the violence and shabby good guys of *film noir*, were abandoned. The 1940s feminist working girls and Jezebels played by Joan Crawford, Bette Davis, and Katharine Hepburn, were replaced by the soda fountains and pony-tails of Annette Funicello, Doris Day, and Debbie Reynolds. No one in Hollywood was willing to take the slightest chance on anybody or anything. Safety, caution, and respectability were the watchwords of the studio chiefs, and controversial or even serious subject matter was avoided at all costs.

West of Eden

A thread of good versus evil that characterized the 1950s was the intelligent Western, typified by George Stevens's *Shane* (1953). I am still ambivalent about *Shane*, particularly as a Christ vehicle. But whether one sees the light of Shane (Alan Ladd) or the dark of Jack Wilson (Jack Palance) as the metaphorical jewel of the film, *Shane* is certainly among the most cinematic. One could set a documentary on garbage-collection in the Grand Tetons and elevate its stature by that fact alone. Put a film of real substance in such a setting and the table is definitely set. *Shane* is beautiful to watch. In some scenes the film's setting, those towering mountain peaks and big sky, over-powers its characters, diffusing them into the vast scenery.

Using his considerable skills as a Christian film critic, Baugh chooses *Shane* as an important cinematic contribution to the mythic realm, in which there is a glorious fusion of theology and film. Baugh sees the film in a more Christian light than I do; he visually and thematically notes the similarities of the Christian story, including the movement through the graveyard to the rising sun as metaphorical of the Paschal mystery. Shane works for me when I decide not to see it as a theologized Western, but rather as a reflection of post-war desires for Americans to return to the myths of fron-tier courage and nation building. Alan Ladd's title character is almost a total non sequitur, as creamy as Doris Day, too clean, too smooth, too unmarked by the broiling sun and the prickly underbrush. In his suede buckskins and well-trimmed hair, he is an improbable outdoorsman. Two Clint Eastwood films, *High Plains Drifter* (1973) and *Pale Rider* (1985), reference *Shane* wholeheartedly (all three films draw on the same fun-damental myth), though flint-faced and implicitly mysterious, Clint Eastwood's char-acters remain rather stereotypic, as though moodiness, squints, and long silences lead to a spectator's definition of goodness and depth of character. Shane is truly mysteri-ous, and perhaps even more unreal, because he is so completely incongruous. As a pos-sibly supernatural guardian of a vast landscape, Ladd's near-flatline characterization is more prayer than person, more ethereal than tumbledown. Less than ten years after this bravura performance he attempted suicide, and died at the age of 51 a year later of 'an overdose of alcohol'. Alan Ladd's blond good looks, charisma and stoic presence never were marred by age. In that way, he is different from the other Western icon, Clint Eastwood.

Many analysts use Clint Eastwood as the parade example of redemption, a move-ment from Dirty Harry, a wooden, wicked action figure, to the Academy-award Western *Unforgiven*. This story worked to redeem Eastwood as well as the Western itself, tagged an 'anti-violence Western', that gave Eastwood forgiveness for his past hard-living film persona. While I know nothing of the real Clint, it seems that his gentleness developed parallel to his aging visage, not to a spiritual transformation.

A buckskin knight, Alan Ladd rides into the middle of a range war in frontier Wyoming between farmers and cattlemen, quickly siding with the 'sod-busters'. The title character is a taciturn former gunslinger who wishes only to settle down and put the past behind him. But as ruthless ranchers bring a diamond-hard hired gunman to the frontier town to scare off his adopted family, Shane realizes that he is the only law available to protect the innocent farmers. Similar to other films in the Western mythog-raphy, the homesteaders represent law and order and civilization. The negative side of the antimony is weighed down by the wicked lawlessness of the restless cattle rustlers.

To illustrate the visceral effect of the violence, director George Stevens had the sounds of gunshots magnified on the soundtrack: nothing like this had been previously attempted in mainstream Hollywood and the results were galvanizing. It is difficult to pretend this is a film about peace when gunfights abound, and characters are visibly hurt, writhing in pain, and frequently killed. The risks and inevitable emotional toll of the profession gives Shane's silence immense power and offers a side of the Western movie hero seldom seen to that point. But try as I will, *Shane* is clearly a *Western*, although the Starrett family in other costumes could have passed for 1950s suburbanites.

Shane discovers the Starretts (Jean Arthur and Van Heflin), a pioneer farm family looking for a hired hand. Suddenly, Ryker and his posse of gun-toting ruffians ride by and threaten to run Starrett off his farm. Ryker, a ruthless businessman, has been trying to rid the valley of homesteaders so he can expand his ranch. After witnessing this brutality, Shane decides to stay on and help out. Provoked by Ryker's boys, Shane joins the homesteader's fight, facing off with a hired gunslinger to make the valley safe for civilized folks like the Starretts. While working on the spread and trying to keep the homestead safe for 'his family,' Shane falls in love with Jean Arthur (who wouldn't?), but showing his transformed goodness, he keeps his distance. One of the best interpreters of Western film genre, Jane Tompkins reads the tension between Shane and Marian Starrett as a genre stereotype of women. Even Marian, Tompkins argues, one of the few women in Western films who we are made to feel is also 'substantial as a person, dissolves into an ineffectual harangue at the end, unsuccessfully pleading with her man not to go into town to get shot. When the crunch comes, women shatter into words' (Tompkins 1993: 63).

As was the case with the Eastwood characters, the disharmony required to call the supernatural guardian into human form has manifested and Shane has appeared. Shane comes from 'nowhere' and eventually returns to that no-place, where even the innocent Brandon De Wilde may not follow. Shane is surely the Other, at least in the culture of range-war mythology. He resembles no one and exhibits few human traits aside from the most superficial. No one, neither sodbuster nor cowpuncher, knows quite what to make of him. He seems friendly but this may be just the side-effect of a complete absence of the reactionism displayed by many of the film's other characters, an entirely different orientation from the merely friendly. Shane is part of no relationship with man or woman and never will be, as he turns from the glorious Jean Arthur and the longing of her young son. Shane clearly returns her love, but from a place as remote and stoic as a calm morning. There are wisps of implication that Shane may have a past but they vanish quickly; subatomic resonances of Shane's transient human form. Shane is there. But in many ways he is not. Of course, director George Stevens probably did not ascribe to any paranormal vision when making the film. But things often happen even when they are not intended, certainly in art.

The film proceeds somewhat formulaically until its chief villains, the cattle-ranching Ryker brothers call up a dark force to oppose Shane's angel of light. The Rykers pioneered the vast valley for open range, against nature and its indigenous inhabitants and are ready to kill to keep their range from being homesteaded. They summon the gunfighter, Jack Wilson, played definitively by the young Jack Palance. His Wilson is a killer of such distilled lethality that just looking at him might turn you to stone. Whenever Wilson is on screen, time seems to slow down as it is refracted by his menacing gravity. The first meeting of Shane and Wilson, at the homestead of Joe Starrett (Van Heflin), is riveting. The Rykers are making the rounds, issuing their final warning to the farmers, accompanied for maximum effect by the recently arrived Wilson. Not a word is exchanged as the two entities unblinkingly size each other up. Dialogue continues in the background but you barely hear it as Wilson, who has dismounted for a drink of water, places a foot in a stirrup then almost levitates back into the saddle, grinning like death, having never taken his eyes off Shane from the first moment, finally backing his horse out of Starrett's yard in order to keep Shane in focus. A later sequence where Wilson meticulously executes Elisha Cook Jr.'s homesteader, a punched-out Civil War veteran with exponentially more pride than sense, probably ranks with the most powerful ever filmed. Rolling thunder clouds open for a moment and bathe the homesteader in bright light as he almost turns back on the way to his doom, then they close and roll on as he rejects his last chance. A number of theologically lensed critics consider this the Christ headed to Golgotha moment. And one can stretch a point, consider Alan Ladd bathed in Jack Wilson's black light, suddenly becomes an avenging angel, if a somewhat diffident 1950s one.

Probably the best study of the Western from a theoretical perspective is Tompkins's *West of Everything*. I particularly recommend her understanding of the finitude of the landscape in the Western – as opposed to the mythic shift to infinite space in the hero-action films that followed, where the hero rode a rocket ship instead of a Palomino. The desert location, she argues, is like the world before Eden, dry, dusty, no people, no trees, brutal. I would push the analogy further to say that the desert landscape sounds like God's punishment to Adam: rife with thistles, unyielding, sweated ground (Gen. 3:17–19).

The location for Everyman seeking to live a moral life resists him; the horizon recedes forever beneath the sky:

> The desert pushes the consciousness of the hero and the reader/viewer beyond itself and into another realm . . . It is not only the body that is tested here; the desert is a spiritual proving ground as well. The landscape, which on the one hand drives Christianity away, ends by forcing men to see something godlike there. (Tompkins 1993: 85)

Much Further West

Charles Ketcham's piece, 'One Flew Over the Cuckoo's Nest: A Salvific Drama of Liberation' had its ups and downs for me. At the outset I should say that aside from his religiosity, Ketcham's work in general is some of the best in finding the religious patterns in film. His work on Ingmar Bergman and Federico Fellini is illuminating and opens up new avenues for discussion for religionists. In his analysis of Milos Forman's *One Flew Over the Cuckoo's Nest* I certainly agreed with Ketcham's characterization of the American audience's appetite for explorations of freedom and human dignity often obtained through violence, and with his observation that the Forman film is more nuanced than the Kesey novel from which it is drawn. However, treating the Jack Nicholson character McMurphy as the Suffering Servant is too romantic for me. Ketcham argues that McMurphy has been crucified by lobotomy:

> Chief Bromden, seeing the stigmata, holds McMurphy in a position reminiscent of the Pieta. Saying 'You're coming with me,' the chief suffocates the persecuted body, pulls the great marble stone water dispenser out of the floor releasing fountains of 'living water,' hurls it through a window and escapes. The jubilation in the ward has all the ringing affirmation of the shouts 'He is Risen!' (May 1992: 132)

Silenced by those in power, the Nicholson character is a martyr, but hardly Christ, whose death and resurrection overturned the powers and principalities forever. That is quite a leap from the victim McMurphy, whose cinematic death is anticlimactic after the lobotomy. Further, Ketcham suggests other Christocentric imagery that seems extreme, for instance, that the patients ingest their daily meds as though they were receiving the Eucharist. In spite of the temptation to draw straight lines from the Christ story to the Cuckoo's Nest, that is just too hard for me to swallow.

Both *2001* and another classic Kubrick film, *Dr. Strangelove or How I Learned to Stop Worrying and Love the Bomb* (1964) focus upon human predilection for designing machinery that functions with perfect logic to bring about a disastrous outcome. The US nuclear deterrent and the Russian doomsday machine function exactly as they are intended, and destroy life on earth. The computer HAL 9000 in *2001* serves the space mission by attacking the astronauts.

Sadly Kubrick's *Dr. Strangelove* does not seem dated or irrelevant 40 years after its release. Peter Sellers in one of his bravura three-for-one performances plays the multiple roles of Dr. Strangelove, Captain Mandrake, and President Merkin Muffley. My favourite scene features George C. Scott, whose character, Gen. Buck Turgidson, is informing the president that it is quite likely a B-52 bomber will be able to fly under Russian radar and deliver its payload even though the entire Soviet air force knows where the plane is headed. 'He can barrel in that baby so low!' Scott says, with his arms spread wide like wings, and his head shaking in admiration at how good his pilots are. While such performances parading the staggering US military might are now found on the Evening News and all day long on Cable, military and civilian player alike seem to reflect the lunatic actors.

When the black comedy was released, according to Terry Southern, who was hired by Kubrick to rewrite the script of *Strangelove*:

> Columbia was embarrassed by the picture and tried to get people to see Carl Foreman's *The Victors* instead. They would steer ticket buyers away from *Strangelove* and try to get them to see *The Victors*. At the time we thought we were going to be totally wiped out. People would call up the box office and be told there were no seats for *Strangelove* and asked if they would like to see *The Victors* instead. Gradually, the buzz along the rialto built word of mouth in our favor.

One can understand the executives at Columbia Pictures being nervous about portraying mad over-the-top Pentagon types with glazed grins and shining eyes, trembling with excitement about world destruction and apocalypse. The end of the film trembles with the uncertainty of the Cold War: after the first nuclear blast, Kubrick cuts back to the War Room, where Strangelove muses that deep mines could be used to shelter survivors, whose descendants could return to the surface in 90 years. The film abruptly ends in a too familiar montage of mushroom clouds, while Vera Lynn sings ''Til We Meet Again.' These sugary lyrics underscore the death-dealing, ironic vision of Kubrick.

> We'll meet again, don't know where, don't know when
> But I'm sure we'll meet again some sunny day
> Keep smiling through, just the way you used to do
> Till the blue skies chase the dark clouds far away.

''Til We Meet Again', written by Ross Parker and Hughie Charles, was a big-band hit in the era of World War II, making the musical reference even more pointed.

Another Kubrick political film was made when the director was only 31 years old, openly defying the Hollywood studio heads by using blacklisted screenwriters. With an intelligent screenplay by then-blacklisted writer Dalton Trumbo, based on a novel by semi-blacklisted writer Howard Fast, its message of moral integrity and courageous conviction is still quite powerful. The all-star cast, including Charles Laughton in plus-size toga, is full of entertaining surprises. Fully restored in 1991 to include scenes deleted from the original 1960 release, the full-length *Spartacus* is a grand-scale cinematic marvel, offering some of the most stunningly choreographed battles ever filmed and a central performance by Douglas that's as sensitively emotional as it is intensely heroic. Jean Simmons plays the slave woman who becomes Spartacus's wife, and Peter Ustinov steals the show with his frequently hilarious, Oscar-winning performance as a slave trader who shamelessly curries favour with his Roman superiors. Significantly the restored version includes a formerly deleted bathhouse scene in which Laurence Olivier (dubbed by Anthony Hopkins) plays a bisexual Roman senator who gets very sweaty over a slave played by Tony Curtis.

Looking for Jesus

There are other concerns that I have with religious patterns and symbols found in films. The primary one is about fashion in interpretation, that sinkhole caused by the suction of sentimentality. In a religionist's eagerness to read through his or her Guilded lens, Christ easily appears whenever a character suffers or appears doomed but likeable. I will illustrate this with two examples from my own rococo readings, both from Scorsese films, since my affinity with his work is apparent from this chapter. It is not much of a stretch to see Christological metaphor in one of Scorsese's earliest films. In *Boxcar Bertha* (1972) the main character Bill Shelby (Keith Carradine) gives his life for the poor and oppressed people with whom he is travelling. After a series of bad-luck actions, Bill and Bertha, the young Barbara Hershey (later to become Scorsese's Magdalene), began robbing trains and living the Bonnie and Clyde life. Be careful. Press the Jesus button and you will get an interpretation that glamorizes the life of youth violence and the hard-scrapple poor, glorifying Shelby for giving everything for the poor, even unto death. Scorsese pushes the redemption button himself: Shelby is nailed by his enemies to the side of the boxcar. Budget crucifixion aside, the film is really more gangster-with-a-heart film, whose main cinematic interest is tracing the antimonies of violence and redemption, poverty and cleansing blood, in Scorsese's work.

The second example comes from one of my students, who found the image of Jesus baked into the celluloid of *Gangs of New York* (2002), arguing that the Leo DiCaprio character takes on his father's mantle of leadership in the community and prepares to risk his life to help the oppressed poor (read rowdy Bowery boys) living in the tenements of the Lower East Side on New York. For me, DiCaprio is biding his time until he can kill the man who killed his father, Daniel Day Lewis, whose violent, but oddly benevolent, character begins a complex relationship with the brash DiCaprio – totally male, stylish, and not riveted with the nails of faith. Glitzier than *Goodfellas*, a spectacle that highlights the growing pains of New York's working class the way *Giant* captured the bitter struggles in nascent Texas between the cattle and oil interests, *Gangs of New York* culminates in a huge street fight with blood and death and very little redemption. Unlike the true films that cause one to generate Christological interpretations, the ending is total Hollywood brawl. This history of Irish and Italian toughs in nineteenth-century slum streets of New York was shot in and around Rome. Like Pasolini, unhappy with the visuals of the Holy Land, Scorsese could not find locations in New York City that were sufficiently pre-industrial to get the look he desired.

A final caveat. Fairy tales are not gospels. Is it valid to look at films such as *Edward Scissorhands* (1990), *The Terminator* (1984), or any other popular film through a religious lens? Can one find suffering, redemption, and, most prized, a 'Jesus figure', behind any camera lens? This trend of swollen metaphors frequently becomes the beast that ate narrative. Sometimes a shy, gentle creature who lives on the outskirts of society is not Jesus, no matter how miraculous his topiary creations. Sometimes a human-looking, apparently unstoppable cyborg is just the governor of California.

References and Further Reading

Babington, B. and Evans, P. W. (1993). *Biblical Epics: Sacred Narrative in the Hollywood Cinema*. Manchester: Manchester University Press.

Bach, Alice (ed.) (1996). *Biblical Glamor and Hollywood Glitz: Semeia 74*. Atlanta, GA: Scholars Press.

Bach, Alice (2004). *Religion, Politics: Media in the Broadband Era*. Sheffield: Sheffield Phoenix Press.

Baugh, Lloyd S. J. (1997). *Imaging the Divine: Jesus and Christ Figures in Film*. Kansas City, KS: Sheed and Ward.

Bliss, Michael (1995). *The Word Made Flesh: Catholicism and Conflict in the Films of Martin Scorsese*. Lanham, MD: Scarecrow Press.

Butler, Ivan (1969). *Religion in Cinema*. New York: A. S. Barnes and Co.

Byars, Jackie (1991). *All That Hollywood Allows*. Chapel Hill, NC: University of North Carolina Press.

Cohen, Sarah Blacher (ed.) (1983). *From Hester Street to Hollywood: The Jewish-American Stage and Screen*. Bloomington, IN: Indiana University Press.

Forshey, Gerald E. (1992). *American Religious and Biblical Spectaculars*. Westport, CT: Praeger Publishers.

Friedman, Lester D. (1987). *The Jewish Image in American Film*. Secaucus, NJ: Citadel Press.

Holloway, Ronald (1977). *Beyond the Image: Approaches to the Religious Dimensions in the Cinema*.

Geneva: World Council of Churches in cooperation with Interfilm.

hooks, bell (1993). *Black Looks: Race and Representation*. Boston, Mass.: Southend Press.

Jasper, David (ed.) (2004). *The Sacred Desert: Religion, Art, Literature, and Culture*. Oxford: Blackwell.

Jewett, Robert (1993). *St. Paul at the Movies: The Apostle's Dialogue with American Culture*. Louisville, KY: Westminster; John Knox Press.

Johnson, Eithne (1998). 'The Emergence of Christian Video and the Cultivation of Video-vangelism', in Linda Kintz and Julia Lesage (eds), *Media, Culture, and the Religious Right*. Minneapolis, MN: University of Minnesota Press, pp. 191–210.

Ketcham, Charles B. (1976). *Federico Fellini: The Search for a New Mythology*. New York: Paulist Press.

Kreitzer, Larry J. (1993). *The New Testament in Fiction and Film*. Sheffield: JSOT Press.

Kreitzer, Larry J. (1994). *The Old Testament in Fiction and Film*. Sheffield: Sheffield Academic Press.

Lyon, David (2000). *Jesus in Disneyland: Religion in Postmodern Times*. Cambridge: Polity Press.

Marsh, Clive and Ortiz, Gaye (1998). *Exploration in Theology and Film: Movies and Meaning*. Oxford: Blackwell.

Martin, Joel W. and Oswalt, Conrad E. Jr., (ed.) (1995). *Screening the Sacred: Religion, Myth, and Ideology in Popular American Film*. Boulder, CO: Westview Press.

Martin, Thomas M. (1991). *Images and Imageless: A Study in Religious Consciousness and Film*. Lewisburg, PA: Bucknell University Press; London Associated University Presses.

May, John R. and Bird, Michael (eds) (1982). *Religion in Film*. Knoxville, TN: University of Tennessee Press.

May, John R. and Bird, Michael (eds) (1992). *Image and Likeness: Religious Visions in American Film Classics*. New York: Paulist Press.

McLemore, Elizabeth (1995). 'From Revelation to Dream: Allegory in David Lynch's *Blue Velvet*', in Martin, J. W. and Oswalt, C. E. Jr. (eds) *Screening the Sacred: Religion, Myth, and Ideology in Popular American Film*. Boulder, Co: Westview Press, pp. 134–41.

Miles, Margaret (1996). *Seeing is Believing: Religion and Values in the Movies*. Boston: Beacon Press.

Owens, Craig (1992). *Beyond Recognition: Representation, Power, and Culture*, edited by Scott Bryson, Barbara Kruger, Lynne Tillman and Jane Weinstock. Berkeley: University of California Press.

Rohdie, Sam (1995). *The Passion of Pier Paolo Pasolini*. Bloomington, IN: Indiana University Press.

Sanders, Theresa (2002). *Celluloid Saints: Images of Sanctity in Film*. Macon, GA: Mercer University Press.

Scorsese, Martin (1989). *Scorsese on Scorsese*. London: Faber and Faber.

Scott, Bernard Brandon (1994). *Hollywood Dreams & Biblical Stories*. Minneapolis, MN: Fortress Press.

Sklar, Robert (1994). *Movie-made America: A Cultural History of American Movies*. New York: Vintage Books.

Stack, Oswald (1969). *Pasolini on Pasolini: Interviews*. Bloomington, IN: Indiana University Press.

Tompkins, Jane (1993). *West of Everything: The Inner Life of Westerns*. New York: Oxford University Press.

Vigano, D. E. (2005). *Gesù e la macchina da presa: Dizionario ragionato del cinema cristologico*. The Vatican: Lateran University Press.

Zeffirelli, Franco (1984). *Franco Zeffirelli's Jesus: A Spiritual Diary*. San Francisco: Harper & Row.

CHAPTER 17
Music

John W. Rogerson

In this brief study of the Bible in music, attention will focus upon works which have used the words of the Bible or which have dramatized stories found in the Bible and the Apocrypha. The reason for this restriction is that there are few pieces of music whose 'programme' is taken from the Bible, that is, instrumental works which seek, without the help of words, to portray or evoke biblical passages, scenes or themes. A notable exception is Joseph Haydn's *The Seven Words of Jesus Christ*, op. 51, nos 1–7, which was commissioned around 1785 to be used in the Cathedral at Cadiz during a service at which a sermon was preached on each of the seven words of Jesus from the Cross. Best known today as a string quartet (the composer also produced versions for full orchestra and for piano solo), the work consists of seven movements, each of which tries to evoke the mood of a particular word of Christ. There is also an introduction, and a concluding movement that seeks to portray the earthquake that immediately followed Christ's death (Matt. 27:51). The works that will be principally discussed will be oratorios and operas, and it must be made clear at the outset that the article is not a piece of music criticism, which would lie outside the competence of the contributor, but an exercise in biblical interpretation. Its aim is to make readers sensitive to what is happening in biblical interpretation where this is a feature of a work of music.

By far the best point at which to begin such an exercise is with what is probably the best known and most popular of all oratorios, G. F. Handel's *Messiah*, first performed in Dublin in April 1742. From the standpoint of a biblical scholar, *Messiah* is a strange work. It does not begin, as does the popular service of Nine Lessons and Carols on Christmas Eve, with the account of the fall of the human race in Genesis 3 and the promise of one who will 'bruise the head' of the serpent (understood traditionally as the devil). It opens with words from Isaiah 40 addressed to the Israelites in exile in Babylon. It contains no account of Christ's passion, although this is presupposed in Part II, and Part III seems to be more concerned with the resurrection of believers than with the resurrection of Christ. Nowhere in the work is the question raised or answered as to what is meant by the title *Messiah*. For most performers and listeners, these problems do not arise. The music is understandably all that matters. However, the strangeness of the selection of the parts of the Bible that were chosen by Handel's librettist, Charles Jennens, becomes explicable when set in the context of the theological controversies that raged at the time (see especially Smith 1995: 145–6).

The late seventeenth and the first part of the eighteenth century in England saw a bitter debate between orthodox Christians and deists. The latter believed in God, immortality and the ultimate punishment of the wicked and the reward of the righteousness, but believed that these truths could be known by human reason. There was thus no need for revealed religions, with belief in miraculous occurrences that made nonsense of science, and dogmas such as the Trinity which offended human reason. The Old Testament was particularly despised by the deists on account of its debased morality (e.g. Joshua's indiscriminate slaughter of the Canaanites) and its lack of a belief in an afterlife. No doubt there were also political motives behind the deist attacks on the Old Testament, because the latter was appealed to in support of the position of the monarchy in England (see Reventlow 1980/1984). For defenders of Christian orthodoxy, the Old Testament was crucial because it was believed to contain prophecies that had been fulfilled in the coming of Christ. The prophecy and fulfilment scheme guaranteed both the divine inspiration of the Bible and the truth of Christianity.

Within the context of this bitter dispute, Jennens's selection of passages becomes understandable. As a defender of orthodoxy, he chose Old Testament passages that were either quoted in the New Testament, or were strongly implied. *Messiah* begins with words from Isaiah 40 because that is where the first three Gospels begin when they describe the public ministry of Jesus. The fullest, and most explicit version is found in Luke 3:4–6 which quotes Isaiah 40:3–5 and 52:10, from which numbers 2 to 4 of *Messiah* are taken (Isa. 52:10 'And all flesh shall see the salvation of God' is very close to 40:5, 'And the glory of the Lord'). *Messiah* continues with Haggai 2:6–7 and Malachi 3:1 with the words 'the Lord whom ye seek, shall suddenly come to his temple', clearly echoing the New Testament incident of the 'Cleansing of the Temple' (Matt. 21:12–13). 'The people that walked in darkness' (number 11) taken from Isaiah 9:2 is quoted in Matthew 4:15–16 while the aria, 'He shall feed his flock', links these words from Isaiah 41:11 with words adapted from Matthew 11:28–9, 'his yoke is easy, his burden is light'. With Part II of *Messiah*, the passages from Isaiah 53:3–6 (numbers 24 to 26 in the oratorio) are quoted and alluded to at Matthew 8:17 and 1 Peter 2:24–5. Smith (1995: 149) does not exaggerate when she says that possibly as many as 51 of the 80 biblical verses in *Messiah* 'are either conscious quotations, or echoes, of the Old Testament in the New'. Seen in this light, *Messiah* was a deliberate attempt to uphold the orthodox view that the coming of Christ had been foreseen by the prophets of the Old Testament, and that this confirmed both the supernatural origin of the prophecies and the truth of Christianity. That none of this will be apparent to almost all performers/listeners of *Messiah* is probably an indication of the fact that *Messiah* contains no overt theological message or significance in today's world, which is perhaps why it remains so popular in a largely post-Christian world.

Whether the same can be said of a work that reached its definitive form only six years earlier than *Messiah*, Bach's *St Matthew Passion* is a matter for debate (the work was first performed in Leipzig on Good Friday 1727 and revised in 1736). But if Bach's masterpiece does not convey a spiritual message in today's world, this is not what Bach and his librettist C. F. Henrici (also known as Picander) intended. Whereas *Messiah* begins with an orchestral overture that could have preceded any oratorio or opera, the 'Passion' begins with an elaborate choral movement whose purpose is to provide the theology in terms of which all that follows is to be understood. This is necessary because the accounts of the passion of Jesus in the first three gospels contain little or no explanation of the significance of the events. It is in the letters of the New Testament, especially those of Paul, that the belief of the early Church is expressed that through Christ's death on the cross, God was reconciling the world to himself by enabling the human race to be forgiven for, and to overcome, human wickedness (2 Cor. 5:19). The passion of Jesus is thus a thoroughly paradoxical set of events. Viewed humanly, it is a crime carried out by humanity on an innocent victim. Viewed divinely and from the perspective of faith, it is God's act of gracious love which takes from evil its power to enslave humanity permanently.

The opening movement of the 'Passion' seeks to explore and resolve these paradoxes. It employs three choirs. One, representing the daughters of Jerusalem, calls upon the other to share its mourning for what is about to happen. However, the second choir can only ask the questions 'whom?', 'where?', 'how?' in response to these entreaties, thus indicating that the meaning of the Passion is not self-evident. As though to answer these questions, a choir of boys' voices, interwoven with the other two choirs, sings the hymn 'O Lamb of God unspotted', which makes it clear that had Christ not died on the cross, the human race would be without hope. Bartelmus (1998: 33 note 86) has argued that the opening chorus draws upon the Song of Songs (6:1), in referring to Christ as the bridegroom, and thus to the ancient tradition that in the Song of Songs the bridegroom is Christ and the bride is the Church or the individual believer. The reference to the Lamb of God in both the hymn sung by the boys' choir and the words used by the first choir joins Isaiah 53:7 with John 1:29. According to Wolff (2001: 302), the reference to the Lamb is also an allusion to the fact that in the book of Revelation it is the Lamb who is the ruler of the eternal Jerusalem (cf. Rev. 22:3). In contrast to *Messiah*, which sets biblical passages to music without comment, the *St Matthew Passion* follows a long line of tradition in interspersing the biblical passages with arias, choruses and hymns that form a running commentary on the biblical text, indicating how it is to be understood and how worshippers/listeners should respond personally. While the transfer of a work intended for devotions in church on Good Friday to the concert hall may offend some, the fact that this is done indicates that both the Passion story and Bach's music have the power to reach beyond the confines of the church to the world outside.

The next work to be considered is Handel's oratorio *Jephthah* which was composed in 1751 (Gunn 2005: 148). Anyone familiar with the biblical story in Judges 11 will be surprised by the version produced by Handel and his librettist, Thomas Morell. In the biblical account, Jephthah vows to God that if he (Jephthah) is successful in defeating the Ammonites, he will offer as a burnt sacrifice the first person who comes to meet him 'from the doors of his house' on his return (Judg. 11:30–1). The first person to meet him turns out to be his only daughter, and after giving her two months in which to bewail her fate with her companions, Jephthah carries out the vow which he had vowed. Handel's *Jephthah* has a 'happy' ending in that the intervention of an angel leads to the modification of Jephthah's action against his daughter. Instead of offering her as a sacrifice, Jephthah consigns her to perpetual virginity and to the service of God. Further, the daughter, unnamed in the Bible, is called Iphis in the oratorio.

In fact, Handel and his librettist were heirs to a lengthy tradition that Jephthah had not carried out his vow to the letter; and the name Iphis is but one of more than 40 names given by different writers to the unnamed daughter (Liptzin 1992: 392). The first interpreter to suggest that the daughter was not sacrificed was the Jewish scholar David Kimchi (1160?–1235?) who wrote, 'he built a house for her and made her live there, and she was separated from human kind and the ways of the world; and it became a decree in Israel that each year the daughters of Israel should go to see her' (Kimchi 1959: 66, my translation). Kimchi's explanation is based on a possible reading of the Hebrew text whereby the words 'and she knew no man. And it was a custom in Israel that the daughters of Israel went . . . four days in a year' are taken as a description of *how* Jephthah fulfilled his vow. Moore (1895:304) lists Jewish and Christian interpreters who had followed Kimchi, and Poole, in his influential commentary of 1685, although not agreeing with such interpreters, felt that their view was sufficiently widespread to deserve discussion and refutation (Poole 1962: 484–5). It is perhaps significant that the Authorized Version had the rendering 'she knew no man' whereas the Revised Version has 'she had not known a man', a translation that rules out the possibility that the daughter's fate was enforced virginity. Bartelmus (1998: 75) draws attention to the possible influence of Genesis 22 on the 'happier' interpretation of the Jephthah story, where the intervention of an angel saves Isaac from the fate of being sacrificed by Abraham. However, in the context of eighteenth-century Europe, the important point is that Handel's oratorio preserves and expresses an interpretation of the biblical text that seeks to ameliorate an otherwise morally difficult episode.

Quite different principles are at work in Handel's oratorio *Belshazzar*, composed in 1744. The only biblical material available occurs in Daniel 5, and deals mainly with the ability of the Hebrew captive, Daniel, to interpret the mysterious writing on the wall which is the divine response to the defilement at a feast presided over by Belshazzar of the vessels taken from the Jerusalem temple. The only historical information given comes at the end of the chapter in the cryptic words 'In that night was Belshazzar the Kings of the Chaldeans slain, and Darius the Median took the Kingdom . . .' (Daniel 5:30–1). Whereas William Walton's *Belshazzar's Feast* of 1931 concentrates on the opening and concluding verses of Daniel 5 together with a setting of Psalm 137 (By the Waters of Babylon), Handel's work is centred upon the battle in which Cyrus, king of Persia, captured Babylon. It opens with recitatives and an aria by Nitocris, the queen mother, in which she bewails the futility of attempts to form vast human empires. Daniel enters, and assures her that while Babylon's fate is sealed, this is part of the divine will, and thus for the good. The scene now switches to Cyrus and his besieging army, and a discussion between the king and a commander, Gobrias, who has deserted from the Babylonians to the Persians following the murder of his son by Belshazzar. The futility of a long siege is acknowledged, and a plan is devised whereby the dams that enable the River Euphrates to protect Babylon will be destroyed. The Persians will enter the city on the night of a great feast in honour of the god Sesach, when Babylonian vigilance will be at a minimum. At the feast called for by Belshazzar, his mother Nitocris reproves the king for misusing the sacred vessels from the Jerusalem temple, and is herself reproved in the words 'is then my mother convert grown to Jewish superstition? Apostate queen!' Meanwhile the Persian plan to drain the Euphrates begins to take effect. At the feast, as Belshazzar sings 'Where is the God of Judah's boasted pow'r? Let him reclaim his lost magnificence . . . and vindicate his injur'd honour!', the hand appears and writes on the wall. To the deeply disturbed king, Nitocris (cf. Dan. 5:10 where 'the queen' exercises this role) draws attention to Daniel's gifts of interpretation, he is summoned and explains the writing. Meanwhile, Gobrias and Cyrus have entered the city and a messenger informs Belshazzar of this. In an ensuing battle (covered by a Sinfonia) Belshazzar and his attendants are slain, Cyrus is greeted by Daniel in the name of the God of Israel, and Cyrus promises to release the Jewish captives and to rebuild Jerusalem and its temple. Nitocris offer her submission to Cyrus and is assured by him that she will remain a queen with Cyrus as her son. A chorus based on Psalm 145:1–2 concludes the work.

The modern listener or performer who is familiar with Daniel 5 will ask where all these details about the battle for Babylon have come from. Although Smith (1995: 429 note 44) and Bartelmus (1998: 150 note 71) rightly draw attention to the use made by the librettist, Charles Jennens, of Xenophon's *Cyropaedia*, they both appear to overlook the most obvious source for Handel's plot, namely, *The Old and New Testament Connected in the History of the Jews and Neighbouring Nations* whose first part was published by Humphrey Prideaux in 1716 (Prideaux 1821). This pioneering attempt to combine biblical history from the eighth century BCE with secular history, drew extensively upon classical sources such as Herodotus and Xenophon and became a standard work. It was reprinted many times into the nineteenth century. On pp. 174–8 (of the 18th edition, 1821) Prideaux gives an account of the fall of Babylon precisely as found in Handel's oratorio, including the names Nitocris and Gobrias. Daniel's relationship to Nitocris (with which the oratorio opens) is explained by Prideaux in terms of Nitocris actually managing the kingdom while Belshazzar concentrated on his pleasures. In this capacity, Nitocris employed Daniel who, however, remained unknown to the king. Prideaux identified Darius the Mede (Dan. 5:31) as Cyaxares, the uncle of Cyrus, to whom Cyrus allowed the title of his conquests (Prideaux 1821: 176). Smith (1995: 262–3, 272–3, 317) has linked Jennens's treatment of Cyrus in *Belshazzar* with the views expressed in Henry Bolingbroke's *The Idea of a Patriot King*. While this may be correct, the fact remains that in *Belshazzar*, there is a setting of a biblical story in the light of what, at the time, was the most up-to-date biblical scholarship, which presented biblical history from the time of the destruction of the kingdoms of Israel and Judah in the context of world history as it was known from classical sources.

To move from Handel's *Belshazzar* to Felix Mendelssohn-Bartholdy's *Elijah* is at first sight, to move backwards in time rather than forward a century (*Elijah* was first performed in 1846 and received its definitive version a year later). While it is true that Mendelssohn greatly admired Bach and Handel and performed a number of the latter's oratorios as well as reviving the *St Matthew Passion* (Todd 2003 *passim*), a glance at the libretto of *Elijah* reveals it to be a strange compositum of biblical passages culled from all over the Bible, apparently regardless of context and of traditional views of the date or provenance of the books of the Bible. This will now be illustrated in some detail.

The work begins with Elijah's prophecy in 1 Kings 17:1, that there will be no rain 'these years'. An overture, presumably meant to indicate the fulfilment of the prophecy, is followed by a chorus in which the people appeal to God for help. Its words are taken from Ezekiel 9:8 ('wilt thou destroy . . .'), Jeremiah 8:20 ('the harvest is past, the summer is ended . . .') and Jeremiah 8:19 ('will the Lord be no more God in Zion?'; see the analysis in Bartelmus 1998: 112–33). A recitative draws upon Isaiah 44:27 (Luther's reading of the Hebrew) and Lamentations 4:4 and a duet of two women with the chorus sings the words of Baruch 2:14b ('hear our prayers, O Lord') and Lamentations 1:17 ('Zion spreadeth forth her hands . . .'). A tenor singing the part of Obadiah (cf. 1 Kgs. 18:3) calls upon the people to rend their hearts and not their garments, in words taken from Joel 2:13, and assures them that if they seek him with their whole heart, they will find him (words taken from Jeremiah 29:13–14). However, the people are sceptical, and sing a chorus drawn largely from Exodus 20:5–6 which rehearses the fact that God punishes the wicked to the third and fourth generation while also having mercy on thousands that love him.

The story of Elijah in 1 Kings 17 resumes with the command to him, given by an angel, to go to the brook Cherith. A double quartet singing Psalm 91:11–12 reassures Elijah that 'he shall give his angels charge over thee . . .'. There follow the incidents of the miraculous barrel of meal and cruse of oil and the restoring to life of the son of the widow of Zarephath, the dialogue between the woman and Elijah being drawn from passages such as Psalm 6:6 ('all night I make my bed to swim in tears'), Psalm 88:10 ('wilt thou show wonders to the dead?') and Psalm 116:12 ('what shall I render to the Lord for all his benefits to me?'). Numbers 10–14 of the oratorio follow the account in 1 Kings 18 of Elijah's encounter with King Ahab, and the contest on Mount Carmel between Elijah and the prophets of Baal, interrupted by the quartet 'Cast thy burden upon the Lord', with the words from Psalm 55:22. God's answer to Elijah in the descent of fire from heaven is answered by an aria from Elijah with words taken from Jeremiah 23:29 ('Is not his word like a fire, and like a hammer that breaketh the rock?') and Psalm 7:11–12 ('God is angry with the wicked every day'). The fate of the prophets of Baal is summed up in an aria based on Hosea 7:13 ('Woe unto them . . .') after which Obadiah uses the words of Jeremiah 14:22 to ask for an end to the drought ('Among the idols of the Gentiles, are there any that can command rain?'). There follows the story, taken from 1 Kings 18, of Elijah telling his servant to look towards the sea for a cloud as big as a man's hand, which will be the sign of coming rain. The dialogue is interspersed with passages such as two verses from Solomon's prayer in 1 Kings 8:35–6 (when the heavens are closed . . . yet if they pray . . . then hear from heaven . . .'). The arrival of the rain is greeted by Elijah and the people in the words of Psalm 106:1 ('Thanks be to God, for he is gracious and his mercy endureth for ever') and Psalm 93:3–4 ('The stormy billows are high, but the Lord is above them, and Almighty').

Part II of the oratorio deals with Elijah's flight from the wrath of Queen Jezebel, his journey to Mount Horeb, and his experience of the presence of God in the 'still small voice'. The action is preceded by an aria and chorus which draw upon passages such as Isaiah 53:1 ('Who hath believed our report?') and 41:10 ('Be not afraid, I am thy

God'), whose purpose is to strengthen Elijah in the ordeal that is to follow. Jezebel now takes centre stage and in words reminiscent of her part in the story of Naboth's vineyard (1 Kings 21 – an incident not included in the oratorio) persuades the people to condemn Elijah to death. Warned by Obadiah (1 Kings 19:2 merely says that Jezebel sent a messenger to Elijah), the prophet flees for his life. His journey is punctuated by reassuring words from angels, including one the best-known pieces from *Elijah*, the trio 'Lift thine eyes, O lift thine eyes' from Psalm 121:1–3. Some of Elijah's remaining uncertainties are expressed by him in a recitative which uses Isaiah 49:4 ('I have spent my strength for naught') and 64:1–3 ('O that thou wouldst rend the heavens . . . and come down'). The angel choir sings from the New Testament the words 'he that shall endure to the end shall be saved' (Matt. 10:22) to which Elijah replies in the words of Psalm 22:11 'be thou not far from me'. The manifestation of the divine presence in earthquake and fire, leading to the 'still small voice' ends not, as in 1 Kings 19:14–18, with the instructions to anoint Hazael as king of Syria, Jehu as king of Israel and Elisha as Elijah's successor. Instead, Elijah hears the seraphim singing the Sanctus from Isaiah 6:3, 'Holy, holy, holy is God the Lord'. All that remains in the oratorio of 1 Kings 19:14–18 is the assurance that God has 7,000 servants in Israel who have not bowed the knee to Baal, and this is the signal to Elijah that he will now be taken up into heaven (2 Kgs. 2). Significantly, he sings words from Psalm 16:9 'my heart is therefore glad . . . and my flesh also shall rest in hope', a passage that is used in the New Testament in Acts 2:26–7 to refer to the resurrection of Christ.

Elijah's role ends at this point in the oratorio, whose remaining five numbers are about Elijah's greatness, beginning with a passage from the Apocrypha (Ecclesiasticus 48:1, 6–7, 9: 'then did the prophet Elijah break forth like a fire . . .') and continuing with passages such as Malachi 4:5–6 ('Behold, God sent Elijah the prophet before the coming of the great and dreadful day of the Lord'), Isaiah 11:2 ('on him the Spirit of God shall rest . . .') and ending with Psalm 8:1 ('Lord, our creator, how excellent thy Name is in all the nations').

Those mainly responsible for the words of *Elijah* were Mendelssohn's friend, Pastor Julius Schubring (1806–89) (Todd 2003: 371) and Mendelssohn himself. Their interpretation of the prophet was entirely spiritual. All references to his political activities or his leadership of groups of prophets were ignored, and it is tempting to see in the overall pattern of triumph, humiliation and ascension an echo of Christ's ministry. What is particularly striking is the seemingly uncritical way in which material was garnered from all over the Bible. While, according to traditional views of the composition of the Bible, Elijah could have known and used the psalms (believed to have been mostly or entirely composed by David), he could hardly have known the words of the prophets Isaiah and Jeremiah, whom he predated by one and two centuries respectively (on the assumption that the eighth-century Isaiah was responsible for the 66 chapters of his book). However, Schubring had studied Theology in Berlin, where he first met Mendelssohn in 1825 (ibid.: 147), and if he attended the lectures of E. W. Hengstenberg, who lectured on the Old Testament there from 1828 to 1869, he will have been introduced to an orthodox view of Theology that saw the Bible as a seamless robe of complementary truths pointing to the atoning sacrifice of Christ. Both Berlin and Leipzig became, during Mendelssohn's lifetime, centres of opposition to the inroads that biblical criticism was trying to make into the academy and church in Germany (see Rogerson 1984: 79–90). In fact, Mendelssohn had to resist Schubring's attempt to make the oratorio end with the Transfiguration scene in the New Testament, where Elijah is seen by Peter, James and John (Matt. 17: 1–8; cf. Todd 2003: 522).

Todd argues that, for Mendelssohn, *Elijah* was a means of expressing his attempt to unite his Jewish family background with the convinced Lutheran faith that he had embraced. Mendelssohn's earlier oratorio, *St Paul*, had contained anti-Jewish elements which Mendelssohn now sought to overcome by presenting the Jewish prophet in ways that were consistent with both Judaism and Christianity (ibid.: 338). There is also the point that Mendelssohn may have avoided Elijah's political confrontations with King Ahab, or the divine command to him (carried out by Elisha) to initiate *coups d'état*, for contemporary political reasons. Todd (ibid.: xxiv) points out that Mendelssohn entertained moderately liberal views that preferred a constitutional monarchy to an absolute one, but he was unlikely to want to present what could be taken as public support for the violent overthrow of established monarchs. In Britain, he was regularly invited to perform before Queen Victoria and Prince Albert, and Racine's play *Athalie* with choruses by Mendelssohn was given its English premiere at Windsor Castle on 1 January 1847. Its theme was the demise of Queen Athaliah, who attempted to usurp the throne of Judah (2 Kgs. 11:1–20). Thus, we have a 'spiritual' Elijah, and although the material is drawn almost entirely from the Old Testament, it is read in a Christian way without giving offence to Jewish feelings.

At the same time that Mendelssohn was wrestling with the composition of *Elijah* (he had begun in 1837), Giuseppe Verdi was composing his opera *Nabucco*, which he finished in 1841. Arguably, the central character in this opera is not Nebuchadnezzar king of Babylon, but his supposed daughter Abigail, who discovers that she is in fact a slave and who, in her anger, usurps the throne of Babylon and condemns the Jewish captives to death including Fenena, Nebuchadnezzar's real daughter, who has meanwhile embraced the Jewish faith. From the biblical point of view, the chief interest lies in the use made of Daniel 2 and 4. The latter chapter takes the form of a letter of Nebuchadnezzar to 'all the peoples, nations and languages' in which he recounts a dream which was interpreted by Daniel. The outcome is that while the king is glorying in the power which has enabled him to build great Babylon, divine judgement is passed upon him. He is driven from human society, is made to eat grass like oxen, and his hair and nails grow like eagles' feathers and birds' claws. This state lasts until Nebuchadnezzar acknowledges the God of Israel as the true king of heaven.

In *Nabucco* this story is adapted to the point where the king successfully wrests the crown from Abigail and then shocks all those present by announcing that he is god, and demanding that all present should bow down and worship him – an allusion to Daniel 3, where worship is demanded of the great image of gold set up by Nebuchadnezzar. There is a flash of lightning, the crown is torn from Nabucco's head and the king descends into madness. His restoration occurs as Fenena is about to be sacrificed. Nebuchadnezzar awakes from a dream in which 'I thought that in the forest I ran before the hunters like a wild beast at bay' (cf. Daniel 4:33). He makes a vow to the God of Judah that if he is restored as king, he will build temples and altars to God's honour. His vow is heard. The idol of Baal before which Fenena and the Hebrews are to be killed falls in ruins (cf. Dan. 2 where Daniel interprets Nebuchadnezzar's dream about a great image destroyed by a stone cut from a mountain without human hands) and Nebuchadnezzar tells the Hebrews to return to their own land and to rebuild the temple. While this latter point is unhistorical and unbiblical in that it was Cyrus who gave permission for the exiles to return (cf. Ezra 1:1–4), it is in keeping with the presentation of Nebuchadnezzar in Daniel 2–4.

The best-known number from *Nabucco* is the chorus of the Hebrew slaves ('Va pensiero, sull'ale dorate': 'Fly, thought, on wings of gold') which is sung at the River Euphrates and alludes to Psalm 137:4 and the silence of the songs of the slaves. This chorus, and the theme of a subject people longing for freedom, rang a chord with an Italian public longing for national renewal and for the freedom of parts of Italy from Austrian rule. Sung spontaneously by the crowd at his funeral, the chorus 'Va pensiero' became a hymn for the emerging national consciousness, and ensured the success of the opera.

It is interesting to compare this function of a biblical story as an expression of national renewal with the remarks made by Smith with regard to Handel's oratorios. It is well known that *Judas Maccabeus* (1747) was dedicated to the Duke of Cumberland, the victor (or butcher, as some would say) at the battle of Culloden in 1746 which ended the Scottish rebellion (Smith 1995: 189). The number 'See the conquering hero comes' had an obvious contemporary reference in this context. Smith also argues that a number of Handel's oratorios were meant to resonate with contemporary events, by means of a series of analogies in which the Israelites represented both Protestants and Britain, threatened by Catholicism and continental foes (Smith 1995: Chapter 9 'Allegorical politics').

Turning to the twentieth century, one of the most significant biblical operas (if it can be called that, see Adorno 1998: 454–75) is Arnold Schoenberg's *Moses and Aaron*. Although the libretto for three acts exists, Schoenberg composed music for the first two acts only, in 1930–1, although in later life he entertained unfulfilled hopes of completing this work as well as *Jacob's Ladder*, a piece that is not as 'biblical' as the title might suggest.

In *Moses and Aaron* the part of Moses is spoken. The work begins with Moses' commission at the burning bush to free his people (cf. Exod. 3:1–4:31) and his great unwillingness to undertake the task. He is promised help in the person of his brother Aaron. When the brothers meet, Aaron cannot conceal his doubt that the people will find it difficult to worship a God they cannot conceive, while Moses insists that God cannot be represented physically in any way. The announcement to the people that God is to set them free, divides them between those who welcome the news, and those who fear what kind of God is involved. The people demand a sign, and Aaron turns the staff of Moses into a serpent, cures Moses' temporary leprosy and turns some water from the river into blood (cf. Exod. 4:1–9 where these signs concern only God and Moses). The people decide to trust and follow Moses.

The second act presupposes the exodus from Egypt and the crossing of the Red Sea and is set at Mount Sinai where Moses has gone to receive the tablets of stone. The absence of Moses is causing unrest among the people and in order to satisfy them, Aaron authorizes the making of the golden calf. The people, in worshipping the idol, relapse into heathendom and indulge in drunken orgies which praise human sacrifice and sexual licence. Moses returns from the mountain and destroys the idol. He accuses Aaron of betraying God, but although Aaron accepts that all representations of God are inadequate, maintains that they are necessary for the people. The people proceed to the promised land led by a pillar of fire by night and cloud by day (cf. Exod. 13:21–2). Moses is left alone. He destroys the tablets of the law. Act 3 begins with Aaron brought as a prisoner to Moses who again accuses him of having betrayed the truth of the only God and the fact of the election of the people. Those who hold Aaron captive ask whether they should kill him. Moses orders his freedom, but Aaron falls dead once he is released.

Quite apart from the significance of *Moses and Aaron* in Schoenberg's personal life, it is a profound interpretation of the biblical narrative. Moses is a tragic figure, largely rejected by the people whom he had freed from slavery, and caught between his own doubts and the conflicting demands of the people and God. Aaron opposes Moses, not only in the incident of the golden calf, but in aligning himself with Miriam in questioning God's exclusive revelation to Moses (Num. 12:2). At the end of the story, Moses is allowed only to glimpse the promised land from afar (Deut. 34:1–4). The deeper theme, that God cannot be represented by any human concept, is not only enshrined in the Ten Commandments (Exod. 20:4) but is implicit in the 'meaning' given to the self-disclosure of God in Exodus 3:14, 'I am that I am'. It is also consonant with a tradition of negative theology in Judaism (also in Christianity and Islam) that God can only be spoken of in terms of what he is not. Adorno notes that in his Songs opus 22, Schoenberg had set the following lines from Rilke: 'all who seek you, tempt you. Those who find you, bind you to picture and appearance (Gebärde)', (Adorno 1998: 454, my translation). One of Adorno's teachers, the theologian Paul Tillich, was to write that 'to argue that God exists is to deny him' (1963: 227).

The problem that *Moses and Aaron* wrestles with is how the Absolute, the ineffable and inconceivable true God can be conceived and understood without this process leading to misrepresentation and denial. Yet to be completely silent and passive is no solution. At one level this is a philosophical problem represented by Moses the 'purist' and Aaron the 'pragmatic'. But there is also a practical and political aspect. If, as the biblical tradition maintains, it is the will of God to choose and to liberate a people, how can this be put into effect without the idea both of God and the liberation being profoundly misunderstood and even corrupted (cf. Freitag 1973: 132 note 284)? The answer is given in the incident of the golden calf. Yet this is not an isolated incident within the narrative parts of Exodus, Numbers and the beginning of Deuteronomy. What are called the wilderness wanderings traditions contain incident after incident in which the liberated people express their dissatisfaction with their freedom and wish for a return to slavery in Egypt. Even the performance of miracles which both save and punish them fails to satisfy the people. The fact that only two representatives of the generation that was freed from slavery are permitted to proceed to the Promised Land (the rest, including Moses, died before reaching it) indicates how the divine will, backed by miracles, can be frustrated by human inability to comprehend the incomprehensible.

Moses and Aaron explores profoundly a theme that is implicit in what, for the biblical tradition, are foundation narratives about the nature of the chosen people as bound up with the inconceivable God. There is no doubt also something biographical in *Moses and Aaron*. Schoenberg, when he wrote the work, had broken with traditional forms of music and innovated twelve-note or serial music in an attempt to escape from previous subjectivity. Yet, as Adorno argues, it was impossible to abandon any resemblance to existing forms (Adorno reflects on the impossibility of a sacred oratorio in a secular world) and in any case, the attempt to convey any sense of the Absolute through the medium of music was bound to fall victim to the paradoxes explored in *Moses and Aaron*. In the opera, Moses as the upholder of the impossibility of representing God in any way is given a speaking part only. Speech has no pictures. Aaron, who is prepared to compromise, has a singing part, the implication being that even music cannot convey the Absolute without distortion. Things have moved a very long way from Mendelssohn's *Elijah* or even Handel's *Messiah*.

The last work to be considered will be Ralph Vaughan Williams's *Sancta Civitas* which was first performed in 1926. Religiously, Vaughan Williams was an agnostic, but perhaps it was his upbringing as the son of an Anglican clergyman that led him to devote so much of his time to writing hymn tunes and setting texts from the Bible, not to mention an almost life-long obsession with Bunyan's *Pilgrim's Progress*. *Sancta Civitas* was partly a response to the composer's first-hand experience of the first World War, the friends he lost, and the chaos that followed it and significantly, it is prefaced with a quotation from Plato's *Phaedo* (114d) in which Socrates discusses the immortality of the soul with his companions before he drinks the poisonous hemlock in accordance with the death penalty imposed upon him. The quotation reads:

> A man of sense will not insist that things are exactly as I have described them. But I think he will believe that something of the kind is true . . . and that it is worthwhile to stake everything on this belief.

In this spirit, *Sancta Civitas* is a setting of texts from the Revelation of St John the Divine, drawn principally from Chapters 18 to 22, which describe the defeat of the earthly powers and armies that oppose God, the fall of Babylon, and the vision of a new heaven and a new earth. Vaughan Williams used the Authorized Version of 1611 and Taverner's Bible, a rare and little-known translation published in 1539 by Richard Taverner. He also used the words of the 'Sanctus', part of which occurs in any case at Revelation 4:8.

From the point of view of biblical interpretation, the most significant fact is that Vaughan Williams systematically removed any reference to Christ from his libretto. This is most obvious at the conclusion, where 'Amen, even so, come, Lord Jesus' (Rev. 22:20) becomes 'Amen, even so come Lord'. At 21:23, where the new city's light is provided by the glory of God and the Lamb, there is no reference in the oratorio to the Lamb; and the same is true in the preceding verse, where only God is the temple as opposed to God and the Lamb in the biblical account. Where 7:16–17 is quoted, 'They shall hunger no more . . .', the words 'For the Lamb which is in the midst of the throne shall feed them' becomes 'For he that sitteth on the throne shall feed them'. This consistent removal of references to Christ also affects the interpretation of 19:11f 'And I saw heaven opened'. There is a description of One who sits upon a white horse and whose name is 'The Word of God' (19:13). This allusion to Christ is omitted, and instead of 'The Word of God' the name is given as 'King of Kings and Lord of Lords' (19:16).

Sancta Civitas, then, rejects the idea predominant in the book of Revelation, that the appearance of a new heaven and a new earth is bound up with the sufferings and exaltation of the Lamb, i.e. Christ. Vaughan Williams uses the words of the Bible to provide a vision of what human reason may hope for, as articulated in the noble words attributed by Plato to Socrates. However, the result is not an anodyne 'everything will be alright in the end' philosophy. As the quotation indicates, such a view requires the courage to live as though the hope were true; and it is an interesting view of the Bible which sees it as providing resources for musical expression of a future hope based upon human reason.

At first sight, Vaughan Williams has a more optimistic view of the possibilities of the human spirit compared with Schoenberg, who also served in the First World War. But Vaughan Williams imports some disturbing dissonances into his portrayal of the heavenly city, nowhere more so than in the Sanctus, where the words 'Lord God Almighty' employ powerful dissonances in both choir and orchestra. Is this the composer's way of questioning the concept of an almighty God in the aftermath of a world war or does he, like Schoenberg, seek to articulate the impossibility of doing justice to the concept, in ways with which humans could be comfortable?

Conclusion

This chapter has only scratched the surface of the subject. Not only have obvious, and well-known works, such as Haydn's *Creation* (1798) or Saint-Saëns's *Samson and Delilah* (1877), not been discussed. There has been no mention of literally hundreds of settings of biblical stories, especially in the eighteenth and nineteenth centuries, by composers whose names have faded into obscurity (cf. Bartelmus 1998: 135 note 3; Smith 1995: 113–19). Readers will also be familiar with other twentieth-century examples such as Benjamin Britten's *Noye's Fludde* (1958), *The Burning Fiery Furnace* (1966), *The Prodigal Son* (1968) and his setting of Wilfred Owen's 'The Parable of the Old Man and the Young' in the *War Requiem* (1961). Nor has there been any discussion of the Bible in music other than classical, such as hymns and even popular music.

The aim of the chapter has been to show that the interpretation of the Bible in oratorios and operas is often a complicated and instructive exercise, affected by personal beliefs and external political and theological circumstances. The chapter will have succeeded if it encourages listeners not only to enjoy and appreciate the music which is devoted to biblical texts and themes, but to realize that the works concerned are also exercises in biblical interpretation, some of which invite deeper reflection upon the biblical material that is employed.

References

Adorno, Theodor W. (1998). 'Sakrales Fragment: Über Schönbergs Moses und Aron', in *Gesammelte Studien*, vol. 16. Darmstadt: Wissenschaftliche Buchgesellschaft.

Bartelmus, Rüdiger (1998). *Theologische Klangrede: Studien zur musikalischen Gestaltung und Vertiefung theologischer Gedanken durch J.S. Bach, G.F. Händel, F. Mendelssohn, J. Brahms und E. Pepping.* Zurich: Pano Verlag.

Gunn, D. (2005). *Judges* (Blackwell Bible Commentaries). Oxford: Blackwell.

Freitag, Eberhard (1973). *Schönberg.* Hamburg: Rowohlt Verlag.

Kimchi, David (1959). 'Commentary on Judges', in *Miqra'ot Gᵉdolot, Nᵉvi'im Rishonim.* Tel Aviv: Schocken Publishing House.

Liptzin, Sol (1992). 'Jephthah and his Daughter', in D. L. Jeffrey (ed.), *A Dictionary of Biblical Tradition in English Literature.* Grand Rapids, MI: Eerdmans.

Moore, George Foot (1895). *A Critical and Exegetical Commentary on Judges.* Edinburgh.

Poole, Matthew ([1685] 1962). *A Commentary on the Holy Bible*, reprint. Edinburgh: Banner of Truth Trust.

Prideaux, Humphrey (1821). *The Old and New Testament Connected, in the History of the Jews, and Neighbouring Nations; from the Declensions of the Kingdoms of Israel and Judah, to the Time of Christ*, 18th edn. London.

Reventlow, Henning Graf (1980). *Bibelautorität und Geist der Moderne: Die Bedeutung des Bibelverständnisses für die geistesgeschichtliche und politische Entwicklung in England von der Reformation bis zur Aufklärung.* Göttingen: Vandenhoeck & Ruprecht; English trans. *The Authority of the Bible and the Rise of the Modern World.* London: SCM Press.

Rogerson, John (1984). *Old Testament Criticism in the Nineteenth Century: England and Germany.* London: SPCK.

Smith, Ruth (1995). *Handel's Oratorios and Eighteenth-Century Thought.* Cambridge: Cambridge University Press.

Tillich, Paul (1963). *Systematic Theology*, vol. 1. London: James Nisbet & Co.

Todd, R. Larry (2003). *Mendelssohn: A Life in Music.* Oxford: Oxford University Press.

Wolff, Christoph (2001). *Johann Sebastian Bach: The Learned Musician.* Oxford: Oxford University Press.

CHAPTER 18

Art

Heidi J. Hornik and Mikeal C. Parsons

Introduction

The reception of the Bible in the visual arts has a complicated, and at times contested, history – a history often effaced and submerged for the contemporary viewer whose experience of visual art, even and perhaps especially religious art, has been limited to a few hours in a modern museum, where the art is displayed on a wall in one of a dozen or so rooms, whose contents are arranged chronologically, or at times, thematically. How easy it is to forget, in that context, that much of the world's great works of art depict religious scenes that were originally intended to be viewed in a house of worship as a liturgical aid, for theological reflection, and as a spiritual guide. Furthermore, all of these works, to varying degrees, reflect the social, political, and/or religious struggles of the day. While experiencing such a work of art as one of several cultural artefacts on the walls of a museum preserving an ancient or antiquated society might prove meaningful, it surely provides only limited access to the work of art as a portal to persons of another time and place. This is certainly true also for those works of art intended to represent scenes and themes from the Bible.

To access the meaning of a visual depiction of the Bible in its historical context, as with any text of the past – especially the remote past – is a notoriously difficult undertaking, as (post-)modern historiography has amply demonstrated. Nonetheless, we are not kept from trying. John Shearman, an art historian, has focused the problem quite clearly: 'It goes without saying, I would have thought, that we cannot step right outside our time, avoiding, as it were, all contamination by contemporary ideologies and intervening histories' (1992: 4). We also agree with Shearman's conclusion:

> such inevitable imperfection ought not to be allowed to discourage the exercise of the historical imagination. In the same way it goes without saying that we will not reconstruct entirely correctly, but it is a sign of an unreflexive lack of realism to suppose that because we will not get it entirely right we had better give up and do something else not subject to error. (ibid.: 4–5)

In this chapter, then, we attempt to understand the ways the Bible has been visually appropriated across the history of art. Thus, we have chosen images from early Christian art, the Byzantine period, the Renaissance and Baroque, and the (largely secularized) nineteenth and twentieth centuries. In each case, the work of art under consideration has both shaped and been shaped by various factors at work in the larger culture. In understanding the way the artist has actualized or concretized the biblical text, we have been greatly assisted by another art historian, Paolo Berdini. In his words: 'Painting is not the simple visualization of the narrative of the text but an expansion of that text, subject to discursive strategies of various kinds' (1997: 35).

These 'discursive strategies' we take to be inextricably intertwined with the artist's social, political, and religious contexts as well as the sources and precedents at the artist's disposal in composing the image. These issues, of course, change from generation to generation, and the same biblical text can speak to very different kinds of problems, as the history of theology shows. In the remaining brief space, this chapter attempts to recount the various ways the Bible has been rendered in the visual arts, and thus received and understood by its audiences at particular and critical moments in its 'career'.

Early Christian

Early Christian art depicts narrative scenes from the Bible that are memorable. Whether it is Jonah being swallowed by a big fish, surviving within its belly, or being cast out and living to tell about it, Jonah's tale is a memorable one! Jonah first appeared on Christian sarcophagi and catacomb paintings in the fourth century.

The Jonah marbles usually are dated to the second-half of the third century CE. Four symbolic sculptures depict the events in the book of Jonah: *Jonah Swallowed* (Figure 18.1a); *Jonah Praying* (Figure 18.1b); *Jonah Cast Up*; and *Jonah under the Gourd Vine* (Figure 18.1c). In addition to these four, a well-preserved *The Good Shepherd* (Figure 18.1d) sculpture completes the group. The Cleveland Museum of Art acquired these works in 1965. The five sculptures, ranging in height from 13 to 20½ inches, were carved from blocks of the same white-grained, well-crystallized marble and are thought to have come from the same source in the eastern Mediterranean. Recent analysis, according to the museum, identifies the Roman Imperial quarries at Docimium in ancient Phrygia (now central Turkey) as the source of the marble (Wixom 1967: 67–88). These quarries supplied the Roman Empire with high-quality marble in the form of unfinished blocks that were used for sculpture, paving, and veneer. The location where the sculptures were originally found remains unknown. The entire group may have been unearthed together from a large pithos, or jar.

All of the figures are finished, except for *Jonah under the Gourd Vine*. We rarely find a group of free-standing sculptures like the Jonah marbles, which were probably meant to be seen in the round. And how do we explain the inclusion of the Christ figure, the good shepherd? Early Christians interpreted Old Testament prophecies and events as announcing and prefiguring the ministry of Jesus or the Church. Their interpretation of the book of Jonah was inspired by Jesus' mysterious rebuke of some religious leaders demanding a prophetic sign: 'You know how to interpret the appearance of the sky,' Jesus warned them, 'but you cannot interpret the signs of the times. An evil and adul-

terous generation asks for a sign, but no sign will be given to it except the sign of Jonah'
(Matt. 16:4). In another passage, Jesus elaborates this typology by identifying his own
ministry as the fulfilment of the sign of Jonah:

> For just as Jonah was three days and three nights in the belly of the sea monster [Jonah
> 2:1], so for three days and three nights the Son of Man will be in the heart of the earth.
> The people of Nineveh will rise up at the judgment with this generation and condemn it,
> because they repented at the proclamation of Jonah, and see, something greater than
> Jonah is here! (Matt. 12:40–1; cf. Luke 11:29–32)

The sculptor integrated motifs from pagan culture in order to supply a piece of Jonah's
prophetic message to Christians. A source for *The Good Shepherd* may be the pagan
criophorus figure; often he was shown bringing an offering to the altar, and, by the

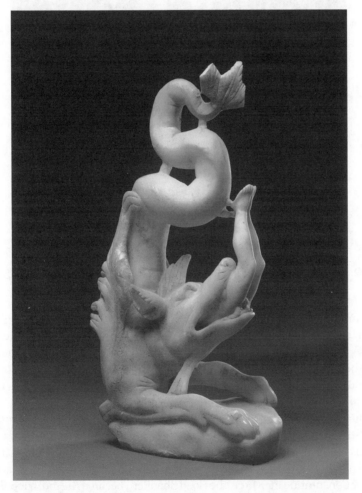

Figure 18.1a   *Jonah Swallowed, Jonah Praying to God, Jonah Under the Gourd Vine. The
Good Shepherd*, Asia Minor, probably Phrygia (central Turkey), Early Christian, c.
270–280. Marble. © The Cleveland Museum of Art, 2002. John L. Severance Fund,
1965.237–241

Figure 18.1b   Jonah Praying to God (see figure 18.1a)

third century CE, he represented the ram bearer with its connotations of philanthropy and loving care. The Cleveland sculpture is one of the best preserved of the 26 extant marbles depicting the Good Shepherd, who commonly is beardless and youthful, and carries a sheep draped over the shoulders. The artist also incorporated the *contrapposto* stance, made known by the Greek sculptor Polykleitos in the fifth century BCE, with one weight-bearing leg straight and the other bent naturally as the weight shifts.

A visual representation of Christ as the Good Shepherd bore rich meaning for the early Christians during times of persecution because it symbolized a leader who would sacrifice his life for his flock; yet, as an already popular image among non-Christians as well, it did not draw attention to the persecuted believers. Later, after the peace brought by Emperor Constantine in 306 CE, the Good Shepherd became the most popular symbol of Jesus Christ.

The rare qualities of this work include the use of a drill to add the contrast of light and dark in the hair. All of the Jonah marbles share this technical characteristic.

Figure 18.1c   Jonah Under the Gourd Vine (see figure 18.1a)

Jonah Swallowed and *Jonah Cast Up* are particularly dramatic representations in marble. They feature a Ketos, or Greek sea monster, that is part land animal and part fish. The early Christian artist likely borrowed from the Ketea found in Greek and Roman sculptures, wall paintings, and mosaics, but found a new narrative in which the sea monster could function. The 'large fish' (Jonah 1:17) is terrifying with such a monstrous body, recoiling back upon itself with its tail high above its head. This strong vertical representation, combined with the circularity of the two forms, helps us to identify the two figures as one.

Jonah within the belly of the fish is a far more difficult subject to depict. In *Jonah Praying*, the sculptor chose to show the sole figure of Jonah in the gesture of an orant, with arms outstretched and palms up, as he prays to God for deliverance. The bearded Jonah wears the same tunic as in the marble showing him under the gourd vine. The *contrapposto* stance, as seen in *The Good Shepherd* marble, invokes a figure at rest. These two pieces and *Jonah under the Gourd Vine* convey a sense of relaxation, meditation, and prayer in contrast to the scenes with the fish that are heightened in drama and action. This alternation of action and calm reflects the biblical story and creates a narrative flow among the five marbles.

In *Jonah under the Gourd Vine*, the prophet reclines and relaxes. He raises his right arm over his head. The body position recalls river god types known throughout the

Figure 18.1d   The Good Shepherd (see figure 18.1a)

Greek and Roman world. The shepherd boy in Greek mythology, Endymion, who slept eternally underneath a tree, may be an inspiration for this depiction of Jonah. Endymion symbolized repose, peace, and well-being; here Jonah has received peace and rests in the calm after the events of the story. Beneath a creeping gourd, which symbolized resurrection in Roman art, Jonah contemplates the miracle of his salvation.

In these Jonah marbles we can glimpse Christian life before its official acceptance in the Roman Empire. When, during the third and early fourth centuries, Christians were threatened by persecution and death, they found hope in the 'sign of Jonah' that promised life would follow death. The parallels between the three-day period of Jonah in the fish and Jesus in the tomb allowed these believers to understand the prophecy of Jonah in a new way, as pointing toward the resurrected Christ who is the shepherd and saviour of those who believe in Him.

After Christianity became an accepted religion in the Empire by the Edict of Milan in 313, artists portrayed Christ less as the simple Good Shepherd and more like a Caesar, with royal attributes such as a halo, purple robe, and throne. A separation occurred between Jonah and Christ in the visual art and theology of Christianity. As Christ became more regal, the popularity of Jonah's story decreased significantly. Perhaps the concerns of the Christians expanded from uncertainty about their own death, which had been a very real issue during the early centuries, to the eternal kingdom of God after resurrection. Jonah's words were not less important to this next generation of Christians, but Christ's triumphant rule over the powers became more prevalent (Hornik 2003:51–4).

Abraham Heschel has pointed out that Hebrew prophets were both *foretellers* and *forthtellers*; their prophetic ministry included both predicting what God would do in the future (foretelling) as well as exposing the injustices of society (forthtelling). Jonah was a reluctant prophet who initially rejected God's command to be foreteller and forthteller to the people of Nineveh. His disobedience led him to spend three days in the belly of a fish before he half-heartedly agreed to deliver God's message to those foreigners.

Jesus, the Son of God, brought God's prophetic message to the residents of Galilee and Judea. Unlike Jonah, Jesus was fully obedient to God's command; in the garden of Gethsemane he prayed, 'Not my will but yours be done,' (Luke 22:42) and this obedience led him to spend three days in the 'belly of Death.' Jesus' message of God's redeeming love, like Jonah's, was intended to be inclusive, inviting Jew and non-Jew alike to become people of God's kingdom (Matt. 28:16–20).

Byzantine

In Byzantine art, the subject of Christ's Resurrection was often coupled with the subject of Christ's Descent into Hell and illustrated in various media (fresco, oil on panel, book illuminations, medallions, etc.) as the Anastasis (Cartlidge and Elliott 2001: 126–7 (Hornik and Parsons 2003)). These images draw presumably on two slender Scriptural references in 1 Peter, where the reader is informed that the crucified Christ 'went and preached to the spirits in prison' (3:19) and that the 'gospel was preached even to the dead' (4:6). In early Christian interpretation (and much subsequent exegesis as well), these two texts were thought to refer to the same event: Christ rescuing the Old Testament saints from Hades, or the so-called 'Harrowing of Hell' or 'Christ in Limbo' (McCulloch 1930; Dalton 1989).

The earliest allusion to the Descent into Hell is found in the writings of Ignatius (early second century):

> If these things be so, how then shall we be able to live without him of whom even the prophets were disciples in the Spirit and to whom they looked forward as their teacher? And for this reason he whom they waited for in righteousness, when he came raised them from the dead. (*Ignatius to the Magnesians*, ix.2: LCL)

In the *Odes of Solomon* (17:9; 42:15), Christ opens the doors of hell and those who were dead rush toward him (see also, e.g., Melito of Sardis, *On the Pasch*, 102). The early Easter liturgy of the church combined reflections on the passages in 1 Peter with interpretations of important Psalm texts (cf. Pss. 16:10; 24:7ff.; 30:4; 107:13–16; and 116:3ff.), that supported this understanding of Christ's descent. As a result of these sustained and various treatments of the theme of Christ's Descent into Hell by early Christian writers, one may rightly conclude that by 'the fourth century, this story had become part of church poetry, the Creed, and liturgy' (Kartsonis 1986: 30).

The fullest description of Christ's Descent into Hell is found in the apocryphal *Gospel of Nicodemus*, which dates from the fifth or sixth century. Here the author attempts to fill in the gaps created by 1 Peter 4:6 regarding the fate of the righteous ones who died before Christ's ministry. Following a conversation between Satan and Hades personified about whether or not the coming of Christ to Hell would be beneficial to them, the author narrates the details of Christ's liberation of the saints from limbo and their delivery to the archangel, Michael. Despite the richness of these literary sources, it is impossible to draw a direct line between them and the development of the image of the Anastasis in Byzantine art. The East's combination of Christ's Resurrection and Descent in the Anastasis illustrates how complicated and convoluted has been the reception of the Bible during certain historical periods.

The earliest extant depictions of the Anastasis are from the eighth century and are found twice in frescoes in S. Maria Antiqua. The fresco at the entrance to the Palatine ramp in S. Maria Antiqua is in very poor condition and its four main figures – Christ, Adam, Eve, and Hades (or perhaps personified Death?) – are barely visible. The figure of Christ is dominant; his glory is depicted by a bright mandorla of light, which almost completely surrounds him. He holds a scroll in his left hand and with his right firmly grasps the wrist of Adam, who is depicted as an old man with one foot still literally in the grave! At the same time, with his right foot Christ rather effortlessly pins the dark, muscular, figure of Death-Hades, who reaches in vain to prevent Adam from leaving the sarcophagus. At Adam's side stands Eve, whose hand is raised in a gesture of petition. Clearly, the focus here, highlighted by Christ's enveloping light, is on Christ's divinity in action.

Extant ninth-century depictions of the Descent into Hell continue the themes established by their eighth-century precedents, while at the same time introducing new innovations. Again, we may consider one of the two frescos in the lower church at S. Clemente, Rome (Figure 18.2). Christ, still with scroll in hand, continues to pull Adam to safety from Hades, though here the sarcophagus of S. Maria Antiqua has been exchanged for an ominous dark hole. Not only has the direction of the action reversed (Christ is now on the viewer's left), the cast of characters now has some interesting variation. Eve disappears in our fresco (and Death-Hades is missing from the other fresco). Here where Death-Hades is present, Christ continues to trample him underfoot, although Hades' efforts to retard Adam's liberation seem even more futile than before. The result in both cases seems to be to suggest that it is the Harrowing of Hell, represented by Christ's rescue of Adam from Hell, and not Christ's triumph over it (represented by Death-Hades underfoot) that occupies centre stage in this (and other) ninth-century representation.

Renaissance

For much of the history of representational art, to miss the specific cultural clues to an image's meaning is almost always to misread the painting. Images are, by their nature,

Figure 18.2   *Anastasis*, Gold and medal. Byzantine icon, 12th century, 9.5 x 8.5 in. Armoury Museum. Kremlin, Russia. Photograph Alinari

emotionally evocative, but the expression of emotions is culturally conditioned. Thus, it is fallacious to assume that an historic viewer of a medieval or Renaissance work of art, in its (usually) liturgical context, would have experienced the same emotion, or range of emotions, as a modern viewer of the same work, now on display on the wall of a modern museum. Yet, without knowledge of the historical context of the art work, this is exactly what we assume.

The Annunciation is one of the most frequently depicted scenes in all the Bible, and as such, the Annunciation scene is a marvellous test case for the ways in which its symbolism and iconography are profoundly shaped by its specific cultural and religious context. While we could demonstrate the complex and multiple ways the Annunciation has been understood in art by looking at scenes across the entire history of art (Robb 1936; Rosenau 1944). Since, however, the Annunciation was especially popular in Renaissance Italy, we may demonstrate this point more forcefully by considering the various ways the scene was depicted pictorially in one particular medium (painting) during one specific period (1440–1460) in one specific place (Florence).

To begin we must briefly consider a sermon by Fra Roberto Caracciolo da Lecce of Florence (Baxandall 1988: 49–56). Fra Roberto's sermon is typical of the theological categories through which visual depictions of the Annunciation would have been viewed by the original audience. Fra Roberto distinguished three mysteries of the Annunciation: the Angelic Mission, the Angelic Salutation, and the Angelic Colloquy

(Fra Roberto 1489). In the last mystery, Fra Roberto attributed five successive spiritual states to Mary and this part of his reflections is most germane to the Florentine Annunciations:

> The third mystery of the Annunciation is called Angelic Colloquy; it comprises five laudable Conditions of the Blessed Virgin:

1	*Conturbatio*	Disquiet
2	*Cogitatio*	Reflection
3	*Interrogatio*	Inquiry
4	*Humiliatio*	Submission
5	*Meritatio*	Merit

While the fifth condition is illustrated in a scene of Mary separate from the Annunciation, examples of each of the first four Laudible Conditions are easily found in mid-fifteenth-century Florentine painting: (1) Disquiet – Filippo Lippi, Florence, S. Lorenzo, Panel; (2) Reflection – Master of the Barberini Panels, Washington, DC, National Gallery of Art, Kress Collection, Panel; (3) Inquiry – Alesso Baldovinetti, Florence, Uffizi, Panel; (4) Submission – Fra Angelico, Florence, Museo di S. Marco, Fresco (Baxandall 1988: 55). As Michael Baxandall has observed: 'The preachers coached the public in the painters' repertory, and the painters responded within the current emotional categorization of the event' (ibid.: 55).

We will consider the first of the laudable conditions, Disquiet, and one of its most famous depictions, that by Fra Filippo Lippi in S. Lorenzo, Florence (Figure 18.3). About this condition, Fra Roberto writes:

> The first laudable condition is called Conturbatio; as St. Luke writes, when the Virgin heard the Angel's salutation – 'Hail, thou art highly favored, the Lord is with thee; blessed art thou among women' – she was troubled. This disquiet, as Nicholas of Lyra writes, came not from incredulity but from wonder, since she was used to seeing angels and marvelled not at the fact of the Angel's apparition so much as at the lofty and grand salutation, in which the Angel made plain for her such great and marvellous things, and at which she in her humility was astonished. (Fra Robertus Caracciolus: cxlix r.–clii r.)

Filippo Lippi (1406–69) took vows at the Carmelite monastery of S. Maria del Carmine in Florence at the age of 15, and within a few short years established himself as one of the most sought-after painters in mid-fifteenth-century Florence. Soon after finishing the altarpiece in 1439, he executed an 'Annunciation' for the church of San Lorenzo in Florence, *c.*1440 (Rowlands 1996: 439–45).

Gabriel greets Mary and evidently interrupts her reading from a tall lectern in the lower right corner. Lippi's surprised Virgin well illustrates the astonishment and wonder with which Mary, in her humility, was said by Fra Roberto to have responded to the angelic salutation. The kneeling angel was, according to Fra Roberto, a gesture of honour bestowed upon Mary. While she keeps Gabriel at a distance with her right hand, Mary raises her left hand in a gesture of surprise. Her body leans away from the angel, partially disappearing behind the lectern.

A modern viewer might puzzle over this response by Mary, but the Renaissance spectator, steeped in the emotional and theological categories that Fra Robert summarizes,

Figure 18.3   Fra Filippo Lippi, *Annunciation*, 1440, San Lorenzo, Florence. Altar panel. Photograph: Alinari

understands these gestures to be rooted in Mary's humility, a humility that, ironically, ultimately justifies her exalted role as the 'mother of God'.

Not all versions of the Annunciation were met with equal approval in the Florentine Renaissance. In fact, Leonardo da Vinci (himself the painter of at least two Annunciations) laments the excessive emotion associated with the laudable condition of Disquiet:

> some days ago I saw the picture of an angel who, in making the Annunciation, seemed to be trying to chase Mary out of her room, with movements showing the sort of attack one might make on some hated enemy; and Mary, as if desperate, seemed to be trying to throw herself out of the window. Do not fall into errors like these. (Leonardo da Vinci: I.58 and II.33 r.; cited by Baxandall 1988: 56)

While not aimed specifically at Lippi, Leonardo's criticism would certainly apply, and his comments demonstrate how the visual interpretation of a biblical scene could be contested even in the same historical time period! Furthermore, interpreting fifteenth-century visual depictions of the Annunciation within the fifteenth-century categories of emotional experience sheds considerable light on the probable impact of the painting on its original audience, and reminds us, when we forget the specific cultural context of the images we are viewing, how easily we may misinterpret the image at hand.

High Renaissance

On 27 May 1993 a terrorist or Mafia car bomb exploded just metres away from the Galleria degli Uffizi in Florence, killing six people. As the glass ceiling of the museum was shattered its shards cut paintings and broke sculptures into pieces. The world held its breath as the list of over 300 damaged objects was published in papers and announced on news channels throughout the world. The world also watched how a city and country famous for its works of art and notorious for its relaxed way of life would respond. After only three weeks of being closed, the Uffizi, the world's largest museum of Italian Renaissance art was ready to re-open its doors (albeit with some galleries still closed) to tourists, scholars and all those concerned to know that what was would be again. Michelangelo's *David* (Figure 18.4), safely exhibited in the Museo dell'Accademia in another zone of the city, became the illustrated symbol on publicity posters and cards that appeared throughout the city on 20 June 1993 with the words 'Firenze riapre. Il Museo degli Uffizi da oggi riapre' ('Florence reopens. The Uffizi Museum reopens today'). It did not matter that *David* was not located (and never was) in the Uffizi, the sculpture symbolized a city that was victim to a terrorist bombing. Instead of sending the world a message of fear, *David* represented a city and its people who 'would not let terrorism remove their dignity or extinguish their desire for beauty, for life, and for peace' ('Gli Uffizi riaprono per far conoscere al mondo che non c'è stato terrore capace di piegare la dignità della popolazione di Firenze e spegnere il desiderio di belezza, di vita, di pace.') The biblical figure of David was the same symbol of the Florentine underdog in the fifteenth century even before Michelangelo (1475–1564) was born and again in the late twentieth century as the city stood strong against terrorism.

The city of Florence, like the biblical character of David, became famous for rising to beat its formidable foes. Florence had a smaller army than Siena, less political power than Rome, and a more difficult access to exportation than the port city of Pisa. Florentines placed a high value upon their city's traditional independence and beauty. Beginning in 1400, Florentines had constant visual references to communal liberty in their architecture and they were increasing the civic works in painting and sculpture (Seymour 1967: 9). The second half of the Quattrocento (1400s) also saw a tremendous spurt in humanistic thinking and influence in all aspects of the arts; the art of sculpture was at this time thought of as a direct parallel to the process of developing the highest good in human nature in general, and in human affairs within the city–state (ibid.: 9–10).

Donatello (1386–1466) sculpted two life-size adolescent Davids, both for the Medici family in 1416 and 1440. The private patronage created a quiet association between Florence and the Medici family as it rose to power within the city. Michelangelo, born

Figure 18.4   Michelangelo, *David*, 1504–8, Museo dell'Accademia, Florence. Marble.
Photograph: Alinari

in 1475, was first and always a Florentine. Lorenzo de'Medici was a friend and patron of Michelangelo in his formative years. The Republican traditions in Florence were strong and never would Michelangelo have thought of himself as 'Italian'.

In 1501, Michelangelo was charged with the task of constructing a colossal David out of a 30-year-old piece of Carrara marble. The figure was intended to be one of a series of 12 prophets to go on the buttresses of the so-called Tribuna – the eastern portion of the Duomo surrounding the cupola (ibid.: 17). This project had been planned for nearly a century among the Florentine sculptors.

Giorgio Vasari's *Life* of Michelangelo was originally published in 1550 and revised in 1568, after Michelangelo's death. Vasari stated that when the David was finished it was placed in front of the Palace of the Signoria (Palazzo Vecchio) as a symbol: just as the Biblical David had 'defended his people and governed it with justice, so he who would govern the city should valiantly defend and justly rule it.' (Seymour 1967: 21).

It should be understood that both editions were printed in Florence by printing houses licensed by the Duke of Tuscany, then Cosimo I de'Medici, and both were dedicated to that ruler. Vasari, who was alive during these events, is a very good story teller but for our purposes of understanding how David is a biblical and civic symbol, a little story-telling still allows the tone of the culture to be correctly understood some five hundred years later.

When the sculpture was completed in 1504, the Operai del Duomo (keepers and patrons of artistic endeavours related to the Duomo) and the Arte della Lana (wool guild who heavily financed such projects) decided to place the work as a civic symbol in front of the governmental palace, the symbolism was clear and strong. Michelangelo, between the ages of 26 and 30, sculpted a colossal symbol of Florence and its people.

Michelangelo's *David* not only possessed the artist's clear sense of dignity, strength, intense thought and *virtu* but was also influenced by the antique sculpture and philosophy that he studied both in Florence and Rome. Michelangelo studied in Rome between 1496 and the Spring of 1501. Collectors, including his own Roman patrons, Cardinal Riario and the banker Jacopo Galli, constantly increased their holdings of antique sculptures as they were unearthed in Rome (Seymour 1967: 46). Prior to this, Michelangelo while in the Lorenzo de'Medici (d. 1492) household was introduced to what was then the major collection of antiquities in Europe. Much of the Roman works were colossal statuary and clearly influenced his own colossal *David*.

Another influence on the artist and the project itself was political. The idea of reactivating the hundred-year-old project for the Duomo sculptures coincided with the hundred-year anniversary of the competition to decorate the bronze doors of the Florence Baptistery. The winner was Lorenzo Ghiberti who decorated the North doors in the 1410. Fillipo Brunelleschi, the runner-up, went on to construct the cupola and dome of the Duomo in the 1460s. The beginning of the sixteenth century in Florence was politically precarious at best. Cesare Borgia's armies from Rome (with the help of the French) were stationed all over Tuscany and posed a threat to Florence itself. The city treasury was far from full and leadership was weak. There was reason to appeal to the support of historical memory: the memory, especially, of consecrated idealism and civic dignity preserved in the medieval Duomo, still vibrant with echoes of the age of Dante and of Giotto, where figures of marble prophets set high were intended to lead the mind upward from the city–state of man to the city–state of God (Seymour 1967: 56).

By 1500, the balance between Church and state had begun to change. In 1494, Savonarola's God-directed form of government had been rejected and concluded with his own execution by burning in front of the Palazzo Vecchio. By the middle of the sixteenth century, Vasari viewed the statue of David as an emblem of the Prince's power (*insegno del Palazzo*). Cosimo I de'Medici had moved himself and his family into the Palazzo Vecchio, and Vasari was in charge of the decoration of the palace at this time. Vasari saw not David the shepherd boy but David the king, whom he related to his patron Duke Cosimo I the princely ideal of justice. There was no longer relevance here to the earlier Quattrocento ideal of republican virtue (ibid.: 58). Michelangelo left for Rome and was very content to be working for the Pope at this time of Medici domination in Florence.

The Davide Falso stands outside the Palazzo Vecchio, still the seat of the mayor of Florence today. Michelangelo's *David* was moved in 1873 to its current location in the Museo dell'Accademia. It was moved to be protected from the environment and until September, 1991 when the second toe of David's left foot was damaged by a deranged assailant during visiting hours. Even though its exhibition space seems cramped to some scholars, it continues to evoke the spirit and the life of the Florentine people and their culture.

Baroque

'No artist has ever depicted the most moving episode from the parable of the Prodigal Son as often or as effectively as Rembrandt' (Hoekstra 1990: 335). Beginning with an etching dating from 1636 until the completion of the famous *Return of the Prodigal* in the last years of Rembrandt's life (1668–69), Rembrandt lovingly worked and reworked various depictions of the Homecoming episode (Figure 18.5). Rembrandt's Hermitage *Prodigal* is one of, if not *the*, most famous depictions of this scene. It is also important to point out that Rembrandt was one of the few great Protestant artists during the Renaissance and Baroque periods. In fact, by the time he painted the *Return of the Prodigal*, he had come profoundly under the influence of the Anabaptist traditions (especially the Waterlanders), a branch of the radical Reformation (Rosenburg 1964: 180–2).

There is much to ponder about the painting, especially the powerful pathos of the elderly, presumably nearly blind, father embracing the beggarly prodigal (Bal 1991). For example, Rembrandt has captured the spirit of the father in his various roles. In the picture, the two hands of the father are quite different. The left hand is strong and masculine; the right is refined, soft, and tender. Most would identify the left hand with traditional masculinity, the right with what is traditionally feminine. So the embrace of the Father is fully male and fully female (Nouwen 1992: 98–9). We will focus our remaining comments on the two male characters to the immediate right of the father.

Though the identity of these two figures has been the object of much debate among Rembrandt scholars, Barbara Joan Haeger has demonstrated that in the biblical commentaries and paintings contemporary with Rembrandt, the parable of the Pharisee and the tax collector (Luke 18) and the parable of the prodigal were closely linked (Haeger 1983). Rembrandt follows that tradition in depicting the seated man beating his breast. Here is the publican or tax collector of the parable beating his breast in repentance, 'God, be merciful to me a sinner' (Luke 18:13). The Elder Brother, on the other hand, stands like the Pharisee in the same parable with hands folded in judgement, 'God, I thank you that I am not like other people: thieves, rogues, adulterers, or even like this tax collector' (Luke 18:11).

In this regard, Rembrandt continues the iconographic and homiletic traditions of identifying the Elder Brother with judgemental Pharisees (Parsons 1996). Every religious tradition must deal with those who stand outside its tradition; that is, every religious tradition must, as it were, deal with the 'Other'. This struggle becomes more convoluted and intense when the 'Other' is a former family member, as is the case with the place of Judaism within Christian thought.

Figure 18.5 Rembrandt, *The Prodigal Son*, St. Petersburg, The Hermitage. Oil on canvas. Photograph: Alinari

The Parable of the Prodigal Son, and especially the role and identity of the Elder Brother focuses this issue poignantly because ever since Augustine, the dominant tendency in both visual and verbal interpretations of the parable has been to identify the elder brother as representative of Jews obdurate to the Christian Gospel. And, as is the case with many religious traditions, the solution to the 'outsider' problem is to exclude the outsider permanently. Thus, Augustine's reading of the parable. 'While meanwhile his elder son, the people of Israel following the flesh, has not in fact departed into a distant region, but nevertheless is not in the house, however he is in the field, namely, he is toiling with reference to earthly things . . .' (*Quaestiones*, lines 106–13). Augustine interprets the father's going out to the Elder Brother as an appeal for Jews to enter the Church 'so that all Israel – to whom . . . blindness has occurred, just as to the one absent in the field may become saved' (Augustine, *Quaestiones*, lines 131–2). As Jill Robbins has put it: 'Augustine, in excluding the elder brother, inaugurates a critical tradition that does not read the elder brother or reads him as outside' (1991: 42).

Rembrandt, however, departs from the biblical account by placing the Elder Brother as the most prominent witness to the homecoming scene. So Rembrandt holds in tension a portrait of the Elder Brother standing in judgement with the possibility that he may in the end join in the feast. Haeger comments; 'Rembrandt does not reveal whether he [the Elder Brother] sees the light. As he does not clearly condemn the Elder Brother, Rembrandt holds out the hope that he too will perceive he is a sinner . . . the interpretation of the elder brother's reaction is left up to the viewer' (1983: 185–6). This open-endedness toward the Elder Brother's response, so rare in the history of inter-pretation, is, we think, a faithful rendering of the parable itself. Thus, by deviating from the details of the account, Rembrandt is able, where many other interpreters have failed, to capture the spirit of Luke's account.

The story ends, not with the Elder Brother departing in disgust never to return, but rather with the father's words ringing in the Elder Brother's ears, 'Son, you are always with me, and all that is mine is yours. It is fitting to make merry and be glad, for this your brother was dead, and is alive; he was lost, and is found.' The response of the Elder Brother is unstated; he is left to choose whether or not to join the banquet. And like stories of the lawyer who questioned Jesus about neighbourliness (Luke 10) and the rich young ruler who sought eternal life (Luke 18), the story of the Elder Brother is left unfinished, or rather left for the hearers of the story to provide their own conclusion(s). Rembrandt's Elder Brother is resentful and stands, with hands folded in judgement over a wastrel prodigal who comes home to unconditional grace. But he does not leave, real-izing that Grace could also be his – 'all I have is yours . . . You are with me always.' Rem-brandt, employing but ultimately subverting the traditional understanding of this parable, makes the daring and seemingly dangerous proposal that Outsiders may finally be included in the great feast, and that the choice is theirs not ours!

Romanticism

The German Romantic painter Caspar David Friedrich (1774–1840) is best known for his symbolic and atmospheric treatment of landscape (Jensen: 778). Friedrich's Crucifixion scene, *The Cross in the Mountains* (Figure 18.6), represents a subject that was intensely the focus of the visual arts in service of liturgy and theology for almost 2000 years. Friedrich's work, dated 1808, is part of a secularized style known as Romanticism which is no less spiritual than a painting of the Crucifixion in the Renaissance world.

As we noted in the introduction, much religious art, especially that inspired by the Christian Scriptures, was created to assist in liturgical worship, theological reflection, and spiritual formation. During the medieval and Renaissance periods, Christian devotional reflection focused primarily on the suffering of the crucified Christ. As MacDonald, Ridderbos, and Schlusemann have observed: 'During the late Middle Ages, devotion to the Passion of Christ, which for centuries had been an important theme in the experience and practice of Christians, was accorded a quite new level of significance' (1998: ix).

To cite one example, consider the work of Fra Angelico, whose cell frescoes in the Dominican monastery of San Marco, Florence, are dominated by scenes from the

Figure 18.6   Caspar David Friedrich, *The Cross in the Mountains*, 1808, Oil. Gemälde-galerie, Dresden, Germany. Photograph: akg-images

scourging and crucifixion of Christ. These frescoes were to serve as devotional aids as the monks contemplated their calling to imitate Christ in his suffering for the world. That one may easily move from the particular example of Fra Angelico to make a more general statement about the medieval and Renaissance focus – one might say obsession – with the Passion, especially in Italian art, is easily demonstrated (Haug and Wachinger 1993; Derbes, 1996). This art assisted in the medieval focus on *imitatio Christi*, the theme of so many medieval manuals from Thomas à Kempis to Ignatius Loyola, and as such was a liturgical aid for communal worship and individual theological reflection (Miles 2004).

As a result of the assault on the visual arts and its ecclesiastical patronage by much of the Protestant Reformation and the scepticism toward traditional theology of the Enlightenment, the visual arts were no longer tethered to the theology of the Church and artists were no longer patronized by the ecclesiastical authorities to produce works of art that supported (or for that matter subverted) the conventional doctrines of traditional Christian orthodoxy. Thus, much religious art from the eighteenth century forward, although still poignantly spiritual, was nonetheless individualized and secularized in the sense that it, for the most part, no longer drew upon the traditional symbols of organized religion for its inspiration.

During Friedrich's study of life drawing and landscape painting, he also became interested in the mythology and the history of Germanic and Scandinavian peoples. Friedrich drew intensively from nature, producing his first landscape etchings using largely symbolic motifs such as paths, bridges, rivers, trees, distant hills and views of cities. These works made marked use of contrast, itself symbolic, between lit and shadowed passages (Jensen: 779). Friedrich's more spiritual and emotional approach to landscape painting occurred while he was visiting the island of Rügen in northern Germany from Spring 1801 until July 1802. It was at this time also that he also expressed his ideas on the times of day in words as well as images, producing four religiously inspired poems in 1803–4 (Hinz 1968: 84). For the next ten years, Friedrich's paintings, many now in oil, thematically create an association of landscape views with the times of day, the seasons or the ages of man (Jensen: 780).

The painting *Cross in the Mountains* (1807–8; Gemäldegalerie, Dresden) represents in surprising monumentality and purity Friedrich's conception of religious landscape (*Friedrich*, 1974: 106). The work fulfils the Romantic requirement of creating a new devotional image in a depiction of landscape. This corresponded with the belief, developed from Lutheran Protestantism, of the kind espoused by the theologian Friedrich Schleiermacher and the poet Gottfried Ludwig Kosegarten (1750–1818), that God manifests Godself in nature and thus humanity views the widening landscape as an act of devotion. Friedrich had met Schleiermacher in Greifswald, and Kosegarten had lived in the nearby Baltic port of Wolgast from 1785 to 1792 (Jensen: 780).

As Friedrich worked in oil, his compositions and meanings changed also. Previously his works had a limited foreground with an unlimited distance in the background. There was a transcendence to his paintings that invited the viewer to meditate on a remote image that seemed to beckon the viewer into it. It was a world of this earth and a world to come. The lack of a middle ground further emphasized this symbolic remoteness. This double-layered picture space is accentuated by the symmetrical arrangement of the objects, as in the painting *The Cross in the Mountains* (Jensen: 782). There are many preparatory studies for the landscape of this painting. Friedrich made studies of the fir trees and other characteristic plants as well as the flow of light in the Bohemian landscape near Tetschen (Monrad and Bailey 2000: 39–40).

The Cross in the Mountains helped Friedrich become known during his time and now as the finest painter of German Romanticism (Börsch-Supan and Jähnig 1975: 300–2). His personal fame only lasted from 1808 to 1818 when he was surrounded by a circle of friends who included university lecturers, artists, and intellectuals. Several of his works produced at this time were purchased by Tsar Nicholas I. His appointment as honorary professor at the academy in Dresden in 1824 was his last mark of public esteem and, at the same time, his failure to secure the appointment as landscape painting teacher was an almost humiliating rejection of the artist by official opinion (Jensen: 783).

The pictures produced after 1825 were considered strange and gloomy despite continued good sales by important artists and noblemen. Friedrich's work remains popular in Germany today although it is superficially understood as painting of mood (Jensen: 783). His paintings were held as a symbol of the spirit of German nationalism during the era of Nazism. His art received wide recognition from inclusion in *The Romantic Movement* exhibition at the Tate Gallery in London in 1959, and since that time his work has become accepted as the most important German contribution to European Romanticism (Tate 1959: 78).

The Cross in the Mountains represents – for the first time in Christian art – an altar-piece conceived in terms of a pure landscape. The cross, viewed obliquely from behind, is an insignificant element in the composition. It is isolated, yet integral form placed majestically amidst the firs and the rays of the setting sun of a Bohemian landscape. Although no body can be seen, the presence of a spiritual being is portrayed through the emotional setting of nature. The setting sun has also been interpreted as the setting of the old, pre-Christian world, in which case the mountain symbolizes an immovable faith, while the fir trees are an allegory of hope. It seems that Friedrich was able to capture the spiritualism without the overt religiosity of one of the most Christian symbols for modern humanity – the cross. This depiction of a Crucifixion by a German Romantic painter further emphasizes the cultural changes in the modern world where a biblically-based story is integrated into (or eclipsed by) an acceptable composition in a nineteenth-century world.

Figure 18.7   Salvador Dalí, *The Sacrament of the Last Supper*, 1955. Oil (65⅝ × 105⅛ in). National Gallery, Washington D.C. Chester Dale Collection 1963.10.115. Image © 2005 Board of Trustees, National Gallery of Art, Washington. © Salvador Dalí, Gala-Salvador Dalí Foundation, DACS, London 2005

Twentieth-Century Art

Salvador Dalí, best known as a Surrealist, executed the painting of the Last Supper (Figure 18.7) during a later period in which he uses classical, religious subjects. Dalí's earlier paintings (prior to 1934) used what he called the 'paranoiac–critical method' (Bradley 1996: 465). They were an attempt to communicate with a viewer the excitement of a world governed by paranoiac misunderstanding (ibid.: 466). He created bizarre dream imagery to create unforgettable imagery from within his mind. He knew Sigmund Freud and became associated with other artists who called themselves Surrealists. Dalí always had a difference of opinion with the other Surrealist artists that may have stemmed from the content of his paintings and the right-wing views he sometimes espoused. He was dismissed from the group in 1934 (ibid.: 466).

Dalí was born in Figueras, Catalonia, and educated at the School of Fine Arts, Madrid. His father was a Republican and an atheist and his mother was Roman Catholic. He was named Salvador in memory of a recently dead brother. This had a profound effect: his subsequent experimentation with identity and with the projection of his own persona may have developed out of an early understanding of himself as 'a reply, a double, an absence' (*Dalí*, 1970: 92).

Dalí spent World War II in the United States. He was very popular in the US and had a retrospective at the Museum of Modern Art, New York in 1941–2. While in the USA he created a dream sequence for Alfred Hitchcock's film *Spellbound*, planned a cartoon, *Destino*, with Walt Disney and wrote his own sensational autobiography, *The Secret Life of Salvador Dalí* in 1942 (Bradley 1996: 468).

Dalí returned to Spain in 1948. The work produced at this time, called his post-war paintings, retained the technical superiority of his earlier works. This renewed eclecticism of technique and style was worked out in paintings and drawings dealing with history, art history, science and religion (ibid.: 468). Dalí was very productive but the works looked very different from his pre-war production. He maintained his desire on the one hand to emulate the achievements of the Old Masters and on the other to pursue visual experiments. *The Sacrament of the Last Supper*, completed in 1955, depicts both these characteristics of the artist.

The National Gallery painting, considered by the artist to be his religious masterpiece, is over 8 feet in length and was painted in nine intense months in a remote village in Spain (*Apollo* 1956: 143). He had been working on religious paintings for the previous eight years. *The Sacrament of the Last Supper* is signed in the lower right on tablecloth: Gala Salvador Dalí / 1955. (His wife's name was Gala.) Speaking about the painting, Dalí said:

> Contrary to the anecdotal and obscure conceptions in paintings on this same subject, I wanted to materialize the maximum of luminous and Pythagorean instantaneousness, based on the celestial communion of the number twelve: 12 hours of the day – 12 months of the year – the 12 pentagons of the dodecahedron – 12 signs of the Zodiac around the sun – the 12 apostles around Christ. (*Apollo* 1956: 143)

This strong numerology immediately recalls Leonardo da Vinci's fresco masterpiece of the *Last Supper* in Santa Maria dell Grazie, Milan. Leonardo, like Dalí, was fascinated with the symbolic and geometric significances of numbers. Leonardo grouped his 12 apostles in four groups (gospel books, seasons of the year) of three (persons of the Trinity). The side panels alternate three black panels with four white panels. The addition of four plus three equalling seven denoted various Christian meaning – seven sacraments, seven gifts of the Holy Spirit, etc. Four multiplied by three equals 12 as noted by Dalí. In addition to the various modes of 12 above, additional religious significance can be given to them by the 12 tribes of Israel.

Dalí stated that this was an 'arithmetic and philosophical cosmogony based on the paranoiac sublimity of the number twelve . . . the pentagon contains microcosmic man: Christ'. Christ is in the centre of the painting blessing the bread as five apostles flank him on either side and two are placed on the opposite side of the table. Leonardo broke convention by placing Judas on the same side of the table as the other eleven apostles. Earlier Last Supper tradition in painting was to have Judas alone and on the opposite side of the table from everyone else. Dalí changes convention yet again in this twentieth-century painting.

The figure of Christ is transparent. The composition of the picture is held together by the architectural form of the dodecahedron – the symbol in antiquity of the heavens (*Apollo* 1956: 143). The shape also leads the viewer's eye upwards to see the ascending chest and arms of Christ. The extended arms also suggest the wings of the dove or third person of the Trinity. The rolling hills in the background seem to ground the painting on Earth while the dodecahedron gives it a spiritual quality despite the almost steel-like beams of its arms.

Dalí was considered an eclectic, and sometimes incoherent, modern artist. The truth may be that he found a way to depict visually the cultural theories of his times (i.e., paranoia, dream therapy, Freudian psychology) in his early works and then returned to his religious upbringing in the post-war paintings. He was fascinated with atoms and the science and military technology used in World War II. His art (and apparent change of subject) may be a direct result of his returning to sources that he knew (the Bible, the Old Master Painters of the Renaissance) and made them his own once again through his religious paintings. Many other contemporary artists of the 1950s and early 1960s returned to religious subjects and found their inspiration in the great artists of the past and in the great literary works of the past – the Bible being at the top of the list!

Conclusion

For the sake of space and in an attempt to give something that resembles adequate coverage of the reception of the Bible in various cultures in differing historical periods, we have focused almost exclusively on the history of the Christian Scriptures (NT and the OT – typologically figured) in Western art. Of course, our first two examples from early Christian and Byzantine art can hardly be considered 'Western' in their origins but these images have been more or less assimilated into the Western collective consciousness. We have been forced to leave unattended a vast amount of Jewish art (for more, see the *Journal of Jewish Art*, published at the Hebrew University in Jerusalem), both ancient and modern – from the amazing synagogue at Dura Europas with its wall-to-wall, three-tiered frescoes (Olin 2000) to the haunting, yet profoundly religious, images in James Freed's Holocaust Memorial Museum in Washington, DC (Miller 1999). Nor have we been able to delve into the complicated ways in which modern concern over gender, class, and race intersects with biblical scenes and imagery (Douglas 1994). Thankfully, some of these issues are taken up in other chapters in this volume.

This all-too-brief tour of the Bible in the visual arts confirms the general thesis of this volume. The biblical text and its interpretations both reflect and challenge the larger cultural assumptions of each historical period and in each specific place. If, as its adherents believe, the Bible is a river from which flow words of life (see Prov. 13:14), viewers of its visual depictions over the past two thousand years seem never to step into the same river twice!

References

Abadie, D. (ed.) (1979). *Salvador Dalí: Retrospective, 1920–1980* exhibition catalogue. Paris: Centre Georges Pompidou.

Bal, Mieke (1991). *Reading 'Rembrandt': Beyond the Word-Image Opposition*. Cambridge: Cambridge University Press.

Baxandall, Michael (1988). *Painting and Experience in Fifteenth-Century Italy: A Primer in the Social History of Pictorial Style*, 2nd edn. Oxford: Oxford University Press.

Berdini, Paoli (1997). *The Religious Art of Jacopo Bassano: Painting as Visual Exegesis*. Cambridge: Cambridge University Press.

Börsch-Supan, Helmut and Jähnig, Karl Wilhelm (1975). Casper David Friedrich: Gemälde, Druckgraphik und bildmäßige Zeichnungen. Munich: Prestel.

Bradley, Fiona (1996). 'Salvador Dalí', in *The Dictionary of Art*, ed. J. Turner, vol. 8: London: Macmillan, pp. 464–8.

Caracciolus, Robertus (1489). *Sermones de laudibus sanctorum*. Naples.

Cartlidge, David R. and Elliott, J. Keith (2001). *Art and the Christian Apocrypha*. London: Routledge.

Dalí par Dalí de Draeger (1970). Paris: Draeger. English trans. 1972.

Dalton, W. J. (1989). *Christ's Proclamation to the Spirits: A Study of 1 Peter 3:18–4:6* (AnBib 23). Rome: Pontifical Biblical Institute.

Derbes, Anne (1996). *Picturing the Passion in Late Medieval Italy*. Cambridge: Cambridge University Press.

Douglas, Sally Brown (1994). *The Black Christ*. Maryknoll, NY: Orbis Books.

Friedrich, Caspar David und sein Kreis (1974). Dresden: Gemäldegalerie Neue Meister.

Haeger, Barbara Joan (1983). 'The Religious Significance of Rembrandt's *Return of the Prodigal Son*: An Examination of the Picture in the Context of the Visual and Iconographic Tradition', PhD dissertation, University of Michigan, Ann Arbor.

Haug, Walter and Wachinger, Burghart (eds) (1993). *Die Passion Christi in Literatur und Kunst des Spatmittelaters*. Tübingen: Max Niemeyer Verlag.

Hinz, S. (ed.) ([1968] 1974). 'Äusserung bei Betrachtung einer Sammlung von Gemälden von grösstenteils noch lebenden und unlängst verstorbenen Künstlern' (1830; MS), Dresden, Kupferstichkab; pp. 84–134, in *Caspar David Friedrich in Briefen und Bekenntnissen*. Munich.

Hoekstra, Hidde (1990). *Rembrandt and the Bible*. Utrecht: Magna Books.

Hornik, Heidi J. (2003). 'The Sign of Jonah', in *Christian Reflection: A Series in Faith and Ethics*, ed. Robert B. Kruschwitz. Waco, TX.: Center for Christian Ethics, Baylor University, 6: 51–54.

Hornik, Heidi J. and Mikeal C. Parsons. (2003). 'The Harrowing of Hell', *Bible Review* (June): 18–26, 50.

Jensen, Jens Christian (n.d.). *Friedrich, Caspar David*. Grove Art Online, Oxford University Press. Available at www.groveart.com.ezproxy.baylor.edu/ (accessed 8 February 2006).

Kartsonis, Anna D. (1986). *Anastasis: The Making of an Image*. Princeton, NJ: Princeton University Press.

Leonardo da Vinci (1956). *Treatise on Painting*, ed. Amos Philip McMahon. Princeton, NJ: Princeton University Press.

Lewis, Elizabeth Bruening (1996). 'Early Christian and Byzantine Art: Religious Iconography', *The Dictionary of Art*, ed. J. Turner, vol. 9. London: Macmillan, pp. 516–19.

MacDonald, A. A., Ridderbos, H. N. B. and Schlusemann, R. M. (1998). *The Broken Body: Passion Devotion in Late-Medieval Culture*. Groningen: Egbert Forsten.

McCulloch, J. M. (1930). *The Harrowing of Hell: A Comparative Study of an Early Christian Doctrine*. Edinburgh.

Miles, Margaret (2004). 'Achieving the Christian Body: Visual Incentives to Imitation of Christ in the Christian West', in Heidi J. Hornik and Mikeal C. Parsons (eds), *Interpreting Christian Art*. Macon, GA: Mercer University Press.

Miller, Naomi (1999). ' "Building the Unbuildable": The U.S. Holocaust Memorial Museum', in Wessel Reinink and Jeroen Stumpel (eds), *Memory & Oblivion*. Dordrecht: Kluwer Academic Publishers, pp. 1091–101.

Monrad, Kasper and Bailey, Colin J. (2000). *Caspar David Friedrich og Danmark*. Oplag: J. P. Moller and Statens Museum for Kunst.

Nouwen, Henri J. M. (1992). *The Return of the Prodigal Son*. New York: Doubleday.

Olin, Margaret (2000). ' "Early Christian Synagogues" and "Jewish Art Historians": The Discovery of the Synagogue of Dura-Europos', *Marburger Jahrbuch für Kunstwissenschaft* 27: 7–28.

Parsons, Mikeal C. 'The Prodigal's Elder Brother: The History and Ethics of Reading Luke 15:11–32'. (1996). *Perspectives in Religious Studies* 23: 147–74.

Robb, David M. (1936). 'The Iconography of the Annunciation in the Fourteenth and Fifteenth Centuries', *Art Bulletin* 18: 480–526.

Robbins, Jill (1991). *Prodigal Son/Elder Brother*. Chicago: University of Chicago Press.

Rosenau, Helen (1944). 'A Study in the Iconography of the Incarnation', *Burlington Magazine* 85: 176–9.

Rosenberg, Jacob (1964). *Rembrandt, Life and Work*. London: Greenwich.

Rowlands, Eliot W. (1996). 'Lippi: (1) Filippo Lippi', in *The Dictionary of Art*, ed J. Turner, vol. 19. London: Macmillan, pp. 439–45.

'Salvador Dalí, His Most Recent Major Work' (1956). *Apollo* 63 (May): 143.

'Salvador Dalí: *The Sacrament of the Last Supper*' (no date). National Gallery of Art, Washington, DC. Available at www.nga.gov/cgi-bin/psearch (accessed 23 June 2004).

Seymour, Charles J. (1967). *Michelangelo's David: A Search for Identity*. Pittsburgh, PA: University of Pittsburgh Press.

Shearman, John (1992). *Only Connect . . . Art and the Spectator in the Italian Renaissance*. Princeton, NJ: Princeton University Press.

Tate (1959). *The Romantic Movement*. Exhibition catalogue. London: Tate Gallery.

Wind, Edgar (2000). *The Religious Symbolism of Michelangelo*. Oxford: Oxford University Press.

Wixom, William D. (1967). 'Early Christian Sculptures at Cleveland', *Bulletin of the Cleveland Museum of Art* March: 67–88.

CHAPTER 19
Architecture

Andrew Ballantyne

Buildings have their roles to play in everyday affairs. The buildings we notice most in documents tend to be those where something extraordinary happens, but often the buildings themselves are too ordinary to be worthy of notice. The buildings that people want to make remarks about, or tell us to go and see, are the exceptions – the special buildings that have had uncommon effort put into them, or which mark the spot where an important event took place. This chapter moves from the commonplace dwellings where people usually did unexceptional things, to monumental buildings that were designed to act as a focus for memories or the collective identity of a culture. The everyday dwellings that are taken for granted in the narratives of many events in the Bible are not the same as the buildings that were around me when I grew up in northern Europe in the twentieth century. Even people who have lived from birth among the places where biblical events took place, around the eastern Mediterranean, will not find these buildings completely familiar, as building methods have changed in recent centuries. There is a degree of strangeness for the modern reader in these buildings that would not have been at all strange for those who first heard the stories. They are presented as part of the furniture of everyday life, and helped to make the stories convincing with their circumstantial detail. They are not there to take one's breath away, and they are never the point of the story. They are part of what is taken for granted in the story that is being told, part of what we all know, or are assumed to know.

For example, there is a house in Jericho, that belonged to Rahab, who sheltered two of Joshua's spies (Josh. 2:1–21). The king heard that there were spies in the town and sent his men to search for them, and when Rahab heard about this she hid the men. That is the point of this part of the story. The detail, which makes the story of interest from an architectural point of view, is that she hid them on the roof of the house, by covering them up with stalks of flax that were drying up there (Josh. 2:6). This detail tells us more than the storyteller might have expected it would, as it is not something that she could have done if she had been living in a house in northern Europe in modern times. First, there is the fact that the house had a flat roof, which a few modern houses have, but those that I am familiar with from personal everyday contact do not. Second, the fact that Rahab was using it as a place to dry flax, which I have never known anyone to do, though I daresay that somewhere it is being done. The flat roof tells us something about the climate of the eastern Mediterranean, and the building materials that were used there in ancient times. The house would have been constructed with walls made of stone, where stone was to be had, or in the sun-baked clay bricks that are mentioned in Exodus (Exod. 5:10). The roof would have sheltered the inhabitants from the rain from time to time, but much more often it would have provided shelter from the scorching sun, and would have kept some air at a comfortable temperature through the oppressive heat of the day and the cold of the clear-aired night.

It would have been made of timbers, and they would not have been sawn following the modern practice, into straight-sided joists, but would have followed the twisting shapes of the olive trees from which they probably came. Such trees are in plentiful supply, and produce a strong timber, but the trees are not large and if one were to cut the branches straight every time, then they would lose most of their strength as well producing much shorter timbers. A modern builder, bound by the conventions of our day, would look at these trees and say that there was no useful timber in them. To complete this story about the likely construction of the house, I should just say that between these larger timbers there would have been smaller ones, easier to come by, and they would probably have supported a layer of flat stones, on which would rest a substantial layer of earth. This earth layer acted as a stable support for the crust of puddled clay that would have kept the house waterproofed for as long as it was properly maintained, and as the layer of earth would have been quite thick, it would also have given good insulation against the extremes of hot and cold during the day and night.

So, the normal houses had flat roofs, which plainly could be used as an upper floor, and they were constructed in such a way that it would be difficult in a small house to make a well-shaped opening in the roof. It would be possible to make a good opening on to the roof if there were a wall on each side of the stair going up to the roof, but to make that happen we have to start imagining a house with at least two solidly constructed compartments, and that would have been a larger-than-normal house in that part of the world at that time. A normal house would have had a single solid wall around it and then lightweight partitions of woven hurdles or curtains inside to make spatial divisions. Space would have been at a premium, and the stairs to the roof would have been outside, perhaps with a single stair being shared by more than one dwelling in places such as Jericho where the inhabitants would have lived close together. In fact, we are told that Rahab's house was part of the city wall (Josh. 2:15), so we can be certain that it was joined by other buildings on each side. This way of making defences continued to be used around the Mediterranean for another 2,000 years and more, although the more important defences came to be made more solidly than this after the invention of cannon.

However, a domestic regime where flax would be dried on the roof is far removed from the practices that we find in the domestic arena in a post-industrial society. The settlement called Jericho was a city in ancient times, but its life would look very rural to us if we were able to revisit it in its ancient condition. The usual means of sustenance would have been agriculture, and Rahab was clearly in touch with a rural culture, despite herself having taken up a more specialized and urban form of employment in prostitution. The drying of flax would not have been a professional activity – taken in for the sake of earning an income – but was part of her domestic activity, which might then have involved her in combing the fibres of flax, spinning them into thread at her spinning wheel, and weaving them into fabrics for her own use. In a more industrialized society we would expect every part of this activity to be carried out by specialists, each with their own highly developed skill (or else working a machine that did the laborious part of the work for them). Such activity happens remotely, and we see nothing of it. There is less subdivision of these tasks in the ancient world, and consequently the dwelling is a place where there is a wider range of activity. The drying of flax is a normal activity in Rahab's world, and the king's men's suspicions are not aroused by the fact that the roof is covered in flax stalks. If for some reason I were to decide that I wanted to dry flax, then I would not be able to do it by spreading it out on my roof, which slopes steeply, and which is likely to be rained on in any case – and the main reason it slopes is so that rain water will run off it efficiently. Guests would not be able to sleep on the roof. I am living in a society that has different habits, different ways of organizing its practices, and that has grown up in a different climate. The house that I occupy is not interchangeable with a house in ancient Jericho. My way of life is very different from Rahab's. However, it would be possible to hide someone here. I can make an imaginative identification easily enough to follow the states of mind of the people in the biblical narrative, but the architectural detail would be worked out differently here.

Thresholds

Similarly, there is a house mentioned in Mark 2:2 that was built in much the same way as Rahab's house. What happens in the narrative is that part of the roof is removed in order to lower a paralyzed man down into the house where Jesus is present. This is odd for a modern audience, in a way that it would not have been for the first people who heard the story. It would have been easy for them to go up on to a roof, whereas it would be difficult and awkward to get up on to my roof, and although it would be possible to remove slates and break through the layers of insulation it would be ludicrous to try to introduce a paralyzed person into the house by such means. Breaking through the roof of the house described in Mark would have been difficult, but far from impossible, given the traditional means of construction, and once the hole had been made it would have been a straightforward matter to make use of it. Not that people did such things on a regular basis. The removal of part of the roof was a seriously damaging thing to do, and it would have taken trouble to repair. It was an act of desperation, and would have been startling for those who witnessed it. Breaking into a modern house through a window would not be disturbing in the same way, because a window already makes a perceptible link between the inside and outside of the building. In the house where Jesus was, there were probably few windows giving light directly into the space. The ferocity of the sun is something to be guarded against in that part of the world, even today, when there is an inclination to have plate glass on display as a signifier of modernity. As there is a need to protect oneself against the effects of earthquakes, the houses are constructed with concrete frames, that support a concrete slab for a flat roof, and it would be inviolate against even desperate intruders. It would be easier to break through the wall of a modern earthquake-resistant house than through its roof. The real shock of breaking through the roof of the old building lies not in its technical impossibility but in the way that it disturbs our sense of security in the home. Something rather fundamental is violated when the confined space of the interior is ruptured and the room flooded with unaccustomed light, as well as a good deal of dusty debris. The effect of this means of entry into the room remains striking and dramatic, and in the narrative it serves to demonstrate how committed these people were to introducing the paralyzed man into Jesus' presence; but the building's role in the narrative is firmly grounded in the everyday experience of the original audience. No extraordinary powers need to be imagined for the deed to be done. The miracle happens a little later in the story.

Where domestic buildings are mentioned in the Bible, they tend to be mentioned for the sake of what the detail tells us about the people involved in the narrative, not for the sake of telling us what the buildings are like. When the roof was broken through, the normal protocols of crossing the threshold were avoided, making the entry to the room extraordinary and remarkable. The normal decorums would not usually be note-worthy, but thresholds are important and charged places in buildings. The unremark-able house is used in a gestural way, so as to allow us to understand the faith and commitment of those who would be in Jesus' presence. By contrast, the time of the orig-inal Passover, as described in Exodus, involves the gestural modification of the build-ings' fabric, when the door jambs and lintels are painted with lamb's blood in order that the Lord will not visit the houses so marked (Exod. 12:7). The blood-marked thresholds will not be crossed. Another important threshold-event was at Christ's tomb, where the threshold had been sealed with a stone so that no one would be able to cross it, but the gospels all tell us that the stone was found rolled away, making the threshold open, but most importantly we read the rolled-away-stone as gestural and indicative of Christ's absence from the tomb. The resurrection was not witnessed directly according to the Gospel narratives, but is to be inferred in the first instance from the condition of the tomb. The threshold has already been crossed, and the emptiness of the interior is the point of the story. The tomb may not be a domestic building, but it has a clear utility as a dwelling for the dead body, as well as its symbolic commemorative function. With the resurrection of the body, the tomb's quasi-domestic function evaporates, and its symbolic commemorative and gestural role takes over.

Christ's burial place was identified and a basilica was built around it. Artistically the most significant 'take' on it is perhaps the Rucellai Sepulchre (c.1467) in the church of San Pancrazio in Florence, which is thought to be the work of Leon Battista Alberti, the author of important treatises on painting and architecture, and the architect of some of the defining buildings of the Renaissance (Tavernor 1998: 110). There is little documentation for the Rucellai Sepulchre, and what there is can be doubted, but Rucellai was Alberti's patron. He may not have sent anyone to Jerusalem to take measurements of the sepulchre there, though there is a document to say that he did (ibid.: 110). The monument is finely worked, half the size of the original, but with its elements reordered. It is rectangular in form with a curved apse at one end. There is a low entrance, placed off-centre at the end opposite the apse, and inside along one of the flanking walls there is a bench which is understood as a resting place for a dead body; but the body is not there. An inscription makes explicit the fact that the Sepulchre at Jerusalem was the model, and its prestige was confirmed when, in 1471, the Pope granted worshippers who visited it on Good Friday and Holy Sundays seven years plenary indulgence (ibid.: 114). Architecture is here being used to focus the thoughts of the pious, and its effectiveness in doing so is recognized in the papal dispensation.

Noah's Ark

We tend to think of Noah's Ark as symbolic and gestural, but it is described in some detail as a practical building project with utilitarian ends. There is nothing symbolic in the form of the ark; it is built simply and directly with a particular function in mind, and is the most ambitious such project mentioned in the Bible. In medieval illustrations it is always depicted as if the builders are labouring on a timber-framed house, and from them we can learn something about medieval domestic architecture, not about ancient boat building. Noah's instruction was to build the ark in Cypress wood, which would mean wood from great trees, which would need to be sawn to shape, but which, when sawn, would be well shaped and not subject to the vagaries of timber from smaller trees. The ark is to be well built, and securely waterproofed – coated with pitch both inside and out. These practical details help to offset the implausibility of the craft's overall dimensions. At 300 cubits long it would have vastly exceeded the length of any boat known to the ancient world. It was to have three superimposed decks, and multiple compartments. The dimensions of the craft were given as an image of what it would take to house the whole animal kingdom. Of the building projects mentioned in the Bible, this one is by far the most familiar in a wider culture. It has been popular as a children's toy, a toy box with a sloping roof-like lid, a door in the side, and a vaguely boat-like lower part that can contain model animals, in matching pairs. In a respectable nineteenth-century household, this was one of the few toys that children were allowed on Sundays, and the story of Noah and the ark still has the presence of a pervasive children's tale, on account of children's fascination with animals rather than for reasons that are more directly theological.

Monuments

There are more building operations described in the Old Testament than in the New, and the New Testament's buildings are not monumental in character. The business of marking significant places with a monument – a pile of uncut stones for example – is firmly established in the Old Testament, and there are traditional biblical sites for New Testament events that are now marked with monuments; but the great cathedrals of the Middle Ages do not spring from any biblical suggestions for places of worship. Their astonishing stone vaults might be taken as a reflection of the vault that separated earth and heaven (Gen. 1:6–8) but there is no direct call for monumental places of worship. The basis of the liturgy of the mass is of course biblical, but it is the re-enactment of domestic events, and it is the actions that define the mass, not the setting in which it takes place. The Last Supper took place in a house with an upper room that was large enough to hold 13 people in a sociable group. The early Christians met in a fairly clandestine way and did not have monumental buildings at their disposal. Early places of worship were built as houses, and are known as places of worship on account of objects that have been excavated from them, not because the buildings were architecturally distinct. The biblical accounts of the Last Supper place it firmly in the domestic realm, and they give no hint of the grandiose settings that would come to be thought of as culturally appropriate for the re-enactment of the event.

In the Old Testament there are descriptions of the construction of three types of monument. The first is the simple commemorative monument – the pile of uncut stones – which marks the spot where a significant event happened. The second is the building of extravagance and excess, represented in the story of the Tower of Babel. The third is the special case of Solomon's temple at Jerusalem, which is presented as an example of appropriate magnificence.

The function of commemoration can be accomplished with a simple cairn and there are examples of altars being built with specifically unhewn stones (e.g. Exod. 20:25; Josh. 8:30). But commemoration is not less effective for being taken on in a more elaborate building, and there are examples of buildings that mark the spot where biblical events took place, or were supposed to have taken place. Eleni, the mother of Constantine – Roman emperor and founder of Constantinople – took an interest in locating the places where Jesus was born and died, and it is thanks to her that we have the basilicas at Bethlehem and Golgotha that mark these places. Whether or not they were identified accurately, in the time since they were built in the fourth century, the buildings have accumulated their own traditions, which make these places the focus of ritual and genuine commemoration. This is where the events are marked on the surface of the Earth, and the commemorative aspect of the stones is fused with a larger building project, so that worship also is incorporated in the monuments' role.

Babel

The idea of building large monuments and impressing people by doing so is a much older idea than anything specifically biblical. The Great Pyramids in Egypt are among the oldest buildings we know, and their reputation in both the ancient and the modern worlds is mainly on account of their immense size. Their function (as burial places) was superseded long ago when they were robbed, but they remained as one of the wonders of the world. In Genesis and Exodus the people of Abraham, Joseph and Moses are nomadic farming communities, and their sheltering tents contrast with the overbearing monuments of the Egyptians, who are presented as powerful and at times cruel. The Tower of Babel would clearly have been a rival for the Egyptians' monuments, had the project been completed and had it survived. The story as told in Genesis 11 is straightforwardly a story of people building for the sake of glory: 'Come, let us build ourselves a city, and a tower with its top in the heavens, and let us make a name for ourselves: otherwise we shall be scattered abroad upon the face of the earth' (Gen. 11:4). There is no mention of any accommodation in the tower: it was not proposed as a way of housing the people, or giving them a better place to work. There is an idea that building the tower will bring these people a reputation, but that might involve some confused thinking. The tower is supposed to be the work of the whole of humanity, which at this time is unified and speaks a single language and can find common cause in the building of the tower. Therefore there is no one outside this community to be impressed by the tower. They might well be pleased with their efforts, but to be pleased with oneself is very different from making a name for oneself. The place chosen for this city and its tower is the plain of Ishtar, which identifies the city as Babylon, a city that is always presented in the Bible as a locus of wrong-headedness (e.g. Jer. 51; Isa. 11:11 and 13–14; Zech. 5:11; Rev. 17). Archaeologists have identified the site of ancient Babylon as being a little to the south of modern Baghdad, and the tower as a ziggurat that has the name Etemenanki – the house of the foundation of heaven and earth (Oates 1986; Hoerth 1998). Before the nineteenth century the existence of Babylon was doubted, as it seemed to be a fabulous and mythical place that surpassed anything that could have been real, but Robert Koldeway's excavations of 1899 uncovered impressive remains, including the Ishtar Gate, covered in reliefs of lions and bulls on a bright blue glazed background, that is now reconstructed in the Pergamon Museum in Berlin. The gate was built of fired clay bricks, as was the Tower of Babel in the biblical account – a much stronger building material than the sun-baked bricks made with straw that the Egyptians had used. '"Come, let us make bricks, and burn them thoroughly." And they had brick for stone, and bitumen for mortar' (Gen. 11:3). So they had building materials that were imperishable and strong and decided to put up a tower that would rise beyond anything previously attempted. There are limits inherent in materials that are exposed when they are used on a large scale. Even a building-shape that is as inherently stable as that of a pyramid can collapse, as the builders of Meydum found in ancient times (Mendelssohn 1974). The fact that there was difficulty and danger in the project was part of the point. Had the building been only expensive, then a certain sort of glory would have attached to it, but the building was in addition something that demanded skill and daring, and the combination of all three qualities would have produced something unrivalled that could not have failed to impress foreigners and to establish Babylon's reputation as the cultural capital of the ancient world. In the Bible's version of events it all went disastrously wrong. God was impressed by the work, but saw it as the precursor of other greater things that he wanted to prevent. So he introduced confusion by multiplying their languages, so they no longer understood one another. They stopped building the city and scattered over the earth (Gen. 11:6–8).

Despite this awful warning, buildings continue to be built that challenge the limits of the possible. There are technologies that can be pressed into service for buildings which make it possible to build in ways that amaze, and if the buildings are expensive and difficult to build, then the fact that they have been built makes them attract admiration and envy. The prestige that attaches to these projects is more important than their commercial viability, and there is a constant risk of ruin. The history of tall building does not stop with the Tower of Babel, but is with us still. We continue to try to work at the limit of what is possible, or safe. The buildings become increasingly dangerous as they reach up ever closer to the skies, as they go beyond the range of fire-fighters' ladders and water jets. The taller a building is, the higher the proportion of its space that will need to be devoted to structure that holds the building up, and fire escapes to allow people to leave the building if difficulties arise, not to mention the additional services that need to be put in place to control the conditions at levels of the building where, if windows were allowed to open, the climate would be found to be unexpectedly cold or windy compared with the conditions encountered down at the ground; and also provisions for emergencies: smoke vents, sprinkler systems and suchlike. In addition to accidental and natural misfortunes, very tall buildings become symbolic and therefore attract hostile attentions, which are countered by security patrols and surveillance systems. We know that these building are dangerous, and these systems are routinely designed into them from the outset. Insurance companies accept money in order to carry the risks that attach to these buildings, and the premiums are high. Statistically speaking, it must be assumed that sooner or later buildings will fail disastrously, though no one could have predicted quite how spectacular and appalling the failure of the twin towers in New York would be, or indeed that it would have been that particular tall building – it was no longer the tallest in the world. Nevertheless, collectively we know that there are in a general way risks, and collectively we are ready to take them. It is because the risks are there that these buildings take the breath away, and make a name for the peoples who build them.

There are alternatives to this way of thinking, and the Bible would seem to exhort us to take them. However, this would involve turning one's back on worldly glory, and giving expression to corporate or national pride, and it is not easily done. There are societies where honour would not be accrued by such means. For example, Gregory Bateson's (1949) analysis of the Balinese value-system presents a society in which a decision to amass the means to construct an enormous building would be seen as a disorder that would disturb the balance of the steady state. It would cause anxiety long before the building came into being, and peer pressure would prevent it from happening. However, as we look round the world at the beginning of the twenty-first century, we see that there are more tall towers than ever coming to completion or being projected for the future, and they are to be found round the globe. We know that there are risks, but there is a stronger imperative that wills people onwards with these projects. They are not inspired by the story of the Tower of Babel, still less warned by it, but they are driven by the same basic human impulses.

The Temple

The building project in the Bible that is described in most detail and at the greatest length is Solomon's building of the temple at Jerusalem. In contrast with the Tower of Babel, this project was designed to glorify God, rather than its builders. The aim is not presented as being to make a building that was larger than any other monument, but to make something that had unparalleled magnificence. The building's dimensions are given twice over, and the two accounts agree in most, but not all, details (1 Kgs. 5–8; 2 Chron. 2–7). The main body of the building was 20 cubits wide and 60 cubits long. The Holy of Holies at one end was 20 cubits long and 20 wide, leaving a space 40 cubits long as the largest volume. These rooms were 30 cubits high (120, according to Chronicles, which seems less plausible). These principal spaces were lined with gold and decorated with images of cherubim, palm trees and flowers. In the Holy of Holies there were two great statues of cherubim, with 5-cubit wings, so that in the confined space their wings spread right across the space, tip to tip. These statues and the altar were also covered in gold. It is programmatically excessive. Moreover, the building process itself was conducted in such as way as to maintain the peace and dignity of the place as far as possible. The noisy part of the work, the shaping of stones with hammer and chisel, was all carried out away from the temple, the stones being brought there fully worked (1 Kgs. 6:7). This was not usual practice, and would have made the carved stones more vulnerable to damage as they were transported to the site in their finished state. The workforce was vast, and was conscripted by Solomon. People were sent to work in Lebanon to provide the timbers: 10,000 would have been there at any one time, working on rotation – one month in Lebanon, two months at home – so 30,000 people were involved. Then there were 70,000 labourers, 80,000 stone cutters and 3,300 supervisors (1 Kgs. 5:14–16). Throughout the descriptions of the work on the temple it is plain that we are to be impressed by the vast cost of the work, as well as by the splendour of the finished results. The house of God was to be a place that had no equal in this world.

Before moving on to take note of the importance of this description, we should recall that the temple's history turned out to be less serene than Solomon would have wanted. Ezra 4–6 records the rebuilding of the temple after it had been sacked by the Babylonians in the sixth century BC. It was the Babylonian kings Cyrus and Darius who from c.520 BC permitted the rebuilding, which was very much less splendid than Solomon's temple had been. The dimensions that are given – 60 cubits high and 60 cubits wide – are different, but retain the pattern of proportions of simple ratios, reminiscent of the proportions in musical harmonies. This temple was itself destroyed in 168 BC, then rebuilt from 19 BC under Herod. It is the temple of this rebuilding that figures in the narratives of the New Testament. It in turn was destroyed in 70 AD.

It is the description of Solomon's temple that gives biblical justification for extravagant building for the house of God: an idea that continued to have currency in the Christian era. There is a particularly notable example of a church built with the model of Solomon's splendour in mind. It was built in sixth-century Constantinople (525–27) and dedicated to St Polyeuktos. The building's patron was a princess, Anicia Juliana, who had ambitions for her family, and the church was a dynastic statement as well as an act of piety. She was said to have surpassed Solomon (Harrison 1989: 40). The church has not survived, but it was excavated in the 1960s, before the site was buried by a motorway. The still-visible fragment of it include niches finely carved with fans of peacock feathers surrounded by delicate twisting vines, and a frieze carrying a text that enabled the remains to be identified with the church that was known about from literary sources. Its dome was lined with gold (perhaps as an expedient to prevent the new emperor Justinian, who acceded to the throne in 527, from taking it from Anicia Juliana) (ibid.: 40). The church was 100-cubit square on plan, and it was the largest and most sumptuous church in Constantinople (ibid.: 137, 139). It would act as a spur to Justinian to surpass it in the rebuilding of Hagia Sophia, which he made half as large again as St Polyeuktos, but in many ways followed its example. When work on that astonishing building was completed (532–7), Justinian is reported to have said, 'Solomon, I have vanquished thee', and in doing so he might have been alluding to the modern Solomon along with the ancient one, though Anicia Juliana had died in 528 (ibid.: 40).

Outdoing Solomon clearly brought with it the risk of falling into the habit of mind that was pursued at Babel. In the twelfth century, St Bernard of Clairvaux famously inveighed against extravagance in churches and monastic buildings (Casey 1970: 63–6). His contemporary the Abbé Suger was rebuilding the abbey church of St Denis, north of Paris, where many of the French kings were buried, in a particularly resplendent manner. It was here under Suger's patronage that the style of architecture that we now know as 'Gothic' was developed. Suger, perhaps feeling the need to justify himself against the accusations of Bernard, wrote about his programme of building of the church, alternating passages which extol the fabulous extravagance of the building and its furnishings, with passages that explain how the aesthetic rapture can be transferred to pious ends. He was reassured to hear that the church of St Denis came second in splendour only to Justinian's Hagia Sophia, and indeed may have been its equal (Panofsky [1948] 1979: 65). In Ezekiel there is a description of a vision of a new temple, a vast and fantastical affair, which shows at least that the description of Solomon's temple did not represent the limit of what could be imagined as suitable for the house of the Lord (Ezek. 40–2). Suger cites Ezekiel's list of precious stones in another place (Ezek. 28:13) in connection with his own decoration of the church:

> Often we contemplate, out of sheer affection for the church our mother, these different ornaments both new and old; and when we behold how that wonderful cross of St. Eloy – together with the smaller ones – and that incomparable ornament commonly called 'the Crest' are placed upon the golden altar, then I say, sighing deeply in my heart: Every precious stone was thy covering, the sardius, the topaz, and the jasper, the chrysolite, and the onyx, and the beryl, the sapphire, and the carbuncle, and the emerald. To those who know the properties of precious stones it becomes evident, to their utter astonishment, that none is absent from the number of these (with the only exception of the carbuncle), but that they abound most copiously. Thus, when – out of my delight in the beauty of the house of God – the loveliness of the many-coloured gems has called me away from external cares, and worthy meditation has induced me to reflect, transferring that which is material to that which is immaterial, on the diversity of the sacred virtues: then it seems to me that I see myself dwelling, as it were, in some strange region of the universe which neither exists entirely in the slime of the earth nor entirely in the purity of Heaven; and that, by the grace of God, I can be transported from this inferior to that higher world in an anagogical manner. (Panofsky [1948] 1979: 63–5)

So Suger's method is to transfer his thoughts from the material world to the spiritual world, and it clearly helps him in his spiritual meditations if the material world before him is at its most resplendent. There is a famous sculpted capital in the basilica of the Madeleine at Vezelay that shows an apparently ordinary scene of some corn being milled by hand. Suger used the same image in one of his stained glass windows. One of these windows, he says:

represents the Apostle Paul turning a mill, and the Prophets carrying sacks to the mill. The verses of this subject are these:

> By working the mill, thou, Paul, takest the flour out of the bran.
> Thou makest known the inmost meaning of the Law of Moses.
> From so many grains is made the true bread without bran,
> Our and the angels' perpetual food.
>
> (Panofsky [1948] 1979: 75)

So the detailed decoration of medieval architecture can often have Bible-derived symbolism, even when the image would not obviously indicate it. For Suger, however, these homely images seem to have been less spiritually efficacious than the presence of large numbers of precious stones:

> To me, I confess, one thing has always seemed pre-eminently fitting: that every costly or costliest thing should serve, first and foremost, for the administration of the Holy Eucharist. *If* golden pouring vessels, golden vials, golden little mortars used to serve, by the word of God or the command of the Prophet, to collect the *blood of goats or calves or the red heifer: how much more* must golden vessels, precious stones, and whatever is most valued among all created things be laid out, with continual reverence and full devotion, for the reception of the *blood of Christ.* (ibid.: 65)

Suger here alludes to – or one could say misquotes – Hebrews 9:13–14: 'for if the blood of goats and bulls, with the sprinkling of the ashes of a heifer, sanctifies those who have been defiled so that their flesh is purified, how much more will the blood of Christ'. Suger takes the analogy and puts it to new use, to justify his vision of a 'super-resplendent' architecture. The implements and settings for Christian worship should be more splendid than Jewish ones (ibid.: 193). The biblical authority for Suger's theological-aesthetic theory is important for the acceptance of his argument's validity by his opponents, who would otherwise have been able to dismiss Suger's tastes as self-indulgent, and as he was the leading protagonist for his position we could expect that the Cistercian attitudes to design would have gained the upper hand and would have held sway, so that the glorious excesses of Gothic architecture would have been checked and would not have come to fruition. It originated in a range of technical accomplishments – rib-vaults, stained glass, flying buttresses, pointed arches – that were brought together by Suger in the realisation of a vision of architecture as a translucent envelope of mystical light in which the divine mysteries could find an appropriate setting. We see that vision being taken up and realized in different ways in different places over the next three centuries, from the gem-like reliquary that was the royal chapel in Paris – the Sainte Chapelle – to the impossibly delicate cages of superimposed traceries that soar to the skies at Strasbourg.

Cities, Gardens and Primitive Huts

Greater than any individual building, the idea of the city reappears in the Bible importantly in connection with their destruction – Sodom and Gomorrah (Gen. 14:10),

Babylon – and annexation. When Joshua took the city of Jericho, he did so by having his troops play music, which made the walls of the city fall flat (Josh. 6). It has been said more recently, by both Schelling and Goethe, for example, that architecture is frozen music. The idea of a rapport between music and architecture seems to be repeated in the proportions of the temple at Jerusalem, and it is there again in the vision of the New Jerusalem in St John's Revelation:

> It has the glory of God and a radiance like a very rare jewel, like jasper, clear as crystal. It has a great, high wall with twelve gates . . . the city lies four square, its length the same as its width . . . fifteen hundred miles; its length and width and height are equal . . . The wall is built of jasper, while the city is pure gold, clear as glass. The foundations of the wall of the city are adorned with every jewel; the first was jasper, the second sapphire, the third agate, the fourth emerald, the fifth onyx, the sixth carnelian, the seventh chrysolite, the eighth beryl, the ninth topaz, the tenth chrysoprase, the eleventh jacinth, the twelfth amethyst. And the twelve gates are twelve pearls, each of the gates is a single pearl, and the street of the city is pure gold, transparent as glass.

> I saw no temple in the city, for its temple is the Lord God the Almighty and the Lamb. And the city has no need of sun or moon to shine on it, for the glory of God is its light, and its lamp is the lamb. (Rev. 21:16–23)

Clearly there are premonitions of this city in Suger's vision of what the church of St Denis should become. Equally the great height of the Gothic spires, invented at Chartres in the twelfth century under Suger's influence, might have been inspired by this description of an unfeasibly tall city. The walls of the great cathedrals swarmed with great multitudes of figures, in the stained glass and in the statuary, many of them figures of biblical origin. One of the most frequently depicted set-pieces in architectural sculpture is the Day of Judgement, which is to be found on the west façade of many a cathedral (Rev. 4ff). The architecture was sometimes, as at Chartres, used to set up parallels between Old and New Testament figures, or prophets and saints, as the row of Old Testament figures on the left side of a portal would be reflected thematically in the row of Christian figures on the right: Abraham with the child Isaac (Gen. 22) on the left, for example, corresponding to the aged Symeon with the infant Jesus in his arms (Luke 2:28) on the right. Going back to the New Jerusalem: it has a river running through it, along the main street, and the tree of life growing on each side of it (Rev. 22:1–2). So at the heart of the city there is something like a garden, not the temple that we might expect, and it will be recalled that Solomon's temple was decorated with the iconography of a garden – palm trees, flowers, pomegranates – also that the first people, Adam and Eve, lived in a garden before they fell from grace and were expelled from it (Gen. 2–3). These figures are often to be found in the architectural sculpture, as they have an important role in the narrative, setting in motion the train of events that culminates in Christ's redemptive sacrificial death. There is a particularly finely designed capital at Vezelay that depicts their crucial moment. Eve is carved standing at one corner of the capital, facing Adam who is on one face (to her right, our left as we look at her) of the capital. She is offering him the fruit of the tree of knowledge to taste. On the other side of Eve, and round the corner of the capital, so out of Adam's sight, is the serpent, wound round a tree. In the Bible there is very little by way of description of the Garden of Eden. 'The Lord God made to grow there every tree that is pleasant to the sight and good for food, the tree of life also in the midst of the garden, and the tree of the knowledge of good and evil' (Gen. 2:9). The description was importantly elaborated by Milton in *Paradise Lost* (1667):

> So on he fare, and too the border comes
> Of Eden, where delicious Paradise,
> Now nearer, Crowns with her enclosure green,
> As with a rural mound the champain head
> Of a steep wilderness, whose hairie sides
> With thicket overgrown, grotesque and wilde,
> Access deni'd; and over head up grew
> Insuperable highth of loftiest shade,
> Cedar and Pine, and Firr, and branching Palm,
> A Silvan Scene, and as the ranks ascend
> Shade above shade, a woodie Theatre
> Of stateliest view. Yet higher then thir tops
> The verduous wall of Paradise up sprung:
> Which to our general Sire gave prospect large
> Into his neather Empire neighbouring round.
> And higher then that Wall a circling row
> Of goodliest Trees loaden with fairest Fruit,
> Blossoms and Fruits at once of golden hue
> Appeerd, with gay enameld colours mixt:
> On which the Sun more glad impress'd his beams
> Then in fair Evening Cloud, or humid Bow,
> When God hath showrd the earth; so lovely seemd
> That Lantskip.
>   (*Paradise Lost*, book 4, lines 13–53)

The garden is rapturously evoked at far greater length than can be transcribed here, and it was admired not only as poetry but also as an inspiration for landscape designers especially in the eighteenth century, and Horace Walpole made comparisons between Milton's description and English gardens that Walpole knew (Dixon Hunt and Willis 1988: 79; Walpole [1780] 1995: 30–). The pre-lapsarian garden was a focus of attention for speculation about the origins of architecture, including various ideas about primitive huts and shelters, and they have been studied by Joseph Rykwert in his book *On Adam's House in Paradise* (1972). In Genesis there is no description of Adam's house, but in Ezra there is a description of a festival that involves the construction of primitive shelters – tabernacles, succoth, or, in the following translation, booths:

> They found it written in the law, which the Lord had commanded by Moses, that the people of Israel should live in booths during the festival of the seventh month, and that they should publish and proclaim in all their towns and in Jerusalem as follows, 'Go out to the hills and bring branches of olive, wild olive, myrtle, palm, and other leafy trees to make booths, as it is written'. So the people went out and brought them, and made booths for

themselves, each on the roofs of their houses, and in their courts and in the courts of the
house of God, and in the square at the Water Gate and in the square at the Gate of Ephraim.
(Neh. 8:1–16)

This festival of primitive architecture – Succoth – is celebrated in autumn and in the
USA is known as the Jewish Thanksgiving. It should properly involve sleeping for seven
nights in a specially constructed shelter, but this can turn into something more like
picnics in the garden. It is supposed to evoke not the Garden of Eden, but the time spent
by the children of Israel as a nomadic people, wandering in the desert after the Exodus
from Egypt. It was then that the identity of the people was formed, and when various
elements of the culture took shape. For example the temple at Jerusalem has its fore-
bear in the Tent of the Presence, and its precinct – an arrangement that is described in
enough detail to be able to make an accurate reconstruction, along with the Ark of the
Covenant, which was designed to be portable, and held Moses' tablets of the law. It was
made of timber and was covered in gold sheet, embossed with seraphim, and the
description of it evokes that of the temple that would later become its home (Exod.
25–7, 30).

Architecture in the Bible and from the Bible

The austerities of a nomadic life seem to inform the generality of thinking about architecture in the Bible. There is a role for legitimate magnificence, for example, in
Solomon's palace and temple, but there is a general suspicion of anything like luxury.
When cities become the seats of luxury, then they invite destruction: Lot's wife, linger-
ingly looking back at the sophistication she was leaving behind turned to salt, while Lot
and his daughters embraced a life of utter simplicity, living in a cave (Gen. 19:26–30).
The vision of the City of God in Revelation is the exception. At its centre, on either side
of the river that runs down the central street, is the tree of life, which makes a counterpart at the end of the Bible to the tree of knowledge at its beginning. The descriptions of its gates outdo any descriptions of the gates of Babylon, which were famously
splendid, though the 'Babylon' in Revelation is identified with the modern Babylon –
Rome – the locus of worldly splendour at the time when St John was writing. The Bible
gives no encouragement to anyone to build magnificently, but the desire to build magnificently is persistent, and it has been reconciled with the desire to build piously by
referring to the exceptional instances of the City of God and Solomon's temple in
Jerusalem. The old pagan city of Rome lost its prestige to the new imperial city of Constantinople – New Rome – whose inauguration was marked by a column that is said to
have various holy relics embedded in it. It came to have as its centrepiece the greatest
church in Christendom – Justinian's Hagia Sophia – where Solomon's precedent was
invoked as showing the way. Similarly the vision of the abbot Suger, which raised the
stakes for medieval church-builders, fused the idea of the city of God with the splendour of Solomon's temple. Many buildings, but especially the medieval cathedrals,
made use of sculpted iconography that had a basis in biblical imagery, and with the
advent of the Gothic style from the twelfth century this iconography migrated into

the extensive stained glass windows. In the hands of skilled craftsmen informed by scholars alert to the signification that could derive from the placing of the images as well as from the choice of images, as at Chartres, sophisticated messages could be encoded, to be unpacked by a learned guide for the enlightenment of pilgrims. The Bible's stories are built into the fabric of some of the greatest monuments in Christendom. While the general tenor of the Bible's coverage of architecture is crystallized in the story of the disaster of the Tower of Babel, its authority has nevertheless been called upon to endorse the most monumental and glorious of structures.

References

Bateson, Gregory ([1949] 2005). 'Bali: The Value System of a Steady State', in *Social Structure: Studies Presented to A.R. Radcliffe-Brown*, ed. Meter Fortes, reprinted in Andrew Ballantyne, *Architecture Theory: A Reader in Philosophy and Culture*. London: Continuum, pp. 74–87.

Casey, M. (trans) (1970). *The Works of Bernard of Clairvaux* (Cistercian Fathers Series IA). Kalamazoo, MI: Cistercian Publications, pp. 63–6.

Dixon Hunt, John and Willis, Peter (eds) (1988). *The Genius of the Place: The English Landscape Garden 1620–1820*, 2nd edn. Cambridge, MA: MIT Press.

Harrison, M. (1989). *A Temple for Byzantium: The Discovery and Excavation of Anicia Juliana's Palace Church in Istanbul.* Austin, TX: University of Texas Press.

Hoerth, A. J. (1998). *Archaeology and the Old Testament.* Grand Rapids, MI: Baker Book House.

Katzenellenbogen, A. (1980). *The Sculptural Programmes of Chartres Cathedral.* New York: Norton.

Mendelssohn, K. (1974). *The Riddle of the Pyramids.* London: Thames and Hudson.

Oates, J. (1986). *Babylon*, rev. edn. London: Thames and Hudson.

Panofsky, E. (ed.) ([1948] 1979). *Abbot Suger on the Abbey Church of St.-Denis and its Art Treasures*, 2nd edn. Princeton, NJ: Princeton University Press.

Rykwert, J. (1972). *On Adam's House in Paradise.* New York: Museum of Modern Art.

Tavernor, R. (1998). *On Alberti and the Art of Building.* New Haven, CT: Yale University Press.

Walpole, H. ([1780] 1995). *The History of the Modern Taste in Gardening.* New York: Ursus Press.

CHAPTER 20
The Theatre

Meg Twycross

This is a series of snapshots, each focused on a different way of dramatizing the Bible. They are arranged chronologically, and reflect some sort of historical process (though they overlap). I have concentrated on the Middle Ages and the Reformation, with a brief coda on the recent past, and confined myself to English, or potentially English, examples, though the earlier ones are in Latin and belong to a pan-European tradition. Overall, they show, as one might expect, that the Bible is not an ordinary book, and that turning any part of it into a play makes a very clear statement about the nature and practice of Christianity at that particular time.

Liturgical Drama: Strengthening Faith

Why dramatize the Bible? The earliest recorded answer in Western Europe is interestingly specific: *ad fidem indocti vulgi ac neofitorum corroborandum* 'in order to strengthen the faith of the uninstructed ordinary people, and of (?)novices' (Sheingorn 1987: 19). It comes from the *Regularis Concordia*, a reforming monastic code of the Benedictine Order drawn up in Winchester in 973, and introduces a description of the Easter ceremony of the Burial and Resurrection of the Cross. The Cross stands metonymically for the body of Christ: on Good Friday it is wrapped in a linen cloth, buried in a 'sepulchre' constructed on the altar, and watched over 'with every reverence' until early on Easter Sunday morning, before Matins, when it is raised by the sacristans, and returned to its appropriate place.

There follows the ceremony of the *Visitatio Sepulchri*, the visit of the Three Marys to the Sepulchre. Three of the brethren, wearing copes and carrying lighted thuribles, representing the Three Marys of Mark's Gospel, come hesitantly, 'as if searching for someone', to the sepulchre where they encounter a fourth brother dressed in an alb and carrying a palm branch in his hand 'in imitation of the angel sitting at the tomb'. There follows a sung dialogue. The 'angel' asks:

> *Quem queritis in sepulchro, O Christicole?*
> 'Whom do you seek in the sepulchre, O worshippers of Christ?'

The 'women' reply:

> *Ihesum nazarenum crucifixum, O celicola.*
> 'Jesus of Nazareth the crucified, O dweller in heaven.'

The 'angel' replies:

> *Non est hic: surrexit sicut predixerat. Ite, nuntiate quia surrexit a mortuis.*
> 'He is not here: He has risen, as He foretold. Go, report that He has risen from the dead.'

The 'Marys' turn to the choir and announce:

> *Allelluia: resurrexit Dominus hodie, leo fortis*
> *Christus filius Dei. Deo gracias, dicite eia.*
> 'Alleluia! The Lord has risen today, the strong Lion,
> Christ, the Son of God. Thanks be to God, cry "Eia".'

The 'angel' calls them back with the antiphon:

> *Venite et videte locum ubi positus erat Dominus, alleluia, alleluia.*
> 'Come and see the place where the Lord was laid, alleluia, alleluia.'

He then raises the curtain on the sepulchre and shows the Marys the empty space, with the discarded linen cloth which represents Christ's shroud. They lay down their thuribles in the sepulchre, and taking up the cloth, display it in the direction of the clergy, 'as if showing that the Lord had risen, since he was no longer wrapped in it', singing the antiphon:

> *Surrexit dominus de sepulchro qui pro nobis perpendit in ligno, alleluia.*
> 'The Lord has risen from the sepulchre, who for us hung on the tree, alleluia.'

They then lay the cloth on the altar, and the prior starts the Te Deum. All the bells ring out.

We might ask how this was to strengthen the faith of the illiterate (which is what *indocti*, 'untaught', would imply in this period). Not through the words, which are in Latin. The effect must have been communicated by other means: the chant; the scent of incense; the ambiguous costuming, half representational, half liturgical; the acting-out of a scene where the gestures were recognizable if hieratic; the memory, presumably, and so the pleasure of identification of a tale they had been told as the lynchpin of their faith; all ending in the triumphant clangour of the bells. We are so used to looking at 'liturgical drama' as a stylized, slightly stiff version of the later mystery plays that we probably underestimate its intense sensory appeal, and, to the *indocti*, its enigmatic quality. The characters are simultaneously human beings and figures of myth.

These were real events but presented so as to invoke the 'religious' emotions of awe and veneration. Even the graveclothes, displayed to show the palpable nature of the evidence, are laid on the altar like a liturgical object.

So a powerful stimulant to faith, but not because dramatization makes it more 'real'. In our terms it is extremely unreal, as the Marys are, in fact, male clergy. It has immediacy because it is enacted, not read. This concentrates the participants and the audience upon the experience of the story. It makes it present to them, as all theatre does; but it also deliberately involves the spectators in a very particular kind of present, since the command *Ite, nunciate quia surrexit*, which ostensibly should send the Marys off to give the news to the disciples as other characters in the story, is in fact answered by the Marys telling/showing the audience. This is not a purely historical message, but an immediate, communal one: 'The Lord is risen, He hung on the Cross *for us*, praise Him.'

Four hundred years later, the clergy in England are still insisting that liturgical drama is chiefly an aid to stirring up the religious emotions of the laity, though these are now focused on *devotion*, a powerful emotional engagement with their faith and especially its major figure, Christ. Dame Katharine Sutton, Abbess of Barking 1363–1376, seeing her lay congregation growing cold in devotion and sluggish in observance (presumably manifested by poor attendance, crucial at Easter, when they should be making their annual communion), agrees with her sisters to mount an Easter ceremony (Young 1993, vol. 1: 164–7). This comprises not only the Burial and Resurrection of the Cross, with a highly elaborated *Quem quaeritis*, but between the two, a *Descensus ad inferos* (Harrowing of Hell). The Abbess and nuns, with certain priests and other clergy, representing the souls of the Patriarchs descending into Hell before the coming of Christ, go into the chapel of St Mary Magdalene and the gate is shut on them. Then the duty priest, dressed in alb and cope, with two deacons, one bearing the processional cross with 'the Lord's banner (the familiar red cross on a white background) hanging from it', other priests, and two choirboys bearing candles, sings outside the gate the antiphon *Tollite portas, principes, vestras* ('Lift up your gates, O ye princes . . .'). He repeats this three times; each time he strikes the gate with the cross, and at the third stroke it opens. The souls in Limbo are released and go in procession to the Sepulchre, where they perform the *Visitatio Sepulchri*.

There is no mention that either the Anglo-Saxon monks or the fourteenth-century nuns might be affected emotionally by the scenes in which they take part. But the Barking *Harrowing of Hell* at least seems aimed largely at the performers, crowded and locked into a side-chapel in the dark, until released by the 'great light' of candles and the cry of *Tollite portas*. Barking Abbey was razed to the ground after the Dissolution, and we cannot currently tell how much the lay congregation might have seen, or whether they only heard it: but the nuns must have been even more affected by the experience than its ostensible target audience.

The *Quem quaeritis* dialogue is not a direct dramatization of any one passage in the Bible. It has been pieced together from the several versions of the narrative which feature in the Easter liturgy. The characters – three women, one angel – are from Mark 16:1–7, the most prominent because it was the Gospel for Easter Day, and also sung during Matins, the original setting for the *Visitatio*. But Mark's angel does not engage in dialogue, for the women are apparently too afraid to speak. He tells them:

6. . . . Be not affrighted: you seek Jesus of Nazareth, who was crucified: he is risen, he is not here, behold the place where they laid him.

7. But go, tell his disciples and Peter that he goeth before you into Galilee: there shall you see him, as he told you.

So where did the famous question-and-answer come from? The angels in Luke 24:5 ask *Quid quaeritis viventium cum mortuis*, but the question is rhetorical. Young suggests that the exchange is a verbal memory of the Good Friday singing of St John's Passion, when in the Garden of Gethsemane Christ asks, twice, those who have come to take him: *Quem quaeritis?* They answer: *Iesum Nazarenum* (John 18:4–5, 7) (Young 1933, vol. l: 204). The rest of the dialogue comes from Matthew 28:1–10, the Gospel for the Vigil of Easter.

We should think of it, like the liturgy in which it is embedded, as a dynamic sequence and interchange of allusions and quotations. Rather than working from a written text, the composer probably drew on his aural memory of familiar words and melodies. These were not even necessarily biblical: more elaborate versions of the *Visitatio* added, for example, the dialogue between the Apostles and Mary Magdalene from the eleventh-century Easter Sequence *Victimae paschali laudes* (Connelly 1957: 96–9). It dramatizes an event, not one account of it. It is almost a dramatization of a picture – compare the *Visitatio* in the *Regularis Concordia* with the contemporary illumination of the Three Marys and the Angel at the Sepulchre in the Benedictional of St Æþelwold. The artist collapses the various stages of the story into one image: the dramatist pulls them out into a moving sequence of three-dimensional images: the angel at the sepulchre, the seeking women, the empty tomb, above all the showing of the evidence of Christ's Resurrection.

The Barking *Harrowing of Hell* is at one further remove. It is not based on a biblical event but on the apocryphal *Gospel of Nicodemus* (Roberts and Donaldson 1870: 439–58). This is a powerfully imagined mythical narrative built on hints from the New Testament (1 Pet. 3:18–20), and fleshed out with prophecy: 'the people that walked in darkness, have seen a great light; to them that dwelt in the region of the shadow of death, light is risen' (Isa. 9:2); 'I will break in pieces the gates of brass, and will burst the bars of iron' (Isa. 45:2; cf. also Isa. 42:7, Hos. 6:2, etc.). *Nicodemus* imagines a dialogue between Christ and Satan at the doors of Hell in the words of Psalm 23 (Vulgate: AV Ps. 24) 7–10:

Lift up your gates, O ye princes, and be ye lifted up, O eternal gates: and the King of Glory shall enter in. Who is this King of Glory? The Lord strong and mighty, the Lord mighty in battle . . . He is the King of Glory.

The Harrowing of Hell became a key episode in the later biblical cycles, though it can never have been quite as theatrically impressive in the open air and daylight as it was in the shadowy echoing inside of the church.

The case of *Nicodemus* is not unique. The cult of the Virgin Mary was sustained by a similar apocrypha, also later dramatized: her childhood was imagined in terms of the infant Samuel's miraculous birth and dedication to the Temple, the portent confirming

Joseph as her husband was a blend of the blossoming of Aaron's rod (Num. 17), and the rod and flower out of the root of Jesse (Isa. 11:1, Vulgate); at her Assumption and Coronation Christ addresses her in the words of the bridegroom of the Song of Songs. But instead of seeing it in these terms, the audience would perceive typology and prophecy fulfilled.

At first 'liturgical drama' is a misnomer: they themselves rightly saw it as part of the liturgy, extraneous perhaps, but the same in texture if distinguished by a degree of impersonation. However, while in some religious houses it remained just that, in others it branched out into all manner of theatrical flourishes: elaborate costume, extended dialogue, individual characterization, striking stage effects and machinery. It becomes detached from the performance of the liturgy. Works like the Beauvais *Ludus Danielis*, and the Tegernsee *Antichrist* are clearly major theatrical events in their own right. But they fall outside my self-imposed remit. We have room for just one play which illustrates a different, arguably modern, approach to its biblical material: the justly admired *Ordo representacionis Ade* ('Order for the representation of Adam').

The Play of Adam and Topicality

Early historians of medieval theatre, seeing it as an evolutionary process towards the theatre of naturalism as exemplified in the works of Shakespeare (itself a curious concept), watched its 'secularization' with approval. 'The condition of any further advance [notice the evolutionary tone] was that the play should cease to be liturgic . . . Out of the hands of the clergy in their naves and choirs, it had passed to the laity in their market-places and guild-halls' (Chambers 1903, vol. 1: 69). E. K. Chambers sees this as a natural result of their increasing length and complexity (one watches fascinated as he struggles to combine this theory with the evidence that a number of very lengthy and complex plays continued to be played in the 'limiting' confines of the church). Two concomitants were, he theorizes, that the dialogue should become spoken rather than sung, and that it should be in the vernacular rather than Latin. 'This was almost inevitable, when laymen performed for a lay audience' (ibid., vol. 1: 88).

Adam is one of Chambers' 'transitional' texts. It seems to have all the prerequisites, apart from the ultimate one: we have no evidence as to whether the laity was involved in acting it. Probably not: it was likely to have been what at the time was called a 'clerks' play'. It dates, probably, from the second half of the twelfth century. It was acted in the open air, outside the church. It is written in Norman French – possibly thus an English production. It is lively, psychologically incisive, and very contemporary. Though it is a biblical play, it must be nearer to secular drama than the liturgical *ordines* which were going on at the same time?

Well, yes and no. What this description misses out is the fact that the first two parts of the play (The Fall of Man, Cain and Abel) are a commentary on the liturgy for Matins at Septuagesima (Muir 1973: 6–8). The modern reader tends to blank out the Latin. In performance, it would be the core of the whole proceeding. In this liturgy, the story of the Fall is divided into six sections, responsories, starting with the creation of Adam and Eve. The play starts with a choir singing the first Responsory: *Formavit igitur*

Dominus hominem de limo terrae . . . 'And the Lord God formed man of the slime of the earth . . .' (Gen. 2:7). The vernacular scenes which follow each chant amplify and explain the text, answering questions like 'Why?' and 'How?' Engagingly, they do it in 'modern' terms: modern language (Norman French), modern social structures (feudalism, the networks of social obligation, land tenure – Adam holds Paradise as God's tenant), modern temptations (Eve is seduced into thinking of herself as a heroine of courtly romance who can allow the flattering attentions of an admirer, and as a result begins to find her husband a bit insensitive, a bit boring). The playwright creates a strong sense of the bonds of reciprocal affection and loyalty which should tie Adam and Eve to God and to each other, and the paramount importance of keeping one's word and thus one's honour. The worst thing that can be said of a person is, as Adam says to Satan, *Tu es traïtres e sanz fei*, 'You are a traitor, without integrity.' Eve is a traitor to Adam: *La coste ad tut le cors traït*, 'The rib has betrayed the whole body'; Adam a traitor to God. The spectator could understand and empathize with the characters, while shuddering as they fell into the trap and cringing with their shame and despair. As a dramatization technique, it is quite different from the *Quem quaeritis*.

This modernization is very much the kind of treatment we might expect nowadays. It has been admired in the works of the sixteenth-century 'Wakefield Master', and made his *Second Shepherds' Play* a persistently anthologized piece. It has its drawbacks, however. Topicality can rapidly lead to obsolescence. Nowadays, the complaints of the Towneley Shepherds still strike a (possibly misleading) Marxist chord; the attempts of the Towneley Cain to avoid tithing can with an effort be translated to tax evasion; but the equally topical sniping of the Towneley *Doomsday* devils at the human legal system has become largely incomprehensible. Many students today find the more rigorous assumptions of *Adam* on the subject of social hierarchy and obligation, especially marital, unpalatable. It is a revelatory comment on the changes in social attitudes that most people nowadays sympathize with the villains (unless, like Annas and Caiaphas, they happen to be in positions of authority) and find the heroes slightly repellent (except for Christ, either because he is wrapped in a veil of residual reverence, or because we have remade him in our own image).

The Urban Cycle Plays: Celebration, Explication, and Empathy

By the time we reach the great civic mystery plays of the fifteenth and sixteenth centuries, the web of relationships between the Bible and drama has become almost too complex to unravel lucidly, because they are carrying so much luggage, devotional, celebratory, and instructional. They were ambitious in scale, covering a vast range of biblical and extra-biblical material. They were truly popular, a major open-air summer event put on at a period when the appetite for corporate display and public participation in religious ceremonial was at its height. They were also a collaboration. The responsibility for the production, the financing, and the overall organization rested squarely in the hands of the citizens and the city. But the scripts as we have them are learned, complex, and theologically sound, almost certainly written by the clergy. Chester attributed its cycle *in toto* to a monk of St Werburgh's Abbey (*Chester Mystery*

Cycle, *EETS SS3* 1974). We do not know who wrote York: it bears evidence of various hands, but it seems likely that it was the work of a group of clerics, whether priests and parish clerks or regular clergy like the Austin Friars of York who gave a home to the Carpenters' confraternity of the Resurrection. These men had close personal relations with the laymen who needed to commission scripts, and as a group had traditionally shown an interest in religious theatre – the clerks of the earlier *clerkes pleyes*.

We have here, then, a collaboration between professionals and amateurs, where the clergy provided the verbal creativity and learning and the laity the practical organiza-tion, production values, and the all-important funding. The two groups will have had the same aims, but different emphases. The Corpus Christi Play did 'honour and rever-ence to our Lord Jesus Christ' (*REED: York* 1979, vol. 1: 11) on the feast which cele-brated the great gift to mankind of His body and blood in the Eucharist. It is theatre as celebration, strengthening faith by participation, whether as actors or as audience. It also affirmed and strengthened the values of the community, not least because the per-formance was an achievement to be proud of. But (which the clergy would have seen as their particular responsibility) it was also an instrument of instruction in the faith. It showed the story of salvation: why it was necessary, how it came about, what it cost, and what the implications were for the individual Christian. Above all, it showed what it was.

Before we look at how this was done, we need to readjust our focus. Any theatrical version of a canonical work is played out against the backdrop of our awareness of the original. But how do we assess what this was for the audience of the mystery plays? We tend unconsciously to assume that the Bible will be available, in our native tongue, to anyone who wants to read it. It will therefore provide a yardstick by which any creative retelling can be judged. Additions will be noted. Differences of interpretation will be foregrounded. We will react to changes in tone. Direct quotations will have a special resonance. But what if this was not in general true for a late-medieval audience?

It is difficult accurately to recreate their knowledge of, and thus attitude to the Bible. One extreme viewpoint is that ordinary people did not really know the Bible at all. To begin with, it was in Latin. Latin was an élite language, the possession of the clergy, who guarded the text of the Bible jealously lest 'the pearl of the Gospel [should be] scat-tered abroad and trampled underfoot by swine' (Knighton [1895] 1965, vol. 2: 151–2). Yes, every time parishioners attended Mass they would hear the Gospel read aloud with the utmost ceremony, and were urged to pay it a special reverence, but this did not mean that they understood it. Handbooks such as *The Lay Folks' Mass Book* (*EETS OS* 71 1879) suggest that the layman should not even try to follow the Latin text, but silently recite a prayer for grace and amendment until the reading was finished. As a four-teenth-century poem on 'Hou mon scholde here hys masse' says,

> þau3 3e vnderstonde hit nou3t
> 3e may wel wite þat god hit wrou3t.
> (lines 431–2)

'though you may not understand it, you can know for a fact that God made it', and points out that a snake does not understand the words that the snake-charmer is using, but she nonetheless feels the power of the enchantment (*The Lay Folks' Mass Book* 1879: 140) In this view, the Latin would be a quasi-magical incantation, possessed of great power, but completely incomprehensible. A modern parallel is some Muslims' experience of the Qur'an.

We clearly need further to redefine our concept of their Bible. For us today, 'the Bible' is that English version with which we are familiar. For them, the authoritative text was the Latin Vulgate. All English translations of the Bible, including those in the plays, were merely second-hand, the next best thing. (Modern critics who attempt to give the plays semi-sacramental status ought to remember this.)

Indeed, in theory, at the time of the cycles, direct translations were forbidden. In 1409, in reaction to the Wycliffite heresy, Archbishop Arundel's *Constitutions* decreed that no-one henceforward was to turn any text of Holy Scripture on his own authority into the English language, *per viam libri, libelli, aut tractatus* ('by means of a book, booklet, or pamphlet'), nor was any such translation, Wycliffite or other, to be read, in part or in whole, in public or in private.[1] From then onwards, officially, there were to be no translations, only retellings.

We might expect, then, that if the Bible were to be quoted directly, with authority, it would be in Latin. On the whole, this is true, though apart from (post-Reformation) Chester, which seems to have a more self-conscious/scholarly relationship with the Vulgate text (Lumiansky and Mills 1983: 99–103), there is not as much as one might expect. Some phrases seem to have been so familiar to the writers that they appear almost automatically, as when the York Pilate presents Christ to the people:

> Sirs, beholde vpon hight and *ecce homo*
> (John 19:5)
> þus bounden and bette and broght you before.
> (33:434–5)

Otherwise, it seems to fall into two major categories. One is prophecy, which seems to have a particular resonance; there is a hint that this is the language that God speaks. Second, by far the greatest number, are the texts of liturgical chants. The use of Latin is virtually equivalent to a music cue, often sung by an angel or angels, presumably choirmen or -boys: *Tunc cantat angelus 'Ascendo ad patrem meum'* (York *Ascension*, Play 42: s.d. after 176). But were these perceived as primarily biblical or primarily liturgical? When in the York *Baptism* the rubric directs *Tunc cantabunt duo angeli 'Veni creator spiritus'* (Play 21: s.d. after 154), there seems to be no difference in status between the biblical antiphon and this ninth-century hymn. They are in Latin because that is how they are sung in church. Any resonances are with the feast day in which they occur.

For some reason, the plays escaped the blanket condemnation of Arundel's *Constitutions*. Peter Meredith suggests that it was because they did not fall under the letter of the law: they were neither *liber, libellus*, nor *tractatus* (Meredith 1995: 61–77). Perhaps as multimedia events they were not considered to be as dangerous as the portable written word. Perhaps it was perfectly plain that any translation was an elucidation, not a substitute, especially where it was aimed at understanding the liturgy. The

N. Town *Mary Play*, which must surely have had the services of professional choristers, takes pains to inform the audience of the meaning and origins of those parts of the Latin liturgy which they might be expected to recite themselves, especially the Fifteen Gradual Psalms and the Magnificat, to which the characters supply a running translation. In York, Chester, and N. Town, Gabriel translates the Ave Maria; Simeon does the same for the Nunc Dimittis. This is something more than informing the audience of the meaning of a biblical text; it elucidates for them the most familiar forms of their worship.

This might suggest that the audience, with nothing on which to base an informed judgement, were peculiarly dependent on an 'official' reading. However, with the increasing literacy of the fifteenth century, many of them were probably more knowledgeable than this extreme scenario suggests. Audiences were socially and educationally highly diverse: in York a high proportion was clergy. We should also draw a distinction between direct knowledge of the text of the Bible and the much more widespread knowledge of its content. This came through other channels: the preaching of their parish priest (sermons in Mirk's *Festial*, based on the *Legenda Aurea* (Mirk 1905; Voragine 1993), for example, very often concentrate on telling the story commemorated on that holy day), through images (again with explication from parish priest or confessor), and through listening to or reading the various retellings of the Bible in English. These ranged from intensive works for private devotion such as Nicholas Love's *Mirror of the Blessed Life of Jesus Christ* (Sargent 2005), in which the Gospel story is harmonized and then parcelled out into a programme of devotional reading for each day of the week, to lengthy romance-like verse retellings such as the *Northern Passion*, the *Stanzaic Life of Christ*, and the comprehensive *Cursor Mundi*. The latter begins:

> Man yhernes rimes for to here,
> And romans red on maneres sere . . .[2]

and goes on to promise the greatest romance of all time, centred on the greatest romantic heroine, the Virgin Mary (Morris 1874: 8). It gives a surprising new slant on the appeal of the Bible, as a treasure house of marvellous stories, full of strong situations and memorable characters.

An astonishing amount of material, adopted by these retellings, had been invented to explain, motivate, or fill in gaps in the narrative. Much of it, like the Harrowing of Hell, and the apocryphal legends of the Virgin Mary, was very old, going back almost to the time of the Gospels themselves, and had acquired semi-canonical status. The tale of the Fall of the Angels, which begins all the surviving English cycles, is similarly compiled from scattered hints, some of which (e.g. Jude 6; Luke 10:18) may refer to a pre-existing myth, some of which have been diverted from their original application: the war in heaven in Revelation 12:7–9; Isaiah 14:12–15 on the fall of the King of Babylon, nicknamed Lucifer after the morning star. As far back as Philo Judaeus, the verse 'And God . . . divided the light from the darkness' (Gen. 1:4) was interpreted as a reference to the separation of the good and disobedient angels. In the grand narrative, it provides a motivation for Satan to engineer the Fall of Man. It might be expected that it would also set up a dualistic struggle between God and Satan, but despite some attempts at this, notably in the N. Town *Passion Play 1*, and of course in the Temptation and the Harrowing of Hell episodes, God's attention is directed firmly towards Man, who has free will and is saveable, not the Devil, who is not.

Other details have become so much part of our culture that we assume they are biblical, even if they are not. Luke's account of the Nativity (2:6–7) was, apparently, felt to be unsatisfying succinct. The most popular attempt to supply this deficit was in the apocryphal *Gospel of Pseudo-Matthew* (Roberts and Donaldson 1885: 368–83).[3] Makers of Christmas cards would be horrified to know that the ox and ass do not appear in Luke: instead they were deduced from Isaiah 1:3: 'The ox knoweth his owner, and the ass his master's crib' and Habakkuk 3:2: 'in the midst of the two beasts wilt thou be known', and were then allegorized as the Jews (the ox) and the Gentiles (the ass).[4] The Habakkuk text only occurs in the Septuagint – in the Vulgate it was translated as 'in the midst of the years' – but the York Joseph knows it as:

> O, nowe is fulfilled, forsuth I see,
> þat Abacuc in mynde gon mene
> And prechid by prophicie.
> He saide oure sauyoure shall be sene
> Betwene [two] bestis lye . . .
> (14:136–40)

This suggests that the playwright was familiar with *Pseudo-Matthew*, which quotes both prophecies. He does not, however, use its story of the midwives, who appear in both Chester and N. Town to bear witness to Mary's continuing virginity.

It is clear that the playwrights knew and used these popular retellings. Sometimes they merely quarry them for plot details or apocryphal episodes; sometimes they use the very words. Lines from the *Northern Passion* are echoed in the York *Crucifixion* and *Resurrection* Plays, not exactly, but as if they were being remembered rather than read. Both the York and N. Town *Joseph's Trouble about Mary* use an early *Life of St Anne* for the spirited defence by her handmaids and Joseph's sour rejoinder (*Life of St Anne* 1928: 20–1); the York *Harrowing of Hell* uses the Middle English *Gospel of Nicodemus* (1907: xix–xxi); N. Town makes extensive use of Nicholas Love; and there are many more.[5] To their clerical authors, the plays were clearly attempting the same goals as the literature: popularizing (in the best sense) instruction.

For both literature and plays provide a value-added reading. Chester was described as 'a play and declaration of divers storyes of the Bible', *declaration* meaning 'explication, clarification' (Lumiansky and Mills 1983: 215; cf. *REED: Chester* 1979: 33). Besides supplying extra material of various kinds, they propounded different modes of interpretation (Twycross 1983: 65–110). This incidentally suggests that the audience was expected to be capable of a fairly sophisticated range of levels of reading, and that even 'the people not learned'[6] would have an appetite for information. We may find much of it fantastic, or quaintly appealing, but very little is the fruit of the playwright's individual imagination: it is solidly based in centuries of scholarly commentary.

This *declaration* is presented in various ways. Chester and N. Town particularly employ a meta-theatrical figure called the Doctor (of Divinity) or the Expositor, who tacitly represents the mediating authority of the Church. Elsewhere the characters themselves comment on the significance of their own or others' actions. Abel in N. Town offers a lamb to God 'Which, in a lombys lyknes / . . . xalt for mannys wyckynes / Onys be offeryd in peynfulnes / And deyen ful dolfoly' (3:75–8) just before he himself become the sacrificial victim – the audience are left to deduce that he also is a type of Christ. Some objects, because of the attention focused on them onstage, cry out to be treated as signs and symbols. The gifts brought by the Magi are read as gold for king-ship, frankincense for Godhead, myrrh for death (Chester 9:136–83, from the *Legenda Aurea*); Noah's dove brings him a branch of olive as 'a signe of peace' (Chester *Noah* 1A:23). Neither of these interpretations is actually biblical, though they persist to this day (Twycross 1988: 589–617).

A 1422 description of the York play states that its aims included 'the rooting out of vices and the reformation of behaviour' (*REED: York* 1979, vol. 1: 37). The clergy had a statutory duty to instruct their flock in those basic practical tenets of the faith, the Ten Commandments and the Seven Corporal Works of Mercy.[7] It is noticeable that in those cycles where Moses does not present the Tables of the Law, the task devolves on the child Christ instructing the Doctors in the Temple. The Doomsday scenario, from Matthew 25:31–46, focuses on the Works of Mercy to such an extent as to suggest that salvation is obtainable purely through works: certainly the evidence of wills suggests that many of the more prosperous members of the audience thought so.

But the main lessons are taught through example. As Nicholas Love asked, 'where salt þou fynde so opun ensaumple & doctrine, of souereyn charite, of perfite pouerte, of profonde mekenes of pacience & oþer vertues, as in þe blessed lif of Jesu crist?' (1995: 12). The characters are eager to point this out:

> All men may take exaunple, lo
> Of lowly mekenes evyn right here . . .
> Be meke and lowe þe pore man to,
> And put out pryde in all manere –
> God doth here þe same.
> (N. Town, *Baptism*, 80–1, 86–8)

One of Christ's reasons for taking on human nature is 'For men schall me þer myrroure make/ And haue my doyng in ther mynde' (York 21:93–4). The Virgin Mary is second only to her Son as an example of patience, charity, humility, and open-eyed submission to the will of God. Mary Magdalene demonstrates passionate repentance and loyalty, Abraham obedience. Their role as exemplary figures means that there is not much attempt to characterize them as individuals, as, for example, Dorothy L. Sayers (in *The Man Born to be King*) individualizes each of her twelve Apostles (Sayers 1943). It is sufficient to recognize and empathize with them in their predicaments, which are merely extreme versions of ours.

There is thus little attempt to historicize them, except where the scenario concerns a conflict between the Old and New Laws. Pilate is not primarily an imperial Roman agent, or Annas and Caiaphas members of the ancient Jewish priestly class; they are the secular and the ecclesiastical arm in a very recognizable power struggle (Horner

1998: 24–76). See, however, Mills (2005). A revealing difference between the fifteenth and the twentieth centuries is the treatment of Judas. Sayers is fascinated by his psychology, and invents a plausible political reason for him to ally himself and then become disillusioned with Christ. The medieval plays are satisfied with the Gospels' 'Satan entered into Judas, who was surnamed Iscariot' (Luke 22:3; John 13:2), and the implied motivation that he was infuriated at the waste of the perfume with which Magdalene anointed Christ, which might have been sold for 300 pence and given to the poor. 'Now he said this,' says John bluntly, 'not because he cared for the poor; but because he was a thief, and having the purse, carried the things that were put therein' (John 12:6). The plays are much more interested in the paradox of the necessary instrument of evil. For them, the problem is theological instead of psychological.

A York civic document of 1426 describes their Corpus Christi Play as *quemdam ludum sumptuosum in diuersis paginis compilatum veteris & noui testamenti* ('a certain lavish entertainment of the Old and New Testament put together in various pageants') (*REED: York* 1979, vol. 1: 42). In 1415, it consisted of a phenomenal 57 pageants, stretching from the beginning to the end of time.[8] Of these, the Old Testament is far outweighed by the New, at 11 pageants to 46. Of the latter, 10 are clustered round the Birth and Childhood of Christ; 7 are events in the Ministry; 18 treat of the Passion, culminating in the Harrowing of Hell; 6 of the Resurrection and beyond; 4 of the later life of the Virgin Mary; and the last of the Day of Judgement. Apart from Coventry, which had no Old Testament plays, this is the general pattern of the other cycles, though no others break them up into quite as many episodes. Why this particular balance? On what criteria was the story of salvation 'put together'?

One obvious model is liturgical drama. In some religious centres, the basic Easter *Visitatio* and its Christmas clone, the Visit to the Manger (*Quem quaeritis in praesepe, pastores, dicite?*) had grown into complex dramas with multiple episodes – from Pilate setting the watch to Doubting Thomas, from the Annunciation to the Massacre of the Innocents. Elsewhere, a range of individual dramatic ceremonies were played during the Christmas period, especially at Epiphany, right up to the Presentation in the Temple (2 February) at the end of the festive season. These clusters are replicated in the 'standard' cycle. There were also free-standing Prophets' Plays (often on Palm Sunday) and Passion Plays. In many cycles, a Prophets' Play links the Old and New Testaments (Young 1933, vol. 2: Chapter 21; Erler 1995: 58–81). There may never be enough evidence fully to investigate the specific relations between liturgical and civic drama, but there is enough to suggest a significant interplay (*REED: York* 1979, vol. 1: 1).[9] For example, the Third Shepherd of the *Shrewsbury Fragments*, clearly liturgical drama, shares a stanza of dialogue with the York Third Shepherd. No-one knows which came first, or what the relationship between them is.[10]

Another model has to be visual. The Corpus Christi Play probably started life as a chronological sequence of pageant tableaux. Presumably it emulated the kind of picture sequences that appeared in Bible picture books, illustrated Psalters, and slightly later, Books of Hours (Kauffmann 2003; Wieck 1988; Wright 2000). These two last became the devotional books *par excellence* of the laity. A standard Book of Hours illustrated the liturgical sequence of the Hours of the Virgin with painted scenes of her life from the Annunciation through to her (non-biblical) Assumption and Coronation –

precisely the pattern of Marian pageants in most mystery-play cycles. In the fourteenth century, this illustrative sequence 'is sometimes supplanted, or accompanied, by another cycle, that of the Passion of Christ' (Wieck 1988: 66). The Penitential Psalms, or the Office of the Dead, are sometimes accompanied by an image of the Last Judgement. Another visual source, though available to the clergy rather than to the laity, is the illustrated Missal, where the images track a narrative through the Church's year. These programmes were replicated by other religious art for public consumption, such as stained glass window sequences and alabaster retables. Anyone trying to create a series of dramatic tableaux would not have far to seek for a model.

It cannot be over-stressed that the playwrights, if they were clergy, were mainly familiar with the Bible from their daily immersion in the liturgy (King 1998: 30–59).[11] To them, the most familiar New Testament stories were those featured in the Gospel of the Mass, supplemented by the readings in the Breviary. They follow a roughly chronological path through the Church's year, from Advent to Pentecost. Whether the civic plays took place, as at York and Coventry, on Corpus Christi Day, or, as at post-1521 Chester, in Whit Week, they acted as a recapitulation of the sacred history which had just been lived through for another year.

This has several effects. It contributes to the habit of mind which sees the Bible as a series of self-contained episodes, in play terms, individual pageants. (Devotional works like Nicholas Love's *Mirror* also followed this pattern.) The embedding of the Gospel in a matrix of other passages from the Bible, from the Lesson (non-Gospel material, sometimes from the Old Testament) to the shorter quotations from the Psalms and Prophets woven into the fabric of the service, fosters the image of the Bible as a seamless web in which prophecy and, through typology, Old Testament events and figures all refer to the Life of Christ. The results range from the anecdotal assumption that the number of massacred Innocents was 144,000,[12] the number of the (male) virgins who accompany the Lamb in the matching Lesson from Revelation 14:1–5, to Christ's use of the love poetry of the Song of Songs to welcome his Mother into heaven.

It may also explain the comparatively very sparse selection of Old Testament episodes. We have seen how the narratives of the Fall and of Cain and Abel in *Adam* were expansions of the Breviary responsories for Septuagesima. The story of Noah follows on Sexagesima Sunday, of Abraham and Isaac on Quinquagesima, and of Moses and the Exodus on Quadragesima. These Old Testament episodes would thus have been associated in the minds of the clergy, and of the pious layman who possessed a Breviary, with the period of preparation for Lent. As Pamela King points out, they were also traditionally considered to be the most significant episodes in the history of man's original alienation from God, and the beginnings of his reconciliation with Him; precisely the argument of the play-cycles (King 1998: 39–40).

Finally, it sets the Bible firmly in the context of an essentially sacramental form of worship. Corpus Christi naturally emphasizes the sacrament of the altar and the magic of transubstantiation. The surviving plays of the Last Supper[13] all comment and instruct as well as showing the Institution as a recognizably ritual act. In the N. Town *Passion Play*, Christ takes 'an oblé in his hand' and declares 'Of þis þat was bred is mad my body'. After a detailed allegorical exposition of the Passover in terms of the new Covenant, he calls on the disciples to 'come forth seryattly [*seriatim*]' (440) to receive 'my body, flesch and blode, þat for þe xal dey upon þe rode' (449–50). Peter makes an act of contrition before receiving it; Judas is challenged 'Judas, art þu avysyd what þu xalt take?' (451). He is not refused, but is warned, 'Yt xal be þi dampnacyon, verylye' (455), reinforcing the belief of *The Lay Folks' Catechism* that

> . . . he that takes it worthily, takes his salvation,
> And who-so unworthily, takes his dampnation.
>
> (1901: 66, lines 326–7)

Other episodes stress the fact that the sacraments directly convey the power of God. In York John the Baptist's objection in Matthew 3:15, 'I ought to be baptized by thee, and comest thou to me?' is turned into a debate on the nature and necessity of the sacrament with a strong emphasis on its mystical powers. One of Christ's reasons is:

> My will is þis, þat fro þis day
> þe vertue of my baptyme dwelle
> In baptyme-watir euere and aye
> Mankynde to taste,
> Thurgh my grace þerto to take alway
> þe haly gaste.
>
> (York 21:100–5)

Virtue means 'efficient power', and it is clear that John's reluctance is partly a terror of touching the divine. In N. Town the Baptist is very specific about how his audience are to repent: 'With contryscyon, schryffte, and penauns, þe devil may ȝe dryve . . . Shryfte of mowth loke þat ȝe make' (Play 22:151, 154). Possibly this emphasis on the sacraments, especially 'shrift of mouth', took on an added urgency in the face of Lollardy, but it is engrained in medieval Catholicism.

This focus must have affected a further perhaps unconscious selection. The liturgical Gospels, especially during Lent and after Trinity, give almost as much prominence to Christ's Ministry, the preaching, the healing, as they do to the other events of His life. This is not replicated in the plays. In York, in 1415, the Ministry pageants were the *Baptism*, the *Marriage at Cana*, the *Temptation in the Wilderness*, the *Transfiguration*, *Christ in the House of Simon the Leper*, the *Woman taken in Adultery*, and the *Raising of Lazarus*. There is no Calling of the Apostles, no Woman of Samaria, no Feeding of the Five Thousand, no exorcism of devils, no walking on the water, no casting out of the traders from the Temple, though all of these feature as Gospels, and most present no difficulties of stagecraft – a dramatist who can show the crossing of the Red Sea should be able to manage walking in water. The healing of the man born blind and of a generic lame man in the *Entry into Jerusalem* acts as a shorthand for all the other miraculous cures, as the Raising of Lazarus is a sufficient token of Christ's own Resurrection and the General Resurrection to come. This economy of selection concentrates on strong events, each with an aura of mystery and the supernatural (what was Christ writing with his finger in the dust?), each with its own specific symbolic or doctrinal resonances.

More mystifying to a modern sensibility, there are virtually no parables, nor is there a Sermon on the Mount, or even the creation of the Lord's Prayer (York had a separate Paternoster Play which may have made this last unnecessary, but the little we know about it suggests that it was a schematic presentation showing the efficacy of its Seven Petitions against the Seven Deadly Sins). Overall, there is remarkably little representation of preaching. This is strikingly different from the emphasis given to Christ's message in the twentieth century by playwrights as different as Dorothy L. Sayers (in *The Man Born to be King*) and Dennis Potter (in *Son of Man*). Both assume that Christ attracted followers, and will attract us, largely through his revolutionary ideas, though their concepts of 'revolutionary' are rather different from each other. Even *Monty Python's Life of Brian* features the Beatitudes, though they fall victim to a major communication failure.

The playwrights are interested in a different kind of convincement. There is debate, but much of it concerns the sacraments, and the mysteries and paradoxes of the faith. Characters such as Joseph, the Baptist, the pilgrims to Emmaus, and Thomas are set up as doubters, and are then convinced by a mixture of argument and miracle. Joseph's Trouble concerns Mary's perpetual virginity; the midwives at the Nativity are convinced of this when the doubter's hand is withered and miraculously cured. The pilgrims and Thomas doubt the Resurrection. The doubters are surrogates for the audience, giving voice to the kind of rationalist arguments they would have used if they had not been convinced of the impossible by the evidence of their own eyes.

The plays do not set out to convert their audiences in our sense, by introducing them to something completely new, but to turn them back to what is already there. *Conversion* to them meant a 'turning back' to the love of God, embodied in Christ. The path to this lay through empathy – which they called *compassion* – with his sufferings and the realization that these were undertaken for you. So far this description of the plays may have suggested a very stylized kind of theatre, in which each biblical incident is milked for its potential for marvels, invoking astonishment and awe, and in which individual character is subjugated to generic moral instruction. But this is balanced by an all-out assault on the audience's emotions. The Passion was an emotional ordeal for audience as well as characters – the unjust accusations, the mockery, the abuse, the flogging, the dragging of the dead-weight Cross, and finally the long-drawn-out tortures of the execution. They were, we are told, 'movyd to compassion and devocion, wepinge bitere teris' bitere teris' (*Of miraclis pleyinge* in Walker 2003: 196–200). The tormentors indulge in an orgy of ingenious brutality, providing a running commentary so that those who cannot, perhaps, see what is going on will be able to hear. The sadistic high point is another scene about which the Gospels were reticent, the 'stretching out and nailing of Christ'[14] to the Cross. It had become a meditational exercise to imagine it step by step, from the horizontal racking with ropes to make his hands and feet fit the bore-holes for the nails, to the raising and dropping of the Cross into its socket: each stage was authenticated by Old Testament prophecy. Seeing this enacted in the everyday setting of their city streets must have given it a raw immediacy not replicated until its exploitation in the cinema.

The Reformation

How much difference did the Reformation make? The picture is only partial because so many of the plays we know existed have disappeared (Blackburn 1971). We have, for example, only five of Bale's thirteen biblical plays, and none by his contemporaries Willey, Radcliffe, and Udall (author of *Ralph Roister Doister*). They tended to draw material from the later books of the Old Testament: Job, Judith, Daniel (the tales of Susanna and Darius), Esther, Jonah, Hezekiah, Tobias. This is partly because most of them were written by semi-professionals for performance in great households or educational establishments, and called for substantial and self-contained plots. As such, they share the fashionable forms. *Jacob and Esau*, probably a school or Inns of Court play, becomes a Terentian comedy with comic servants. Early Tudor secular drama was fond of allegory as a mode of psychological and political analysis, so that abstractions rub shoulders onstage with biblical characters. In Thomas Garter's *Susanna* (printed 1569) the heroine is undermined by a character called Ill Report and assaulted by two Elders called Voluptas and Sensualitas; the realm of Ahasuerus in *Godly Queen Hester* (later 1520s) is inhabited by Pride, Adulation, and Ambition; while Lewis Wager's *Mary Magdalene* (1566) ceasing to be a Catholic saint, becomes a Prodigal Daughter, seduced by Infidelity (in a religious sense) and his satellite vices.

John Bale (1495–1563) is a model of what we would expect Protestant drama to be but actually rarely is. An ex-Carmelite, he seems to have identified with his namesake the Baptist (Bale 1985, vol. 1: 8), and seized on theatre as an ideal tool of Protestant polemic. He combines the exposition of Lutheran doctrine with virulent and often very funny anti-Popish satire. He appears to have attempted a comprehensive Protestant reading of the Old and New Testaments. Both *Three Laws* and *God's Promises* give a bird's eye view of the Scriptures. *Three Laws* (1538) shows how the laws of Nature, Moses, and Christ's Gospel were 'corrupted by the Sodomytes, Pharysees and Papystes' – the first two are also explicitly Papists. *God's Promises* is a Protestant Prophets' Play, from Adam to John the Baptist.

His surviving New Testament plays, *John the Baptist's Preaching in the Wilderness* and *The Temptation of Christ*, provide an alternative reading to the 'Popish' cycle pageants on the same subjects. They expect their audience to be capable of following, and presumably passionately interested in, some pretty complex doctrinal argument. Bale intends conversion in our sense. The Baptist, a proto-Protestant, preaches the coming of a new dispensation; his hearers cry, 'At these newe tydynges, whom thys good man doth brynge, / My hart within me for joye doth leape and sprynge' (50–1). But instead of using the real audience, he supplies an intermediary stage audience in the form of three allegorical figures: *Turba Vulgaris* (the common people), *Publicanus* (a tax-collector), and *Miles Armatus* (a professional soldier), all deduced from Luke 3:10–14, but topical as well. Each asks for and receives personalized guidance following his conversion. This is clearly not a new realism, or even the beginning of the self-enclosed world of the modern stage, but the need to control the audience's response by providing surrogates for them: the same technique as the cycle plays' Joseph, midwives, and Doubting Thomas, but with widely different ends.

The Baptist's 'newe lernynge' (207) concerns the outward and visible sign of an inward and spiritual grace: his baptism of water is the outward sign of repentance, to be confirmed and quickened by the spiritual grace of Christ's baptism of faith. A Pharisee and Sadducee (Matt. 3:7–11) attempt to undermine this doctrine and are roundly condemned for their outward pretence of holiness, and their 'pestilent [and clearly Roman] traditions':

> Neyther your good workes, nor merytes of your fathers,
> Your fastynges, longe prayers with other holy behavers
> Shall yow afore God be able to justyfye.
>
> (265–7)

Despite the newness of the doctrine, however, Bale uses techniques from the plays he is trying to supersede. God appears unselfconsciously on stage, even if his self-introduction is bafflingly abstract:

> I am Deus Pater, a substaunce invysyble
> All one with the Sonne and Holy Ghost in essence.
>
> (*Three Laws*, 36–7)

Bale mocks at ritual but uses the Advent antiphons to sum up each of the scene in *God's Promises*. He himself frames the plays as a Prolocutor, like the cycles' Expositor figure, another way of ensuring control.

Bale's doctrinal emphasis may be a function of the newness of the Reformation in England. In later Protestant plays, references are more oblique. *Jacob and Esau* (1568) is an exception in foregrounding the Calvinist doctrine of predestination: before either of them was born, 'Jacob was chosen, and Esau reprobate' (Mal. 1:2; Rom. 9:13), thus explaining why the younger brother is given rule over the older. Most biblical drama, however, was aimed at moral improvement (especially in school plays) or covertly political ends. It is sometimes difficult to tell what the playwright's sectarian stance was. *Godly Queen Hester* (late 1520s) may be a surrogate for Catherine of Aragon, but the play is largely anti-Haman, who may or may not stand for Cardinal Wolsey, as the Jews may or may not stand for the religious orders (Walker 2003: 408–31). *The Most Virtuous and Godly Susanna* (printed 1568 but possibly 1550s) celebrates 'how prone God is to help such as are just' (Garter 1937, line 8) under persecution, but the plight of the heroine might allude to that of Anne Boleyn, or of Protestants under Queen Mary, or even of the Catholics under Edward. It is in fact far more interested in the corruption of the judiciary and the establishment of the two-witness principle, which suggests an Inns of Court play. The rise of the school drama leads to a whole rash of Prodigal Son plays in both Latin and English. The shape of the plot very nicely fits the traditional *Mankind* scenario. Biblical drama was still popular at the end of the century, though most of the texts are lost: they were almost all Old Testament subjects. In *A Looking Glass for London and England*, Thomas Lodge and Robert Greene threaten the capital with the same downfall promised to Nineveh.

Meanwhile the urban biblical cycles were apparently thriving. It is not generally realized that only two of the manuscripts of the cycle plays, York (*c*.1463–77) and N. Town

(1490s?) actually date from the fifteenth century (Meredith and Kahrl 1977: xiii–xiv and note 4). The rest are post-1500. The Chester Whitsun Plays only existed in the form in which they are recorded from 1531. The manuscripts are very late, copied out by local antiquaries at least a generation after the final performance in 1575. The two surviving pageants of the Coventry Play were updated in 1535 (King and Davidson 2000). The Towneley manuscript, a miscellany, was written down in the 1550s, probably for devotional reading by a recusant family in Lancashire (Palmer 2002: 86–130). The random surviving plays from other cycles (Newcastle, Norwich) are also late.

In all these manuscripts, the pageants themselves must necessarily predate the copying, but it is impossible to say whether this was by a matter of years, decades, or even centuries. The interesting thing from our point of view is that, except for York and N. Town, they are all situated in the period of the English Reformation. They should surely show a wholesale readjustment of doctrine or, failing that, at least reflect contemporary attitudes to the translation of the Bible: 'Matthew's Bible' was licensed in 1537, Henry VIII's Great Bible was published in 1539 and 'set up in some convenient place' in every parish church for the use of parishioners.[15]

At first, this looks plausible. The second text of the Norwich Grocers' Play, 'The Storye of the Temptacion of Man in Paradyce, being therin placyd, and the expellynge of Man and Woman from thence', is said to be 'newely renvid and accordynge unto the Skripture, begon thys yere Anno 1565', and its prologue makes it clear that conformity with the Scriptures is a key issue (*Non-Cycle Plays*, 1970, 11). This protestation did not save it from extinction: 1564/5 was the last year in Norwich in which 'Souche pagentes as were wonte to go in the tyme of whitson holydayes' were set forth (*REED: Norwich* 1984: 51).

For the cycle plays seem to have been too popular and too traditional to change. Rewriting them would in any case have been a daunting undertaking. One solution was to leave the most offensive out. In Edward VI's reign (his father's Reformation had no discernible effect on the biblical plays) production of the Marian plays was suspended, to be restored at the accession of his sister. By Elizabeth's time, however, the plays were inexorably associated in the official mind with Roman Catholicism, and therefore, if nothing more, as providing a forum in which potentially disaffected crowds might gather together on an occasion where sectarian feeling might run high. Those who wanted to keep them resorted to special pleading designed to show that the product complied with official guidelines; or at least, where it did not, that it could be excused on the grounds of antiquarian interest and local patriotism.

Chester's *Late Banns*, possibly written in Edward's reign and revised again in the 1560s and 1570s (Lumiansky and Mills 1983: 192), are an excellent barometer of the pressure of public and official opinion. They apologize profusely, not for outmoded doctrine, but for the apocryphal content of some of the pageants:

> Now yow worshipfull Tanners, that of custome olde
> the fall of Lucifer did trulye sett out,
> some writers awarrante your matter; therefore be bolde

> lustelye to playe the same to all the route,
> and if anye therefore stande in anye dowbte
> your author his author hath; youre shewe let bee
> good speeche fine playes with apparel comlye . . .
>
> (Late Banns, 69)

'Some writers' – all the commentators on the *Hexameron* from Augustine onward – 'awarrante your matter', so the playwright may take confidence from his authorities, while the producers can be satisfied that at least its production values make it a sensational start to the cycle. Similarly, in the *Nativity*, 'the Scriptures a warraunte not of the midwives reporte' (*Late Banns*, 94), so the audience is merely to 'take hit in sporte' (*Late Banns*, 95). *The Entry into Jerusalem*, however, is thoroughly Scriptural: 'a commendable true storye and worthy of memorye' (130), while the *Last Supper* is to use 'the same words . . . as Criste himselfe spake' (133–4) – though they are not in fact a verbatim translation of any Gospel or of the Eucharist.

The writer of the *Late Banns* reflects the views of his age about monkish darkness by creating a scenario in which the original playwright, traditionally a monk in St Werburgh's Abbey, becomes a sort of Wycliffe or Tyndale. He is described as a 'moncke – not moncke-lyke, in Scriptures well seene', a monk who was, unlike the rest of his kind, skilled in the Scriptures, and risked martyrdom[16] to place this information in the hands of the people:

> These storyes of the testamente at this tyme, you knowe,
> in a common Englishe tonge [were] never reade nor harde.
> Yet thereof in these pagiantes to make open showe,
> this moncke – and noe moncke – was nothinge affrayde
> with feare of burninge, hangeinge, or cuttinge of heade
> to sett out that all maye deserne and see,
> and parte of good belefe, beleve ye mee . . .
>
> (Late Banns, 27)

The burning, hanging, and decapitation sound like an echo of Foxe's *Book of Martyrs*,[17] but may be a distant remembrance of Arundel's *Constitutions*.

None of this special pleading, however, saved these 'popish plays' from suppression. Their final performance in Chester was Midsummer 1575, when some plays were omitted 'for the superstition that was in them': the exact nature of this 'superstition' is unspecified (*REED: Chester* 1979: 110). In 1609 the antiquarian David Rogers wrote their epitaph:

> we have all cause to power [pour] out oure prayers before God that neither wee nor oure posterities after us maye nevar see the like abomination of desolation [as the plays], with suche a clowde of ignorance to defile with so highe a hand the moste sacred scriptures of God. But, oh, the mersie of God: for the tyme of oure ignorance, he regardes it not.
> (Lumiansky and Mills 1983: 194, 265–6)

The Recent Past

This was also effectively the epitaph of full-blooded English biblical drama. It had a strange afterlife as a puppet-show entertainment – a particularly striking one which toured in the 1620s and 1630s was called *The Chaos of the World*, and showed 'The history of some parts of ye bible, as of ye creation of ye world, Abrahams sacrificing his sonne, Ninevah besieged & taken, Dives & Lazarus' as well as Jonah and the Whale, and Shadrach, Meshach, and Abednego in the burning fiery furnace (Butterworth 2005: 134–5). It could perhaps be said to have risen again as oratorio. But tastes had changed, and official censorship tightened. The 1605 Act against 'the great abuse of the holy name of God in stage plays, interludes, May games, shews and such like' became the nucleus of a theatrical myth which maintained that it was against the law for God or Christ to be impersonated on the stage (Horner 2001: 34–96). This was extended at the whim of the Lord Chamberlain's office and under the pressure of public opinion to 'any biblical personages'. Oscar Wilde's *Salome* (Wilde 1894), which succeeds in making not only Ezekiel's wanton Aholibah and the Harlot of Revelation but even the Song of Songs sound as decadent as his heroine, was refused a licence on these grounds in 1892, and is still most familiar as the libretto to Richard Strauss's 1905 opera.[18]

In the inter-war period, religious drama had what appeared at the time to be a promising revival. The Religious Drama Association of Great Britain (RADIUS) was set up in 1929. A festival culture fostered by the Anglican church, especially at the cathedrals of Canterbury and Chichester by George Bell, Dean of the first and Bishop of the second, brought together a network of dramatists including T. S. Eliot, Charles Williams, Dorothy L. Sayers, and, slightly later, Christopher Fry. The practical moving spirit was the director E. Martin Browne. At a weekend conference organized by Bell in 1932, it was agreed

> that the Authorized Version of the Bible was especially suitable for text as well as subject of religious plays; that the Old Testament was notably rich in dramatic possibilities; and that authors must be allowed freedom of interpretation and treatment. With respect to plays written specifically for production in churches, they regarded the most appropriate form as the masque accompanied by music and ceremonial; but they felt that great reserve should be exercised in representing the Deity.[19]

Murder in the Cathedral (directed at Canterbury by Browne in 1935) is only the most famous of the resulting plays. They were largely performed in cathedrals and churches, which gave them a particular flavour, and presumably authorized the use of 'biblical personages' and themes; some were even later transferred to the commercial theatre, apparently without objection. Their attachment to the language of the Authorized Version meshed with the experimental revival of verse drama in the mid-century years. They moved from the celebration of Christian themes to the use of archetypal Old Testament figures and situations which allowed writers to explore the anxieties raised by the spread of the Nazi hegemony, and then the experience of war and its lengthy aftermath. Christopher Fry, for example, started writing *The Firstborn*, about Moses and the Exodus, in 1935, when the British became aware of the plight of the Jews under Hitler, though it was not produced professionally until 1948 (Fry 1952).[20] His *A Sleep of Prisoners* (of war) (Fry 1951) written for the 1951 Festival of Britain, uses the fiction of a sequence of dreams in which each soldier becomes a different Old Testament character caught up in an apparently inescapable pattern of familial aggression and violence: Cain and Abel, David and Absalom, Abraham and Isaac. Lastly, all four walk, tormented but unscathed, in the burning fiery furnace of 'the human shambles'. This theme had a continuing resonance in the post-war years when we all expected imminent extermination by the H-Bomb.

Meanwhile the days of censorship were numbered. When back in December 1941 the first episode of Dorothy L. Sayers's *The Man Born to be King* was broadcast on BBC Radio, to a public furore of praise and contumely and after a question asked in the House, it was announced that the Lord Chamberlain had been consulted, and had replied 'that he had no objection to the broadcasts provided an audience was not present, since all that was involved was the reading, before a microphone, of words attributed to Our Lord'. Another authority suggested that it was no different from a minister reading the Gospel in church (Sayers 1943: 15). But a hole had been made in the dyke, and when in 1951 E. Martin Browne produced an abbreviated and modernized version of the Corpus Christi Play in York to celebrate the Festival of Britain, Christ and God the Father appeared on stage, though not in the programme.

1957 saw two influential musical treatments of medieval plays. Noah Greenberg's revival of *The Play of Daniel* (New York 1959), performed annually thereafter by the New York Pro Musica, had a great influence on both sides of the Atlantic. Benjamin Britten used the Chester play of Noah as the libretto for his *Noyes Fludde*, first performed in Orford Church at the Aldeburgh Festival in 1958. The ballad-like stanzas proved immensely singable, and Britten wove familiar hymns into the musical fabric: Tallis's Canon, and 'Eternal Father strong to save' where the original called for the metrical Psalm 69, 'Save me O God'. With an infinitely extensible cast of animals allowing every available child to play a part, it has remained a favourite with churches and schools ever since. It has also confirmed the popular belief that mystery plays are simple, charming, and mainly suitable for children. Britten's later settings of biblical libretti by the South African writer William Plomer were the 'church parables', *The Burning Fiery Furnace* (1966) and *The Prodigal Son* (1968).[21] Also premièred in Orford, they were experiments in translating oriental stylization into an English mode, in a blend of Noh theatre and medieval music drama.

After the Theatres Act of 1968, the way was open in the professional theatre for a handful of Christs cast in different moulds, but each again reflecting the preoccupations of the time: in this case the role and fate of the charismatic leader and the movement that he creates. Malcolm X (murdered 1965), Che Guevara (murdered 1967), and Martin Luther King (murdered 1968) quickly became iconic anti-establishment figures. Though Dennis Potter's 1969 television play, *Son of Man* (Potter 1969),[22] and *Jesus Christ Superstar*, the 1970 'rock opera' by Tim Rice and Andrew Lloyd Webber,[23] superficially seem very different, each presents a Christ who is arguably more man than God, carried to his death by an impetus he cannot control, only consent to. Potter's revolutionary Christ, a man of the people, is tormented to the very end by doubts about his role. *Superstar*'s Christ is the victim of his own celebrity, battered by the demands of those who love him, those who want him to cure them, and those (including his accusers) who want him to explain himself. Judas, again, acts as interpreter and cata-lyst, fearful that Christ has begun to take his image seriously, that the adulation of the crowd will become lethal. Both plays end with the Crucifixion: the Resurrection is, apparently, deemed to lie in the unexpected success of the movement.

Both *Superstar* and *Godspell* (1971), in which the Passion of Christ is told by a group of flower-children clowns, drew their energy, visual imagery, and music from the current alternative culture. They were seen at the time as potential shots in the arm for Christianity, appealing to a youth audience which had been alienated from formal reli-gion. 'Jesus is cool', as Caiaphas sings in *Superstar*. Christianity comes over very much as a youth movement, heavy on love and peace, light on theology. Popular culture has since moved on: other disciplines than mine are better qualified to assess how far this phase has affected popular religion. The musicals, together with Rice and Lloyd Webber's children's *Joseph and the Amazing Technicolor Dreamcoat* (1972),[24] are still being revived.

The subsequent history of biblical drama in Britain has been overshadowed, perhaps unhealthily, by revivals of the cycle plays. Martin Browne's York productions made them popular, but his presentation in the Museum Gardens encouraged a host of poorer imitations in which ersatz medievalism became a substitute for serious thought. The need to compress a day's (or in the case of Chester, three days') theatre into three hours emphasized the narrative line at the expense of texture and detail. Popular versions like John Bowen's *Fall and Redemption of Man* (1968) cherry-picked episodes from all the extant cycles, destroying their particular flavours (Bowen 1968). The bulk of revivals have been amateur or community theatre, but some professional productions helped to raise their public profile even further. Tony Harrison's 1985 National Theatre version of *The Mysteries* (Harrison 1985) was an exciting and imaginative theatrical event, and equally distorted, set in an proletarian Eden that never was – Arts and Crafts with a touch of Trades Unionism instead of medievalism. It has also recently been revived. The most successful recent production, *Yiimimangaliso The Mysteries* (2001),[25] based on the Chester Whitsun Plays, came from South Africa: vibrant, inventive, musical, convinc-ing, multilingual – and leaving us with the regretful sense that the baton has been handed on, and we no longer know how to do this.

Where does biblical drama go next? It is hard at the moment to see a trend, other than endless revivals. The odds seem stacked against serious new work. The decline in church attendance, however token it may have been, and the multi-culturalization of education means that a playwright can no longer assume that the audience will have a background knowledge of biblical stories, let alone be able to pick up quotations and allusions. In 1951, the Festival of Britain assumed that religious drama would be a major and appropriate feature of the celebration of Britishness. Half a century later, society has changed. It is not surprising that the Passion has been politicized. One of the telling features of *Yiimimangaliso* was that it translated so well to the recent South African past, or at least our perception of it. Some images, however, still have an atavis-tic power, even if the Crucifixion now speaks of man's inhumanity to man rather than his rejection of God.

It has, however, a captive audience among the convinced, where the emphasis has shifted from spectatorhood to participation, and to drama rather than theatre: integrated into worship (the new liturgical drama), and moving into the streets for Easter re-enactments (the new processional drama). Whether this is essentially ephemeral remains to be seen. It is naturally prone to all the dangers of its special status, from unthinking emotionalism (a danger stressed six hundred years ago by the writer of *A Tretise of Miraclis Pleyinge*) to the 'pious conformity' (Martin Browne's description of Oberammergau) wickedly sent up by the traditional Passion Play in Denis Arcand's *Jesus of Montreal*. This film suggested two alternative treatments of the material: one in the play confected by the actors, a historical investigation into the 'real' Jesus; the other the contemporary parallels being played out in their offstage lives.

This raises the interesting question: are biblical stories naturally archetypal, either in terms of human relationships (Cain and Abel, Joseph and his brothers, David and Absalom) or metaphor (the Garden of Eden, the Burning Fiery Furnace), or has our culture been so radically shaped by them that they appear to be so? Is the Bible still 'notably rich in dramatic possibilities' for the present day?

The unseen and so far unmentioned presence in this narrative is of course film. The screen can display greater marvels, create greater emotional intimacy, torture more graphically. It can also provide an arena for subversion and analysis, from *The Last Temptation of Christ* to *Monty Python's Life of Brian*. And it has the mass audiences. Biblical drama has, after all, had a relatively short life on the professional stage. Maybe this is its natural home.

Notes

1   *Concilia* (1737, vol. 3: 314–19). Cf. Watson (1995: 822–64).
2   'People are keen to listen to rhymes, and read romances of many kinds.'
3   The earlier *Book of James* or *Protevangelium* has no Latin version (James 1924: 38).
4   First seen in Origen (third century) and in art as early as the fourth century: Schiller (1971, vol. 1: 59–61).
5   See Lumiansky and Mills (1983: Chapter 2); the *Mary Play* (1997: 14–19); the *Passion Play* (1990: 19–23); and *The York Plays* (1982: 40–1); cf. Woolf (1972).
6   N. Town, 'Procession of Saints', line 9.
7   For an account of Archbishop John Thoresby's version of Archbishop John Peacham's *Ignorancia sacerdotum*, and its Englishing by Gaytrigge as *The Lay Folks' Catechism*, see Hughes (1988: 149–51).
8   See *REED: York* (1979, vol. 1: 16–26) and Beadle and Meredith (1983: li–lxi).
9   For Easter sepulchres, see Raine (1955: 37, 125, 161, 191, 196, 214, 231, 235, 250, 254, 295).
10   The *Shrewsbury Fragments* are one actor's part, with cue tags, for a Shepherds' Play, a *Visitatio*, and a *Peregrini* (the Supper at Emmaus); ed. Davis (1970: 1–7).
11   On the York Corpus Christi Play and the liturgy, see also Pamela M. King, *The Worship of the City* (forthcoming).
12   *Towneley Plays* (1994, *Massacre*, 703–5); cf. Oosterwijk (2003: 3–53).
13   The York pageant has lost a leaf, possibly 'deliberately removed during the religious controversies of the sixteenth century' (*York Plays* 1982: 231).

14 This is the title of the 1415 York Painters' and Stainers' pageant. See Meredith (1995: 62–3).

15 The Great Bible was finally published in April 1539, but the injunction to display a large-volume English Bible in churches was issued in September 1538. Matthew's Bible seems to have filled the gap. See Hammond (1982: 67–72).

16 Marginalia in Rogers' *Breviary*; *REED: Chester*, p. 240: 'This moncke without fere of marterdome sett out in enlishe the storye of the testament, the bible that men mighte vnderstand and beleue.'

17 First published in English in 1563: John Foxe, *Actes and Monuments of these Latter and Perillous Dayes, Touching Matters of the Church* . . . (London: John Daye, 1563).

18 Swinburne's medievalizing *Masque of Queen Bersabe* (1862) was not meant for the theatre; Swinburne (1904, vol. 1: xxxi–296).

19 Ronald Jasper, quoted in E. Martin and Henzie Browne, *Two in One* (1981: 72); taken from Bennett (1999).

20 First broadcast 1947 (Children's Hour); produced at the Edinburgh Festival 1948.

21 Benjamin Britten and William Plomer, *The Burning Fiery Furnace: Second Parable for Church Performance*, by William Plomer, set to music by Benjamin Britten op. 77 (London: Faber Music, 1966); *The Prodigal Son: Third Parable for Church Performance*, by William Plomer, set to music by Benjamin Britten, op. 81 (London: Faber Music, 1968).

22 Performed as BBC Wednesday Play, 16 April 1969; staged 22 October 1969 at Phoenix Theatre, Leicester.

23 First produced as record album in 1970, first stage production 12 October 1971 at the Mark Hellinger Theatre, New York; opened in London on 9 August 1972; film 1973. Andrew Lloyd Webber and Tim Rice *Jesus Christ Superstar: [a rock opera]*, music by Andrew Lloyd Webber; lyrics by Tim Rice (London: Leeds Music, 1970); film directed by Norman Jewison (Universal Studios, 1973; video 1998, DVD 2004).

24 'Pop cantata' for St Paul's Junior School, 1968; first production Edinburgh Festival, 1972. Andrew Lloyd Webber and Tim Rice *Joseph and the Amazing Technicolor Dreamcoat* (Borough Green: Novello, 1975, revised edition of [1969]).

25 Adapted by Mark Dornford-May, son of Peter Dornford-May, director of the Chester Mystery Plays at Chester, and Charles Hazlewood. Video by Heritage Theatre (2001).

References

Bale, John (1985). *The Complete Plays of John Bale* ed. Peter Happé, 2 vols. Tudor Interludes; Cambridge: D. S. Brewer.

Beadle, Richard and Meredith, Peter (1983). *The York Play: A Facsimile of British Library MS Additional 35290, together with a Facsimile of the 'Ordo Paginarum' Section of the A/Y Memorandum Book*. Leeds: University of Leeds School of English.

Bennett, Helen (1999). 'Norah Lambourne's Designs for the York Mystery Play Revivals of 1951, 1954 and 1957', unpublished electronic MA dissertation, Lancaster University.

Blackburn, Ruth (1971). *Biblical Drama under the Tudors*. The Hague: Mouton.

Bowen, John (1968). *The Fall and Redemption of Man: Selected, Arranged and Rendered into Modern English from the Chester, Coventry, Lincoln, Norwich, Wakefield and York Mystery Plays*. London: Faber.

Browne, E. Martin and Browne, Henzie (1981). *Two in One*. Cambridge: Cambridge University Press.

Butterworth, Philip (2005). *Magic on the Early English Stage.* Cambridge: Cambridge University Press.

Chambers, E. K. (1903). *The Medieval Stage,* 2 vols. London: Oxford University Press.

The Chester Mystery Cycle (1974). Ed. R. M. Lumiansky and David Mills. *EETS SS* 3.

Concilia Magnae Britanniae et Hiberniae (1737). Ed. D. Wilkins, 4 vols. London.

Connelly, Joseph (1957). *Hymns of the Roman Liturgy.* London: Longmans, Green.

The Coventry Corpus Christi Plays (2000). Ed. Pamela M. King and Clifford Davidson (Early Drama, Art and Music Monograph Series 27). Kalamazoo, MI: Western Michigan University, Medieval Institute Publications.

Cursor Mundi: Part 1 (1874). Ed. Richard Morris. *EETS OS* 57.

Erler, Mary (1995). 'Palm Sunday Prophets and Eucharistic Controversy', *Renaissance Quarterly* 48: 58–81.

Foxe, John (1563). *Actes and Monuments of these Latter and Perillous Dayes, Touching Matters of the Church . . .* London: John Daye.

Fry, Christopher (1946). *The Firstborn.* Cambridge: Cambridge University Press.

Fry, Christopher (1951). *A Sleep of Prisoners.* London: Oxford University Press.

Garter, Thomas (1936). *The Most Virtuous and Godly Susanna.* Ed. B. Ifor Evans and W. W. Greg. (Malone Society Reprints). London: Oxford University Press.

The Gospel of Nicodemus (1885). In *The Ante-Nicene Fathers: Translations of the Writings of the Fathers down to A.D. 325,* vol. 8. Ed. Alexander Roberts and James Donaldson, rev. A. Cleveland Coxe. Grand Rapids, MI: Eerdmans. Reprint of Edinburgh: T. & T. Clark, 1870, pp. 439–58.

The Gospel of Pseudo-Matthew (1885). In *The Ante-Nicene Fathers: Translations of the Writings of the Fathers down to A.D. 325,* vol. 8. Ed. Alexander Roberts and James Donaldson, rev. A. Cleveland Coxe. Grand Rapids, MI: Eerdmans. Reprint of Edinburgh: T. & T. Clark, 1870, pp. 368–83.

Hammond, Gerald (1982). *The Making of the English Bible.* Manchester: Carcanet New Press.

Harrison, Tony (1985). *The Mysteries.* London: Faber.

Horner, Olga (1998). ' "Us Must Make Lies": Witness, Evidence, and Proof in the York *Resurrection*', *Medieval English Theatre* 20: 24–76.

Horner, Olga (2001). 'The Law that Never Was', *Medieval English Theatre* 23: 34–96.

Hughes, Jonathan (1988). *Pastors and Visionaries: Religion and Secular Life in Late Medieval Yorkshire.* Woodbridge: Boydell and Brewer.

The Interlude of the Virtuous and Godly Queen Hester (1966). In *Six Anonymous Plays,* 2nd series. Ed. John S. Farmer (Early English Dramatists). Guildford: Traylen. Facsimile reprint of London: Early English Drama Society, 1906, pp. 245–87.

Jacob and Esau (1966). In *Six Anonymous Plays,* 2nd series. Ed. John S. Farmer (Early English Dramatists). Guildford: Traylen. Facsimile reprint of London: Early English Drama Society, 1906, pp. 1–90.

James, M. R. (1924). *The Apocryphal New Testament.* Oxford: Clarendon Press.

Kauffmann, C. M. (2003). *Biblical Imagery in Medieval England, 700–1550.* London: Harvey Miller.

King, Pamela M. (1998). 'Calendar and Text: Christ's Ministry in the York Plays and the Liturgy', *Medium Ævum* 67: 30–59.

King, Pamela M. (forthcoming). *The Worship of the City.* Woodbridge: Boydell and Brewer.

Knighton, Henry ([1895] 1965). *Chronicon Henrici Knighton,* ed. Joseph Rawson Lumby, 2 vols (Rolls Series 92B). London: HMSO, 1895, reprinted Kraus.

The Lay Folks' Catechism (1901). Ed. T. F. Simmons and H. E. Nolloth. *EETS OS* 118.

The Lay Folks' Mass Book (1879). Ed. T. F. Simmons. *EETS OS* 71.

Love, Nicholas (2005). *The Mirror of the Blessed Life of Jesus Christ*. Ed. Michael G. Sargent. Exeter: University of Exeter Press.

Lumiansky, R. M. and Mills, David (1983). *The Chester Mystery Cycle: Essays and Documents*. Chapel Hill, NC: University of North Carolina Press.

Mary Magdalene (1982). In Donald C. Baker, J. L. Murphy and L. B. Hall (eds), *The Digby Plays*. EETS 283.

The Mary Play from the N. Town Manuscript (1997). Ed. Peter Meredith, 2nd edn. Exeter: University of Exeter Press.

Medieval Drama: An Anthology (2003). Ed. Greg Walker. Oxford: Blackwell, pp. 196–200.

Meredith, Peter (1995). 'The Direct and Indirect Use of the Bible in Medieval English Drama', *Bulletin of the John Rylands University Library of Manchester* 77(3): 61–77.

The Middle-English Harrowing of Hell and Gospel of Nicodemus (1907). Ed. William Henry Hulme. EETS ES 100.

The Middle English Stanzaic Versions of the Life of Saint Anne (1928). Ed. Roscoe E. Parker. EETS OS 174.

Mills, David (forthcoming). 'I Know My Place', *Medieval English Theatre 27*.

Mirk, John (1905). *Festial Part I*. Ed. T. Erbe, *EETS ES* 96.

Muir, Lynette R. (1973). *Liturgy and Drama in the Anglo-Norman Adam* (Medium Ævum Monographs NS 3). Oxford: Blackwell.

Muir, Lynette R. (1995). *The Biblical Drama of Medieval Europe*. Cambridge: Cambridge University Press.

Le Mystère d'Adam (Ordo representacionis Ade) (1963). Ed. Paul Aebischer, *Textes littéraires français* 99. Geneva: Droz. Trans. Richard Axton and John Stevens, *Medieval French Plays*. Oxford: Blackwell, 1971, pp. 1–44.

The N-Town Play: Cotton MS Vespasian D. 8 (1991). Ed. Stephen Spector, 2 vols. *EETS SS* 11 and 12.

The N-Town Plays: A Facsimile of British Library MS Cotton Vespasian D VIII (1977). Ed. Peter Meredith and Stanley J. Kahrl (Leeds Texts and Monographs Medieval Drama Facsimiles 4). Leeds: University of Leeds School of English.

Of miraclis pleyinge (2003). In Greg Walker (ed.), *Medieval Drama: An Anthology*. Oxford: Blackwell, pp. 196–200.

Ogden, Dunbar H. (2002). *The Staging of Drama in the Medieval Church*. Newark, NJ: University of Delaware Press; London: Associate University Presses.

Oosterwijk, Sophie (2003). ' "Long lullynge haue I lorn!": The Massacre of the Innocents in Word and Image', *Medieval English Theatre* 25: 3–53.

Palmer, Barbara (2002). 'Recycling "The Wakefield Cycle": The Records', *Research Opportunities in Renaissance Drama* 41: 86–130.

The Passion Play from the N. Town Manuscript (1990). Ed. Peter Meredith. London: Longman.

The Pepysian Gospel Harmony (1922). Ed. Margery Goates. *EETS OS* 157.

The Play of Daniel: A Thirteenth-Century Musical Drama (1959). Ed. for modern performance by Noah Greenberg; based on the transcription from British Museum Egerton 2615, by Rembert Weakland; narration by W. H. Auden. New York: Oxford University Press. Audio records: *The Play of Daniel: A Twelfth Century Musical Drama* (London: Brunswick, 1955); *The Play of Daniel: A Twelfth Century Musical Drama* (New York: Decca, 1958).

Potter, Dennis (1971). *Son of Man*. Harmondsworth: Penguin.

Raine, Angelo (1955). *Medieval York*. London: Murray.

(REED) *Records of Early English Drama: Chester* (1979). Ed. Lawrence M. Clopper. Toronto: Toronto University Press.

(REED) *Records of Early English Drama: Norwich 1540–1642* (1984). Ed. David Galloway. Toronto: Toronto University Press.

(*REED*) *Records of Early English Drama: York* (1979). Ed. Alexandra F. Johnston and Margaret Dorrell, 2 vols. Toronto: Toronto University Press.

Regularis Concordia ([*c*.973] 1987). In Pamela Sheingorn, *The Easter Sepulchre in England* (EDAM Reference Series 5). Kalamazoo, MI: Medieval Institute Publications.

Sayers, Dorothy L. (1943). *The Man Born to be King.* London: Gollancz.

Schiller, Gertrud (1971a). *Christian Iconography*, trans. Janet Seligman, 2 vols. London: Lund Humphries.

Schiller, Gertrud (1971b). *Ikonographie der christlichen Kunst, Band 3: Die Auferstehung und Erhöhung Christi.* Gütersloh: Gerd Mohn. Text at http://copac.ac.uk/wzgw?id=1133492& field=ti&terms=Ikonographie+der+christlichen+Kunst

The Shrewsbury Fragments (1970). In *Non-Cycle Plays and Fragments*, ed. Norman Davis. *EETS SS* 1 (1–7).

Swanson, R. N. (1993). *Catholic England.* Manchester: Manchester University Press.

The Towneley Plays (1994). Ed. Martin Stevens and A. C. Cawley. *EETS SS* 13.

Twycross, Meg (1983). 'Books for the Unlearned', in James Redmond (ed.), *Drama and Religion.* Cambridge: Cambridge University Press, pp. 65–110.

Twycross, Meg (1988). 'Beyond the Picture Theory', *Word and Image* 4: 589–617.

Voragine, Jacobus de (1993). *The Golden Legend: Readings on the Saints*, trans. William Granger Ryan, 2 vols. Princeton NJ: Princeton University Press.

Watson, Nicholas (1995). 'Censorship and Cultural Change in Late-Medieval England: Vernacular Theology, the Oxford Translation Debate, and Arundel's Constitutions of 140', *Speculum* 70: 822–64.

Wieck, Roger S. (1988). *The Book of Hours in Medieval Art and Life.* London: Sotheby.

Wilde, Oscar (1894). *Salomé: A Tragedy in One Act.* London: Elkin Mathews and John Lane; Copeland and Day; text at http://etext.lib.virginia.edu/subjects/salome/prod.html

Woolf, Rosemary (1972). *The English Mystery Plays.* London: Routledge and Kegan Paul.

Wright, Rosemary Muir (2000). 'Introducing the Medieval Psalter', in Brendan Cassidy and Rosemary Muir Wright (eds), *Studies in the Illustration of the Psalter.* Stamford, CT: Shaun Tyas, pp. 1–11.

The York Plays (1982). Ed. Richard Beadle. London: Edward Arnold.

Young, Karl (1933). *The Drama of the Medieval Church*, 2 vols. Oxford: Clarendon Press.

CHAPTER 21
The Circus

Burke O. Long

On the morning of 25 April 1892, bursts of cold rain assaulted Philadelphia, threatening to keep spectators away from the opening of the Adam Forepaugh Circus. Trying to reassure the public and outdo the competition, ad writers had boasted that fourteen thoroughly waterproof tents protected the 'oldest, largest, richest exhibition in the world' (Forepaugh 1892a: cover). The boast worked. By afternoon, wrote one reporter, every available horse-drawn conveyance was pressed into service, as some 10,000 Philadelphians, making the streets 'black with pedestrians', made their way to show grounds near the corner of present-day Huntington and Broad Streets (*Daily News*, 26 April 1892).[1]

City residents were accustomed to being the first to see each year's new show, since the circus had wintered over in Philadelphia for many years. This year, however, spectators sought the additional thrill of witnessing a simulated catastrophe: *The Sublime Historic Bible Spectacle, Fall of Nineveh*, a production designed and directed by Cincinnati artist, John Rettig.

Although inured by the exaggerations of brightly coloured circus posters, many of those who made their way to north Philadelphia registered astonishment at what they saw. The main tent was filled nearly to capacity, despite the threatening weather. The stage was as wide as a modern American football field is long. And Nineveh's fall, enacted in pantomime, took up half of the circus's two-hour running time.

To one awed reporter, 'nothing so beggared description in magnificence and extravagance' as Nineveh itself. 'The ancient buildings were of full size, and there was plenty of room for the vast glittering armies to fight, the hundreds of pretty women to dance, and the festivities and races to be held' (*Evening Star*, 26 April 1892). 'Upwards to 1000 persons,' wrote another, acted in the pantomime drama. There were 'scores of handsomely caparisoned horses and gorgeous chariots . . . exquisite music . . . costumes rich, elegant, and appropriate in design . . . mechanical effects . . . [all were] admirably constructed and handled' (*The Times*, 26 April 1892).

The printed programme promised spectators scrupulously historical re-enactment, 'thousands of correct and costly gorgeous costumes', as well as indiscreet abandon, the 'Bacchanalian Revels . . . , Dances, Orgies, Games, Races . . . , [and] Sacrifices' (Forepaugh 1892a: 3). On display were the royal court – its opulence, games and feasting – and a voluptuous, self-indulgent Sardanapalus, Nineveh's last ruler. In a side area, traders at the 'Oriental slave market' closely inspected female chattel and bid for their choices. Moorish acrobats performed feats of endurance. Undulating lines of veiled and gossamer clad women, the Astronomical Ballet, showed leg and danced allegory as they aligned the sun, moon, comets, and stars in worshipful attendance before Sardanapalus. Through all this, the biblical prophet Jonah declaimed God's dire warnings on Nineveh (Figure 21.1) until, facing invading armies and collapsing walls, the unrepentant Sardanapalus threw himself onto a funeral pyre. In a burst of pyrotechnics

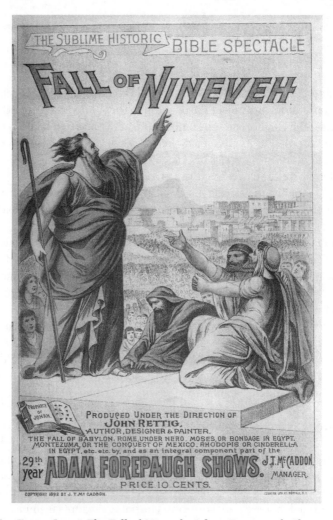

Figure 21.1   Front Cover, *The Fall of Nineveh*. Adam Forepaugh Shows, 1982. From the Collection of the Public Library of Cincinnati and Hamilton County, Ohio

and prolonged applause, the city walls collapsed and Sardanapalus died, taking with him the voluptuous beauties who had once served his every desire.

'The lesson is a solemn one,' wrote one reporter, 'and most impressively told, though not a word is spoken' (*Daily News*, 26 April 1892). The city's demise was witnessed *en masse*, but privately too, as though one looked into the enticing heart of depravity, at least as deeply as public sensibilities could permit.

Such extravagant productions were not unusual in the late nineteenth century. Historical and patriotic pageants were popular in post-Civil War America (Zellers 1955: 40–60), but by the late 1880s and early 1890s, the public was demanding much more ambitious efforts. Urban growth, electrification of city buildings and streets, new mechanical technologies and rising prosperity made possible an immense expansion of commercial amusements (Nasaw 1993; Lynes 1985). Managers of established theatres raced to satisfy audiences with large-scale productions that emphasized scenic spectacle (Booth 1981; Brockman 2002: 92). Other producers abandoned the indoor proscenium for huge open-air venues where they could wrap their pageants around visual effects impossible to achieve on smaller stages (Glassberg 1990; Prevots 1990). Meanwhile, entertaining and educational displays became enormously popular. Huge exhibition halls, such as the Crystal Palace in London, and idealized cityscapes at world fairs drew tens of millions to choreographed celebrations of empire, cultural progress, industrial invention, and nationalist achievement (Beaver 1970; Burris 2002; Hoffenberg 2001; Rydell 1984).

In this competitive context, circus owners lured audiences with full size architectural sets, glittering processionals, ballet corps, equestrian drills, acrobatic tournaments, scenes of racing horses and combat, fireworks, mayhem, and elaborate *tableaux vivants*. Producers drew material chiefly from fairy tales, nursery rhymes, and myths of classical antiquity, famous battles and popular fantasies of the 'Orient'. In the United States, many shows dramatized nationalistic epics of American settlement and expansion.

Quite a few spectacles drew on the Bible and Christian history. In 1851, the G. F. Bailey Circus presented *The Crusades*, and in 1903 the Ringling Brothers revived the theme for its US tour. During the intervening 50 years, King Solomon and the Queen of Sheba, perhaps the most popular of biblical figures among circus audiences, appeared with the John Robinson Shows in 1891 and 1899. Barnum and Bailey featured them in 1901 and 1903 under the title, *Tribute to Balkis*. Trying to reclaim such success a decade later, the Ringling Brothers headlined their 1914 tour of Europe with Solomon and the Queen of Sheba, and brought them to the United States the following year. As late as 1928, the famous pair featured in the John Robinson Circus.

Meanwhile, Imre and Bolossy Kiralfy achieved worldwide fame with dance and pantomime extravaganzas on patriotic, historical and biblical themes (Gregory 1988; Barker 1988). Their first Bible-based spectacle was *The Deluge, or Paradise Lost* (1874), produced at Niblo's Theater in New York City (*New York Times*, 27 October 1874: 7). Next was Imre Kiralfy's *The Fall of Babylon* (1887) which toured with the Barnum and Bailey Circus in 1890. Imre then created *Nero and the Burning of Rome* in 1888 and licensed the show to Barnum and Bailey for the years 1889–91. In the first of two summer seasons, 1891 and 1893, Bolossy Kiralfy's *King Solomon or, the Destruction of Jerusalem* drew over one million people to Eldorado, an amusement park near Jersey

City, NJ (Barker 1988: 251). Finally, the Barnum and Bailey shows of 1901 and 1903, hired Bolossy Kiralfy to present Solomon and the Queen of Sheba under the title *A Tribute to Balkis.*[2]

Although opening parades and spectacles would continue to be regular features of circus entertainment well into the twentieth century, these epical pageants, whether or not circus based, faded rather quickly after about 1910. Labour troubles, rising costs and the advent of motion pictures – better suited for creating operatic spectacles – doomed all but the more modest, mostly regional productions (Zellers 1955).

It is not surprising, then, that in 1892, thousands of Philadelphians primed for spectacular entertainment came out to witness the last days of Nineveh. The show's designer and director, John Rettig, was already famous for several pageants, among them the Bible-based *Fall of Babylon* (1886 and 1888) and *Moses; or the Bondage in Egypt*, produced in 1890 (Gregory 1988: 61–80; Haverstock 2000: 719–20; Ramsay 1895).

Audiences received *Nineveh* as entertainment, of course, but also as biblical drama. One reporter wrote that the show was firmly 'founded on the Biblical account of the destruction of this great capital of the ancient world' (*Daily News*, 26 April 1892). It did not matter that the Bible only alluded to Nineveh's destruction. Or that the Book of Jonah reports the city spared rather than destroyed (Jonah 3:10). The pageant was taken as a living Holy Book anyway, fraught with the assurances of true history and the immediacy of divine instruction. Possibly following the Forepaugh company's promotional literature, one reporter noted that the story had been 'reproduced with the utmost fidelity as to historic facts' (*The Press*, 26 April 1892). Said others, the show made 'the on-looker think he was back in old Bible times' (*Buffalo Inquirer*, 17 May 1892) seeing old-time prophecy fulfilled (*Wilkes-Barre Record* , 14 May 1892).

Researcher and librettist Evelyn Milligan, wife to John Rettig (Haverstock et al. 2000: 720) had of course taken her cues from the Bible. Perhaps just as important was her attachment to the idea of Bible as fundamentally prophetic. Since the founding of the United States, Scripture functioned this way, as the Republic's iconic book whose essence was fulfilled in on-going national experience. Early settlers fashioned the 'New World' as a landscape of biblical names (Davis 1995). Essayists saw the revolutionary wars as a millenarian exodus of God's church into 'A Canaan here, another Canaan [that] shall excel the old, and from a fairer Pisgah's top be seen' (Bercovitch 1975: 145–6). In the nineteenth century, this typology was adapted to Westward expansion and commercial advertising with Daniel Boone, for example, like a new American Moses, surveying the Promised Land of infinite possibility (Long 2003: 304–9). Other writers at the time transformed this 'new Israel' into an ever-adaptable 'call for order in a (Christian) community committed to progress, mobility, and free enterprise'. The new commonwealth was a biblical people destined to triumph over paganism, the white race over the dark, the enlightened over primitive societies (Bercovitch 1983: 221–3).

This malleable myth was embodied in the Rettig–Milligan tale of Nineveh's fall. Although related to the written Bible, the drama took substance in the dynamic spaces of performance and reception where, night after night, performers re-enacted a theatrical, heavily didactic version of biblical history. But they also portrayed America's mythic self to fellow citizens of that new 'Canaan' who viewed (and applauded) the passing of a great, but lesser civilization.

In the set-up, pack-up and move-on world of travelling mass entertainment, the show celebrated capitalist success and American nationalism. At the same time, it reinforced specific cultural attitudes about the Bible, Western 'Occidental' civilization and the 'Orient'. The 'sublime historic Bible spectacle' (Forepaugh 1892b: cover) offered moral uplift and populist education while lending middle-class respectability to commercial mass entertainment. Yet, that same respectability also permitted the indulgence of private, otherwise illicit, pleasures, judged of course, by biblical morality.

Focusing on this one drama, *The Fall of Nineveh*, I attempt in this chapter to recover something of the vibrant mix of national myth, mass entertainment and theatrically realized Bible. To do this, neither the written Bible nor its ephemeral realization on stage claims priority in critical analysis. Rather, I reconstruct a Bible/bible, what Exum and Moore called a moment of 'unceasing mutual redefinition' in which 'cultural appropriations constantly reinvent the Bible, which in turn constantly impels new appropriations' (1998: 35).

An 'Oriental' Fantasy

When John Rettig and Evelyn Milligan were preparing their outdoor drama, a particular image of Nineveh was already firmly planted in popular imagination. Classical Greek and Roman writers, followed by early Christian authors, perpetuated an image of Nineveh's last ruler Sardanapalus as an effeminate voluptuary whose weakness led to Assyria's defeat (Frahm 2003: 39–41). Lord Byron transformed that fragmentary tradition into a romantic tale of heroic self-immolation (Byron 1821) which was performed on stage in 1834. By then, and inspired by Byron, Eugène Delacroix painted 'The Death of Sardanapalus' (1826–27). At first harshly criticized, Delacroix's huge painting soon came to epitomize Orientalist renderings of the 'East' as a fantasy place of opulent and languid decadence (Spector 1974; Said 1978). Following its 1853 and 1867 performances in London, Byron's play travelled to the United States. There, Charles Calvert vivisected Byron's elegant verse into what one viewer called 'admirable barbaric splendor' pleasing to large audiences in New York and Boston (*New York Times*, 15 August 1876: 4, 27 August 1876: 7; Calvert [Lord Byron] 1876a).

It seemed that nothing, except perhaps the legendary debauchery of ancient Rome and Babylon, could rival the power of Nineveh to excite the imagination, whether romantic or scholarly, or both. Austen Henry Layard's engagingly heroic tale of discovering the sand-covered ruins of ancient Nineveh (Layard 1849, 1856) sparked enormous interest, especially in England (Kildahl 1959). Layard's accounts were reprinted many times and inspired imitators (Newman 1876). The monumental statuary and *bas-reliefs*, having been removed for Queen and Empire, made for a triumphal display in the London's Crystal Palace (Layard 1851). Some years later, a new generation of archaeologists took up Layard's quests (Smith 1875), while readers continued to seize upon reports of fresh discoveries as proof of the Bible and lessons in morality (e.g., *New York Times* 10 January 1875: 8).

The popular fever was largely unaffected by excavators and university-based historians who by about 1875 had dismissed the lurid traditions of Sardanapalus as fiction (Frahm 2003: 43). Sober history was one thing, Nineveh's seductive appeal quite another. Her power to excite lay in centuries-old fantasies of fabulous luxury and unspeakable dissipation which, by the nineteenth century, had been visualized in illustrated Bibles, paintings, oratorios, and staged melodramas. Fortunately, for the feverish and properly poised viewer, warnings about the perils of moral weakness could always redeem these glimpses of exotic degeneracy.

Rettig–Milligan took up this titillating image of Nineveh and Sardanapalus while pointedly using first-hand study of archaeological reports to create the meticulous realism of their costumes and architectural sets. Indeed, the authors went some lengths to display scholarly authority in an illustrated 'Short History of Assyria' that was included in the 10¢ programme. The Bible, classical writers, and the 'wonderful discoveries of the present century, by Layard, Botta, Rawlinson, and Rich' provided the sources. Scientific spirit (the god of modern progress) supplied the energy. Expressing a common opinion about emergent archaeology, Rettig–Milligan assured readers that the new discoveries 'revealed to us the buried records of this earliest civilization, which not only confirm the Scriptures, but fill in the missing links which now make hitherto obscure passages intelligible' (Forepaugh 1892b: 10–11).

Education and *apologia* aside, the dramatized story presented entertaining spectacle that unfolded in a series of five pantomimed *tableaux*, each with musical accompaniment and several action-filled scenes. The souvenir programme included a one-page synopsis (Forepaugh 1892b: 2), which I reproduce with original typeface emphases to help us imagine the enticing effects of melodrama, colourful display, and showman's hyperbole:

Tableau 1. **WALLS AND WATCHTOWERS OF NINEVEH.** Bustling commerce, camels, cows, military movements. **JONAH** preaches the destruction of Nineveh, the people scoff and deride him. Armies appear, a stupendous, thrilling, exciting battle ensues. **SARDANAPALUS** and his army rush out of Center gate and a hand-to-hand conflict ensues. Enemy routed.

Tableau 2. Walls move away. **INSIDE CITY OF NINEVEH. GORGEOUS TRIUMPHAL PROCESSION** . . . captives led by reins drawn through their lips, populace, musicians, priests carrying images, the Queen of the Harem, eunuchs, dancing girls . . . **AN ASSYRIAN FETE DAY** . . . lion tamers, jugglers, gladiators, acrobats, snake charmers, wild animals in dens, spear throwing, lance and shield contests, all manner of races, sports and games. **AN ORIENTAL SLAVE MARKET** . . . female slaves . . . spirited bidding . . . slaves crouch before the auctioneer's stand and all other details faithfully produced . . . great chariot races. Jonah again warns city of its approaching doom and when scoffed at, heavy peals of thunder . . . vivid flashes of lightning . . . Populace scatters terrified.

Tableau 3. Walls of Nineveh close. Throne Room and Palace. Sentinels placed. Meanwhile, inside the palace, a festival and sacrifice to **ASSHUR**, the Deity of Nineveh.

Tableau 4. **BACCHANALIAN REVELS.** Sardanapalus, surrounded by harem . . . Grandees, Nobles, generals, etc., dining, drinking, feasting . . . **GRAND SATURNALIA.** Female slaves press the juice of grapes into golden bowls . . . They paint his lips and tint his eyelids and place garlands of flowers upon his brow . . . entrancing music, girls with golden harps and lutes and pipes sing paeans of praise to the King . . . Arbaces (governor of Media) disgusted with the effeminacy of Sardanapalus immediately leaves. Then . . .

GRAND ASTRONOMICAL BALLET Grand march of celestial bodies, waltz of the moon, dance of the sun, *Pas de Seul* of the comet; grotesque dance by the astrologers, flight of the celestial bodies, apotheosis . . . Mounted warrior interrupts the feast and warns the king of the presence of the enemy . . . Arbaces and Nabopolassar . . .

Tableau 5. CONSTERNATION. Trumpets in distance . . . warriors rush to defend the King . . . Sardanapalus defiant . . . messenger brings awful intelligence that walls of city undermined by flood in river . . . knows prophecy of Jonah is being fulfilled . . . Orders erection of funeral pyre, his wives, concubines, slaves, eunuchs, jewels and riches are placed on the pyre . . . enemy enters city . . . Sardanapalus mounts the funeral pyre, fires it . . . perishes with his treasures amid smoke and flame.

DESPAIR! DESTRUCTION! DEATH!

SUBLIME FINALE

In the end, spectators were meant to see both heroism and admonition. As Rettig–Milligan explained in their foreword or 'Argument', Sardanapalus deprived his enemies of their greatest prize while 'redeeming his past ignominious life by a heroic death' (Forepaugh 1892: 8). Rettig–Milligan allowed Byron the last word:

> Time shall quench full many
> A people's records, and a hero's acts:
> Sweep empire after empire, like this first
> Of empires, into nothing; but even then
> Shall spare this deed of mine, and hold it up
> A problem few dare imitate, and none
> Despise – but, it may be, avoid a life
> Which led to such a consummation.
> (Forepaugh 1892b: 8; Byron 1821:
> Act V, Scene 1)

That 'life', the librettist wrote, was one of material excess and moral weakness epitomized by self-indulgence, effeminacy and idolatry. Wickedly contrary to nature, Sardanapalus 'secluded himself in his palace, with his harem, assumed the garb of a woman, handled the distaff, painted his face, and abandoned himself to a life of idleness and folly' (Forepaugh 1892b: 5). Worse still, the 'entire populace' gave itself up to similar 'dissipation and depravity' and moreover, to idolatrous bowing before 'colossal images of stone' (ibid.: 5, 17). This people of 'dyed eyebrows [and] fastidiously arranged toilets' would inevitably fall as would the 'weak effeminate' king so 'steeped in voluptuous indolence [that] he desired no fame or glory as a conqueror . . . and spent his time in feasting and dissipation' (ibid.: 15, 23).

This picture of a loathsome, gender-confused Sardanapalus probably played well to audiences familiar with nineteenth-century taxonomies of civilization. At once confident and anxious, these narratives often championed a Darwinian notion of cultural progress, but treated the calls for equality among the sexes with caution, if not alarm. Political philosopher and journalist Jean-Pierre Proudhon, for example, believed that nations arise with austere, virile energy. However, they collapse if they take on woman's qualities of pity, charity, grace and love. These naturally female characteristics 'testify – from the point of view of pure justice – to her (woman's) inferiority' (Proudhon 1875: 38–9, cited in Dijkstra 1986: 211). Men, and nations run by men, must choose. Keep women in their place, or subject all men, and nations, to evolutionary regression and pornocracy.

Discussing 'national character and laws' as essential elements of civilization, George Harris was only a little less harsh. He argued that in primitive societies, 'the occupations and habits of the softer sex are more refined and civilizing than are those of the men'. However, in more advanced societies, women have done 'little . . . for the advancement of learning and science (and) much to encourage and to foster luxury'. In an age of 'voluptuousness', Harris added, men become 'slaves of women' and their 'superior wisdom and sagacity' give way to the 'whims and frivolities of the feebler sex'. In short, 'men degenerate into women'. Although women deserve the vote, Harris concluded, men should beware their weaknesses while encouraging the innate female traits of 'caution, refinement, and tenderness' (Harris 1873: 256–7).

That advice, and not always from men, could be found in many a Victorian self-improvement booklet. 'Whatever a woman is,' wrote Mary Melendy, PhD, MD, 'there should be a sweet, subduing, and harmonizing influence of purity, truth, and love, pervading and hallowing . . . the entire circle in which she moves'. Since men are given to savagery, women should 'soften their manners, and teach them all needful lessons of order, sobriety, and meekness, and patience, and goodness' (Melendy 1903: 41).

Fearing that such exhortations were becoming less persuasive, novelist E. Lynn Linton expressed a nearly hysterical fear of unnaturally reversing gender roles and thus hastening the decline of civilization. 'Wild women' feminists, 'in their desire to assimilate their lives to those of men', were introducing into the cultured classes 'certain qualities and practices hitherto confined to the uncultured and – savages'. These perversions, Linton added, are steps 'downwards in refinement and delicacy – wherein lies the essential core of civilization' (1891: 597–8).

One contemporary example of such a slide into feminized decadence was Ottoman Turkey. The Sultans, a worrisome danger to European political interests after the Crimean War, were regularly portrayed in gossipy, sexualized accounts as having surrendered to abhorrent appetites, fanaticism and unseemly luxury. 'The Sultan's Extravagance', as one article headlined, included 5,500 palace servants, a fabled menagerie, and 1200 wives and concubines, '500 more than Solomon's family' (*New York Times*, 27 December 1875: 3). Other reports detailed 'A Sick Man's Amusements' (*New York Times*, 21 May 1876: 6) and misspent wealth, 'Thousands for the Harem and Nothing for the Army' (*New York Times*, 7 October 1878: 8). Another news account excoriated – on page one – the 'enemy to all progress' who, born in 'Mohammedan fanaticism', gave rise to a 'simple disbelief in anything, to an indifference to aught, save the pursuit of pleasure and gain' (*New York Times*, 5 June 1876: 1).

Visual artists in Europe and America realized that pursuit in lush images of 'Oriental' life (Ackerman 1994) which, in a dialectical dance with social conditions in the West, often depicted eroticized violence against women (Dijkstra 1986: 111–16).

Popular entertainment often confirmed accepted opinion by serving up its own version of the envied and degraded Arab as specimens of 'distorted physicality' (beauty as well as grotesque deformity) and 'insatiable sexuality' (Salem 1995: iv–v).

The Rettig–Milligan *Fall of Nineveh* can hardly be understood apart from its entanglement with such constructions of Orientalism and deep anxieties about the durability of Anglo-European, Christian, civilization. The drama re-created an ancient Nineveh that was grander than its own legend, surpassing 'in splendors the wildest, most gorgeous phantasies (*sic*) of Oriental fabulists' (Forepaugh 1892a: 5). It also presented a fantasy-enhanced ancient/modern 'Orient', a place of opulence, arrogant defiance of the one true God, and debauched effeminacy – all symptoms of a society's weakness and decline, then and now. Nineveh's destruction had been prophesied by biblical truth-sayers, yes. That upholds biblical truth. But her catastrophic entombment in the desert sands of the 'East' was also a consequence of transgressing the order of civilization. And that reasserts the power of natural law, and of those social orders that endure.

In the Forepaugh Bible/bible, these matters were distilled into one moralizing moment of military onslaught and self-immolation (Figure 21.2). Imagining the scene in monumental style, an artist positioned Sardanapalus, lighted torch in hand, atop a tiered platform whose foundation is engulfed in flames. As rapacious armies advance, the King heroically gestures over all that is his: richly decorated palace implements, a statue (perhaps of himself or a god), bejewelled and finely dressed women – countless numbers of them, wives, slaves, concubines arrayed in a tableau of female anguish. (The scene is stiffly heroic and chaste compared to Delacroix's highly sexualized

Figure 21.2   Back Cover, *The Fall of Nineveh*. Adam Forepaugh Shows, 1982. From the Collection of the Public Library of Cincinnati and Hamilton County, Ohio

fantasy.) Some of the women appear grief-stricken, others seem to be in a dead faint, some are swooning, or twisted by paroxysms of wailing, while others pitifully clutch at the king's robes. Possessions all, they submit to this weak voluptuary who, even as a defective man, asserts masculine power over all he commands. The thrilling climax, wrote one reporter, 'holds the spectator breathless, so realistic does it appear' (*The Record*, 26 April 1892).

As historiography, this dramatic climax recreates the demise of an ancient civilization, or as the admen wrote, of the former 'capital of the entire civilized world' (Forepaugh 1892a: 5). As performance, the fall of Nineveh insinuated triumph for the manly and masculine. It re-enacted the terrible dangers of enervating (female) luxury, while reaffirming the prophecies of a trustworthy, and patriarchal, Bible. It celebrated a fierce warrior code: the (rightfully) invading armies; the path of suicide, rather than surrender; the principled Arbaces who, explained the printed programme, had been so 'disgusted with the effeminacy of Sardanapalus' that he joined the Babylonians with the 'determination to overthrow the voluptuous monarch' (Forepaugh 1892b: 3).

A Respectable Place

As one Philadelphia reporter implied, one should take from the sublime biblical spectacle a solemn lesson (*Daily News*, 26 April 1892). However, middle-class audiences did not just simply appear at the tent ready for instruction. They had to be assembled and convinced, perhaps given permission, to seek amusement in places of good repute. These venues had to be seen (and marketed) as safe, respectable, and decidedly distinct from the dimly lit, male-oriented theatres that were common before the electrification of cities (Nasaw 1993: 5–6). The reclamation was well underway in mid-nineteenth-century America, as impresarios of public entertainment increasingly appealed to women, particularly wives and mothers, who were the primary carriers and signifiers of middle-class respectability (Butsch 2000: 66–7). Such transformations required slick salesmanship, a revised moral taxonomy of shows and audiences, and a strong dose of agreeable self-deception.

The Adam Forepaugh management purveyed hyperbole as utterly 'truthful advertising' (Forepaugh 1892a: 19) and packaged its shows as both high-brow entertainment and safe, family education. Artists' credits listed a *Maître de Ballet Signor* Luca Resta and luxurious costumes by 'Lavilleaux of Paris'. News accounts – perhaps encouraged by company admen and free tickets given to reporters and clergy – frequently noted attendance by leading citizens or people of the 'highest social grade'. These presumably could pay $1.50 for comfortable high-backed chairs in reserved boxes and appreciate the fine European arts (*The Record*, 27 April 1892; *Buffalo Courier*, 17 May 1892). Like other circuses, the Forepaugh Shows enforced (and advertised) rigid rules of 'demeanor and deportment' for its employees. The company also claimed to have made efforts to protect the public from 'gamblers, confidence men, and swindlers' known to 'prey on the good' at large public gatherings (Forepaugh 1892a: 15). Nothing, it seems, would be allowed to detract from the salutary 'treasures of entertainment and instruction' that would be found fit for parents and their 'dear little ones' and even the 'most learned and pious clergymen' (Forepaugh 1892a: 3, 17, 21).

The Fall of Nineveh was first, wholesomely biblical. An advertising brochure, *The Book of Wonders*, as well as programme and libretto assured patrons that the sublime spectacle would acquaint 'the people of to-day with the lives, the customs, the religion of the oldest of all earth's peoples'. For those tempted by Darwin and historical criticism to doubt the Bible's veracity, the show would illustrate 'many of the historical teachings of the Scripture' and reassure the 'pious public' of the truthfulness of Scripture (Forepaugh 1892a: 5, 7; Forepaugh 1892b: 24). Indeed, the 'most learned and pious' clergy (who were typically won over with free tickets and solicitous invitations) would find in the Forepaugh Bible/bible 'most valuable information and instruction which they can in turn impart to their respective congregation' (Forepaugh 1892a: 17; Barker 1988: 144).

Moreover, the spectacle was not simply a trifling amusement. It was sold as part of the Adam Forepaugh Shows' mission of educational uplift. Indeed, admen claimed, the biblical pageant was 'an extraordinary addition . . . to the curriculum of the Forepaugh University' and a 'veritable collection of priceless jewels and gems which incrust the tiara that crowns the popular university of the people, the Adam Forepaugh Shows'. No one, not even the most dense, could afford to let pass this opportunity to be schooled by 'centuries of classic research by prophets, antiquarians, scientists, savants and historians' (Forepaugh 1892a: 3, 24).

Furthermore, claimed the *Book of Wonders*, consider the menagerie, the 'most famous collection of animals ever brought together since Noah'. Its value cannot be overestimated, and no parent 'can afford to have children kept in ignorance'. A 'student' of any age will find here the 'rarest of Nature's fanciful animate creations'. Study Forepaugh's animal kingdom, patrons were told, and receive 'more real, genuine, practical information than the most exhaustive study of zoology from books' (Forepaugh 1892a: 14).

Similarly, a Moorish Bedouin Circus Company both entertained and, in their exotic 'Oriental' otherness, displayed vestiges of ancient Nineveh. First, stated the *Book of Wonders*, the group included the 'only genuine and Arabian women ever seen in America' and among these, 'two of the most famous beauties of the (Sultan's) royal harem', the first to 'have ever been permitted to visit foreign shores'. These titillating claims would have been enough to excite fantasies of the 'East' and Sardanapalus. But there was more. Among the acrobats were the 'Kabyles and Assions', tribal groups believed (by whom is left unclear) to be 'direct lineal descendants' from the Ninevites. Shocking habits offer the proof. Honouring the dove and fish, rites of animal sacrifice; self-torture; wild dancing amid fire; handling deadly reptiles – all these practices mark the 'Kabyles and Assions' as vestigial and degraded links to a lost antiquity. Simply put, 'these (people) are the true offsprings (sic) of a race (the Assyrians) once great in its civilizing influence' (Forepaugh 1892a: 23).

Yet, staged domesticity was on display, too. Milling about a Bedouin village strategically placed on the way to the main Forepaugh tent, show goers (in the manner of educational exhibits at world's fairs) could view the Moorish Circus Company at home. Camels, mules and donkeys; women grinding grain, weavers working at their looms; sword makers and carpenters; guns, saddles, tools, and cooking utensils. There were flutes, pipes and tom-tom players (making 'the most diabolical music' reported the *Daily News*, 26 April 1892). Although captive to the benignly imperialistic gaze of specta- tors, these 'thirty-five strange people' were said to be 'utterly oblivious to any and all observers' (Forepaugh 1892a: 23). And as close to authentic Nineveh as one could get – that is, before the show.

The Spirit of America

The Adam Forepaugh Shows spent lavishly to bring its entertainment to the public. Nor, boasted company admen, did so 'vast an addition . . . as the sublime spectacle' curtail the 'satisfying programme of former years' (Forepaugh 1892a: 17). There were daily expenses of $5,000, and $3 million were invested, roughly $100,000 and $60 million respectively in today's dollars. *The Book of Wonders* itemized what the money bought. Employees, 1,250, including 200 circus performers and another 200 'premiers, secondas and coryphées in the corps de ballet'. Animals, 400 horses plus 250 wild creatures in the menagerie and 60 thoroughbreds for the hippodrome races. Two acres of moving panorama, 300,000 sq ft of scenery, a 300 ft grand spectacle stage, 2,000 costumes and 2,000 'spears, javelins, scimitars, battle-axes, battering rams and swords'. Fourteen tents, including the main show tent, seats for 12,000, one quarter of which were 'high-backed, numbered and actually reserved'. And for trans- port, 54 railroad cars stretching three quarters of a mile (Forepaugh 1892a: 13).

Although akin to the brash profligacy that the Bible spectacle condemned, such excess – and boasting about it – were permissible and even admired in the American and male-dominated pursuit of capitalist enterprise. Illustrated biographies of Adam Forepaugh and John Rettig, surrogates for America, assuaged any doubt about the matter.

In so doing, the Forepaugh writers followed a well-established literary tradition. In the 'new Canaan' of loosely bound colonies reaching for a common sense of nation- hood, the lives of public figures, told and re-told, constituted an ongoing spiritual biog- raphy of America (Bercovitch 1975: 148–9). Accordingly, Adam Forepaugh and John Rettig were presented as ideal Americans, leaders who in moral character and self-made accomplishment embodied the iconic values and true spirit of the Republic.

For 26 years, the *Book of Wonders* asserted, Adam Forepaugh conducted his mammoth travelling shows, growing larger, adapting and 'keeping time to the music of progress'. Living values that were both 'constructive' and 'conservative', Forepaugh 'builded (sic) his Shows upon the indestructible foundations of an honesty which gained for him the solid support of public admiration and confidence'. Any additions to the entertainment were 'the real thing', quality goods that 'would not wear out in a day, a week, a month, a year, a decade of years'. Known to all as an 'ever true friend', Forepaugh was justly the most famous man in America – 'with the possible exception of the Father of his country', the writer added, at once awarding Forepaugh modesty and apotheosis (Forepaugh 1892a: 1).

In 1889, Adam Forepaugh received 'the inevitable summons to the Great Beyond'. Nevertheless, readers were assured, the legacy of George Washington – magnetic leadership, conservatism, constructive initiative, thrift and concern for honest value – persisted in the show of 1892. Indeed, wearing stylish mutton chop side burns and dignified mien, the great Forepaugh himself ruled over the cover of the *Book of Wonders*. He was the first wonder it seems, the founding patriarch and prodigy who had sired everything now on display before the public. Faintly invoking biblical allusion, the admen concluded that manager J. T. McCaddon, 'upon whom the mantle of the great Forepaugh has fallen', would ensure that the shows' respectability and the founder's gifts would unquestionably be 'perpetuated in all their vast extent and merit' (Forepaugh 1892a: 1).

John Rettig also was styled as an exceptional man of genius and virtue. A testimony to egalitarian possibility, Rettig's life demonstrated that anyone with industry and talent could achieve great success, of course within the racially and gender-based boundaries set by custom and law at the time. Rettig, claimed the biographer, 'is an American by birth, by education, by artistic training, by the scenes of his triumphs, all American. He is undoubtedly THE BEST REPRESENTATIVE OF THE GENIUS OF AMERICAN ART'. Moreover, the earlier spectacle that he had created in Cincinnati 'laid the foundation of the TEMPLE OF WESTERN CLASSICAL POPULAR EDUCATION' (Forepaugh 1892a: 11, emphases in original).

Bearing letters of introduction from 'many of the most eminent men of the nation' (one, from the Governor of Ohio, was reproduced in the *Book of Wonders*), Rettig made a 'personal visit to the exhumed ruins of the buried city (Nineveh)'. He was received like a visiting dignitary in famous museums of London, Paris and Cairo. Now, back home, the 'well-nigh inexhaustible resources and surplus capital of the great Adam Forepaugh Shows' had been placed at Rettig's command (as he readily acknowledged, according to the *Boston Post*, 7 June 1892). At last, he could 'execute his long cherished designs' and produce his 'masterpiece', *The Fall of Nineveh*. The Bible show is a 'spectacle, a drama, a tragedy, a comedy, an opera, a ballet, a poem, a study' that rivals Homer and surpasses in its 'gorgeous displays of wealth the riches conjured by Aladdin's lamp' (Forepaugh 1892a: 11).

In this happy marriage of 'all American' privilege, art, populist education and capitalist enterprise, John Rettig's genius found its consummate expression. And the Adam Forepaugh Shows were its greatest attraction. Unfettered commercialism, honesty, pure genius, wealth, fame, capitalist dominance – all these themes of America's collective narratives fell together in the circus that was entertainment, historical instruction, and display of industrial production. The biographies of Forepaugh and Rettig, and the works they created singly and together, reflected America's story, or one version of it. The Forepaugh Bible/bible added moralistic warning, but ostensibly without undermining any spectator's aspiration to share in the spirit and rewards of national destiny.

The Real Show

Opening day of the Forepaugh Shows in Buffalo, New York, left one reporter overwhelmed, 'almost dazed' at the drama 'made virile by imposing pageantry and ceremonial':

A maze of distracting divertissements, a glory of spectacular radiance – on the ground and in the air, near and distant – now graceful, now floating motion, anon the rush of the hurricane; constantly changing effulgence of color; the glittering panoply of antique armed hosts; swarthy faces of Asiatic cast; entrancing music; the beasts of the desert and the jungle; voluptuous oriental beauty; incidental achievements of indescribable daring or preternatural art – not strange is it that the mind is in a whirl as when one is awakened from a dream in which all the entertainments of the Arabian Nights were compressed into one. (*Buffalo Courier*, 17 May 1892)

The reporter may have been almost dazed, but certainly not speechless.

Apparently not everyone was so enthralled. When the circus reached Boston about three weeks later, Nineveh's walls collapsed at the beginning, not at the end, of the evening's performance. To one Bostonian at least, the 'virile' story was 'but a prelude to the great circus show . . . and all those things so dear to the hearts of men, women and children who can't keep away from the circus' (*Boston Post*, 7 June 1892). Wrote another reporter, *The Fall of Nineveh* is now the opening attraction 'instead of being dragged in at the close, to be interrupted by those who are impatient to leave early in order to secure seats in the (street) cars'. The change, he added, was 'to the evident satisfaction of the public' (*Saturday Transcript*, 11 June 1892).

This small detail is a reminder that despite its pretensions to populist education and moral uplift, the Adam Forepaugh Shows and its Bible/bible were fundamentally vehicles of mass, for-profit entertainment. They were commodities of an increasingly consumerist, industrialized society which valued economic productivity and systematic generation of capital. In the years before the appalling economic downturn of the mid-1890s, the titans of big business, above all, sought to build efficient money-making machines and hold on to satisfied customers. In this setting, the Holy Book of circus spectacle was created over and over again in performance – as Orientalizing entertainment, socially conservative instruction, and nationalist affirmation. It was a Bible/bible that enjoyed cultural reverence, like that due a trustworthy and revered ancestor. But it was sold and consumed just like the raucous pandemonium of acrobats, bareback riders and performing elephants 'so dear to the hearts of men, women and children who can't keep away from the circus' (*Boston Post*, 7 June 1892).

Notes

1 News accounts of the 1892 Forepaugh show are taken from clippings in Rettig (n.d.).
2 There are as yet no complete inventories or comprehensive studies of these spectacle dramas. Smith (1943) briefly surveys circus spectacles, mostly by title. The Circus World Museum, Baraboo, Wisconsin, and the Milner Library of the Illinois State University at Normal, Illinois, hold extensive circus archives. For the work of Imre Kiralfy, see Gregory (1988) and Barker (1994). Barker (1988) offers an edited version of Bolossy Kiralfy's unfinished autobiography. Haverstock (2000) and Siegrist (2002) deal with aspects of John Rettig's work, which is further documented in materials held by the Cincinnati Historical Society and the Cincinnati Public Library.

References

Ackerman, Gerald (1994). *American Orientalists*. Paris: ACR.

Adam Forepaugh Shows (1892a). *Book of Wonders*. Philadelphia, PA: Morrell Brothers Show Printers.

Adam Forepaugh Shows (1892b). *The Sublime Historic Bible Spectacle Fall of Nineveh*. Buffalo, NY: Courier Lithograph Co.

Barker, Barbara (ed.) (1988). *Bolossy Kiralfy, Creator of Great Musical Spectacles*. Ann Arbor, MI: University of Michigan Press.

Barker, Barbara (ed.) (1994). 'Imre Kiralfy's Patriotic Spectacles: Columbus and the Discovery of America (1892–1893) and America (1893)', *Dance Chronicle* 17: 149–78.

Beaver, Patrick (1970). *The Crystal Palace, 1851–1936: A Portrait of Victorian Enterprise*. London: Hugh Evelyn.

Bercovitch, Sacvan (1975). *The Puritan Origins of the American Self*. New Haven, CT: Yale University Press.

Bercovitch, Sacvan (1983). 'The Biblical Basis of the American Myth', in Giles Gunn (ed.), *The Bible and American Arts and Letters*. Philadelphia, PA: Fortress Press, pp. 219–29.

Booth, Michael R. (1981). *Victorian Spectacular Theatre 1850–1910*. London: Routledge & Kegan Paul.

Brockman, C. Lance (2002). 'Setting the Stage for Motion Pictures', in Patricia McDonnell (ed.), *On the Edge of Your Seat: Popular Theater and Film in Early Twentieth-Century American Art*. New Haven, CT: Yale University Press, pp. 92–105.

Burris, John (2002). *Exhibiting Religion: Colonialism and Spectacle at International Expositions, 1851–1893*. Charlottesville, VA: University Press of Virginia.

Butsch, Richard (2000). *The Making of American Audiences: From Stage to Television, 1750–1990*. Cambridge: Cambridge University Press.

Byron, George Gordon (1821). *Sardanapalus, a Tragedy; The Two Foscari, a Tragedy; Cain, a Mystery*. London: John Murray.

Calvert, Charles [Lord Byron] (1876a). 'Sardanapalus', *New York Times*, 15 August, p. 4.

Calvert, Charles [Lord Byron] (1876b). 'Sardanapalus', *The Ray*. 26 December, p. 1.

Davis, Moshe (1995). 'Biblical Place Names in America', in Moshe Davis (ed.), *With Eyes Toward Zion*, vol. IV: *America and the Holy Land*. Westport, CT: Praeger, pp. 135–46.

Dijkstra, Bram (1986). *Idols of Perversity: Fantasies of Feminine Evil in Fin-de-Siècle Culture*. New York: Oxford University Press.

Exum, Cheryl and Moore, Stephen (eds) (1998). *Biblical Studies/Cultural Studies: The Third Sheffield Colloquium* (JSOTSup, 266). Sheffield: Sheffield Academic Press.

Frahm, Eckart (2003). 'Images of Ashurbanipal in Later Tradition', in Israel Eph'al, Ammon Ben-Tor and Peter Machinist (eds), *Eretz-Israel (Hayim and Miriam Tadmor Volume)*. Jerusalem: Israel Exploration Society, pp. 37–48.

Glassberg, David (1990). *American Historical Pageantry: The Uses of Tradition in the Early Twentieth Century*. Chapel Hill, NC: University of North Carolina Press.

Gregory, Brendan Edward (1988). 'The Spectacle Plays and Exhibitions of Imre Kiralfy, 1887–1914', PhD dissertation, University of Manchester.

Harris, George (1873). *Civilization Considered as a Science, in Relation to its Essence, its Elements, and its End*. New York: D. Appleton and Co.

Haverstock, Mary S., Vance, Jeannette and Meggitt, Brian (eds) (2000). *Artists in Ohio, 1787–1900: A Biographical Dictionary*. Kent, OH: Kent State University Press.

Hoffenberg, Peter H. (2001). *An Empire on Display: English, Indian, and Australian Exhibitions from the Crystal Palace to the Great War*. Berkeley, CA: University of California Press.

Kildahl, Phillip Andrew (1959). 'British and American Reactions to Layard's Discoveries in Assyria (1845–1860)', PhD dissertation, University of Minnesota (photographic reproduction, Ann Arbor, MI, UMI, 1997).

Langstroth, T. A. (no date). 'The Colorful World of John Rettig: A Scrapbook', unpublished MS, Cincinnati Public Library, Cincinnati, OH.

Layard, Austen Henry (1849). *Nineveh and its Remains: With an Account of a Visit to the Chaldean Christians of Kurdistan, and the Yezidis, or Devil-Worshippers; and an Inquiry into the Manners and Arts of the Ancient Assyrians*. New York: G. P. Putnam.

Layard, Austen Henry (1851). *The Nineveh Court in the Crystal Palace*. London: Crystal Palace Library and Bradbury & Evans.

Layard, Austen Henry (1856). *A Popular Account of Discoveries at Nineveh*. New York: Derby & Jackson.

Linton, E. Lynn (1891). 'The Wild Women as Social Insurgents', *The Nineteenth Century* 30: 596–605.

Long, Burke O. (2003). 'Holy Persuasion: The Bible as Advertising', in J. Cheryl Exum and H. G. M. Williamson (eds), *Reading from Right to Left: Essays on the Hebrew Bible in Honour of David J. A. Clines*. Sheffield: Sheffield Academic Press, pp. 301–19.

Lynes, Russell (1985). *The Lively Audience: A Social History of the Visual and Performing Arts in America, 1890–1950*. New York: Harper and Row.

Melendy, Mary R. (1903). *Perfect Womanhood for Maidens – Wives – Mothers*. Chicago: Monarch Book Company.

Nasaw, David (1993). *Going Out: The Rise and Fall of Public Amusements*. New York: Basic Books.

Newman, John P. (1876). *The Thrones and Palaces of Babylon and Nineveh: From Sea to Sea, a Thousand Miles on Horseback*. New York: Harper and Brothers.

New York Times (1875). 'Nineveh: Its Past Glory and Present Desolation. The Rise and Fall of the Assyrian Empire, Its Record in Sacred and Profane History, Kings of Nineveh, Wars with the Jews, Final Destruction', 10 January, p. 8.

Prevots, Naima (1990). *American Pageantry: A Movement for Art and Democracy*. Ann Arbor, MI: UMI Research Press.

Proudhon, P.-J. (1875). *La Pornacratie, ou les femmes dans les temps modernes*. Paris: A. Lacroix.

Ramsay, Alexandrina (1895). 'The Art of a Scene Painter', *Monthly Illustrator* 4: 329–35.

Rettig, John (n.d.). 'Scrapbook', unpublished MS, Cincinnati Historical Society, Cincinnati, OH.

Rydell, Robert (1984). *All the World's a Fair: Visions of Empire at American International Expositions, 1876–1916*. Chicago: University of Chicago Press.

Said, Edward (1978). *Orientalism*. New York: Vintage.

Salem, Lori (1995). ' "The Most Indecent Thing Imaginable": Sexuality, Race and the Image of Arabs in American Entertainment, 1850–1990', PhD dissertation, Temple University, Philadelphia, PA.

Siegrist, Sarah E. (2002). 'Rettig's (1858–1932) "Montezuma or the Conquest of Mexico" (1889): A Case Study of American Pageantry in Cincinnati', MA thesis, University of Cincinnati, OH.

Smith, A. Morton (1943). 'Spec-ology (sic) of the Circus', *Billboard* 50: 51, 55.

Smith, George (1875). *Assyrian Discoveries: An Account of Explorations and Discoveries on the Site of Nineveh during 1873 and 1874. Illustrated with Photographs and Woodcuts*. New York: Scriber Armstrong & Co.

Spector, Jack J. (1974). *Delacroix: The Death of Sardanapalus*. New York: Viking Press.

Zellers, Parker (1955). 'A Survey of American Pageantry from 1753 to 1955', MA thesis, Indiana University, Bloomington, IN.

CHAPTER 22
The Body

Gerard Loughlin

The Bible is like a body. It is a whole composed of many parts, in the pages of which we find other bodies, identities which even now haunt the Western imagination: like so many dead bodies in a library. The biblical body is not singular, but many: malleable and multiform. St Paul imagined that the Christians to whom he wrote in Corinth constituted a body, whose head was Christ (1 Cor. 12:12–31). Making Christ head changes the body of the Bible, both in form and in meaning. When the Bible no longer ends with the second Book of Chronicles, as in the Hebrew Bible, but with the Book of Revelation, at the end of the Christian New Testament, and when the Bible no longer witnesses to the Messiah who is to come but to the Messiah who, having arrived and departed, is to come again, then we are dealing with very different books. We are dealing with different textual bodies, and different orderings of the bodies inside them – the bodies who live in the texts as characters and encounter them as readers, the believers who are bound over and into their bindings. And while both Jewish and Christian Bibles open with apparently the same book – Bereshith/Genesis – they are in fact different texts, for when Christ is head, all other bodies are ordered to his flesh; they become figures of his physique. And this even includes the Bible's first human bodies, those of Adam and Eve, who, it turns out, were already too late; imperfect copies of a humanity that would succeed them.

In the Bible, God's Torah is written on stone (Exod. 24:12) and flesh, in the hearts of the people (Jer. 31:33; 2 Cor. 3:2–3), and in the Gospels it arrives in a body, in the life of Jesus (Luke 4:16–21). The Bible writes our flesh, its meanings and possibilities. But writing is nothing if it is not read, and the distinction between writing and reading opens a space for movement, for a field of energy. This, indeed, is the field of religion, in which believers are bound (*religare*) over to the reading, again and again (*relegere*), of the texts by which they are both bound and set free. The divine Hermes lives in this space, as its *energeia*, as the movement of bodies who read themselves differently. How we understand ourselves determines our reading of the texts by which we are written.

As already suggested, to think about the bodies in the Bible is to think about the Bible itself, and its hold on our imaginations. This chapter will mention only a few of the Bible's bodies, and offer the merest sketch of their effects on later culture(s). Many of the most significant bodies go unmentioned, or if mentioned, undiscussed, and of those discussed only some of their modalities are explored. As Averil Cameron notes, all 'the central elements in orthodox Christianity – the Incarnation, the Resurrection, the Trinity, the Virgin Birth, and the Eucharist – focus on the body as symbolic of higher truth' (1991: 68). Indeed, for all these elements, the body is not just a symbol of their truth, but the site where it is realized. But this chapter can only touch on a few of these elements. In particular, this chapter does not attend to those biblical bodies whose lives are largely lived outside the texts. In one sense this is true of all biblical bodies, which live not just in the Scriptures, but in their interpretation. But this is more true of some than of others. It is more true of the New Testament's women, especially the Virgin Mary and Mary of Magdala. Moreover, in leaving these bodies out of account, we curtail the lives of those bodies we do discuss, for all biblical bodies are interrelated. Just as one cannot understand Christ without Adam (1 Cor. 15:20–8, 45–9) – and so Adam without Christ – so one cannot understand Eve without Mary, since in Christian tradition Mary is Eve's repetition, her second life, as Christ is Adam's (Gambero [1991] 1999: 51–8). Nor can one understand Christ without Eve–Mary – from whom Christ takes his flesh, and to which he returns the church (John 19:26–7), which is also his own body as well as his bride (Eph. 5:25–32), the body-bride that will become Eve–Mary herself (Gambero [1991] 1990: 117–18, 198–9, 296–7; see further Beattie 2002). Christian symbolics are utterly incestuous and conceptually vertiginous.

Biblical bodies are never discreet and self-enclosed. There are places in the Bible where attempts are made to police borders, as in Leviticus, which is one of the Bible's most anxious books, being concerned with the ritual purity of ancient Israel's priestly class. The holy is pure and its priests have to be perfect, with undefiled bodies, free of those flows that unsettle the boundaries between one thing and another: between male and female, inside and outside, us and them. Polity and purity were intimately related because the security of the social body was maintained through the due order of the priestly body, as it served the Lord who in turn protected Israel from her enemies. 'The Israelites were always in their history a hard-pressed minority ... The threatened boundaries of their body politics would be well mirrored in their care for the integrity, unity and purity of the physical body' (Douglas 1966: 124). Thus, the priestly concern with purity became an obsession with the body's porosity, with the seepages and ejaculations of its fluids, which could cross the borders of skin and country. Human flesh is always traversing and transgressing boundaries; its fluids seeping out; its skin touching other skins, its limbs entangling aliens – human and divine. It leaves one land and enters another, travelling from one book to the next, and, above all, it slips beyond the scrolls in which it was first written, beyond the pages of its inception, to live in the imaginations of those traditions we call religions, and, beyond them, in the cultures they once wrote and still write.

If nothing else, this chapter is intended to show that the Bible as body inhabits the bodies that come after it and live within it. Present bodies – in whatever age or culture – become biblical bodies, and biblical bodies become present lives. And sometimes this is for good, and sometimes for ill. The Bible can irradiate flesh with God's glory and condemn it to hell's fires. It was Eric Auerbach who imagined the Bible as a voracious, all-consuming text. 'Far from seeking, like Homer, merely to make us forget our own reality for a few hours, it seeks to overcome our reality: we are to fit our own life into its world, feel ourselves to be elements in its structure of universal history' (1953: 13). But the Bible does not do this by itself. It has to be fed by those communities – Jewish and Christian – upon which, in a sense, it feeds.

As bodies changed over the centuries, formed and reformed by changing cultures, different biblical texts were written (read) upon them, or old texts in new ways. Thus, when homosexual bodies were discovered in the nineteenth century, and, in their wake, heterosexual ones also – in 1869 and 1887 respectively (Foucault [1976] 1984; Halperin 1990: 15–40) – the Bible had to be newly read, its writing of flesh descried anew. Before there were homosexuals there had been sodomites – whose predilection, *sodomia*, was first coined by Peter Damien in the eleventh century (Jordan 1997) – and, before the sodomites, in the ancient Greco-Roman world, there had been *molles* and *tribades*, soft men and hard women. The soft men were passive when they should have been active, enjoying penetration rather than penetrating; while the women were the reverse, assuming an inappropriate, dominant role in sexual relationships (Brooten 1996: 143–73). But though these sexual 'characters' bear some relationship to the modern 'homosexual', it is a very distant one, for the determining criterion was not whether you desired your *own sex*, but whether you desired to be the *other sex*, and the other sex was never just a biological form, but always also a social role. It was reprehensible for a man to (want to) be penetrated, but not for him to penetrate a boy, since a boy's standing – until he became a man – was akin to that of a woman, and woman was made for penetration. This ancient way of thinking – which always understood sexual congress to be asymmetric, between a dominant and a submissive, with one *using* the other, and their relationship coded as that between man and woman (Halperin 1990: 29–38) – is even further removed from modern conceptions of gay and lesbian people, who understand themselves as wanting to be their own sex, while also desiring members of it. Gay men are thus very different from those men in Leviticus who sleep with other men *as if with women*, as also from the *malakoi* and *arsenokoitai* in Paul (1 Cor. 6:9–11; 1 Tim. 1:9–10), whose sexual practices – whatever they were – may have resembled modern ones, but which would have had very different meanings, and so have been different acts.

Past biblical bodies are continually being written into present gay and lesbian ones, while at the same time the latter are being read back into the Bible. Thus homosexuals appear in the Bible, but only in modern, twentieth-century Bibles, as when the New English Bible finds 'homosexual perversion' in Corinth, or the New Revised Standard Version discovers 'sodomites' in the same place (1 Cor. 6:9). These are careless, ideological translations, passing off modern personages as ancient, biblical bodies, which thus seem to appear in the present, or rather, not so much the ancient bodies themselves – which have been replaced with modern ones – as the ancient, Levitical and Pauline antipathies to those past bodies.

The chief focus of this chapter, however, is the body of God and its sex. It is often asserted – in both Jewish and Christian traditions – that God has no sex, and that concern with God's gender, as raised in feminist thought and theology, is beside the point. And indeed one can use the distinction between sex and gender, as between biological and social categories, to argue that God has no sex but is gendered, and gendered predominately, though not exclusively, as male in both Jewish and Christian traditions. But while the distinction between sex and gender, biology and culture, serves a purpose, it rests on the fallacy that biology escapes its mediation, and is not itself a social category: the myth that science is not a cultural product. But biology is cultural, and our ideas of sex are gendered, and God's gender affects his sex, and this becomes all too evident when divinity is used to underwrite certain human orderings, and most notably those that exclude women from certain kinds of power. It is then that we discover that women are not fully human because not really divine – in the way that men are. We discover that gender neutrality is a ruse of male partiality. This is the legacy of the biblical tradition with which Western culture – both religious and secular – is now engaged, and it would seem that only the Bible's hesitations and indeterminacies will allow it and its culture(s) to think God beyond gender, and so free the bodies that live within it for a more fluid life (Loughlin 1998).

Omphalos

Philip Gosse (1810–88), a member of the Plymouth Brethren and a marine zoologist, famously argued, in his book *Omphalos* (1857), that though Adam did not need a navel – having been born of the earth rather than a woman – he nevertheless had one (Philip Gosse [1857] 2003). Adam gave every appearance of being a normal body, even though he had never been born, had never been a baby, nor grown and gone through puberty to become the father of the human race. In just the same way, the trees in the garden of Eden gave every appearance of having grown from seed, rather than having been recently planted, fully limbed and leafed; just as the earth's sedimented rocks, with their fossilized bones, give every appearance of vast millennial age, when in fact only a few thousand years old. In this way, Gosse sought to reconcile the body of the biblical text with the dead bodies in the body of the earth. 'This "Omphalos" of his,' as Gosse's son, Edmund, observed, 'was to bring all the turmoil of scientific speculation to a close, fling geology into the arms of Scripture, and make the lion eat grass with the lamb . . . But, alas! atheists and Christians alike looked at it, and laughed, and threw it away' (Edmund Gosse [1907] 1949: 77).

But if Gosse had been less of a zoologist and more of a theologian, he might have argued that Adam had a navel because, being made in the image (*tselem*) and likeness (*demuth*) of God, he was made in the *image of the image* of God – the deity embodied in Christ – who not only had a navel, being the son of his mother, but was also the Omphalos of the world.[1] By this circularity – Christ made in the image of Adam (and Eve) made in the image of Christ – one can overcome the biblical conundrum of how bodies can image that which has no body. Adam and Eve are belated. Chronologically, they precede Christ, but ontologically, they come after him, as types of his prototype, repetitions of the one true 'image of the invisible God, the firstborn of all creation' (Col. 1:15), the embodied deity. But of course this would not have answered to Gosse's real problem, which was the existence of relics seemingly older than the earth which contained them; a problem that he could only have answered by learning to read the Bible better than he did.

Bones

The Bible – in all traditions – begins with the making of bodies. Out of primal chaos God forms the bodies of the heavens and the earth and on the earth the bodies of plants and animals, and in the sea the 'great sea monsters,' and in the air the birds of 'every kind' (Gen. 1:21–3). And then God makes humankind (*adam*) in God's own image, after God's own likeness: humankind in two kinds, 'male and female he created them' (Gen. 1:26–7). God makes by speaking; God's words form matter, their meaning bodied forth. God makes like from like, humankind from the dust of the ground, *adam* from *adamah*, and then breathes life into the earthlings (Gen. 2:7).

The bodies of Adam and Eve are the most protean in the Bible, since they will become figures for all other bodies, the templates for all future generations, giving dignity and decrepitude to all following flesh. The only other biblical body that is more significant is Christ's, and, as we have already seen, his body will encompass theirs. The order of Adam and Eve will become the order of men to women, and all later orderings of the sexes will be judged by how far they adhere to or depart from that of the primal couple. Eve made from Adam's bone has suggested her secondariness – woman's dependency – down the ages, even to the day when 'natural selection' replaced God as the maker of humankind.

> The greater size, strength, courage, pugnacity, and energy of man, in comparison with woman, were acquired during primeval times, and have subsequently been augmented, chiefly through the contests of rival males for the possession of the females. The greater intellectual vigour and power of invention in man is probably due to natural selection, combined with the inherited effects of habit, for the most part able men will have succeeded best in defending and providing for themselves and for their wives and offspring. (Darwin [1879] 2004: 674)

Even when the Bible had been reduced to myth, its culture was being written onto the bodies of its now doubtful readers. Previously, people had thought the difference between the sexes to be one of degree rather than of kind, the woman being but a 'cooler' version of the 'hotter' man. This ancient, 'one-sex' biology – in which male and female were but permutations of a single sex, polar moments of an altogether fungible flesh – lasted throughout the Middle Ages and into the early modern period (Laqueur 1992). Eve's flesh was not different in kind from Adam's, and their difference from one another was not ontological but spectral. A woman could become a man; and a man might fear to become a woman, to become effeminate, losing that balance of humours which women could only hope to enjoy through the guidance of their husbands (Brown 1988: 5–32).

But with the arrival of modernity and the emergence of new interests, pressing for the entry of women into male domains, a new biology was needed to establish and maintain the difference between the sexes, so that women could become something altogether different from men, from a newly discrete male body and its privileges. By the end of the nineteenth century, the eminent Scottish physician Patrick Geddes (1854–1932) found that male and female bodies were composed of fundamentally different cells, and for theologians the same became true for Adam and Eve, so that the removal of Adam's rib was understood to have constituted a new creation, a different species altogether (Balthasar 1990: 365–6; John Paul II 1981: 155–6).

Adam and Eve were expelled from Eden for eating forbidden fruit, and this story tells us more about the ordering of the sexes, since they were expelled with a differential curse which marks their 'fall' as a fall into patriarchal order. The woman will bring forth children in pain, and yet still desire to have more of them with her husband, who will rule over her; while he will toil to wrest food from the earth, out of the dust from which he was made and to which he will return (Gen. 3:16–19). Modern readers have recognized that this subordination of the woman to the man is a disorder, consequent upon their learning the difference between good and evil (Gen. 3:22). But Augustine, who did not doubt that women were more bodily than men, and men more rational than women, did not find here a story about how women are properly or improperly subordinate to men, but about how learning good habits is painful and requires subordinating the flesh to reason, as if to its 'husband' (Augustine 2002: 91). For Augustine, the 'carnal' meaning of the story makes little sense – something about women turning to their husbands after giving birth, when everyone knows that husbands are rarely present at the 'delivery' – and so it must be read 'spiritually', allegorically, and the curses as commands rather than punishments.

When Genesis first narrates the making of humankind the text becomes uncertain as to whether this is the making of one thing – humankind – or two things – man and woman – and this equivocation extends to, or flows from, a similar trembling over the singularity of the divine, which is signified with a plural name, 'elohim (Gen. 1:26–30). This uncertainty will resonate in later hesitations over human identity, whether it is one or two, man or woman-and-man. For many men – for Tertullian (On the Apparel of Women, I.i–ii) and Palladius in the third century – it seemed that women must first become men if they were to be saved; that in being saved they will become the 'selfsame sex as men', for man alone was made in the image of God (Tertullian 1994: 14–15). In learning virtue (virtus), woman becomes man (vir); she becomes – as Palladius had it – a 'female man of God' (Cloke 1995: 214; see also Miles 1992: 53–77). And if this language seems merely rhetorical – the use of strong metaphor for an androcentric ideal of virility – we have Augustine's testimony in the City of God (XXII.17) that many imagined a change of body, 'because God made only man of earth, and the woman from the man'. It is thus reassuring to learn that 'the sex of a woman is not a vice, but nature', and that God, 'who instituted two sexes will restore them both' in the resurrection. And this much is taught by Christ when he denied that there would be marrying or giving in marriage in the resurrected life, and so implied the presence of both men and women in heaven (Matt. 22:29; Augustine 1998: 1144–6).

Later commentators find in Genesis a story of bodily complementarity: Eve is the difference that complements Adam's singularity, his aloneness. But in fact, while Eve is numerically distinct, she is ontologically the same as Adam – 'bone of my bones and flesh of my flesh' (Gen. 2:23) – and so not his complement but his companion, the same-but-different who will breach his solitariness. But this companionability is almost immediately undone by the insinuation of the serpent that leads to the fall into hierarchy. Henceforth – from Aristotle to *When Harry Met Sally* (USA 1989) – friendship between men and women will seem impossible. The attempt to establish the equality necessary for true friendship will become a paradisal project: the attempt to live ahead of – in preparation for – the arrival of a promised restoration, the coming of a Messianic equilibrium.

Mouths

In the Bible God's body is not so much seen as heard, for God speaks, and speaking is the voicing of a body: exhalation become semantics. God's body is everywhere because God is always speaking, from the first to the last page. God speaks in the speaking of others – 'The Lord your God says . . .' But God must first speak (to) them, draw close and breathe upon them, before they can speak after him. We may of course imagine God speaking with a *disembodied* voice, as when a speaker is out of sight, in another room, another space. But by its nature, the dis*embodied* voice bespeaks a bodily origin, even if it is now only the body of the text, which breathes when it is read, given voice in the singing of the cantor in the synagogue, the reader in the church.

God, being mouthless, must speak through the mouths of others. But in the Christian Bible, God gains a mouth in the person of Jesus, who speaks not just in God's stead, but as God. He is God speaking. But no sooner spoken, than he too, like all speaking, passes away, like breath on the wind. But in finding Christ the Omphalos of the world, Christianity finds the world spoken into being by Christ (John 1:3), so that the Logos – God's utterance – speaks the world, and is its breathing, and all mouths can be – because in some sense they already are – the mouth of God.

But mouths, like the body itself, are manifold; multiple organs. Mouths are not just for speaking, but also for eating, and, indeed, kissing. And these uses are not absent from the Bible and its reading. Indeed, the Bible itself is like a mouth, for it speaks the Word of God and is to be spoken; and it is to be eaten, like food; and kissed like lips. Both Jews and Christians kiss their Scriptures, in church and synagogue and in private devotion; an intimate sign of their love for God's word.

There are many kisses in the Bible – from those of David and Jonathan, who 'kissed each other, and wept with each other' (1 Sam. 20:41) to Judas, who betrays his 'friend' with a kiss (Matt. 26:49–50); from Naomi, Orpah and Ruth, who kissed and 'wept aloud' together (Ruth 1:9) to the 'holy kiss' with which the early Christians were enjoined to greet one another (Rom. 16:16; 1 Cor. 16:20; 2 Cor. 13:12; 1 Thess. 5:26; 1 Pet. 5:14) – but perhaps the most significant kiss, because the most potent for later readers, is the kiss importuned at the beginning of the Song of Songs: 'Let him kiss me with the kisses of his mouth' (1:2)! More than any other verse in the Song of Songs, more than any other biblical kiss, this entreated intimacy would become an enduring symbol for the soul's union with God in the Christian mystical tradition, which is to say, the theological tradition, at least until the fourteenth century, when theology began to be torn from spirituality. This tradition, being infatuated with the incarnation, with the conjunction of divine and human in Christ, was deeply paradoxical, using the body and its amours to explore the soul's embrace in the arms of a bodiless God.

For Bernard of Clairvaux (1090–1153), in his *Sermons on the Song of Songs*, the entreated kiss evokes multiple intimacies: between the bride and her bridegroom, the (monkish) soul and Christ, the church and her Saviour, and between Christ and the Father. This kiss is first the kiss of incarnation, when the Word's mouth was pressed to the mouth of Jesus. 'A fertile kiss therefore, a marvel of stupendous self-abasement that is not a mere pressing of mouth upon mouth; it is the uniting of God with man' (2:3; Bernard 1971: 10). And having kissed Jesus on the lips, the Word in Jesus kisses the ascending soul, who, however, must start her ascent with first kissing Christ's feet. 'Prostrate yourself on the ground, take hold of his feet, soothe them with kisses, sprinkle them with your tears and so wash not them but yourself. Thus you will become one of the "flock of shorn ewes as they come up from the washing" [Song of Songs 4:2]' (3:2; Bernard 1971: 17). Then, when you have received forgiveness for your sins, you may aspire to kiss the hands of Christ – as he raises you up – and then, at last, to receive the kiss of his mouth (3:5–6; Bernard 1971: 19–20). For Bernard, the soul ascends to Christ by ascending his body with kisses, a ladder of arousal that rises to a returned kiss on the mouth, 'at the summit of love's intimacy' (4:1; Bernard 1971: 21). It is because the bride asks for a kiss on the mouth, rather than just a kiss, that Bernard inserts the other kisses (of feet and hands) before the first kiss of the Song. And it is because the bride asks to receive *the kisses* of his mouth, rather than to be kissed on her mouth or by his mouth, that Bernard is led to find the kiss at the heart of God. Bernard distinguishes between mouth and kiss because the lips that kiss and are kissed become for him the lips of the Father and the Son, with the Spirit the kiss itself that flows between the lips of the divine lovers. The soul participates in the erotic life of the Trinity when she receives the kiss which is the Spirit, and which Christ gave to the Church when he breathed upon the disciples (John 20:22). 'That favour, given to the newly-chosen Church, was indeed a kiss.'

> Hence the bride is satisfied to receive the kiss of the bridegroom, though she be not kissed with his mouth. For her it is no mean or contemptible thing to be kissed by the kiss, because it is nothing less than the gift of the Holy Spirit. If, as is properly understood, the Father is he who kisses, the Son he who is kissed, then it cannot be wrong to see in the kiss the Holy Spirit, for he is the imperturbable peace of the Father and the Son, their unshakeable bond, their undivided love, their indivisible unity. (8:2; Bernard 1971: 46)

Augustine, in his book on *The Trinity*, famously likened the divine triunity to the relationship of lovers. Carnal love is the 'coupling or trying to couple' of two things, namely the 'lover and what is being loved'. And if we raise this image to a spiritual plane, to love of the spirit in the friend, rather than of the friend's body, we will arrive at a more fitting triad for modelling the divine relationships: 'the lover, what is being loved, and love' (8.5.14; Augustine 1991b: 255). In a sense, Bernard returns this image to the carnal, even as he finds in it the soul's perfecting: as she kisses the lovers' kiss that moistens their pressed lips. It is perhaps only in the twentieth century that we will find a revered theologian offering a theology as sexualized as Bernard's.

Hans Urs von Balthasar (1905–88), who died shortly before he was to become a Roman Cardinal, was steeped in the Christian tradition of 'sacred eroticism' (Rambuss 1998), and, like Augustine and Bernard before him, found the triune God to be the 'lover, responding beloved, and union of the fruit of both' (Balthasar [1989] 1990: 32). The Spirit as fruit of the union between Father and Son is an obviously sexual metaphor. Picking up on the Song of Song's 'well of living water' (4:15), in which Gregory of Nyssa (c.330–c.395) had seen the bridegroom's mouth, gushing with the words of eternal life (quoted in Balthasar [1988] 1995: 157–8), Balthasar does not hesitate to imagine the divine life as an ejaculatory flow; 'a flowing wellspring with no holding-trough beneath it, an act of procreation with no seminal vesicle, with no organism at all to perform the act'. It is just a 'pure act of self-pouring-forth' (Balthasar [1989] 1990: 30). The same biblical image informs Balthasar's (masturbatory) vision of the bridegroom's return to life on the first Easter morning; but now the fountain's mouth is a wound, from which the seminal flow gushes forth:

> Is it the beginning? It is small and undefined as a drop. Perhaps it is water. But it does not flow. It is not water. It is thicker, more opaque, more viscous than water. It is also not blood, for blood is red, blood is alive, blood has a loud human speech. This is neither water nor blood. It is older than both, a chaotic drop. Slowly, slowly, unbelievably slowly the drop begins to quicken . . . But look there: it is indeed moving, a weak, viscous flow. It's still much too early to speak of a wellspring. It trickles, lost in the chaos, directionless, without gravity. But more copiously now. A wellspring in the chaos. It leaps out of pure-nothing-ness, it leaps out of itself . . . The spring leaps up even more plenteously. To be sure, it flows out of a wound and is like the blossom and fruit of a wound; like a tree it sprouts from this wound . . . Deep-dug Fountain of Life! Wave upon wave gushes out of you inexhaustible, ever-flowing, billows of water and blood baptizing the heathen hearts, comforting the yearning souls, rushing over the deserts of guilt, enriching over abundantly, over-flowing every heart that receives it, far surpassing every desire. (Balthasar [1954] 1979: 151–3; see further Crammer 2004 and Loughlin 2004: 146–61)[2]

The mouth is not only for kissing, it is also for eating, and as such is associated with bodies in the Bible and with the Bible as food. 'My soul is satisfied as with a rich feast, and my mouth praises you with joyful lips when I think of you on my bed, and medi-tate on you in the watches of the night' (Ps. 63:5–7). In the Book of Revelation (10:8–10), John is given the word of God to eat, on a little scroll. 'So I took the little scroll from the hand of the angel and ate it; it was sweet as honey in my mouth, but when I had eaten it, my stomach was made bitter' (10:10). It is a word of judgement, just like the scroll-food given to Ezekiel for his eating and prophesying, a word of 'lamen-tation and mourning and woe', but as sweet as honey in his mouth (Ezek. 2:8–3:3). As both the Word of God, Bible and Christ are one, scroll-flesh and scroll-food, since Christ is the word–body given for eating:

> Then he took a loaf of bread, and when he had given thanks, he broke it and gave it to them, saying, 'This is my body, which is given for you. Do this in remembrance of me.' And he did the same with the cup after supper, saying, 'This cup that is poured out for you is the new covenant in my blood.' (Luke 22:19–20)

In one fourteenth-century illustration of the meal that the angel gives John to eat, the Eucharistic aspect of the scroll-book is suggested by the postures of the messenger and the visionary, who have become celebrant and communicant. The angel supports John's arm as he raises the book to his mouth, as if it were a chalice (see Loughlin [1996] 1999: frontispiece). It is above all in the Christian Eucharist – performed, interpreted and contested throughout the centuries and across the world – that we see the Bible's most audacious body realized in the bread-become-flesh and community-become-Christ; in Christ become food and embrace.

Phallus

When pushed, most people will admit that God has no body, but they will still think that he does, and how could they not when they think *him* a 'he'. For popular piety the learning of the theologians is neither here nor there, let alone the teaching of the Church's mystical tradition that if we are to understand God we must begin to abandon the images by which we strive to comprehend God. We must learn to let them fall away, like the rope that helps to hoist a glider aloft, and which the glider must release in order for it to spiral upwards on nothing but rising air. Unless the rope is released, the glider will never rise, but fall back to the ground. In order to know the God of the Bible we have to let the Bible go. When Augustine and his mother Monica looked out on the garden in Ostia, and, through their conversation, ascended together to the divine wisdom, they did so by moving beyond – if only for a moment – the words and bodily images by which they climbed, and with which Augustine afterwards recalled their ascent in his *Confessions* (9.10.24):

> Step by step we climbed beyond all corporeal objects and the heaven itself, where sun, moon, and stars shed light on the earth. We ascended even further by internal reflection and dialogue and wonder at your works, and we entered into our own minds. We moved up beyond them so as to attain to the region of inexhaustible abundance where you feed Israel eternally with truth for food. There life is the wisdom by which all creatures come into being, both things which were and which will be . . . And while we talked and panted after it, we touched it in some small degree by a moment of total concentration of the heart. (Augustine 1991a: 171)

The description that has done most to establish God as a body, as an old man with a white beard – an image of patriarchy with an almost pathological hold on the popular imagination – is that of the Ancient of Days in the Book of Daniel. 'His clothing was white as snow, and the hair of his head like pure wool' (Dan. 7:9). William Blake's 1794 picture of the Ancient of Days engraved this image on the modern mind. It shows a strong, naked deity, half-squatting on his haunches and leaning forward to set the bounds of the firmament with his compasses, while his white hair and beard (which is not directly mentioned in Daniel) streams in the winds of creation. This is Daniel's Ancient turned into the Creator God of John Milton's *Paradise Lost* (1667/1674), who comes forth, 'golden compasses' in hand, 'to circumscribe/This universe, and all created things' (VII: 224–6). Milton, as Blake saw, had turned the Creator into a demi-urge, who comes forth from heaven in order to calm and order the 'vast immeasurable abyss/Outrageous as a sea' that washes up against the shores of heaven (VII: 210–12). For Blake, Milton had succumbed to the newly forming scientism of the seventeenth century, that reduced the world to the material and measurable, and which Blake asso-ciated with John Locke and Isaac Newton. As named in Blake's *Milton* (1804–8), the God of these deists had become 'Satan': 'Newton's Pantocrator weaving the woof of Locke' (I.iv.11; see further Raine 1968, vol. II: 53–83). The path that would lead from the unseen God of the Bible to the demiurge of modern deism was taken as soon as people began to imagine the Bible's God as an old man in the sky.

The Bible is very reticent about seeing God. But instead of refusing us sight of God's body, it shows it variously, first one way, then another, so that in this way – a *via posi-tiva* brimming over with images – the Bible becomes a *via negativa*, obscuring (and so revealing God's hiddenness) by showing us too much; too many fragmentary images. In Deuteronomy (4:12–24), the Israelites are reminded that they cannot picture God because God has no form to be seen. Moses, in the Book of Exodus (33:20–3), wanted to know God (*da'ath 'elohim*; Exod. 33:13) – like the men of Sodom, who wanted to know Lot's visitors (Gen. 19) – a subtle, or not so subtle, intimation that to know God is to sleep with him. But Moses is told that he cannot see God's face and live, so that when God makes his 'goodness' to pass before Moses, he covers Moses with his hand, so that Moses sees only God's departing back (see also Judg. 13:22). And yet Moses has already seen God and lived, because only a few verses before he was in the tent of meeting, speaking to God, 'face to face, as one speaks to a friend' (Exod. 33:11; see also Num. 12) – up close and personal – and a few chapters further back, Moses, and Aaron and Nadab and Abihu, and 70 elders, sat down and ate a covenant meal in God's presence, and they all saw God and lived (Exod. 24:9–11).

But what did they see? Perhaps they saw only a part of God? 'Under his feet there was something like a pavement of sapphire stone, like the very heaven for clearness . . . [T]hey beheld God, and they ate and drank' (24:10). Perhaps they saw only God's feet? Perhaps God can be seen only in parts? As in other visions and sightings of the deity (Amos 9:1; Job 42:5; 1 Kgs. 22:19; Isa. 6:1–2; Ezek. 1:26–8), divinity is oddly indis-tinct or dismembered in the strange stories of Moses in the cleft of the rock and eating with the elders and God; a pointer, it might be thought, to the metaphorical nature of God's body.

For St Thomas Aquinas in the thirteenth century, in his *Summa Theologiae*, God is not even a being, let alone a body, and so the Bible's bodily metaphors for God – includ-ing references to God's eyes, arm and hand (Ps. 33:16; Job 40:4; Ps. 117:16) – have to be taken as symbols of God's power (1a.3.1 ad 1; 1a.1.9). 'Parts of the body are ascribed to God in the scriptures by a metaphor drawn from their functions. Eyes, for example, see, and so, we call God's power of sight his eye, though it is not a sense-power, but intellect. And so with other parts of the body' (1a.3.1 ad 3; Thomas Aquinas 1964: 23). God is no more a man, or like a man, than he is a lion or a bear or a rock (Hos. 13:8; Deut. 32:4).

But there is something uncanny about these stories, as also about the story of Jacob wrestling throughout the night with the man he meets by the Jabbok (Gen. 32:22–32), and whom he takes to be God (32:30); the man/God who gives him the new name of Israel (32:28). Howard Eilberg-Schwartz (1994) has argued that the reason why Moses is only allowed to see God's back, and why those with whom God eats only see his feet, is because to see more, or to be told more of what they saw, would be to see, or to be told about, God's front, and so God's sex: the divine phallus. God's member is often intimated, but never seen, and this despite the fact that God's relationship to Israel is like that of a cloth that clings to his loins (Jer. 13:11). Ezekiel, who does not hesitate to tell us about the Egyptians 'whose members were like those of donkeys, and whose emission was like that of stallions' (Ezek. 23:20), is teasingly coy when it comes to his vision of God, his sighting of the 'something that seemed like a human form.' He tells us what every part of this body looked like, except for its loins:

> Upward from what appeared like the loins I saw something like gleaming amber, something that looked like fire enclosed all around; and downward from what looked like the loins I saw something that looked like fire, and there was splendour all around. Like the bow in a cloud on a rainy day, such was the appearance of the splendour all around. This was the appearance of the likeness of the glory of the Lord. (Ezek. 1:27–8)

The Bible, and later rabbinical commentaries, hesitate over God's sex – Ezekiel looks upwards and downwards from God's loins, but not at them – and this is because to see God's genitals is to remember that the divinity who commands his creatures to reproduce (Gen. 1:28) does not himself do so. God has no consort, and so no use for the genitals that he yet gives to his human likenesses. It was in order to solve this conundrum – Eilberg-Schwartz argues – that ancient Israel imagined herself as God's consort. The patriarchs of Israel are wife to God's husband, who has entered into a marriage contract with them – as the prophets Hosea, Jeremiah and Ezekiel testify – and who ravishes them. God has watched over Israel from infancy, when no one else would have her. And when she is old enough, he 'takes' her for his own:

> [O]n the day you were born your navel cord was not cut, nor were you washed with water to cleanse you, nor rubbed with salt, nor wrapped in cloths. No eye pitied you, to do any of these things for you out of compassion for you; but you were thrown out in the open field, for you were abhorred on the day you were born. I passed by you, and saw you flailing about in your blood. As you lay in your blood, I said to you, 'Live! and grow up like a plant of the field.' You grew up and became tall and arrived at full womanhood; your breasts were formed, and your hair had grown; yet you were naked and bare. I passed by you again and looked on you; you were at the age for love. I spread the edge of my cloak over you, and covered your nakedness: I pledged myself to you and entered into a covenant with you, says the Lord God, and you became mine. Then I bathed you with water and washed off the blood from you, and anointed you with oil. (Ezek. 16:4–9)

God washes away the blood of Israel's 'deflowering'; and male circumcision becomes the mark, in her flesh, of God's possession; the mark, on each man, of his deflowering. Prudish commentators overlook the euphemism of the spread cloak (see Ruth 3:3–9), and like to describe God's 'bedding' of the girl Israel as a marriage. It is, but Israel becomes more nearly a 'kept woman' than a wife, dressed in fine clothes and adorned with jewellery – bracelets on her arms, a chain on her neck, a ring in her nose, earrings in her ears, and a crown on her head (16:10–13). She herself becomes a piece of jewellery: the girl on the arm of her 'sugar daddy', reflecting his power back to him. 'Your fame spread among the nations on account of your beauty, for it was perfect because of my splendour that I had bestowed on you, says the Lord God' (16:14). But this girl is Israel – the *men* of Israel; and this solution to the problem of finding a use for God's sex now has the result of queering Israel's men – as we might say, but they could not. The men of Israel must either acknowledge that they are like men who sleep with men as if with a woman (Lev. 18:20), or imagine that they are women. It is then this dilemma that is partly overcome – hidden – by hiding God's phallus; by averting one's gaze.

As Eilberg-Schwartz notes, the same kind of discomfort afflicts Christian men who are enjoined to think of Christ as their bridegroom (Eph. 5:30; Eilberg-Schwartz 1994: 237). If only at a symbolic level, all Christian men are queer, as when St Bernard and his monks yearn for the kiss of Christ. This truth can be occluded in several ways. On the one hand, the early Church's enthusiasm for celibacy (see Clark 1999) – enjoined on those who would be perfect, if not on all – enabled the use of erotic language and imagery, its spiritualization being underwritten by the celibate's spiritualization of his or her own body through chastisement of its fleshly desires. And when celibacy lost its attraction, and marriage – especially in Protestant Christianity – became more desirable, the homoeroticism involved in men loving a 'male' God was secreted away by an increased discernment and destruction of all sodomitical bodies. This is why twenty-first-century debates about (male) homosexuality and same-sex marriage are so unsettling for the Christian churches.

Once men can marry men – can lie with a man *as with a man* – the relationship between men and the 'male' Christian God is fully revealed as queer. (This is why Hans Urs von Balthasar is such an unsettling theologian, for he locates 'sodomy' within the Trinity when he imagines the Father 'fertilizing' the Son; Balthasar [1989] 1990: 78.) Once gay relationships are allowed, the pretence that a man can really only lie with a woman, and a woman can really only lie with a man, are revealed as pretences. But these pretences are but modes of an even deeper pretence: that women depend on men, as Israel depends on God in Ezekiel's tender but terrifying vision. This, finally, is the deep pretence at the beginning of the Bible, in the story of woman made from man. It is the great mystifying reversal at the heart of all biblical cultures and their secular successors: the myth of a man without an omphalos.[3]

Notes

1   Though some have thought that Christ was born by a kind of miraculous Caesarean section, which left Mary perfectly intact.

2   I am grateful to Tina Beattie for bringing this text to my attention.

3   Christianity, of course, rewrites this myth by finding Adam but an image of the true man – Christ – who is indeed born of a woman. But then Christianity seemingly makes the woman dependent on a 'male' deity. It is only when Christianity acknowledges that incarnation is

not one but two, and not two but many – in the co-redeemers of Mary and her son, and in those incorporated in him and so in her (see D'Costa 2000: 32–9, 196–203) – that God can be released from the constraints of gender (the differential valorization of sexed bodies), and men and women from sexual hierarchy. And this is what is at stake in acknowledging that men can lie with men as men, and women with women as women, and that (at the altar) women as well as men can represent the man who gave himself away for *all*.

References

Auerbach, Eric (1953). *Mimesis: The Representation of Reality in Western Literature*, trans. Willard R. Trask. Princeton, NJ: Princeton University Press.

Augustine (1991a). *Confessions*, trans. Henry Chadwick. Oxford: Oxford University Press.

Augustine (1991b). *The Trinity*, trans. Edmund Hill, OP. New York: New City Press.

Augustine (1998). *The City of God against the Pagans*, ed. and trans. R. W. Dyson. Cambridge: Cambridge University Press.

Augustine (2002). *On Genesis* ('On Genesis: A Refutation of the Manichees; Unfinished Literal Commentary on Genesis; The Literal Meaning of Genesis'), trans. Edmund Hill, OP and Matthew O'Connell, *The Works of St Augustine*, vol. 13. New York: New City Press.

Balthasar, Hans Urs von ([1954] 1979). *Heart of the World*, trans. Erasmo S. Leiva. San Francisco: Ignatius Press.

Balthasar, Hans Urs von ([1988] 1995). *Presence and Thought: An Essay on the Religious Philosophy of Gregory of Nyssa*, trans. Mark Sebanc. San Francisco: Ignatius Press.

Balthasar, Hans Urs von ([1989] 1990). *Credo: Meditations on the Apostles' Creed*, trans. David Kipp. Edinburgh: T. & T. Clark.

Balthasar, Hans Urs von (1990). *Theo-Drama: Theological Dramatic Theory*, vol. 2: *The Dramatis Personae: Man in God*, trans. Graham Harrison. San Francisco: Ignatius Press.

Beattie, Tina (2002). *God's Mother, Eve's Advocate: A Marian Narrative of Woman's Salvation*. London: Continuum.

Bernard of Clairvaux (1971). *Sermons on the Song of Songs I*, trans. Kilian Walsh, OCSO, *The Works of Bernard of Clairvaux*, vol. 2. Kalamazoo, MI: Cistercian Publications.

Blake, William (1969). *Complete Writings*, ed. Geoffrey Keynes. Oxford: Oxford University Press.

Brooten, Bernadette J. (1996). *Love between Women: Early Christian Responses to Female Homoeroticism*. Chicago: University of Chicago Press.

Brown, Peter (1988). *The Body and Society: Men, Women and Sexual Renunciation in Early Christianity*. London: Faber & Faber.

Cameron, Averil (1991). *Christianity and the Rhetoric of Empire: The Development of Christian Discourse*. Berkeley, CA: University of California Press.

Clark, Elizabeth A. (1999). *Reading Renunciation: Asceticism and Scripture in Early Christianity*. Princeton, NJ: Princeton University Press.

Cloke, Gillian (1995). *'This Female Man of God': Women and Spiritual Power in the Patristic Age AD 350–450*. London: Routledge.

Crammer, Corrine (2004). 'One Sex or Two? Balthasar's Theology of the Sexes', in Edward T. Oakes, SJ and David Moss (eds), *The Cambridge Companion to Hans Urs von Balthasar*. Cambridge: Cambridge University Press, pp. 93–112.

Darwin, Charles ([1879] 2004). *The Descent of Man*, ed. James Moore and Adrian Desmond. London: Penguin.

D'Costa, Gavin (2000). *Sexing the Trinity: Gender, Culture and the Divine*. London: SCM Press.

Douglas, Mary (1966). *Purity and Danger*. London: Routledge.

Eilberg-Schwartz, Howard (1994). *God's Phallus: And Other Problems for Men and Monotheism*. Boston: Beacon Press.

Foucault, Michel ([1976] 1984). *The History of Sexuality*, vol. 1: *An Introduction*, trans. Robert Hurley. Harmondsworth: Penguin.

Gambero, Luigi ([1991] 1999). *Mary and the Fathers of the Church: The Blessed Virgin Mary in Patristic Thought*, trans. Thomas Buffer. San Francisco: Ignatius Press.

Gosse, Edmund ([1907] 1949). *Father and Son: A Study of Two Temperaments*. Harmondsworth: Penguin.

Gosse, Philip ([1857] 2003). *The Evolution Debate 1813–1870*, vol. 4: *Omphalos: An Attempt to Untie the Geological Knot*, ed. David Knight. London: Routledge.

Halperin, David M. (1990). *One Hundred Years of Homosexuality and Other Essays on Greek Love*. New York: Routledge.

John Paul II (1981). *Original Unity of Man and Woman*. Boston: St Paul Books.

Jordan, Mark (1997). *The Invention of Sodomy in Christian Theology*. Chicago: University of Chicago Press.

Laqueur, Thomas (1992). *Making Sex: Body and Gender from the Greeks to Freud*. Cambridge, MA: Harvard University Press.

Loughlin, Gerard ([1996] 1999). *Telling God's Story: Bible, Church and Narrative Theology*. Cambridge: Cambridge University Press.

Loughlin, Gerard (1998). 'Baptismal Fluid', *Scottish Journal of Theology* 51: 261–70.

Loughlin, Gerard (2004). *Alien Sex: The Body and Desire in Cinema and Theology*. Oxford: Blackwell.

Miles, Margaret R. (1992). *Carnal Knowing: Female Nakedness and Religious Meaning in the Christian West*. Tunbridge Wells: Burns & Oates.

Raine, Kathleen (1968). *Blake and Tradition*, 2 vols. Princeton, NJ: Princeton University Press.

Rambuss, Richard (1998). *Closet Devotions*. Durham, NC: Duke University Press.

Tertullian (1994). *On the Apparel of Women*, trans. S. Thelwall, in A. Roberts, J. Donaldson and A. C. Coxe (eds), *The Ante-Nicene Fathers*, vol. IV. Edinburgh: T. & T. Clark, pp. 14–25.

Thomas Aquinas (1964). *Summa Theologiae*, vol. 2 (1a.2–11), trans. and ed. Timothy McDermott, OP. London: Eyre & Spottiswoode.

PART IV
Reading in Practice

CHAPTER 23
Contextuality

Gerald West

All interpretations of the Bible are contextual. This statement would have aroused the ire of the vast majority of biblical scholars a decade or so ago. While it may be true for ordinary readers of the Bible, they would have retorted, it was false with respect to biblical scholarship, which seeks to provide an objective and ideologically neutral reading of the Bible. This was the fundamental difference between 'ordinary' interpretations and scholarly interpretations: the former are subjective while the latter are objective.

The past couple of decades have destroyed any lingering notion of an 'objective' interpretation of the Bible (or any text for that matter). Some still stamp their feet and shout, 'But the Bible says . . .' However, the Bible itself says nothing. A reader is required before the Bible says anything, and once we acknowledge a real reader as an active participant in the process of interpretation, we must abandon any strict claim to neutrality and objectivity. Readers always bring their concerns and questions to their readings of the Bible, even if they are scholarly questions and concerns. Our contexts, therefore, always shape our reading practice.

The most prominent context that we bring to the Bible is our theological context. Our beliefs about God and the world play a significant role in how we approach the Bible and what we find there. Theological contexts have exerted such a significant influence on biblical interpretation over the centuries that modern biblical scholarship could be said to have arisen as a response to this theological dominance. However, in attempting to free itself from theological control, biblical scholarship made overstated claims about neutrality and objectivity, whereas what they were really doing was bringing different contexts to bear on the Bible. Instead of reading the Bible from a theological context, biblical scholarship read the Bible from a historical context. Instead of asking theological questions, biblical scholarship asked historical questions.

The great contribution of biblical scholarship has been that it has made us aware of the historical contexts that produced the Bible. The Bible, biblical scholarship has demonstrated, is a product of the social, political, economic, cultural and religious contexts of the Ancient Near East. Historical concerns and questions have sought to explore and reconstruct this complex context and in so doing have enhanced our understanding of the contexts from which the Bible emerged and to which the Bible originally spoke.

But the Bible is not only about the past, it is also a book that speaks to the present. While it is worth trying to reconstruct what the Bible might have meant in its original contexts, the vast majority of Bible readers want to know what the Bible means for their current contexts. And while biblical scholars might not have been interested in establishing lines of connection between the biblical contexts and contemporary contexts, ordinary readers of the Bible are considerably interested in doing so.

But historical concerns and questions are not the only ones that biblical scholars have brought to the Bible. Dissatisfied with the neglect of the Bible as text, as literature, increasing numbers of biblical scholars have turned their attention to literary questions and concerns. Instead of asking historical questions, they have asked literary questions. The Bible, after all, is literature, and while we have to reconstruct the history that lies behind the Bible, we already have the Bible as literature before us. Literary concerns and questions have led to a close and careful reading of the biblical text. The gospel of Mark, for example, is more than the product of a particular historical context; it is also a finely wrought piece of literature, and in order to understand it we must pay as much attention to how it works as text as we do to its historical context.

Again, biblical scholars have been slow to acknowledge the potential literary approaches to the Bible have for contemporary contexts. Most biblical scholars are embarrassed to make the move from ancient text to current context. But here too ordinary readers of the Bible are far less reticent. They have eagerly embraced the available literary resources, finding fertile lines of connection between, for example, Mark's narrative world and their own.

Ordinary readers of the Bible do not need the resources of biblical research, whether historical or literary, in order to hear the Bible speaking into their contexts. They have always been able find lines of connection between the Bible and their lives. But, I will argue in this chapter, the resources of biblical scholarship provide substantial additional ways of establishing connections between the Bible and the ordinary interpreter. Indeed, the historical and literary resources of biblical scholarship offer the ordinary Bible interpreter a host of potential places of connection for the many questions and concerns that they have in their daily lives.

Contextual Bible Study

In many contexts around the world today, there are initiatives which attempt to link the Bible in its contexts with Bible readers in their contexts. One way that has developed for doing this, formulated in many contexts around the world, though in diverse forms, has been through community-based Bible study. This is not the place for a history and categorization of this family of practices, suffice to say that the following form a part of it: the Centro de Estudios Bíblicos (CEBI) in Brazil (Dreher 2004), with whom socially engaged scholars like Carlos Mesters worked and which included the 'Four

Sides' approach of Gilberto Gorgulho (Mesters 1984, 1989); the See–Judge–Act method of the Young Christian Workers and the Institute for Contextual Theology (among others) in South Africa (Cochrane 2001; Dumortier 1983; Speckman and Kaufmann 2001); the Ilimo Community Project Bible studies in Amawoti, South Africa (Philpott 1993); and the Contextual Bible study method of the Institute for the Study of the Bible and Worker Ministry Project (now Ujamaa Centre) in Pietermaritzburg, South Africa (Wittenberg 1993; West 2003).

The Ujamaa Centre – a merger of the Institute for the Study of the Bible and the House of Studies for Worker Ministry – operates in the interface between socially engaged biblical scholars and ordinary poor, working-class, and marginalized readers of the Bible (West 2003). This interface provides a number of sites in which the Bible becomes a resource, among other resources, for social transformation. One of the key concerns confronting us in South Africa (and in the world more generally) are economic concerns. By doing Bible study together – the core work of the Ujamaa Centre – we establish a sacred and safe space in which important contextual issues like this can be broached, and where we can begin to use biblical resources to engage with contextual issues.

Central to work of the Ujamaa Centre is a Bible reading process that has come to be called 'contextual Bible study'. The phrase is formed by both historical and methodological impulses. Methodologically, 'contextual Bible study' begins with, but admits to more than, the contextual nature of all interpretation. The many disruptions of modernity's masterly march have taken their toll. We have lost our interpretative innocence. As David Tracy aptly shows, 'There is no innocent interpretation, no innocent interpreter, no innocent text' (1987: 79). But contextual Bible study is not content with an admission of contextuality. Contextual Bible study embraces and advocates context. Commitment to rather than cognizance of context is the real concern. Because, as Elisabeth Schüssler Fiorenza has argued, 'Intellectual neutrality is not possible in a historical world of exploitation and oppression', biblical scholars and theologians are called to an intellectual conversion that enables them to become committed to the context of the poor and marginalized (1983: xxi). So implicit in the notion of 'contextual' as it is used in the phrase 'contextual Bible study' is commitment to a particular context, the context of the poor, the working class, and the marginalized.

For example, the prevailing public theology in our context proclaims that poverty (and now HIV and AIDS) are a punishment from God. This predominant theology is derived from deuteronomistic and related theological trajectories, colloquially known as the theology of retribution. Briefly, the theology of retribution argues that what a person sows, so will they reap. As the saying suggests, the metaphor for this form of theology comes from agriculture, and the saying (like the theology) probably has its origins in the early agricultural experience of ancient 'Israel' (Wittenberg 1991). In a context in which each family had its tribal land, experience would generally show that those who worked diligently and hard would reap plentiful crops, while those who were lazy and neglectful of their land would suffer hardships. This reality of agricultural life was generalized into other aspects of community life. Given that God was in control of all spheres of life, the argument would go, and not just agriculture, those who lived good lives would reap goodness and those who lived bad lives would reap badness.

However, as Gunther Wittenberg has carefully argued (Wittenberg 1991), this community wisdom became distorted as the context changed. With the rise of the monarchy and centralized state, new pressures were brought to bear on the relatively settled and stable agricultural life of ordinary 'Israelites'. Before the monarchy, communities would have had to deal with some unpredictable external factors, such as drought, locusts, and invasions from neighbouring peoples (e.g. the Philistines). While the monarchy brought with it security against invasions by providing a standing army, the king, his court and the army all had to eat, and they were not producers. So, as Samuel warns the people in 1 Samuel 8 when they come to him to ask for a king to govern them 'like other nations', the centralized monarchic state must extract food and labour in the form of tribute and taxes from those living on the land. Now it is no longer true that what you sow you reap! You sow, but others in addition to you and your family take and consume what you have produced. In other words, the experience of ordinary people living on the land is no longer the same as it was; it was now possible to work diligently and hard and still not to live well because your resources were being taken by the centralized monarchic state to sustain itself.

However, as Wittenberg shows, this change in experience did not lead to a change in theology, at least not initially. As we know, theological systems are slow to change! What happened, according to Wittenberg, is that the theology remained but became inverted. Before, when people worked diligently it was generally accepted that they would reap the benefits of conforming to God's order. In order to sustain this theology of retribution under the new centralized monarchic system a shift in perspective was required. Now those who showed signs of prosperity were assumed to have done what is right before God. Now, it was argued, what you reaped indicated what you must have sown!

The problem with this theology, of course, is that those who prospered by unjust means were presumed to have lived justly. Many houses and full barns, fine clothes and livestock, and extravagant imported goods were seen by society as signs of God's blessing for a good life. Remarkably, even though there was clear evidence to contrary, this distorted theology of retribution endured. God, it was assumed, was in control, and so those who prospered must have pleased God by living according to God's order.

This kind of theology has little understanding of structural injustice, and those who have advocated it tend to be those who benefit from systemic privilege, be it the racial privilege of apartheid, the middle-class privilege of capitalism, or the male privilege of patriarchy. Such a theology is also prevalent among those who stigmatize and discriminate against those who are HIV-positive or living with AIDS. This distorted deuteronomistic theology is familiar to many of us, for it has been championed not only from many pulpits, but also by world leaders like Margaret Thatcher, Ronald Reagan and George W. Bush. The Ujamaa Centre refuses to allow this theology to take a hegemonic hold, and so we contest it at every opportunity through what we call contextual Bible study (West 2000a). Daily our collaboration with organized groups of the unemployed (many of whom are also HIV-positive) confronts us with the theology of retribution's legacy of guilt. Most of the unemployed young men and women we work with believe they are somehow responsible for their plight. They have little understanding of the systemic effects of neo-liberal capitalism in its various globalized forms. One of our tasks, as we see it, is to provide some understanding of the systems that oppress them.

Because the Bible is such a pervasive and important text in the lives of most South Africans, it can be used as a resource. Though we are careful not to move too quickly from the Bible to our current context, the contextual Bible study process as a whole does provide a safe space in which the pooled interpretative resources of both local communities and collaborating biblical scholars can be used to generate lines of connection between the Bible and our present. These lines of connection then provide opportunities for further analysis and action. For example, one of the debates in South Africa at present is our government's shift from an economic policy that favoured social-ist principles – the Reconstruction and Development Programme – to an economic policy that has bowed the knee to neo-liberal capitalism – the Growth, Employment and Redistribution policy. Young black Africans who fought and then voted for our African National Congress-led government struggle to understand this shift. While some are prepared to attend workshops which analyse this shift and other related macro-economic issues, most remain overwhelmed by their unemployment and the guilt that comes with it, particularly the young men, who face not only a future of unemploy-ment, but as a consequence also a future that denies them the resources to marry and so attain full manhood (in a strongly patriarchal society).

In a context such as this we do Bible study as a way of engaging with unemployed youth. Our approach is based on questions, beginning and ending with what we call community consciousness questions. These are questions that draw explicitly on the local knowledge of the community. In-between these framing questions, we ask text-based questions as an entry point into the text, and these questions in turn lead into socio-historical questions which probe the world that produced the text. So, for example, we have used Mark 11:15–13:2 as a means of probing the relationship between the poor widow and the systems that have made her poor, including the scribes 'who devour widows' houses' and the temple institution (see West 2000a). Here unem-ployed youth are able to see the connections, both in the text and socio-historically, between poverty, gender and oppressive systems like the temple.

Another example which deals explicitly with destructive deuteronomic theologies, and which I will discuss more fully, begins with a simple comparison between two texts. In Proverbs 22:2, we read: 'The *rich* and the *poor* have this in common: the Lord is the maker of them all'. However, in Proverbs 29:13, we read: 'The *poor* and the *oppressor* have this in common: the Lord gives light to the eyes of both'. What is the relationship between these texts and how are we to understand the difference in phrasing? As Gunther Wittenberg points out, the two sayings are almost identical, but there is a sig-nificant difference (1991: 163). While the second lines of both proverbs affirm the pres-ence of God as creator and sustainer of all, the first lines show a significant shift. In the first saying it is possible to speak of the 'the rich and the poor' in non-relational terms; the rich and poor are descriptive, neutral, terms. In the second saying the neutral 'rich' is replaced by the pejorative 'oppressor' (ibid.: 163). The rich and poor are here linked relationally, and the relationship is one of oppression. There is a shift in analysis implicit here: a shift from wealth as a desirable asset and a blessing from God to wealth as the product of the oppression of the poor (ibid.: 163).

What is going on here? What social realities underlie this shift? The answer, we discover by pooling our interpretative resources, is the system of debt, a system that remains with us today. Textual discussion leads into a socio-economic analysis of biblical realities and our own.

The Socio-Economic Context

Each of these sayings has its own socio-economic location. The first saying probably reflects an early period in Israel's history. Early 'Israel', according to Norman Gottwald, emerged as a social formation through the successful resistance of various groups against the Canaanite city-states that dominated Canaan (Palestine) in about 1300–1200 BCE. For some centuries prior to this period 'Canaan had been dominated by city-states with hierarchies of aristocratic warriors and bureaucrats who took over the agricultural surplus of the villages where the majority of the populace lived and primary production was based' (Gottwald 1985: 272). The socio-economic system that sustained the city-states was a tributary mode of production which was almost entirely dependent on rural peasant communities. Local Canaanite kings and other ruling elites, living in the cities, extracted taxation, forced labour, and military service from peasant farmers and herders.

Various sectors of Canaanite society struggled against the city-state system in variety of ways. The peasant majority resisted surrendering their produce and labour whenever and however they were able. Sometimes they went further, supporting an invading army or joining a rebel faction in an attempt to change or at least modify the oppressive system. An alternative, taken up by many peasants, Gottwald argues, was to withdraw to the highland or steppe regions 'where they would be less vulnerable to state power'. The seasonal movement of pastoral nomads made it more difficult for the state to control them, and also gave them more room for manoeuvre in forming alliances with forces opposing the oppressive city-state system. Social outsiders, or *'apiru* (perhaps the origin of the term Hebrew), often turned to robbery or offered themselves as mercenaries; they too sometimes retreated to or based themselves in the more mountainous regions (ibid.: 273):

> During the fourteenth and thirteenth centuries, as warfare among the city-states increased and as population apparently declined (for reasons unknown at present), restive peasants, pastoral nomads, *'apiru*, and other disaffected elements [victims of the city-state system], were drawn toward closer cooperation, even alliances, in order to fend off the control of the city-states. In time, probably with the arrival of the exodus Israelites, the religion of Yahweh became the socioreligious ideology and organizational framework that won over these rebellious peoples and helped to forge them into an effective revolutionary movement that expelled the tributary mode of production from the highlands and substituted a system of free peasant agriculture within a loose tribal design. (ibid.: 273)

One of the mechanisms that made the Canaanite city-state system work was debt, because debt established a systemic link between the rich and the exploited. Debt made peasants dependent on the rich in one of two ways. Either peasants were repaying debt at interest or, as often happened, debt led to slavery, and slaves were the labour force that sustained the system of wealth generation for the rich. Taxation, forced labour, and military conscription all placed enormous pressures on the peasant community. These pressures, together with unpredictable weather conditions, were enough to begin the cycle of borrowing, repayment with interest, further debt, the forced selling of the land held as collateral, and eventual enslavement.

However, the slaves who had fled Egypt with Moses brought with them an unusual god – Yahweh, a god who heard the cry of slaves (Exod. 3:7). This god became the God of the poor and marginalized in Canaan, working with them to forge an alternative to the city-state system of oppression.

What we call 'Israel' emerges, therefore, according to Gottwald, as 'an ethnically and socioeconomically mixed coalition composed of a majority of tribally organized peasants (80 per cent or more of the populace), along with lesser numbers of pastoral nomads, mercenaries and freebooters, assorted craftsmen, and renegade priests', over and against 'the imperial and hierarchic tribute-imposing structures of Egyptian-dominated Canaan' (1985: 284). 'Within the momentum of the Israelite movement' (and this is an appropriate understanding of the term 'Israelite'), diverse segments of the Canaanite underclasses, previously divided and at odds in their struggles, gathered in the hill country and united in free agriculture ' (ibid.: 285). In order to survive the drafting and taxing powers of the tributary state system which dominated the entire region 'Family and village networks of self-help and mutual aid were revived and extended to larger social groupings, gaining strength and experience in proportion as the military and political dominion of the city-states was expelled from the hill country' (ibid.: 285).

In order to establish themselves securely, this egalitarian project called 'early Israel', Gottwald argues,

> needed to gather enough people, well-enough fed and housed and skilled enough in the new methods of upland agriculture, to be able to extend mutual aid to one another, to absorb and encourage newcomers, and finally to defend themselves collectively against efforts of the declining city-states to reestablish their control. (ibid.: 285)

A vital element in reconstituting themselves was their egalitarian socio-economic practice. The socio-economic relations of Israelites were egalitarian, says Gottwald 'in the sense that the entire populace was assured of approximately equal access to resources by means of their organization into extended families, protective associations of families (sometimes called clans . . .), and tribes . . .' (ibid.: 285). Furthermore,

> efforts were made to ensure the self-sustaining integrity of the household productive units. Many laws and stories allude to or describe some of these measures. Land was to be held continuously within extended families and never sold for speculation. It was obligatory to extend aid to other Israelites in need and no interest was permitted on such emergency loans. Strict limits were placed on contract servitude. Special provisions for the socially vulnerable (widows, orphans, strangers) were insisted on. An even-handed judicial system was highly prized. (ibid.: 287)

It is from within such a socio-economic context, we suggest, that our first saying probably comes. In such a society there are those who can be described as rich and those who can be described as poor, but the rich are not rich because of an exploitative and oppressive socio-economic system. 'Rich' and 'poor' are relative terms, not relational terms. It is also from within such a socio-economic context that the basic vision of the Jubilee was born (Lev. 25; see also Deut. 15:1–3, 12–15, Jer. 34:8–16), though in its final form, as we now have it, it has been reworked, probably during the postexilic period, when other agendas were at work (Grabbe 1993), though we can still catch glimpses of the initial liberatory impulses. The Jubilee was a legal, structural, mechanism to ensure that there was no systemic relationship between wealth and poverty, between the rich and the poor. Implicit in the Jubilee laws is the recognition that through a variety of circumstances people may become poor; for example, through drought, crop diseases, sickness on the part of those working the land, laziness, loans, etc. people may become indebted, and may even be forced to sell their land and perhaps themselves. However, the Jubilee laws are designed to prevent poverty becoming entrenched structurally. Debt and enslavement can never be the final word within an egalitarian socio-economic system (and vision). The Jubilee laws provide for the land itself to rest (Lev. 25:4–6), for the restoration of land to those who lost their land (Lev. 25:7–34), for aid to those in difficulty (Lev. 25:35), for interest-free loans to those in need (Lev. 25:37–8), for the release of those who have been forced to sell themselves into slavery (Lev. 25:39–55). In sum, the Jubilee laws provide legal protection for those who have become poor (including the land) and in so doing they break the cycle of debt and enslavement; the Jubilee laws prevented the rich from becoming 'the oppressor' (and the poor from becoming 'oppressed'). Such laws had their inception in early egalitarian Israel, but as we will see, the socio-political situation changed, and with it the socio-economic system, and so the Jubilee laws were probably never implemented.

So, unfortunately for our young unemployed contextual Bible study participants, the biblical story does not end happily ever after. The external pressures on early Israel continued to increase, particularly with the rise of the Philistine presence in the region. The Philistines gained 'a solid hold on the southern coastal plain after 1150 BCE and by 1050 BCE were posing a serious threat to the mountainous heartland of Israel' (Gottwald 1985: 319). Their oligarchic form of leadership and their iron weaponry and mobile military made them effective fighters in the hill country. Internally, there was an erosion of the egalitarian commitment, particularly in the socio-economic sector, with 'the accrual of prosperity and influence to certain regions and families, particularly in Manasseh, Ephraim, Benjamin, and Judah'. For example, we read of priestly abuses by Eli's sons (1 Sam. 2:12–17) and of bribery and perversion of justice among Samuel's sons (1 Sam. 8:1–3) – it would seem that later generations were not as committed to the values of the struggle as those that went before them!

These external and internal pressures combined to bring about change. Perhaps the most graphic description of this change is to be found in 1 Samuel 8. The elders of the Israelites caucus and then persuade Samuel to change their socio-political system. 'We are determined', they say, 'to have a king over us, so that we also may be like other nations, and that our king may govern us and go out before us and fight our battles'

(1 Sam. 8:19–20). Samuel is reluctant to participate in this (counter-revolutionary) change, but the elders are insistent, and so Samuel agrees to participate, but only after having warned them of the nature of this socio-political system, and its related socio-economic mechanisms:

> These will be the ways of the king who will reign over you: he will take your sons and appoint them to his chariots and to be his horsemen, and to run before his chariots; and he will appoint for himself commanders of thousands and commanders of fifties, and some to plow his ground and to reap his harvest, and to make his implements of war and the equipment of his chariots. He will take your daughters to be perfumers and cooks and bakers. He will take the best of your fields and vineyards and olive orchards and give them to his courtiers. He will take one-tenth of your grain and of your vineyards and give it to his officers and his courtiers. He will take your male and female slaves, and the best of your cattle and donkeys, and put them to his work. He will take one-tenth of your flocks, and you shall be his slaves. (8:10–17)

Here we have a clear picture of the city-state system! Early Israel had been formed through their struggle against such a system, now they embrace it! We must not be too harsh on them, however. There were benefits from a centralized state structure; for example, under this system there would be a centralized standing army that would defend them against the aggressive Philistines. But there would also be a cost, and Samuel portrays this cost in graphic detail.

A city-state structure, as we have seen, leads ultimately to enslavement, whether this be the Egyptian, Canaanite, or Israelite version. Samuel is clear about this too. But, unfortunately, Israel followed the path that led gradually, via Saul and David, who were more like the old tribal chiefs than city-state kings, to Solomon, who established a fully fledged city-state structure, complete with a central temple, priesthood, administration, and army, and a tributary socio-economic system. It is no wonder, therefore, that after Solomon's death the kingdom of Israel divides into two, a kingdom formed by the northern tribes (called Israel) and a kingdom formed by the southern tribes (called Judah). The burden of taxation, military conscription, and forced labour placed on the people by Solomon eventually oppressed them to such an extent that the northern tribes revolted (1 Kgs. 12). But they were unable to implement a stable alternative social system, partly because of internal tensions but also largely because of growing Assyrian imperial pressure. The excesses of Solomon and the rise of the Assyrian and then the Babylonian Empire left the people with few resources to build something different. Our second saying probably comes from sometime during the days of the divided monarchy, from within a system of taxation, conscription, and forced labour, where the subsistence farmers were driven from their land by debt and became slaves of the city-state system. Within this system there is a systemic relationship between the rich and the poor and it is called 'oppression'.

The picture which emerges from our contextual Bible studies can be summarized as follows. Early Israelite society in the pre-monarchic period was based on an egalitarian association of clan and tribal groups. The land was distributed equally among the people, with periodic reallocations of land. Extended families worked together for labour-intensive tasks and the community owned all of its produce. Warfare was largely defensive, and each tribe provided resources (human and material) in the event of having to form an army. However, under the threat of Philistine domination a centralized monarchy developed following the Canaanite model of kingship. The Canaanite system was based on a central temple, seen as the home of the god. The king was seen as the son of the god, whose duty it was to collect the agricultural produce of the peasants on behalf of the god. The agricultural surplus of the peasants was gathered in as their tribute to the god. This enabled the king to pay a standing army, administrators, and priests. The king was also entitled to conscript for military service and labour (see Gottwald 1979, 1985; Pixley 1991).

Similarly, during the time of the united monarchy, under Solomon, one of the functions of the temple was to gather the surplus from the peasant farmers in order to maintain the military, administrative, and religious structures of centralized government (see Chaney 1993). This economic (and political) function of the temple continued into the New Testament period. From the time of Solomon, therefore,

> the temple [in Jerusalem] . . . functioned as the control center of the tributary mode of production that appropriated the agricultural surplus of the peasant cultivators and shepherds of the rural countryside and redistributed it among its priests, Levites, and lay officials. In time it became the hub of all commercial enterprise and activity – at least in the province of Judea – although it was always subject to the imperial power that dominated the country and drew off much of its profits in the form of taxes and tribute. Additionally the temple received a vast income from the temple tax which the law required every Jew to pay annually, gifts from the wealthy individuals, revenues from its landholdings, and profits from the sale of sacrificial animals and money exchange. In effect, it served as the central bank of worldwide Judaism, and all of its assets and dispersements were controlled and administered by the priestly aristocracy. (Waetjen 1989: 183)

The temple, then, was not merely a religious institution, but economic and political as well:

> Indeed, the religious dimension served to legitimate the political-economic aspects of the Temple and high priesthood. The Torah provided both the divinely given 'constitution' of the political-economic-religious rule of the Temple and the high priesthood along with the fundamental traditions through which the people were governed.

Because it was understood that the ultimate head of the society was God, and because the Torah taught that the people owed tithes and offerings to God, it was relatively easy for the high priests to legitimate a system that served their interests and 'in which the peasant producers supported the Temple apparatus and priestly aristocracy'. Furthermore, 'It was this religiously sanctioned economic support from the people's tithes and offerings that enabled the high priests to exert political power over the peasant producers' (Horsley 1994: 73). It is no wonder that Jesus devoted so much of his ministry to challenging the few (about 5 per cent of the population) who maintained and benefited by from this system and in undermining their biblical interpretations (see Mark 11:27–13:2). However, Jesus was not only standing against the injustice of the temple system, he was also standing with the masses – 'the crowd' (Mark 12:37b) – who were being oppressed and dispossessed by this system. According to Jesus' analysis, and our second saying, wealth and poverty are systemically related.

From Reading the Bible to Reading Reality

Doing contextual Bible studies takes time and careful facilitation, for the process is as important as the product. The unemployed are not used to having their voices taken seriously, and so we are careful to allow for enough time for everyone to participate as fully as they are able. Furthermore, ordinary Christians are not used to reading the Bible closely and carefully, either in its literary or its socio-historical dimensions, so by enabling a more careful reading process we develop 'reading' strategies that are not only useful for reading the Bible but that are also useful for 'reading' reality.

Young unemployed black South Africans are not used to the Bible being of relevance to their plights, for the churches are strangely silent when it comes to economic issues (ICT 1991). Yet here is a reading of the Bible that drips with relevance! The temple in Jerusalem sounds just like the World Bank or the International Monetary Fund! More significantly, they are able to see the systemic dimensions of wealth and poverty as well as the systems that sustain this systemic relationship between poor and oppressors. And it is precisely this kind of connection between text and context that creates the space for creative and agentive participation in the present. The contextual Bible study does not 'solve' the problems of the unemployed, but it does provide a sacred and safe place in which to analyse and reflect on their reality from a theological perspective.

The process does not end, however, with Bible study. Typically, the Ujamaa Centre's contextual Bible study is only one element of a weekend long workshop. Surrounding the Bible study are other activities, including economic analysis from trained economists like Sampie Terreblanche and Margaret Legum. People like this provide their analyses of current economic context, furnishing additional resources for unemployed black youth to both understand and act.

In his economic analysis, Terreblanche provides a detailed history of the systemic relationship between power, land, and labour in South Africa spanning a period of more than 350 years (Terreblanche 2002). He identifies a number of successive systemic periods in South African history, beginning with 'the mercantilistic and feudal system institutionalized by Dutch colonialism during the second half of the 17th and most of the 18th century (1652–1795)' (Terreblanche 2002: 14). This was followed by the system of British colonial and racial capitalism (1795–1890) and a related system of British colonial and mineral capitalism (1890–1948) (ibid.: 15). Unfree labour patterns were intensified when the Afrikaner-oriented National Party won the general election of 1948, and although they 'did not drastically transform the economic system of racial capitalism institutionalised by the English establishment, it used its political and ideological power to institutionalise a new version of it' (ibid.: 15). 'Since 1990', continues Terreblanche, 'we have experienced a transition from the politico-economic system of white political domination and racial capitalism to a new system of democratic capitalism' (ibid.: 15). South Africa's economic system has moved, Terreblanche argues, 'over the past 30 years from one of colonial and racial capitalism to a neo-liberal, first-world, capitalist enclave that is disengaging itself from a large part of the black labour force' (ibid.: 422). This transformation, though it has 'coincided with the introduction of a system of representative democracy which is effectively controlled by a black, predominantly African, elite', still exhibits 'an ominous systemic character' (ibid.: 422–3):

> In the new politico-economic system, individual members of the upper classes (comprising one third of the population) profit handsomely from mainstream economic activity, while the mainly black lumpenproletariat (comprising 50 per cent of the population) is increasingly pauperised. Ironically, individual members of the black and white upper class in the new system seem as unconcerned about its dysfunctionality as individual members of the white elite were about that of the old. The common denominator between the old and the new systems is that part of society was/is systemically and undeservedly enriched, while the majority of the population were/are systemically and undeservedly impoverished – in the old system through *systemic exploitation*, and in the new system through *systemic neglect*. (ibid.: 423)

Fortunately, as Margaret Legum has argued, 'It doesn't have to be like this!' What she means by this, the title of a recent book (Legum 2002), is that the consensus of the 'Old Economics' no longer holds. Typified by the what is known as the Washington Consensus, and reflected in the Structural Adjustment regimes foisted on many African and other developing countries, the premises of this Old Economics were as follows. First, South Africa has a high growth potential; second, integration into the benign global economy will enhance economic growth; third, a high economic growth rate will unlock the labour-absorptive capacity of the economy; fourth, the benefits of a high economic growth rate will 'trickle down' to the poor; and fifth, the restructuring of the economy should be entrusted to market-led economic growth (Terreblanche 2002: 424–5). The economic policy of our new democratic government 'was formulated under strong pressure from the corporate sector and its global partners' is based on these questionable premises, and much of Legum's and Terreblanche's work does just this – it questions them.

While Terreblanche and Legum provide important theoretical analysis, the participants in our Bible studies have their own direct experience with the effects of the economic policies founded on these premises. Young black African South Africans, 50 per cent of whom are unemployed (Legum 2002: 14), can testify to the economic as well as the psycho-social effects of current policy. The economic effects are clear. First, we are experiencing jobless growth. While in 2000 we had a laudable economic growth rate of 3 per cent, unemployment fell by 2.2 per cent, or 126,500 jobs (ibid.: 13). Second, globalized capital determines who works where, by shifting itself to locations where it can garner the highest and quickest profits. 'Work can be moved from one area to another in search of labour prepared to work for less money' (ibid.: 15). Capital is not kept at home, and the only thing that 'investment' is vested in is profit, not people. Third, money has become de-linked from productive enterprise. Between 90 and 98 per cent of all money traded internationally on the foreign exchange markets is purely speculative. It does nothing except flit around the globe in search of profit (ibid.: 16–17). Fourth, the system currently in place is unable to connect work and income.

Technological growth and the centralization and consolidation of multinational corporations result in wage-based work for fewer and fewer; and yet there is plenty of work that needs doing, but it is work for which there is no income in the present system (ibid.: 18–19). Fifth, and finally, the very real limits to growth are becoming more and more apparent. The earth is unable to sustain the dream of wealth for all – the vision of capitalism. 'Even if the global market could spread wealth, the planet cannot continue to absorb the toxins that even current levels of consumption produce' (ibid.: 19).

All this and more our contextual Bible study participants know from first-hand experience, as do many like them in the United States of America, Russia, Argentina, Brazil and Uruguay, to mention a few (ibid.: 21–4). They also know of this economic system's pyscho-social effects (ibid.: 24–6). Growing insecurity in every facet of life, delinquency and crime, the globalization of crime, the rise of religious fundamentalisms and xenophobia, and a general tensions and disease in society as the gulf between the rich and poor widens. Fortunately, as Margaret Legum's input would go on to explain, it doesn't have to be like this! But before we can do anything about it, we must understand the dynamics of this 'system'. Contextual Bible study shows the systemic relationship between the poor widow and the Jerusalem temple and between the poor and the oppressor.

With understanding comes the desire to participate in change. Clearly macro-economic reform is necessary, but for this to happen the governing elite must 'change its thinking about the nature of the South African problem and about possible solutions to that problem' (Terreblanche 2002: 439). We need a people-centred rather than a profit-centred society. To accomplish this, Terreblanche suggests, we require, first, a new vision of the dignity and humanity of all South Africans (ibid.: 441–4); second, a new vision for healthy social relations and social justice (ibid.: 444–6); third, a new vision of the role the state has to play in a post-apartheid South Africa (ibid.: 446–9); fourth, a new vision of the role of civil society in our democratic system (ibid.: 449–51); and fifth, we need a new vision of what constitutes or defines social welfare (ibid.: 451–5).

While work begins, and there are signs that it has, at the macro-economic level, there are initiatives with which we can all engage. For example, a simple starting point is to lobby for and work towards the implementation of a Basic Income Grant (BIG) in South Africa. 'This is an income paid from cradle to grave, unconditionally, to all citizens, as individuals, without a means test or work requirement. It is a right of citizenship. It represents a person's entitlement to a small part of the fruits of the society in which they live; and their stake in its success' (Legum 2002: 32). Among its many advantages (see ibid.: 32–4) is that it would deal with chronic destitution; it would provide minimal means to look for work, by providing money for clothes, bus fares, a CV, etc.; it would allow people to take low paid work or to resist exploitative rates of pay and conditions; it would enable people living with AIDS to eat and so be able to take their antiretroviral treatment (when it is eventually available); it would treat people equally; and it would give people the dignity of being able to pay for their basic services like electricity and water.

Initiatives such as this capture the imagination and energies of the unemployed youth we work with in the Ujamaa Centre. Understanding why they are unemployed is part of the solution to doing something about it, and both Bible study and economic analysis play a role in this process. They both also play a role in moving into action.

Conclusion

Contextual Bible study is a process which seeks for lines of connection between the biblical text and its contexts and today's readers and their contexts. By locating the biblical text in its literary and socio-historical contexts, we not only allow the text to speak to us out of its ancient past, we also provide today's readers of the Bible with additional lines of connection between their contexts and the Bible. Ordinary readers of the Bible will have already found their own ways of establishing lines of connection with the Bible, but what the contextual Bible study process adds to their resources is access to the riches of the Bible in its literary and socio-historical contexts. In doing this we are attempting both to be responsible to the discipline of biblical scholarship and to Bible readers in our communities. Contextuality, in both its past and present forms, is central to this process.

References

Chaney, Marvin L. (1993). 'Bitter Bounty: The Dynamics of Political Economy Critiqued by the Eighth-Century Prophets', in N. K. Gottwald and R. A. Horsley (eds), *The Bible and Liberation: Political and Social Hermeneutics*. Maryknoll, NY: Orbis.

Cochrane, James R. (2001). 'Questioning Contextual Theology', in M. T. Speckman and L. T. Kaufmann (eds), *Towards an Agenda for Contextual Theology: Essays in Honour of Albert Nolan*. Pietermaritzburg: Cluster.

Dreher, Carlos A. (2004). *The Walk to Emmaus*. São Leopoldo: Centro de Estudos Bíblicos.

Dumortier, J. M. (1983). *Many in This City Are My People: Young Christian Workers*. Durban: Young Christian Workers.

Fiorenza, Elizabeth Schüssler (1983). *In Memory of Her: A Feminist Theological Reconstruction of Christian Origins*. London: SCM.

Gottwald, Norman K. (1979). *The Tribes of Yahweh: A Sociology of the Religion of Liberated Israel, 1250–1050 B.C.* Maryknoll, NY: Orbis.

Gottwald, Norman K. (1985). *The Hebrew Bible: A Socio-Literary Introduction*. Philadelphia, PA: Fortress.

Grabbe, Lester L. (1993). *Leviticus: Old Testament Guides*. Sheffield: Sheffield Academic Press.

Horsley, Richard A. (1994). *Sociology and the Jesus Movement*, 2nd edn. New York: Continuum.

ICT (Institute for Contextual Theology) (1991). 'Workers, the Church and the Alienation of Religious Life', in J. R. Cochrane and G. O. West (eds), *The Threefold Cord: Theology, Work and Labour*. Pietermaritzburg: Cluster.

Legum, Margaret (2002). *It Doesn't Have to Be Like This! A New Economy for South Africa and the World*. Kenilworth: Ampersand Press.

Mesters, Carlos (1984). 'The Use of the Bible in Christian Communities of the Common People', in N. K. Gottwald and R. A. Horsley (eds), *The Bible and Liberation: Political and Social Hermeneutics*. Maryknoll, NY: Orbis.

Mesters, Carlos (1989). *Defenseless Flower: A New Reading of the Bible*, trans. F. McDonagh. Maryknoll, NY: Orbis.

Philpott, Graham (1993). *Jesus Is Tricky and God Is Undemocratic: The Kin-dom of God in Amawoti*. Pietermaritzburg: Cluster.

Pixley, George V. (1991). 'A Latin American Perspective: The Option for the Poor in the Old Testament', in R. S. Sugirtharajah (ed.), *Voices from the Margin: Interpreting the Bible in the Third World*. Maryknoll, NY: Orbis.

Speckman, McGlory T. and Kaufmann, Larry T. (2001). 'Introduction', in M. T. Speckman and L. T. Kaufmann (eds), *Towards an Agenda for Contextual Theology: Essays in Honour of Albert Nolan*. Pietermaritzburg: Cluster.

Terreblanche, Sampie (2002). *A History of Inequality in South Africa, 1652–2002*. Pietermaritzburg: University of Natal Press.

Tracy, David (1987). *Plurality and Ambiguity: Hermeneutics, Religion, Hope*. San Francisco: Harper & Row.

Waetjen, Herman C. (1989). *A Reordering of Power: A Socio-Political Reading of Mark's Gospel*. Minneapolis, MN: Fortress Press.

West, Gerald O. (2000a). 'Contextual Bible Study in South Africa: A Resource for Reclaiming and Regaining Land, Dignity and Identity', in G. O. West and M. W. Dube (eds), *The Bible in Africa: Transactions, Trends, and Trajectories*. Leiden: Brill.

West, Gerald O. (2000b). 'Kairos 2000: Moving beyond Church Theology', *Journal of Theology for Southern Africa* 108: 55–78.

West, Gerald O. ([1999] 2003). *The Academy of the Poor: Towards a Dialogical Reading of the Bible*. Pietermaritzburg: Cluster. Originally published by Sheffield Academic Press.

Wittenberg, Gunther H. (1991). 'Job the Farmer: The Judean *am-haretz* and the Wisdom Movement', *Old Testament Essays* 4: 151–70.

Wittenberg, Gunther H. (1993). *Prophecy and Protest: A Contextual Introduction to Israelite Prophecy*. Pietermaritzburg: Cluster.

CHAPTER 24

Politics

Tim Gorringe

'What have Christians to do with the *res publica?*' Tertullian answers his own question with a critique of idolatry, drawing largely on the prophets and Paul, which goes to the very heart of Rome's claim for political legitimacy. In doing so, he warns us not to define politics too narrowly. When Ched Myers, in 1988, offered 'a political reading of Mark's story of Jesus' in terms of a 'war of myths', the pointed contrast of two opposed views of the world, he was continuing Tertullian's agenda. Myths, Myers argued, referred to any meaningful symbolic discourse and 'politics' to the whole range of concrete relationships, economic, military and cultural (Myers 1988: 16). Our concern with the political reaches much further than the *res publica*, the affairs of the State, narrowly conceived. The 'kingdom' which lies at the heart of Jesus' discourse presupposes the *shalom* of the Hebrew Bible, in the sense that that is God's will. *Shalom* is cultural wholeness, the harnessing of economics to the needs of the community so that fullness of life – education, health, housing, music, dance, theatre and all the rest – is possible, so that people flourish. The societal process which sees that communities either flourish or disintegrate is what I shall mean by 'politics'. Overtly political action *presupposes* culture before it shapes it. Karl Marx makes this point in his third thesis on Feuerbach. The dialectic between the intentional shaping of society in accordance with what is taken to be God's will, and culture as we find it, whether in Canaan or the Roman Empire, is the theme of almost the entire Scriptural witness. According to John, the 'word' – teaching, doctrine, story, narrative, intention – became cultural *flesh* as an account of how it might be possible to talk about God in a world where the powerful wash their hands of inconvenient decisions and the poor are crucified. The signs in John's gospel, said Stewart Headlam talking to the Fabian Society in 1892,

> were all distinctly secular, socialistic works: works for health against disease, works restoring beauty and harmony and pleasure where there had been ugliness and discord and misery; works taking care to see that the people were properly fed, works subduing nature

to the human good, works shewing that mirth and joy have a true place in our life here, works also shewing that premature death has no right here. (*Christian Socialism* 1892)

Headlam grasps the way in which the cultural and the political intermesh. John Yoder does the same in arguing that the believer's cross is the price of their social nonconformity (Yoder 1972: 97). The profound interrelation between faith, culture and politics is also the theme of the Vatican II Encyclical *Gaudium et Spes* (Tanner 1990: 57–62).

Christopher Hill argued that the heyday of the political use of Scripture, in Britain at least, was in the period from 1520 to 1660. 'Because church and state were one, religion became politics, with the Bible as the text book for both'. Changing intellectual currents and the realization that you could prove anything from it meant that it was 'dethroned' as a political resource (Hill 1993: 51, 413ff. As Marx put it, 'Cromwell and the English people had borrowed speech, passions and illusions from the Old Testament ... When the bourgeois transformation had been accomplished, Locke supplanted Habbakuk' (Marx 1979: 105). In fact, some of the most important political developments in the twentieth century were argued text by text from Scripture exactly as they were in the fourth, fourteenth or seventeenth centuries – one only has to mention Barmen, the Kairos Document, the growth of Protestantism in Korea, and the contribution of bible study to the Latin American base communities to realize that (Hill 1993: 447ff.).

The Christian community never lived *sola scriptura* but appealed for its political, cultural and economic understandings to the whole range of human tradition known to it: to Stoicism, Platonism and later to Aristotle; to the great Roman historians and moralists like Cicero; to what was taken to be common sense; later to psychology and sociology. For the most part, even for Protestants, Scripture was not the major court of appeal in political arguments and of course the understanding of Scripture and the mode of appeal to it varied from age to age. At the same time, right up to the present, it is these particular texts which remain constant for the Church as other intellectual fashions come and go and as the common sense of one age becomes the barbarity of another (Kelsey 1975). The texts contain huge swathes of overtly political material: histories of kings, wars, palace revolutions, super-power rivalry, political execution. They contain swingeing prophetic critiques of injustice, and laws dealing with property, slavery, and the appointment of kings. At the very heart is a cultural politics which has always constituted a temptation to sectarianism: 'You shall not do as they do in the land of Egypt, where you lived, and you shall not do as they do in the land of Canaan, to which I am bringing you. You shall not follow their statutes' (Lev. 18:3).

The tradition of drawing a distinction between the religious and the political, goes back, as we have seen, to the second century and this tradition sometimes argued that the New Testament, as opposed to the Old, had exclusively spiritual concerns. To the contrary, we have to object, an account of the political use of Scripture could almost be given in terms of the reception history of four New Testament texts: Mark 12:17 and parallels ('Render to Caesar'); John 18:36 ('My kingdom is not of this world'); Romans 13:1 ('The powers that be are ordained of God') and 1 Peter 2:13 ('For the Lord's sake accept the authority of every human institution'). No texts are more frequently cited and by and large they are cited in favour of the status quo. At the same time, all these texts received vigorous counter-interpretations, especially from the Reformation on. If there is no such thing as *sola scriptura* equally there is no such thing as 'the plain sense of Scripture'. As an anonymous pamphleteer put it in 1649, 'Hypocritical tyrants can alter and wrest the Scriptures how they will have it' (Hill 1993: 230). In the vehement debates of the seventeenth century, writes Christopher Hill, the Bible produced no agreed new political philosophy: 'it came to be used as a ragbag of quotations which could justify whatever a given individual or group wanted to do'. This contributed to pragmatism, lack of theory, the rise of empiricism (ibid.: 188). Equally, it contributed to the urgent search for an adequate hermeneutic, one of the key themes of political theology throughout the twentieth century which, while conceding that there is no escape from the conflict of interpretations, is at least much clearer about what constitutes a proper appeal to Scripture (Barth 1975, 1956; Rowland and Corner 1990; Segundo 1976).

Because the texts understand politics as a cultural task, or culture as a political task, no aspect of life is 'apolitical'. It follows that to elucidate political commentary is to pay attention to the whole work of Christian reflection, and therefore any short article on the political use of scripture is bound to fall short. With that caveat I shall focus on just four themes. The first I shall call 'The cry for justice'. The prophetic writings of the Hebrew Bible still retain their power to move hearts and stir passions more than two and a half millennia after they were written. They speak with a directness matched by scarcely any other ancient text. In origin, they are political and they have consistently, and up to the present, generated political commentary. The second theme I shall refer to as 'authority', for some the very heart of any political theology (O'Donovan 1996: 6). The Hebrew Bible set a puzzle for later interpreters by both supporting and critiquing the idea of kingship. According to John, Jesus claimed a kingdom 'not according to the standards of this world'. Volumes of commentary have followed these ideas. Third, Paul claimed that 'for freedom Christ has set us free' (Gal. 5:1). Freedom, clearly, is a potent political idea, especially in relation to its opposite, slavery. In places, the Christian Scriptures seemed to endorse slavery, but elsewhere it was much less clear. Finally, no account of the political impact of Scripture can ignore the visionary side of the prophetic writings and of the Book of Revelation. Many other questions would need to be dealt with in a full account: the nature and role of law; the question of the use of force, vital to the maintenance of authority; the question of economics, including property and work, only touched on here; the notion of being 'a chosen people' (Schama 1988); the idea of exile; the question of the true nature of community. The themes I have chosen are crude enough as an interpretive grid for the vast extent of Christian commentary but they will give us some insight into the way Scripture has shaped politics and culture over the past two millennia.

The Cry for Justice

For the 'social Christianity' of the early twentieth century the critique of the eighth-century prophets was the canon within the canon. Who could not see that when Amos, Micah and Isaiah spoke they had the evils of industrial society in mind (e.g. Ward 1910; Scott 1944)? 'Let justice roll down as waters'. The thrilling words of the prophets pronounced God's verdict on a class-divided society and on conspicuous consumption. The early Church Fathers had an equal passion for justice but what appears curious to us is that these texts play very little part in their preaching. Far more popular were gospel texts like Luke 16, and the Psalms, texts to which John Bunyan later appealed in much the same way (Bunyan 1658). These texts were used within a rather loose appeal to Stoic natural law theory. 'How far, you rich people, do you push your mad desires?' asks Ambrose. 'Shall you alone dwell upon the earth?' (Isa. 5:8) 'Why do you cast out the fellow sharers of nature and claim it all to yourselves? The earth was made in common for all . . . Nature . . . does not know the rich' (Avila 1983: 62). Expounding Luke 16, John Chrysostom argues:

> This is robbery: not to share one's resources . . . Do not be astonished. I shall offer you the testimony of the Sacred Scriptures, which say that not only to rob others' property, but also not to share your own with others, is robbery and greediness and theft . . . 'Bring the whole tithe into the storehouse that there may be food in my house' (Malachi 3:10). (*De Lazaro Concio* 2.4; Avila 1983: 83)

Augustine introduces an *ad hominem* argument: 'God gives the world to the poor as well as to the rich. Will the rich person have two stomachs to fill because of being rich?' But he also appeals to Scripture:

> Speaking through Haggai, the Lord said, 'Mine is the silver and the gold' (Haggai 2:8), so that those who do not wish to share what they have with the needy . . . should understand that God commands sharing not as being from the property of them whom he commands . . . but as being from his own property. (Sermon 39.2; Sermon 50.1 Avila 1983: 115)

The Church Fathers refrain from drawing the moral that these arguments demand redistribution and an egalitarian society, though Basil of Caesarea and Ambrose both argue that (to use Balzac's phrase) 'behind every great fortune there lies a crime', and that true care for the poor would dispose of large fortunes (appealing to Mark 10:20). Such sentiments reappear in John Ball and in Lollard preaching. Clement of Alexandria, on the other hand, followed by Augustine and most of the Church Fathers, anticipates the main medieval argument in urging that it is important not to be possessed by possessions and that the rich must give alms.

The radical implications of the appeal to common ownership, supported by Acts 4, eventually surface in Radical Reformation when 'the Common Treasury' becomes a political cliché. Furthermore, the prophetic writings, as well as Jesus' hostility to Mammon, constitute a critique of extremes of wealth and poverty which it is difficult to gloss over and which the medieval Dooms were well aware of.

As was classically documented by R. H. Tawney, the Church from the Patristic period to Luther took it for granted that usury was immoral and cited the Levitical texts to prove it (Tawney 1938). Well into the seventeenth century this understanding was normative as, for example, in Bishop Sanderson's *XXV Sermons* (1681). By the beginning of the eighteenth century, however, these texts quietly dropped out of use until, strangely enough, the late twentieth century when the appeal to the Levitical Jubilee legislation became the platform for a massive popular campaign for the remission of Third World Debt in which the Church and various NGOs, though not successful, certainly forced politicians on to the back foot and extracted rhetorical concessions.

One of the most remarkable documents of Christian political history is the anonymous appeal of the German peasants in 1525. It is argued from Scripture texts point by point in relation to their particular demands. Citing Romans 10, they note that they are grievously oppressed by the free labour they have to provide to their lords and ask 'that we be dealt with graciously, just as our ancestors were, who provided these services according to the word of God'. Citing Luke 6, they oppose enclosures asking that common land be returned into the hands of the community. Such demands, and their political reference points, did not spring out of nowhere but show that the political bearing of the Scriptural texts was well understood by the European peasantry (Schultz 1967: 13, 15). 'The forms rebellion took', wrote Marc Bloch of medieval Europe, 'were also traditional: mystical fantasies: a powerful preoccupation with the primitive egalitarianism of the Gospels, which took hold of humble minds well before the Reformation' (1966: 169). Diarmid MacCulloch argues that the newly translated Psalms provided explosive political texts in Reformation Europe (2003: 307).

The text of the Apocalypse played an especially important role here, shredding the taken-for-granted consensus about the way things had to be (Rowland and Corner 1990: 87). With its baroque imagery the Apocalypse, Rowland and Corner argue, helped people to see that the dominant powers were not the ultimate point of reference for the world. In the Book of Revelation, 'The grandeur of Rome, which seems to be invincible and even divine, is revealed for what it really is. It is a bombastic sham maintained by vicious and diabolical means. This is a stunning critique of the accepted order and received wisdom' (Rowland and Corner 1990: 135; cf. MacCulloch 2003: 553).

Throughout Christian history, though especially after the rise of vernacular translations, this Apocalyptic imagery proved polyvalent, standing for every kind of tyranny from the Holy Roman Empire to Charles I to Cromwell to Napoleon and later to both communism and free market capitalism. Noting the way the biblical text worked in situations of oppression, Johan Baptist Metz, and the liberation theologians argued that the Church had to recover the 'dangerous memory' of the biblical texts – dangerous because they motivate for action against prevailing hegemonies.

Authority

Any politics has to come to terms with the issue of authority. What is the origin of this? The so-called 'household texts' of the New Testament preached the law of the father in a way which, from Augustine to Filmer, seemed to indicate that patriarchy was the fundamental building block of society, the model of all authority. Thus, in *The City of God*, Augustine appeals to 1 Timothy 5:8 to argue that domestic peace begins with the ordered harmony of giving and obeying orders. To be sure, he radicalizes this so that in the household of the just 'even those who give orders are the servants of those whom they appear to command. For they do not give orders because of a lust for domination but from a dutiful concern for the interest of others, not with pride in taking precedence over others, but with compassion in taking care of others' (Augustine, *City of God* 19.14). In the late twentieth century Yoder appealed to this and other 'household texts' to plead for 'revolutionary subordination', willing servanthood in the place of domination (1972: 163ff.). He distinguishes between submission (*hypotasso*) and obedience (*hypakouo*) arguing that it is the acceptance of order, rather than obedience, which is at stake (ibid.: 175). The difficulty of doing this is illustrated by Augustine's reference, a little later, to the blows which may be necessary to keep authority in place. For St Thomas, woman's subordination is proved not from Scripture (Gen. 2:24 seems to speak against it) but from natural law (ST 1a 92.1). By the time we get to Filmer, Augustine's evangelical gloss has gone. We see from the patriarchal narratives that fathers have the power to judge in capital cases, make war and conclude peace. From there he is able to argue that kings are the fathers of their people (Sommerville 1991: 7).

Authority was a key issue both in ancient philosophy and in Christian political reflection and three of the texts mentioned earlier – 'Render to Caesar', Romans 13 and 1 Peter 2 – stood at the heart of the debate (O'Neill 1975: 209). The issue of the relative position of secular and ecclesiastical authority emerged more or less as soon as the empire became Christian. Ambrose uses the 'Render to Caesar' passage to insist on a distinction of realms: 'To the emperor belong the palaces; to the bishop, the churches. You have been entrusted with jurisdiction over public buildings, but not over sacred ones' (Phan 1984: 183). Basil of Caesarea uses Roman 13 for the same purpose. The earthly empire, he argues, is always subordinate to God's law and if the State is opposed to the divine law, the Christian must resist it. This argument appears again at the Reformation in the hands of Calvin, John Knox and many others who gloss Romans 13 with Acts 5:29 ('We must obey God rather than any human authority').

It was, of course, Augustine who gave classical shape to two kingdom theory with his great contrast of the heavenly city and the earthly city in *The City of God*. The earthly city is characterized by the lust for domination, the other by love for God. Augustine goes on to quote Romans 1 to characterize the perverse idolatry of the earthly city (Augustine, *City of God* 14.28). Of course he does not have in mind a division between sacred and secular realms: the two 'cities' run through every stratum of society. A city is a body of people joined in concord and the Church makes its political contribution because the 'precepts of concord' contained in its Scriptures offer a sure foundation for civil society (Augustine, Letter 138). Against Augustine's intention the habit of thinking in terms of two kingdoms as sacred and secular realms became ingrained because of the natural tension between secular authorities and those who claim a higher authority. The Church's increasingly vocal claim to authority over the emperor made sure that it became a major fault line in Christendom. Medieval controversialists like William of Ockham argue the case against papal supremacy rigorously from Scripture. The fanciful use of texts like Luke 22:38 ('behold there are two swords') or Genesis 1:16 ('God made two great luminaries') forced him to challenge the allegorical reading of Scripture. Mystical senses are allowable, he argues, but 'if it is not in divine Scripture explicitly in itself or in something which implies it, it should not and cannot be adduced to prove and confirm disputable and doubtful things about which Christians disagree' (Ockham 1992: 134). At the close of six books of detailed exegesis he concludes that those who argue for the subordination of emperor to pope 'have not read the sacred Scriptures, or have not understood them' (ibid.: 134).

The emergence of two kingdoms theory at the Reformation is, therefore, well prepared. In his pamphlet on secular authority (1523) Luther argues from a pessimistic reading of human nature that without force the world would become a desert.

> And so God ordained the two governments, the spiritual which fashions true Christians and just persons under Christ, and the secular (*weltlich*) which holds the Unchristian and wicked in check and forces them to keep the peace outwardly and be still, like it or not.

As so often, he appeals to Romans 13 and 1 Peter 2:14 to justify his case (Höpfl 1991: 11). Arguing with the peasants the following year he insists: 'You want power and wealth so that you will not suffer injustice. The gospel, however, does not become involved in the affairs of this world, but speaks of our life in the world in terms of suffering, injustice, the cross, patience, and contempt for this life and temporal wealth' (Schultz 1967: 35). This kind of appeal, which led Marx to dismiss Christianity contemptuously as 'opium of the people', has continued up to the present (Norman 1979). Over against it is the insistence that:

> The Kingdom of God is a social order and not a hidden one . . . it is that concrete jubilary obedience, in pardon and repentance, the possibility of which is proclaimed beginning right now . . . It does not assume time will end tomorrow; it reveals why it is meaningful that history should go on at all. (Yoder 1972: 108)

As we have seen, Basil has already argued in the fourth century that failure to obey God's law invalidates earthly authority. Early medieval authors allowed tyrannicide (Sabine 1937: 11). John of Salisbury, in the twelfth century, appealed for this both to Plutarch and to Jerome's reading of the Books of Kings and to Judith (Nederman 1990: 206). Earlier he has appealed to Romans 13 to argue that even bad princes exercise divine authority and must be understood as 'scourges of God' (the example he gives is of Attila) (ibid.: 28ff.). He cites Deuteronomy 17 to argue that the true prince, as opposed to a tyrant, will rule by the law and have the law always before him (ibid.: 41). Aquinas is more circumspect about dealing with tyrants. He allows that there is a certain Old Testament precedent for tyrannicide but, appealing to 1 Peter 2:20, argues that it does not agree with Apostolic teaching. The proper course is to seek help from whoever is superior to one's ruler, and ultimately from God. On the one hand (citing Prov. 21:1), God has the power to change the hearts of tyrants and on the other (citing Hos. 13:11), tyrants must be understood as a punishment for sin.

Luther began by agreeing with the conventional view that even unjust authority must be obeyed but changed his mind over time. In 'Against the Robbing and Murdering Hordes of Peasants', he cites both 'Render to Caesar' and Romans 13 to argue that the peasants must be obedient.

> It does not help the peasants when they pretend that according to Genesis 1 and 2 all things were created free and common, and that all of us alike have been baptized. For under the

New Testament, Moses does not count; for there stands our Master, Christ, and subjects us, along with out bodies and our property, to the emperor and the law of this world, when he says, 'render to Caesar'. (Schultz 1967: 51)

As late as 1530 Luther could write to the Elector of Saxony, 'According to Scripture, it is in no way proper for anyone who would be a Christian to set himself against his government, whether it acts justly or unjustly'. Later in the same year, in his 'Warning to his dear German People', we find him arguing that in certain circumstances resistance to a prince should be understood as self-defence. 'A Christian knows very well what he is to do – namely to render to God the things that are God's and to Caesar the things that are Caesar's, but not to render the bloodhounds the things that are not theirs' (Sherman 1971: 6, 19). Much more robust was an anonymous pamphleteer from the time of the peasant war who noted that 'to knock people such as Moab, Agag, Ahab, and Nero from their thrones is God's greatest pleasure . . . Go to it!' (Baylor 1991: 118).

> Joshua 1:7f commands the principle that no lord has the power to act according to his own will, but only on the basis of divine law. If he does not, simply get rid of him . . . St Paul provides us the second saying from the divine law in 2 Corinthians 10:8 where he says, 'Power is given to build up and not to destroy'. And what does St Paul intend with his punishing and mocking words other than that a harmful ruler should not be tolerated? (Baylor 1991: 119)

Calvin himself, although he believed that subjects should never hold the authority of magistrates in contempt, nevertheless argued that resistance was allowable if anything contrary to the will of God was ordered. This, of course, left wide open what was meant by the will of God. Catholic uses of the apocryphal book of Judith are another example of how Scripture authorizes violent resistance to tyranny (MacCulloch 2003: 469).

A further question which was central to Christian political reflection was the type of authority one ought to have. That Roman history remained a staple of European education right up to the nineteenth century meant that people were always aware that a republic was a possibility, and great Republicans like Cato the elder were widely admired. The case for monarchy, then, could not quite be taken for granted. Eusebius of Caesarea appealed to the deuteronomic history, and especially 1 Kings 8, to argue that monarchy was God's chosen means of government. Aquinas considered Aristotle's arguments for the various forms of government and endorses monarchy principally by appealing to common-sense arguments, though also, somewhat disingenuously, to 1 Samuel 13:14 ('The Lord has sought out for himself a man after his own heart') and, arguing that rule by one has proved better in experience, to Jeremiah 12:10 ('Many shepherds have destroyed my vineyard'). Counter-arguments were increasingly developed from the early sixteenth century. The anonymous *To the Common Peasantry* of May 1525 appeals to 2 Corinthians 10 to argue that authority may be vested in any member of the community, 'tailor, shoemaker or peasant', and that once vested it must be obeyed (Baylor 1991: 107). The author argues that hereditary rule is not Christian but had its origins in Babylon with Nimrod. Finally 1 Samuel 8 comes into its own:

> When that elect race, the children of God, the Israelites, had a communal government and no king then God dwelled cordially among them . . . But then heathen desire enticed and charmed them to establish a powerful king among them . . . as is clearly shown in 1 Samuel 8. God was greatly displeased by this and he foretold great misery and grief, with serfdom and other things which would bind their hands as a result of hereditary kings. (ibid.: 114–15)

A common stratagem in the magisterial Reformation was to distinguish between higher and lower magistrates. All exercised power, and if there was a conflict between higher and lower it might be in order to support the latter. Calvin felt that debate about the right form of government was dangerous, speculative and unfruitful but that, on balance, aristocracy was the best form of government in that it involved shared authority. 'Experience has always borne this out, and the Lord confirmed it by his own authority when he instituted an aristocracy bordering on a polity among the Israelites, since he wished to keep them in the best possible condition until such time as he would bring forth an image of Christ in David' (Höpfl 1991: 57). John Hall, in *Of Government and Obedience* was clear that 'unto my strictest enquiry, there could not be found one text in the Bible countenancing and maintaining any other form' of government than monarchy (Hill 1993: 179). John Harrington, by contrast, was equally clear that Scripture warranted a commonwealth.

Anabaptism, as witnessed by the Schleitheim Articles, rejected the holding of any position of governmental authority by Christians:

> Christ should have been made a king, but he rejected this (Jn. 6:15) . . . We should do likewise and follow him. In this way we will not walk into the snares of darkness. For Christ says, 'Whoever wants to follow me should deny himself and take up his cross and follow me' (Mt 16:24). (Baylor 1991: 117)

It is not fitting for a Christian to be a magistrate because

> the authorities' governance is according to the flesh, but the Christian's is according to the spirit. Their houses and dwellings remain in this world, but the Christians are in heaven . . . Their weapons of conflict and war are carnal and only directed against the flesh, but the Christian's weapons are spiritual and directed against the fortifications of the devil. (ibid.: 178)

The Levellers argue that, in virtue of human equality, no human being has '(by nature) any authority, dominion or magisterial power, one over or above another' (ibid.: 31). Milton takes up this argument in a piece of close scriptural reasoning. Moses was a king but he shared his power. Further, the divine appointment of kings stopped with the Davidic dynasty. 'All the rest, anywhere in the world, I assert, have been established by the people alone' (Milton 1991: 92, 100). Deuteronomy 17 showed that God vests the right of choosing and changing governments in the people (ibid.: 13). Milton's treatment of the 'Render to Caesar' passage is highly original. He asks:

> Who does not know that those things which belong to the people should be given back to the people? Render to all men what you owe them, says Paul, Rom 13. So not all things

are Caesar's. To give back to any Caesar what we did not receive from him would be most base and unworthy of the origin of man. For if upon beholding the face and countenance of a man, someone should ask whose image is that, would not anyone freely reply that it was God's? Since then we belong to God, that is, we are truly free and on that account to be rendered to God alone, surely we cannot, without sin and in fact the greatest sacrilege, hand ourselves over in slavery to Caesar, that is to a man, and especially one who is unjust, wicked and tyrannical? (ibid.: 107–8)

Paul does not set out what he means by the powers and does not intend to do away with rights and constitutions. The command not to resist power applies also to kings. Everything depends on the proper exercise of power.

Without magistrates and civil government, no commonwealth, no human society, no life can exist. But if any power or magistrate acts in a fashion contrary to this, neither the former nor the latter has been properly ordained by God. Thence subjection is neither owed or taught to such a power or magistrate, nor are we prevented from any sensible resistance to them, for we will not be resisting the power or the magistrate . . . but a robber, a tyrant, and enemy. (Milton 1991: 113, 115, 116)

This is not so far from the view of Vatican II on this text (Tanner 1990: 1122).

At the beginning of the twentieth century we are back with the conventional reading when the school catechism in Russia, prepared by the Holy Synod and appealing to Romans 13, taught that those who violated their duty to the Sovereign violated also their duty to God (Figes 1997: 63). The double Reformed Church in South Africa likewise appealed to this text to discountenance any rebellion against the apartheid state. Responding to this, the Kairos Document glosses Romans 13 with Revelation:

The Jews and later the Christians did not believe that their imperial overlords, the Egyptians, the Babylonians, the Greeks or the Romans, had some kind of divine right to rule them and oppress them. These empires were the beasts described in the Book of Daniel and the Book of Revelation. God allowed them to rule for a while but he did not approve of what they did. It was not God's will. His will was the freedom and liberation of Israel. Romans 13:1–7 cannot be contradicting of all this. (Villa-Vicencio 1986: 253)

Theologians including Karl Barth, H. Berkhof and John Yoder all developed the theme of the 'principalities and powers' of Ephesians 6:12, but perhaps none so powerfully as Walter Wink, arguing that the powers are the internal expression or spirituality of social groups or movements, and that they have to be engaged and exposed (Wink 1984, 1986, 1992). A quite new approach to authority emerges from this, much more sceptical of divine warrant.

Freedom

From the second to the sixteenth century Christian theologians have been preoccupied with authority. The scales begin to tip towards the priority of freedom in the sixteenth century when the perception that the Bible was subversive became commonplace. 'Our holy prelates [say that God's Word] causeth insurrection', said Tyndale, 'and teacheth the people to disobey, . . . and moveth them to rise against their princes, and to make all common, and to make havoc of other men's good' (Hill 1993: 3). Parliament sought to prevent women who did not belong to the gentry reading it and Bishop Jewel felt that it was providential that it had hitherto not been put in the hands of ordinary people (ibid.: 335, 406). A history of Presbyterianism written in 1670 felt that the marginal notes of the Geneva Bible savoured 'of sedition . . . destructive of the persons and powers of kings, and of all civil intercourse and human society' (ibid.: 58). From the seventeenth century on freedom becomes a truly dominant theological theme, above all in the twentieth century with Karl Barth and then with Liberation theology.

Just as the concern with authority began with the household and went on to the state, so the concern with freedom began with reflection on slavery. The Torah prohibited slavery among Israelites. Paul argued that a slave who was also a Christian must be respected as a brother. For most of Christian history, however, slavery has been taken for granted. Augustine argues that human beings were born free and that slavery is the result of sin (appealing to Dan. 9:3–15). Although slavery is not intended by God:

> it remains true that slavery is a punishment ordained by that law which enjoins the preservation of the order of nature, and forbids its disturbance . . . That explains the Apostle's admonition to slaves, that they should be subject to their masters and serve them loyally and willingly. (Eph. 6:5)

What he means is that if they cannot be set free by their masters, they themselves may thus make their slavery, in a sense, free, by serving not with the slyness of fear, but with fidelity of affection, until all injustice disappears and human lordship and power is annihilated, and God is all in all (Augustine, *City of God* 19.15). The closeness to Yoder's 'revolutionary subordination' is evident. Augustine's great opponent, Pelagius, interestingly, advocates human equality much more vigorously, appealing to 1 Corinthians 12 (Bradstock and Rowland 2002: 16–19).

Aquinas could not follow Aristotle in considering a slave 'an animated instrument'. Slaves were not free to make up their own mind, to be sure, but they remained rational animals (ST 2a 2ae 47.13; 50.2). He distinguishes two types of subjection, one in which people are subjected for someone else's advantage, which is the result of sin, but the other in which people are ruled for their advantage. 'For the human group would have lacked the benefit of order had some of its members not been governed by others who were wiser. Such is the subjection in which woman is by nature subordinate to man' (ST 1a 92.1). Though Genesis 1:26 seemed to speak against this, 1 Peter 4:8 was summoned to its aid, as vindicating the proper use of our gifts. This kind of subjection would have applied in the state of innocence because all social groups need leaders and some are naturally equipped for leadership (ST 1a 96:4). In the next century John Ball cannot have been an entirely isolated voice in appealing to the Creation narrative to argue social equality: 'We are all descended from one father and mother, Adam and Eve. What reasons can they give to show that they are greater lords than we, save by making us toil and labour, so that they can spend?' (Bradstock and Rowland 2002: 41).

Luther's 1520 treatise, 'On the Freedom of a Christian Man', followed Augustine in exploring the dialectic of bondage and freedom. Expounding Philippians 2:5f., he writes: 'Thus from faith flow forth love and joy in the Lord, and from love a cheerful, willing, free spirit, disposed to serve our neighbour voluntarily, without taking any account of gratitude or ingratitude, praise or blame, gain or loss' (*Luther's Primary Works* 1883: 128). Four years later, the German peasants cited a whole string of texts, including Romans 13, to appropriate this dialectic somewhat differently: 'We willingly obey our chosen and appointed rulers (whom God has appointed over us) in all Christian and appropriate matters. And we have no doubt that since they are true and genuine Christians, they will gladly release us from serfdom, or show us in the gospel that we are serfs' (Schultz 1967: 12). A decade or so earlier, Bartoleme de las Casas had appealed to Ecclesiasticus 34:18ff. to condemn the treatment of the Indians in what is now Haiti (Gutiérrez 1993).

The Levellers argue for equality appealing to Genesis 1. Adam and Eve are

the earthly, original fountain, as begetters and bringers forth of all and every particular and individual man and woman that ever breathed in the world since; who are, and were by nature all equal and alike in power, dignity, authority and majesty.

Filmer derived precisely the opposite from the same text. Biblical discussion groups in the 1640s concluded that 'the relation of master and servant had no ground in Scripture; that peerage and gentry were 'ethnical and heathenish distinctions' (Hill 1993: 199). The Royalist Sir Thomas Aston noted sourly the habit of citing 'the old seditious argument, that we are all sons of Adam, born free; some of them say, the Gospel hath made them free . . . They will plead Scripture for it, that we should all live by the sweat of our brows' (ibid.: 156).

In the eighteenth-century debate on slavery, both sides appeal to Scripture as well as to 'justice, humanity and sound policy'. The Revd Raymond Harris, in his *Scriptural Researches* of 1788, argued that both the Mosaic Dispensation and Christian Law allowed slavery. Abolitionists, by contrast, argued that the Mosaic law was now superseded and that Christ taught that all men are now brethren (*sic*). Thus Granville Sharp argued that Christ taught 'that all mankind, even our professed enemies . . . must necessarily be esteemed our neighbours . . . so that the same benevolence . . . is indisputably due, under the Gospel, to our brethren of the universe' (Turley 1991: 20, 23, 24).

The famous appeal to the exodus made by liberation theology did not, of course, begin there. Negro slaves sang 'Go down, Moses, tell old Pharaoh to let my people go' long before liberation theology existed. Joseph Arch understood his situation in the Agricultural Labourers Union in these terms in England (Arch 1966: 42–4). In Korea under Japanese occupation the authorities banned the translation of the Old Testament, and they were especially worried about Exodus, the significance of which was self evident to the Korean people. A Sunday School primer from 1907 noted: 'The Book of Exodus is written about the God who, with his power, saved the people from suffering and enslavement.' Analogies between Egypt and Japan, Pharaoh and the Emperor, were explicitly drawn. 'The Book of Exodus teaches that the enemy of justice persecutes the people of God and oppresses them, but it cannot ruin the witness to the truth, nor can it prevent it' (Yong-Bock 1983: 107). In Guatemala in the 1970s the Exodus story played a similar role. Rigoberta Menchu recalls studying the Exodus story:

> It talks a lot about the life of Moses who tried to lead his people from oppressions, and did all he could to free his people. We compare the Moses of those days with ourselves, the 'Moses' of today . . . We began looking for texts which represented each of us. We tried to relate them to our Indian culture. We took the example of Moses for the men, and we have the example of Judith, who was a very famous woman in her time and appears in the Bible . . . She held her victory in her hands, the head of the King. This gave us a vision, a stronger idea of how we Christians must defend ourselves. (Menchu 1984: 131–2)

In Korea, the translation of the Bible into Hangul, the vernacular script, was instrumental in the revival of Korean culture, and the formation of a political consciousness just as the English translations had been in sixteenth- and seventeenth-century England (Yong Bock 1983: 84). Lamin Sanneh finds similar processes at work in many African countries in the late nineteenth and twentieth centuries. Vernacular translations, he argues, set in train movements to overthrow colonial overlordship (Sanneh 1993: 74). Similarly, Paul Landau (1995) shows how missionary preaching was harnessed by an African kingdom to underwrite its power.

Characteristically, we can find the theology of freedom which is the hallmark of Karl Barth's work in his exposition of Romans 13. 'Let every man be in subjection' means, said Barth, that we must be aware of the falsity of all human reckoning as such.

> It is evident that there can be no more devastating undermining of the existing order than the recognition of it which is here recommended, a recognition rid of all illusion and devoid of all the joy of triumph. State, Church, Society, Positive Right, Family, Organized Research, etc, etc, live of the credulity of those who have been nurtured upon vigorous sermons-delivered-on-the-field-of-battle and upon other suchlike solemn humbug. (Barth 1933: 483)

What was meant by 'subjection' Barth insisted, was the resolution to starve the authorities of their pathos. Romans calls neither for revolution nor for the status quo, but for 'the great positive possibility' of learning what it means to love. As he developed this theme in his *Church Dogmatics*, he characterized God as 'the One who loves in Freedom', who elects the creature and asks for response. Barth's emphasis on freedom has led some to argue that his is a theology of revolution (for example, Lehman 1972; Marquardt 1972). The huge scriptural indices of the *Church Dogmatics* sufficiently indicate that Barth derived his political theology from the whole of Scripture and strenuously resisted adopting any canon within the canon.

Liberation theology, as it was formulated at Medellin in 1968, proclaimed:

the God whom we know in the Bible is a liberating God, a God who destroys myths and alienations, a God who intervenes in history in order to break down the structures of injustice and who raises up the prophets in order to point out the way of justice and mercy. He is the God who liberates slaves (Exodus), who causes empires to fall and raises up the oppressed. (Gutiérrez 1974: 116)

The new theology famously used the exodus as a paradigm of God's intention for humankind: 'The God of Exodus is the God of history and of political liberation more than he is a God of nature . . . The Exodus experience is paradigmatic. It remains vital and contemporary due to similar historical experiences which the People of God undergo' (ibid.: 157, 159). This had simply not occurred to the Fathers: for Augustine it is simple history with no contemporary significance (Augustine, *City of God* 16.43).

This emphasis on liberation of course chimed in with the dominant political rhetoric since the Enlightenment. It was taken up in a similar way by both Black theology and Dalit theology. It did not universally characterize Church teaching, to be sure, but it represented a very different emphasis to that of the pre-Reformation period.

Vision and Hope

Prophetic and apocalyptic texts inspired the call for justice, but they equally inspired visions of a new order. 'The Apocalypse can remind readers of early Christian literature that the hope for a reign of God on earth, when injustice and oppression will be swept away and the structures of evil society broken down, is an important component of the Christian gospel' (Rowland and Corner 1990: 148–9). Without 'utopia', it has been argued, without the possibility of negating an order beyond the point that we are able to threaten it, there is no possibility at all of the constitution of a radical imaginary – whether democratic or of any other type (Laclau and Mouffe 1985: 190). From the beginning the Christian hope had millenarian tendencies, looking for a thousand year reign on earth, and therefore not other-worldly in the sense which Marx castigated. Irenaeus appeals to more than twenty texts, including Isaiah 26:19, 30:25–6, Ezekiel 37 and Luke 12:37–8, to defend the view that the just will reign in a literal earthly kingdom (*Adversus Haereses* H 5 32.1–36.3). Tertullian appeals to Revelation 20 and 21 to make the same point (*Against Marcion* 3.24). Augustine offers his own reading of the apocalyptic texts in Book 20 of the *City of God*, reading the millennial kingdom of Rev. 20:4–6 as the age of the church. Although he emphasized that the church was a *corpus mixtum*, and had constantly to resist the devil, this opened the way to an identification of the church with the kingdom. The present age, in which wheat and tares are sown together, will last to second coming. Famously, it was Joachim of Fiore, in the twelfth century, who found in the book of Revelation both 'the key to the reading of the Bible as a whole and to the interpretation of history', who changed this reading, proposing a threefold rather than a twofold periodization of history (Rowland and Kovacs 2004: 19). The impact of this was, Karl Löwith (1949) argued, to open up a sense of history as an arena for potentially revolutionary change.

Whilst the apocalyptic texts were quarried both for readings of history and for denunciation of opponents throughout the Reformation and after it could be argued that it was in the twentieth century that the political reading of this literature came into its own. Concretely both Dorothy Day, of the Catholic Workers Movement, and the Kairos Document, appeal to Revelation 21 to ground their hope for a real change in the near future, a change, moreover which will be accomplished by reconciliation rather than by violence. On a more theoretical level we find a complex process of transmission by which the Marxist Ernst Bloch was inspired by Thomas Müntzer, his writings in turn inspired the theology of hope, which then had an immense impact on liberation theology. 'The God of exodus and resurrection', wrote Moltmann, ' "is" not eternal presence, but he promises his presence and nearness to him who follows the path on which he is sent into the future.' The resurrection is the heart of Moltmann's early eschatology. The resurrection of the crucified is the heart of the contradiction in an unredeemed world:

> Any kind of docetic hope which leaves earthly conditions or corporeal existence to the mercy of their own contradictoriness and restricts itself to the Church, to the cultus or to believing inwardness, is therefore a denial of the church. The hope that is born of the cross and the resurrection transforms the negative, contradictory and torturing aspects of the world into terms of 'not yet' and does not suffer them to end in 'nothing'. (Moltmann 1967: 30, 197)

In the earlier work he valued eschatology above apocalyptic, which he read negatively. When he returned to the theme 20 years later, he had learned better, partly under the impact of a growing apocalyptic exterminism in Western society and in the United States in particular. Appealing not just to the resurrection narratives but to both political and cosmic apocalyptic texts in Scripture, he argues that the ground for hope in the downfall of the world in God's faithfulness, not optimism 'God will remain faithful to his creative resolve even if the world he has created founders on its own wickedness . . . "God is faithful for he cannot deny himself" (2 Tim. 2:13)' (Moltmann 1996: 229). The apocalyptic ideas about the end of the world in the New Testament are subordinated to the expectation of Christ's *parousia* and to the completion of his saving work (ibid.: 231). The eschatological message of the New Testament – 'The end of all things is at hand' (1 Pet. 4:7) 'is geared towards resistance and against resignation' (ibid.: 137). Life born out of the hope of resurrection means being prepared to act in accord with God's promised new world of justice, righteousness and peace, contrary to all historical chances of success a but in hope for 'the life of the world to come', the rebirth of the cosmos (ibid.: 234). It is a theology of hope in resistance, a theology of exile in a very different sense to which Augustine intended (ibid.: 192).

The Bible and Politics

How important has the appeal to Scripture been in the wider scheme of things? Marx poured scorn on those who thought they could change things simply by changing ideas, but on the other hand no one was quicker to grant the dialectical interplay of idea and reality. No simple formula gives us the answer to how these texts functioned politically but one plausible suggestion is that they bore on what Raymond Williams called 'structures of affect', seeping into the emotional and intellectual bloodstream of a culture and thereby changing what passed as common sense (Gorringe 1996). Is this still the case?

'Today', wrote Christopher Hill in 1993, the political authority of the Bible 'exists only in dark corners like Northern Ireland or the Bible belt of the USA' (1993: 428). I hope it is clear from this brief chapter that this is simply not the case. Throughout the twentieth century, from Russia to Africa, from Europe to Asia, the Bible remained a profoundly disturbing political text. This was so even though reactionary appeals to Scripture continued to be made. In other words, Hill's view that the polysemy of Scripture undermined its political power does not seem to have been the case. Karl Barth in 1916 was neither the first nor the last to discover 'the strange new world of the Bible' in which the judgement of God is announced 'on all the unrighteousness of men'. Partly because of the density of views contained within them, but even more because of the central thrust of their contents, the texts continue to speak and to shape culture and polity (Gorringe 2004: Chapter 5). To use a metaphor of Gutierrez, humans drink from their own wells, and these wells include especially the Christian Scriptures. These texts continue to shape our social imaginary, calling rulers to account and inspiring visions of societies in which God's *shalom* may be realized.

References

Arch, J. (1966). *Autobiography*. London: MacGibbon & Kee.

Augustine (1998). *The City of God against the Pagans*, ed. and trans. R. W. Dyson. Cambridge: Cambridge University Press.

Avila, C. (1983). *Ownership*. Maryknoll, NY: Orbis.

Barth, Karl (1933). *The Epistle to the Romans*. Oxford: Oxford University Press.

Barth, Karl ([1956] 1975). *Church Dogmatics*, 2 vols. Edinburgh: T. & T. Clark.

Baylor, M. (ed.) (1991). *The Radical Reformation*. Cambridge: Cambridge University Press.

Bloch, M. (1966). *French Rural History*. London: Routledge.

Bradstock, A. and Rowland, C. (2002). *Radical Christian Writings*. Oxford: Blackwell.

Bunyan, John (1658). *A Few Sighs from Hell*.

Christian Socialism (1892). Fabian Tract No. 42.

Figes, O. (1997). *A People's Tragedy*. London: Pimlico.

Gorringe, T. (1996). *God's Just Vengeance: Crime, Violence and the Rhetoric of Salvation*. Cambridge: Cambridge University Press.

Gorringe, T. (2004). *Furthering Humanity: A Theology of Culture*. Aldershot: Ashgate.

Gutiérrez, G. (1974). *A Theology of Liberation*. London: SCM.

Gutiérrez, G. (1993). *Las Casas: In Search of the Poor of Jesus Christ*. Maryknoll, NY: Orbis.

Hill, C. (1993). *The English Bible and the Seventeenth Century Revolution*. Harmondsworth: Penguin.

Höpfl, H. (1991). *Luther and Calvin on Secular Authority*. Cambridge: Cambridge University Press.

Kelsey, David (1975). *The Uses of Scripture in Recent Theology*. London: SCM.

Laclau, E. and Mouffe, C. (1985). *Hegemony and Socialist Strategy*. London: Verso.

Landau, P. (1995). *The Realm of the Word: Language, Gender, and Christianity in a Southern African Kingdom*. London: Currey.

Lehman, P. (1972). 'Karl Barth: Theologian of Permanent Revolution', *Union Theological Seminary Review* 28(1): 67–81.

Löwith, K. (1949). *The Meaning of History*. Chicago: University of Chicago Press.

Luther's Primary Works (1883). Ed. H. Wace and C. Bucheim. London: Murray.

Marquardt, F. W. (1972). *Theologie und Sozialismus*. Munich: Christian Kaiser.

Marx, K. (1979). *The 18th Brumaire of Louis Bonaparte*, vol. 11 of *Collected Works*. Moscow: Progress.

MacCulloch, Diarmid (2003). *Reformation: Europe's House Divided*. London: Allen Lane.

Menchu, R. (1984). *I Rigoberta Menchu*. London: Verso.

Milton, J. (1991). 'A Defence of the People of England', in M. Dzelzainis (ed.), *J. Milton: Political Writings*. Cambridge: Cambridge University Press.

Moltmann, J. (1967). *Theology of Hope*. London: SCM.

Moltmann, J. (1996). *The Coming of God*. London: SCM.

Myers, C. (1988). *Binding the Strong Man: A Political Reading of Mark's Story of Jesus*. Maryknoll, NY: Orbis.

Nederman, C. J. (trans.) (1990). John of Salisbury, *Policraticus*. Cambridge: Cambridge University Press.

Norman, E. (1979). *Christianity and the World Order*. Oxford: Oxford University Press.

Ockham, William of (1992). *A Short Discourse*, ed. A. McGrade, trans. J. Kilcullen. Cambridge: Cambridge University Press.

O'Donovan, O. (1996). *The Desire of the Nations*. Cambridge: Cambridge University Press.

O'Neill, John (1975). *Paul's Letter to the Romans*. Harmondsworth: Penguin.

Phan, P. (1984). *Message of the Fathers of the Church: Social Thought*. Wilmington, DE: Glazier.

Rowland, C. and Corner, M. (1990). *Liberating Exegesis*. London: SPCK.

Rowland, C. and Kovacs, J. (2004). *Revelation*. Oxford: Blackwell.

Sabine, G. (1937). *A History of Political Thought*. London: Harrap.

Bishop Sanderson's *XXV Sermons* (1681).

Sanneh, L. (1993). *Encountering the West*. London: Marshall Pickering.

Schama, S. (1988). *The Embarrassment of Riches*. London: Collins.

Schultz, R. (ed.) (1967). *Luther's Works*, vol. 46: Philadelphia, PA: Fortress Press.

Scott, R. (1944). *The Relevance of the Prophets*. New York: Macmillan.

Segundo, J. L. (1976). *The Liberation of Theology*. Maryknoll, NY: Orbis.

Sherman, F. (ed.) (1971). *Luther's Works*, vol. 47. Philadelphia, PA: Fortress Press.

Sommerville, J. (ed.) (1991). *Patriarchal and Other Writings*. Cambridge: Cambridge University Press.

Tanner, N. (ed.) (1990). *Decrees of the Ecumenical Councils*. London: Sheed & Ward.

Tawney, R. H. (1938). *Religion and the Rise of Capitalism*. Harmondsworth: Penguin.

Thomas, Aquinas (1963–75). *Summa Theologiae*, New Blackfriars edn, 60 vols. London: Eyre & Spottiswoode.

Turley, D. (1991). *The Culture of English Antislavery, 1780–1860*. London: Routledge.

Villa-Vicencio, C. (ed.) (1986). *Between Christ and Caesar*. Grand Rapids, MI: Eerdmans.

Ward, H. (1910). *Social Ministry: An Introduction to the Study and Practice of Social Service*. New York: Eaton & Mains.

Wink, W. (1984). *Naming the Powers*. Philadelphia, PA: Fortress Press.

Wink, W. (1986). *Unmasking the Powers*. Philadelphia, PA: Fortress Press.

Wink, W. (1992). *Engaging the Powers*. Philadelphia, PA: Fortress Press.

Yoder, J. H. (1972). *The Politics of Jesus*. Grand Rapids, MI: Eerdmans.

Yong-Bock, K. (1983). 'Korean Christianity as a Messianic Movement', in *Minjung Theology: People as the Subjects of History*, edited by the Commission on Theological Concerns of the Christian Conference of Asia. Maryknoll, NY: Orbis.

CHAPTER 25
Ecology

Anne Primavesi

In 1769, English naturalist the Reverend Gilbert White applauded zoologist Thomas Pennant's scientific expedition to Scotland as that of a 'philosopher investigating the works of nature'. This attitude to the study of natural history disdains present distinctions between philosophers, professional ecologists and clerics such as White himself and the Reverend William Buckland, Charles Lyell's Oxford mentor in mineralogy and geology. For them, research and observation of living organisms in particular environments and of their fossil ancestors were a natural and ancient human preoccupation dating back to Aristotle. His *History of Animals*, especially Books VI, VIII and IX, displayed an impressive knowledge of animal demographics and of its link with the friendship and enmity between wild animals and the abundance of their food supply (Acot 1998: 151ff.).

White saw his own study of nature, the 'great economist', as furnishing further proof of the wisdom of God in creation. This consciously echoed the language and religious presuppositions of his Swedish contemporary, botanist Carl Linnaeus. His widely admired 1749 essay, 'The Oeconomy of Nature', was a rationalist religious tract whose underlying purpose was to find the hand of God there. Detailed scientific classification of plant–animal associations and systematic treatment of the gap between the theoretical birthrate of a population and its actual increase was explained through a metaphysics of divine providence. This presupposed that 'Nature's economy' was established by God to sustain a just proportion among species and so prevent any one of them increasing to an extent detrimental to human needs (Worster 1977: 33; Acot 1998: 152; White [1789] 2004: 72).

Twenty-four centuries after Aristotle, ecologists now consider themselves engaged in a practical discipline whose complex principles can be rationally defended and its data empirically attested. Presumed independent of philosophical preoccupations and religious presuppositions, ecology is defined as 'the study of patterns in nature, of how those patterns came to be, how they change in space and time and why some are more fragile than others'. Its subject-matter is the relationships among living beings and their environment and its aim is to develop a 'practical ecology'. Based primarily on case studies, natural history and rules of thumb, this type of ecology is considered a possible basis for environmental philosophy even though it cannot yield precisely defined concepts or theories. It is also seen as an indispensable alternative to the inspirational 'soft ecology' of interest to backpackers, birders and scuba divers. The opposite of this soft version, 'hard ecology', focuses on ecological structures and is based on predictive and explanatory principles. It is most useful in resolving environmental controversies and providing a precise foundation for answering courtroom challenges on environmental protection or development rights (Shrader-Frechette 2003: 304–5).

To understand this cultural shift away from White's approach to the study of natural history (he was certainly a 'birder'), it is necessary to look in some detail at the Linnaean model of natural economics he and others used to study patterns in nature. In spite of later scientific dissatisfaction with its errors and disassociation from its premises and conclusions, it played a vital role in the development of the concept of ecology and in its expansive cultural impact. The following brief history of that concept's invention and definition also highlights some scientific and cultural developments that both determined the course of ecological science and at the same time affected Christian biblically based presuppositions about nature and our place and role within it.

Invention and Scientific Definition of Ecology

As Linnaeus's 1749 tract was translated and read throughout Europe and America so his use of the concept of 'Nature's economy', with and without its Christian metaphysics, became an accepted part of the study of natural history. In 1866 the German biologist and philosopher Ernst Haeckel incorporated the concept into the science he classified as 'oekologie'. The word combines the Greek *oïkos* (house, habitat) and *logos* (study, reason) to describe the science of 'the economy, mode of life and external vital relationships of organisms'. (After the International Botanical Congress of 1893 it assumed its modern spelling as 'ecology'.) Haeckel proposed it as a replacement for the word 'biology', for by ecology he meant 'the entirety of the *science of the relationship of the organism with the environment*, including in a broad sense all the conditions of existence'. In 1868 he offered a still broader definition that linked ecology with biogeography and both of them specifically to the Linnaean concept of the 'economy of nature':

> The *ecology of organisms* [is] the knowledge of the sum of the *relations of organisms to the surrounding outer world*, to organic and inorganic conditions of existence; the so-called '*economy of nature*'; the correlations between all organisms living together on one and the same locality, their adaptation to their surroundings, their modification in the struggle for existence, expecially the circumstances of parasitism, etc. (Acot 1998: 672, 703)

Ecology therefore presupposes that the whole of earth's living organisms constitute a single, natural economic unit resembling a household or family. This exists in and through a web of complex relationships with the environment and no individual organism or species can survive independently of those relationships. The environment is defined as being composed of all the 'organic and inorganic conditions' on which the organisms' lives depend. They include the correlations between organisms within that environment, their adaptation to it and their modification by it in their struggle for existence. The interrelationships between these conditions mean that life on earth for all organisms, including ourselves, is defined in terms of interdependence.

The contemporary understanding of ecological interdependence follows from understanding those interrelationships as Haeckel understood them. He saw, as did his contemporary Darwin, that individual organisms exist only because of a shared dependence on others, even the most apparently insignificant. Today, through use of the electron microscope and other technological advances, this understanding is reinforced for us by knowledge (unavailable to Haeckel or his contemporaries) of the vital role played within all species' lives by subvisible organisms. Then and now, species survival also depends on the place or niche each one occupies within the local environment and the contribution each makes to the welfare of their conjoining and congening species. This requires them to adapt to each other and to their common surroundings. The parasitic mistletoe, for instance, takes its nourishment only from certain species of trees; its seeds are dispersed only by certain birds and its flowers pollinated only by a particular group of insects. Those species who fail to adapt to these circumstances die out and are replaced over time by others (Worster 1977: 156).

Haeckel's definition of ecology not only marked a significant scientific advance in our understanding of the essential interdependence of life forms and of the role played by environmental conditions in the evolution of all life on earth, including our own. It also brought together the work of a number of disciplines, such as botany, geography, geology, animal chemistry, and evolutionary biology. Together they led to the development of concepts that are now part of an international cultural resource base: ecosystem, species extinction, climate change and biodiversity, for example. Above all, the concept of 'environment' has become a household as well as a scientific commonplace; one used across disciplinary boundaries and invested with multivalent meaning.

It is also the case that even though Haeckel's understanding of ecology made no direct reference to the long-term effects of organisms on their environments, it did open the way to the present understanding of those effects. It is now accepted that we ourselves, especially since the Industrial Revolution of the past two centuries, have affected and do affect the local and planetary environment in an unprecedented fashion. We are becoming conscious, in varying degrees, of the correlations between the effects of our lives over time on the 'organic and inorganic' elements comprising our environments; of our impact on the planetary atmosphere and of its reciprocal impact on us and on our environments in what we call global warming.

By 1869 Haeckel had also offered a theoretical basis for the reconciliation of economics with ecology and for linking both of them with Darwinian evolutionary theory. His understanding of economics was based on a kinship of etymologies (*oïkos-logos* and *oïkos-nomos*) that resonated with the earlier Linnaean connection between the art of household management and Nature's 'management' of earth's resources. But Haeckel brought it up to date by quoting Darwin's comments on possible types of relationship within the household, on their complexity and on their context: that of the 'struggle for existence':

[Ecology is] the body of knowledge concerning the economy of nature – the study of all the relationships of the animal to its organic and inorganic environment. This includes, above all, the friendly or hostile relations with those animals and plants with which it enters into direct or indirect contact-in short, ecology is the study of the complex inter-relationships Darwin referred to by the expression, the conditions of the struggle for existence. (Acot 1998: 672)

Religious and Cultural Significance

For Haeckel and Darwin, as previously for White, the concept of the 'economy of nature' referred not only to the art of household management in the widest possible sense of both natural and human organization and use of resources. It referred specifically to the Linnaean system of natural order conceived of as comprising intricate, interconnected cyclical systems. Linnaeus based his understanding of their operation on the perpetual circulation of water from the heavens to the earth and back again. For him, this created unending interlocking processes of 'propagation, preservation and destruction' contrived by God to perpetuate the established course of nature. Our similarly 'established' role within this economy was to use nature's products to enrich the human economy. This, for him, lay at the centre of the grand organization and government of life on earth; at the heart of the rational ordering of all material resources in an interacting, interdependent whole. Linnaeus saw God 'both as the Supreme Economist who had designed the earth household and as the housekeeper who kept it functioning productively' (Worster 1977: 33–9).

Neither Haeckel nor Darwin, however, agreed with Linnaeus that God played this or any other role within nature's economy. Nor did either of them agree with him, against Aristotle, that God 'set up an enduring community of peaceful coexistence'. And nor did they accept the Linnaean religious presupposition that the economy of nature is a permanent, divinely ordained cycle of change from which nothing really new ever appears. For Linnaeus, it was an 'immutable' ecology ordered by God to serve our needs. But the 'immutability' of species had been comprehensively challenged by Charles Lyell through his study of changes in the earth's surface that showed the living world to be in a state of dynamic equilibrium; and that fluctuations in the balance of nature can lead to the extinction of species. There was now an understanding, taken for granted by Darwin and by Haeckel, that over long periods of time geological and other processes slowly altered physical factors in the environment of species and that this, together with relationships with other species, creates sharp competition for 'living space'. So as it became clear that some species disappear or are modified through adaptation, 'Linnaean mechanisms were secularized' (Acot 1998: 154).

This necessarily challenged the biblical understanding that those mechanisms were created by God to serve our needs. The Linnaean appeal to divine providentialism relied on a literal understanding of the Genesis text in which every beast of the earth, and every bird of the air, everything that creeps on the ground and all the fish of the sea were delivered into our hands; and every moving thing that lives was to be food for us. For as God gave us the green plants, everything is given to us (Gen. 9:2–3).

So Linnaeus wrote:

> All these treasures of nature, so artfully contrived, so wonderfully propagated, so provi-
> dentially supported throughout her three kingdoms, seem intended by the Creator for the
> sake of man. Everything may be made subservient to his use; if not immediately, yet medi-
> ately, not so to that of other animals. By the help of reason, man tames the fiercest animals,
> pursues and catches the swiftest, nay he is able to reach even those which lye hidden in
> the bottom of the sea. (Worster 1977: 36)

The break with these Linnaean presuppositions of a cyclical, unchanging order created by God in nature, by which living beings all aim at the same end, marks a decisive move in the secularization of the natural world. What it does not mark, however, is a move away from Linnaeus's conclusion: i.e. that aim and end are to serve us. There-fore, even though the theological legitimation for this assumption is no longer invoked, the natural economy was and is still assumed to be subservient to the human economic system; not only locally, but globally. And as its impact on the natural economy becomes more evidently lethal, efforts to reduce that impact are routinely, indeed almost solely justified in terms of human benefit.

Another notable feature of the 1869 definition is its echo of Aristotle's analysis of intra-species competition for food and the resulting friendly or hostile relationships between animals. Brought up to date as the Darwinian 'struggle for existence', compe-tition for scarce food resources has become the dominant metaphor for understanding our own financial economic systems. Practically as well as etymologically connected now is our perception of ecological relationships between and within species and between them and ours as one of competition. Competitive metaphors, of some winning and many losing in the pitiless struggle for existence, have shaped not only our view of the market economy but our perception of relationships between ourselves. They too are portrayed as a constant, often violent competition for resources ranging from water and oil provided by the natural economy to love and security within the family home (Primavesi 2000: 108–16).

However, even as competition and progress-through-struggle have become domi-nant themes of both natural and social sciences, a powerful undercurrent of political and intellectual critique of this model of relationship has also developed. Analyses of domination, whether of nature, women, other races, religions, the poor or other living beings, have given rise to diverse non-governmental movements ranging from ecofem-inism and anti-militarist campaigns to liberation theologies, social ecologies and anti-globalization rallies. These movements can and often do work actively together to implement a partnership ethic between us and nonhuman nature that they hope might lead to a sustainable ecological relationship with our global environment.

Intellectual movements based on the process philosophy of Alfred North Whitehead support a view of the world as an organism comprising individual organisms, each of which is constituted by its set of relations with all the rest. An ecological systems view of life such as that proposed by physicist Fritjof Capra emphasizes the whole over the parts, process over structure, the relative knowability of the external world, the idea of networks of knowledge and information and the recognition of the necessity of approximation (Merchant 1994: 1–28). Within the life sciences there is a growing emphasis on co-operative models based on symbiotic relationships within species and on symbiotic associations of organisms with different abilities and potentialities (Primavesi 2000: 116ff.).

Holism and Its Implications

The ecological world-views briefly summarized in the preceding paragraph all reflect the comprehensive nature of Haeckel's terms. Ecology is 'the entirety of the science of the relationship of the organism with the environment'; 'of all the conditions of existence', 'the knowledge of the sum of the relations of organisms to the surrounding outer world' and 'the correlations between all organisms living together on one and the same locality'. As with Darwinism, this is a definitive move toward including ourselves within the sum of relations between organisms and the surrounding outer world. In *Natürliche Schöpfungsgeschichte* (The Natural History of Creation), published in Berlin in 1868, Haeckel not only defined ecology as I have it above. He underlined the comprehensiveness of its subject-matter by advising naturalists not to restrict their research to a very narrow field lest they lose sight of nature as a whole. Rather, as with the theory of evolution, they are to keep the unity of the whole in mind (Acot 1998: 707). To do this consistently means, of course, understanding ourselves in the light of that theory: as a dependent species within that interdependent whole. We belong within the entire household of nature in the widest possible sense and therefore, like all those within it, we depend absolutely on its natural resources and natural economy to sustain our existence, propagation and evolution.

Nearly 150 years later, Christian acceptance of our proper place within that whole is by no means complete. The continued growth in adherents of 'creationism' as a doctrine that rejects human evolution through natural selection is the most obvious sign of its incompleteness. The theological reasons for this are integrally connected to the central Christian paradigm of personal salvation, based largely on an Augustinian hypothesis that presumes our descent from a prototypical male, Adam, at a particular moment in time. This hypothesis is itself based on Augustine's interpretation of the opening chapters of Genesis. His theological anthropology brings together doctrines of creation and salvation in such a way as to reinforce our perception of ourselves as uniquely created in the image of God and that therefore, as Linnaeus presumed, all things on earth are given to us by God for our use and are subservient to us because we alone are endowed with reason by the Creator (Primavesi 2003: 91–8; 2004: 129–43).

Given this traditional perception of ourselves, backed up by religious authorities throughout the Christian era, small wonder that we resist being reminded, in the most uncompromising manner, that we are not an exception to the rules of evolutionary biology. And further, that our relationships with our environment and interrelationships with those with whom we share it are such that we cannot, without grave consequences for ourselves, assume the right to use its resources for our sole benefit. All this is highly disorienting, indeed disturbing, for a species that has believed and preached for centuries that God has given it dominion over all living creatures. Or in a secular version of this belief, based on the supremacy of human rationality, that our brains, technologies and higher consciousness have given us the ability and the right to dominate every other life form.

In the latter case resistance to accepting our ecological identity and status remains all the stronger for being generally tacit: a hidden product of the 'push–pull' relationship between ecology, religion and culture. The scientific data push us toward a self-perception that leaves no room for human exceptionalism or for taking up any position 'outside' the natural economy. Yet the pull of centuries of religious and cultural legitimizing of ourselves as being made in the divine image, or now, of being given a covert mandate by science to rule the earth and to use all its creatures for our own benefit, remains strong enough for us to behave as if our ecological interdependence is outweighed by our right to disregard it.

Darwin, like Haeckel, found that the constant placing of man (*sic*) at the centre of scientific explanation replicated the most exasperating characteristic of providential and natural theological writing. He considered the reflexive nature of such explanations instances of arrogance. Yet as Gillian Beer notes, the essential anthropocentricity of his own language places us at the centre of signification in evolutionary terms. Natural history remained imbued with the presupposition from natural theology that there is a 'plan of creation' evident in natural laws. So while Darwin's deliberate omission in *The Origin of Species* of any reference to human beings as the crowning achievement of the natural and supernatural order made that text radical and disquieting, the entire absence of humans as a point of reference or a point of conclusion would have rendered it nihilistic and therefore unreadable (Beer 2000: 44–56). So the tacit assumption that we are at the centre of any 'plan' evident in natural laws remains and is no less powerful for being unstated.

There are also epistemological issues attached to the call from Haeckel to ecologists not to lose sight of nature as a whole and not to restrict their research in such a way as to lose sight of the unity of the whole. While Shrader-Frechette makes no reference to Haeckel, she takes issue with his holistic view of ecology. It would, she says, make it one of the most controversial and difficult sciences in which to achieve unifying and successful laws and predictions. For as there are communities of different species as well as abiotic and biotic elements of the environment, there is no precise, empirically confirmed ecological whole. This for her makes scientific appeals to holism at best problematic. So she concludes that while most well-known ecologists regard James Lovelock's Gaia theory, the basis of many accounts of holism, as possibly correct, they remain agnostic about it, or, as she does herself, they reject it as unproved speculation. For her, as ecosystems are not agents in any meaningful sense, Dobzhansky, Lovelock, Rolston and others are wrong to suggest that they are holistic units engaged in maximizing their well-being. Her final objection to holistic explanations is that, despite their heuristic power, they are neither falsifiable nor even testable (Shrader-Frechette 2003: 304, 308–10).

It is certainly true that we cannot experience, test or falsify any unit in nature as a whole; all our experiences of it and data culled from that experience are partial and fragmentary at best. But abstractions from that data to a framework within which they can be examined by and discussed with others can, so to speak, help fill in the gaps between the parts under discussion. This relationship between an implied whole and observable phenomena or instances of behaviour is, pace Shrader-Frechette, one of ecology's strengths as a scientific discipline. It is certainly true that the idea of a whole, whether of a whole ecosystem, or of the whole of a person or of the world, is, as John Dewey reminds us, an imaginative and not a literal idea (Crosby 2002: 26). But through such imaginative extensions of our observations of, for example, organic or inorganic conditions within an animal's environment; or of the particular type of relationship (friendly or hostile) between the animals and between them and plants, ecological concepts such as that of an ecosystem can fill the gaps and enable us to see animals, plants and environmental conditions as an interacting, interdependent whole.

In his *Steps to an Ecology of Mind*, Gregory Bateson points to the cultural significance of such concepts. In lecturing students on subjects as diverse as psychiatry, anthropology, ecology and cybernetics, he found that the problem they had with learning from him was that they had been trained to think and argue *inductively* from data to hypotheses; whereas he tested hypotheses against knowledge derived by *deduction* from the fundamental concepts of science or philosophy (Bateson 1972: xvii f.). In a later book, *Mind and Nature: A Necessary Unity*, he argues for the relationship between data and hypothesis as that between what he calls the two great contraries of mental process, rigour and imagination. The hypothesis he invokes (as does Shrader-Frechette) is that of connective pattern. 'What pattern', he asks, 'connects the crab to the lobster and the orchid to the primrose and all four of them to me?' (Bateson 1985: 16f.). For him, the patterns can and must ultimately connect in the unity of the whole. As a practical ecologist, Shrader-Frechette presumes that the study of patterns in nature, which is how she defines ecology, requires keeping them separate from each other.

This is the case even though the term 'ecology' began life as a holistic hypothesis built on a similar concept, that is, the economy of nature. But that concept too had a very specific content, the study of certain interrelationships, that made and still makes it extremely useful, both philosophically and scientifically. For the study presupposes that neither the concept nor the experience, the data nor the hypothesis of the economy of nature is ever wholly or sharply separate one from the other. But nor can they be simply identified one with the other. The two often meld together indistinguishably in our minds, but one can challenge the other in unexpected ways. New theoretical models, such as the ecological one, can prompt us to question hitherto accepted or unanalysed attitudes regarding experience; just as new experiences, now often aided by new technologies, may lead us to question, revise or abandon established theories (Crosby 2002: 17–27).

There is another important methodological link between Linnaeus, Darwin and Haeckel. Darwin's theory of evolution and Haeckel's ecological theory presupposed Linnaeus's organization and classification of species into a coherent plan, in spite of errors detected in it later. Therefore even though some of ecological science's current practitioners might see it differently, the historic link between Linnaeus, Darwin and Haeckel still holds true (Acot 1998: 373). As does Haeckel's historic link with ecologists today. Despite Shrader-Frechette's doubts about its untestability, most would agree with Haeckel's postulate of Nature as an interrelated whole; although perhaps not many of them would accept his monist philosophical basis for it. Also despite its traditional Christian premise, in practice, most of them appear to agree with Linnaeus's conclusion that all these treasures of nature, so artfully contrived, so wonderfully propagated, so providentially supported throughout her three kingdoms, '*seem intended* by the Creator *for the sake of man. Everything may be made subservient to his use, if not immediately, yet mediately*' (Worster 1977: 35–6; my italics).

Rejection of the Linnaean religious premise was strong enough in 1998 for the editors of *The European Origins of Scientific Ecology* to exclude Linnaeus from the group of those considered founders of the discipline of ecology because of the 'providentialism of his analysis' (Acot 1998: xviii). There was, too, an important scientific reason for this exclusion. His tract on 'The Oeconomy of Nature' presents a thoroughly static portrait of the geo-biological interactions within it. Like the classical Greek naturalists, Linnaeus allowed only one kind of change in the natural economic system, that of a cyclical pattern that keeps returning to its point of departure (Worster 1977: 34). Yet while this scientific presupposition may rightly disqualify him as a major contributor to ecological science, his assumption that we have the right to vigorously pursue the work of categorizing, adapting and utilizing our fellow species to our own advantage has neither disappeared from scientific practice nor from traditional Christian views of our role within the natural economy.

Given this cultural consensus, ecology as a scientific discipline has developed without any of the conspicuous disagreements between its proponents and upholders of religious doctrine that marked the emergence of Darwinism. One possible reason for this is that its necessarily integrated and implicitly holistic view of nature prevents any one aspect of it from being taken as grounds for battle between opposing professional bodies within science and religion. Nevertheless, it can and does function, as I have intimated, as a radical critique of the religious legitimation of oppressive power structures and of a literalist biblical creationism. So what aspects of an ecological paradigm support such a critique?

The Idea of Nature

The most important, perhaps, in spite of (and increasingly highlighted by) cultural and religious resistance to it, is that a perceptible increase in ecological understanding of our dependence on other life forms and on the environments we share with them fosters a sense of our belonging within rather than dominating nature. In theory, that understanding can either lead to or can follow from Haeckel's view of nature as a unified whole: a view that might seem beyond doubt or question. But as Shrader-Frechette has shown, for some ecologists at least it remains questionable because untestable by us. Her view also resonates with some aspects of postmodern deconstructionist theories that can be shown to have clear implications for a wide range of environmental issues and policies.

In *Reinventing Nature?* (1995), editors Michael Soulé and Gary Lease respond to these theories and at the same time illustrate the extremes to which some theorists will go to assert our independence from, and therefore our control over the natural world. Their

primary assertion is that the natural world as described by scientists and conservationists, if it exists, is a human artefact produced by our economic activities. As such it
is, therefore, grist to the mill of further material reshaping by us. Not only is it there for
us: it is produced by us. And its potential for further use by us is seen as the proper aim
of scientific research into the interrelationships between plants and animals and their
interactions with the organic and inorganic elements in their local surroundings. Naturally opposed to this view is one that assumes that the world as a whole, including its
living components, really does exist apart from humanity's perceptions of it, our impact
on it and beliefs about it (ibid.: xv). The problem with this view, as we have seen,
is how to test it: a problem compounded by the fact that as part of it, we cannot test
the whole.

Either position, if held to an extreme, loses sight of the fact already mentioned: that
we cannot consider ourselves in any real sense as existing 'apart from' the world. Therefore we cannot hold with any consistency that the world really does exist apart from
us. But this means that our grasp of it as a whole is necessarily an abstraction: the work,
as Bateson says, of our imagination. On the other hand, the absolutizing of human
experience of nature to the extent that it becomes an extension of ourselves serves to
support updated humanist versions of the Linnaean religious conclusion that nature
exists for our sole use and benefit. Conservationists rightly find this alarming because
it supports our continuing abuse of nature by undermining arguments for conserving
life forms and habitats that are not deemed immediately or proximately useful to us.
Scientists too can find it upsetting to be told that nature is, so to speak, our invention,
because it seems to imply that science and scientific data do not play an objective role
in discovering the truth about reality (Soulé and Lease 1995: 47).

Historian of ecological ideas Donald Worster addresses the deconstructivist position
by allowing for the fact that environmental history tells the story of a changing bio-
physical environment altered by forces of nature and human technologies working
together in a complicated dialectic. While the resultant change in our environment,
Worster notes, is now clearly discernible, change is never all there is to nature. Change
leads somewhere: it has a discernible direction, conventionally called 'progress'. The
founders of the science of ecology were all intensely aware of the biological and geological past. Like Darwin, however, they believed that the change from past to present
is not all disorderly or directionless. Change unmakes order but also makes it anew.
Nature has its great regularities, its great coherences that persist over time. This act of
balancing a sense of historical change with a sense of stability, of finding within
the swirl of history a normative state, persisted in ecology, says Worster, well into
the 1960s.

Then a portrayal by ecologists such as Eugene Odum of ecosystems tending towards
equilibrium rather than development gained ground. This left us no model of development for human society to emulate. In reaction to that, ecologists developed an
increasing interest in the phenomenon of environmental disturbance. By the 1990s,
revisionist ecologists had succeeded in leaving little tranquillity in nature. Instead they
regarded it as a landscape of patches of all sizes, textures and colours, changing continually through time and space, responding to an unceasing barrage of perturbations.
This is a nature, Worster says, that looks remarkably similar to, indeed reflects back the

human communities of that time: none of which now appears as a stable entity and about which academic departments of history and historians of social change have been writing extensively (Worster 1995: 69–74). Examples are to hand in post-imperial Africa and Asia, and worldwide following the collapse of the Soviet Union.

This mirroring of human societies in our view of nature is neither new nor surprising. Looking at the idea of nature inherited by nineteenth-century Europeans and persisting since in some form or other, R. G. Collingwood argued that whether seen as organism or machine, such views of Nature were based on an analogy with the human person. For the Greeks, the analogy was between macrocosmic nature and the microcosmic human being; for later thinkers, between nature as God's handiwork and machines that are human handiwork. For Christians like Linnaeus and White, as a clockmaker is to a clock, or a millwright to a mill, or a potter to clay, so God is to nature.

Gradually, however, throughout the eighteenth century and the advancement of natural science, the idea of 'progress' and therefore of change gained momentum and was established, in Haeckel's day, as synonymous with the Darwinian notion of 'evolution'. Wherever and by whoever employed, the concept of evolution attempts to resolve the observable tension between what are (to us) changing and unchanging elements in the world of nature. It does so by maintaining that what had hitherto been regarded as unchanging is in reality subject to change. It places the concept of process, change and development in the centre of the picture as the fundamental category in our thinking about the world.

For the Greeks, it had been axiomatic that nothing is knowable unless it is unchanging. But the world of nature, again according to them, is a world of continual and all-pervading change. This would seem to make a science of nature impossible. Post-Renaissance thinkers avoided this conclusion by distinguishing between the world of nature as it appears to our senses and the 'substance' or 'matter' lying behind it. This was the true object of natural science, knowable because unchanging, but whose changing arrangements and dispositions were the realities open to our senses. There were also the 'laws' according to which these arrangements changed. So matter and natural law were the proper, unchanging objects of natural science. This sought to strip away from nature-as-we-perceive-it whatever is obviously changeable. Scientist Evelyn Fox Keller (2000) acutely observes the same perennial human need for stability in the face of change in regard to the discovery of DNA.

But by the beginning of the nineteenth century, historians had trained themselves to think scientifically about a world of constantly changing human affairs in which there is no unchanging substrate behind the changes and no unchanging laws according to which the changes take place. Once more, historical human consciousness provided an analogy for thinking about nature. The historical concept of scientifically knowable change or process was applied, under the name of evolution, to the natural world. Two important shifts in the concept of nature followed that are directly relevant to the emergence of ecology as a science and as a philosophy.

The first, which involved a change in how the ecologist thinks about change, was to see it as no longer cyclical but progressive. The cyclical view of natural change saw one from state *a* to state *b* as part of a process that completes itself by a return from state *b* to state *a*. Any sort of non-cyclical change, such as that from youth to old age, was regarded as a mutilated fragment of one that, if completed, would have been cyclical; or was regarded as incompletely known. This was an aspect of Linnaeus's work that led to its being rejected as a basis for scientific ecology. For modern thought, dominated by the idea of progress or development, reverses this state of things and, on the principle that history never repeats itself, regards the world of nature as characterized by the constant emergence of new things.

Second, the model of nature as a machine became untenable. It is impossible to describe one and the same thing in the same breath as a machine and as developing and evolving. A machine is essentially a finished product or closed system. It cannot function as a machine until it is completely built and once that is done, it cannot develop, for developing means working at becoming what, as yet, one is not (Collingwood 1960: 3–14).

What we now have, as noted already, is a culture of ceaseless change in which industrial capitalism promises a 'new world order' of the endless accumulation of wealth with no promise of ever achieving a steady state in social, economic or ecological terms. Nature is again turned into a mirror of society, reflecting back to us the chaotic energies of capital and technology. There follows from this an abundance of post-modern, deconstructivist ecological models that emphasize competition and disturbance within nature and so not only reflect the effects of global capitalism and ideology but are highly compatible with that force dominating the earth (Worster 1995: 77). The extent of that disturbance is laid out authoritatively in the aptly titled *Something New under the Sun*. It concludes that over the past two centuries our species has become the equivalent of a geological force in the changes we have wrought on the earth's surface (McNeill 2000).

Having glimpsed the connection between the science of ecology and its cultural and economic conditions, Worster concludes that the most recent models of ecology are sure to be superseded just as Odum's model of the ecosystem was superseded. This acceptance of their historical relativism does not, however, lead to complete cynicism any more than it does to rigid adherence to any one model. Nor does it lead back to a pre-historical or pre-modern consciousness. Instead, he suggests several conclusions that transcend present circumstances and, on the basis of substantial evidence drawn from the intertwined study of nature and humanity, acknowledge that we cannot set up any impermeable barrier between them. They are, he says, conclusions about reality that not only can but must constrain our choices and inform our values if we want to survive as a species.

First, he returns to the principle of interdependency and to the fact that modern knowledge reveals that living nature, for all its private, individualistic strivings, works by that principle and in fact, can work in no other way. He offers extraterrestrial travel as an example: send any individual organism into outer space alone, without any of the services provided by other kinds of organisms, from soil fertility to oxygen generation, and it will not survive. Knowledge of the manifold forms of this interdependency has been accumulating since Lucy walked across the plains of Ethiopia. All the changes we discern in civilization are only changes in the patterns of interdependency, not in the reality or necessity of interdependency itself. What we call the environmental movement of the post-World War II period has been essentially a reawakening to its truth, although its implications have yet to work their way into the heads of economic and political leaders (Worster 1995: 78–9). And indeed, into those of religious leaders.

Second, Worster advocates the study of societies that have managed to fit themselves to their ecological niche for impressively long periods of time, that are less destructive of the living creatures around them and have acquired vital knowledge of the place they inhabit. Such enduring communities have one dominant characteristic: they have made and kept rules to govern their behaviour based on intimate local experience. They have not tried to 'live free' of nature or of the group; nor have they resented restraints on individual initiative but have accepted many kinds of limit on themselves and enforced them on one another. Their methods may not meet modern standards of privacy, or be compatible with a sense of personal rights; and they can stifle original-ity. 'But throughout history, having these rules and enforcing them vigorously seems to be a requirement for long-term ecological survival' (Worster 1995: 80–1).

Religious Holism

Anthropologist Mary Douglas offers a powerful, indeed startling, biblical parallel to Worster's counter-cultural vision of the role played by rules and rule-keeping in an eco-logically sustainable society. She analyses the religious rules governing the community addressed in the book of Leviticus and the motivation for obeying them. Injunctions to be compassionate would not be necessary because kindness would be predicated in the rules of behaviour as well as exemplified in the narratives. The book is to be read in line with Psalm 145:8–9: the God of Israel has compassion for all that he has made. His love for his animal creation lies behind laws that legislate for justice between persons, between God and his people and between people and animals. The idea of goodness in Leviticus is encompassed in the idea of right ordering. Being moral would mean being holy as God is holy: being in alignment with the universe, working with the laws of cre-ation which manifest the mind of God. In this case the laws were given by God to Moses:

> Thou hast made the moon to mark the seasons;
> The sun knows its time for setting.
>   (Ps. 104:14–29)

In this psalm, right judgement, correct time and place, and correct behaviour would incorporate all that is needful for knowing the moral law (Douglas 2000: 44).

Her argument for this reading and how its rules worked rests on her account of the society as one imbued with analogical rather than rational-instrumental thinking. The latter creates contexts in which 'human nature' or 'human rights' can be ordered and legislated for within a linear, hierarchical model. Analogical thinking, however, is cor-relative. It places an item or event within a scheme organized in terms of analogical relations among the items selected and then reflects on them and acts in terms sug-gested by the relations. The meaning of one item or element

> would now always have to be sought in whole systems of meanings . . . No more is it useful
> to consider what separate items such as bread or blood symbolize. It is not just a change

in our methods of work, but a change in our understanding of human thinking . . . [W]hat is important is not the one-to-one relations of group to species but the overall confrontation of human society and nature. (ibid.: 22–3)

This, for her (and, after Worster, for us) throws new light on how the 'rules' operate within such a society. Surprisingly, she says, even though Leviticus is self-described as a collection of commandments or laws, examining its language discloses that instead of straight imperatives we read expressions that can be variously translated as: 'He shall bring his offering . . .' or 'Let him bring his offering.' She quotes John Sawyer's suggestion that in this 'imaginary community receiving this oblique information about its obligations', the language seems almost to avoid normal direct means of stating obligations. The author wants us to imagine a state or a society in which some things are to be done and others not done, as everyone knows what is to be done. So, according to Douglas:

we look in vain for an explanation of what it is about the hoofs of camels and pigs that puts them in the prohibited class of animal, or what it is about water animals without fins and scales, or those that crawl on land or in the water, that they must not be eaten, or why honey must not be burnt in sacrifice.

The priestly writer is teaching the people of Israel to honour the order of creation in their lives and by doing so to share in its work. 'The living body is his paradigm' (ibid.: 35, 37).

This contemporary biblical reading gives some idea of what Worster means by the type of society that fits its ecological niche because it makes and keeps rules that govern human behaviour in the light of a greater whole: in this instance, the order of creation that manifests the mind of God. Their lives are to be ordered in such a way as to honour and share in the work of creation by behaving properly towards all its members. While the society that would live according to such laws may not, as Worster remarks, be compatible with present-day cultural, social or individual perceptions of human identity or standards of conduct, that in itself highlights the ecological problems cited already, ranging from Linnaean presuppositions to postmodern assumptions, that are created by religious and cultural emphases on human exceptionalism.

One possible remedy is the cultivation of what I call ecological humility (Primavesi 2004: 5–7, 119–28). It is supported epistemologically by Shrader-Frechette's acknowledgement of human inability to know, and therefore to test or to falsify, any concept of nature as a whole. At the same time it presupposes the self-confidence needed to learn and to benefit from the knowledge of others. As science now enjoys the public epistemological privileges previously enjoyed by the Church, ecologists and religious leaders need to proclaim the message of our interdependence in order to counteract the usually unstated message of our exceptionalism. And as our understanding grows of the complexity of all the interactions that sustain our lives, and how necessarily deficient our explanations or descriptions of them must be, we become more aware of the all-encompassing reality that holds us together. We know in part, and can only express in part, that of which we are part; and by virtue of which we know or express anything.

The religious analogue would be the awareness that as the greatness and goodness of God surpasses everything by which we move towards God, so our knowledge of the world in which we seek to know God is always surpassed by its reality.

As Job was reminded by God:

> Where were we when the foundations of earth were laid? . . . When the sea was shut in with doors? . . . Have we commanded the morning and caused the dawn to know its place? . . . Does the eagle soar at our command? (Job 38:4, 8, 12; 39:27)

Confronted with his ignorance, Job's exemplary answer still rings true: 'I have uttered what I did not understand, things too wonderful for me to know' (Job 42:3).

Post-Haeckel, however, we are learning, slowly and rather painfully, that what we know and, above all, what we do not know about nature's economy, is of great account.

References

Acot, P. (ed.) (1998). *The European Origins of Scientific Ecology (1800–1901)* (The History of Science, Technology and Medicine). Amsterdam: Overseas Publishers Association.

Bateson, G. (1972). *Steps to an Ecology of Mind*. New York: Ballantine Books.

Bateson, G. (1985). *Mind and Nature*. London: Flamingo.

Beer, G. P. K. (2000). *Darwin's Plots*. Cambridge: Cambridge University Press.

Collingwood, R. G. (1960). *The Idea of Nature*. Oxford: Oxford University Press.

Crosby, D. A. (2002). *A Religion of Nature*. Albany, NY: State University of New York Press.

Douglas, M. (2000). *Leviticus as Literature*. Oxford: Oxford University Press.

Fox Keller, E. (2000). *The Century of the Gene*. Cambridge, MA: Harvard University Press.

Habel, N. (ed.) (2000–2002). *The Earth Bible*, vols 1–5. Sheffield: Academic Press.

McNeill, J. R. (2000). *Something New under the Sun: An Environmental History of the Twentieth-Century World*. New York: W. W. Norton.

Merchant, C. (ed.) (1994). *Ecology*. Atlantic Highlands, NJ: Humanities Press.

Primavesi, A. (2000). *Sacred Gaia*. London: Routledge.

Primavesi, A. (2003). *Gaia's Gift: Earth, Ourselves and God after Copernicus*. London: Routledge.

Primavesi, A. (2004). *Making God Laugh: Human Arrogance and Ecological Humility*. Santa Rosa, CA: Polebridge Press.

Shrader-Frechette, K. (2003). 'Ecology', in D. Jamieson (ed.), *Blackwell Companion to Environmental Philosophy*. Oxford: Blackwell, pp. 304–15.

Soulé, M. E. and Lease, Gary (eds) (1995). *Reinventing Nature?: Responses to Postmodern Deconstruction*. Washington, DC: Island Press.

White, G. ([1789] 2004). *The Illustrated Natural History of Selborne*. London: Thames and Hudson.

Worster, D. (1977). *Nature's Economy: A History of Ecological Ideas*. Cambridge: Cambridge University Press.

Worster, D. (1995). 'Nature and the Disorder of History', in M. E. Soulé and Gary Lease (eds), *Reinventing Nature? Responses to Postmodern Deconstruction*. Washington, DC: Island Press, pp. 65–87.

CHAPTER 26
Psychology

Ilona N. Rashkow

Until recently, reading the Bible was thought to be a rather straightforward procedure. The goal was to respond 'properly' by trying to 'understand' the text and grasp *the* 'meaning'. This changed once psychology became a more accepted form of biblical exegesis, although as D. A. Kille has pointed out, psychological biblical criticism has been one of the hidden avenues of biblical interpretation, unfortunately made inaccessible by the lack of organization and coherence within the literature. However, recent shifts in the discipline of biblical studies, along with the increasing influence of psychological perspectives on culture in general, have made psychological approaches to the Bible more visible (Kille 2002).

Of course, the use of psychology in interpreting biblical texts is no more a conceptually unified critical position in biblical studies than in literary studies generally. The term is associated with scholars who examine the writer (D. J. Halperin), the biblical characters (D. Clines, Y. S. Feldman, I. N. Rashkow, D. Zeligs), or the reader (D. Clines et al.). Further, the approaches are neither monolithic nor mutually exclusive. But biblical scholars who use psychology seem to agree that 'meaning' does not inhere completely and exclusively in the text and that the 'effects' of reading Scripture, psychological and otherwise, are essential to its 'meaning'. Ultimately, this type of literary criticism yields in biblical studies a way of looking at biblical narratives *and* readers which reorganizes both their interrelationships and the distinctions between them. As a result, recognizing the relationship of a reader to the biblical text leads to a more profound awareness that no one interpretation is intrinsically 'true'. That is, the 'meaning' of biblical narratives is not waiting to be uncovered but evolves, actualized by readers (as interpreters).

Recent Works in the Area

The most recent (and comprehensive in terms psychology and religion in general) is Volume 2 of *The Destructive Power of Religion*, entitled *Religion, Psychology, and Violence*

(Ellens 2004). The volume consists of fourteen chapters dealing with various aspects of the interface of religion, psychology, and violence and confronts a panoply of issues attempting to address religiously-inspired violence around the world from a psychological perspective.

W. Rollins's *Soul and Psyche* (1999) is probably the most definitive survey of the field of psychological biblical criticism to date. Indeed an entire issue of *Pastoral Psychology* (2002) was devoted to a review of it. Rollins (1999) provides a comprehensive examination of the past, present and future of the field, and includes an extensive bibliography.

Many scholars in the field apply specific psychological approaches to specific biblical texts. For example, D. A. Kille (2001) provides an introduction to psychological biblical criticism in general and his primary focus is Genesis 3 from the perspectives of Freudian, Jungian, and developmental psychologies. E. Edinger (2000) uses a Jungian perspective when analysing the prophetic books of the Bible. N. J. Cohen (1998) applies the developmental theory of Erik Erikson, moving from Adam and Eve as illustrations of Infancy, to Cain and Abel as early childhood. R. J. Solomon (2000) uses Bruno Bettelheim's concept of the 'context of community'. According to Solomon, reading the Bible elucidates a group's problems which can be 'helped' by identification with biblical characters. P. A. Kruger (2000) applies the cognitive model of anger suggested by Lakoff and Kovecses to the expressions of anger in the Hebrew Bible. According to Kruger, the application of this paradigm 'allows a clearer comprehension of the conceptual organization of these expressions and their respective relationships to one another' (2000: 181). P. Watson uses the work of René Girard who says that humans learn to desire specific objects through a process of imitation ('mimetic desire') which leads inexorably to violence. Girard's theory holds that human communities were established when this violent desire was discharged in the murder of an innocent human scapegoat; this process is evident in primitive religion and myth and continues to operate within the structure of all human society. According to Watson (1998), the Bible is centrally important in unmasking this bloodshed, and he uses Girard's thoughts to reveals why a peaceful postmodernity absolutely requires foundations in a mimesis. Y. Kluger and N. Kluger-Nash (1999) look at the book of Ruth as an expression of a return of the Feminine to Israelite religion after it had been displaced by the cult of YHWH.

It should be noted that there is another aspect of 'Bible and Culture', namely, the impact of the Bible *on* psychology. Indeed, given Freud's extensive writings in this field, any attempt to summarize his essential view of religion in general and the Bible specifically is open to charges of oversimplification and of neglecting the significance of statements that appear to run contrary to what is presented as his fundamental or overall views. Nevertheless, it appears that throughout his writings Freud emphasizes the *defensive* rather than the *adaptive* aspects of religion. Although acknowledging its contribution to civilization in promoting and justifying instinctual renunciation and to some extent, compensating for it through the promise of a heavenly reward, his appreciation of the creative and sublimatory functions of religion appears minimal.

For example, in *Totem and Taboo* (1913), Freud argues that the primitive prohibitions against sexual relations with women of the same clan and against the killing of the totem animal (the representative of the father) derived from the sons' remorse at the murder of a loved object. The ritual sacrifice of the totem animal once a year, however, 'not only comprised expressions of remorse and an attempt at atonement, it also served as a remembrance of the triumph over the father' (ibid.: 145). Thus, the biblically mandated animal sacrifice comprised a defence which simultaneously permitted the easing of guilt and the disguised expression of the repressed wishes. Freud saw Christianity, with its prohibition against murder and incest and its sacrifice of the divine son, as an updated version of the primitive totemic defence against oedipal ambivalence. In *From the History of an Infantile Neurosis* (1918), Freud offers an individual example of religion's social function. Speaking of his patient's religious piety, which, he writes, turned into an obsessional neurosis, he suggests two reasons that 'civilization runs a greater risk if we maintain our present attitude to religion than if we give it up' (ibid.: 35). First, in grounding prohibitions in the biblical authority of God, 'we are investing the cultural prohibition with a quite special solemnity, but at the same time we risk making its observance dependent on belief in God' (ibid.: 41). In the modern, scientifically-inclined world, diminishing belief in God reduces the power of religion to promote social integration. Furthermore, the general 'character of sanctity and inviolability' with which religion invested cultural regulations is plainly contradicted, for

> not only do [these regulations] invalidate one another by giving contrary decisions at different times and places, but apart from this they show every sign of human inadequacy . . . Eventually, the criticism which we cannot fail to level at them also diminishes to an unwelcome extent our respect for other, more justifiable cultural demands. (ibid.: 41)

More recently, Polka (2001) makes a cogent (though not highly elaborated) case for the Bible as the effective source of the therapeutic ideals implicit in Freud's psychoanalytical protocol. On the other hand, Dominian, a psychiatrist, writes in 1998: 'I accept [the details of the stories of the Christ of Faith] at face value and analyze them as I would any revelation made to me by my patients.' Unlike Miller, who takes key events from Jesus life (the conflict with his family, the decisive events of his baptism followed by the struggle with Satan, and certain features of his teaching and relationships with others) and proposes, for example, that Jesus had positive early experiences with his father, but his father's death when Jesus was still an adolescent left him with feelings of loss and the responsibility as firstborn son to take on the care of the family and that Jesus passed through crisis of identity and faith, coming into his own unique ministry, 'at about thirty', Dominian does not hypothesize about Jesus' childhood.

While these examples are interesting (and certainly relevant) I am focusing on the influence of psychology on biblical interpretation primarily because I am not a practising psychotherapist, but rather, trained in psychoanalytic literary theory. Given this caveat, the remainder of this chapter is devoted to psychoanalysis and the Bible from the perspective of psychoanalytic literary theory.

Psychoanalysis and the Bible

Sigmund Freud once acknowledged that most of his discoveries about the unconscious mind had been anticipated by the poets of the past. Thus, it should not be surprising that psychology in general (and psychoanalytical approaches in particular) have been used in an effort to explain the origins, character, and effects of biblical literature. Generally speaking, there are three points at which psychoanalysis can enter the study of a literary work: (1) examining the mind of the author; (2) examining the minds of the author's characters; and (3) examining our own minds. There is a long tradition of Freudian criticism that examines the text for buried motives and hidden neurotic conflicts that generated the writer's art: in writing *Hamlet*, for example, it is claimed that Shakespeare was working over the death of his son (Jones 1949); and in writing *The Gambler* Dostoevsky was drawing upon the prohibitions placed upon masturbation in his childhood (Freud 1928). Because the hazards of examining an author's mind are inversely proportional to the amount of material available on the writer's life and private thoughts, it is never completely safe to guess at the psychoanalytic significance of a work of art, even that of a candid living author, and for some major writers (like Chaucer, Shakespeare, and the biblical writers), we have only the most minimal sense of what their private lives may have been; more often, none at all. Thus, this form of psychoanalytic literary criticism is viewed generally as speculative.

Most of Freud's own ventures into literature involved the analyses of literary characters. His initial remarks on the Oedipus complex were literary, involving both Hamlet and Oedipus. Hamlet, according to Freud, is 'the hysteric' who delays because he is paralysed by guilt over Claudius' enactment of his own unconscious wishes (1916–17: 335). A stream of essays by additional analysts followed, mostly on other fictitious textual characters, writing what might be described as 'case studies' of literature dealing with those characters whom they categorized as 'neurotic'. Most of these analysts emphasized Freudian themes as the Oedipus complex, anality, schizoid tendencies, latent or expressed homosexuality, guilt, etc., and the roles they played among literary characters.

Psychoanalytic fictional character analysis has not fallen into as deep a disrepute as concentrating on the writer, in great part because fictional characters are viewed as representatives of life and as such can be understood only if we assume that they are 'telling a truth'. This assumption allows us to find 'unconscious' motivations, albeit in literary characters. For example, Abraham's actions and language reveal a great deal about him, despite the fact that all we will ever 'know' is contained in the 1,534 verses of Genesis.

On the other hand, literary characters are both more and less than humans. This presents a problem. While one aspect of narrative characterization is to provide a *mimetic* function (to represent human action and motivation), another aspect is primarily *textual* (to reveal information to a reader or to conceal it). This situation has no precise parallel in life, although it can be argued that people often resemble literary characters in the masks we present to the world. As a result, examining a narrative character is not risk-free either. For instance, contradictions in Abraham's character may result from the psychic complexities the biblical writer imagined; or, they may result from the fact that Abraham is an agent in a literary narrative with a highly developed system of conventions – his 'traits' may be more a function of the requirements of the story-line than his personality.

Since authors may not provide much material for the theorists and since characters are not people, many scholars have shifted their focus from the interpretation of meanings embedded within a text to the processes of writing and reading. Rather than attempting to determine *objective* meanings hidden within a text (meanings a reader needs to extricate) these scholars concentrate on the *subjective* experience of the reader (interactions between reader/text/author) and the values and premises with which a reader approaches interpretation of a text. As within psychoanalysis itself, their foci are problems of indeterminacy, uncertainty, perspective, hermeneutics, and subjective (and communal) assumptions and agreements.

Objections to Freudian Literary Theory

M. B. Schwartz and K. J. Kaplan (1998) concentrate on the psychological 'meaning' of Hebrew Bible narratives and how the characters dealt with challenges of family, handicap, depression, etc. and include actual clinical research which parallels the biblical narratives. However, they reject a psychology based on the Freudian system because, they write, in the Hebrew Bible, depression is dealt with successfully. They argue that the focus of the Hebrew Bible is far more optimistic in that it encourages people to hope and teaches that day to day human effort has purpose and meaning and that heroism is not a useful aim for man to set himself. On the other hand, K. J. Kaplan (1997) discusses why Freud employed Greek rather than Hebrew foundation legends, specifically the story of Oedipus, as a basis for psychoanalysis. According to Kaplan, Freud's choice of Oedipus emanates from his deterministic view of the universe, paralleling the Greek rather than the biblical story of creation. Thus, in the Greek account, nature precedes the gods and the Oedipal conflict is inherent which Kaplan writes is the fundamental basis for Freud's view of human psychology.

J. Boyd (2000) uses a particularly unusual approach among psychologically-oriented biblical scholars. He writes that a 'true' biblical psychology must *refute* the several assumptions of secular psychology, particularly psychoanalysis. According to Boyd:

> True psychology is profoundly theological; the covenantal relationship between man and God must lie at the heart of any biblical psychology. Secular psychology maintains, contrary to Scripture, the view that 'self care' is primary, rather than care for others. Biblical psychology maintains that wisdom lies in understanding the Word of God. Further, the diagnostic system must be re-written. An understanding must be predicated upon the basic dysfunction between man and God. While secular psychology may be helpful, for a Christian psychologist, the Word of God must be the primary textbook, not the writing of secular psychologists. (2000: 3)

Similarly, W. Cole writes that the integration paradigm of 'psychoanalytic' and 'biblical' psychology has served as an assumptive framework for much of the effort to relate psychology and the Bible. He reviews and evaluates (negatively) the assumptions of this paradigm and offers an alternative approach – the Creation narrative (Cole 1959).

However, a primary objection to psychological literary theory among biblical scholars, feminists and others, is the Freudian idea of penis envy (Wright 1984). M. Torok,
for example, argues that 'penis envy' is not based on biological fact but is a miscon-
ception: a common phallic phase does not characterize the infantile development of
both sexes. One psychoanalyst who seems to bridge the Freudian and anti-Freudian
schools of thought is Jacques Lacan who reinterprets Freud in the light of structuralist and post-structuralist theories of discourse (Davis 1983; Felman 1981; Muller and
Richardson 1982; Rashkow 2000a; Torok 1964; Wright 1984). Since Lacan focuses
on the mutual interaction among society and the self with the use of language as an
intermediary, that is, language is the pivotal concept linking self and society, he shifts
from Freud's biological penis to the phallus as signifier, and as a result, many biblical
scholars find his writings more relevant to both males and females.

Jacques Lacan, the French psychoanalyst whose thought has had such a broad influence on literary theory since the 1960s, considered psychoanalysis as much a part of
philosophy as of medicine. Ironically, although Lacan deviated from the mainstream
of psychoanalytic thought and was expelled from the International Psychoanalytic
Association, he believed himself to be returning *to* Freud rather than departing *from*
him. Briefly, where Freud views the mechanisms of the unconscious as generated by
libido (sexual energy), Lacan centres the theory of the unconscious on the sense within
us of something being *absent*. Lacan describes two 'levels' of absence: (1) the less intense
awareness of absence which can take the form of mere lack (*manque*) or of need (*besoin*);
and (2) the perception of an unmet need or an unmet desire which is more profound
and hence, more urgent. Both of these levels of absence force the psyche to make
demands. A deeper feeling of absence takes the higher form of desire (*désir*). Lacan
defines *désir* as two-fold: first, it is a feeling towards an object which is unconscious;
second, this object can and does desire us in return. Lacan's terms for the universal
symbol, or signifier of *désir* is the *Phallus*. It is important not to confuse the Phallus in
this sense with the male sexual organ, the penis. According to Lacanian theory, *both*
sexes experience the absence of and desire for the Phallus – which may be one reason
Lacan's restructuring of Freud has appealed to feminists such as L. Irigaray (1977).
Indeed, the sexually critical and liberatory potential of Lacan is that although one sex
has an anatomical penis, neither sex can possess the phallus. As a result, sexuality is
incomplete and fractured for *both* sexes. Moreover, although men and women must
line themselves up on one or another side of the linguistic/sexual divide, they need not
align themselves with the side which is anatomically isomorphic.

Lacan's theory of psycho-sexual development is also a revision of Freud's in that
Lacan shifts the description of mental processes from a purely biological model to a
semiotic one. For example, Freud discusses the first phase of childhood as the oral
phase, in which the child's pleasure comes largely from suckling; the anal phase follows,
when the child learns to control and to enjoy controlling the elimination of faeces. For
Lacan, the analogue of the oral phase is the 'mirror stage', from six to 18 months, in
which the child's image of its bodily self changes from mere formlessness and fragmentation to an identification with a unified shape it can see in the mirror. During this
development, the child experiences itself as '*le désir de la Mère*', the desire of the mother
(in both senses – as an object that is itself unconscious and can desire us in return).

That is, the baby not only knows that it needs its mother but also feels itself to be what completes and fulfils the mother's desires. From this phase Lacan derives the psychic field of the 'Imaginary', the state in which a person's sense of reality is grasped purely as images and fantasies of the fulfilment of his or her desires. This stage, begun during the child's second year of life, continues into adulthood.

In Lacanian thought, repression, and unconscious content occur together with the acquisition of language, at around 18 months (when Freud's anal stage begins). Lacan derives his ideas of language and the unconscious from the semiotician Ferdinand de Saussure, as he was interpreted by the structuralist anthropologist Claude Lévi-Strauss who considered the unconscious as 'reducible to a function – the symbolic function', which in turn was merely 'the aggregate of the laws' of language (1967: 198). The primary laws of language in structural linguistics are those of the selection and combination of primary basic elements. *Metaphor* is a mode of symbolization in which one thing is signified by another that is like it, that is part of the same paradigmatic class (for example, 'a sea of troubles' or 'All the world's a stage'). Lacan sees metaphor as equivalent to the Freudian defence of 'condensation' (in which one symbol becomes the substitute for a whole series of associations). *Metonymy*, on the other hand, is a mode of symbolization in which one thing is signified by another that is associated with it but *not* of the same class (for example, the use of 'Washington' for 'the United States government' or of 'the sword' for 'military power') – a syntagmatic relationship which Lacan regards as equivalent to Freudian 'displacement'.

As the child learns the names of things, his or her desires are no longer met automatically; now the child must ask for what he or she wants and can not request things that do not have names. As the child learns to ask for a signified thing by pronouncing a signifier, he or she learns that one thing can symbolize another and has entered what Lacan calls the 'field of the Symbolic'. As J. P. Muller and W. J. Richardson describe:

> From this point on the child's desire, like an endless quest for a lost paradise, must be channeled like an underground river through the subterranean passageways of the symbolic order, which make it possible that things be present in their absence in some ways through words. (1982: 23)

At this stage, desires can be repressed, and the child is able to ask for something that metaphorically or metonymically replaces the desired object. Lacan punningly calls this stage of development '*le Nom-du-Père*' – 'the Name-of-the-Father' – because language is only the first of the negations and subjections to law now beginning to affect the child. In French, the phrase '*le Nom-du-Père*' 'the Name-of-the-Father' is pronounced exactly the same as '*le Non-du-Père*' the '*no*-of-the-Father' – hence its connection to negation and subjection to law.

Another Lacanian field, less discussed in his writings than the others, is that of the 'Real'. By this Lacan refers to those incomprehensible aspects of experience that exist beyond the grasp of images and symbols through which we think and constitute our reality. That is to say, adult humans are always inscribed within language, but language does not constitute the ultimate reality. Since in Lacan's dialectic of desire one object may symbolize another (which is itself a substitute for still another), Lacan says that 'the unconscious is structured like a language'.

Like Freud, Lacan approaches literature primarily as material which properly interpreted illustrates the major concepts of his psychology. His indirect influence on literary theory and criticism has been considerable, primarily because his psychology has affected the philosophy and literary theory of the many French scholars who attended his seminars (and then by extension, British and American scholars who were influenced by the French). But a strain of direct Lacanian biblical criticism has begun to appear as well in the past several years and is, in great part, the approach which I use (along with that of Freud's).

An Example of Psychology and the Bible: A Psychoanalytic Perspective

It is almost a commonplace to state that psychoanalysis *and* the Hebrew Bible deal with many aspects of human sexuality (Freud 1905: 135–243; 1925). In the remainder of this chapter I provide an example of a psychoanalytic reading of a biblical incest narrative which seems almost anachronistically Freudian and Lacanian: that of Noah and Ham. I would like to make it perfectly clear that my theoretical approach is literary, albeit *influenced* by psychoanalytic theory (Rashkow 1993; 2000a). Unfortunately, the relationship between 'literature and psychoanalysis' usually implies a relationship of subordination rather than coordination. Literature is submitted to the 'authority' or the 'prestige' of psychoanalysis (Felman 1981: 5). The literary text is considered as a body of language to *be* interpreted, while psychoanalysis is a body of knowledge used *to* interpret. What I have tried to do is read Freud, Lacan, and the Bible concurrently rather than to provide a hierarchical positioning. That is, I have not been reading the Bible *in the light* of these psychoanalysts but rather *while reading* them. Certainly, I do not consider either a biblical scholar. Rather, I appropriate their *approaches* as a tool for biblical interpretation.

Genesis 9:18–27 narrates the 'unconventional' behaviour of an inebriated Noah and his sons Shem, Ham, and Japheth:

> The sons of Noah who went forth from the ark were Shem, Ham, and Japheth. Ham was the father of Canaan. These three were the sons of Noah; and from these the whole earth was peopled. Noah was the first tiller of the soil. He planted a vineyard; and he drank of the wine, and became drunk, and lay uncovered in his tent. And Ham, the father of Canaan, saw the nakedness of his father, and told his two brothers outside. Then Shem and Japheth took a garment, laid it upon both their shoulders, and walked backward and covered the nakedness of their father; their faces were turned away, and they did not see their father's nakedness. When Noah awoke from his wine and knew what his youngest son had done to him, he said, 'Cursed be Canaan; a slave of slaves shall he be to his brothers.' He also said, 'Blessed by the LORD my God be Shem; and let Canaan be his slave. God enlarge Japheth, and let him dwell in the tents of Shem; and let Canaan be his slave'. (Gen. 9:18–27; all translations are my own)

This short episode, which constitutes a link between the story of the Flood and the Table of Nations, is puzzling. Because of its brevity and textual inconsistencies, a number of scholars have suggested that this narrative is merely a 'splinter from a more substantial tale' (E. Speiser 1964: 62). If so, it might account for some of the many unanswered questions. A fuller account, for example, might address why Ham is spoken of as the youngest son in verse 24 and listed as the second of three sons in verse 18; or exactly what Ham 'had done to' Noah which incurred such wrath; or how Noah 'learned' what occurred; or why, if it was Ham who was guilty of some significant misdeed, Noah's curse is directed at Canaan; or why this particular punishment was selected; or why Japheth is allied with Shem; or why a threefold emphasis on Ham's paternity of Canaan; or, or, or . . . many obvious elements of critical importance that need clarification. Have two different stories been merged? Is a part of the text missing? Although 'text critics' (scholars who 'correct' one text in light of another) and 'source critics' (scholars who do not view the Masoretic Text as a unified entity, but rather examine narratives as disparate units) have much to say about the linguistic and literary development of this text, I prefer the approach of psychologically-oriented biblical scholars who view it as a puzzling, but unified whole. As such, I assume that even *this* narrative in its present state is intended to 'make sense'. That is, there is a coherence in the narrative that a psychoanalytic 'reading' helps explicate.

The narrator of this enigmatic tale begins with a seemingly inconsequential piece of information in presenting the genealogy of Noah: Genesis 9:18 tells us the names of Noah's sons, reasonable enough, and then casually mentions that Ham is the father of Canaan. Typical of biblical narrative, this off-hand comment is an example of a frequently-used literary technique of the biblical writer – introducing information presumably irrelevant to the immediate context yet crucial to the understanding of subsequent developments. Without it, we would be as ignorant of the identity of the *object* of Noah's curse as we are of its *cause*. Significantly, it is typical also of that of an analysand.

Then the story begins. After the Deluge, Noah was 'the' tiller of the soil. According to *Tanhuma* Genesis 11, Noah invented the plough: that is, Noah was the initiator of true agriculture as opposed to hoe agriculture or horticulture (*Midrash Rabbah* Gen. 22:3). The article 'the' implies something well-known about Noah, possibly a tradition as a folk hero – or perhaps by initiating viticulture, Noah was the first to discover the soothing, consoling, and enlivening effects of wine! Indeed, many commentators who discuss this passage excuse Noah's excessive drinking exactly because he *was* the first wine-drinker. For example, John Chrysostom, a Church Father, writes that Noah's behaviour is defensible: as the first human being to taste wine, he would not know its after-effects. According to Chrysostom, Noah 'through ignorance and inexperience of the proper amount to drink, fell into a drunken stupor' (cited in Hamilton 1990: 202–3). Philo, a Hellenistic Jewish philosopher, goes even further in exonerating Noah. He notes that one can drink in two different manners and goes on to explain that Noah was not 'drinking to excess' but 'merely . . . partaking of wine':

> For there is a twofold and double way of becoming drunken: one is to drink wine to excess, which is a sin peculiar to the vicious and evil man; the other is to partake of wine, which always happens to the wise man. Accordingly, it is in the second signification that the virtuous and wise man is said to be drunken, not by drinking wine to excess, but merely by partaking of wine. (Philo 1971: 160)

The Rabbis place Noah in a somewhat more ambiguous light:

> Satan thereupon slaughtered a lamb, and then, in succession, a lion, a pig and a monkey. The blood of each as it was killed he made to flow under the vine. Thus he conveyed to Noah what the qualities of wine are: before a man drinks of it, he is innocent as a lamb; if he drinks of it moderately, he feels as strong as a lion; if he drinks more of it than he can bear, he resembles a pig; and if he drinks to the point of intoxication, then he behaves like a monkey, he dances around, sings, talks obscenely, and knows not what he is doing. (*Midrash Rabbah* Gen. 36:3)

It was not only the ancients who felt it necessary to exonerate Noah, at least partially. Indeed, this kind of apologetic permeates the work of most contemporary scholars. For example, when N. Sarna discusses Noah's drinking, he says that 'no blame attaches to Noah since he was oblivious to the intoxicating effects of his discovery' (1989: 65). Similarly, G. Knight writes that:

> Under no circumstances are we to bring a moral judgment to bear upon Noah as he falls drunken in his tent. Man learns only from experience. In our day, every material discovery brings its compensatory disadvantages, road deaths from the development of the internal combusion [*sic*] engine, unspeakable devastation from the discovery of nuclear fission. Noah is the 'guinea-pig', so to speak, from whom all mankind has been able to learn that along with drunkenness goes moral laxity, and that the drugging of the higher powers of human consciousness leads to sexual license. (Knight 1981: 105)

But back to the story. The narrator relates two facts: first, having become inebriated, Noah 'uncovered himself within his tent' and second, Ham 'saw his father's nakedness'. At this point, the text takes on several additional layers of ambiguity, all of which revolve around sexuality.

There appears to be little question that Noah's 'uncovering himself' means exposure of his genitalia. In fact, Habakkuk 2:15 and Lamentations 4:21 mention such exposure by the inebriated and associate it with shame and loss of human dignity: 'Woe to him who makes his neighbors drink of the cup of his wrath, and makes them drunk, to gaze on their shame!' (Hab. 2:15); 'Rejoice and be glad, O daughter of Edom, dweller in the land of Uz; but to you also the cup shall pass; you shall become drunk and strip yourself bare' (Lam. 4:21).

Further, there is little doubt that Ham saw his father's exposed genitalia. It should be noted in passing that the Levitical prohibitions are against 'uncovering' one's father's nakedness, not merely 'seeing' his genitalia. Not surprisingly, there have been several interpretations of what actually occurred within the confines of Noah's tent but little unanimity. For example, the Babylonian Talmud has an interesting 'dialogue' on the episode and Rabbinic sources are divided on whether Ham castrated his father or engaged in a homosexual act, the former interpretation relying upon the fact Noah had no children after the flood. Rav maintains that Ham castrated his father, while Samuel claims that he sexually abused him:

[With respect to the last verse] Rav and Samuel [differ,] one maintaining that he castrated him, whilst the other says that he sexually abused him. He who maintains that he castrated him, [reasons thus:] Since he cursed him by his fourth son, he must have injured him with respect to his fourth son. But he who says that he sexually abused him, draws an analogy between 'and he saw' written twice. Here it is written, *And Ham the father of Canaan saw the nakedness of his father*, whilst elsewhere it is written, *And when Shechem the son of Hamor saw her [he took her and lay with her and defiled her].* Now, on the view that he emasculated him, it is right that he curse him by his fourth son; but on the view that he abused him, why did he curse his fourth son: he should have cursed him himself? – Both indignities were perpetrated. (*Sanhedrin* 70a)

More recently, W. G. Cole suggests that although Genesis 9:22 cites 'looking' as Ham's only crime, Ham did more than mere looking, and thinks the words 'what his younger son had done to him' reveals a sexual attack on the father (Cole 1959: 43). Along these lines, J. M. Robertson draws attention to the similarity of this story to that of the castration of Uranus by Kronos (Robertson 1900: 44). F. W. Bassett suggests that the idiomatic expression 'saw his father's nakedness' could mean that Ham 'had sexual intercourse with his father's *wife* [my emphasis]' (Bassett 1971: 235). However, other scholars disagree. E. A. Speiser notes that while the term 'saw his father's nakedness' relates to genital exposure (contrast Gen. 42:9 and 12) it does not necessarily imply a sexual offence (cf. Gen. 2:25 and Exod. 20:26) (Speiser 1964: 61).

Similarly, C. M. Carmichael writes:

for those who think the incident between Ham and Noah involved a homosexual act . . . they speculate – wrongly, I think – that because the act was so abhorrent the biblical author did not spell it out. My view is that a lawgiver found the narrative *suggestive* of the topic of sexual encroachment on a father. (1997: 99)

N. Sarna takes Ham's actions quite literally, that is, Ham is 'guilty' of having seen Noah's genitalia and then compounds his crime (lack of modesty and filial respect) by leaving his father uncovered and 'shamelessly bruiting about what he had seen' (Sarna 1989: 66). Sarna seems to backtrack, however, by adding that verse 24 ('Noah knew what his younger son *had done to him*' [my emphasis]) and the severity of Noah's reaction suggest that the Torah has 'suppressed the sordid details of some repugnant act' (Sarna 1989: 66 cf. Phillips 1980: 39–40 Kunin 1995: 173–5). S. Brandes's position is that anthropological evidence suggests that in many cultures fathers make every effort to ensure that they do not reveal their genitals to their sons (1980: 99).

But *whose* 'repugnant act'? As I stated earlier, based on psychoanalytic literary theory, other literary representations of the incest motif, and clinical situations involving father–son incest, the act could have been either Noah *fantasizing* about the homosexual activity or possibly actually *initiating* such a liaison with his son, Ham. While the narrator is silent as to what actually occurred between Noah and Ham, the text does report that Ham told his brothers about the encounter. Having 'learned what [?] his youngest son had 'done to him,' Noah curses Canaan (!?), condemning him to be (literally) a 'slave of slaves' (a grammatical construction that expresses the extreme degree of servitude) and blesses Shem and Japheth. This is the first example of the biblical genre of parental blessing and cursing (cf. Gen. 27:4; 27:29; chap. 49). The text is silent as to how Noah became aware of the situation and why Canaan, not Ham, is cursed. Saadia and Ibn Janah construe the curse to mean 'Cursed be [the father of] Canaan', a phrase that has appeared twice already in this brief narrative. Ibn Ezra has an interesting reading of this verse. He claims that 'his youngest son' does not refer to Ham as *Noah's* youngest son but rather to Canaan as *Ham's* youngest son (Sarna 1989: 66). Thus, Ham is the offended party, and *his* son Canaan the perpetrator of some base deed. Accordingly, Noah, as grandfather, blames Canaan for 'defiling' Ham. All that can be said with any surety about Ibn Ezra's reading is that Noah remains 'pure', the righteous man saved from the deluge by the deity and from condemnation by most commentators.

Although source critics might argue that in the fuller story Canaan, son of Ham, was a participant in the offence against Noah, there are so many questions and ambiguities relating to this narrative in general that perhaps we can look for explanations within the text itself by using the approach of psychoanalytic literary theory. As in the psychoanalytic process, one way to arrive at possible answers is to raise (perhaps obvious) questions.

Question 1: How did Noah 'uncover himself within his tent'? Did he intentionally remove his clothing and *then* lie down or did he accidentally expose himself while sleeping?

Question 2: If Noah intentionally removed his clothing, rather than accidentally kicking off his garment while asleep, can we assume that he was relatively sober (as Philo maintains, quoted above), at least sober enough to disrobe? Or, in the words of Genesis Rabbah, was Noah a lamb, lion, bear, pig, or monkey?

Question 3: When did Ham enter the tent? Was Ham *already* in the tent when Noah arrived or did Ham wander in sometime later?

While these questions might seem meaningless, bear with me and hopefully the questions will become more relevant and lead to the ultimate issue: if Ham entered the tent first and Noah intentionally removed his clothing in Ham's presence, was Noah initiating, either consciously or unconsciously, an incestuous encounter?

Since the text does not state explicitly that Noah lost consciousness and because it requires at least some coordination to remove clothing, I am assuming that Noah was probably not drunk enough to pass out. If Noah disrobed *aware* that Ham was in the tent, again, there are (at least) three possible scenarios, each of which could be said to rely upon Noah's reduced inhibitions due to the effects of the wine. All three of these readings are based on the premise that under the influence of alcohol, Noah was more likely to act upon repressed desires or frustrations. As Joseph Conrad wrote, 'It is a maudlin and indecent verity that comes out through the strength of wine' (Conrad 1912: 194).

Option 1:   Noah undressed before his son arrived and when Ham arrived Noah
             initiated a forbidden fantasy – an incestuous liaison with his son.
Option 2:   Noah disrobed in his son's presence, and by doing so, Noah's hereto-
             fore repressed fantasy of an incestuous, homosexual encounter with
             his son was brought to the surface of his consciousness but *not* acted
             upon.
Option 3:   Ham, seeing his naked father, is the one who initiated a sexual
             encounter (as most commentators suggest).

The third scenario, the one which most Rabbinic authorities seem to favor, appears
to be the *least* reasonable. If Ham either had castrated his father or initiated a homosexual act, it seems rather unlikely that he would then run outside looking for his brothers Shem and Japheth as witnesses. Indeed, clinicians report that children who have
had incestuous homosexual relations generally do not discuss the incident until many
years later (Medlicott 1967: 135). More likely, therefore, are either of the first two readings, options which help explain the extreme nature of Noah's curse: his guilt and
his shame.

While many elements of the conventional vocabulary of moral deliberation (such as
'ethical', 'virtuous', 'righteous' and their opposites) are largely alien to the psychoanalytic lexicon, the concepts of 'guilt' and 'shame' do appear, albeit in technical (and
essentially non-moral) contexts (Smith 1986: 52). 'Guilt' and 'shame' are described as
different emotional responses, stemming from different stimuli, reflecting different patterns of behaviour, and functioning in different social constructions (although the two
are often related). Their primary distinction lies in the norm that is violated and the
expected consequences.

Guilt relates to internalized, societal and parental *prohibitions*, the transgression of
which creates feelings of wrongdoing and the fear of punishment (Piers and Singer
1953). Shame, on the other hand, relates to the anxiety caused by 'inadequacy' or
'failure' to live up to internalized societal and parental *goals and ideals* (as opposed to
internalized prohibitions), expectations of what a person 'should' do, be, know, or feel.
These feelings of failure often lead to a fear of psychological or physical rejection, abandonment, expulsion (separation anxiety), or loss of social position (Alexander 1948:
43). The person shamed often feels the need to take revenge for his or her humiliation,
to 'save face'. By 'shaming the shamer', the situation is reversed, and the shamed
person feels triumphant (Horney 1950: 103).

If the Freudian theory that the primary incest scene (the Oedipal relationship) must
be successfully resolved for the 'healthy' mental development of every individual or the
repressed desire may return in another setting can be applied correctly to this narrative, when Noah 'awoke from his wine' either he realized that an *actual* incestuous,
homosexual encounter with his son, Ham, had occurred; or he recognized his *repressed*
desire for such a relationship. Presumably as a result, Noah understandably felt guilt
(for having violated the societal norms which prohibit homosexuality) and shame.
Hence Noah's need for revenge in order to maintain his dignity and self-esteem. In other
words, Noah 'shamed the shamer'. Using what reads like classical Freudian defence
mechanisms, Noah attempted to alleviate his own anxiety by using methods that would

deny, falsify, or otherwise distort his heretofore repressed fantasy. First, Noah sublimated the obviously dangerous memory or idea – his desire for Ham. Next, Noah rejected *himself* as the source of his uncomfortable feelings and attributed the origin of these emotions to Ham. That is, instead of saying 'I wanted Ham' Noah said, 'Ham wanted me.' Essential here is that by displacing his emotions, Noah, the *subject* of unresolved incestuous, homosexual desires changes himself into the *object* of these desires. By doing so, Noah is able to provide a rationalization for his curse. As a result, Ham is forced into the position of shouldering Noah's displaced guilt and shame.

But why curse Canaan and not Ham? Looking at artistic and literary representations of this narrative in the light of psychoanalytic literary theory might provide an insight into Noah's actions, different from that of non-psychologically-oriented biblical scholars. Renaissance painters appear to display a rather playful approach to this biblical episode, one which echoes psychoanalytic thought and recent clinical data. Generally speaking, the pictures portray the obviously masculine naked patriarchal figure lying in a drunken state. However, significant from the perspective of a psychological approach to the Hebrew Bible (as well as actual reported incest cases), there is considerable sexual confusion in the representation of the three brothers, Japheth, Shem, and Ham. A twelfth-century mosaic, for example, shows Ham without a beard beside his two bearded brothers, perhaps suggesting the oft-used theme that beards and masculinity are equated, as in the well-known Samson narrative of Judges 13–16. Jacopo della Quercia (c.1430) shows only two brothers, one carrying a cloak with averted eyes and behind him (presumably) Ham with his garments drawn up to expose his own genitalia. Hiding in the vines is a mysterious feminine figure. Might she represent a feminized portrayal of Ham? Giovanni Bellini portrays a nude, heavily bearded Noah cavorting about. Ham, smooth-skinned, is pictured in the middle of the scene.

For purposes of this article, I am most interested in Michelangelo's reading of the text. Michelangelo shows all three brothers with feminine hair arrangements. However, the brother nearest to Noah is the most masculine, with clearly identifiable male genitalia. The second brother has male genitalia but a rather protuberant feminine-like abdomen and is being embraced from behind by the third brother, a dark Ham without any male genitals to clearly identify his sex. The decreasingly masculine representations of each of the brothers suggests that Michelangelo's reading of the narrative portrays the first brother as sufficiently secure in his own masculinity not to hurry to look at his father's genitals, the second brother as confused and Ham *as* a female. Why would Ham be portrayed in such a feminized style? Noteworthy for purposes of my reading is the fact that clinically it has been generally accepted that homosexual seduction by the father threatens the son's masculinity and overwhelms him with a passive feminine identification (Medlicott 1967). That is, the father who makes sexual approaches to his son symbolically castrates him by 'making a woman' of him, which is consistent with my interpretation of the Renaissance artists. In other words, these painters are portraying Ham from *Noah's* perspective – as feminized.

But this still does not explain fully why Canaan, and not Ham is cursed. On to Lacan. Lacanian theory suggests that by consigning Ham's son and further progeny into abject slavery, Noah *symbolically* castrates Ham. As stated above, although the word 'Phallus' is interchangeable with 'penis' in ordinary usage, this is not the case in that branch of psychoanalysis which concerns itself with psychosexual development. In the discourse of psychoanalysis, the word 'Phallus' does not denote the anatomical organ 'penis', but rather the signifier or symbol of what we desire but lack, and is most often associated with the concept of *'power'*. Canaan becomes powerless, lacking a phallus, in effect having the same standing as females. Ham, while not *physically* castrated, is *symbolically* castrated by the enslaving of Canaan and his progeny. Noah, on the other hand, is exonerated and can maintain his status as 'righteous'.

Conclusion

Whether Freudian, Lacanian, feminist, or any combination thereof, as D. Clines has observed, 'what has happened . . . in the last three decades can be represented . . . as a shift in focus that has moved from *author* to *text* to *reader*' (1990: 9–10); readers *'use the Bible today . . . in terms of their values, attitudes, and responses'* (McKnight 1988: 14–15, emphasis added). Thus, perhaps wittingly or otherwise, more biblical scholars seem to be reading using some form of psychological theory – dissenters notwithstanding. Many of these works have taken the form of interpenetrative readings of various psychological approaches and the Bible. This seems to be a workable compromise since psychology in biblical exegesis is relatively new, and Lacan's ideas in particular are still relatively unfamiliar. I suspect, however, that as psychological criticism becomes more widely accepted, the focus will change. Like psychology itself, psychologically-based readings will be centred more intensely on the Word and the chain of associations that are developed within the text – an approach which seems particularly relevant for biblical scholars.

References

Alexander, F. (1948). *Fundamentals of Psychoanalysis*. New York: Norton.

Bassett, F. (1971). 'Noah's Nakedness and the Curse of Canaan: A Case of Incest?', *Vestus Testamentum* 21: 236–74.

Boyd, J. (2000). 'Biblical Psychology: A Creative Way to Apply the Whole Bible to Understanding Human Psychology', *Trinity Journal* 21(1): 3–16.

Brandes, S. (1980). *Metaphors of Masculinity: Sex and Status in Andalusian Folklore*. Philadelphia, PA: Westminster/John Knox Press.

Carmichael, C. M. (1997). *Law, Legend, and Incest in the Bible: Leviticus 18–20*. Ithaca, NY: Cornell University Press.

Clines, D. J. (1990). *What Does Eve Do to Help? And Other Readerly Questions to the Old Testament* (Journal for the Study of the Old Testament Supplement Series, vol. 94). Sheffield: Sheffield Academic Press.

Cohen, N. J. (1998). *Voices from Genesis: Guiding Us through the Stages of Life*. Woodstock, VT: Jewish Lights Publishing.

Cole, W. (1959). *Sex and Love in the Bible*. New York: Association Press.

Conrad, J. (1912). *A Personal Record*. New York: Harper & Brothers.

Davis, R. C. (ed.) (1983). *Lacan and Narration: The Psychoanalytic Difference in Narrative Theory*. Baltimore, MD: Johns Hopkins University Press.

Dominian, J. (1998). *One Like Us: A Psychological Interpretation of Jesus*. London: Dartman, Longman, and Todd.

Edinger, E. (2000). *Ego and Self: The Old Testament Prophets from Isaiah to Malachi*. Toronto: Inner City Books.

Ellens, J. H. E. (2004). *The Destructive Power of Religion: Violence in Judaism, Christianity, and Islam*, vol. 2: *Religion, Psychology, and Violence*. London: Praeger, pp. 155–76.

Feldman, Y. S. (1994). *Freud and Forbidden Knowledge*. New York: New York University Press.

Felman, S. (ed.) (1981). *Literature and Psychoanalysis: The Question of Reading: Otherwise*. Baltimore, MD: Johns Hopkins University Press.

Freud, S. (1905). *The Standard Works of Sigmund Freud*, vol. 7: *Three Essays on the Theory of Sexuality*, ed. and trans. J. Strachey. London: The Hogarth Press and the Institute of Psycho-Analysis.

Freud, S. (1913). *The Standard Works of Sigmund Freud*, vol. 13: *Totem and Taboo*, ed. and trans. J. Strachey. London: The Hogarth Press and the Institute of Psycho-Analysis, pp. 1–161.

Freud, S. (1916–17). *The Standard Works of Sigmund Freud*, vol. 15: *Introductory Lectures on Psycho-Analysis*, ed. and trans. J. Strachey. London: The Hogarth Press and the Institute of Psycho-Analysis, pp. 15–239.

Freud, S. (1918). *The Standard Works of Sigmund Freud*, vol. 17: *From the History of an Infantile Neurosis*, ed. and trans. J. Strachey. London: The Hogarth Press and the Institute of Psycho-Analysis, pp. 7–122.

Freud, S. (1925). *The Standard Works of Sigmund Freud*, vol. 19: *Some Psychical Consequences of the Anatomical Distinction between the Sexes*, ed. and trans. J. Strachey. London: The Hogarth Press and the Institute of Psycho-Analysis, pp. 241–60.

Freud, S. (1928). *The Standard Works of Sigmund Freud*, vol 21: *Dostoevsky and Patricide*, ed. and trans. J. Strachey. London: The Hogarth Press and the Institute of Psycho-Analysis, pp. 177–94.

Halperin, D. J. (1993). *Seeking Ezekiel: Text and Psychology*. University Park, PA: Pennsylvania State University Press.

Hamilton, V. (1990). *The Book of Genesis: Chapters 1–17*. Grand Rapids, MI: Eerdmans.

Horney, K. (1950). *Neurosis and Human Growth*. New York: W. W. Norton.

Irigaray, L. (1977). *Ce Sexe qui n'en est pas un (This sex which is not one)*, trans. C. Porter and C. Burke. Ithaca, NY: Cornell University Press.

Jones, E. (1949). *Hamlet and Oedipus*. London: Victor Gollancz.

Kaplan, K. J. (1997). 'Freud, Oedipus and the Hebrew Bible', *Journal of Psychology and Judaism* 21(3): 211–16.

Kille, D. A. (2001). *Psychological Biblical Criticism*. Minneapolis, MN: Fortress Press.

Kille, D. A. (2002). 'Psychology and the Bible: Three Worlds of the Text', *Pastoral Psychology* 51(2): 125–34.

Kluger, Y. and Kluger-Nash, N. (1999). *A Psychological Interpretation of Ruth*. Einseideln, Switzerland: Daimon.

Knight, G. (1981). *Theology in Pictures: A Commentary on Genesis, Chapters One to Eleven*. Edinburgh: Handsel Press.

Kruger, P. A. (2000). 'A Cognitive Interpretation of the Emotion of Anger in the Hebrew Bible', *Journal of Northwest Semitic Languages* 26(1): 181–93.

Kunin, S. (1995). *The Logic of Incest: A Structuralist Analysis of Hebrew Mythology*. Sheffield: Sheffield Academic Press.

Lévi-Strauss, C. (1967). *Structural Anthropology*. New York: Anchor Books.

McKnight, E. V. (1988). *Post-Modern Use of the Bible: The Emergence of Reader-Oriented Criticism*. Nashville, TN: Abingdon Press.

Medlicott, R. (1967). 'Lot and his Daughters', *Australian and New Zealand Journal of Psychiatry* 1: 134–9.

Midrash Rabbah: Genesis (1983). Eds H. Freedman and I. Epstein. London: Soncino Press.

Miller, David L, (ed) (1995). 'Biblical Imagery and Psychological Likeness', in *Jung and the Interpretation of the Bible*. New York: Continuum.

Muller, J. P. and Richardson, W. J. (1982). *Lacan and Language: A Reader's Guide to Écrits*. New York: International Universities Press.

Pastoral Psychology (2002). 51(2).

Phillips, A. (1980). 'Uncovering the Father's Skirt', *Vestus Testamentum* 30: 39–40.

Philo (1971). *Philo in Ten Volumes*, Vol. Supplement I: *Questions and Answers on Genesis: Translated from the Ancient Armenian Version of the Original Greek*, trans. R. Marcus. London: William Heinemann.

Piers, G. and Singer, M. (1953). *Shame and Guilt*. New York: W. W. Norton.

Polka, B. (2001). *Depth Psychological Interpretation and the Bible: An Ontological Essay on Freud*. Montreal: McGill-Queen's University Press.

Rashkow, I. N. (1993). *The Phallacy of Genesis: A Feminist-Psychoanalytic Approach*. Louisville, KY: Westminster/John Knox Press.

Rashkow, I. N. (2000a). 'Lacan', in *A Handbook for Postmodern Biblical Interpretation*. St Louis, MO: Chalice Press, pp. 151–5.

Rashkow, I. N. (2000b). *Taboo or Not Taboo: The Hebrew Bible and Human Sexuality*. Minneapolis, MN: Fortress Press.

Robertson, J. (1900). *Christianity and Mythology*. London: Watts Publishers.

Rollins, W. G. (1999). *Soul and Psyche: The Bible in Psychological Perspective*. Minneapolis, MN: Augsburg Fortress.

Sanhedrin: Hebrew-English Edition of the Babylonian Talmud (1969). London: Soncino Press.

Sarna, N. (1989). *The Jewish Publication Society Torah Commentary: Genesis*. Philadelphia, PA: Jewish Publication Society.

Schwartz, M. B. and Kaplan, K. J. (1998). 'Toward a Hebraic Psychotherapy', *Journal of Psychology and Judaism* 22(3): 161–239.

Smith, J. H. (1986). 'Primitive Guilt', in J. Smith and W. Kerrigan (eds), *Pragmatism's Freud: The Moral Disposition of Psychoanalysis*. Baltimore, MD: Johns Hopkins University Press, pp. 52–78.

Solomon, R. S. (2000). 'Bruno Bettelheim and the Chazon Ish: Toward a New Jewish Psychotherapy', *Journal of Psychology and Judaism* 24(3): 223–31.

Speiser, E. (1964). *Genesis*. Garden City, NY: Doubleday Press.

Torok, M. (1964). 'L'envie du pénis sous la femme', in *La Sexualité féminine: Nouvelle recherche psychanalyse*. Paris: Payon.

Watson, P. (1998). 'Girard and Integration: Desire, Violence, and the Mimesis of Christ as Foundation for Postmodernity', *Journal of Psychology and Theology* 26(4): 311–21.

Wright, E. (1984). *Psychoanalytic Criticism: Theory in Practice*. London: Methuen.

Zeligs, D. F. (1988). *Psychoanalysis and the Bible: A Study in Depth of Seven Leaders*. New York: Human Sciences Press.

CHAPTER 27
Gender

Deborah F. Sawyer

In the Introduction to the *Woman's Bible* published at the end of the nineteenth century, Elizabeth Cady Stanton explains that the impetus for her and her associates to produce this two-volume work stemmed from a need to present alternative interpretation regarding the status of women in the Bible. This was essential since the pervading interpretation up to this point had provided justification for social, political and legislative treatment of women as the second sex:

> When in the early part of the Nineteenth Century, women began to protest against their civil and political degradation, they were referred to the Bible for an answer. When they protested against their unequal position in the church, they were referred to the Bible for an answer. (1985: 8)

This publication represents a milestone in the subject of gender studies and the Bible. In presenting an alternative interpretation of 'woman' these pioneers within the movement for women's suffrage destabilized and deconstructed the given biblical concepts of masculinity and femininity, and, by extension, inevitably produced a critique of the role of 'man'.

The habit of turning to biblical texts to justify a particular interpretation of the roles of men and women is as old as some biblical texts themselves. Christian scripture draws on the Hebrew Bible to support its prohibition of women teaching (1 Tim. 2:8–15). This passage defines behavioural expectations for both women and men, that are endorsed by a particular interpretation of Genesis 2–3: 'For Adam was formed first, then Eve; and Adam was not deceived, but the woman was deceived and became a transgressor' (1 Tim. 2:14). Interpretations of this kind recur consistently in Christian tradition from antiquity to modernity. With the dawn of what is now known as first-wave feminism, however, these interpretations were not only challenged but also exposed as simply interpretations, albeit pervasive ones, and not definitive, objective meanings for the text. The pioneering work of early feminist biblical scholars was supported by the prevalent biblical 'scientific' exegesis of their day. German scholarship from a Liberal Protestant stance in particular served the work of these women by allowing them, for example, to argue that two accounts of creation can be discerned in Genesis, one of which presents an equal and complementary relationship between the first couple (Gen. 1:26–7).

Feminist Hermeneutics

The critique of biblical texts and the history of their interpretation from the perspective of a feminist hermeneutical stance, through the process of gender analysis, intensified with the advent of second-wave feminism, which began in the late 1960s. A range of hermeneutical tools was applied to biblical texts, reflecting the range of exegetical methodologies that evolved in biblical scholarship from around the middle of the twentieth century. The hermeneutical stance taken by scholars approaching the text from the perspective of gender analysis, reflected the move in the wider sphere of biblical studies away from the pursuit of a single objective meaning of the text towards subjective awareness. A comment made by Elisabeth Schüssler Fiorenza gives us a glimpse into the battle being fought at that time for the academic recognition of feminist hermeneutics:

> Anyone identified with the 'feminist cause' is ideologically suspect and professionally discredited, while scholars who do not articulate their theoretical pre-understandings and political allegiances are 'objective' exegetes, free from bias, non-partisan and absolutely scientific. (1982: 35)

This tendency to articulate a particular standpoint, or bias, was a key feature in the work of both feminist and liberation theologians from the late 1970s.

The work of Phyllis Trible neatly reflects the combination of contemporary exegetical methodology with a feminist hermeneutical stance. Trible resisted the interpretation of 'feminism' as a narrow focus on women, but rather described her work as 'a critique of culture in the light of misogyny' (1978: 7). She applied rhetorical criticism to the biblical text, following James Muilenburg, where, 'the major clue to interpretation is the text itself' (1978: 7). Trible's hermeneutical stance singled out, not only feminist issues raised by the text, but also the possibility for a relationship of complementarity between men and women. Her analysis of Genesis 2–3, entitled 'A Love Story Gone Awry' and published in *God and the Rhetoric of Sexuality* (1978), remains a landmark in the history of biblical exegesis. Her work has been criticized for its optimism (Clines 1990: see below), but it succeeded in foregrounding aspects of the text and even narratives that had been bypassed by generations of men in the academy. Her exegesis of Judges 19, 'An Unnamed Woman: The Extravagance of Violence' in *Texts of Terror* (1984), lays bare the horror of a woman gang-raped, left for dead, her body subsequently desecrated. Trible concludes her exegesis by reminding the reader: 'Woman as object is still captured, betrayed, raped, tortured, murdered, dismembered, and scattered. To take to heart this ancient story, then, is to confess its present reality' (1984: 87).

While Trible's work is ahistorical, in contrast, Bernadette Brooten's work is essentially historical applying a very different methodology, although sharing the same hermeneutical stance. Brooten utilizes all types of material in an attempt to reconstruct women's history ('*herstory*'), particularly in the period of late antiquity. The Bible is one source among many that can be instrumental in her project. Brooten draws attention to the huge silences that exist within our historical accounts: 'the lack of sources on women is part of the history of women' (1985: 66). Rather than taking the biblical evidence as normative, Brooten uses external sources to expose its idiosyncrasies. She also shows how clues to actual practice can be gained by reading biblical teaching 'against the grain'. For example, if Paul teaches that women should veil their heads (1 Cor. 11:5–6), then this tells us that some did not; if he exhorts wives to be subject to their husbands (Eph. 5:22), then some were not; if he bids women to remain silent in the congregations (1 Cor. 14:34), then some did not.

Of particular significance is Brooten's early work on the interpretation of archaeological data which provided invaluable evidence for both early Judaism and early Christianity. Her thesis was based on nineteen Greek and Latin inscriptions dating from 27 BCE to possibly as late as the sixth century CE. In these inscriptions women are given the titles 'head of the synagogue', 'leader', 'elder' and 'mother of the synagogue'. A number of these inscriptions had been known to scholars for some time, and Brooten notes, 'According to previous scholarly consensus, Jewish women did not assume positions of leadership in the ancient synagogue. Scholars have therefore interpreted the titles borne by women in these inscriptions as honorific' (1982: 1). She offers an alternative interpretation, suggesting that these women did actually hold the offices ascribed to them. On the tomb of one individual, Rufina, she is described as 'head of the synagogue', which would mean that she would have been learned in matters of Jewish law, she would have particular responsibility for the spiritual direction of the community, she would have taught in the community, and she would have been involved in decisions relating to the building and restoration of the synagogues (1982: 10). Such interpretation brings new light into the debate regarding the biblical evidence for female leadership in early Christianity.

Elisabeth Schüssler Fiorenza's seminal work, *In Memory of Her: A Feminist Theological Reconstruction of Christian Origins* (1995a), which first appeared in 1983, combines historical, sociological and theological approaches to the text, working from a feminist standpoint and a 'hermeneutic of suspicion'. Fiorenza identifies women's 'counter-tradition', a term used by Elisabeth Gössmann to describe the unbroken chain of women's experience that can be uncovered down the centuries of Christian history (1999), as beginning with the ministry of Jesus, and evident in the ministries of female contemporaries of the first apostles. She uncovers a 'golden age' for women in terms of their inclusion in the radical theological visions of that time. While there were tensions and alternative, more exclusive versions of earliest Christianity (or Christianities), Fiorenza identified a clear affirmation of women's roles within the new movement. This is echoed in the title of her book. *In Memory of Her* is an allusion to an incident in Bethany during Jesus' his final journey to Jerusalem, where an unnamed woman anoints his head with expensive ointment, much to the chagrin of his male disciples:

But Jesus said, 'Let her alone; why do you trouble her? She has performed a good service for me. For you always have the poor with you, and you can show kindness to them whenever you wish; but you will not always have me. She has done what she could; she has anointed my body beforehand for the burial. Truly I tell you, wherever the good news is proclaimed in the whole world, what she has done will be told in remembrance of her.' (Mark 14:6–9)

The baptismal formula articulated in the writings of Paul is for Fiorenza the true egalitarian vision of Church or 'ecclesia': 'There is no longer Jew or Greek, there is no longer slave or free, there is no longer male and female; for all of you are one in Christ Jesus' (Gal. 3:28).

Certainly, Fiorenza sees in later gnostic and patristic writings a type of androgyny that has little to offer women in terms of equality, 'becoming a disciple means for a woman becoming "male", "like man", and relinquishing her sexual powers of procreation, because the male principle stands for the heavenly, angelic, divine realm, whereas the female principle represents either human weakness or evil'. But she continues, 'Gal. 3.28 does not extol maleness but the oneness of the body of Christ, the church, where all social, cultural, religious, national, and biological gender divisions are differences are overcome, and all structures of domination are rejected' (1995a: 218). Her interpretation of Gal. 3:28 has been challenged, particularly by the work of Dale Martin.

He has explored the notion of becoming 'one' in the baptismal formulas and theology of Paul, and concludes, contrary to Fiorenza, that Paul, in his context within the ancient world, presents an 'unequal androgyny' (Martin 1995: 230). He demonstrates that 'androgyny was invariably described in male terms' (ibid.: 231). In sum, redemption for a woman meant losing her female nature and being subsumed in the gender hierarchy to maleness. Fiorenza's interpretation is perhaps more rooted in the idealism of second-wave feminist theology than the realities of ancient perceptions of gender and androgyny.

Second-Wave Feminism

Feminist criticism represented a variety of stances across a spectrum from within and without the traditions of Judaism and Christianity, from post-traditional through to conservative. The conservative positions on the spectrum could be described in terms of religious apologetics with commentators maintaining their religious stance whilst accommodating biblical values and feminism accordingly. One example was the publication of Mary Evans's (1983) work, *Woman in the Bible*, where no biblical text, however challenging, was rejected. Instead terms are re-interpreted: the headship of the husband over his wife for example, (Eph. 5:23), is explained in terms of 'source' rather than dominance (1983: 66), a wife's prescription to be subject in everything to her husband (Eph. 5:24) is understood as 'a voluntary putting first of the will and desires of the husband, seeking his benefit' (1983: 68). While the credibility of these interpretations has to be left to the discernment of the reader, the work of some such Christian feminists attracted severe criticism from Jewish feminist writers, who criticized the tendency to ascribe negative attitudes to women found in Christian scripture to the Jewish 'background' of the early figures, such as Paul of Tarsus (Plaskow 1994).

Moving along the spectrum of second-wave feminist biblical hermeneutics we discover scholars who, while maintaining an allegiance to a particular tradition, display a more liberal attitude towards the text. They argue, for example, that texts that appear to denigrate women and have a history of supporting misogyny, are not universally prescriptive: they are 'time-bound' in the same way that biblical teaching on slavery was put aside in cultures that reject the practice. This radical reformist stance can be seen as a clear point of continuity between first-wave and second-wave feminist biblical hermeneutics, where a strong biblical faith stands side by side with an agenda to lay bare the text, stripped of its outward clothing of interpretative layers of patriarchal bias. This stance can be discerned in the work of three eminent feminist second-wave scholars: Rosemary Radford Ruether and Elisabeth Schüssler Fiorenza within a Christian context, and Judith Plaskow from a Jewish one. Fiorenza's scholarship on the Pauline literature clearly demarcates between texts that are inclusive and affirm women, and those that marginalize and discriminate against them (Fiorenza 1995a). In broader terms, her comments in the formative days of feminist biblical hermeneutics, as it emerged as a discipline of the academy (gaining recognized status in the Society of Biblical Literature), detail the repercussions for the existing canon of scripture in the light of this critique:

> A feminist theological hermeneutics of the Bible that has as its canon the liberation of women from oppressive sexist texts, structures, institutions, and internalized male values, maintains that solely those traditions and texts of the Bible that transcend their patriarchal culture and time have the theological authority of revelation, if the Bible should not continue to be a tool for the patriarchal oppression of women. (1982: 43)

This concept of a 'new canon', a more exclusive version of sacred texts, was prevalent also in the work of Rosemary Radford Ruether, whose *Womanguides* she described as, 'a working handbook from which such a new canon might emerge, much as early Christians collected stories about their experience from which they preached the "good news" and from which, eventually, fuller texts were developed and ratified as the interpretive base for the new community' (1985: ix). Radical re-thinking of the canon would exclude biblical texts identified as misogynist and include ancient texts that affirm rather than marginalize women, and contemporary feminist 'midrash'. Thus, a canon for 'womanchurch' (Ruether) or 'ecclesia' (Fiorenza) would begin to emerge. In 1994, Fiorenza edited a two-volume work, *Searching the Scriptures*, in which she and other feminist scholars demarcate and interpret a set of texts that suggests a new emerging feminist canon, marking the centenary of the publication of Elizabeth Cady Stanton's *The Woman's Bible*.

At the other polarity of the spectrum we find radical positioning where biblical texts are rejected along with the traditions they represent. A key figure at the height of second-wave feminism in the 1970s and 1980s was Mary Daly, who rejected the possibility of reforming either the traditional religions of Judaism and Christianity or the texts that bear witness to them. In the light of her far-reaching critique of Christianity

(1973), Mary Daly moved from a radical position within that tradition to being a post-Christian, concluding that the traditions based on the Bible were created by men and for men. Thus, if women wish to be truly liberated they must put aside traditional religion and reconfigure spirituality on their own terms. Naomi Goldenberg published *Changing of the Gods: Feminism and the End of Traditional Religions* in 1979, in similar vein to Daly from a Jewish standpoint. Whilst the conclusions of both Daly and Goldenberg were rejected by reformist feminists, their critiques have proved invaluable to many within traditional religions, in that they articulate extremely useful diagnoses of the problems inherent in those religions. In fact, they present an agenda for reform, particularly in terms of language and structure.

The Male God

Two major issues emerged for feminist theologians and biblical scholars at this time, namely the maleness of God and the patriarchal nature of biblical literature. The maleness of God was a challenge to feminist theologians, philosophers of religion and biblical scholars alike. The solution could never be a mere tweaking of male pronouns. Mary Daly's maxim: 'If God is male, then the male is God' (1973: 19), could be reversed to demonstrate the endemic nature of the problem: if the male is perceived as God, then God will be perceived in male terms. However, this re-writing of the diagnosis is more reminiscent of third-wave rather than second wave feminism with its echo of Foucault in the suggested instability of a given meta-narrative.

In biblical texts, Hebrew and Greek alike, God is invariably male in terms of the gender of the language used for 'him'. The biblical God might explode the given categories for acceptable or possible male behaviour, but throughout it all he remains, in linguistic terms, male. Perhaps the most striking example in the Bible of divine transcendence of male categories is Deuteronomy 32:18: 'You were unmindful of the Rock that bore you; you forgot the God that gave you birth'. Here we find the unique example of the Hebrew verb 'to give birth' appearing in the text in the form of the third person masculine singular. Indeed, the motherhood of God does appear as a biblical theme to depict God's unswerving care and option for Israel, for example, in Jesus' lament over Jerusalem, 'How often have I desired to gather your children together as a hen gathers her brood under her wings' (Matt. 23:37; cf. Isa. 42:14; 66:13; Ps. 131:2). These examples serve the purposes of biblical authors to depict both the unconditional love God has for his people and his omnipotence. God can be a mother to Israel because, unlike humans, he transcends gender. But in consistently using male language, despite the nature of the actions described, God is not simply transcending human capacity, but more specifically, he transcends human male capacity.

Despite exceptional passages such as those mentioned above, the overriding language and imagery used for God in the Bible are male, and this has been consistently repeated by commentators down the centuries. God in the Bible has a special relationship with the first man, suggesting a unique bond between the God described in male language and the human male he creates with his own hands (Gen. 2:7). The main purpose for the creation of the human creature bearing the image of God is to

'Be fruitful and multiply, and fill the earth and subdue it' (Gen. 1:28). Thus Adam needs a partner to fulfil this purpose. Before creating Eve, God creates all the rest of the living creatures, parading them in front of Adam, and Adam exercises his authority over them by naming them. But there is no creature that adequately reflects his likeness – no creature that can be his partner and helper (Gen. 2:20). When God does create Eve out of Adam's side a form of parity between man and woman seems evident: 'bone' of his 'bone', 'flesh' of his 'flesh' (Gen. 2:23), or even complementarity, as Phyllis Trible has argued (1978: 94–105). Although woman clearly images man, she is neither identical nor equal (Clines 1990: 25–48), despite the exegetical attempts of feminist theologians. Although she is recognized as the same species as Adam, as opposed to the other creatures he was presented with, she is different. And it is in her difference from Adam that she is subordinate: created specifically for his need, and help him to fulfil the purpose of his existence. As Adam is ontologically unable to be God's equal, so Eve cannot be Adam's equal. So the hierarchy of creation as set out in the opening chapters of Genesis, and as such providing the blueprint for successive biblical relationships, is clearly God, man, woman, creatures. Man is closest to God, and so male imagery comes closest to capturing the essence of the divine.

For many feminist theologians the biblical use of male language for God is dealt with by contextualization, by recognition of the relative nature of the societies that produced these texts. Although biblical texts cover numerous centuries of the ancient world, a consistent characteristic throughout this history is the patriarchal structure of the societies which were responsible for the texts. Whether agrarian or urban, these societies might have variations in terms of the extent and impact of their values in social, political and legislative terms; but they were all characterized by patriarchy. If this characteristic is judged to be 'time-bound', and relative to a particular ancient society, then it could be put to one side. For radical feminists moving beyond the traditions, this is an impossible task since patriarchy is part of the essential identities of Judaism and Christianity. If they lose that characteristic, their core, then they cease to exist in any real sense.

Turning to Christian scripture, the most common articulation of God in male language is the image of 'father', intensifying, or channelling, the divine being without ambiguity into male form. Mary Rose D'Angelo is among feminist biblical scholars who have confronted this issue, but rather than taking the radical stance of rejecting the tradition as essential patriarchal, she attempts to situate the earliest Christian articulations of God as father within the framework of the Roman Empire in the first century and thereby expose the limitations of such an image:

> Neither Jesus nor the NT can be shown to have used the word 'father' in a way that constitutes a transhistorical revelation that is unique and will be irreparably lost if twentieth century theology and practice choose other imagery for God. (D'Angelo 1992: 630)

But she warns against any simplistic attempt to drop the title 'father' for God that takes Christianity out of the reality of its origins:

> But the use of 'father' in the NT cannot be ignored; it is important not only to diversify language and imagery for God but also to attend to the patriarchal and imperial horizons

within which Christianity was born and has lived, and to continue to ask how they have limited our visions of the divine. (1992: 630)

A variety of means emerged from feminist theology to deal with the issue of the 'maleness' of God. Reformist feminist Christians have problematized the concepts of the fatherhood of God and the maleness of Jesus that infers the exclusion of the feminine, and have suggested solutions that attempt to stay true to the religion while offering less exclusive models for God. One of the most influential scholars in this field is Sallie McFague, who offers the model of 'friend', or 'friendship' as a more constructive and inclusive metaphor for the divine/human relationship, and one that allows for human autonomy:

> Rather than stressing the protection, comfort, and redemption of individuals *apart* from others and the world, a friendship model emphasizes sacrifice, support, and solidarity *with* others and the world. God's saving. God's saving activity is seen in an 'adult' not a 'father/child' mode. God is our friend who suffers with us as we work with God to bring about a better existence for suffering humanity. (McFague 1982: 186)

Feminist theology and biblical interpretation have developed new ways of understanding the biblical images of God. Rather than uncritically translating the concept of 'father' from ancient cultures to our own time, the image has been deconstructed to disclose a spectrum of meanings that go beyond traditional interpretation.

The biblical God does not need to be diluted to fit the liberal patriarch we have tended to meet in commentaries written since the rise of historical criticism, or to be modified to become the champion of the dispossessed. The biblical deity can be all these things, as well as being the God who slays the enemies of Israel, who can demand child sacrifice from Abraham, kill the innocent Job's wife and children as part of a wager, encourage Rebecca to deceive her husband and deny the rights of her eldest son. God's love is undeniably attested throughout the Bible, but the character of that love is contingent upon the meaning, and limitations, of the metaphors and imagery drawn on by the biblical authors in their times. The concept of paternal love in the context of the Roman Empire is inevitably and inextricably bound up with absolute authority and power. 'Fatherhood' as understood in the first century can be a loving and caring image, but it can also demand the exposure of new-born babies, or the brutal massacre of children in the arena. In translating this metaphor uncritically to our own time, levels of meaning intrinsic to the metaphor in its biblical context were neither confronted nor challenged.

A biblical critique that examines the text from the stance of its use of gendered language can explore the meaning of 'fatherhood' in the light of its context in biblical times and add insight for the work of contemporary theologians and philosophers of religion, in divulging new language for human experience of the divine. The concept of divine love that readers of the Bible today identify with – spiritually and materially – will be, as ever, a concept that resonates with their own situation.

The Male Saviour Figure

In the Christian tradition the male imagery for God intensifies through the belief in the incarnation. The extent to which this has been problematized is dependent on the level of significance that is placed on God 'becoming' a man, or God 'becoming' Jesus of Nazareth. In other words, the question is whether Jesus' maleness is central to his ministry. For radical feminists this has been a key issue in that Jesus, the Son of God, completes and affirms an essentially male Godhead that excludes any possibility of female representation: 'The image itself (God-Man) is one-sided, as far as sexual identity is concerned, and it is precisely on the wrong side, since it fails to counter sexism and functions to glorify maleness' (Daly 1973: 72).

For reformist feminist Christian scholars the maleness of Jesus is secondary to the liberative power of his message. This conclusion was reached after much theological speculation. From among the vanguard of reformists in the 1980s, Ruether was probably the most radical thinker on the issue of Christology, and it was she who voiced the classic question, 'Can a male savior save women?' in the title to the chapter on Christology in her book *Sexism and God-Talk* (1983). Her Christology has been questioned as to whether it remains 'orthodox' in Christian terms, since she appears to foreground Jesus' role as the prophet of a new humanity at the expense of his unique nature as formulated in the creeds:

> In this sense Jesus as the Christ, the representative of liberated humanity and the liberating Word of God, manifests the kenosis of patriarchy, the announcement of a new humanity through a lifestyle that discards hierarchical caste privilege and speaks on behalf of the lowly. (1983: 137)

For Fiorenza, Ruether's Christology is problematic on other grounds in that it fails to go beyond Jesus' maleness, 'in other words, stories about Jesus the liberator continue to function for religiously inculcating feminine romance attitudes and to legitimate kyriarchal relations of dominance and submission' (Fiorenza 1995b: 47).

Fiorenza is less critical of the Christology that has emerged from non-first world contexts. In commenting on the work of the African-American Jacquelyn Grant (1989), she agrees that, 'Scripture, tradition, theology, and Christology must therefore be critically analyzed and tested for their ideological-political functions in legitimating or subverting kyriarchal structures and mind-sets of domination' (1995b: 49). For Fiorenza, however, Grant's widening of the lens of critique to allow that patriarchy is part of the bigger problematic of oppression, blurs the focus of the struggle:

> I do not think that we can derive the criterion and norm of a feminist Christian theology from the option of the historical Jesus for the poor and outcast. Rather, we must ground feminist theology in wo/men's struggles for the transformation of kyriarchy. (1995b: 48)

Fiorenza's Christology eludes an easy definition: it is visionary, it is embedded in feminist liberation movements and at the same time it is universalistic in seeking the liberation of all. It escapes the 'kyriarchal' trinitarian image by incorporating female ingredients. Jesus is situated as Miriam's child and Sophia's prophet, thereby surpass-ing the problem of an exclusive male saviour figure (1995b: 190). According to Fiorenza, the message articulated by Mary in the Magnificat (Luke 1:46–55) explains dynamically, Christologically and evangelically, the theological core of the Christian message.

The figure of 'Christa' is one of the most challenging images to have emerged from feminist Christology. This is the name given to a statue sculpted by Edwina Sandys of Jesus in female form, with arms outstretched as though being crucified. This image, linked to the Pauline formula of oneness in the body of Christ (1 Cor. 12; Gal. 3:28), became an icon for feminists constructing Christologies, particularly those arguing for a relational model: 'We are the Christa' (Heyward 1989: 84). In the person of Christa, the connectedness of humanity, the concept of community, can be realized inclusively. For Carter Heyward, becoming one in Christa allows for authentic existence, allowing individuals to be themselves whatever their gender, colour or sexuality. Mary Grey's notion of relationality focuses both on the cross and the resurrection (1990). Christ/Christa on the cross identifies with the experience of women in mutual broken-ness, woundedness, and through the resurrection is the promise of wholeness and healing. Christ on the cross personifies, through sacrificial love, the connectedness that is part of women's experience. Redemption lies in the connectedness, 'redemptive mutuality', rather than in the challenge to hierarchical ecclesiology (or, in Fiorenza's terminology, 'kyriarchal' structures).

As we can see from this discussion, the maleness of Jesus, far from being an obsta-cle in terms of feminist analysis, has in fact prompted important developments in Chris-tological thinking that go beyond the immediate interests of feminist theology. It takes Christology beyond the man/God debate and exposes and questions the essentiality of Christ's manhood. When that manhood is deconstructed, and replaced by crucified womanhood, this radical paradigm shift reveals, at the very least, how embedded male imagery is within traditional Christianity, and how far it needs to go to be comfortable with a truly inclusive symbol of redemption.

The patriarchal nature of biblical texts obviously extends beyond the imagery used to describe God or the Son of God. Eve, the mother of the human race, is told her husband will rule over her. Biblical law codes presume a male audience that is instructed, among many other matters, in the ways of getting and maintaining wives, giving daughters to husbands, and how to deal with adulteress wives and wayward daughters. Wisdom is personified as a women so that men can hear her call. Male off-spring are preferred over female, male circumcision is the mark of being in covenant with God, Jesus chose 12 male disciples, women are commanded by Paul of Tarsus to remain silent in the congregations. These are merely a few examples of the overt patri-archy in biblical literature which articulate man as the first sex and woman as the second, the clear 'other' from whom he can clearly differentiate himself. Reformist feminists have questioned whether patriarchy is an essential part of the biblical tradi-tion. As we have observed, for Mary Daly and other radical feminists, patriarchy lies at the core of its identity, and by extension, the identities of religions of the Bible. For the reformists, however, it was deemed possible to dig beneath the layers of patriarchy and expose a 'depatriarchalised' text (Trible 1978), and find the liberating essence of biblical theology (Ruether 1983). In the Jewish tradition, the feminist scholar Judith Plaskow interprets the Exodus community as a dynamic, time-less phenomenon that goes beyond the time-bound historical moments of patriarchal societies and allows the religion to be radically inclusive of women and men (1990). The reformist agenda echoes that of the first-wave pioneer, Elizabeth Cady Stanton:

> The canon law, the Scriptures, the creeds and codes and church discipline of the leading religions bear the impress of fallible man, and not of our ideal great first cause, 'the Spirit of all Good,' that set the universe of matter and mind in motion, and by immutable law holds the land, the sea, the planets, revolving round the great centre of light and heat, each in its own elliptic, with millions of stars in harmony all singing together, the glory of creation forever and ever. (1985: 13)

Third-Wave Feminism

There is no hard and fast division between second-wave and third-wave feminism in the area of biblical hermeneutics. It is interesting to note the conscious decision to entitle one of the volumes that marked the centenary of the publication Elizabeth Cady Stanton's *Woman's Bible*, the *Women's Bible Commentary*. As the editors, Carol Newsom and Sharon Ringe, put it in their Introduction:

> whereas she [Stanton] entitled her work the 'Woman's Bible', we have chosen the plural, 'Women's Bible'. The reason for this is our recognition of the diversity among women who read the bible and study it. There is no single' woman's perspective' but a rich variety of insight that comes from the different ways in which women's experience is shaped by culture, class, ethnicity, religious community, and other aspects of social identity. (1992: xv)

If we measure the difference between the second-wave and third-wave feminism, crudely but concisely in terms of essentialism versus relativism in relation to women's experience/s, then the two positions have co-existed since the late 1980s and continue to do so at the present time. Not only are they concurrent but they are at times confused. Fiorenza, for example, can on the one hand state, 'feminist theologians must no longer articulate wo/men's identity in essentialist universalistic terms' (1995b: 188). But at the same time she universalizes the 'struggle for liberation' so that it becomes an abstract rather than concrete reality. Catherine Keller is particularly critical of Fiorenza's positioning; pointing out that her use of imperatives in writing could be construed as one 'kyriarchy' replacing another (1997: 73). For many women, the term 'feminist' is exclusivist and remains the currency of white middle-class Western women. As Keller points out, 'While she [Fiorenza] like other U.S. feminists prefers "feminist" as a political-epistemological term to "women" with its potential biologism, the women of color to whom they appeal against other white feminists prefer "women's movement" to feminism' (1997: 70).

Jacquelyn Grant epitomized the critique of second-wave feminism with the title of her book *White Women's Christ and Black Women's Jesus*, where she argues that:

The significance of Christ (for black women) is not his maleness, but his humanity. The most significant events of Jesus Christ were the life and ministry, the crucifixion, and the resurrection. The significance of these events, in one sense, is that in them the absolute becomes concrete. (1989: 220)

Grant's standpoint here is 'womanist' rather than 'feminist', a position defined, seriously and, at the same time, playfully, by Alice Walker as:

1 . . . From *womanish* . . . from the black folk expression of mothers to female children, 'You acting womanish,' i.e., like a woman. Usually referring to outrageous, audacious, courageous or *willful* behaviour . . .

. . . *Also* A woman who loves other women, sexually, and/or nonsexually. Appreciates and prefers women's culture, women's emotional flexibility, . . . and women's strength. Sometimes loves individual men, sexually and/or nonsexually. Committed to survival and wholeness of entire people, male *and* female. Not a separatist, except periodically, for health . . .

. . . Womanist is to feminist as purple to lavender. (1984: xi–xii)

The womanist positions are juxtaposed to the exclusivist position of many second-wave feminists, secular and non-secular, epitomized in the position taken by the radical feminist Mary Daly who at one and the same time universalizes woman's experience and diagnoses it as oppression from patriarchy, and its cure, liberation from patriarchy by means of separationist tactics, in every sphere, from spirituality to sexuality. Dolores Williams is very sceptical about how convincing a white middle-class woman's critique of patriarchy can be:

It is silent about the positive boons patriarchy has bestowed upon many white women, for example, college education; the skills and credentials to walk into jobs the civil rights movements obtained for women; in some cases the *choice* to stay at home and raise children and/or develop a career – *and* to hire another woman (usually a black one) to 'help out' in either case. (1993: 185)

The heroes of biblical narrative for womanist theologians reflect their bias and their awareness of 'triple oppression' through being part of the underclass, poor and female. The story of Hagar, from the Hebrew Bible has been foregrounded by these writers:

Hagar's and Ishmael's life-situation was like that of black female slaves and their children. Like Hagar they experienced harsh treatment from slave mistresses. Slave women were raped by slave masters. Slave masters fathered children by slave women, and then disclaimed and sold them away to other plantations. (ibid.: 193)

While there are clear points of identification between the biblical narrative on Hagar and black slavery contexts, what are lacking, as Williams points out, in any credible exegesis of Hagar's story, are the resources to develop a positive vision of a productive quality of life (ibid.: 193):

When our principle is God's word of survival and quality of life to oppressed communities (or families) living in a diaspora, we put different emphasis upon biblical texts and identify with different biblical stories. (ibid.: 194)

For Williams, a vision such as that described by the prophet Jeremiah (29:4–7) offers a 'survival and quality of life' paradigm that is more liberating than that found in the Hagar story. Through the mouth of Jeremiah God commands the captive Jews in Babylon to build houses, plant gardens, build extended families, and most importantly, 'seek the welfare of the city where I have sent you into exile, and pray to the Lord on its behalf, for in its welfare you will find your welfare' (Jer. 29:7). In contrast to Hagar and Ishmael, these exiles can exercise autonomy, they are not totally dependent on an 'other', albeit God, for their survival.

Biblical exegesis executed from a womanist hermeneutical standpoint reveals the fragmentation of the notion of women's experience. Just as there can be no monolithic 'woman's movement', neither can womanism speak for all non-first world women. Asian women and Hispanic women have found their own voices, and foreground texts that resonate with their standpoint. The Asian feminist theologian, Chung Hyun Kyung, for example, offers an exegesis of the figure of Mary of Nazareth that reveals her perpetual virginity, not as a passive state of being, but as a sign of her empowerment, 'Virginity lies in her true connectedness to her own self and to God. It is an inner attitude, not a psychological or external fact.' And thus, 'when a woman defines herself according to her own understanding of who she really is and what she is meant for in this universe (and not according to the rules and norms of patriarchy), she is a virgin' (1990: 77). These words are reminiscent in the existentialism of Carter Heyward's theology of connectedness, or relationality (see above), although using the oneness of Christ/Christa rather than Mary, which must start with the self and then work for others.

For many womanist writers, patriarchy cannot be seen purely as the woman's enemy, it is also the enemy of oppressed black men, or any man disempowered by oppressive systems that subvert his identity and autonomy. While it can be clearly understood why feminist biblical and theological scholarship has clustered around particular issues and texts, this has worked to restrict the scope of contemporary feminist theology, and, at times, blinded it from asking more searching questions as to why certain texts do in fact challenge the boundaries. Phyllis Trible describes a 'depatriarchalized' Bible (1973) that presumes an a-cultural level of existence for biblical texts – or rather, certain texts. There is a level of meaning, according to Trible, that transcends the culture in which it was produced, and in which it was transmitted. This level of meaning exists in a space that can only exist, can only be explained, at the level of faith. It is contingent on the reader's particular situation within a community of faith, and in that acknowledged space it is a reality, but obviously it is not a universal one. For those outside the community of faith there can be no 'depatriarchalized' Bible – however large or small that imagined text might be. When we stand outside that community of reformist feminist believers, and ask why these texts challenge patriarchal boundaries, we may not conclude with Trible that they are the challenge of a 'depatriarchalized' god, but rather they are the ultimate finesse of a very patriarchal god.

The essentially patriarchal nature of biblical texts has long been identified, although opinion still divides on the question of what might be recovered or 'depatriarchalized' for those with a reformist feminist theological agenda. Feminist critique has uncovered many examples of narratives where biblical writers have employed female characters for pragmatic purposes – often to underline the omniscient power of the deity. In narratives that allow pre-eminence to particular women, male characters can be denigrated to positions of powerlessness. In the biblical context where male supremacy is assumed, this process of emasculation functions to destabilize the audience's expectations, and allows the author to apply the surprise tactic of a male deity using female vehicles to ensure his plan is accomplished. Narratives employing this tactic include the account of Sarah, Hagar and Abraham; Rebecca and Isaac; Rachel and Jacob; Tamar and Judah; Naomi, Ruth and Boaz. And this theme carries on into the apocryphal literature, presenting us with the supreme example: Judith and Holoferenes. It is discernible also in early Christian texts where the male disciples are outshone by the faith of the women around Jesus. Even – or especially – the account of the first couple in paradise allows for such a reading. Biblical scholars have revealed how the recurring theme of overturning primogeniture characterizes the story of Genesis, and this process is usually abetted by female collusion. Furthermore, these consistent key moments of female empowerment characterize not only Genesis, but also stories throughout the Jewish and Christian canons and apocryphal texts.

When contemporary gender theory is applied to this particular theme within biblical literature, it becomes evident that both masculinity and femininity have been destabilized within the patriarchal framework, and not with the intention to undermine this world-view, but rather to reinforce it. The supreme manifestation of patriarchy – the power of the male god – is triumphant and remains assured. Mere male mortals can be ridiculed in this scheme in the service of this higher purpose.

This widening of the lens, and the move towards relativism have taken feminist theology out of an academic ghetto as well as breathing fresh air into Western academia. Women's studies have become gender studies, but what must not be forgotten is that without the hermeneutical battles having been fought by feminists on the grounds of bias versus objectivity, acceptable exegesis carried out through the male gaze on historical grounds would have remained normative for the academy. The variety of standpoints represented at the Annual General Meetings of the Society of Biblical Literature today stands as testimony to those battles won.

References

Anderson, P. S. (1998). *A Feminist Philosophy of Religion*. Oxford: Blackwell.

Brooten, B. J. (1982). *Women Leaders in the Ancient Synagogue: Inscriptional Evidence and Background Issues* (Brown Judaic Studies). Atlanta, GA: Scholars Press.

Brooten, B. J. (1985). 'Early Christian Women and Their Cultural Context: Issues of Method in Historical Reconstruction', in A. Y. Collins (ed.), *Feminist Perspectives on Biblical Scholarship*. Chico, CA: Scholars Press.

Chopp, R. S. and Davaney, S. G. (eds) (1997). *Horizons in Feminist Theology: Identity, Traditions, and Norms*. Minneapolis, MN: Fortress Press.

Clines, D. J. A. (1990). *What Does Eve Do to Help? And Other Readerly Questions to the Old Testament*. Sheffield: Sheffield Academic Press.

Collins, A. Y. (ed.) (1985). *Feminist Perspectives on Biblical Scholarship*. Chico, CA: Scholars Press.

Daly, M. (1973). *Beyond God the Father: Toward a Philosophy of Women's Liberation*. Boston, MA: Beacon Press.

Daly, M. (1975). 'The Qualitative Leap beyond Patriarchal Religion', *Quest (Women and Spirituality)* 1: 20–40.

D'Angelo M. R. (1992). '*Abba* and "Father": Imperial Theology and the Jesus Traditions', *Journal of Biblical Literature* 111(4): 611–30.

Evans, M. (1983). *Woman in the Bible*. Exeter: Paternoster Press.

Fiorenza, E. Schüssler (1982). 'Feminist Theology and New Testament Interpretation', *Journal for the Study of the Old Testament* 22: 32–46.

Fiorenza, E. Schüssler (1993). *Discipleship of Equals: A Critical Feminist Ekklesia-logy of Liberation*. London: SCM Press.

Fiorenza, E. Schüssler (ed.) (1994). *Searching the Scriptures*, vol. 1: *A Feminist Introduction*, vol. 2: *A Commentary*. New York: Crossroad.

Fiorenza, E. Schüssler ([1983] 1995a). *In Memory of Her: A Feminist Theological Reconstruction of Christian Origins*, 2nd edn. London: SCM Press.

Fiorenza, E. Schüssler (1995b). *Jesus: Miriam's Child, Sophia's Prophet: Critical Issues in Feminist Christology*. London: SCM Press.

Goldenberg, Naomi R. (1979). *Changing of the Gods: Feminism and the End of Traditional Religions*. Boston: Beacon Press.

Gössmann, E. (1999). 'The Image of God and the Human Being in Women's Counter-Tradition', in D. F. Sawyer and D. M. Collier (eds), *Is There a Future for Feminist Theology?* Sheffield: Sheffield Academic Press, pp. 26–56.

Grant, J. (1989). *White Women's Christ and Black Women's Jesus: Feminist Christology and Womanist Response*. Atlanta, GA: Scholars Press.

Grey, M. (1990). *Feminism, Redemption, and the Christian Tradition*. Mystic, CT: Twenty-Third Publications.

Heyward, I. C. (1989). *Speaking of Christ: A Lesbian Feminist Voice*. New York: Pilgrim Press.

Keller, C. (1997). 'Seeking and Sucking: On Relation and Essence in Feminist Theology', in R. S. Chopp and S. G. Davaney (eds), *Horizons in Feminist Theology: Identity, Traditions, and Norms*. Minneapolis, MN: Fortress Press.

Kyung, Chung Hyun (1990) *Struggle to be the Sun Again: Introducing Asian Women's Theology*. Maryknoll, NY: Orbis.

Lorde, A. (1983). 'An Open Letter to Mary Daly', in C. Moraga and G. Anzaldúa (eds), *This Bridge Called My Back: Writings by Radical Women of Color*. New York: Kitchen Table, Women of Color Press, pp. 94–7.

Martin, D. B. (1995). *The Corinthian Body*. New Haven, CT: Yale University Press.

McFague, S. (1982). *Metaphorical Theology: Models of God in Religious Language*. London: SCM Press.

Newsom, C. A. and Ringe, S. H. (eds) (1992). *The Women's Bible Commentary*. London: SPCK.

Plaskow, J. (1990). *Standing Again at Sinai: Judaism from a Feminist Perspective*. San Francisco: HarperCollins.

Plaskow, J. (1994). 'Anti-Judaism in Feminist Christian Interpretation', in E. Schüssler Fiorenza (ed.), *Searching the Scriptures*, vol. 1: *A Feminist Introduction*. London: SCM Press, pp. 117–29.

Ruether, R. R. (1983). *Sexism and God-Talk: Towards a Feminist Theology*. London: SCM Press.

Ruether, R. R. (1985). *Womanguides: Readings Toward a Feminist Theology*. Boston: Beacon Press.

Sawyer, D. F. (1992). 'Resurrecting Eve?', in P. Morris and D. F. Sawyer (eds), *A Walk in the Garden: Biblical, Iconographical and Literary Images of Eden*. Sheffield: Sheffield Academic Press, pp. 273–89.

Sawyer, D. F. (1996). *Women and Religion in the First Christian Centuries*. London: Routledge.

Sawyer, D. F. (2002). *God, Gender and the Bible*. London: Routledge.

Sawyer, D. F. and Collier D. M. (eds) (1999). *Is There a Future for Feminist Theology?* Sheffield: Sheffield Academic Press.

Stanton, E. C. (1985–98). *The Woman's Bible Part 1 and Part 2*. New York: European Publishing Company. Abridged edition (1985) Edinburgh: Polygon Books.

Trible, P. (1973) 'Depatriarchalizing in the Biblical Tradition', *Journal of the American Academy of Religion* 41: 30–48.

Trible, P. (1978). *God and the Rhetoric of Sexuality*. Philadelphia, PA: Fortress Press.

Trible, P. (1984). *Texts of Terror*. Philadelphia, PA: Fortress Press.

Walker, A. (1984). *In Search of Our Mothers' Gardens*. London: Women's Press.

Williams, D. S. (1993). *Sisters in the Wilderness*. Maryknoll, NY: Orbis.

CHAPTER 28
Nationalism

Jo Carruthers

Because the nation-state is for many synonymous with secularism, it is therefore presumed to be inherently antithetical to religion. The enacting of a law against 'conspicuous' religious items in French schools in 2004 has been seen as the fulfilling of France's commitment to secularism as constituted in the laws separating state and religion in 1905. For many theorists the very definition of what constitutes a 'nation-state' is precisely this distancing of secondary facets of identity in the attempt to create an authentic citizenship, what Benedict Anderson has termed 'deep, horizontal comradeship' (1995: 7). What makes the 'nation-state' differ from the more loose term of 'nation' is that it is an identity that is defined by being a 'state', an entity governed by an unbiased system of administration that enacts the rational principles of equal rights for each individual.

For a theorist such as Anderson, as well as other leading figures like Ernest Gellner and Eric Hobsbawm, nationalism becomes a signal of the renunciation of religion in its embracing of Enlightenment, rational norms for the construction of society. 'Modernist' theorists of nationalism – what Anthony D. Smith calls the 'dominant orthodoxy in the field' (1998: xii) – date it to the French Revolution, a time, Smith explains, that the modernists see as 'marking the moment when nationalism was introduced into the movement of world history. It was then that the ideal of the sovereignty of the people was fused with the drive to cultural homogeneity, to forge self-determining nations of co-cultural citizens' (1999a: 6). As such, nationalism is distanced from religious influence and located in a rationalist era, becoming its very epitome. The assumption at the heart of such theorizing is that religion is – and encourages – archaic forms of community groupings because it is itself, at heart, very unmodern. Liah Greenfeld, although not a modernist, also places the rational, modern nation-state at odds with religion. Like many other historians and theorists, she sets the beginnings of nationalism at the English Civil War, but regards the use of the Bible and religious discourse as merely a tool – a language 'in which they could express the novel consciousness of nationality' (1992: 52). Her conclusion – that pushes religion out of the realm of national thinking – is that 'it was only natural that at the time of the centrality of religion in every sphere of social existence, nascent nationalism was clothed in religious idiom' (ibid.: 63).

For Greenfeld, religion is merely apparel that has contributed nothing to the core of national thinking. This separation of religion and nationalism is only possible, however, if religious discourse can be conceived as co-existing alongside the emergent discourse and logic of nationalism and democracy in hermetic coherence. However, religious discourse never exists in a pure form separate from cultural influences; moreover, religious conviction, assumptions and logic were especially intrinsic to seventeenth-century thinking, the era to which Greenfeld dates the nascent nation-state. Christopher Hill, perhaps the most prominent historian of the seventeenth century, is at pains to reiterate in his book, *The English Bible and the Seventeenth-Century Revolution*, that 'the vernacular Bible became an institution in Tudor England' and it 'was, or should be, the foundation of all aspects of English culture' (1993: 4, 7). Logically, therefore, Adrian Hastings insists on the inclusion of religion within the discussion of nation, ethnicity and nationalism: 'These four are, moreover, so intimately linked that it is impossible, I would maintain, to write the history of any of them at all adequately without at least a fair amount of discussion of the other three' (1997: 1).

The equating of nationalism with modernity (and the subsequent distancing of religious influence) has been challenged in more recent years, not least by theories of diaspora and globalization that undermine the assumption that it is, exclusively, the nation-state, as conceived in the eighteenth century, that is the ideal model for modernity. These theories contest the neat fit between parochial nationalism and a rationally structured society (see Bauman 2004; Boyarin and Boyarin 2002). In suggesting that global conceptions of identity may be more suitable bedfellows of the modern era, Hastings undermines any unquestioning fusion of the nation-state and modernity:

> The nation-state does not inherently belong to modernity and if Britain, for long the prototype of modernity, pioneered the nation-state, it also pioneered the non-national world empire . . . Indeed it may be the political reality of Britain's global empire which looks in another fifty years' time more like the real prototype for the political restructuring of modernity. (1997: 6–7)

On closer inspection, the insistence on the modernity of the 'nation-state' does seem doubtful, especially because in many of its modern forms, nationalism often seems more archaic than modern.

The neat fit between nationalism, modernism and secularity espoused by the modernist theorists of nation-states has nonetheless started to unravel. Returning to the image with which I opened this chapter, the move to ban 'conspicuous' religious symbols from schools in France may be generated by a desire to impose secularism, but has been received by much of the Muslim community as discriminatory. Despite the rationalist nation-state representing itself as a defender of individual rights and freedoms, secularism has nevertheless failed some of its citizens. Perhaps the problem lies in a secularism that imposes homogeneity in the public realm and thus banishes religious identity to the private, a move that at heart assumes the polarity of rationalism and religion. For example, Julia Kristeva's (1993) evocation of secularist France as a promise of equality is one that sets the sacred against the rational, dismissing it as a quality inherently antithetical to the nation-state:

> the French national idea, which draws its inspiration from the Enlightenment and is embodied in the French Republic, is achieved in a *legal and political pact* between free and equal individuals. If it be true that it thus causes the *sacred* to be absorbed by the *national* identified with the *political*, it does not do so only to ensure the most rational conditions for the development of capitalism, but also and above all to put forward its dynamics towards accomplishing the rights of man. (ibid.: 40)

A convincing challenge to this assumption has come from Jacques Derrida, a critic from a similar philosophical tradition to Kristeva, who instead insists upon the inherent religiosity of the rational: 'the imperturbable and interminable development of critical and techno-scientific reason, far from opposing religion, bears, supports and supposes it'. Furthering his project of undermining the presumptions of Western metaphysics, he breaks down the assumed radical disparity between religion and reason which, he argues, 'develop in tandem, drawing from this common resource: the testimonial pledge of every performative, committing it to respond as much *before* the other as *for* the high-performance performativity of technoscience' (1998: 28). Thus at the heart of reason – of language and of all communication in fact – lies the fiduciary: 'belief, trustworthiness or fidelity, the fiduciary, "trust" in general, the tribunal of faith' (ibid.: 29). He concludes:

> in principle, today, there is no incompatibility, in the said 'return of the religious', between the 'fundamentalisms', the 'integrisms' or their 'politics' and, on the other hand, rationality, which is to say the tele-techno-capitalistico-scientific fiduciarity, in all of its mediatic and globalizing dimensions. (ibid.: 45)

The faith, the fiduciary, that lies at the heart of rationality thus draws religion and the nation closer than modernist critics consider possible. Belief is thus

> an idiom that is above all inseparable from the social nexus, from the political, familial, ethnic, communitarian nexus, from the nation and from the people: from autochthony, blood and soil, and from the ever more problematic relationship to citizenship and to the state. In these times, language and nation form the historical body of all religious passion. (ibid.: 4)

Conceptually, then, the nation and religion perhaps have more in common than modernist theorists are comfortable with admitting. On a more practical level, the conceptual distancing of rationalism from religion results in clearly discriminatory actions such as the banning of 'conspicuous' religious symbols from the supposedly secular educational environment. Returning to Kristeva, such an action can be defended because practices such as 'religion, sexual, moral and educational' differences are banished to the private realm, while the 'neutrality of educational, medical and similar spheres' means that the expressions of such 'private' practices must give way to the '*esprit général*' (1993: 61–2). Although not commenting directly on the banning of Muslim headscarves here, Kristeva's viewpoint nonetheless reveals the problem at the heart of such legislation. By equating neutrality with secularism, Kristeva ignores that the secular is inherently antithetical to religion: it is by no means neutral. As such, secularity does not encourage equality but merely relegates the (religious) differences between individuals away from view – the very differences that are the basis for the need for equality legislation (the two entities on either side of an 'equal' sign are rarely identical).

Nevertheless, there are undeniable connections between modernity and nationalism that have served to simplify, in many theorists' minds, the complex (and often contradictory) factors that contribute to the construction and perpetuity of nation-states. Key theorists of nationalism who have insisted on the importance of understanding nationalism's roots in religious discourse include A. D. Smith and Adrian Hastings. Smith has traced the sense of mission at the heart of the nation-state to religious discourse: 'The idea of a chosen people', he asserts, 'is an essentially religious concept' (1999b: 335). These theorists give more emphasis to the heritages, the leftovers, from the pasts of nation-states and maintain that any undue neglect of such legacies distorts our understanding of the logic and rationale of nationalist thinking. Smith insists that the 'expression of the ideals of a national mission and national destiny among so many peoples', 'attests to the continuing role of pre-modern ties, sentiments and symbols in the modern world, and the way in which modernization has revitalized those ties and sentiments' (ibid.: 351). He traces this specifically back to the narrative of Israel (as do Hastings and Kohn), a key contributor to emergent nationalist rationales that has been neglected in much mainstream theorizing. Hastings insists:

> The specific root of nationalism does not lie in the circumstances of post-Enlightenment modernity. On the contrary. It lies rather in the impact of the Bible, of vernacular literature and of the two combined in creating a politically stable ethnicity, effectively 'imagined' by its members across a unique mythology. (1997: 151)

He goes on to insist: 'Nation-formation and nationalism have in themselves almost nothing to do with modernity' (ibid.: 205).

Although Anderson dates the emergence of the nation-state to the eighteenth century and rational Enlightenment (conveniently side-stepping the issue of religion's place in emerging nationalism), he nevertheless recognizes the debt to the past that nation-states owe. However, unlike Hastings and Smith, he sees the role of the nation-state as inhabiting a space left by the death of religion; religion metamorphoses into the nation-state:

> With the ebbing of religious belief, the suffering which belief in part composed did not disappear. Disintegration of paradise: nothing makes fatality more arbitrary. Absurdity of salvation: nothing makes another style of continuity more necessary. What then was required was a secular transformation of fatality into continuity, contingency into meaning. As we shall see, few things were [are] better suited to this end than the idea of nation. If nation-states are widely conceived to be 'new' and 'historical', the nations to which they give political expression always loom out of an immemorial past. (1995: 19)

While it is true that nationalism assumes a mythic role in an individual's life that resembles the part religion plays – bringing continuity and meaning – Anderson's pronouncement of the death of religion is, to say the least, exaggerated. The waning of religious belief as *the* core component of political construction does not equate with the disappearance of religious belief from political life. As Bauman affirms: 'The modern mind was not necessarily atheistic . . . What the modern mind did, however, was to make God irrelevant to human business on earth' (2004: 72). Although the modern nation-state has in most cases separated state and religious institutions, Anderson assumes an homogeneity of belief across that state that certainly does not fit the composition of England, even since the eighteenth century. Rather, religious conviction continued to influence politics in significant ways: religious belief still played a huge role in the composition of parliament as well as in many political decisions.

Anderson neglects the more tangible links between nationalism and religion: the latter does not merely fill the space left empty by the former, although some transition is evident. Rather, nationalism owes much of its narrative and rationale to essentially religious concepts that are then never fully banished even by the most virulent of secularisms. Tracing the nation-state and nationalism to its religious roots in the biblical narrative of Israel is not claiming a consistent and explicit religious element. Rather, it reveals that the specific mythic constituency of nation-states are indebted to religious narrative and that nation-states and nationalisms retain more than a residue of a religious savour. As Ernest Renan claims, writing from within the ultra-secular French nation: 'A nation is a soul, a spiritual principle' (1990: 19).

Kohn, in his *The Idea of Nationalism*, an early and influential study, identifies three main ideas that Jewish thinking as expressed in the Bible has contributed to nationalism: 'the idea of the chosen people, the consciousness of national history, and the national Messianism' (1945: 36). The concept of chosen people is also for Smith – one of the most prominent theorists of nationalism – central to the character of the nation-state and contributes to the endurance of nationalist doctrine. Its essentially religious character provides much that rationalism cannot: it confers on a group 'a sense of their moral superiority over outsiders' and endows them with hope that their 'hitherto lowly or marginal status' will be reversed as well as hardening the boundaries between the group and outsiders (1999b: 336–7). Even Kristeva recognizes the heritage of what she calls 'a sacred nationalism' as residing in the 'alliance with God' that 'constitutes the Jewish people as a chosen nation' (1993: 23). Kohn also traces to Hebrew society a sense of nascent democracy, unique among ancient monarchical cultures, that emerges from the Bible, the legislation of which 'was animated by constant care and consideration for the dignity of every member of the people and for brotherly relations among them' (1945: 28).

Adrian Hastings has published perhaps the most detailed account of the influence of the Bible on nationalism in his *The Construction of Nationhood*. His claims for the importance of the Bible are great: 'Without it and its Christian interpretation and implementation, it is arguable that nations and nationalism, as we know them could never have existed . . . Biblical Christianity . . . undergirds the cultural and political world out of which the phenomena of nationhood and nationalism as a whole developed' (1997: 4). It is not merely religion, in Hastings' view, that constructs a sense of a 'chosen people' but the Christian interpretation of biblical narrative that evokes nationalism:

> Islam advances trade, education and even state-formation as well as monotheism and reli-
> gious devotion but it does not advance nations or national languages. On the contrary its
> specific socio-cultural impact, noticeable throughout Africa, is to draw people into a single,
> far more universalist, community whose sole language of direct encouragement is Arabic
> and whose consciousness is fuelled by pilgrimage to Mecca. Every genuine example of
> nation-construction one can find in Africa seems dependent upon Christianity and bibli-
> cal translation, never upon Islam. (1997: 158)

If nationalism owes its existence to the Bible, then, why did nationalism only emerge in the early modern period when the Bible – and Israel – had been around for over a millennium? Why did nationalism emerge at this time and place and why did the Bible generate such new perspectives on national identity?

The first group to take the biblical model to heart was England and so the answer to these questions is necessarily contained within its history. The context of the English Reformation seemed to have been the perfect climate for the propagation of biblical nationhood. The presence of the new vernacular Bible in this newly and virulently Protestant country enabled the emergence of a horizontalist and autonomous national identity, at least in its most embryonic of forms. As Christopher Hill explains:

> the seventeenth century was a crucial turning-point in the evolution of England from a
> monarchy which structurally had much in common with the great absolutisms of the con-
> tinent – though far weaker – into a state in which power resided with a parliament repre-
> sentative of the propertied classes. (1990: 20)

England has not been the only nation to have read its identity in the pages of the Old Testament (see examples later in the chapter) but it is perhaps one of the most impor-tant because of the influence it has had on later conceptions and practices of nation-alism and nationhood. Timothy Brennan characterizes nationalistic thought in the English Civil War as the consciousness of 'individual liberty', as expressed in Milton, that then 'found its way through the French *philosophes* of North America, where it raised its head in the form of attacks on authoritarianism, censorship and the stran-gling of free trade' (1990: 52). This exporting – or what Anderson calls 'pirating' – of national identity has become almost all-pervasive with Western nationalism providing the primary model for postcolonial states. Although recognizing England's heritage, Brennan ignores the imaginative birthplace of Milton's virulent nationalism: the pages of the Bible which directly influence English and American forms of nationalism, as well as indirectly those secular nationalisms epitomized by the French Revolution. Peter Van der Veer traces the influence of Western practices, which he claims 'are partly rooted in Christianity', on Eastern nationalisms. His study claims that the presence of modern-day Hinduism and Hindu nationalism is the result of the imposition of 'reli-gion' and 'nation' – both Western concepts – onto a more heterogeneous group iden-tity. The nationalist impetus of Hinduism evident in India this century is, he claims, 'not quite a rhetoric of "chosen people", but to the extent that it is, this is the result of the influence of both Orientalism and Christianity' (1999: 430).

The Bible's influence on early modern England's short-lived republic is not surprising: over a million Bibles were sold in England between the Reformation and 1640 (Hill 1993: 8). Its contents are easily mined for narratives that resemble what we now know as nationalism. Its Old Testament compellingly dramatized the history of God's people – the nation of Israel – through tribulations and victories:

> The Bible . . . presented in Israel itself a developed model of what it means to be a nation – a unity of people, language, religion, territory and government. Perhaps it was an almost terrifyingly monolithic ideal, productive ever after of all sorts of dangerous fantasies, but it was there, an all too obvious exemplar for Bible readers of what every other nation too might be, a mirror for national self-imagining. (Hastings 1997: 18)

Protestantism saturated England with this narrative, but it was the context of England itself that resulted in the nascent nation-state of Civil War England. The newly fragmented world following the schism of England from Rome resulted in fears of invasion. A more defensive mentality and the desire for autonomy and continuity made the epic of Israel a narrative that became a welcome explanation for the current turbulence. The conditions were perfect for the creation of a new way of conceiving of the self in nationalist horizontalist terms as opposed to the subjection of monarchy. Although overestimating the climate of toleration and ignoring the radically politicized nature of Puritanism, Kohn reads the Civil War as nationalism's birthplace:

> There in the civil war of the seventeenth century, in the first great surge of nationalism which embraced a whole people, religion was depoliticized and deterritorialized; religious tolerance was established, as was the supremacy of Parliament over the king. There the individualism of the Reformation asserted itself against authoritarianism, and the foundations were laid for a new epoch into which essential elements of Renaissance and Reformation were transformed and incorporated, an epoch whose light was to dawn upon the Continent only in the eighteenth century. (1945: 125)

The economic and technological changes in early modern England were clearly constituent of the increased nationalist impetus. Due to the printing press, the growing dissemination of texts across England in the fifteenth and sixteenth centuries made the English language – and as a result, England – a centripetal force for the construction of English identity. Hastings concurs: 'Once an ethnicity's vernacular becomes a language with an extensive living literature of its own, the Rubicon on the road to nationhood appears to have been crossed' (1997: 12) The emergence of a horizontality of self-conception is the result of a community of readers: 'fellow-readers, to whom they were connected through print, formed, in their secular, particular, visible invisibility, the embryo of the nationally imagined community' (Anderson 1995: 44). In the seventeenth century, the book that this visible–invisible community was reading was the Bible. Its influence on the minds and lives of the English at this time was massive, not only for its content but also because the influx of the printed vernacular in England had a huge influence on the status of this language. As Christopher Hill explains, the prevalence and authority of this book were hugely important 'in asserting the supremacy of the English language', in a country that for the previous four centuries had been dominated by Norman French (1993: 7).

Despite her hostility to the Bible's influence upon English nationalism, many qualities that Greenfeld cites as being essential to the emerging national consciousness parallel changes in Christian religion itself: it seems that Protestantism, nascent capitalism and nascent nationalism went hand in hand. Greenfeld cites concepts central to nationalist thinking – free and equal citizenship, the belief 'in man as an active, essentially rational being' – that are characteristic of the new Protestantism, a religion emerging from the margins of society and proclaiming equal access to God for all. As Linda Colley states in her study of British national identity, *Britons: Forging the Nation 1707–1837* (2003), Protestantism was central to the new nationalistic concepts of individual liberty: 'they still had access to the word of God in a way (they believed) that Roman Catholics did not, and for this reason, if for no other, Protestants, even the poorest of them, were free men' (2003: 42). Hill also sees Protestantism as invoking democratic principles: 'The logic of Protestantism called social hierarchy into question. In the 1530s some of Thomas Cromwell's protégés preached the equality of man and advocated a career open to the talents. Under Oliver Cromwell these doctrines were put into practice' (1990: 50). Even Greenfeld herself concedes that the Reformation was 'perhaps the most significant among the factors that furthered the development of the English national consciousness' (1992: 84). The attitudes of the rulers of England in the seventeenth century witness to precisely the democratic principles that were eked from the Bible at this time. Interpretation was often helped along in the Protestant Bibles with marginal notes. James I, for example, thought the Geneva Bible's notes were seditious because they suggested that in the case of the Egyptian midwives, 'disobedience herein was lawful' (Exod. 1:19) (Hill 1993: 60).

Hans Kohn locates these 'democratic' impulses in the Bible's representation of Israel:

> The attitude towards kingship and kingly power is one of the most characteristic traits of the Bible. Here the roots of later democracy can be found in the feeling of equality and common destiny of the whole people, a feeling at first limited to the members of the group and denied to outsiders, barbarians or gentiles. (1945: 28)

Although Israel was, for much of the biblical narrative, a monarchy, the people's request for a king is depicted in the Bible as a choice of an inferior monarchy over a superior theocracy. A humanly hierarchical society is by no means the model that the Bible portrays. Rather, the hierarchy it encourages is one of God above a 'nation of priests'. As well as espousing proto-democratic principles, the Bible also presents a nation with a shared history. The God of the Bible is, Kohn claims, the God of the historical deed, and thus:

> the fundamental condition of national consciousness, a common stock of memories of the past and of hopes for the future, which permeates the whole people and determines their mind and aspirations, grew among the Jews for the first time, and was expressed more firmly then ever thereafter. (1945: 34–5)

Kohn also cites the notion of the Covenant as an important one for inspiring a sense of national identity because it 'was not concluded between God and the kings or leaders of the people, but between God and the whole people, every member in complete equality' (ibid.: 37). It thus acts as one example of the distance of Judaism from monarchism: 'The elements of its [Covenant] constitution were one God, one law, one people. No earthly ruler interfered between God and the people' (ibid.: 39).

The unique instance of the emergence of nationalism at so early a date is perhaps due to the prevalence of Calvinist doctrine among the dominant factors in the Civil War. Calvinist doctrine is best known for its emphasis upon predestination, the belief that God has always already preordained who will be saved and who condemned. Because of Calvin's insistence on the inherent sinfulness of humanity and a person's inability to turn to God, salvation is envisaged as a result of God's calling and action. The logical conclusion that Calvin, and his followers, drew was that it was only the elect who could be saved. This notion of a preordained elect – this hierarchy of the chosen few – encourages a sense of cosmic structuring in which individuals (and individual nations) are chosen. This leads very easily to a view that Protestant nations – those that exhibit the signs of being the elect – are elevated because of their chosen state. The *Institutes*, Calvin's hugely influential work, presents the individual's conscience as above monarchical or political demands: 'We are subject to men who rule over us, but subject only in the Lord. If they command anything against Him, let us not pay the least heed to it' (*Institutes* 4.20.32) (Kohn 1945: 136–7).

Early modern Puritan doctrine was also characterized by its intense personalization of biblical interpretation, an emphasis that led the Protestant English to read the Bible as solely applicable to their specific situation, as a story about their very own history. All events are thus viewed through the framework of a omnipotent God who preordains the fates of nations; victory and defeat are thus equally the result of Providence. Speaking of Israel and thus biblical theology, the Jewish historian Martin Sicker explains: 'if these nations, which failed to perceive the true God, were able to defeat Israel, it was only because they were being used as vehicles by the God of all to punish Israel for its perfidy' (1992: 25). Thus, calls for public fasts in England which began in the 1620s and occurred monthly from November 1641 (see Hill 1993: Chapter 3) were recognitions that, precisely because they were (at least in most Puritans' minds) the chosen nation, 'contrition and repentance by the people would still bring about the ultimate redemption of the nation in the land of Israel' – interpreted by the Puritans as the new Israel, England (Sicker 1992: 27).

The English translation of a German Protestant commentary from 1584 and its English-composed Preface illustrates the uniqueness of the English position on national identity and appropriation of the Bible. This commentary juxtaposes a German position, as expressed by John Brentius, alongside an English gloss, by the translator, a schoolmaster, John Stockwood. The commentary is on the Book of Esther: the story of a Jewish girl who becomes queen of the Persian Empire and saves her people from the genocidal attempts of the Persian courtier Haman. Esther thus personifies, in Jewish and Christian religion, a self-sacrifice on behalf of the people of God. In Catholic tradition she is a precursor of Mary – Esther approaches the emperor to save her people, just as Mary acts as an intercessor to Christ, her king, for her people. Although conventionally read in terms of the community of faith, in the late sixteenth century, English appropriations of this book, more often than not, become an assertion of national – not religious – patriotism; an assertion evident in Stockwood's, but not Brentius's, comments on the biblical book. German Protestantism was characterized not by nationalism but by universalism. Salvation was private and was not subject to any earthly barriers. Kohn explains the lack of national fervour in early modern Germany as a result of conservatism: 'Luther's attitude of passivity towards political and social questions led him to an acquiescence in and affirmation of the existing order . . . Salvation, the central problem for him, was strictly an individual concern which could be solved only by faith' (1945: 136). Brentius expresses a conventional opposition towards Jews because they are rejecters of Christ, however prompted by his nationalist impulses, Stockwood reads the story allegorically. The English thus have a closer relationship to the Jews and identities become fused. Linking the details of the Book of Esther to specifics of English society means the line between the Jews and English becomes problematically blurred.

Stockwood's Preface – as long as the translated German commentary itself – is really a second commentary. His conflation of England with the biblical Israel is apparent as he refers to 'the wealth of the church, and wellfare of Israell' (1584: 3), a conflation of the modern Christian Church and the biblical Jewish nation. Thus the Old Testament chosen people are appropriated for Stockwood as they are now prefigurations of the English Church, a new chosen, Protestant, people. He compares the two states, insisting that the current church has urgent responsibilities because of its superior state:

> What excuse then shall those be able to alledge, which hauing the chifest places of credit, and countenance vnder Christian kinges and princes, not in the persecution, but the peace of the Gospell, not in the thraldome, but in the libertie of the church, not in the cloudes of ignorance, and in the darke mist of superstition, but in the cleere light of the trueth, and bright shyning sunne of sincere religion. (1584: 6)

Protestantism is here the 'trueth' and 'sunne of sincere religion' as compared with the ignorance and 'darke' superstition of a redundant Judaism. With chosenness comes responsibility and for Stockwood, the English have no excuses to fail God because they have the 'chifest places of credit'. The application here is not specifically English, but national – those who have no excuse are those who are under Christian kings and princes, a sign of a peculiarly – but not exclusively – chosen state.

Stockwood moves on to discuss persecution and the prevalence of enemies to the true Church – a subject close to Protestants' hearts after the reign of 'bloody' Mary. As a jumping off point, he uses the example of Haman's accusations against the Jews (that results in the king handing over control of the Jews to Haman, and means he can go ahead with his genocidal plans). The wrongful accusations against Jews in the Book of Esther pre-empts his reflections on wrongful accusations against Protestants (and Stockwood wants to highlight this because the explicit purpose of his publishing is to ask Walsingham – to whom the Preface is dedicated and whom Hastings calls 'an anti-Catholic of the most unyielding sort' (1997: 81) – to further protect wrongfully accused Protestants). However, Stockwood is very aware of not wanting to venerate Jews as a people and so quickly moves to remind the reader that Jews after the advent of Christianity are now themselves accusers (of Christ and Christians) and rightfully persecuted for real acts of treason (Elizabeth's Jewish doctor was accused of and executed for attempted poisoning (see, for example, Berek 1998: 149–53)). The Jews are thus discredited for their persecution of Christians in order to emphasize the supersession of Christians over Jews. The hierarchy is established. Stockwood goes on to highlight England as a place of persecution in which godly Protestants had known their share of wrongful accusation in recent years:

> the Iewes, which so often accuse Christ, and his Apostles of sedition, of strange religion and newe doctrine, are in the ende themselues as seditious and rebelles put to the sword and slaughter by the Romane Emperours. But hereof there is I thinke no nation that euer hath had more notable experience, then this little Iland of ours. For whether you looke vnto our godly Ester herselfe, or vnto the chiefe gouernours vnder her, I meane of the common wealth, or of the Church, or whether you looke vnto her poore subjects, which then were as the scattered and dispersed Iewes, the time is not long since, nor the yeres manie, in which not onley one, but diuerse *Amans* occupying the highest roomes as well in the ciuil government, as also in the policie of the Church, accused both our godly *Ester* her selfe, togither with Mordecai, that is such as vnto her then were most deare, and not onely so, but also the rest of the poore Iewes, I meane all such as were knowen to be the true followers of Iesus Christ, of as great crimes, as *Mardocheus* is here charged with, but falsely. (1584: 19–20)

The finely drawn line between the Jews and the English is here blurred as Stockwood not only sympathizes with the 'poore' Jews but also fuses them with Christians: 'I meane all such as were knowen to be the true followers of Iesus Christ'. The reason for this blurring is Stockwood's allegorical reading in order to overwrite the Jews and Israel with England itself. England is special in this logic because of her suffering – no other nation has ever had 'more notable experience' of false accusation and persecution. Embattled and marginal to all who look on, in the divine scheme the English are nevertheless the chosen people precisely because of this persecution. Stockwood's allegory refers to Elizabeth as 'our godly Ester' and '*Mardocheus*' is Walsingham. The enemies, the Catholics, are *Amans* and following this logic the 'true followers of Iesus Christ' are therefore the English, who are also the Jews – a jarring logic. Although tying himself up in knots, Stockwood is here expressing what will become a common practice: reading the stories of the Bible as though they were directly relating to contemporary political practice and more specifically to the nation of England itself.

Brentius, conversely, reads 'the trve Israelites' as 'are as many as beleeue in the seede of Abraham, which is Jesus Christ' (1584: 139). The German Brentius, having a much weaker sense of national identity, is subsumed by his loyalty towards Protestantism. Because his comparison between Israel and the new Israel is a simple passing on of religious identity – not national – Brentius can even demonize the Jews, perversely reading them as a type of Haman:

> For this story perteyneth unto the people and Church of God. But the Iewes, because they have cast of Christ, the true seede of Abraham, they are no more the people, nor his

Church, but they apperteine unto *Ismael*, and *Esau*, who always persecuted the true seede of Abraham. And because that they hate the true Israelites, which are the Christians, with ye same hatred, wher-with *Aman* in times past hated them, it is plain, that they are the coosins and kinred of *Aman* the Amalechite, which nation alwayes with extreme hatred thirsted after the utter distruction of the Israelites. Wherefore so far of is it, that the Iewes which now are, may promise unto themselves any hope of their deliverance, and of the destruction of the Christians, out of this booke, that rather in *Aman* there is extant and remaining a manifest example, that in as much as once they have begun to fall before the Church of Christ, they can never rayse up themselves againe, unless they convert to Christ, who only is our salvation. (1584: 166–7)

Because of the use of a spiritual rather than a national mapping, the Jews in Brentius's taxonomy have been superseded by Christianity and are, in their now unregenerate state, utterly abhorrent, but redeemable through belief in Christ. In Stockwood's paradigm, however, the Jews must remain ancient relics, ambivalent as models and yet inferior to Christianity, so that he can superimpose superior 'Englishness' onto the pages of the Bible. It is necessary that they remain an historical artefact, locked in a binary relationship with English Protestantism, guaranteeing English identity.

It was not only England who interpreted itself in light of biblical narrative. Smith lists an array of groups who have read themselves as being in a special covenantal relationship with God: 'the Armenians, the Copts, the Amharic Monophysites, the Greek and Russian Orthodox, Irish Roman Catholics, Ulster Protestants, Presbyterian Scots, New England Protestants and Afrikaners' (Smith 1999b: 336). Modern 'Israels' share a practice of interpreting contemporary events as the fulfilment of now symbolic Old Testament occurrences. Thus battles and victories are interpreted – and justified – in the light of divine Providence. For Kruger, the leader of the Boers of South Africa in the 1870s, the Great Trek (to escape British rule) and the Battle of Blood River (in which the Boers defeated a key African enemy that enabled them to establish a settlement) were signs of the Afrikaners' chosen status. On their establishment in their new land, they thus made a covenant with God in which their part was to build the new Jerusalem on African soil. The sense of moral and ethnic superiority that they had as the 'chosen people' resulted eventually in the racial apartheid that nationalists effected after 1948 (see Smith 1999a; Templin 1999). Ironically, it is the sense of being an embattled, persecuted minority that engenders this self-interpretation as a chosen people – bringing hope of a reversal of fortunes – but that results in tyranny. Ruled by the British and outnumbered by the Africans, the Afrikaners created themselves as a chosen nation, rightfully ruling over the native inhabitants of what became their new Jerusalem. Interestingly, it is the emphasis upon the Old – not the New – Testament that allows such direct interpretations of Israel without any reference to Christ and more spiritual, less literal, interpretations. J. Alton Templin in his *Ideology on a Frontier* notes that the 'assumption that Christ is prefigured in all Old Testament narratives disappeared' in late nineteenth-century South Africa (cited in Akenson 1992: 61). A Calvinistic doctrine of the elect rationalized the Afrikaners' interpretation of their 'chosenness' as being a responsibility to rule the land. Akenson explains the thinking of Abraham Kuyper (1837–1920), an influential Dutch theologian:

when one is called (elected, or predestined) through particular grace, one gains the ability to see the true order and purpose of God's entire creation. Thus the social and the individual are melded: for it is first an ability, and, now a responsibility, of those who are elected through particular grace to lead the church, the nation, the world in the discovery of the order and law that God had preordained for all creation. The church, both its clergy and laity, acquires the task of leading the nation. (ibid.: 71)

The most obvious use of Israel as a model is in the formation of the State of Israel itself, in 1947. Despite Israel containing only a minority of orthodox believers, the state nevertheless draws upon its mythic past, taking the rationale for its nationalism from the pages of the Bible. As Dan Jacobson explains: 'It is in the very nature of the Jewish state that the Hebrew Scriptures will always be a source of pride and reassurance to its inhabitants, whether they are believers or not. To no other people does the Bible speak so intimately, or in such a directly inspiriting fashion' (1982: 13).

For each of these examples of chosen peoples, Kohn's warning in 1945 seems pertinent:

In the knowledge of a special bond uniting God and His people lies the danger of a possible justification for all arrogance and for an assumed leadership of other peoples. God will place His people above all others. When His people fight, He fights with them; they fight for Him. National greatness and expansion become the duty towards God, are sought for His glorification. All these later ideas of a God-ordained national imperialism originated in one of the possible interpretations of Jewish nationalism. (1945: 38)

This is indeed a danger that has been repeatedly realized. Even in a technically secular context, such as in US foreign policy, the belief in a 'national mission to preserve freedom and democracy' resulted in an impulse to 'follow through her destiny by military intervention' (Smith 1999b: 348). The move from a marginal status that gains strength from being 'chosen' to becoming tyrannical is a short one despite its obvious paradoxes: 'Nationalism is to be justified as an appropriate protest against a universalizing uniformity, dominance by the other, but its consequence is too often precisely the imposition of uniformity, a deep intolerance of all particularities except one's own' (Hastings 1997: 33–4).

But, as Kohn himself acknowledges at the end of the above indented extract, this was only one interpretation of Jewish identity open to interpreters, and more especially open to Protestants. As Hastings insists, 'There is nothing inherently nationalist about Protestantism' (1997: 55). Protestants who read themselves as the chosen Israel did so ignoring that the 'New Testament universalized the idea in a church sent to "all nations" (Matthew 28:19) where there is neither Jew nor Gentile (Galatians 3:28)'. He asks the obvious question: 'How can one get back from that to any sense of a single Christian nation set apart as chosen by God?' (1999: 386). The seeming anomaly of Protestants interpreting the Bible in such a way that makes them its – national – subject is exacerbated by the fact that universalism is even present in the Old Testament. Although Hastings sees universalism as an exclusively New Testament attribute – the Old Testament is instead characterized by chosenness – there are strands of Jewish tradition that see the Hebrew Bible as espousing universalism. Martin Sicker traces the concept of the nation in the Jewish Bible and tradition in his *Judaism, Nationalism, and the Land of Israel* (1992). Throughout the Hebrew Bible, Israel is set apart precisely to be a model to the nations and universal salvation shall come through the Jews:

> according to biblical teaching, Israel is not a natural social phenomenon, but a nation that was deliberately brought into existence for a specific universal purpose, namely, to serve as a national model of a moral community worthy of emulation by the other nations of the world. (ibid.: 19)

He points to Isaiah 2:2–3: 'And it shall come to pass in the end of the days that the mountain of the Lord's house shall be established as the top of the mountains, and shall be exalted above the hills; and all nations shall flow into it.'

The particularity of the Protestant interpretation – that the Bible need not be read in this way – returns us to Hastings's question: 'How can one get back from that to any sense of a single Christian nation set apart as chosen by God?' The answer must be that cultural pressures asserted themselves upon the Protestant readers so that they were inclined towards a nationalistic interpretation – one that emphasized chosenness, moral supremacy, distinctiveness and superiority – rather than a universalist one. Why a specific interpretation is chosen over another has to be reflective of the historical and social context of the readers. The English obviously were not open to the possibility that they could – or rather should – be defeated by the Catholic Spanish, that they should submit to Rome or that they should link themselves to the Continent. Although reading the Bible could have challenged such attitudes – and for some they did – the prejudices in the reader were stronger than the alternatives presented from outside. The influence of the biblical narrative upon nationalism cannot therefore be seen as in any way inevitable, or as intrinsic to the Bible itself. As Hent de Vries asserts, the categories and practices of religion are 'always parasitic upon – and shot through with – notions that resonate with the larger culture' (2002: xi). The situation of the reader and the narrative of the Bible were melted together so that both could co-exist in mutual redefinition: England's impulse for independence and the rising power of the middle classes could be rationalized through a selective retelling of the narrative of the nation of Israel. In such a way, those impulses were both reconciled with the dominant religion as well as ultimately defended by it.

Tracing nationalist impulses back to the pages of the Old Testament does not imply that modern nationalisms are inherently Protestant, but as Smith explains, the stories 'spawned, or were transformed into, strong nationalist ideas' (1999b: 343). What is found in rationales of the nation-state and nationalism, therefore, are residues of religious logic. It should not be surprising, therefore, that the basic characteristics of the nation-state are both utterly representative of modernity and in stark contrast to it. The importance of myth to the stability and continuance of nationalist sensibility – its inherently irrational character – is precisely the consequence of nationalism's roots in a biblical narrative based on a supernatural view of history. The tracing of national identity and its sense of a 'chosen people' to the Bible makes greater sense of the essentially combative sense of the nation: that the nation constructs itself antagonistically through its enemies. The mythic qualities of nationalism are revealed in its dependence upon the creative arts in order to fire and stabilize the imagination. Reflecting the assumptions of a number of theorists, Hastings insists that, 'Nationhood can survive only through an exercise in the imagination, both collective and personal' (1997: 27). Hence, the importance of artistic representations of the nation for national sentiment.

Steven Grosby traces the inherently contradictory impulses at the centre of nationalisms more precisely to specifics of the narrative of Israel. He identifies at the symbolic centre of ancient Israel 'heterogeneous orientations', namely 'primordial' and 'universal' orientations (1999: 362). He explains further that: 'There are the primordial attachments to kinship and land coexisting with the rationalization of both law and religion.' This duality also exists in the unconditional and conditional covenants in the Hebrew Scriptures that on the first-hand emphasize lineage (unconditional commitment to Abraham's descendants) yet on the other hand emphasize fidelity – contradictory impulses that stress ethnicity on the one hand and contract on the other (ibid.: 366). It is this dual nature of the core of the biblical Israel that Grosby suggests is echoed in the modern nation-state's duality of ethnie and state: of both primordial and modern impulses. What Grosby calls 'heterogeneity' is also reflected in Protestantism itself and the modern nation: Protestantism preaches a gospel of universality and yet its emphasis upon the vernacular and upon individual interpretation and divine relationship has, perversely perhaps, encouraged – even created – nationalistic tendencies. The inherent dualism of the nation-state which both looks back to a shared past, emphasising ethnic community, at the same time as declaring a rational basis for citizenship and nationhood, and is therefore perhaps best understood in the light of this biblical model.

Acknowledgements

I would like to thank Dr Arthur Bradley for his advice during the preparation of this article. I am also indebted to the Leverhulme Trust and St Deiniol's Library for their support.

References

Akenson, Donald Harman (1992). *God's Peoples: Covenant and Land in South Africa, Israel and Ulster*. Ithaca, NY: Cornell University Press.

Anderson, Benedict (1995). *Imagined Communities: Reflections on the Origins and Spread of Nationalism*, 2nd edn. London: Verso.

Bauman, Zygmunt (2004). *Identity: Conversations with Benedetto Vecchi*. Cambridge: Polity Press.

Berek, Peter (1998). 'The Jew as Renaissance Man', *Renaissance Quarterly* 51(1): 128–62.

Bhabha, Homi (ed.) (1990). *Nation and Narration*. London: Routledge.

Boyarin, Jonathan and Boyarin, Daniel (2002). *Powers of Diaspora: Two Essays on the Relevance of Jewish Culture*. Minneapolis, MN: University of Minnesota Press.

Brennan, Timothy (1990). 'The National Longing for Form', in H. Bhabha (ed.), *Nation and Narration*. London: Routledge, pp. 44–70.

Breuilly, John (1993). *Nationalism and the Nation State*. Manchester: Manchester University Press.

Colley, Linda (2003). *Britons: Forging the Nation 1707–1837*. London: Pimlico.

Derrida, Jacques (1998). 'Faith and Knowledge: The Two Sources of "Religion" at the Limits of Reason Alone', in Jacques Derrida and Gianni Vattimo (eds), *Religion*. Cambridge: Polity Press.

der Veer, Peter van (1999). 'Hindus: A Superior Race', *Nations and Nationalism* 5(3): 419–30.

De Vries, Hent (2002). *Religion and Violence: Philosophical Perspectives from Kant to Derrida*. Baltimore, MD: Johns Hopkins University Press.

Eagleton, Terry, Jameson Fredric and Said, Edward W. (1990). *Nationalism, Colonialism and Literature*, intro. Seamus Deane. Minneapolis, MN: University of Minnesota Press.

Finn, Margot C. (1993). *After Chartism: Class and Nation in English Radical Politics, 1848–1874*. Cambridge: Cambridge University Press.

Gellner, Ernest (1983). *Nations and Nationalism*. Oxford: Blackwell.

Greenfeld, Liah (1992). *Nationalism: Five Roads to Modernity*. Cambridge, MA: Harvard University Press.

Grosby, Steven (1999). 'The Chosen People of Ancient Israel and the Occident: Why Does Nationality Exist and Survive?', *Nations and Nationalism* 5(3): 357–80.

Hastings, Adrian (1997). *The Construction of Nationhood: Ethnicity, Religion and Nationalism* (The 1996 Wiles Lectures Given at the Queen's University of Belfast). Cambridge: Cambridge University Press.

Hastings, Adrian (1999). 'Special Peoples', *Nations and Nationalism* 5(3): 381–96.

Hill, Christopher (1990). *A Nation of Change and Novelty: Radical Politics, Religion and Literature in Seventeenth-Century England*. London: Routledge.

Hill, Christopher (1993). *The English Bible and the Seventeenth-Century Revolution*. Harmondsworth: Allen Lane.

Hobsbawm, E. J. (1990). *Nations and Nationalism since 1780*. Cambridge: Cambridge University Press.

Jacobson, Dan (1982). *The Story of the Stories: The Chosen People and Its God*. New York: Harper & Row.

Kohn, Hans (1945). *The Idea of Nationalism: A Study in its Origins and Background*. New York: The Macmillan Company.

Kristeva, Julia (1993). *Nations without Nationalism*, trans. Léon S. Roudiez. New York: Columbia University Press.

Pecora, Vincent P. (ed.) (2001). *Nations and Identities: Classic Readings*. Oxford: Blackwell.

Renan, Ernest (1990). 'What Is a Nation?', in H. Bhabha (ed.), *Nation and Narration*. London: Routledge.

Sachar, Howard M. (2001). *A History of Israel from the Rise of Zionism to Our Time*, 2nd edn. New York: Alfred A. Knopf.

Sicker, Martin (1992). *Judaism, Nationalism and the Land of Israel*. Boulder, CO: Westview.

Smith, Anthony D. (1991). *National Identity*. Reno, NV: University of Nevada Press.

Smith, Anthony D. (1998). *Nationalism and Modernism: A Critical Survey of Recent Theories of Nations and Nationalism*. London: Routledge.

Smith, Anthony D. (1999a). *Myths and Memories of the Nation*. Oxford: Oxford University Press.

Smith, Anthony D. (1999b). 'Ethnic Election and National Destiny: Some Religious Origins or Nationalist Ideals', *Nations and Nationalism* 5(3): 331–55.

Stockwood, John (1584). 'Preface' to *A Right Godly and Learned Discourse Upon the Booke of Ester Most Necessary for this Time and Age, to Enstruct all Noble Men, and Such as God Hath Advanced Unto High Places about Princes, that God Looketh for this as an Especiall Duety at Their Handes, Principally to Endevuour themselves to procure the Wealth of God His People, and the Benefite and*

Good of His Church, and Withall to teach the Servants of the Lord that are in Daunger and Misery, with Pacience and Prayer to Attend upon the Lord untill he Send them Deliverance, Written in Latin by Iohn Brentius a German, and Newly Turned into English for the Comfort of God His Children, by Iohn Stockwood Schoolemaster of Tunbridge. London.

Templin, J. Alton (1999). 'The Ideology of a Chosen People: Afrikaner Nationalism and the Ossewa Trek, 1938', *Nations and Nationalism* 5(3): 397–417.

CHAPTER 29
Post-colonialism

Sharon A. Bong

In this chapter, I elucidate the primacy of post-colonial deliberation in the context of Asia, where Christianity is both its colonial heritage and its burden – the point of contention being that colonization effects a historical, conceptual and spiritual dehumanization. I also show the ways in which Asian theologians practise post-colonialism through their theologizing premised on the Bible, the colonial text, in resonance with their lived realities. The post-colonial condition illuminated by Edward Said (1978), Homi Bhabha (1994), Gayatri Spivak (1990) and Sara Ahmed (2000), find eloquent expression in the theologizing of Asians, in protestation against the crippling forces of oppression: their colonial past, internal colonization and neo-colonization. Thus, the culpability of the Church is two-fold: as an ally (in the politic dispensation of 'divine sanction') to Western imperialism in absolutizing the binarism of God/servant, and as an insidious parallelism to the civilized West/primitive East. Asian resistances are manifest in the rise of nationalism (collective identity) and conscientization of the individual, in repudiation of '[the induced and illusionary complacency of] a happy slave' to that of 'an individual gifted with human dignity and salvific splendour' (Gnanadason 1994: 74).

The critique of the prefix 'post' affords a cautionary assessment to the reflexive zeal of 'discursive self-presentation' (Mohanty et al. 1991: 74). In its privileging of the insurgency of the colonized, it inadvertently reconstitutes the binarism of colonial/post-colonial. It thus re-inscribes the latter category as a derivative of and subordinated to the former category, the very facile distinctions that it purports to dismantle. The prefix 'post' is further contested in Ahmed's thesis of 'post-coloniality as *failed historicity*'. 'Post-colonial' is problematic on three grounds. First, 'post-colonial' attributes centrality to (Western) colonialism as 'marker of historical difference' and by derivation, marginality to (Third World) post-colonialism, for instance, when used interchangeably with independence (from colonial rule). Second, colonialism is made a 'marker of time' that foregrounds the linearity of progress (of the Western variant) accentuated not only by 'capitalist modernity' but also globalization, the accelerated flux of persons, commodities (particularly the objectification of women and children) and ideologies. Third, 'post-colonialism' suggests that 'colonialism has been overcome in the present' (Ahmed 2000: 10). This runs counter to the vestiges of colonialism that are prevalent in the form of internal colonization and neo-colonization – the exacerbation of unequal encounters within the matrix of multi-ethnicity, multi-culturalism and multi-religiosity of 'post-colonial' nation-states.

The implication of problematizing 'post-colonial' is evident as the historicity of Christianity in Asia starts off as a colonial heritage: for 'the missionaries came alongside the military, mercenaries and merchants [and] the crucified Christ has come to be perceived as a conquering Christ' (Chia 2004). As such, Ahmed argues for 'strange encounters', the eliding of closures (hence the qualifier 'strange') in opening up meaning within the interface of cultures and religions in a heterogeneous context. Theologizing in a 'post-colonial' context thus involves 'strange encounters':

> Ways of encountering what is already encountered – in order to engender ways of being and acting in the world that open the possibility of the distant in the near, the unassimilable in the already assimilated, and the surprising in the ordinary. (Ahmed 2000: 164)

The diverse and nascent indigenous articulations of Asian theologizing in a post-colonial context encompass: Asian feminist spirituality (Chung 1990; Mananzan 1992), 'theology of the womb' (Katoppo 1980), theology of the 'poor woman' in Asia (Wong 2000), Christian Dalit theology (Devi 1994; Nirmal 1994), 'theology shoes-off' (Fung 1992), *Minjung* theology (Park 1988; Chung 1991), 'theology of unification' (Suh 1994), 'theology of Buraku liberation' (Teruo 1994), 'third-eye theology' and 'flat-nosed theology' (Song 1980, 1982). Yet:

> It is clear that neither of these theologies is Asian. Nor is Asia independent enough to work out its own theology, because even in major conferences organized in Asia the theological mood and method remain Western. (Pieris 1990: 39)

The irrefutable element of truth in Pieris' objective but potentially provocative admission, accounts for the defensive stance of some proponents of Asian theologies, that is it not only distinctive (from Western Christianity, even its oppositional theologies such as liberation theology and feminist theology), but also imbued with distinction. A point of illustration is gleaned in the final statement of the sixth conference of the Ecumenical Association of Third Word Theologians (EATWOT) in 1983, who in attesting to the irruption of 'Third World' theologies, perceive the reactionary rise of 'feminist theology, theology of resistance, European theology of liberation, theology of conversion, theology of crisis, political theology, and radical evangelical theology' as symptomatic of 'the fresh air of repentance and renewal in the First World' (Fabella and Torres 1985: 192–3).

The primary objective of this chapter is to afford a strategic and calculated assessment of the rather volatile dynamics between the 'original' (however contested a category that is) Biblical Christianity and its apparent 'Asianized' derivative (the pejorative implication being the very point of contention). Without recourse to expedient simplification, partiality or romanticization which impinge on the intellectual and spiritual integrity of both discourses, the ensuing conceptual framework is three-fold: (1) the functionalism of binary opposition between colonizer and colonized); (2) its problematization as a focus of critical inquiry and differentiation and (3) the subversion of binarisms and the reconstruction of an alternative paradigm. The following is an exegesis of how and why God is not only white.

Binarism as Politics of Identity

> We were made all white, baptised from head to toe, all white as flour-packers or as homeless nomads roaming in the dust . . .
>
> This is how my 'freedom' and my 'dignity' began. This is how my 'politics' awoke in me.

This poignant extract from Sun Ai Lee-Park's poem, *The Wish*, recounts the paradoxical triumph and defeat of the Korean 'exodus', reminiscent of the journey of faith through the spiritual desert in Exodus 16, re-counted in Hebrews 11:22. The Koreans crossing the North–South border in peril of their lives are a people at once liberated, yet derelict – without a name, home and country (Fabella and Torres 1985: 172). The humiliation of a physical cleansing – sprayed with disinfectants and being at the mercy of their 'saviours', the 'Yankee soldiers' (whose provisional bases proliferate in South Korea) – is analogous to their purgation through baptismal rites of initiation into a foreign realm, where the means and ends of both allusions are alienating.

The politicization of spirituality – a faith-based activism that engenders social justice – and its corollary, the spiritualization of politics – good governance that is imbued with a spiritual ethos – are necessarily partisan in order to effect desired change in the divided world of Asia. The heterogeneity of Asia, unique and healthy on the one hand, is disruptive on the other, with regard to the reality of its political factions, economic disparity, racial, ethnic, cultural and religious divisions. The initial phase of theologizing of, for and by Asians is therefore reactionary to the convergent weight and suffocating presence of its antecedents, Western imperialism and Christianity. The mutually cohesive and complicit political agendas of both, the one blatant, the other insidious, are held accountable by Asian theologians for colonialism, from the proprietorial appropriation of the Other to its sinful dehumanization.

To facilitate a paradigm shift from the margins to the centre, Asian theologians are unapologetically partial towards indigenous expressions of faith and by the same token, hostile to 'Western' elements deemed transgressive of an Asian sensibility and disposition. Binarisms are thus utilized as expedient 'articulate categories' of differentiation (McClintock 1995: 5). This evinces an Asian/non-Asian dichotomy of essence/derivation and purity/pollution: a polemic that admittedly affords a cathartic release of anger, hurt and despair, but which remains defeatist at worst and unconstructive at best.

Contemporary Asian theologians, in rising to vindicate their people against the (un)holy civilizing missions of both Empire and Church, nevertheless temper their collective voices of protest with tolerance, objectivity and resilience. An illustration of this is the final statement of the sixth EATWOT conference that locates sinful structures of oppression not only in 'westernization and christianization', but also in 'neocultural domination', 'anthropological poverty' and 'internal domination' (Fabella and Torres 1985: 185). However, distinctions are accorded due significance: C. S. Song's postulation of a 'flat-nosed theology' (Song 1982) invests the anthropomorphized God with an Asian (albeit stereotyped) visage. Jojo M. Fung's 'theology of shoes-off' (Fung 1992) sacralizes, with biblical justification (Exodus 3), a cultural practice that is characteristically Asian: the removal of one's shoes upon entry into a place of refuge or worship.

Chung Hyun Kyung's seminal formulation of an emerging Asian feminist spirituality seems almost didactic in its prescriptive stipulation of a 'new understanding of theology' as a 'cry, plea and invocation', 'God-praxis' and 'vision quest', a 'new understanding of the identity of theologians' and a 'new methodology' (Chung 1990: 99–109). The emphasis on restoration from the burden of westernization/'christianization' is evident in Yong Ting Jin's espousal of a 'new creation' involving messianic happiness and radical renewal for a 'new earth' as prophesied for the future by the prophet Isaiah (Isa. 65:17–25). This 'new creation' manifests itself as a 'new lifestyle', a 'new exercise of power', a 'new theological reflection', a 'new faith community' and a 'new pattern of relationship' (Fabella and Odduyoye 1994: 104–7). The binarism of Asian/non-Asian thus elucidated, reverses the hierarchy of Western/Asian and redeems the 'second (minority) term' of Asian, 'temporality', 'difference', from being colonized by 'the first (majority) term' of Western, 'universality', 'culture' (Mohanty et al. 1991: 73). This is how we may understand such prophetic re-visioning of dominant/subjugated subjectivities as the following: 'You will see my servants eating while you go hungry; you will see my servants drinking while you go thirsty' (Isa. 65:13); and 'the wolf and the young lamb shall feed together' (Isa. 65:25). Though the basic structural relation of superior/inferior is not yet sufficiently undermined in lived realities, the re-positioning of Asian above that of its nemesis, serves as a reminder that 'it is not the centre that determines the periphery, but the periphery that, in its boundedness, determines the centre' (Mohanty et al. 1991: 73–4).

Such a disjunction of Occident/Orient (West/East) is exemplified by Edward Said in his ground-breaking thesis, *Orientalism* (1978), where he expounds the naturalization and destabilization of the colonial construct of the post-Enlightenment period:

> The Orient is not an inert fact of nature . . . just as the Occident itself is not just *there* either . . . the Orient was Orientalised not only because it was discovered to be 'Oriental' . . . but also because it *could be* – that is, submitted to being – *made* Oriental. (Said 1978: 4–6)

Disparities between Christianity, the 'handmaiden of foreign aggression' (Kwok 1989: 95), and 'so-called Oriental religions' (Pieris 1990: 8), are first characterized by over-simplification: 'the West *studies* all the world religions, whereas the East simply *practises* them'. Second, it is coloured by romanticization whereby religion in the West is merely 'a "department" in life' as opposed to the East, where 'religion *is* life'. And thirdly, it is marred by inferiorization wherein the 'caricature of Asian religiousness . . . [is exclusively represented by the] navel-gazing yogi . . . or the Zen Buddhist seated still in lotus posture' (Pieris 1990: 12). This 'flexible *positional* superiority' of the Occident over the Orient (Said 1978: 7), is amplified in the antignostic bias of the 'monastic tradition of the West. . . . [which circulates] beneath a thick encrustation of Occidentalism', and reduces gnosticism to a 'world-denying asceticism [that is deemed] the distinctive mark of all "Eastern" religions (Said 1978: 10–12). I would add that 'Eastern religions' includes Christian theologizing of, for and by Asians.

Problematization of Binarisms

Homi Bhabha, in his important article, 'Of Mimicry and Man: The Ambivalence of Colonial Discourse' (1994: 85–92), affords a pertinent theoretical basis to account for the ambivalence inherent in the inevitable need to problematize binarisms. The 'epic intention of the civilizing mission, "human and not wholly human"' (ibid.: 85), is the crass justification for the dehumanization of colonial people under the tyranny of the State or Church. The ignominy of mimicry imposed on primitives or heathens, in projecting affectations of 'a reform of manners' and 'religious reform' (Bhabha 1994: 85), is unconsciously subverted in the very performance of mimicry itself. The seemingly benevolent colonial desire for a 'reformed, recognizable Other, as a subject of a difference that is almost the same, but not quite' (ibid.: 86), entails the fetishistic spectacle of mimicry, the interminable rehearsal of approximation, of impersonation (at the risk of fragmenting the self) – yet, remaining 'almost the same but not white [Christian]' (ibid.: 89).

The very act of assembling a façade that is alien (and potentially offensive) to one's being, paradoxically dissembles; for mimicry:

> does not merely destroy narcissistic authority through the repetitious slippage of differ-
> ence and desire. It is the process of the *fixation* of the colonial as a form of cross-
> classificatory, discriminatory knowledge within an interdictory discourse, and therefore
> necessarily raises the question of the *authorization* of colonial representations. (Bhabha
> 1994: 90)

To that end, there is a discernible shift in tone with regard to representations which are '*almost the same, but not quite*' (Bhabha 1994: 86) in cognizance of the ambivalence of their form and matter in dialogue and confrontation with Christianity and Western-ization. Song with much candour, argues that a 'first-hand transposition of faith' from its originating point, Jerusalem, to the rest of the world, in particular, the 'so-called Third World', is contingent on having 'a negotiable [air] ticket:

> A journey from Israel to Asia – needs to be undertaken all over again. For one thing, the
> airplane ticket purchased for us . . . was a non-negotiable discount ticket. The journey was
> cut down to economy size. It had many intermediary stopovers. The most frustrating part
> of it was that the itinerary could not be altered. (Song 1982: 5–7)

His humorous analogy shows a sensitivity and sense of regret towards the transmis-sion of a superimposed, distilled faith and the infantilization of Asian Christians by

Western missionaries. With resilient hope however, he departs from such reductive 'second-hand transpositions' (Song 1982: 7), and calls for Asians, as subjects of their own history, to encounter Christianity 'first-hand'. This is significant given that Asia, from current 'missiological forecasts' in the light of the rise of Christian evangelism in the region, is now undisputedly Christianity's 'centre of gravity, in quantitative and qualitative terms' (ibid.: 6).

Similarly, constructive is Dulcie Abraham's conviction that Malaysian Christians, in recognition of Christianity as both their colonial heritage and their burden, both liberating and oppressive, have 'appropriated the Christian ethos of compassion and caring . . . and are in the forefront of action on behalf of the disadvantaged as well as human rights movements in the nation, in particular, women's human rights' (Norani 1995: 22). As such, Abraham draws on a 'theology of equivalence' that takes as its foundational premise, the creation story of Genesis 1: 27 where both male and female are created in God's divine image, *Imago Dei* (Norani 1995: 17). Kuribayashi Teruo denounces certain churches in Japan that perpetuate colonial mimicry, 'by uncritically borrowing [North American and European] theologies, institutions, canon laws, spirituality, and even lifestyles' and discriminate against Burakumin peoples or indigenous outcasts. This solidarity with outcasts emulates Christ's preferential option for the poor: 'How blessed are the poor in spirit, the Kingdom of heaven is theirs' (Matt. 5:3); '[God] has sent me to proclaim liberty to captives, sight to the blind, to let the oppressed go free' (Luke 4:18); and 'it was those who were poor according to the world that God chose, to be rich in faith and to be the heirs to the kingdom' (James 2:5). What is interesting is that Teruo's denunciation is legitimized by the 'liberating praxis' that is the crux of the Gospel: where 'a new church . . . [will be modelled upon] the figure of Jesus Christ who was born as and died as an outcast and was resurrected for the despised' (Teruo 1994: 24). And Chung Hyun Kyung urges 'second-generation liberationists' to employ with discernment, the 'coloniser's tools and the space to create' that is the legacy of the 'first-generation liberationists', who, though primarily reactionary, paved the path of struggle towards self-actualization and authentication (Chung 1994: 53).

Conciliatory dispositions like these afford a welcome interlude and mature alternative to mere contests of power between competing Western and Asian theologies. But the crystallization of the latter is a manifestation of autonomy which becomes itself a re-formulation of former ecclesiastical dominance and exegetical dogmatism. Where universal claims to Truth are ahistorical and apolitical, Asian theologies are historicized and politicized. Thus, the dynamic paradigm shifts which are alluded to by the following theologian are characterized by a dialectical tension between 'mimicry – a difference that is almost nothing but not quite – [and] menace – a difference that is almost total but not quite' (Bhabha 1994: 91). A Sung Park juxtaposes *Minjung* and Process hermeneutics, in an effort to weigh the credibility of one against the other (Park 1988: 118–26). Having contrasted the different problems, goals and methodologies of *Minjung* and Process hermeneutics, he concludes that the potential realization of each can be achieved by assimilating something of the other:

> In its encounter with Minjung theology, process theology may learn primarily the depths of human suffering shown in the abyss of Han and the necessity of the active involvement in the world for maximizing the intensity of experience. (Park 1988: 126)

He writes of the mutually informative and beneficial, almost symbiotic relationship involved in espousing the creation of 'new heavens and a new earth' (Isa. 65: 17):

> From process theology, Minjung theology may learn chiefly its idea of radical openness of the eschaton and its coherent idea of freedom. With the complementarity of these ideas, Minjung theology will be better equipped for its historical vocation to advance the millennium on earth. (Park 1988: 126)

By logic of extension, the Bible is similarly treated with ambivalence: an unsettling combination of implicit reverence and critical distance:

> As 'signs taken for wonders' – as an insignia of colonial authority and a signifier of colonial desire and discipline . . . [it undergoes], as well, a process of displacement that, paradoxically, makes the presence of the book wondrous to the extent to which it is repeated, translated, misread, displaced. (Bhabha 1994: 102)

First, Kwok Pui-Lan attests to the androcentric and Eurocentric bias of the Bible, thus de-legitimizing its transcendence for the people of Asia (Fiorenza 1993: 101–16). For instance, she contends that the '(culturally conditioned) biblical images of bread-making and yeast-rising, as well as predominant representations of "God as Baker-woman", are alienating to the Chinese, whose staple diet is rice, not bread' (Kwok 1994: 152). Alienating biblical texts would include passages where bread is a metaphor for spiritual food (Deut. 8:3, Neh. 9:15, Ps. 78:25), or where Wisdom, the feminine personification of God, offers 'bread' for the conversion of fools (Prov. 9: 5), or where the 'bread of suffering' symbolizes the ingestion of the body of Christ as the 'bread of life' (John 6:35) through the Eucharistic meal (Mark 14:22), shared among the faith community (1 Cor. 10:17). Second, Teruo's censure of ecclesiastical double standards, in its mistreatment of Burakumin peoples, justifiably extends to its exegetic source, thus de-stabilizing 'the credibility of the gospel' itself (Teruo 1994: 24).

Third, Song's position is less severe, as he maintains the 'enormous changeability of the gospel' as the living Word (1982: 11). The translation of the Bible into the vernacular testifies to its accessibility, relevance and mutability of meaning: wherein 'mutual transposition of languages . . . [is invested] with communicative power' (ibid.: 8). This is in fulfilment of the biblical prophecy of a transformation from 'the spirit of Babel (Genesis 11: 9) to the [apocalyptic] spirit of Pentecost (Acts 2)', where diverse speech not violent silence is celebrated as 'a language of liberation, connection and unification from below' (Chung 1991: 41–2). It is evident that the Bible, contextualized within oppressive lived realities and polyvalent narratives of faith communities, is thus 'detranscendentalised, contextualised, historicized, genderised' (Benhabib 1992: 224). Essentially, the Bible 'can neither be "original" – by virtue of the act of repetition that constructs it – not "identical" – by virtue of the difference that defines it' (Bhabha 1994: 107). The Bible is thus demystified.

As such, the construction of the Bible warrants dispute, for in the context of 'non-biblical culture[s] of Asia, the emblem of the English book – "signs taken for wonders" – [is] an insignia of colonial authority and a signifier of colonial desire and discipline' (Bhabha 1994: 102). The supercilious myths of the 'white man's burden' (Kwok 1993:

102) and the (no less complicit) 'white woman's other burden' (Jayawardena 1995), in undertaking the glorified mission of civilizing 'heathens', are justifiably debunked by Asian Christians today who are authorized, equally elected as the people of God, to appropriate the central, liberating biblical message of the risen Christ heralding salvation within their historical, material and cultural specificities (Matt. 28:7, Mark 9:9, Luke 24:34, John 20:10 and 2 Tim. 2:8). An involved, subjective, praxis-centred theologizing from the grassroots is fore-grounded as a corrective to the 'historical-critical method of interpretation' that is founded on a 'Eurocentric positivist approach' (Bhabha 1994: 103). This is a departure from 'ideological correlatives of the Western sign – empiricism, idealism, mimeticism, monoculturalism . . . that sustain a tradition of English "cultural" authority' (Bhabha 1994: 105). Embraced is a 'dialogical imagination' (Kwok 1993: 103) which, by privileging a feminist and inclusive re-interpretation of the Bible, decolonizes Christianity. Such hermeneutics recover biblical images of God as mother (e.g. Isa. 49:15; 66:13), God as Wisdom, regenerating and sustaining (Prov. 1:20, 3:19–20, 8) and God as Spirit, the Source of life (Gen. 1:1–2; Ps. 104:30).

A further illustration of such discursive dynamics is the cross-cultural rehabilitation of Hagar (Gen. 16 and 21:8–21), who by virtue of being a 'foreigner, a slave and a woman [bears] the triple burden of oppression' (Abraham 1996: 5). Re-claimed by 'Third World' feminists, she becomes 'paradigmatic of the intersections of racism, classicism and sexism by women of colour in different continents' (Kwok 1993: 105). Where Western feminist theologians have lauded Sarah's chuckle as a mark of dissent at hegemonic male domination, feminist postcolonial theologians foreground Hagar from the margins and privilege her standpoint as an alien surrogate mother victimized by Abraham and Sarah, the stalwart ancestors of the Christian faith who are nonetheless not above scrutiny (Kim 1993: 23–5, Lung 1997: 34–5, Chung 1994: 392). As such, African-American, Asian-American, Latin American, African and Asian feminist theologians highlight Hagar's slavery, destitution, prostitution (sold into polygamy) and loss of cultural identity in an act of solidarity against compounded forces of oppression that is the reality of many 'Third World' women. Essentially, the 'English book', the Bible, de-constructs itself, as it is paradoxically 'a moment of originality and authority' as well as 'a process of displacement . . . to the extent that it is repeated, translated, misread, displaced' (Bhabha 1994: 102). The 'colonial text' as such 'can neither be "original" – by virtue of the act of repetition that constructs it – nor "identical" – by virtue of the difference that defines it' (Bhabha 1994: 107). The Bible as a living Word, thus facilitates its own fluidity and plurality of meaning, as its presence is impinged, made relevant by the lived experiences of its 'colonized' people, the faithful of the Church.

A corollary to the demystification of the Bible is the deconstruction of God as a pre-eminent Being. The biblical tradition and weight of scholarship of two centuries afford a grand meta-narrative of Christianity and its transcendent claim to Truth, upon which the binary God/servant is premised. The category of 'God' is seemingly pre-discursive (to the point of being predestined in a religious context), not only naturalized but aggrandized and (Its supremacy) intractable. The second category of 'servant' is derivative from and utterly subordinate in its subservience to the former. The absolutist dialectic is systematically destabilized not only through the demystification of the Bible, but also the deconstruction of a pre-eminent God and by extension, de-stigmatization of indigenous cultures and religiosities.

The multiple revelations of God in the Bible lend a mutable conception of God in the disavowal of God's transcendence: the fullness of revelation in Jesus (John 1:1) and the Word of God as active and alive in believers (Heb. 4:12). In articulating a particularized and personalized theology of and for Malaysian Christians, Jojo M. Fung, a Malaysian Jesuit, reinstates the Asian cultural practice of removing one's shoes (for sanitary, aesthetic and reverential purposes), as symptomatic of a disciple's total self-abandonment, vulnerability and penitence in the presence of God and for the fulfillment of God's will. From the story of God's command to Moses to take off his sandals 'for the place where you are standing is holy ground' (Exod. 3:5–6), 'shoes-off' becomes symbolic of one's 'human response in the face of the awe-inspiring manifestation of the Divine [which] evokes sentiments of humility, nakedness and a need for inner cleanliness in the hearts of Malaysian believers' (Fung 1992: 14).

More significantly, it parallels the biblical narrative of Moses' 'shoes-off' experience before the burning bush, as a prelude to the emancipation of the Israelites in the Exodus event (Exod. 3:1–5) and the Apostle Peter's 'shoes-off' encounter with Jesus (Epiphany) who walked barefoot on water (Matt. 14:25–33) (Fung 1992: 16–22). Manifestations of the Hebrew God through Self-disclosures of 'I am Who I am' to both Moses and Peter (the latter through Jesus, son of God), is testimony of God's compassion and immanence. God is not impervious to the cries of the oppressed as evidenced by Its divine interventions in human history.

God's all-encompassing nature is further humanized 'in the person of Jesus who is Emmanuel (God-with-us), the Word made flesh' (Matt. 1:23–4, John 1:14) (Fung 1992: 40). Its infinite variety of Being, though fundamentally un-representable, is embodied in the opacity of 'I shall be who I shall be': thereby authenticating the face of Jesus the Nazarene (of the triune God) as 'black, brown and yellow' (Fung 1992: 40). By extension of 'divine inspiration' based on the biblical affirmation of the Incarnation of Jesus in the human person of each believer, the 'Shoes-off barefoot Jesus is the Malaysian manifestation of the Hebrew God in our history' (ibid.: 41). The colonized personification of God as white and male, are not only refuted but also personalized, Malaysianized in this instance, to celebrate the divinity of each human person, which transcends the 'articulated categories' or identity markers of race, gender and class, as made in the image of God.

The very principle of *Imago Dei* (made in God's image or likeness), approximates Bhabha's notion of 'colonial mimicry [which] is the desire for a reformed, recognizable Other, *as a subject of a difference that is almost the same, but not quite*' (Bhabha 1994: 86). On one level, the intent of the colonizer is to erase inequities through effecting sameness between non-equals or the colonized and themselves. On another level, the colonizer insists on preserving essentialized and often eroticized differences (i.e. Christian/pagan, white/Asian, modernized/infantilized) so that the Other is rendered 'almost the same, but not quite'. The mutually exclusive and disproportionate categories of colonizer/colonized are analogous to that of the God/servant dialectic, as divinely ordained, or seemingly so. The religious compulsion to mimic a deity, through anthropological identification with Christ, frustrates one's sense of self and agency because one invariably falls short. Proliferating images of God are representations of the material conditions of living, at once an assimilation and transcendence of humanity's historicity, temporality, even mortality, witnessed through Christ in allusion to the Triune God. In emulation, not mere mimicry, of Jesus, the Shoes-Off Barefoot who embodies God, Malaysian Christians do theology as a proactive response to God's call. In doing so, they embody the God who introduces himself to Moses as 'I am he who is' (Exod. 3:14–15). Such a 'Theology of Shoes-off' as practised by Asian-Malaysian disciples proliferates the image of God as 'I shall be who I shall be', re-constructs the binary of Master/slave and reclaims agency in continuing the mission of salvation entrusted to them (Fung 1992).

Subversive Digressions

> Hybridity . . . is the name for the strategic reversal of the process of domination through disavowal . . . [It] is the revaluation of the assumption of colonial identity through the repetition of discriminatory identity effects . . . the colonial hybrid is the articulation of the ambivalent space . . . making its objects at once disciplinary and disseminatory. (Bhabha 1994: 112)

The displacement of the neo-colonialism of State and Church by the materialization of an Asian spirituality approximates Bhabha's categorization of the deconstructive presence of the hybrid subject, in which the slippage of identity is evinced by its assimilation and the avoidance of objectification. The extent of subversion is manifest in the de-authorization of colonial ascendancy. The 'colonial hybrid' challenges the colonizer's abstraction of Christianity as atemporal, ahistorical and apolitical. Hybrid subjects such as Asian theologians refract abstract faith through the prism of the basic needs of its most disenfranchised communities.

Pieris cogently describes the 'disoriented West' as paralysed by a 'decadent culture of technocratic imperialism' (1990: 13). This stands in bleak contrast to churches of Asia that are rejuvenated by a 'new Orientalism' or the 'third reformation' of the church (ibid.: 8). The regeneration of the East as arbiter of 'powerful religious forces shaping the destiny of Asian masses' (ibid.: 31), is truly revolutionary in its hybridization or syncretic embrace of Christological and Buddhological paths to truth (ibid. 1990: 12). For it is 'the spirit of Buddhist wisdom and Christian love' which embodies the dialectical mutuality of 'silence [as] the *word unspoken* and the word [as] *silence heard*' (ibid.: 41). And that 'Christian love' embodies not only 'Word' that was with God and is God but also flesh who 'lived among us' attesting to the transcendence and immanence of God that continues to be present in our lived realities (John 1:1, 13–14). The church is challenged to rebirth through the double baptism (in emulation) of Jesus (re-birthing in Matt. 3:13–17, Mark 1:9–11, Luke 3:21–2): first, with the humility 'to be baptized by its precursors in the Jordan of Asian religion' and second, with the courage 'to be baptized by oppressive systems on the cross of Asian *poverty* [both voluntary and forced]' (Pieris 1990: 41). Ultimately, as Pieris contends, 'theology in Asia [as] the Christian apocalypse of the non-Christian experiences of liberation', is the apotheosis of the redemptive death of the Church (life through death in Matthew 28:6–7, Mark 16:6, Luke 24:34, John 20:10) (1990: 41).

Song's formulations of a 'third eye theology' (Song 1980), exercises the 'metonymy of presence' that is the inadvertent (and undesirable) colonial effect of hybridity: where 'its peculiar "replication" terrorises authority with the *ruse* of recognition, its mimicry, its mockery' (Bhabha 1994: 115). Essentially, the re-enactment of biblical truths serves as points of origin yet departure for theologies of Asia. It radicalizes Christianity by transforming the negativity or lack of 'almost the same, but not quite' (ibid.: 86) into the genesis of a spirituality that is (providentially) distinct from that of its colonial heritage. A graphic illustration of this is Song's espousal of 'doing theology with a [Buddhist] third eye', which reincarnates Christ 'through Chinese eyes, Japanese eyes, Asian eyes, African eyes, Latin American eyes'. It thus heralds a revivalism very different from that of the '[German] Reformation' (Song 1980: 12). For those, 'clothed in Christ (i.e. baptized) . . . there can be neither Jew nor Greek, there can be neither slave not free [person], there can be neither male nor female – for you are all one in Christ Jesus' (Gal. 3:28–9).

Such a faithful appropriation is contingent on his perceptive observation that 'each portrait of Christ is at once a representation and a misrepresentation' (Song 1980: 12). This in turn concretizes Spivak's advocacy of strategic essentialism premised on her distinction between '*Vertretung*' and '*Darstellung*' – the political and aesthetic representations, respectively (Landry and Maclean 1993: 198). Thus, the Asian recovery of the image of Christ, *Imago Dei*, in allusion to his 'flat-nosed Christ' (Song 1982: 3), is both a spiritual testament and a political affirmation.

The politics of self-representation is synonymous with one's assertion of agency, as being empowered with self-determination towards self-actualization. Theologies reformulated for and by Asians are profound and compelling refutations of Spivak's haunting conviction that the 'truly "subaltern", most truly marginalized, cannot "speak" [for themselves]' (Landry and Maclean 1993: 289). In retrospect, the insurgency of Asian Christians or Christian Asians disrupts not only hegemonic, Eurocentric constructs of Christianity, but also invalidates the colonization by faith itself. This is substantiated through the seemingly sacrilegious two-pronged revolutionary praxis: the de-transcendentalization of God, from the aggrandizement of God/servant to a 'servant-God – a God who serves', and the sacralization, by extension, of the grassroots, human agency (Nirmal 1994: 35). This is premised on the radicalization of servitude preached by Jesus and epitomized in the de-construction of the binary of Master/servant (Mark 10:42–5, Luke 22:26–7), his emphasis on loving servanthood as an extension of observing commandments, (Gal. 5:13), and ultimately, by the actualization of this in his redemptive death (Mark 10:45). Thus, in repudiation of epistemological and structural violence (Emberley 1993: 5; Landry and Maclean 1993: 199; Spivak 1990: 71, 138), it resolutely embraces Chung's articulation of the 'epistemology from the broken body' (Matt. 27:26–50, Mark 15:15–34, Luke 23:26–46, John 19:1–30) in the passionate and compassionate response to feed the hungry, heal the sick and clothe the naked, in fulfilment of an eschatological faith (Chung 1990: 104).

The irrepressible irruption of 'Third World' theologies exemplifies the 'inauguration of politicization for the colonized' (Guha and Spivak 1988: 3). It risks essentialism, both strategic and polemical, rather than deliberations over political correctness or global diplomacy, even politic manoeuvres (Marchand and Parpart 1995: 6; Landry and Maclean 1993: 198). It relinquishes the violent abstraction of intellectualism and guards jealously, its fidelity to the oppressed masses. Admittedly, its earnest representation may seem intimidating to those who deem themselves uninitiated, regardless if one is an Asian or not. As such, Chung Hyun Kyung's 'gentle but radical' message epitomizes the essence of theologies of, for and by Asians, in its prophetic vision of the epiphany of an emerging Asian spirituality: 'Listen to us for a while! It will be liberating, healing. Don't take our claims as threat. It's an invitation, a gift.'

'Third World' theologies of liberation are thus controversial because they essentially liberate doctrinal, dogmatic and Eurocentric theology. Intrinsic to 'Dalit', 'Mujerista', 'Womanist', 'Minjung' and 'Shoes-Off' theologies, is the politicization of spirituality and the spiritualization of politics. It is an inspired and courageous vocation to fulfill God's eschatological promise on earth as in heaven as articulated in the Lord's Prayer (Matt. 6:10, Luke 11:2). The question of agency is inseparable from the commitment to praxis – doing theology from the grassroots and thus repudiating the 'epistemic violence of imperialist [theology]' (McClintock 1995: 16). It also epitomizes 'subaltern insurgency', an indefatigable attempt at self-representation in the face of failure and in defiance of pre-determined rules of recognition (Landry and Maclean 1993: 306).

Malaysian 'Shoes-Off' theology is an exposition of a transformative faith consolidated by its ' "theological shift" away from Europe toward the South and East Asia' in solidarity with the 'young, vibrant and dynamic churches' of the Third World (Fung 1992: 75). Based on five phases of discernment in the form of a spiral movement (ibid.: 76), this nascent spirituality is creative, integrative, inclusive and prophetic. Its corresponding praxis involves, first, localizing the liturgy by, for example, translating the Bible and the liturgy into the vernacular, which in Malaysia incorporates Malay, Chinese and Indian cultural symbolisms into the liturgy. Second, it involves converging faith (sacred) and nationalism (secular) so that the church participates in the independent nation-state's formative vision of holistic development for this millennium. Third, it involves promoting inter-religious dialogue and championing justice for the marginalized. In so doing, the Malaysian Christians claim a subject position that is reminiscent of Bhabha's 'colonial hybrid [who] is the articulation of the ambivalent space where the rite of power . . . [makes] its objects at once disciplinary and disseminatory . . . a negative transparency' (Bhabha 1994: 112).

The fulfilment of the Malaysian Church's liberating mission as proposed by Fung's 'Shoes-Off' theology culminates in an ' "eruption from below", gushing forth, spilling over the top, flowing down, reshaping the life of our people at the grassroots' (Fung 1992: 79). It thus approximates to the 'colonial hybrid's' subversive potential of dismantling hierarchical, sinful, oppressive structures. As God poignantly mirrors the human face in anguish, the dialectic of God/servant is de-legitimized. Salvific acts in history initiated by God such as Creation (Gen. 1:1), Exodus from enslavement to deliverance (Exodus, Isa. 40:3), Embodiment in Jesus (John 1:1), the Crucifixion and Resurrection (Matt. 26–8), are perpetuated by human agency as covenantal partners in the re-creation of God's eschatological promise to create heaven on earth. Essentially, humanity is not a hapless, passive entity awaiting salvation or damnation. Rather, they are an elected vessel, both 'disciplinary and disseminatory', akin to Bhabha's 'negative transparency', which concretizes God's will to feed the hungry, clothe the naked and heal the sick. A Christian then becomes 'not a source, but a re-source of light [and God]' (Bhabha 1994: 110). The elected vessels become a 'light for the world' (Matt. 5:14), emulating Jesus who is 'the light of the world' (John 8:12), so that others can 'see shining the light of the gospel of the glory of Christ, who is the image of God' (2 Cor. 4:4).

A further transgression of Western hegemony of thought and expression is thus evinced through the subversion of binarisms, tantamount to a breakthrough in faith, in relation to syncretism and theologies from Asia and the Western backlash that this entails. The foundational logic of the 'A/Not-A' binarism of western metaphysics, which privileges 'A' over its derivative 'Not-A', its inferiorized other, is characterized by absolutism and intractability. This is because it precludes the 'Law of the Excluded Middle [which] makes the boundary between A and Not-A impermeable' (Magee 1995: 109) and feeds the religious bias of anti-syncretism. There is a plethora of terms used to signify the liminal space that blurs the boundaries in syncretic encounters: enculturation, acculturation, inculturation, bricolage, amalgamation, symbiosis, assimilation, identification, coherence and dissolution (Shorter 1988; Stewart and Shaw 1994; Gort 1989).

Kwok Pui-Lan disclaims 'western [exclusionary] symbolic logic [of] the opposite of "A" is "negation A"', in fidelity to the oriental wisdom of yin–yang philosophy and Buddhism'. The former deems 'A/Not-A' as 'correlated, interdependent and interpenetrating. While the latter radically maintains that 'all reality is neither one nor many but is not-two (non-dualistic)' (King 1994: 69). Her prophecy of religious syncretism challenges the unrelenting myopia of religious fundamentalists: 'the ultimate challenge for all of us is to create a sociopolitical reality, a cultural matrix, and a way of speaking about God, Tao, Allah, or Nothingness so that we can all live, and live abundantly' (ibid.: 69): in the words of Jesus, 'I have come so that they may have life and have it to the full' (John 10:10).

Consider Chung Hyun Kyung's invocation of the spirits:

> Let us prepare the way of the Holy Spirit by emptying ourselves . . . [and] by taking off [our] shoes . . .
> Come. The spirit of Hagar, Egyptian, black slave woman exploited and abandoned . . .
> Come. The spirit of indigenous people of the earth . . .
> Come. The spirit of Korean women in the Japanese 'prostitution army' . . .
> Come. The spirit of the Amazon rain forest now being murdered every day . . .
> Come. The spirit of the Liberator, our brother Jesus, tortured and killed on the cross . . .
> (Chung 1991: 38–9)

Her supplication to the sacred spirits of the marginalized, persecuted and annihilated, traversing spatial, temporal and cultural differences, concretizes her preferential and revolutionary option for 'the survival-liberation centered syncretism' (Chung 1990:

113). This is an expression of theologizing of, for and by Asians within multi-ethnic, multi-cultural and multi-religious lived realities. As such, Minjung hermeneutics, a theologizing that starts off with the Minjung, the most down-trodden of Korean society, 'transcends the perimeter of Christianity and appropriates Korean history, culture, religions and tradition . . . (with) stories, songs, mask dances, socio-biography, socio-economy, rumours, literature, history, shamanism, Buddhism, and Chondokyo (an indigenous religion)' (Park 1988: 125).

The repudiation of syncretism stems from fear and intolerance of difference. Asian theologians have unwittingly resuscitated '*synkrasis*, a mixing together, a compound' and its derivative, '*kretoi* [that is] a strategically practical, morally justified form of political allegiance' from the periphery of disapprobation (Stewart and Shaw 1994: 3). As we saw, Aloysius Pieris of Sri Lanka calls for a 'double baptism': baptism in the 'Jordan of Asian Religiosity' and baptism in the 'Calvary of Asian poverty' (Pieris 1994: 143). Sugirtharajah advocates the Indian attitude 'sarvadharmasambhava' or acceptance of all religious experience (Sugirtharajah 2002: 205). Jojo M. Fung of Malaysia, in his fusion of shamanic healing and Catholic sacramental anointment of the sick, knowingly renders God as the 'Ultimate Enabler of the process of new syncretism' (Fung 1996: 30). Fung develops this in his multifaceted model of cross-cultural solidarity with the Orang Asli, an indigenous marginalized people of West Malaysia, envisioning mission as a dialogue with them and their religious beliefs and cultural traditions (Fung 2003: 212–13). In so doing, the hyphenated space of both-and, both Christianity and Asian spiritualities, is fore-grounded as a departure from the either/or positioning of 'A/Not-A'.

The assimilation of the 'wild wind of the Holy Spirit' with *han*-ridden spirits invoked (Chung 1991: 393–4) parallels the symbiosis of the politicized 'contemplative heritage of Asia's great religions' (i.e. Zen meditational breathing) and Biblical Hebrew *Ruah* 'the Breath of God' (Gen. 1:2) (Mananzan 1992: 71). The Indonesian feminist theologian, Marianne Katoppo, in affirmation of the 'metacosmic soteriologies of Asia, such as Hinduism', asserts that 'it is unthinkable to dichotomize male and female to the extent that the Christian West has done, any more than it is possible to dichotomize life and death' (King 1994: 246). Chung Hyun Kyung poignantly captures the essence, impulse and sanctity of reclaiming syncretism as an Asian heritage and the re-creation of living abundantly in faith (John 10:10), in ourselves, our communities and our God(s). In doing theology, she prophetically relativizes the essence of Christianity:

> Because of warnings against syncretism, I once asked myself: how can I be a Christian and yet Buddhist? Through time . . . my question changed. I now ask: 'How can I be Christian without being Buddhist?' . . . I discovered my bowel is a shamanic bowel, my heart is a Buddhist heart and my head is a Christian head. (Sugirtharajah 1994: 5)

Post-colonialism: Negation or Empowerment?

> It is not the centre that determines the periphery, but the periphery that, in its boundedness, determines the centre. (Mohanty et al. 1991: 73–4)

This brings to light the de-colonized 'second (minority) terms' of Asian spirituality, namely, immanence, praxis, localization, truths or partiality, which are no longer subordinate to the privileged 'first (majority) terms' (ibid.: 73) of Eurocentric Christianity, transcendence, doctrine, abstraction, universalism and unitary Truth. Such hegemonic de-stabilization is reminiscent of the new spirit of the Kingdom of God: 'blessed are the poor in spirit: the kingdom of Heaven is theirs' (Matt. 5:3). Post-colonialism as an expedient academic, spatial and temporal periodization of history and genre, ironically reinstates the structures of domination that it purports to avoid (de la Campa et al. 1995: 30; McClintock 1995: 10–12). In the context of Asia, it bears the weight of a colonial conglomerate that includes the tyrannical Japanese Occupation during the Second World War, not to mention the Portuguese, Dutch, Spanish and British colonization across centuries of subservient mimicry. It bears the weight of the internal colonization of indigenous peoples by inimical and unsustainable national development policies in the name of modernization and progress. It bears the weight of neo-colonialism in the form of economic dependency on multi-national corporations and foreign donors such as the International Monetary Fund which widens the gulf between the haves and the have-nots. The notion of a 'globalised transhistoricity of colonialism', far from obfuscating 'determinate histories of determinate structures' (de la Campa et al. 1995: 31), makes transparent the proliferation and compression of oppressive forces that are political, socio-economic, cultural and religious.

Yet in theologizing from the standpoint of the poor of Asia, in fidelity to Jesus' preferential option for the poor, do Asian theologians run the risk of romanticizing the poor? Chia's contention that Christianity remains a ' "ghetto" religion in Asia' refutes this in his 'theologising from Easter'. In the context of the widespread and crippling poverty of the masses, he maintains that, 'before one can expect Asians to understand Easter and appreciate the Resurrection, justice and the liberation for the poor have to be realities evidenced in Asian societies' (Chia 2004). In saying this, he challenges the 'fantasies of absolute distance and absolute proximity' of universalisms, the Truth of the Good News in this instance (Ahmed 2000: 166). In the former, where universal Truth *'judges from afar by reading "the other" as a sign of the universal'*, he privileges the materiality of feeding the hungry, clothing the naked, healing the sick over the eschatological promise of the (abstract and inedible) Word (Matt. 25:35–7). In the latter, which *'assumes that the language of [the] universal [Word] has got "close enough" to the truth of the other's (well) being'*, he insists that the light of Easter (Matt. 28:6–7, Mark 16:6, Luke 24:8, John 20:10), as the foundational basis of Christianity, be refracted through the prism of the needs of Asia's poor in their particularized contexts of disenfranchisement. This serves as a touchstone in authenticating theologizing by, of and for Asians.

In conclusion, theologies from Asia are a successor epistemology – evolutionary and revolutionary – to post-Enlightenment Liberation Theologies from Latin America and Africa. Through dialectical encounters between theologizing by Asians and post-colonial theorizing, I have delineated the ways in which theologizing from Asia is first, knowledge that counts in drawing from the wellsprings of multi-ethnicity, multi-culturalism and multi-religiosity of Asia. Second, those who theologize are those who know, those invested with social and cultural capital because they start thought from

Asia's poor, those who live theology within the rubric of oppression and agency. Third, in doing so, Asian theologians see from above and below: they insist on hyphenating the categories of universalism–particularity, transcendence–immanence, doctrinal Truth–living truths, singularity–plurality, spirituality–materiality and Christianity–Asian spiritualities. Theologizing from Asia that breaks down unified and uncontested meanings of the Bible, first received as a colonial text, when translated within the plurality of cultures and religions of Asia, is a paradoxical breakthrough.

Finally, Asian theologians have it both ways, partial knowledge in resisting the abstraction of universalisms at the cost of incurring the wrath of Rome (the violence of silencing Asian theologians such as Tissa Balasuriya). They achieve this by insisting on the particularities of what it means to theologize from the heterogeneous bowels of Asia that is differentiated from Latin America and Africa within the common condition of post-coloniality. In doing so, they politicize spirituality in responding 'Here I am' (Exod. 3:4) to the call of engendering social justice. And they spiritualize politics in insisting on good governance at local and global levels: development that is sustainable and equitable in begetting a heaven on earth.

Will the new millennium be the 'Asian Millennium' invigorated by the great spiritual traditions of the East' (Crowell 1997)? The signs of the times allude to this potentiality by virtue of the dynamism of churches of Asia. The greater contention inferred in this prophecy is that Christianity has become a spiritual tradition of the East, an Asian religious tradition that is not only a re-source but also a source of light to the world.

References

Abraham, Dulcie (1996). 'A Home for Hagar', in *Voice of Christian Women*, May: 4–5.

Ahmed, Sara (2000). *Strange Encounters: Embodied Others in Post-Coloniality*. London and New York: Routledge.

Benhabib, Seyla (1992). *Situating the Self: Gender, Community and Postmodernism in Contemporary Ethics*. Cambridge: Polity Press.

Bhabha, Homi (1994). *The Location of Culture*. London and New York: Routledge.

Chia (2004). 'Easter and Asian Theology', *National Catholic Reporter*, 14 May, 40(28): 18.

Chung Hyun Kyung (1990). *Struggle to Be the Sun Again: Introducing Asian Women's Theology*. Maryknoll, NY: Orbis Books.

Chung Hyun Kyung (1991). 'Come, Holy Spirit – Break Down the Walls With Wisdom and Compassion', in Ursula King (ed.), *Feminist Theology from the Third World: A Reader*. Maryknoll, NY: Orbis, pp. 392–4.

Chung Hyun Kyung (1994). ' "Han-pu-ri": Doing Theology from Korean Women's Perspective', in R. S. Sugirtharajah (ed.), *Frontiers in Asian Christian Theology: Emerging Trends*. Maryknoll, NY: Orbis, pp. 52–62.

Crowell, Todd (1997). 'In Search of an Asian Path'. *Asiaweek*, 19 December, p. 1.

De la Campa, Roman, Kaplan, E. Ann and Sprinkler, Michael (eds) (1995). *Late Imperial Culture*. London and New York: Verso.

Devi (1994). 'The Struggle of Dalit Christian Women in India', in Ursula King (ed.), *Feminist Theology from the Third World: A Reader*. London: SPCK, pp. 135–7.

Emberley, Julia V. (1993). *Thresholds of Difference: Feminist Critique, Native Women's Writings, Post-colonial Theory*. Toronto: University of Toronto Press.

Fabella, Virginia and Oduyoye, Mercy Amba (eds) (1994). *With Passion and Compassion: Third World Women Doing Theology*. Maryknoll, NY: Orbis.

Fabella, Virginia and Torres, Sergio (eds) (1985). *Doing Theology in a Divided World: Papers from the Sixth International Conference of the EATWOT*. 5–13 January, Geneva, Switzerland. Maryknoll, NY: Orbis.

Fiorenza, Elisabeth Schüssler (ed.) (1993). *Searching the Scriptures: A Feminist Introduction*. vol. 1. London: SCM Press.

Fung, Jojo M. (1992). *Shoes-Off Barefoot We Walk: A Theology of Shoes-Off*. Kuala Lumpur, Malaysia: Vivar Printing.

Fung, Jojo M. (1996). 'A Local Theology of Healing: Temiar Shamanism, Syncretism, and Mission of the Local Church', unpublished, DMin paper, Chicago: University of Chicago Press.

Fung, Jojo M. (2003). *Ripples on the Water: Believers in the Orang Asli's Struggle for a Homeland of Equal Citizens*. Masai, Malaysia: Majodi Publication, Diocesan Office for Social Communications.

Gnanadason, Aruna (1994). 'Women's Oppression: A Sinful Situation', in Virginia Fabella and Mercy Amba Oduyoye (eds), *With Passion and Compassion: Third World Women Doing Theology*. Maryknoll, NY: Orbis, pp. 69–76.

Gort, Jerald et al. (1989). *Dialogue and Syncretism: An Interdisciplinary Approach*. Amsterdam: Editions Rodopi.

Guha, Ranajit and Spivak, Gayatri Chakravorty (eds) (1988). *Selected Subaltern Studies*. New York and Oxford: Oxford University Press.

Jayawardena, Kumari (1995). *The White Woman's Other Burden: Western Women and South Asia During British Colonial Rule*. New York and London: Routledge.

Katoppo (1980). *Compassionate and Free: An Asian Women's Theology*. New York: Orbis.

Kim, Sangwha (1993). 'The Story from Hagar's Perspective', in *In God's Image* 12(4): 23–5.

King, Ursula (ed.) (1994). *Feminist Theology from the Third World: A Reader*. Maryknoll, NY: Orbis.

King, Ursula (1995). *Religion and Gender*. Oxford: Blackwell.

Kwok Pui Lan (1989). 'The Emergence of Asian Feminist Consciousness of Culture and Theology', in Virginia Fabella and Sun Ai Lee-Park (eds), *We Dare To Dream: Doing Theology as Asian Women*. AWRC and EATWOT Women's Commission in Asia.

Kwok Pui Lan (1993). 'Racism and Ethnocentrism in Feminist Biblical Interpretation', in Elisabeth S. Fiorenza (ed.), *Searching the Scriptures: A Feminist Introduction*, vol. 1. London: SCM Press, pp. 101–16.

Kwok Pui Lan (1994). 'Mothers and Daughters, Writers and Fighters', in R. S. Sugirtharajah (ed.), *Frontiers in Asian Christian Theology: Emerging Trends*. Maryknoll, NY: Orbis, pp. 147–55.

Landry, Donna and Maclean, Gerald (eds) (1993). *Materialist Feminisms*. Oxford: Blackwell.

Lung, Ngan Ling (1997). 'The Cries of Hagar', in *In God's Image* 16(2): 34–5.

Magee, Penelope M. (1995). 'Disputing the Sacred: Some Theoretical Approaches to Gender and Religion', in Ursula King (ed.), *Religion and Gender*. Oxford: Blackwell, pp. 101–20.

Mananzan, Mary J. (1992). *Woman and Religion: A Collection of Essays, Personal Histories and Contextualised Liturgies*, rev. edn. Manila: Institute of Women's Studies.

Marchand, Marianne H. and Parpart, Jane L. (eds) (1995). *Feminism/Postmodernism/Development*. London and New York: Routledge.

McClintock, Anne (1995). *Imperial Leather: Race, Gender and Sexuality in the Colonial Context*. London and New York: Routledge.

Mohanty, Chandra Talpade, Russo, Ann and Torres, Lourdes (eds) (1991). *Third World Women and the Politics of Feminism*. Bloomington, IN: Indiana University Press.

Nirmal, Arvind P. (1994). 'Toward a Christian Dalit Theology', in R. A. Sugirtharajah (ed.), *Frontiers in Asian Christian Theology: Emerging Trends*. Maryknoll, NY: Orbis, pp. 27–40.

Norani Othman and Ng, Cecilia (eds) (1995). *Gender, Culture and Religion: Equal Before God, Unequal Before Man*. Kuala Lumpur, Malaysia: Persatuan Sains Social Malaysia.

Park, A. Sung (1988). 'Minjung and Process Hermeneutics', *Process Studies* 1(2): 118–26.

Pieris, Aloysius, SJ (1990). *Love Meets Wisdom: A Christian Experience of Buddhism*. Maryknoll, NY: Orbis.

Pieris, Aloysius, SJ (1994). 'Two Encounters in My Theological Journey', in R. S. Sugirtharajah (ed.), *Frontiers in Asian Christian Theology: Emerging Trends*. Maryknoll, NY: Orbis, pp. 141–6.

Said, Edward (1978). *Orientalism*. London: Routledge and Kegan Paul.

Shorter, Aylward (1988). *Toward a Theology of Inculturation*. London: Geoffrey Chapman.

Song, C. S. (1980). *Third-Eye Theology: Theology in Formation in Asian Settings*. Guildford and London: Lutterworth Press.

Song, C. S. (1982). *The Compassionate God: An Exercise in the Theology of Transposition*. London: SCM Press.

Spivak, Gayatri Chakravorty (1990). *The Post-Colonial Critic: Interviews, Strategies, Dialogues*. Ed. Sarah Harasym. New York and London: Routledge.

Stewart, Charles and Shaw, Rosalind (eds) (1994). *Syncretism/Anti-syncretism: The Politics of Religious Synthesis*. London: Routledge.

Sugirtharajah, R. S. (1994). *Frontiers in Asian Christian Theology: Emerging Trends*. Maryknoll, NY: Orbis.

Sugirtharajah, R. S. (2002). *Postcolonial Criticism and Biblical Interpretation*. Oxford: Oxford University Press.

Suh, David Kwang-sun (1994). 'Theology of Reunification', in R. S. Sugirtharajah (ed.), *Frontiers in Asian Christian Theology: Emerging Trends*. Maryknoll, NY: Orbis, pp. 196–205.

Teruo (1994). 'Recovering Jesus for Outcasts in Japan', in R. S. Sugirtharajah (ed.), *Frontiers in Asian Christian Theology: Emerging Trends*. Maryknoll, NY: Orbis, pp. 11–26.

Wong Wai Ching (2000). 'Negotiating for a Postcolonial Identity: Theology of "the Poor Woman" in Asia', *Journal of Feminist Studies in Religion*, Fall, 16(2): 1–21.

CHAPTER 30
Postmodernism

Andrew Tate

Introduction: Postmodernism and the 'Book of Books'

This chapter explores the multiple manifestations and interpretations of the Bible in our own complex historical moment, an epoch frequently identified with the name 'postmodern', one of the most notoriously slippery epithets in the English language. 'Unfortunately, "postmodern" is a term *bon à tout faire* . . . applied today to anything the user of the term happens to like', states Umberto Eco (1985: 64). The misgivings of the Italian novelist-philosopher embody the frustration of a vast body of critical thinkers including sociologists, architects and theologians who have dared to define postmodernism. 'The new sensibility is defiantly pluralistic', Susan Sontag once proclaimed: 'it is dedicated both to an excruciating seriousness and to fun and wit and nostalgia'. Sontag's analysis, pregnant with ecstatic zeal in 1964, remains oddly prophetic regarding the 'high-speed and hectic' atmosphere of the early twenty first century (1990: 304). Privileged societal hierarchies – between high and low culture, for example – are regarded with suspicion in postmodern thought. Fittingly, this conveniently fuzzy term is associated with indeterminacy, ambivalence, irony and detachment. Paradoxically, it is also used to diagnose the pathology of a world violently divided by fundamentalisms, fanatical political creeds, and the (not unrelated) remorseless exigencies of global capitalism. Such unsettling contexts might not be entirely new to human society – bloodshed, belief and business form the dark materials of world history – but these frameworks are currently structured in ways quite alien to the traditions of understanding with which previous generations have narrated their world-views. The prospects of identifying shared beliefs that straightforwardly define trans-national communities such as the Church are undermined by the bruising realities of life in a belligerent, fragmented world. This palpable lack of unity or what Stanley Hauerwas calls the 'current sparsity of agreements about agreements' shapes our reception of all texts and particularly one as crucial to the history of the West as the Bible (1997: 1).

Eco suggests that 'postmodernism is not a trend to be chronologically defined, but, rather an ideal category – or better still . . . a way of operating': 'every period has its own postmodernism' (1985: 66). For the American Marxist critic, Frederic Jameson, postmodernism is emphatically 'a periodizing concept' through which we might 'correlate the emergence of new formal features in culture with the emergence of a new type of social life and a new economic order' in the six decades since World War II (1998: 3). The postmodern era is synonymous in Jameson's view with the advent of 'multinational capitalism' and is characterized by

> New types of consumption; planned obsolescence; an ever more rapid rhythm of fashion and styling changes; the penetration of advertising, television and the media generally to a hitherto unparalleled degree throughout society; the replacement of the old tension between city and country, centre and province, by the suburb and by universal standardization; the growth of the great networks of superhighways and the arrival of automobile culture (1998: 3, 19–20)

How then does the present-day 'cultural logic' – to use Jameson's terms (1991) – of plurality and changefulness connect with the Bible, the book that the poet Emily Dickinson once sceptically named 'an Antique Volume'? Christopher Deacy claims that the language of biblical faith is now 'articulated through radically different vehicles of expression and outside traditionally demarcated boundaries of religious activity' and insists that these new agents be taken seriously (2001: 2). Similarly, this chapter argues against a simplified, tabloid-style consensus that twenty-first-century civilization is irrevocably estranged from its biblical inheritance. Indeed, Vanhoozer has argued that with the collapse of 'secular reason', a social force that 'repressed . . . the notion of divine revelation', '[p]ostmodernity has opened up breathing space' that 'creates . . . space to hear, once again, the voice of God, the wholly "other," speaking in Scripture' (2003c: 167). Yet many of the old orthodoxies have been tested: our epoch is bewildering, morally turbulent and, as Walter Brueggemann claims, readers of the Bible are working in a 'wholly new interpretative situation' (1993: vii).

The canonical Jewish-Christian writings, collectively known as the Bible, might well appear uncanny to a contemporary reader without specific religious commitments. As Robert Alter and Frank Kermode have commented, '[t]o most educated modern readers the Bible probably seems familiar and strange, like the features of an ancestor' (1989: 1). This dizzyingly plural book figures so heavily in our shared past, that it demands constant reappraisal. In the late nineteenth century, John Ruskin, a polymathic prophet for the age, exhorted his readers to examine the significance of biblical writing for their own, increasingly materialistic culture. For Ruskin, the Bible was more than a grimly monolithic volume; it was the 'Book of books':

> Think, so far as it is possible for any of us – either adversary or defender of the faith – to extricate his intelligence from the habit and the association of moral sentiment based upon the Bible, what literature could have taken its place, or fulfilled its function, though every library in the world had remained, unravaged, and every teacher's truest words had been written down. (1908: 109–10, 118)

Today relatively few people readily refer to this most commonplace and mysterious of texts as a guide in matters either of morality or political conduct. Yet the Bible is quoted, deconstructed, appealed to, denounced and appropriated almost relentlessly in our perplexing, detradtionalized world; faith, past or present, is no prerequisite for access to this legacy. Daniel Bell contends that contemporary capitalist life is characterized by an 'extraordinary freedom to ransack the world storehouse and to engorge any and every style it comes upon'. Pop culture is witness to this blithe boundary-crossing in which 'nothing is forbidden, all is to be explored' (1979: 13–14; quoted in Woodhead and Heelas 2000: 376) when novelists, theorists, movie directors and musicians revisit the Bible as a rich seam of images to be exploited and revised, parodied and praised. The trope of boundary-crossing movement – between disciplines, cultures and spiritualities – is a recurrent motif in recent interrogations of postmodern theology (Exum and Moore 1998a; Bauman 1998; Ward 2000). Tom Beaudoin, for example, a self-styled 'Generation X' theologian, narrates his spiritual return to Catholicism via Baptist meetings and Jewish Synagogues as typical of his contemporaries' 'irreverence' (2000: 18). Spiritual tourism, in which the liberty to flirt evasively with multiple faith traditions becomes a kind of fetish, is one of the idiosyncrasies of late capitalism.

Fragments of biblical quotation continue to litter the transactions of contemporary life: half-remembered parables and scriptural figures shadow dance in our shared but near amnesiac cultural consciousness. Language deemed sacred is rarely contained by the narrow spaces of organized belief: Carroll observes that placards bearing the slogan John 3:16, potentially the most recognizable verse in the gospels, are frequently flourished by devout fans at major sporting events (1998b: 50). Surprisingly the same quotation can inspire a quasi-devout essay by a non-religious cultural theorist (Žižek 2001). Students of cultural history will discover the Western tradition's reliance on a reservoir of imagery derived from the Old and New Testaments. At the other end of the aesthetic spectrum, scheming soap-opera characters can be branded 'Judas' and, regardless of faith tradition, the audience will understand the indictment, but perhaps be unaware of its obnoxious historical associations. If a once disgraced politician returns to government, (s)he might easily be described as a 'prodigal' figure by the mass media in a secular echo of Jesus' parable of the lost son (Luke 15:11–32). In the most secular of contexts, an ancient metaphor of divine love can be intuitively deployed to lend magnitude, however specious, to the transitory sphere of political affairs.

For all this mystical mischief, the constitutive influence of the Bible on the Western imagination should not be underestimated; it exists as more than a ghostly half presence in the (post)modern world. 'The Bible has invited endless exegesis not only because of the drastic economy of its means of expression,' Alter asserts, 'but also because it conceives of the world as a place full of things to understand in which the things of ultimate importance defy human understanding' (Alter and Kermode 1992: 22). Biblical interpretation persists in the official arenas of Jewish *midrash* and Christian hermeneutics, but, just as vitally, it is also at play in the unsanctified spaces of everyday experience. Understanding sacred texts becomes part of the democratic, unruly rituals of reading and argument undertaken by ordinary individuals and communities: by believers, doubters and unabashed sceptics. Although the postmodern mind is wounded and forgetful, traumatized by violence and anxious about the future, trace memories of ancient narratives assist in the process of imagining a more just society.

The chapter will emphasize the extraordinary resilience of the 'Book of books' in our so-called 'postmodern' era. The sequence of headings around which the chapter is structured is designed to represent the diverse fields of contemporary society in which the Bible remains a vital and challenging presence. These comprise an evaluation of the generative tension between postmodern and biblical reading strategies; the significance of narrative and acts of story-telling as both postmodern and biblical practice; and, finally, an exploration of the escalating, vibrant correlation between popular culture and biblical literature.

Reading in the Dark: Babel, Interpretation and a Confusion of Tongues

> But the LORD came down to see the city and the tower that the men were building. The LORD said, 'If as one people speaking the same language they have begun to do this, then nothing they plan to do will be impossible. Come, let us go down and confuse their language so they will not understand each other.'

> So the LORD scattered them from there over all the earth, and they stopped building the city. That is why it was called Babel – because there the LORD scattered them over the face of the whole earth. (Gen. 11:5–9)

The story of the construction and fall of the Babel tower, a narrative delineating how human arrogance might precipitate both divine punishment and social atomism, has become one possible paradigm for postmodern experience. Zygmunt Bauman, for example, describes contemporary culture as a 'cacophony of moral voices' (1992, xxii). Echoes of disorderly, deafening post-Babel tongues can be heard everywhere: in the clash of cultures and the rise of fundamentalisms – both secular and sacred – we are witnesses to a stunning plurality of cultural idioms and an aggressive struggle for domination; bound by the limits of what Benedict Anderson famously named 'imagined communities' (1983) we find ourselves alienated from those who conceive of reality differently.

A complex, image-driven society such as our own demands sophisticated modes of interpretation; readers are required to be more, not less, literate. In an era characterized by global communication we are relentlessly bombarded with the seductive imagery of adverts, the urgency of 24-hour news channels and the instantaneous text-messages. Rival stories – commercial, political and religious – fight for attention and supremacy. The internet, with its seemingly infinite links and the interminable choices offered by satellite television, have both become aesthetic and interpretative paradigms: we rapidly move from image to image and between fragments of stories – fictional and real – swiftly making our judgements. For Valentine Cunningham, the act of reading 'is never innocent' because the 'reader' carries with them a set of cultural rules for textual understanding and 'is always in some sense already fallen into knowledge': 'Reading is . . . a postlapsarian business. It has always eaten of the tree of theoretical knowledge' (2002: 5). This allusion to the fall of humanity in Genesis 3 is a powerful metaphor for interpretation. By necessity, younger generations have become adept at non-linear modes of reading. As Detweiler and Taylor, two theologians of contemporary culture, argue '[p]ostmodernity cuts and pastes, scans and surfs . . . We're interactive and interrelated, practicing a different form of thinking' (2003: 34).

In a crucial episode in Mark Haddon's *The Curious Incident of the Dog in the Night Time* (2003), Christopher Boone, the novel's adolescent narrator, absconds to London. When he arrives at Paddington Station, Christopher is overwhelmed by the nightmarish and exhilarating overload of information. The station is an exemplary space of late capitalism, pulsing with human traffic and a multitude of seductive advertisements, all competing for the subjective desires of the traveller-consumer. It embodies what Guy Debord in 1967 identified as the 'society of the spectacle' and it is another iteration of Babel. However, Christopher – as his name suggests, a Christ figure, lost in a postmodern desert – is not an average 'consumer of illusions' (Debord 1983: 47). He suffers from Asperger's syndrome and, coupled with a brilliant ability to rationalize, he 'sees everything' and has a profound antipathy for new situations. Instead of passively absorbing the multitude of signs, he is viscerally confused and upset by the Babel of inducements to insatiable consumption. In this defamiliarizing passage, the novelist evokes the confused, subconscious mind of the postmodern citizen who, as David Lyon observes, is taught to forget 'the idea that who we are is given by God . . . we shape our malleable image by what we buy' (2000: 12).

Appropriately, the story of the construction and fall of the Babel tower appeals to diverse intellectual sensibilities, both radical and conservative, whose writings have been influential in shaping the emerging world-views of the past 20 years. Jacques Derrida, for example, has produced what Hart calls one of the writer's 'most winning accounts of deconstruction' via 'an allegory of mankind's second fall' in Genesis 11:1–9 (Derrida et al. 1985a, 1985b; Hart 1989: 109). *The Postmodern Bible*, in response to Derrida's commentary on this biblical passage, describes deconstruction itself as a 'Babelian intervention': 'it challenges the erection of any concept of reality unscathed by interpretation, by translation, whether it take the form of a historical reconstruction, a literary reading, a scientific hypothesis, or a philosophical system' (Castelli et al. 1995: 129). Derrida's resolutely unsystematic analysis of the complex relation between language and meaning and the challenge to the dominant traditions of Western philosophy have been crucial for contemporary articulations of biblical theology. Graham Ward is one of the leading contemporary theologians to engage with Derrida's critique of 'the metaphysics of language itself which continually deceives us into believing that words are merely windows on the world' (1995: 5). Where Ward explores the potential of Derrida's theories of difference to recuperate an orthodox theology, others, like Don Cuppitt and Mark C. Taylor have appropriated deconstruction to define radical 'atheologies', abandoning realism. Gavin Hyman (2001) and Gerard Loughlin (1996) contrast these nihilist theologies with the work of other contemporary theologians including Ward and John Milbank whose work offers a thorough critique of secular culture via the great theological tradition and a Christian engagement with Derrida. Similarly, Hart challenges what he names the 'often unspoken assumption that there is a natural or inevitable link between deconstruction and atheism' (1989: 42). Other significant readings of Derrida and theology include studies by Arthur Bradley (2004) and John D. Caputo who argues that 'far from being the last nail in the coffin prepared for the death of God, the deconstructibility of things is one of the hallmarks of the kingdom of God' (2001: 478).

Alongside the deconstruction of Derrida, the babble of Babel is also a trope invoked by Michel Foucault, another crucial voice in post-structuralist philosophy, in his interrogation of archaeology and episteme, *The Order of Things* (1989: 36). Other explicit citations of this story of vanished linguistic and social unity are made in the titles of George Steiner's *After Babel: Aspects of Language and Translation* (1992) and A. S. Byatt's novel *Babel Tower* (1995). In *Roger's Version* (1986), John Updike's theologian narrator invokes the ghost of Babel as he repudiates a student's quasi-heretical attempt to prove the existence of God (1986: 22).

The cultural diversity of our postmodern moment is accompanied by a yearning to recuperate a mythic linguistic transparency, a desire to overcome our sense of what Foucault, invoking Babel, terms a sense of 'lost similitude' (1989: 36). Bauman argues that '[t]he allure of fundamentalism stems from its promise to emancipate the converted from the agonies of choice' and insists that this mode of extremism is 'a legitimate child of postmodernity, born of its joys and torments and heir to its achievements and worries alike' (1998: 74). However, the varieties of fundamentalism extend well beyond the borders of the major world religions; the monotheism of mammon, the apparent victory of consumerist culture, with its strict creed of the open market, is the most successful of fundamentalisms. After the totalitarian regimes of the last century, a new Babel has been erected: the language of global capitalism, in which all nations and individuals are now expected to be fluent, supposedly effaces any ethnic, social or religious differences, so that once more the world is supposedly unified in a single tongue. 'The norm now is money', states Terry Eagleton, suggesting that the collapse of anything resembling a coherent social order in the West has produced a vacuum that capital enjoys rather than abhors (2000: 16–17).

How does the contemporary imagination respond to the seductive pleasures of capital? In Douglas Coupland's first novel, *Generation X: Tales for an Accelerated Culture* (1991), one of his characters commits a minor, random act of vandalism against a high-priced car: 'I'm just upset that the world has gotten too big – way beyond our capacity to tell stories about it, and so all we're stuck with are these blips and chunks and snippets on bumpers' (ibid.: 6). The next section of the chapter will focus on the postmodern yearning for narrative and its possible connections with the Bible.

What's the Story?: 'Denarration' and the Bible

'Humanity surrounds itself with narrative', claims John Sutherland. 'We marinade, embalm and poach ourselves in the stuff' (2004: 11). The postmodern world is teeming with stories: as Sutherland suggests we are all storytellers and listeners; we trade in fictions, real and imagined, which are produced, consumed and reused in countless novels, films and shared anecdotes. Michael Edwards asserts that this need for narrative is essentially theological: 'Story offers an otherness, of unity and purposive sequence. It also offers, in particular, beginnings and ends . . . The specific of story is that it appeals to the desire for a new beginning' (1984: 73). What role does the Bible play in this quest for origins and endings, for renewal and a sense of purpose? Historically, Christians and Jews have used their sacred writings as a lens through which to view the problematic relation between material reality and spiritual truth. The books of what Christian culture names the Bible – problematic and misleadingly harmonizing title though it is for such a diverse collection of writings – have been viewed as a locus of authority, in its many versions, and as foundational for Western society.

However, in his contentious secularization thesis, Callum Brown concludes that: '[i]f a core reality survives for Britons, it is certainly no longer Christian':

> Whereas previously, men and women were able to draw upon a Christian-centred culture to find guidance about how they should behave . . . from the 1960s a suspicion of creeds arose that quickly took the form of a rejection of Christian tradition and all formulaic constructions of the individual. (2001: 193)

Douglas Coupland, one of the sharpest narrators of contemporary experience, insists that 'our lives need to be stories, narratives' and 'when our stories vanish, that is when we feel lost, dangerous, out of control and susceptible to the forces of randomness'. For Coupland, this becomes 'the process whereby one loses one's life story: "denarration"' (1997: 179). This logic might be applied to Brown's model of a post-Christian society, one that has lost its sense of belonging to a biblical – and originally Jewish – narrative of fall, exile and redemption. Gerard Loughlin suggests that a faithless contemporary world has become estranged from the 'plot' that previously shaped it:

> The medievals conceived the world as a book written by God, the plot of which is given God's other book, the Bible. Today, however, the world is plotted by different narratives, either humanly authored (modernism) or authorless (post-modernism). Now the world writes itself; or better, is writing itself. (Loughlin 1996: 29)

Loughlin stands in a dynamic tradition of narrative theology and his work negotiates the necessity of reclaiming a divinely authored storyline from the ruins of contemporary secularity. Alienation from a narrative that confers meaning and identity is fundamental to one of the most influential – if not specifically theological – accounts of postmodernity. 'Simplifying to the extreme, I define *postmodern* as incredulity toward metanarratives' (Lyotard 1984: xxiv). The metanarratives or '*grand récits*' identified by Lyotard are those self-legitimating stories – including science and, implicitly, religion and politics – that explain and justify the limits of knowledge and understanding. The Bible *per se* is not a metanarrative, despite its claims to truth and its constitutive influence on Western culture. However, Christianity, the broad and politically powerful interpretative framework that names the Bible and provides its major interpretative context, *is* a classic grand narrative. In these terms, as David Lyle Jeffries suggests, the 'purpose' of biblical writing 'was thought to assist in the reestablishment of right relationship between God, the ultimate Author, and his fallen, alienated readers' (1996: xv).

Consumer capitalism has become a rival metanarrative to those offered by transcendent, text-focused religions; it is a story that justifies itself and which demands veneration. A culture driven by inexorable acquisitiveness and dependent upon incessant
greed surely conflicts with Judaeo-Christian doctrines of holiness, community, spiritual
aspiration and the injunction against the worship of false idols. In the postmodern age
we both prize mobility and mourn the loss of home; we pursue transient thrills and
ache for the eternal. The apparent confusion of our era – a pathological duality that
Jameson has described as 'schizophrenia' – might be a product of postmodernity's lack
of a stable identity (1998: 3). Linda Hutcheon, for example, writes of the 'grand flourish of negativized rhetoric' and the 'disavowing prefixes' connected with contemporary
aesthetic and critical theory: 'we hear of discontinuity, disruption, dislocation, decentring, indeterminacy, and antitotalization' (1988: 3). Similarly, Gavin Hyman states
that '[p]ostmodernism is . . . a negative and parasitic term that depends on the negation
of something else for its self-definition' (2001: 11). This 'something else' is the confident culture of modernity that emerged in the European Renaissance of the fifteenth
and sixteenth centuries and gained momentum with the eighteenth-century Enlightenment. Modern Western culture celebrated the power of human intellect, and superstition and ambiguity were banished to the forgotten wastelands of history: the world
apparently became a wholly knowable space that could be measured, understood and
conquered.

Religion did not simply disappear with the advent of modernity but its social dominance was undermined by the cultural ascendancy of the newly empowered universities. 'The withdrawal of God meant a triumphant entry of Man', Zygmunt Bauman has
observed of this paradigmatic shift (1992: xii). Biblical scholarship underwent a revolution during the eighteenth and nineteenth centuries as it sought to reconcile values
of secular reason with the traditions of faith. Theological method, inflected, in particular, by historical criticism was modernity's gift to the Church (Stiver 2003). In a
pioneering study, Hans Frei describes 'the break-up of the cohesion between the literal
meaning of the biblical narratives and their reference to actual events' precipitated by
the emergence of historical criticism (1974: 4). The long-tradition of 'realist' Bible
reading, exemplified in Frei's view by Augustine, 'envisioned the . . . world as formed
by the sequence told by the biblical stories' (ibid.: 1). The individual reader was expected
to interpret 'the shape of his own life as well as that of his era's events as figures of that
storied world' embodied in the Bible (1974: 3). In the enlightened world of eighteenth-
century Europe, however, a belief in progress and human perfectibility became the
dominant world-view that supplanted an eschatological hope for salvation by a transcendent God.

Yet, in spite of its apparent triumph, contemporary critiques suggest that modernity
was merely a powerful fiction that masked a lack of certainty about the contingent
foundations of human knowledge (Bauman 1992; Ward 2003). Modernity proved to
be a temporary state rather than an achieved utopia. Faith in the infallibility of human
reason – indeed in the quasi-sanctity of progress – was devastated by the unimaginable
and unrepresentable horrors of the Holocaust and later genocides in the twentieth
century. '[T]he Enlightenment itself collapses under the weight of its own aspirations',
observes Rowan Williams (2000: 164). What began as a democratic impulse to

demystify an allegedly immutable sacred order that protected the interests of a ruling elite itself contained a 'hidden investment in certain sorts of power and enslavement' (2000: 164). Secular reason is no less politically and economically innocent than a social order based around monarchical and ecclesiastical hierarchies. Indeed, Bauman suggests that the cult of reason took on a sacred aura as '[m]odernity was . . . [the Western Man's] *mission*, proof of moral righteousness and cause of pride' (1992: xiv).

Postmodern culture, whether it represents either the culmination or final repudiation of modernity, certainly has different implications for biblical interpretation and narrative theology. Where modernity was characterized by confidence in the integrity of systems of interpretation, its contemporary sequel is far less trusting and, indeed, becomes radically aware of the artificial status of all method. Understanding and interpretation are condition, subject to prejudice and the limits of vision; as Exum and Moore observe: 'there is no neutral place from which interpretation may occur . . . social locations are always interpreted, not given.' (1998b: 35).

Bauman suggests that, from one perspective, this new culture 'is a state of mind marked above all by its all-deriding, all-eroding, all-dissolving *destructiveness*' (1992: vii–viii). Taken in isolation, this diagnosis would suggest that a postmodern approach to the Bible is necessarily characterized by corrosive scepticism. Yet Bauman suggests that contemporary iconoclasm is not a 'destructive destruction' (ibid.: ix). Postmodernism might be seen as a '*re-enchantment* of the world modernity tried hard to *dis-enchant*' (ibid.: x). This is not to suggest that the contemporary suspicion of methodology, order and reason facilitates a simplistic return to a pre-critical naïvety, in which the difficult questions that might be inspired by an authentic, mature wrestling with the Bible are silenced.

In a peculiar late essay, D. H. Lawrence, the fractious Romantic-Modernist author, reviewed the routines of reading that he learned during his non-conformist childhood. *Apocalypse* (1931) considers the persuasive force of having 'the Bible poured every day into my helpless consciousness, till there came almost a saturation point' (ibid.: 9). 'The Bible', argues Lawrence, 'has been temporarily killed for us . . . by having its meaning arbitrarily fixed. We know it so thoroughly, in its superficial or popular meaning, that it is dead, it gives us nothing any more' (ibid.: 15). Do the interpretative 'instincts' of contemporary readers resemble those of Lawrence?

Postmodern world-views might, in fact, recuperate the holy strangeness of biblical discourse. Julian Barnes' novel *A History of the World in 10½ Chapters* (1989) parodies the Jewish-Christian grand narrative by contrasting belief in purpose and moral order with what he suggests is the absurd and hazardously contingent nature of human experience. The book begins with a re-writing of the flood narrative from Genesis 6–9. Barnes' subversive short story is narrated neither by an omniscient figure nor by Noah but via the tale's titular 'stowaway': a woodworm. This dispossessed, unlovely creature argues that its account 'you can trust' because it has no need to glorify humanity or religious tradition (1989: 4). Readers committed to an orthodox religious position might be offended by Barnes' appropriation of a sacred text but equally 'The Stowaway' can be construed as an act of defamiliarization that engenders a new, constructive encounter with biblical literature. In turning to a story of origins, Barnes memorializes the imaginative vision of Genesis and metaphorically confronts the abuses of religious belief.

Barnes' playful re-imagination of the authorized religious history of the world is one of many re-interpretations of biblical tradition produced by the ambivalent spiritual imagination of the postmodern world. In the sequence of 'Pocket Canons' published in the late 1990s, the canonical collided with voices of dissent when individual books of Bible in the Authorized King James Version were republished, each coupled with a short introductory commentary by a contemporary novelist, artist or scientist. Many of these introductions were most notable for their lack of reverence for the source material and reflect atheist world-views. Louis de Bernières, for example, describes the Book of Job as 'insidiously subversive': God, for de Bernières, emerges from the narrative appearing 'like an unpleasantly sarcastic megalomaniac' (1998: xiii) and as 'a frivolous trickster' (ibid.: xiv). Where the 'Pocket Canons' series demonstrated respect for the language of the Authorized Version but a degree of resentment towards its substance, a new iteration of the scriptures, *The Street Bible* (2003), transforms biblical language into contemporary vernacular in an attempt to salvage its meaning. Rob Lacey's project, which he notes 'is not meant to replace the real thing' and uses 'an absolute minimum of religious language' exemplifies a mode of contemporary missiology that recognizes the necessity of negotiation with new cultural vocabularies (2003: 11).

Similarly, contemporary critical theory, much of it associated with sceptical strands within postmodernism, has opened up new horizons for biblical interpretation. All serious readers – regardless of creed – need to engage with those theorists whom one philosopher has named 'secular postmodernists who so often evoke nothing but fear and loathing from people of faith' (Westphal 1999: 2). The self-styled Bible and Culture Collective, co-authors of the *The Postmodern Bible*, a daring attempt to synthesize radical theory and biblical scholarship, argue against a simple evaluation of postmodernity that offers either 'unthinking repudiations or mindless approbations' of the trend. The collective calls instead for 'a critical engagement with its substances – its debates, its theories, and its practices in all of their aesthetic, social, and political aspects' (Castelli et al. 1995: 9).

In the revolutionary year of 1968, Roland Barthes published his epoch-making essay 'The Death of the Author', a cultural manifesto with radical implications for all acts of reading:

> We know that a text is not a line of words releasing a single 'theological' meaning (the 'message' of the Author-God) but a multi-dimensional space in which a variety of writing, none of them original, blend and clash. The text is a tissue of quotations drawn from the innumerable centres of culture. (1977: 146)

This fundamental 'decentring' of texts, in which the 'author-god' is no longer perceived as the ultimate arbiter of meaning has particular resonance for biblical interpretation. Barthes even describes this 'poststructuralist' shift as 'anti-theological' since it involves a 'revolutionary', readerly resistance to 'God and his hypostases – reason, science, law' (1977: 147). However, the alleged death of the author is not necessarily synonymous either with the death of God or the end of Judaeo-Christian 'grand narratives'.

Theologians might elucidate previously repressed elements of biblical narrative via the 'post structuralism' of Barthes and others. As Brueggemann observes, 'Church inter-pretation . . . has tended to trim and domesticate the text not only to accommodate regnant modes of knowledge, but also to enhance regnant modes of power' (1993: vii). Traditions of social justice vital in Jewish and New Testament teaching are no guar-antee that contemporary readers can transcend the delicately veiled ideologies of self-interest that might govern any epoch. Readers convicted by the call in Isaiah 58:6 to 'true fasting' ('loose the chains of injustice and untie the cords of the yoke . . . set the oppressed free') are obliged to confront interpretative modes that exclude, subjugate or silence particular individuals or groups who do not belong to the established commu-nity of faith.

Perspectives ostensibly hostile to religious interpretation including Marxist, Feminist and deconstructive modes of criticism might alert readers to the ways in which some interpretations of the Bible are invested in modes of power struggle (Carroll 1998a; Castelli et al. 1995). Robert Carroll has given particular emphasis to the potential of New Historicist literary theory that seeks to give voice to 'the repressed and excluded' and 'to redress history in favour of the silenced and repressed of (somebody else's) history, usually the wretched of the earth' (1998a: 55).

Vanhoozer has identified a crucial ambiguity in the relationship between the con-flicted *Zeitgeist* of the early twenty-first-century West and the traditions of religious understanding as represented in Scripture. As Wolterstorff – a key figure for Vanhoozer's work – argues, '[t]he common, though nonetheless audacious, claim that God speaks' is a fundamental creed for Christian, Jewish and Muslim believers, in their many distinctive traditions and communities (1995: 16). The argument that God might act as 'a communicative agent' via the written word is a still more complex and poten-tially divisive conviction but it has not merely evaporated with the progress of science, technology and apparent parallel secularization of Western society (Vanhoozer 2003c: 165). Indeed, postmodernity, for all its suspicion of absolutes, is no synonym for a con-fidently secular culture that happily evades all religious interference. Ward, for example, has argued that 'with postmodernism God emerges from the white-out nihilism of modern atheism' and that the postmodern turn 'has fostered post-secular thinking – thinking about other, alternative worlds' (1997: xxi–xxii).

Proponents of 'secularization theory', including Bruce (1996) and Brown (2001), differ in their accounts of the origins of religious decline, but broadly concur that Western societies have progressively abandoned adherence to institutional spiritual practice. Yet alternative models of religious change, equally robustly defended, have emerged in recent years. '[T]he myth of secularization is dead,' Harvey Cox has com-batively stated (1999: 143). Lyon is also critical of standard sociological accounts that conclude religion is in terminal decline, offering the 'paradoxical' view that the process of secularity may have even become the 'stimulus for religious growth' since the frag-mentation of 'old religious monopolies' including Christianity are 'now compelled to reassess their vision, mission and strategies' and 'may well find new vigour in a plu-ralistic situation of competition' (2000: 33).

'Competition', a term most readily associated with free-market economics, now informs every area of cultural life in the West, including ostensibly sacred acts such as religious commitment. In what Lyon calls a 'detraditionalized world of deregulated religion' (2000: 17), individuals are faced with a seductive diversity of rival choices in a gaudy, bewildering spiritual marketplace. York argues that, far from constituting a point of resistance to consumerism, 'religion itself often becomes simply one more commodity and one more "tool" in the overall process of globalized homogeneity' (2001: 363). According to this model, the Bible loses its aura of authority and mutates into just one more option to be selected or rejected by the individual consumer according to their needs and desires. Dare we turn to a body of holy writings deeply embedded in our cultural memory but apparently utterly removed from what Jameson names the 'fundamental materiality' of our world (1991: 67)?

'Even Better than the Real Thing': The Bible, Popular Culture and the Post-Secular Imagination

Biblical figures preoccupy the early twenty-first-century imagination. 'The implosion of the secular', argues Graham Ward, 'has . . . facilitated a new return to the theological and a new emphasis upon re-enchantment: a return not signalled by theologians but by filmmakers, novelists, poets, philosophers, political theorists, and cultural analysts' (2001a: xv). Where modernity made an idol of 'meaning-legislating reason' and insisted that 'the world had to be *de-spiritualized*, de-animated and denied the capacity of the *subject*', today's prevailing atmosphere welcomes the mystical and the sublime in their numerous forms (Bauman 1992: x). This final section will identify a number of examples of biblical allusion in contemporary culture including critical theory, literature, music and cinema.

The turn to the sacred is often ambivalent: Slavoj Žižek, a self-styled 'fighting materialist', both deplores 'the return of the religious dimension in all its different guises' and argues that 'there *is* a direct lineage from Christianity to Marxism . . . the authentic Christian legacy is much too precious to be left to the fundamentalist freaks' (2000: 2). Literary criticism (McClure 1995; Tate 2002) and philosophy of religion (Blond 1999) also reflect the so-called turn to the 'post-secular'. The concept remains rather controversial, however, and Brian D. Ingraffia believes that, in apologetic terms, postmodern philosophy 'moves no further toward a recovery of the central scandal of the Christian faith' (1999: 64).

Consciously or otherwise, narratives central to the Bible are appropriated and reshaped by the eclectic contemporary imagination. Visions of divine judgement and miracle stories pervade recent Hollywood films and serious literary fiction. What is less apparent, however, is the authenticity of this new culture of scriptural allusion: are we faced with a monstrous mass of sacred simulacra that mimic shapes of spiritual substance but signify nothing? '[W]hat becomes of the divinity when it reveals itself in icons, when it is multiplied in simulacra? Does is remain the supreme power that is simply incarnated in images as a visible theology?' asks Baudrillard, in impishly apocalyptic mood (1994: 4). The famous essay from which this question is taken, 'The Precession of Simulacra' (1981) begins with a quotation from Ecclesiastes: it is, however, a fake, a biblical red herring that playfully suggests fundamental problems regarding representation, reality and the sacred.

Anxiety regarding the legitimacy of re-presentations of the holy in 'worldly' or irreligious forms such as film, pop music and the novel originates in the nineteenth-century elevation of creativity to the status of religion. Eagleton's claim that 'culture itself in the modern age comes to substitute itself for a fading sense of divinity and transcendence' suggests that culture is burdened with the responsibilities previously shaped by religious faith (2000: 2). Paul Heelas argues that 'dedifferentiation has . . . taken place with regard to the secular-sacred boundary. In measure, the religious has become less obviously religious, the secular less obviously secular' (Heelas et al. 1998: 3). Similarly, Grace Davie observes that '[t]he sacred starts to spill over into everyday thinking' and that during the 'last decade of the twentieth century . . . the sacred [was] plundered by the secular. At the very least, the lines between the two categories are undoubtedly becoming increasingly blurred' (1994: 41). The collapse of stable distinctions between religious practice and secular culture reflects wider social transformations. Jameson suggests that one of the defining features of postmodernity 'is the effacement in it of some key boundaries or separations, most notably the erosion of the older distinction between high culture and so-called mass or popular culture' (1998: 2). In the realm of the entertainment industry, a contested space where an unholy trinity of the aesthetic, the sensuous and the intellectual collide with the callous logic of commerce, religious identity frequently blurs. As Mazur and McCarthy observe, 'quasi-religious popular culture sites serve as points of intersection – sometimes harmonious, often conflictual – for people of very diverse and disparate identities' (2001: 3). Ostensibly 'secular' public events often achieve highly charged 'sacred' atmospheres: the vast crowd at a major football match or ecstatic dancers in a club might experience an intense sensation of communion; the darkened, holy hush of a cinema can be compared with the rituals of religious ceremony or, if the film is particularly poignant, to a moment of epiphany.

For Beaudoin, popular culture is much more than a surrogate religious tradition for his spiritually destitute contemporaries. He seeks the divine in unexpected places and argues that generations immersed in the songs and stories created by almost anybody but those who lead the Church, are intensely spiritual. 'During our lifetimes . . . pop culture was the amniotic fluid that sustained us. For a generation of kids who had a fragmented or completely broken relationship to "formal" or "institutional" religion, pop culture filled the spiritual gaps' (2000: 21). According to Beaudoin, this sustaining 'amniotic fluid' has generated a sharp awareness of the holy strangeness of biblical narrative.

Postmodern fiction is drawn into this perpetual wrestling with the plot of the Bible. James Wood's confrontational debut novel, *The Book Against God* (2004), for example, takes its epigraph from Paul's epistle to the Hebrews: 'For whom the Lord loveth he chasteneth, and scourgeth every son whom he receiveth' (12:6; cf. Prov. 3:12). Despite its apostate title, the novel becomes a highly spiritual – and arguably Christian – reworking of the parable of the prodigal son. Douglas Coupland's *Hey Nostradamus!* (2003), a fictional response to the motiveless mass-murders of North American high school students, has coincidental but strong parallels with Wood's novel: it too is intro-duced by an epigraph from Paul (1 Cor. 15:51–2 ('Behold, I tell you a mystery: we shall not all sleep but we shall all be changed . . .') and concludes with an explicit re-imagination of the same parable of sin, exile and redemption. Wood and Coupland are not unambiguously religious writers (indeed the former has written of his adolescent unconversion from Christianity) but both novels are animated by their sophisticated exploration of scriptural intertexts.

If the relationship between literature and Bible has been privileged, pop music is too easily dismissed as the most hedonistic art form to emerge in the 'value free' world of postmodernity. Lynch (2002) and Beaudoin (2000) both explore the significance of music to youth culture as a kind of surrogate for orthodox spirituality. Biblical imagery is often at play in pop music and sometimes in the most surprising of places. John Sutherland has observed that 'the narrative of [The Streets'] A Grand Don't Come for Free is constructed around Christ's parable of the lost piece of silver' (2004: 11). The album could not be described as religious or even spiritual by any conventional stan-dards but it takes its origin, subconsciously or otherwise, from Luke 15:9 and illustrates the persistence of parables in the popular consciousness.

Subversive artists sometimes employ biblical allusion with surreptitious playfulness. For example, on the cover of their album, *All that You Can't Leave Behind* (2000), the Irish rock band U2 – whose ambivalent relationship with Christian spirituality is well documented (Turner 1995; Stockman 2001) – are photographed in a departure lounge at Charles de Gaulle airport, standing in front of a digital screen displaying what is apparently a flight number, J333. This figure is, in fact, a coded reference to the prophet Jeremiah: 'Call to me and I will tell you great and unsearchable things you do not know' (Jer. 3. 33). The black and white portrait of the band – characteristic of their iconog-raphy – framed by a space that embodies global mobility and transience, is destabilized by the veiled reference to a biblical call to prayer.

Bruce Springsteen, one of the most ambivalent icons of American cultural life, has negotiated with an imaginative biblical inheritance throughout his three-decade career. Kate McCarthy (2001) assiduously traces the ways in which Springsteen's songs narrate the legacies of Puritan aspirations from the perspective of struggling, working-class men and women living in a viciously competitive country, far from the grace of a 'Promised Land'. His early work, in particular, is infused with the language of Genesis and Exodus. *Darkness on the Edge of Town* (1978), for example, dramatizes the ways in which original sin haunts the protagonists of 'Adam Raised a Cain' and 'Racing in the Street', people desperate to escape the overwhelming unhappiness of powerless, small-town life. The later lyrics are more infused with a New Testament theology but these appropriations are never blithely optimistic. The title track of the John Steinbeck-influenced album, *The Ghost of Tom Joad* (1995), a bitter hymn to America's dispossessed migrant workers, is charged with a disruptive biblical spirit: the destitute, desperate nar-rator resembles nothing less than a contemporary Christ, a suffering servant, kenoti-cally divested of earthly power and might. This incarnational imagery is intensified when Springsteen whispers 'And the last shall be first and the first shall be last', echoing the recurrent image of power reversal from the gospels (Matt. 19:30, 20:16; Mark 9:35, 10:31; Luke 13:30). On *The Rising* (2002), Springsteen responded to the national grief precipitated by the destruction of the World Trade Center in New York on 11 September 2001. This consciously 'post-9/11' album resists jingoistic diatribes, focusing instead on laments for the dead and bereaved and prayers for peace. Significantly, the album's recurrent motif, heard particularly on the title track but also on the Gospel-inflected final track, 'My City of Ruins', is of the resurrected body, an echo, conscious or otherwise, of 1 Corinthians 1:15.

Film has become the prevailing narrative medium of the early twenty-first century. An iconoclastic Protestant mistrust of the pictorial is replayed in contemporary culture (Baudrillard 1994). Postmodernity, so dependent on technologies of reproduction and repetition, has created a world in which the image seems to overwhelm the word. Despite these anxieties, the relationship between film and the Bible is now widely explored (see, for example, Miles 1996; Deacy 2001; Aichele and Walsh 2002; Higgins 2003; Reinhartz 2003).

Contemporary cinema is drenched with quests for redemption and visions of judgement. This applies not only to self-consciously devotional work like Mel Gibson's contentious *The Passion of the Christ* (2004) but also to superficially 'secular' films such as the confused, explicitly messianic dystopian world of *The Matrix* (1999) and its sequels. The miraculous, mythic literature of the Bible continues to invigorate and problematize the imaginative terrain of our historical moment. Violent apocalyptic fantasies such as *End of Days* (1999) make explicit use of Revelation but are rarely characterized by spiritual profundity. However, other films use biblical allusion in more sensitive and spiritually challenging ways: P. T . Anderson's epic, strange compendium of Los Angeles tales, *Magnolia* (1999) ends with an absurd sequence in which an Exodus-like plague of frogs rains down on the city, as a compelling image of judgement and grace (Reinhartz 2003: 24–38).

My final example is Kevin Smith's satire *Dogma* (1999): the film is insulting, irreverent and flawed but it is also provocatively biblical. In an interview, Smith stated with a rare lack of irony that he made the film not to offend but as a genuine 'celebration of faith'. As a committed – if unlikely – Roman Catholic, Smith confronted aspects of his spiritual tradition that he found most disturbing. The work with which the iconoclastic writer /director connects his film is neither Monty Python's *The Life of Brian* (1979) nor Martin Scorsese's *The Last Temptation of Christ* (1988) but, perhaps surprisingly, the Psalms. In connecting a superficially sacrilegious work of entertainment with an ancient book of prayer, praise and spiritual longing, Smith embodies the creative tension between the chaotic, evolving and eclectic spirituality of the contemporary world – however we choose to label it – and the great and troubling 'Book of books'.

Conclusion: Postmodern Jubilee

'The world speaks of holy things in the only language it knows, which is a worldly language' (Buechner 1992: 63). The stories, images and theologies drawn from the books of the Bible for centuries are appropriated and exploited in the era of late Capitalism. Out of the waste of our rapacious consumption, sometimes in barely comprehensible shapes, arise rituals and stories that articulate a need for mystery and sanctity. If postmodern culture is considerably more suspicious of institutions and individuals who claim to have a monopoly on truth, it is no less exercised by the pursuit of transcendence and what one novelist has recently named the necessity to 'speak of remarkable things' (McGregor 2002).

At the end of the twentieth century, multiple organizations – including Christian, Jewish and secular relief agencies – united under the name Jubilee 2000, derived from the biblical tradition of ending debt and freeing slaves every 50 years (Lev. 25:11; Isa. 61:1–2). The global pressure group – that later partially evolved into the Make Poverty History campaign – succeeded in engendering the cancellation of a vast amount of iniquitous Third-World debt. In a bewildering world, violently divided by creeds, rendered absurd by extremes of wealth and poverty, the Bible might, in fact, 'radically reconstrue and recontextualize reality' (Brueggemann 1993: 26). The Bible, claims Alter 'is a literature steeped in the quirkiness and imperfection of the human that is ultimately oriented toward a horizon beyond the human' (1992: 20–1). The postmodern pursuit of this strange, unsettling literature opens up new perspectives and offers a constant challenge to injustice, visible and veiled.

References

Aichele, G. and Walsh, R. (eds) (2002). *Screening Scripture: Intertextual Connections between Scripture and Film*. Harrisburg, PA: Trinity Press International.

Alter, R. (1992). *The World of Biblical Literature*. New York: Basic Books.

Alter, R. and Kermode, F. (eds) (1989). *The Literary Guide to the Bible*. London: Collins.

Anderson, B. (1983). *Imagined Communities*. London: Verso.

Barthes, R. (1977). *Image-Music-Text*, trans. Stephen Heath. London: Collins.

Barton, J. (ed.) (1998). *The Cambridge Companion to Biblical Interpretation*. Cambridge: Cambridge University Press.

Baudrillard, J. (1994). *Simulacra and Simulation*. Ann Arbor, MI: University of Michigan Press.

Baum, G. (ed.) (1999). *The Twentieth Century: A Theological Overview*. London: Geoffrey Chapman.

Bauman, Z. (1992). *Intimations of Postmodernity*. London: Routledge.

Bauman, Z. (1998). 'Postmodern Religion?', in P. Heelas, D. Martin and P. Morris (eds), *Religion, Modernity and Postmodernity*. Oxford: Blackwell, pp. 55–78.

Beaudoin, T. (2000). *Virtual Faith: The Irreverent Spiritual Quest of Generation X*. San Francisco: Jossey-Bass.

Blond, P. (1998). *Post-Secular Philosophy: Between Philosophy and Theology*. London: Routledge.

Bradley, A. (2004). *Negative Theology and Modern French Philosophy*. London: Routledge.

Brown, C. G. (2001). *The Death of Christian Britain: Understanding Secularisation, 1800–2000*. London: Routledge.

Bruce, S. (1996). *Religion in the Modern World: From Cathedrals to Cults*. Oxford: Oxford University Press.

Brueggemann, W. (1993). *The Bible and Postmodern Imagination: Texts under Negotiation*. London: SCM Press.

Buechner, F. (1992). *A Room Called Remember: Uncollected Pieces*. San Francisco: HarperCollins.

Caputo, J. D. (2001a). 'The Poetics of the Impossible and the Kingdom of God', in G. Ward (ed.), *The Blackwell Companion to Postmodern Theology*. Oxford: Blackwell, pp. 469–81.

Caputo, J. D. (2001b). *On Religion*. London: Routledge.

Carroll, R. P. (1998a). 'Poststructuralist Approaches: New Historicism and Postmodernism', in J. Barton (ed.), *The Cambridge Companion to Biblical Interpretation*. Cambridge: Cambridge University Press, pp. 50–66.

Carroll, R. P. (1998b). 'Lower Case Bibles: Commodity Culture and the Bible', in J. C. Exum and S. D. Moore (eds), *Biblical Studies/Cultural Studies: The Third Sheffield Colloquium*. Sheffield: Sheffield Academic Press, pp. 46–69.

Castelli, E. A., Moore, S. D., Phillips, G. A. and Schwartz, R. M. (eds) (1995). *The Postmodern Bible*. New Haven, CT: Yale University Press.

Coupland, D. (1992). *Generation X: Tales for an Accelerated Culture*. London: Abacus.

Coupland, D. (1997). *Polaroids from the Dead*. London: Flamingo.

Coupland, D. (2003). *Hey Nostradamus!* London: Flamingo.

Cox, H. (1999). 'The Myth of the Twentieth Century: The Rise and Fall of Secularization', in G. Baum (ed.), *The Twentieth Century: A Theological Overview*. London: Geoffrey Chapman, pp. 135–43.

Cunningham, V. (2002). *Reading after Theory*. Oxford: Blackwell.

Davie, G. (1994). *Religion in Britain since 1945: Believing Without Belonging*. Oxford: Blackwell.

Deacy, C. (2001). *Screen Christologies: Redemption and the Medium of Film*. Cardiff: University of Wales Press.

De Bernières, L. (1998). 'Introduction', *The Book of Job*. Edinburgh: Canongate.

Debord, G. (1983). *Society of the Spectacle*. Detroit, MI: Black and Red.

Derrida, J. et al. (1985a). *The Ear of the Other*, ed. C. V. McDonald, trans P. Kumf and A. Ronnell. New York: Schocken Books.

Derrida, J. et al. (1985b). 'Des Tours de Babel', in J. F. Graham (ed.), *Difference in Translation*. Ithaca, NY: Cornell University Press, pp. 165–77.

Detweiler, C. and Taylor, B. (2003). *A Matrix of Meanings: Finding God in Pop Culture*. Grand Rapids, MI: Baker Academic.

Eagleton, T. (2000). *After Theory*. London: Allen Lane.

Eco, U. (1985). *Reflections on the Name of the Rose*. London: Secker and Warburg.

Edwards, M. (1984). *Towards a Christian Poetics*. London: Macmillan.

Exum, J. C. and Moore, S. D. (eds) (1998a). *Biblical Studies/Cultural Studies: The Third Sheffield Colloquium*. Sheffield: Sheffield Academic Press.

Exum, J. C. and Moore, S. D. (1998b). 'Biblical Studies/Cultural Studies', in J. C. Exum and S. D. Moore (eds), *Biblical Studies/Cultural Studies: The Third Sheffield Colloquium*. Sheffield: Sheffield Academic Press, pp. 19–45.

Foucault, M. (1989). *The Order of Things: On the Archaeology of the Human Sciences*. London: Routledge.

Frei, H. W. (1974). *The Eclipse of Biblical Narrative: A Study of Eighteenth and Nineteenth-Century Hermeneutics*. New Haven, CT: Yale University Press.

Hart, K. (1989). *The Trespass of the Sign: Deconstruction, Theology and Philosophy*. Cambridge: Cambridge University Press.

Hauerwas, S. (1997). *Wilderness Wanderings: Probing Twentieth-Century Theology and Philosophy*. Boulder, CO: Westview.

Heelas, P., Martin, D. and Morris, P. (eds) (1998). *Religion, Modernity and Postmodernity*. Oxford: Blackwell.

Higgins, G. (2003). *How Movies Helped Save My Soul: Finding Spiritual Fingerprints in Culturally Significant Films*. Orlando, FL: Relevant.

Hutcheon, L. (1988). *A Poetics of Postmodernism: History, Theory, Fiction*. New York: Routledge.

Hyman, G, (2001). *The Predicament of Postmodern Theology: Radical Orthodoxy or Nihilist Textualism?* Louisville, KY: Westminster/John Knox Press.

Ingraffia, B. (1999). 'Is the Postmodern Post-Secular? The Parody of Religious Quests in Thomas Pynchon's *The Crying of Lot 49* and Don De Lillo's *White Noise*', in M. Westphal (ed.), *Postmodern Philosophy and Christian Thought*. Bloomington, IN: Indiana University Press, pp. 44–68.

Jameson, F. (1991). *Postmodernism, or the Cultural Logic of Late Capitalism*. London: Verso.

Jameson, F. (1998). *The Cultural Turn: Selected Writings on the Postmodern, 1983–1998*. London: Verso.

Jeffreys, D. L. (1996). *The People of the Book: Christian Identity and Literary Culture*. Grand Rapids, MI: Eerdmans.

Lacey, R. (2003). *The Street Bible*. Grand Rapids, MI: Zondervan.

Lawrence, D. H. (1931). *Apocalypse*. Florence: G. Orioli.

Loughlin, G. (1996). *Telling God's Story: Bible, Church and Narrative Theology*. Cambridge: Cambridge University Press.

Loughlin, G. (2003). *Alien Sex: The Body and Desire in Cinema and Theology*. Oxford: Blackwell.

Lynch, G. (2002). *After Religion: 'Generation X' and the Search for Meaning*. London: Darton, Longman and Todd.

Lyon, D. (1999). *Postmodernity*, 2nd edn. Buckingham: Open University Press.

Lyon, D. (2000). *Jesus in Disneyland: Religion in Postmodern Times*. Cambridge: Polity Press.

Lyotard, F. (1984). *The Postmodern Condition: A Report on Knowledge*, trans. G. Bennington and B. Massumi. Manchester: Manchester University Press.

Mazur, E. M. and McCarthy, K. (eds) (2001). *God in the Details: American Religion in Popular Culture*. New York: Routledge.

McCarthy, K. (2001). 'Deliver Me from Nowhere: Bruce Springsteen and the Myth of the American Promised Land', in E. M. Mazur and K. McCarthy (eds), *God in the Details: American Religion in Popular Culture*. New York: Routledge, pp. 23–45.

McClure, J. A. (1995). 'Postmodern/Post-Secular: Contemporary Fiction and Spirituality', *Modern Fiction Studies* 41(1): 141–63.

McGregor, J. (2002). *If Nobody Speaks of Remarkable Things*. London: Bloomsbury.

Miles, M. R. (1996). *Seeing and Believing: Religion and Values in the Movies*. Boston: Beacon.

Morgan, R. (1998). 'The Bible and Christian Theology', in J. Barton (ed.), *The Cambridge Companion to Biblical Interpretation*. Cambridge: Cambridge University Press, pp. 114–28.

Reinhartz, A. (2003). *Scripture on the Silver Screen*. Louisville, KY: Westminster/John Knox Press.

Ruskin, J. (1903–12). *The Works of John Ruskin*, library edn, ed. E. T. Cook and Alexander Wedderburn, 39 vols. London: George Allen.

Schad, J. (ed.) (2001). *Writing the Bodies of Christ: The Church from Carlyle to Derrida*. Aldershot: Ashgate.

Schwartz, R. M. (1998). 'Teaching the Bible "as" Literature "in" Culture', in J. C. Exum and S. D. Moore (eds), *Biblical Studies/Cultural Studies: The Third Sheffield Colloquium*. Sheffield: Sheffield Academic Press, pp. 190–202.

Sontag, S. (1990). *Against Interpretation and Other Essays*. New York: Anchor/Doubleday.

Stiver, D. R. (2003). 'Theological Method', in K. J. Vanhoozer (ed.), *The Cambridge Companion to Postmodern Theology*. Cambridge: Cambridge University Press, pp. 170–85.

Stockman, S. (2001). *Walk On: The Spiritual Journey of U2*. Orlando, FL: Relevant.

Sutherland, J. (2004). 'Ripping Yarns', *The Guardian*, 30 April, pp. 10–11.

Tate, A. (2002). ' "Now – Here is My Secret": Ritual and Epiphany in Douglas Coupland's Fiction', *Literature and Theology* 16(3): 326–38.

Turner, S. (1995). *Hungry for Heaven: Rock 'N' Roll and the Search for Redemption*. Illinois: Intervarsity Press.

Vanhoozer, K. J. (ed.) (2003a). *The Cambridge Companion to Postmodern Theology*. Cambridge: Cambridge University Press.

Vanhoozer, K. J. (2003b). 'Theology and the Condition of Postmodernity: A Report on Knowledge (of God)', in K. J. Vanhoozer (ed.), *The Cambridge Companion to Postmodern Theology*. Cambridge: Cambridge University Press, pp. 3–25.

Vanhoozer, K. J. (2003c). 'Scripture and Tradition', in K. J. Vanhoozer (ed.), *The Cambridge Companion to Postmodern Theology*. Cambridge: Cambridge University Press, pp. 149–69.

Ward, G. (1995). *Barth, Derrida and the Language of Theology*. Cambridge: Cambridge University Press.

Ward, G. (ed.) (1997a). *The Postmodern God: A Theological Reader*. Oxford: Blackwell.

Ward, G. (1997b). 'Introduction, or, A Guide to Theological Thinking in Cyberspace', in G. Ward (ed.), *The Postmodern God: A Theological Reader*. Oxford: Blackwell, pp. xv–xlvii.

Ward, G. (2000). *Theology and Contemporary Critical Theory*, 2nd edn. Basingstoke: Macmillan.

Ward, G. (ed.) (2001a). *The Blackwell Companion to Postmodern Theology*. Oxford: Blackwell.

Ward, G. (2001b). 'Introduction: "Where We Stand" ', in G. Ward (ed.), *The Blackwell Companion to Postmodern Theology*. Oxford: Blackwell, pp. xii–xxvii.

Ward, G. (2003). *True Religion*. Oxford: Blackwell.

Westphal, M. (ed.) (1999). *Postmodern Philosophy and Christian Thought*. Bloomington, IN: Indiana University Press.

Williams, R. (2000). *Lost Icons: Reflections on Cultural Bereavement*. Edinburgh: T. & T. Clark.

Wolterstorff, N. (1995). *Divine Discourse: Philosophical Reflections on the Claim that God Speaks*. Cambridge: Cambridge University Press.

Wood, J. (2004). *The Book Against God*. London: Vintage.

Woodhead, L. and Heelas, P. (eds) (2000). *Religion in Modern Times: An Interpretive Anthology*. Oxford: Blackwell.

York, M. (2001). 'New Age Commodification and Appropriation of Spirituality', *Journal of Contemporary Religion*, 16(3): 361–72.

Žižek, S. (2000). *The Fragile Absolute – or, Why Is the Christian Legacy Worth Fighting For?* London: Verso.

Žižek, S. (2001). 'Christ's Breaking of the "Great Chain of Being" ', in J. Schad (ed.), *Writing the Bodies of Christ: The Church from Carlyle to Derrida*. Aldershot: Ashgate, pp. 105–10.

Index of Biblical References

General Index